Conflicting Worlds

NEW DIMENSIONS OF THE AMERICAN CIVIL WAR

T. Michael Parrish, *Editor*

D1551384

REFORGING THE WHITE REPUBLIC

Race, Religion, and American Nationalism, 1865–1898

EDWARD J. BLUM

LOUISIANA STATE UNIVERSITY PRESS

BATON ROUGE

Published by Louisiana State University Press
Manufactured in the United States of America
Louisiana Paperback Edition, 2007
First printing

DESIGNER: *Amanda McDonald Scallan*
TYPEFACE: *Whitman*
TYPESETTER: *G&S Typesetters, Inc.*

Library of Congress Cataloging-in-Publication Data

Blum, Edward J.
    Reforging the White Republic : race, religion, and American nationalism,
1865–1898 / Edward J. Blum.
        p. cm.—(Conflicting worlds)
    Includes bibliographical references and index.
    ISBN 0-8071-3052-4 (hardcover : alk. paper)
    1. United States—History—1865–1898.   2. Nationalism—United
States—History—19th century.   3. United States—Race relations
—History—19th century.   4. United States—Church history—19th
century.   I. Title.   II. Series.
E661.B68 2005
973.8—dc22

                                            2004021168

ISBN-13: 978-0-8071-3248-7 (paper : alk. paper)

Chapters 4 and 5, respectively, appeared previously in slightly different form as "Gilded Crosses:
Postbellum Revivalism and the Reforging of American Nationalism," *Journal of Presbyterian History*
79, no. 4 (Winter 2001): 277–92; and "The Crucible of Disease: Trauma, Memory, and National
Reconciliation during the Yellow Fever Epidemic of 1878," *Journal of Southern History* 69 (November
2003): 791–820. Used by permission.

The paper in this book meets the guidelines for permanence and durability of the Committee on
Production Guidelines for Book Longevity of the Council on Library Resources. ∞

God wept; but that mattered little to an unbelieving age;
what mattered most was that the world wept
and still is weeping and is blind with tears and blood.
— W. E. B. DU BOIS, *Black Reconstruction in America* (1935)

Contents

Acknowledgments   ix

INTRODUCTION
Race, Religion, and the Fracturing of the White Republic   /   1

1.   THE LAST AND GREATEST BATTLE OF FREEDOM:
Race and the American Nation after the
Assassination of Abraham Lincoln   /   20

2.   ON THE VERGE OF HEAVEN:
Religious Missions, Interracial Contact, and the
Radicalism of Radical Reconstruction   /   51

3.   THE APOSTLES OF FORGIVENESS:
Religion and National Reunion in Northern Society,
Popular Culture, and National Politics, 1865–1875   /   87

4.   INVENTOR OF LEGENDS MIRACULOUS:
National Reconciliation and Racial Segregation
during America's Third Great Awakening   /   120

5.   THE WHITE FLAG WAVES:
Spiritual Reunion and Genocidal Visions during the
Yellow Fever Epidemic of 1878   /   146

6.   NO NORTH, NO SOUTH, NO SECTIONALISM IN
POLITICS, NO SEX IN CITIZENSHIP:
Race, Nationalism, and Gender Politics in the Rise
of the Woman's Christian Temperance Union   /   174

7.   TO THE PERSON SITTING IN DARKNESS:
Global Missions, Religious Belief, and the Making
of the Imperial White Republic   /   209

EPILOGUE:
Dreaming of the White Republic, Defending
the Souls of Black Folk   /   244

Notes   /   251
Bibliography   /   303
Index   /   345

Illustrations follow page 150

Acknowledgments

Writing this book has brought me great joy and great sorrow. I have been confronted by an America both beautiful and terrible. Along the way, my travels have been heartened by many generous, caring, and gifted scholars. The history department at the University of Kentucky was a place of great learning and spiritual striving for me. My director and friend, Kathi Kern, provided unsurpassed mentoring. Mark Wahlgren Summers and Philip Harling pushed me to read widely. Joanne Pope Melish taught me to read deeply. The many hours we shared to discuss writing, racial constructions, and religious faith not only made this book possible, but also changed my life. In addition, I must thank Tracy Campbell, Patricia Cooper, Steven Weisenburger, Bob Flynn, Richard Bailey, Erin Shelor, Carolyn DuPont, Rebecca Bates, Melanie Beals Goan, and Julie Sweet for their support during my sojourn in Kentucky.

At Baylor University, I have once again been surrounded by a host of bright minds and singular personalities. I have never encountered so many individuals so interested in religion. Sociologists Paul Froese, Chris Bader, Rodney Stark, Byron Johnson, Charlie Tolbert, and Diana Kendall have been wonderful colleagues and friends. Likewise, historians Kim Kellison, Thomas Kidd, David Hendon, and Barry Hankins have been astute critics and pleasant companions. Even the Dean for Student Learning and Engagement, Frank Shushok, showed an interest in my manuscript. And Tom Hibbs, Dean of the Honors College and perhaps the most down-to-earth philosopher I have ever met, is a scholar worthy of much emulation. I am thankful that I have the opportunity to learn from him.

Numerous other comrades contributed time and energy to this project. Gaines Foster and Jim Findlay were excellent conversation partners, while Scott Poole endured countless conference panels with me. There will be most likely many more. I will never be able to repay my intellectual debt to Scott. As an undergraduate at the University of Michigan, Susan Juster taught me to appreciate American religious history, and, always with a smile, John Carson suffered through far too many chapters on Dwight Moody. James Moorhead, Joanne Meyerowitz, Clarence Walker, Matt Gallman, and Gardiner Shattuck offered substantial criticisms of the text, and I trust they will think this a better work for their efforts. My colleagues in the Pew Younger Scholars Summer Program, especially Laura Veltman and Scott Stabler, made for two weeks of intense dialogue and grand cheer. Mike Parrish, my colleague at Baylor and editor, helped transform this manuscript into a book, while Derik Shelor, my copyeditor, was immensely helpful. Finally, Sarah Hardin poured over every page. Together we laughed and cried. I cannot thank her enough. Sarah is a brilliant scholar and a wonderful person. Chances are her work on racism and politics in twentieth-century Louisville will cause quite a stir. I hope that each reader will see sides of America in this book that inspire and that haunt, for ultimately the nation is what we envision it to be and what we make it.

REFORGING THE WHITE REPUBLIC

INTRODUCTION

Race, Religion, and the Fracturing of the White Republic

In 1867, the New York artist J. L. Giles engraved the image of a dream for the future of the United States. Its title, "Reconstruction," was simple, but its vision was extraordinary. Giles conceived of an American nation reborn after four years of bloody civil war. The days of death were now past, and northerners and southerners enjoyed a land of peace, equality, and brotherhood. Although sectional rivalries and the institution of slavery had cost more than a half million lives, Yankees and Confederates now shook hands in fraternal unity. Flanked by angels in the clouds, deceased sectional opponents Daniel Webster of New Hampshire and John C. Calhoun of South Carolina cordially greeted one another. In the land of the living, abolitionist Horace Greeley and Confederate president Jefferson Davis embraced, while Union general Ulysses S. Grant and Confederate general Robert E. Lee clasped hands.

Sectional reconciliation, however, was but one of the print's major themes. Two other more startling images were racial justice and racial harmony. The old pillars of "Slavery" that upheld the national pavilion were being replaced with new ones of "Justice," "Liberty," and "Education." Former Confederates and former slaves agreed to work amicably side by side, and in the bottom center of the print, a black baby and a white one slept soundly in their cribs. The eagle of liberty soared over them carrying a banner that read, "All men are born free and equal." Above the entire scene, Jesus Christ approvingly looked down. He bestowed his blessings on the American people and implored them to "Do Unto Others As You Would Have Done Unto You." Giles's "Reconstruction" was an amazing expression of hope for America's future. In this imaginary realm, love and respect transcended sectional and racial hatred, and God smiled. (See figure 1.)

When Giles engraved "Reconstruction," the destiny of the United States was anything but certain. The long and grueling Civil War and the years immediately following it brought a host of questions to the minds of white and black Americans. What would become of the nation? Would Confederates be punished for their rebellion? Would they ever have full citizenship rights and privileges again?

What would happen to the millions of recently emancipated, yet hardly free, men and women in the South? How far would the social revolution inaugurated by emancipation proceed? How would the nation ever become united and on whose terms? Already by 1867 there had been substantial change. Four million people of color had achieved their liberation, the federal government had constitutionally guaranteed citizenship rights for African Americans throughout the country, and even universal manhood suffrage appeared imminent. At the same time, Congress discussed further disempowering former Confederates and redistributing land in the South. As one African American in California put it, "The Revolution had begun, and time alone must decide where it is to end."[1]

As in Giles's print, the image of God and Christ observing and evaluating America's Reconstruction continued to be a powerful one even in the early twentieth century, long after Reconstruction had ended. Two competing memories of the postwar era emerged, but both relied on heavenly figures. In 1915, film director D. W. Griffith adapted several novels by the minister-turned-author Thomas Dixon Jr. into the nation's first modern motion picture, *The Birth of a Nation*. In this movie, the era of Reconstruction stood as a chaotic time when vindictive northern radical Republicans and sexually driven blacks conspired to demoralize the white South after the Civil War. The South and the nation were redeemed, however, when the men of the former Confederacy banded together to form the Ku Klux Klan and to vanquish "Negro rule." At the end of Griffith's sweeping drama, Jesus Christ hovered over the newborn American nation. He seemed to sanctify the Klan's protection of white supremacy and the reunification of the North and the South.[2]

But God was not so pleased with the United States in the scholarly imagination of W. E. B. Du Bois, the most prominent African American intellectual of the first half of the twentieth century. To him, the idea that God approved of an America created by violence and terrorism was ludicrous and a moral travesty. His own interpretation of the history of post–Civil War America stood in direct defiance of that offered by Griffith, Dixon Jr., and a contingent of white historians of the early twentieth century. In Du Bois's work, the era of Reconstruction was marked by the grand quest of freed African Americans for racial justice and the grotesque betrayal of democracy by northern and southern whites who refused to offer genuine freedom to people of color. Ultimately, the defeat of racial justice and democracy "was a triumph of men who in their effort to replace equality with caste and to build inordinate wealth on a foundation of abject poverty have succeeded in killing democracy, art and religion." The United States that emerged out of Reconstruction was not one over which God smiled; it was one over which "God wept."[3]

Du Bois's and Griffith's competing views of Reconstruction demonstrated that Giles's original vision of postwar America was never fully realized. In the decades following the Civil War, certain aspects of his print were accomplished, while others went tragically unfulfilled. Northern and southern whites did largely forgive one another for the devastating war, and national unity eventually triumphed over sectional animosity. In fact, national reunion helped pave the way for the rise of an overseas American empire at the end of the century. Racial equality and justice, however, remained elusive dreams. By 1900, a dark cloud of racial terror had descended upon the land. Although the Fourteenth and Fifteenth Amendments to the Constitution offered all African Americans full citizenship and black men the right to vote, white supremacist organizations, such as the Ku Klux Klan and the White Leagues, bulldozed away those privileges. Railroads, hotels, and other public and private institutions became more and more segregated, and even the Supreme Court affirmed racial separation. In the closing decades of the century, a wave of violence drenched America with blood. Between 1882 and 1900, whites from New Orleans to Maine lynched more than seventeen hundred African Americans. How did the beautiful dreams of the mid-1860s devolve into the hellish nightmares of the 1890s? Why did northern whites reconcile with their former opponents and discard their concerns for protection and justice for people of color?

Reforging the White Republic traces the tragedy that followed the Civil War. It focuses on how the post–Civil War reunification of whites, the decline in American race relations, and the rise of a militarized, imperialistic nation were permitted, and even encouraged, by northern whites, who abandoned the hopes for racial equality and brotherhood that were given graphic form in Giles's "Reconstruction." Based upon a wide variety of sources from the postwar years—including newspapers, magazines, personal diaries and letters, convention minutes, sermons, hymns, missionary tracts, travelogues, poems, popular novels, short stories, school primers, children's literature, political speeches, congressional reports, Supreme Court opinions, and political caricatures—this book explores the ways Protestant Christianity in the North helped to forge a new sense of white American nationalism after the Civil War that sanctified the segregation of African Americans and their political disenfranchisement. From the end of the Civil War to the War of 1898, northern religion—its spokesmen and spokeswomen, practitioners, ideologies, and movements—played a critical role in reuniting northern and southern whites, in justifying and nourishing the social and spiritual separation of whites and blacks, and in propelling the United States into global imperialism. Northern white Christians, in short, were essential to the reforging of the white republic.[4]

I

Long before the Civil War and Reconstruction, Protestantism, American nationalism, and whiteness had been bound together tightly in the imaginations of Euro-Americans. As early as the colonial and revolutionary periods, colonists and their children conceived of their new land and nation in religious and racial terms. While Samuel Adams hoped to create a "Christian Sparta" after the American Revolution, Thomas Jefferson proposed a seal for the new United States where "the children of Israel in the wilderness" were "led by a cloud by day and pillar of fire by night" on one side, "and on the other side, Hengist and Horsa, the Saxon chiefs from whom we claim the honor of being descended, and whose political principles and form of government we have assumed." The Revolutionary generation and the leaders of the United States in the early nineteenth century created a nation that granted unprecedented rights to white men, but brutally oppressed people of color. The northern states gradually emancipated their slaves, but in turn passed laws that restricted the political, legal, and social rights of African Americans. Several Midwestern states, in fact, banned the entrance of any African American, whether free or slave, and in the majority opinion of *Dred Scott v. Sanford* (1857), Chief Justice Roger Taney of the U.S. Supreme Court declared that blacks were in no way citizens of the United States. At the same time, southern state legislators made slave manumissions far more difficult after the Revolution, and many even outlawed the education of African Americans. During these years, northern and southern whites continued to view their country as a "redeemer nation" called by God to serve as a beacon of liberty and economic prosperity to the world. This view of their national identity proved useful in justifying slavery, expropriating Native American lands, and warring with Mexico in the 1840s. By the mid-nineteenth century, the United States was a nation marked by its deep commitment to whiteness and to Protestant Christianity.[5]

The Civil War thoroughly fractured this white republic—both literally and figuratively. For decades preceding the war, northern and southern whites had come to view themselves as fundamentally different peoples with distinct origins, traits, cultures, and economic systems. Origin myths, which suggested that austere Puritans had populated the North while hot-blooded Cavaliers had settled the South, emerged to explain sectional differences. As northerners and southerners grew further and further apart during the antebellum era, sectional antagonism heightened. One Civil War soldier from Michigan put it this way: "A '*genera-tion* has been educated to hate *the South*' & most earnestly is the hate returned." In seceding from the Union and forming their own nation-state, Confederate south-erners demonstrated that they no longer viewed themselves as national brethren with northern whites. The Confederate South was convinced that Abraham Lincoln and the Republican Party would not uphold the tenets of the white repub-lic—a nation in which the rights, privileges, and liberties of white men, espe-cially slaveholders, were vigorously protected. As one Louisiana writer put it, "The present conflict in America is not a *civil* strife, but a war of *Nationalities* . . . a war of alien races. . . . Cavalier and Roundhead no longer designate parties, but *nations*."[6]

The war provided both sections with an opportunity to demonize one another and for northern and southern religious leaders to further imbue their under-standings of national identity with religious beliefs. Southern church leaders ral-lied to the Confederate cause and depicted northerners as inherently irreligious, overly materialistic, and even the tools of the devil. In the opening weeks of armed conflict, Presbyterian minister Benjamin Morgan Palmer of New Orleans told one group of southern whites that "history reads to us of wars which have been bap-tized as holy; but she enters upon her records none that is holier than this in which you have embarked." In the North, preachers and politicians also employed bibli-cal rhetoric to call northerners to uphold the Union. They denounced any political dissent as irreligious, they conflated the fate of the Union with the fate of God's kingdom, and they asserted that the war was God's way of purifying the nation of its sins.[7]

Also devastating to the chief tenets of the white republic was the emergence of a new northern appreciation for African Americans as important members of the nation. The exigencies of the war and the heroism of African American soldiers, who demonstrated amazing patriotic allegiance to the Union, forced a reevaluation of the conflation of whiteness and American nationalism. As nearly two hundred thousand blacks joined the Union's forces and helped turn the tide of the struggle, many northern whites expressed greater willingness to admit African Americans into the body politic. Radical abolitionists, who had once been widely despised, were now heralded as beloved prophets. Even President Abraham Lincoln, who had shown little interest in bringing about emancipation early in the war, openly met with black leaders and discussed the merits of black suffrage before the South surrendered.[8] Northern African Americans perceived this drastic shift in the pub-lic temper and began to imagine that a new era of racial justice and fraternity was

about to commence. Early in the war, African American minister Sella Martin proclaimed that the conflict provided the nation its greatest opportunity to eliminate
racial injustice and exploitation. If radicalism carried the day, he believed, then
whites and blacks would join Christ with God:

> And ascend the nation's Tabor,
> To remain transfigured there,
> With the white man and the negro,
> Standing one on either side.[9]

By the spring of 1865, the antebellum white republic lay in shambles. Southern
whites were outside of the nation, and a host of northern whites sought to include
African Americans as full citizens.

In the decades following the Civil War, the United States underwent another titanic struggle. This one was not to save the nation, but to determine who constituted the "nation" and who did not. During the immediate postwar years, northern radicals continued to challenge the conflation of whiteness and American
citizenship. A coterie of northern white Protestants advanced a racially egalitarian
ideology that viewed former slaves as full American citizens. Radical ministers
denied the existence of inherent differences between African Americans and
northern whites, and they called for universal brotherhood to transcend racial
parochialism. In this way, they evinced a type of civic nationalism, in which shared
political commitments to the Union, democracy, Christianity, and human liberty
constituted the essential basis for citizenship.

From the end of the Civil War to the turn of the century, however, growing
numbers of white Protestants abandoned their commitments to civic nationalism.
They came to authorize, rationalize, and at times lead the process of racial and national formation that left people of color disfranchised, segregated, and without legal protection. Northern white Protestants helped re-create and re-sanctify the
ethnic nationalism that had been in place before the war, in which racial categories
defined national citizenship. By the turn of the century, northern religious leaders
encouraged whites to view peoples of color—both within the United States and in
other parts of the world—as unsuited for full inclusion in the nation. This great reversal in racial imaginations played a pivotal role in constructing a multitiered understanding of American nationalism, one that positioned peoples of color as subordinate citizens and separated them from northern and southern whites both
physically and spiritually.

The reforging of the white republic involved not only the disempowerment of
African Americans. It also entailed the re-solidification of a national whiteness that

papered over sectional divisions. This book situates northern Protestants at the center of this process, religiously legitimizing a national identity premised upon whiteness. Recently, the works of scholars such as David Roediger, Alexander Saxton, Matthew Frye Jacobson, and Grace Elizabeth Hale have demonstrated innumerable links between whiteness and sectional and national imaginations. As these historians and others have shown, ideas of racial differences and categories are not based on objective, observable, physical differences relating to skin color or any other biological factor. Rather, concepts such as "whiteness" and "blackness" are social and historical constructs that shift and change over time. They are continually being made and remade. As race theorists Michael Omi and Howard Winant maintain, "racial categories themselves are formed, transformed, destroyed and re-formed" quite regularly. Racial ideologies are any structures of meaning that describe perceived differences among peoples as innate, immutable, and located on and in the body. Racial constructions, furthermore, are created in order to make, sustain, and legitimate hierarchies.[10]

For all of their contributions to American history and critical race theory, however, studies of the making and transforming of whiteness in the nineteenth century have tended to ignore that a national schism took place. They have largely neglected that the white republic fell, shattered, and was eventually put back together again. Although one of the most enduring transformations of the nineteenth century, the remaking of national whiteness was so successful that it appeared as if it had never been ruptured. The fiction of a monolithic and national whiteness has masked the fact of a fractured and reconfigured whiteness that followed the Civil War. It was not, as historians often claim, that "the North won the war, but the South won the peace." Rather, whiteness prevailed. The white ethnic nationalism that had been prevalent in the antebellum North and South re-ascended in the decades following the Civil War and transcended sectionalism.

Reforging the White Republic contributes to the critical (d)evaluation of whiteness. It shows how northern religious leaders and ideologies helped institute whiteness, rather than loyalty to the federal Union or American political principals, as the fundamental prerequisite for full national citizenship. By 1900, in the minds of many northerners, American nationalism, whiteness, and Protestant Christianity had been powerfully bound together once again, and the beginning of the century witnessed northern white Protestants thoroughly embracing and propagating an ethnic nationalism that privileged whiteness at the direct expense of the radical civic nationalism of the mid-1860s.[11]

Focusing on the ways northern Protestants helped re-create a sense of American nationalism among whites, while they marginalized African Americans, this book offers a completely new perspective on sectional relations and racial ideologies after the Civil War. Although a variety of scholars have demonstrated the critical importance of religion on the northern home front during the war, northern religion has been largely ignored or trivialized in studies of America's racial, social, and cultural Reconstruction.[12] The scholars who have shaped the field—William Dunning, Eric McKitrick, John Hope Franklin, Kenneth Stampp, Eric Foner, James McPherson, Laura F. Edwards, and Heather Cox Richardson—have generally neglected northern religious leaders and beliefs. When they have dealt with Protestantism, they have made only cursory or vague statements.[13] Those scholars who have examined the influence of religion in postwar America, such as Gaines Foster, Charles Reagan Wilson, and W. Scott Poole, have tended to concentrate on the South. While they have delineated with much brilliance the relationships among southern religious ideologies, the myth of the Lost Cause, and the emergence of the "New South creed," northerners and Protestants have been left out of most discussions of the remaking of the nation. Only recently have historians attempted to tie religious leaders in the North to fundamental issues in postwar America, but none have drawn direct connections between race, religion, American nationalism, and imperialism.[14]

Likewise, students of sectional reunion have almost completely downplayed religious leaders and ideologies. These historians have investigated national reconciliation in terms of literary traditions, economic interests, historical memories, and racial and gender ideologies, but rarely in terms of faith. In *The Road to Reunion*, Paul Buck offered a largely cultural evaluation of national reunion, maintaining that northerners and southerners linked arms as northerners grew enamored with southern literature, southern soldiers, and southern customs. Alternatively, in *Origins of the New South*, C. Vann Woodward detailed the ways in which northern and southern businessmen drove reconciliation by creating integrated national markets. Northern capital and southern parvenus, he suggested, tied the nation together. Complicating the economic interpretation of reunion and building upon Buck's original work, Nina Silber, Cecilia O'Leary, and David Blight have drawn connections among gender metaphors, racial attitudes, historical memory, and national reconciliation. To them, as northerners selectively "forgot" the radical implications of emancipation during the Civil War, and as they creatively "remembered" the sectional conflict as a shared national experience of bravery, Yankees bonded with former Confederates in a love feast of virile white manhood. In this way, *fin-de-siecle* northern and southern whites formed a unified and powerful phalanx committed to the restoration and maintenance of the white republic. All of these scholars implicitly assume that religion was not a salient feature of postwar America.[15]

Positioning northern religion at the center of postwar reunion and the reconsolidation of national whiteness, *Reforging the White Republic* not only offers a new window into reconciliation and Reconstruction, but also challenges the bedrock assumption of nearly a century of religious historiography on the postbellum years. For the most part, historians of late nineteenth-century white Protestantism have followed Arthur Schlesinger Sr. in describing American Protestantism as a reactive force. These scholars, including Henry F. May, Sidney Ahlstrom, and Martin Marty, have focused on how social changes forced Protestants to transform themselves from upholders of the capitalistic status quo to Social Gospelers battling for reform. Confused by large cities, class conflict, and Catholic and Jewish immigrants, late nineteenth-century Protestants were propelled to change or forfeit their social relevance. To most historians, the story of postwar Protestantism is a tale of reaction and reform, of industrial challenge and religious response.[16]

This book turns the assumption of the "reaction thesis" on its head by exploring how Protestants drove, solidified, and often sanctified changes in American society. Religion during Reconstruction and the Gilded Age was not just relegated to churches and chapels, prayer meetings and parlor halls. It played a vital role in political meetings and press rooms, city streets and country farms. Christian idioms and ideologies touched all parts of American society and life. Congressmen quoted scripture as fervently as Sunday school teachers; popular novelists drew upon Protestant narratives with the gusto of evangelical missionaries; and political cartoonists used scenes from the Bible to comment on current politics as readily as Protestant ministers. Novelists, poets, politicians, and statesmen alike considered Christian metaphors, narratives, and ideologies to be powerful and compelling tools to sway public and personal opinions. *Reforging the White Republic*, thus, winds and twists through a wide array of venues and media, seeking to show religious ideologies at play in virtually every aspect of American life.[17]

Although this is not specifically a study of Protestant denominations or theology, readers interested in those topics will find much here to contemplate. During the nineteenth century, almost every aspect of American Protestantism was permeated by whiteness. From the theological association of whiteness with godliness to the racial segregation of blacks and whites in churches, American religious history cannot be rightly comprehended without attention to the dynamic interactions among religious belief, racial ideologies, and national imaginations. For these reasons, some of the contours of denominational histories and theological shifts are meshed together here with larger themes in American religious, political, and social life.

Visitors to the United States during the late nineteenth century certainly considered religious beliefs and figures to be crucial players in American society. After touring the North in the mid-1860s, British novelist Anthony Trollope observed, "One hardly knows where the affairs of this world end, or where those of the next begin." He perceived that all the people held strong religious beliefs, concluding, "Everybody is bound to have a religion." Echoing Alexis de Tocqueville, who had commented extensively on the importance of religious faith in the United States after his trip to America in the 1830s, French political thinker Ernest Duvergier de Hauranne called Americans "the most religious people in the world." "They [Americans] feel that to separate religion from human affairs would condemn it, so to speak, to suffocate in a vacuum," he continued. "The religious ideal . . . is rather a school of active morality associated with all aspects of life." More than two decades later, Great Britain's James Bryce concluded his appraisal of American society by suggesting that "Christianity is in fact understood to be, though not the legally established religion, yet the national religion."[18]

To Bryce, de Hauranne, Trollope, and a host of prominent American leaders during Reconstruction and the Gilded Age, religion stood at the core of America's national identity. They viewed the United States as a "Christian nation," but by "Christian" they meant a decidedly Protestant land. Both de Hauranne and Trollope considered religion a defining characteristic of the nation. While de Hauranne claimed that "[a] nation that includes prayer in all parts of its public and private life is certainly a religious nation," Trollope contended that "the nation is religious in its tendencies, and prone to acknowledge the goodness of God in all things. A man there is expected to belong to some church, and is not, I think, well looked on if he profess that he belongs to none." Near the end of the century, Supreme Court Justice David J. Brewer also drew connections between Christianity and Americans' national identity in his opinion for *Church of the Holy Trinity v. The United States* (1892). Citing American state constitutions, legal decisions, common customs, and the general mood of society, Justice Brewer proclaimed that it was "historically true that the American people are a religious people. . . . [T]his is a Christian nation."[19]

In a similar vein, one of America's foremost historians during the late nineteenth and early twentieth centuries, J. Franklin Jameson, lectured his colleagues of the American Historical Association that "of all means of estimating American character from American history, the pursuit of religious history is the most complete." The influence of religion, he maintained, was ubiquitous in the United States. "Millions have felt an interest in religion where thousands have felt an interest in literature or philosophy, in music or art," Jameson continued. "Millions have known little of any book save one, and that one the most interesting of religious books, the most influential, the most powerful to mould and transform." If Jameson, Brewer, and these others are to be believed, religion in late nineteenth-century America served as a primary matrix through which many Americans interpreted, evaluated, and articulated their experiences and ideas.[20]

II

This book seeks to untangle some of the intersections among religion, nationalism, race relations, and American imperialism from the end of the Civil War to the turn of the century. In the mid-1860s, white Protestants helped fan the flames of sectional hostilities, while they pushed vigorously for justice for African Americans. The Civil War and Abraham Lincoln's assassination in April 1865 thoroughly destabilized northern whites' racial and national imaginations. The ways in which northern ministers, newspaper editors, political cartoonists, and travelers to the South sought to make sectional and racial sense of the assassination of President Lincoln indicated that the white republic had been deeply fractured. A wide variety of Yankees perceived both African Americans and Confederates in new ways, challenging the whiteness of Confederates and asserting the essential national sameness of southern blacks and northern whites. Put another way, two kinds of muddied racial and national distinctions existed for many northerners by the war's end: one between "Confederate" and "Yankee" and the other between "white" and "black." For these northern whites, ideas of racial difference were not necessarily fixed in binary opposition, with whites on one side and blacks on the other. Instead, ideas of racial and national difference sat in a triangular arrangement—with Yankees, Confederates, and African Americans occupying distinct positions. The story of postwar Reconstruction was, in part, the tale of how this triangular racial and sectional structure appeared momentarily and then quickly lapsed again into a white-black binary.

Debates in the mid-1860s over whether northerners should align with freedpeople or with former Confederates were fierce and racialized. A handful of pastors invoked common whiteness as a strategy to downplay sectional antagonisms. They called for peace and urged northern leaders to shepherd the former rebels gently back into the national fold. The northern and southern Episcopal churches, for instance, reunited institutionally after the war as an expression of national goodwill and solidarity. Cries for amnesty, however, were met by a righteous indignation from other ministers. Angry clerics believed that the assassination heralded a divine mandate for retribution against the South. Several prominent and vocal northern white ministers, journalists, and cartoonists characterized Confederates as innately and immutably different from and inferior to Yankees, and they perceived these distinctions to reside on and within the body. In short, they considered Confederates a "race" distinct from Yankees. This racialized view of southerners never gained political or religious ascendancy in the postwar era, but it was an extreme manifestation of a prevalent feeling in the North—that Confederates should not be considered full citizens because of their rebellion and that northerners and southerners were no longer brothers.

While northern ministers debated the racial and national position of Confederates, many of them actively supported the drive to make African Americans full members of the national community. Several of these pastors waged a holy war against notions of racial difference between whites and blacks. In so doing, they demonstrated deep commitments to a northern civic nationalism, where shared commitments to the federal Union and principles of democracy constituted the essential right to citizenship. These ministers implored their congregations to help African Americans rise from slavery through education and enfranchisement and hoped that people of color would be fully included in the new nation.

The possibilities of an alliance between northern whites and freedpeople that stood in opposition to southern whites after the war became a reality when thousands of northern whites traveled south as missionaries to the former slaves. Racial radicalism and egalitarianism moved from the pulpits of the North to the fields, schoolhouses, and villages of the postbellum South. The postwar educational crusade demonstrated that "radical Reconstruction" was not as restrained and limited as historians have recently asserted. Commitments to civic nationalism did not recede immediately after the war. Dozens of influential benevolent associations sought to use schools and churches to invite people of color into the nation. Persistent and regular contact with freedpeople, moreover, had the power to dramatically transform the racial imaginations of some northern whites. Several female missionaries not only challenged racial and gendered etiquette regarding relationships between white women and black men, but also came to identity themselves as part of African American society, blurring distinctions between "white" and "black." The radicalism of these missionaries may not have reflected the opinions of the majority of northern whites, but the intensity of their attempt to incorporate people of color into the nation indicated a radical and dynamic national milieu. At the same time, Yankee interactions with southern blacks heightened animosities between northerners and southern whites. Former Confederates largely despised this second wave of Yankee "invaders" and sought to drive them away through violence and cultural coercion. But scores of missionary-teachers refused to be bullied, and they showed a sense of racial egalitarianism well ahead of their time.

Hopes and efforts for an integrated nation were largely betrayed in the decades following the war, however. Religious beliefs, leaders, and movements did a great deal to rebuild the white republic during Reconstruction and the Gilded Age. Northern proponents of national reunion in the late 1860s and 1870s, especially minister Henry Ward Beecher and his sister Harriet Beecher Stowe, implored northern audiences to forget past sectional strife, to forgive former Confederates for the war, and to forge a new sense of national solidarity with southern whites. Beecher, Stowe, and other religious leaders endeavored to shift the North's moral imperative away from racial uplift and toward national conciliation. Depicting the South as an idyllic land of racial harmony and economic prosperity, they encouraged northerners to view former Confederates as national brethren. At the same time, the major Protestant denominations in the nation—the Baptists, Methodists, and Presbyterians, all of whom had divided over sectional disputes in the antebellum era—showed an increasing interest in reconciling with one another. Religious rhetoric and metaphors also played key roles in literary and political calls for reconciliation, permeating a broad "culture of conciliation." Writers and politicians, including the eccentric editor and presidential candidate Horace Greeley, regularly cloaked reunion in sacred garb and claimed that God ordained solidarity among whites.

In the middle of the 1870s and the 1880s, the shoe salesman-turned-evangelist Dwight Lyman Moody further encouraged sectional reunion and the rise of the postwar white republic with his massive revivals. Hailed by contemporaries as the era's preeminent religious leader, Moody played an important role in justifying the northern rejection of radical Reconstruction and in linking northern and southern whites in fraternal unity. In a political and social atmosphere depressed by financial hard times, class conflict, and seemingly interminable sectional bickering, Moody discouraged Protestants from taking an active interest in social reform and instead focused on the conciliatory message of the Christian gospel. The great evangelist also embraced southern Protestant leaders and appealed to southern white audiences. In so doing, Moody entreated northern and southern whites to forget their past and present grievances. His sermons revealed a northern amnesia regarding the Civil War that effaced memories of the importance of slavery and racial issues in the terrible conflict. Instead, he highlighted similarities between northern and southern whites. Moody invented a mythical "War Between the States" in which the fact of northern and southern soldiers' bravery and a shared experience of combat obscured the reality of their fundamentally antagonistic convictions about the essential organization of society.

During the summer and fall of the year immediately following Moody's large-scale urban revivals, 1878, the United States experienced the worst medical disaster Americans had ever endured. In less than six months, more than one hundred thousand Americans contracted yellow fever and twenty thousand perished from it. The epidemic provided a traumatic moment that allowed northern and southern whites an opportunity to enact reconciliation. As northerners provided funds to the South and prayed together for southern whites, Yankees collectively performed sectional goodwill. At the same time, the outbreak supplied northern and southern whites a moment to reconstruct images and memories of one another. Northerners consciously effaced memories of former Confederates as uncivilized traitors. Southerners now became heroic and Christian martyrs. Southern whites, for their part, echoed northern sentiments of national reconciliation in poetry, political proclamations, mass demonstrations, and newspaper editorials. Northerners and southerners alike sought to reconceptualize the epidemic from a horribly devastating event into a grand moment of spiritual rebirth for the nation. Although the major Protestant denominations failed to reunite institutionally, the outbreak and Moody's revivals were moments for northern and southern Protestants to join together in common cause. The actions and responses of northern and southern whites during the summer and fall of 1878 suggest that it was a crucial year for solidifying the national consciousness that northern Protestants like Moody, Beecher, and Stowe sought so fervently.

In the decades following the yellow fever epidemic, the Woman's Christian Temperance Union (WCTU), especially its dynamic leader, Frances Willard, helped further cement national reunion by rallying thousands of northern and southern white women in a common cause. WCTU leaders in the 1880s and 1890s hoped that, by casting their crusade as a holy war against alcohol and the mistreatment of women and children, they could unify white women from all over the nation. Encouraging northern and southern women to forget the bitterness and pain of the Civil War, Willard endeavored not only to create a national temperance organization, but also to lead women of both sections into third-party politics. To her, temperance stood as the only means to destroy the twin demons of sectional animosity and sectional politicking. Largely because of her efforts, the WCTU became the largest women's organization in the United States and one of the only reform organizations in the country to maintain a genuinely national constituency. By the turn of the century, it boasted a membership of almost two hundred thousand women from the North and the South. At national conventions and local meetings, in their correspondence and their diaries, white women in the WCTU proclaimed that they had obtained a new sense of national solidarity through their religious battle against the saloon and the drunkard.

Temperance reform, the yellow fever outbreak, and the Great Awakening were crucial to remaking the American nation in the late nineteenth century. They helped forge a new national identity that eased the pain of the Civil War and ameliorated deep-seated sectional bitterness. As geographer Benedict Anderson and other theorists have shown, "nations" are "imagined political communities," in which individuals experience a sense of shared identity with one another and commitment to one another. To Anderson, feelings of "deep, horizontal comradeship" stand as the hallmark of national solidarity. In the post–Civil War United States, Beecher's preaching, Stowe's writing, Moody's revivals, the medical epidemic of 1878, and the rise of the WCTU helped create that type of American identity among whites. Religious revivals, benevolence, common suffering, and religious reform provided many of the needed opportunities for northern whites to imagine former Confederates as equal partners in the nation and to treat them as such.[21]

National reconciliation, however, did not only entail the forgiveness of southern whites. Forgetting and abandoning commitments to racial justice were essential to the remaking of the white republic. Rejecting the civic nationalism of the mid-1860s, northern Protestant leaders and ideologies played a critical role in the resurrection of an ethnic nationalism of whiteness. Drawing upon white supremacist doctrines that had been prevalent in the antebellum North and seeking to forge stronger ties with former Confederates, the northern apostles of national forgiveness explicitly rejected racial equality and depicted African Americans as social, cultural, and religious aliens in the nation. In the early 1870s, white Protestants withdrew spiritual, economic, and political support from African Americans, and Beecher and Stowe justified this retreat by asserting that black Americans could best serve the United States as a permanent laboring underclass. Moody accepted race-based segregation at his revivals and thereby offered religious legitimacy to Jim Crow. Amid the virulent epidemic of 1878, northern and southern whites generally denied relief to southern blacks, and systematic medical negligence resulted in the deaths of countless African Americans. Finally, leaders of the WCTU undermined rights for African Americans and lent their moral authority against immigrants and Catholics. In an effort to win the vote for white women and expand their political power, white temperance organizers demonized African Americans and immigrants as unworthy of national citizenship. Some WCTU leaders even hoped that people of color would emigrate from the United States to nations that would more readily accept them. Ultimately, the legacy of racial prejudice in the North and the desires of northern white Protestants to reach out to southern whites in the 1870s, 1880s, and 1890s led them to repudiate their Civil War–era commitments to building an integrated nation of racial equality. By the end of the century, most white Protestants not only accepted racial segregation and disfranchisement, but also sanctified them as part of God's divine order for the nation. Racial justice had been crucified at the altar of white reunion.

This religiously inspired postwar nationalism played a vital role in the rise of the American global empire in the 1880s and 1890s. National reconciliation at home and imperial efforts abroad had a dialectical relationship. Reunion enabled the United States to focus its energies on foreign lands and in turn created stronger feelings of national identity at home, and northern white Protestants were pivotal in the outward and militaristic thrust of the nation. During the Gilded Age, they committed themselves to "the evangelization of the world in this generation" and, in the process, diverted their eyes from problems in the South and toward global militarism and domination. Missionary organizations encouraged American political leaders to intervene in the affairs of other nations and provided the American public with intensely racialized views of foreign peoples. When the United States went to war against the Spanish Empire in 1898, white Protestants were some of the most rabid jingoists. They hailed the war as the Lord's way of solidifying post–Civil War national solidarity. Missionary idioms and rhetoric, moreover, supplied top-ranking politicians and writers, including President William McKinley, Senator Albert Beveridge, Theodore Roosevelt, and novelist Thomas Dixon Jr., with a *lingua franca* for national reconciliation and imperialism. The War of 1898 stood as the culmination of the postbellum reforging of the white republic, a nation whose imperialism was ordained by God. By the turn of the century, the radical civic nationalism of the 1860s had been almost completely destroyed. The vast majority of whites, whether they endorsed imperialism or opposed it, agreed that whiteness was a prerequisite for national citizenship—and therefore African Americans and people of color in Cuba and the Philippines could not be full-fledged "Americans."

The epilogue examines the conflation of whiteness, American nationalism, Protestant Christianity, and global imperialism in a variety of writings at the turn of the century, especially Arthur Bird's utopian novel *Looking Forward*, written immediately after the War of 1898, and Edward Bellamy's *Equality: A Novel*. These works show how drastically northern whites' racial and national imaginations had shifted from the end of the Civil War. Bird imagined that the United States would conquer the entire Western Hemisphere, that differences between northerners and southerners would be completely obliterated, that missionaries would spread the gospel of Protestant Christianity and American capitalism throughout the world, and that all people of color would be relegated to Venezuela. Like Edward Bellamy, who also imagined a segregated utopia, Bird presented an image of the nation that resonated with countless northern whites. Unlike the radical ministers and missionaries of the mid-1860s, Bird mirrored the prevailing sentiments of northern white Protestants in conceiving of whiteness as the supreme measure of national identity and citizenship. The hopes for a nation of sectional and racial fraternity in Giles's 1867 print had been thoroughly defeated and erased. An America of sacred white supremacy and global aspirations had been born.

III

Reforging the White Republic is not just concerned with the attitudes and actions of northern white Protestants. Southern whites and African Americans were also essential to and influenced by the process of reunion. Each chapter and the epilogue, therefore, includes the responses of southern whites and African Americans to national events. By and large, southern whites continued to maintain a cultural commitment to Confederate nationalism in the years following the war, and only embraced American nationalism when their understanding of race relations was nationalized. They venerated the "Lost Cause"—the belief that God was with the South even though it had failed to prevail during the military conflict—and refused to accept national reconciliation as long as northern whites demanded apologies for slavery or secession. Southern whites defied, often violently, any attempts to alter race relations in the South, and they were deeply committed to restricting African American independence. The white South surrendered its plans for an independent nation in 1865, but it refused to allow the North to dictate the terms of the peace. Only as northern whites rejected their plans for radically reforming the nation, honored the ghosts of the southern lost cause, and promoted second-class status for African Americans did white southerners en masse embrace offers for national reunion. By the turn of the century, southern whites had few problems squaring their southern-ness with their American-ness, because white supremacy had become a national faith.

At the same time, the effects of sectional reunion and the rise of an American "empire" were disastrous for African Americans and people of color throughout the world. White racism was an intensely moral issue that had spiritual ramifications for many African Americans. As W. E. B. Du Bois told students at the Philadelphia Divinity School in 1907, American prejudice and greed were moral and spiritual problems at their core. Racism "is a problem not simply of political expediency, [or] of economic success," he lectured, "but a problem above all of religious and social life; and it carries with it not simply a demand for its own solution, but beneath it lies the whole question of the real intent of our civilization: Is this civilization of the United States Christian?"[22]

To black leaders like Du Bois, racism, segregation, lynching, and imperialism proved that the American nation was anything but Christian. African Americans served as the most astute and brilliant critics of the spiritual state of the nation and repeatedly highlighted connections between northern Protestantism, sectional reconciliation, and the formation of an American nationalism premised upon whiteness. Black leaders created an oppositional discourse that turned the trope of America's "Christian nationhood" against whites. Depicting civil rights as a sacred obligation, denouncing Jim Crow as anti-Christian, railing against the silence of white Protestant leaders over racial injustice, and condemning racial violence as immoral, these African Americans drew upon and constructed their own interpretations of Christianity to combat racism. They upheld a social gospel that prized justice, liberty, and equality. They assailed racial disfranchisement and violence whether within the United States or perpetuated by the U.S. government throughout the world. From leaders like Frederick Douglass, Frances E. W. Harper, Alexander Crummell, W. E. B. Du Bois, and Ida B. Wells to untutored sharecroppers and anonymous poets, African Americans censured northern Protestants for accepting reunion with southern whites and failing to defend the rights of people of color. Du Bois carried these arguments and a commitment to civic nationalism into the twentieth century, serving as the leading opponent of the conflation of whiteness, Protestant Christianity, and American nationalism. For Du Bois and for many other black Americans, religious faith was not merely a "haven in a heartless world" or a shield of defense. Religion provided eloquent tools of resistance with which they endeavored to stave off the reforging of the white republic. Their lack of success was not due to a lack of effort. The authority of white religious leaders was simply too great, and the appeal to white solidarity too powerful.[23]

Reforging the White Republic, then, tells one part of the story of how the two belligerent "nations" of the Civil War reunited and took up an imperialistic enterprise in less than four decades. It is a tale of how most northern whites abandoned their Civil War–era pledge to "die to make men free" in Julia Ward Howe's "Battle Hymn of the Republic" in favor of the War of 1898's "white man's burden" that warned against calling too loudly for freedom and characterized peoples of color as "half devil and half child." It is a tale of how whites claimed a new national solidarity at the expense of racial reform, how ministers and politicians marshaled religious and white supremacist rhetoric in order to wield social power, and how imperialism wrapped itself in sacred cloth. Authorized and sanctified by Protestantism, whiteness and American nationalism once again became powerfully knotted together in the years following the Civil War, and neither American Protestantism, nor the United States, has yet to be redeemed from this legacy.

But a tale of dissent also runs throughout these pages. The voices of opposition to the white republic were never silenced completely. In subtle and not-so-subtle ways, thousands of African Americans consistently challenged white reunion and racial inequality. They forced white supremacists to refashion and repackage their racist ideologies and arguments. The defiance of these blacks and that of their few loyal white friends demonstrated that national reconciliation without racial justice was not inevitable. Avenues and ideas of racial equality could have been followed. An America of interracial harmony and fraternity, as imagined by J. L. Giles in 1867, could have been born. Listening to the voices of religious protest is a way to hear anew the "note of warning," as William Dean Howells put it, in Rudyard Kipling's "The White Man's Burden":

> Be all ye will or whisper,
> Be all ye leave or do,
> The silent sullen peoples
> Shall weigh your God and you.[24]

Black leaders like Du Bois may have been sullen, but they were certainly not silent. The image of a weeping God haunted Du Bois's *Black Reconstruction in America* as it does this book. Giles's vision has yet to be realized. Vestiges of Griffith's nation still remain. Whiteness, godliness, and American nationalism continue to be deeply ingrained in the imaginations of many Americans. The light of liberation has yet to pierce the darkness of discrimination.

1

THE LAST AND GREATEST BATTLE OF FREEDOM

Race and the American Nation after the Assassination of Abraham Lincoln

Northerners had little to celebrate on Easter Sunday in 1865. A day usually set aside for cheer became an occasion for mourning and sorrow. New York City was draped in black, and newspapers printed thick black lines around their columns to express their grief. Countless churches, businesses, and homes were covered with funeral cloth, while businessmen joined children in the streets to weep. On Good Friday two days earlier, an assassin had cut down President Abraham Lincoln.[1] The savior of the Union and the liberator of the slaves was now dead. The North had lost so many soldiers over the past four years of devastating civil war. Now it had lost its leader. Herman Melville attempted to describe the passionate and conflicted feelings he and numerous others felt and to put the assassination into cosmic perspective in his poem "The Martyr" (1866):

> Good Friday was the day
> Of the prodigy and crime,
> When they killed him in his pity,
> When they killed him in his prime
> . . . .
> He lieth in his blood—
> The father in his face;
> They have killed him, the Forgiver—
> The Avenger takes his place,
> The Avenger wisely stern,
> Who in righteousness shall do
> What the heavens call him to,
> And the patricides remand;
> For they killed him in his kindness
> In their madness and their blindness,
> And his blood is on their hand.

> There is sobbing of the strong,
>   And a pall upon the land;
> But the People in their weeping
>   Bare the iron hand;
> Beware the People weeping
> When they bare the iron hand.[2]

For African Americans, the assassination was particularly devastating. Upon hearing of Lincoln's assassination, one freed man in Charleston, South Carolina, directly connected the death of the president with that of Jesus Christ: "Lincoln died for we, Christ died for we, and me believe him de same mans."[3] When the news of Lincoln's death reached a convention of African Methodist Episcopal ministers in Ohio, the men wept "like children." One attendee reported, "There never was such an hour in the history of our Church. God grant we may never see the like again."[4] A black poet gave voice to the sadness and anger of many African Americans in a poem printed in the *Christian Recorder*:

> I cannot write, my heart's too full of grief,
> Because the dastard's hand has slain our honored Chief
> Him whom the nation loved, it now must mourn,
> And the avenging rod throughout the land be borne.[5]

The North's most prominent black leader, Frederick Douglass, felt especially troubled. Preaching at a memorial service in Rochester, New York, he told his audience that it was "a day for silence and meditation; for grief and tears." Like so many others, he was bewildered by the dizzying array of recent events: the collapse of the Confederacy; General Robert E. Lee's surrender only days earlier; Lincoln's death; and the attacks upon Secretary of State William Seward and his son that also occurred on the night of April 14. Amid the trauma and confusion, however, Douglass proclaimed that the North could take solace in one fact: it had achieved a newfound solidarity. "To-day, to-day as never before this North is a unit," he announced. This eloquent former slave was not merely interested in alleviating the pains of his audience. By 1865, he had become a savvy political orator, and he recognized that the emotions generated by the assassination could be directed to generate greater concern for racial justice. Douglass offered a providential interpretation of John Wilkes Booth's crime, maintaining that God permitted the evil deed to warn the Union against forgiving Confederates too quickly. "The inscrutable wisdom of Him who controls the destinies of Nations" allowed Booth to slay Lincoln, Douglass contended. God desired to teach the North. It must punish the rebellious South and bring full liberation and equality to African Americans. "Let us not be in too much haste in the work of restoration," Douglass thundered. "Let us not be in a hurry to clasp to our bosom that spirit which gave birth to Booth." Instead, the North must complete the work it had started with emancipation. It must maintain the alliance it had forged with people of color during the Civil War. It must reward African Americans for their loyalty and discipline southern whites for their disloyalty. "Let us not remember our enemies and disfranchise our friends," he concluded.[6]

Douglass was not alone in calling Yankees to support greater rights for African Americans and to endorse severe punishments for Confederates. A significant number of northern ministers and politicians declared that the war had not ended with Lee's surrender or Lincoln's death. Justice was still to be meted out. For them, a strict and stern punishment was in order. Slaveholding, secession, and now the assassination of Lincoln provided evidence that southern whites needed to feel the chastening rod. While several leading northerners advocated the executions of chief Confederates, a small group of ministers, journalists, and artists maintained that southern whites were in fact not "white" at all, but a "race" separate from and inferior to Yankees. For this group, Confederate disloyalty and rebellion indicated that they had no place in the national fraternity and that they should be relegated to second-class citizenship.

At the same time, a number of ministers joined the radical Republicans in demanding a complete transformation of the nation with regard to people of color. A cadre of Yankee preachers championed the cause of civil rights for freedpeople, inveighing with all of their moral might against prejudice and racism. Rejecting and even ridiculing scientific and theological claims that whites and blacks constituted separate species, they encouraged northern whites to recognize the "universal brotherhood of man." These ministers characterized their martyred president as a friend to all humanity, hoping that their parishioners would follow Lincoln's alleged egalitarianism. Ultimately, these ministers articulated a growing conviction in the North that inclusion in the national body should be based on beliefs and principals, specifically on commitments to the Union, rather than on whiteness or blackness.

Religious arguments for racial justice did a great deal to further radicalize the North, and leading newspapers, magazines, and politicians drew upon biblical justifications for civil rights and universal manhood suffrage. In turn, people of color reveled in the belief that a new day had dawned in the nation. They commented widely upon the ways in which religious leaders and ideologies were propelling the North to assail the bulwarks of prejudice. The end of the war, they believed, had ushered in a brand new nation, one that included them as full citizens. Southern whites, alternatively, recognized that a more radical North appeared to be emerging and braced themselves for a new attack. They were prepared to continue to defy the North and the federal government.

Frederick Douglass was wrong about one point. The North did not become "a unit" after Lincoln's death—religiously or politically. In the days, weeks, and months after that fateful night at Ford's Theatre, a small but vocal group of northern white pastors and politicians argued against punishing the South. These advocates of reconciliation—some of whom were Democrats, while others were Republicans—constructed memories of Lincoln as a forgiving martyr who in death atoned for the sins of the South and the nation. They did not challenge the whiteness of Confederates, but hoped instead that southern whites would be quickly received into the postwar nation.

Divisions among the Protestant clergy reflected and exacerbated a much larger political and social fracture in the Civil War North. During the sectional division, competing factions had emerged within both the Democratic and Republican parties over the course of the war and the procedures for Reconstruction. Although Democrats split between "purists," who generally opposed the war, and "legitimists," who were willing to align with conservative Republicans and to work for a Union victory, the Democrats almost unanimously called for a quick reconciliation with the South when the war was over. In unison, they also denounced the extension of political rights to African Americans. "This is a white man's government" and "the Union as it was; the Constitution as it is," served as their dual rallying cries.[7]

Republicans failed to offer a united front in opposition to the Democrats. In grappling with wartime Reconstruction of the South, the Republican Party feuded over a host of issues, including whether President Lincoln or Congress had the legal and constitutional authority to direct the process, how stern the punishment of Confederates should be, and how far the federal government should proceed in supporting the freedpeople. The "moderate" Republicans generally hoped to give southern blacks enough rights to become free laborers, but not so many privileges that southern whites would be enraged. In their effort to bring the South back into the Union quickly, the moderates committed themselves to political expediency, rather than principles of civil rights for former slaves. They were willing to compromise parts of their program in order to gain enough votes to pass specific pieces of legislation. The "radical" Republicans, who drew much of their support from the abolitionists, were far more interested in completely transforming the

South. By and large, they wanted to punish Confederates for their disloyalty, confiscate some of their property to distribute to people of color, and empower African Americans throughout the country with equal rights before the law. The radicals were committed to assuring that African Americans had a meaningful role in the postbellum government, regardless of how southern whites felt about it. Congressman Thaddeus Stevens may not have spoken for all radicals when he proclaimed that "the whole fabric of southern society *must* be changed," but the belief that the South should be substantively overhauled was a common one among radicals.[8]

When Lincoln was murdered in April of 1865, however, neither Congress nor the new president, Andrew Johnson, had the ability to articulate their vision for Reconstruction before northern ministers and editors had their say. Congress would not convene until December 1865, while Johnson did not pronounce any semblance of a coherent plan for Reconstruction until late May 1865. In the immediate aftermath of Lincoln's assassination, the battle over the place of southern whites and freedpeople in the postwar nation was waged in the churches and the press. The struggle for the northern conscience was, in part, a religious one that pitted pastor against pastor, congregation against congregation, and northerner against northerner. Ultimately, the northern response to Lincoln's assassination demonstrated just how fractured the white republic had become by the end of the war, as the northern public wrangled over who would constitute the nation. As African American author Paul Laurence Dunbar put it regarding the end of the war, "It was not flesh and blood, but soul and spirit that counted now."[9]

I

Unlike any other moment of the nineteenth century, the days and weeks following Lincoln's assassination provided northern pastors unprecedented opportunities to offer their moral guidance to the people. Northerners flocked to their houses of worship on Easter Sunday, April 16, seeking explanations for the tragedy and hope for the future. "An Easter Sunday unlike I have seen," penned New York lawyer and diarist George Templeton Strong. "Trinity [Church] was never filled so full. . . . The crowd packed the aisles tight and even occupied the choir steps and the choir itself nearly to the chancel rails."[10] The *Cincinnati Gazette* noted that many churches in the city were filled "almost to suffocation."[11] On two subsequent national days of prayer and fasting, April 23 and June 1, Yankees once again packed their churches to honor the martyred president. Hundreds of Troy, New York, residents attended services every day for two weeks after the calamity, and New England Congregationalist George Walker recorded in his diary that "[a] full hall & attentive audience" filled his church on several days in late April.[12]

Millions of northerners, moreover, paid their respects for Lincoln and heard eulogies while they observed his body as it traveled by train from Washington, D.C., to Springfield, Illinois. Sociologist Barry Schwartz has recently suggested that the ritualization of Lincoln's death through sermons and specifically through the funeral procession elevated him into the pantheon of America's civil religion. Lincoln became more than a beloved leader. He was now venerated as a sacred figure.[13] Religion seemed to be everywhere in mid-April, even affecting the stock market. When news of the assassination reached Wall Street on Saturday, April 15, 1865, "all business was stopped," and the brokers joined together in prayer to ask God for help. One merchant remarked, "For forty years . . . I have been in Wall Street, but this is the first time I ever heard it praying!"[14]

Whether during Easter commemorations or more regular Sunday ceremonies, the climactic moment of northern Protestant worship services was "the sermon," and this was never more true than in the days and weeks following that fateful night at Ford's Theatre. Most nineteenth-century ministers considered the sermon their most potent weapon in shaping the lives of their parishioners and in driving public discourse. Since the Protestant Reformation in the sixteenth century, the sermon stood as the central element of Protestant worship.[15] While music, scripture readings, and prayers served as moments when Protestants enacted their belief in God and their status as "His people," sermons instilled personal growth and enrichment. Preachers motivated their audiences to follow Christ; they inspired their parishioners to make right social and political choices; and, ultimately, they shaped public debates, moods, and emotions.[16]

Nineteenth-century professors of homiletics explicitly instructed theology students to focus their energies on their sermons. All the elements of the Sabbath discourse should be honed, the professors insisted, from the appropriate placement of texts to the proper methods of breathing. "The preparation and delivery of sermons is in fact to be the great business of his life," wrote Daniel P. Kidder, professor of preaching at the Garrett Biblical Institute in Evanston, Illinois. "*Preaching must be the GREAT business of all who would wield the power of the pulpit.*"[17] Other ministers and professors agreed with Kidder. Even those generally opposed to "political sermonizing," such as Austin Phelps, professor of homiletics at Andover Theological Seminary for more than three decades, viewed the sermon as a powerful, indeed revolutionary, tool: "Its genius is that of practical agitation and change. It is transforming and subversive, it is revolutionary. It cometh to send a sword on earth. Its destiny is to overturn and overturn and overturn."[18]

Many sermons, especially those responding to Lincoln's assassination, had impacts that extended far beyond the walls of chapels and churches. Published in newspapers, pamphlets, and book collections, post-assassination sermons became part of a broad nineteenth-century Protestant print culture that shaped public discourse and ultimately helped to create what historian Richard Brown has called an "informed citizenry." These ministers believed that the reading of religious literature could instill proper virtues into American citizens. To maintain a powerful cultural voice in the growing and expanding nation, Protestants of the nineteenth century put an enormous amount of time, energy, and capital into publishing and distributing books, tracts, and journals. Printed sermons proliferated and were often reprinted in secular periodicals.[19] After Lincoln's death, for instance, countless newspapers carried sermons and hundreds of the ministers' discourses were transformed into pamphlets at the express desire of a local congregation. "The secular press never acknowledged God so distinctly as now," gloried Presbyterian Robert Sample. Everywhere, "public proclamations and official dispatches record His name."[20]

Ministers, editors, and congregants sought not only to memorialize Lincoln's death by printing these sermons, but also to assert their interpretations of the tragic event over northern society. Members of C. B. Crane's Hartford Baptist Church praised their minister for capturing the social mood: "[F]ully endorsing the sentiments of the discourse, we respectfully solicit a copy for the press, believing that its circulation in a permanent form will subserve [sic] the interests of justice and freedom."[21] Another group wrote to their minister that "a large and intelligent congregation of citizens" approved of his sermon. They hoped that wider publication would "shape the popular opinion."[22] One publishing editor acknowledged this point in a preface to a compilation of New York sermons after Lincoln's assassination. "[T]his volume treasures up the utterances of those who were the mouth-pieces of the people," he maintained, "and thus conveys to the readers of the future a better idea of the wonderful effects produced on the national heart."[23]

Because sermons functioned as instruments of persuasion, they served as a battleground for competing ideas and visions of the American nation.[24] Pastors offered a variety of conflicting interpretations of how northerners should view the defeated South. Some ministers, who endorsed the radical Republican hopes to punish the South, pinned the blame for Lincoln's assassination squarely on the shoulders of the Confederacy. Dubbed the "Bloodhounds of Zion" by the

Democratic *Easton-Sentinel* of Pennsylvania, these clerics interpreted Lincoln's assassination as God's divine call for vengeance.[25] Preaching in Brooklyn's South Presbyterian Church, Samuel Spear recommended a stern punishment for Confederates. "I would hang them by the neck till they are dead," he exclaimed, "and keep hanging the leading rebels till justice in this form had fully met the demands and wants of the public safety."[26] Other ministers, like Buffalo's Joel Bingham, condemned the South for wartime atrocities and the evils of slavery.[27] For some, hopes for violent reprisals did not abate even after the initial shock of the assassination wore off. Claiming to be in a "calmer mood" than he had been on Easter, Illinois Presbyterian preacher Isaac Carey commented, "I find myself unwilling to take back or modify the strong language then used or the sentiments then expressed." Carey clearly invoked sectional hatred. "[T]he blood of a hundred thousand rebels," he thundered, "would not atone" for the president's death.[28] For these ministers, the wrathful God of the Old Testament reigned supreme and demanded retributive justice.

Pastors such as Carey, Bingham, and Spear interpreted Lincoln's death in ways similar to Frederick Douglass. They maintained that God had permitted the assassination for two main reasons. First, the president had completed his divine mission of "saving the Union." Lincoln's death, they assumed, merely meant that he would make his way to paradise sooner than they had expected. Second, they claimed that God intended the assassination as a note of warning to the North. It should not forgive the South too quickly, for the Lord desired to punish Confederates for disunion and slavery.[29] George Templeton Strong, a moderate Republican who was more interested in sound currency and protective tariffs than justice for freedpeople, recounted that he found this interpretation compelling when his minister voiced it. "He [Reverend Vinton] brought out clearly the thought that had occurred to me and to many others," Strong penned in his diary. "Perhaps Lincoln had done his appointed work; his honesty, sagacity, kindliness, and singleness of purpose had united the North and secured the suppression of rebellion. Perhaps the time has come for something beside kindliness, mercy, and forbearance, even for vengeance and judgment."[30]

In an effort to prove that southerners did not deserve full national citizenship, some northerners went so far as to depict Confederates as fundamentally alien from northern whites. Rejecting the antebellum ethnic nationalism that privileged whiteness, these northerners offered a revised ethnic nationalism that redrew racial lines in order to exclude rebellious southerners. For the New School Presbyterian Reverend Charles Robinson of Brooklyn, taking Lincoln's life confirmed that

Confederates constituted a different "race" than Yankees. "Talk to me no more of the same race, educated at the same colleges, born of the same blood," he fumed. The stain of murder irrevocably tainted Confederates with a collective guilt that transformed their essential nature in Robinson's estimation. He underscored his racialized and religious understanding of America's national identity by describing the sectional difference with a cosmic metaphor. "Satan was of the same race as Gabriel," he maintained, "and educated at the same celestial school of love and grace; but one became a rebel, and between them ever thereafter was 'a great gulf fixed.'" The southerner, Robinson concluded, "cannot be brother of mine, [for] he belongs to no race of mine." Robinson's comparison of Confederates to the Prince of Darkness, his insistence that southern whites had different "blood" than northern whites, and his claim that a "fixed" gulf separated them suggest that his use of the word "race" was not merely a synonym for "nations" or "peoples." [31] The demon Satan and the angel Gabriel were immutably, essentially, and permanently different. Like Lucifer, Confederates had earned expulsion from the sacred community because of their rebellion and had been transformed in the process. They now belonged to a netherworld of spiritual, racial, and national otherness. [32]

Robinson was not alone in describing Yankees and Confederates as different in "blood" or in associating Lincoln's opponents with demonic forces. Several artists, for instance, portrayed either Booth or Confederate president Jefferson Davis in the company of the devil. (See figures 2 and 3.) In the South during the Civil War, several writers had promoted the theory that northern and southern whites were two separate races with separate historical lineages. The irascible southern diarist Mary Chesnut clearly viewed Yankees as an ethnic group that differed from southern whites and from immigrants when she wrote in 1864, "In all these years [of the war] I have seen no Yankees. All the prisoners, well or wounded, have been Germans, Scotch regiments, Irish regiments—most Germans, however." Discussions of racial differences between northerners and southerners gained currency within the Confederacy during the first two years of the war, but faded as the battle continued. [33]

But in the North at the end of the war, several northerners portrayed southerners as racially different. In two prints from *Frank Leslie's Illustrated Newspaper* of New York, artists employed a variety of gender-, race-, and class-based images to depict Confederates as uncivilized barbarians who did not belong in the national community. Confederate president Jefferson Davis became an especially poignant symbol of Confederate depravity after he was captured, allegedly disguised in women's clothing. Effeminizing Davis with a bonnet and skirt, northerners not only gloated over their victory, but also contradicted claims of southern martial mastery and manhood.[34] The features on his face and head connoted rebelliousness, lack of civilization, and ultimately racial inferiority. Contrasted with an image of Union general Benjamin Butler in *Harper's Weekly,* the *Frank Leslie's Illustrated* print clearly depicted Davis as not white. While Butler's face appeared smooth and his hair and mustache groomed, Davis had deep lines on his elongated and simianized face. He had an extended brow and nose, and his hair was disheveled. The image of southern women in another caricature from *Frank Leslie's Illustrated* indicated similar notions of southerners' barbarity. These women were clearly impoverished. Some lacked shoes, and some wore tattered dresses. Rioting over bread, they broke windows and wielded sticks, knives, and pistols while they stood defiantly or crouched mischievously in opposition to law and order. Like the image of Davis, their faces had deep lines and they appeared belligerent. Davis and these women looked similar to the depictions of nineteenth-century Irish men and women that racialized them as nonwhite.[35] Seen as racially inferior and culturally alien, Confederates had lost all control of themselves and their society—so much so, in fact, that their men dressed like women and their women behaved like men. (See figures 4, 5, and 6.)

Several northern journalists who toured the South immediately after the war also described southerners as biologically and morally inferior to northern whites. Traveling throughout Georgia and the Carolinas to observe political and social conditions, New England journalist Sidney Andrews perceived southern bodies as revealing degenerate internal qualities. In an observation that resonated with the works of some nineteenth-century scientists who suggested that differences in the sizes and shapes of men's and women's skulls proved that white men were innately more intelligent than white women and people of color, Andrews viewed the "heads" of men in the South Carolina state legislature to be indicative of their mental deficiencies. "The average Southern head," he wrote, "doesn't show near as much intellectual force and vigor as the average Northern head." At other moments, he referred to southerners as inherently lazy and barbarous, tropes that were commonly used to denigrate African Americans and Irish immigrants.[36]

Notions of racial difference between northerners and southerners persisted into the late nineteenth century, although they took no systematized fashion. In 1868, Gertrude Thomas of Georgia recorded listening to a lecture in which "Mr Adams defines the characteristics of the Northern people to be 'cold cautious and thoughtful.' Those of the South to be 'warm impulsive and impetuous.'" As late as the 1880s, the editor of the *Louisville Courier-Journal,* Henry Watterson, lamented that many northerners and southerners had viewed and continued to view one another as separate peoples. "For my own part," he told a group of bankers, "I have never believed in isothermal lines, air-lines, and water-lines separating distinct races. I no more believe that the river yonder, dividing Indiana and Kentucky, marks off two distinct species than I believe that the great Hudson, marks off distinct species." Watterson's explicit rejection of ideas that environmental peculiarities of the North and the South had spawned two separate races showed that such conceptions retained some degree of currency even after the Civil War. In the days immediately following Lincoln's assassination, descriptions of Confederates and Yankees as distinct races stood as perhaps the most powerful means to maintain sectional animosities and to bar southern whites from full national inclusion.[37]

But not all northern Protestants disputed the whiteness of Confederates or even believed that southerners should be kept out of the national body for very long. Several ministers who came from a variety of political backgrounds defied the assertions of southern separateness and stressed brotherhood instead. They wanted the past forgotten and Confederates quickly readmitted into the national body. They sought to heal sectional wounds, rather than aggravate them. Abolitionist-turned-moderate Henry Ward Beecher, one of the most influential nineteenth-century preachers, sympathized with the South and denounced the advocates of retribution. "The idea of emphasizing the warning against treason by the execution of one or two men . . . when every other family in those states is broken up . . . is preposterous," he declared.[38] Lutheran and Democrat J. G. Butler concluded his Easter sermon by asking God "to forgive, to heal, to help, and bind in one common brotherhood all the states of this Union."[39] Other pastors made similar appeals. Methodist John McClintock pleaded for peace by depicting Lincoln as a Christ-like figure whose blood had washed away the nation's sins. If "anything that you read or hear in these sad days, breeds within you a single revengeful feeling, even towards the leaders of this rebellion," he proclaimed, "then think of Abraham Lincoln, and pray God to make you merciful. Think of the prayer of Christ, which the President said, after his Saviour, 'Father, forgive them, they know not what they do.'"[40] Even one African American minister invoked clemency. Jacob Thomas of New York encouraged his congregation to think of the "Great Emancipator" as a prince of peace: "One of the most prominent features in the character of our departed friend was his merciful disposition even toward his foes."[41] Like northern Democrats who hoped that the North would now spread "a Broad mantle of mercy" over the South, Beecher, Butler, McClintock, and Thomas thought that there had been enough carnage. To them, Lincoln's death was an atoning sacrifice that should serve to end all hostilities.[42]

Still another group of clerics either admitted that they could not determine the cosmic meaning of Lincoln's death, or claimed that forces other than sectional hatred were at work. Some asserted that Booth's career had impaired his moral judgment and led him to commit the heinous deed. Since he was an actor, they maintained, Booth had difficulty distinguishing reality from fantasy. This confusion warped his mind and led him to believe that his actions were part of a new performance. "That one word 'theatrical' explains it all," claimed Reverend Thomas Laurie. "No other could express such commingled wickedness and insensibility."[43] Pennsylvania's Robert Sample lamented, "God deals strangely with the State. We do not know His purpose, and cannot see the wisdom which has permitted the sad event we mourn to-day. Moreover, we do not know the relation which one event sustains to another, or the influence which one nation is designed to exert upon another."[44] Another minister told his New York congregation that he did not know the meaning of the events: "[M]ysterious are the ways of Providence."[45] These Protestant leaders heard no authoritative decree from heaven and offered no moral guidance to their parishioners. These were not admissions of ignorance so much as they were acceptances of divine mysteries.

II

The debate over whether to treat Confederates with leniency or severity continued to rage into May, June, and July of 1865, especially after President Andrew Johnson clarified his plan for Reconstruction, which favored the quick and easy readmission of the southern states. Of the Protestant denominations, northern Methodists and Congregationalists leveled the most vehement attacks against the South, although these two denominations had quite different relationships with southern whites before and during the war. The vast majority of Congregational churches were located in New England, and their association with abolitionism and liberal theology meant that they failed to garner a large following in the South. Because they had a very limited ecclesiastical history with southern whites and because many of their parishioners were committed to emancipation, they had little to lose and much to gain by denouncing the Confederate South. Northern Methodists, in contrast, had hundreds of thousands of denominational brethren below the Mason-Dixon Line. But from the 1840s to the time of the Civil War, interactions with southerners had become increasingly contentious. In 1844, the denomination split over slavery and a battle for the allegiance of the border states commenced. Northern Methodists became increasingly aggravated that they had lost control over the property rights to churches in the South. During the war, Methodist editors repeatedly referred to the southern church as "this degenerate, bastard Methodism" and looked to "disintegrate and absorb" the southern congregations. When the federal government allowed northern Methodist preachers to occupy the pulpits of disloyal southern Methodists, the northerners jumped at the chance. They took over Methodist churches in New Orleans, Charleston, Nashville, Memphis, Baton Rouge, and several other locations. In some cases, they refused to return the churches to southerners even after the South had surrendered.[46]

Hopes for punishing Confederates were high within northern Methodist and Congregational circles during the months following Lincoln's assassination. On April 20, the central Methodist weekly, the *Christian Advocate and Journal*, commented, "We hope hereafter to hear much less of public clemency toward public enemies than we have heard for some weeks past. It is quite time that the enemies of law and government should be taught, and, through their punishment, the whole nation learn, that treason is a crime to be punished by the judges."[47] In early June, the journal maintained its predictions of sectional discord: "The war may be ended, but our troubles are not. The rebels have laid down their arms, but the great majority of them are mailed with sharp prejudice and bitter hatred."[48] The Congregationalist *New York Independent* agreed with the Methodist journal. As some southern states passed laws in July and August that restricted African American liberties—the infamous black codes—the *Independent* warned against mercy: "From every quarter of the South comes a warning to the people of the North against a too rapid and a too lenient process of reconstruction. The evidence that the rebels, though conquered, are not subdued, and that their hearts are rankling with hatred to their conquerors and hostility to the emancipated slaves, is overwhelming."[49]

Unlike the Methodists and Congregationalists, the northern Old School Presbyterians were far more inclined to favor a speedy national restoration. They met calls for sectional enmity with appeals for reconciliation. Although the Presbyterian Church had splintered into several groups during the antebellum era, it was not until the Civil War that any of the divisions were accomplished strictly along sectional lines. The denominational spilt of 1837 into "New School" and "Old School" branches had resulted in the majority of southern Presbyterians entering the Old School ranks. But they were not without their northern allies. There were many Old School Presbyterian churches in the North, and most of the faculty of the Princeton Theological Seminary stood firmly by the Old School branch. Old Schoolers believed that the church should remain separate from the realm of politics and other "worldly" affairs. They held fast to the "doctrine of the spirituality of the church" and the belief that slavery, "like the family relations, was a divine institution." Only when the Civil War made intersectional fraternity nearly impossible did the Old School denomination split along sectional lines, and when the war was over, some northern Old Schoolers saw no reason to remain enemies.[50]

Several northern Old School Presbyterians sought to reforge their relationships with southern Presbyterians, but they insisted that southern whites repent for the sins of secession and slaveholding. Preaching in June, Henry Boardman believed that northern Christians and leaders must help ameliorate antagonisms. "It is the province of the minister of the gospel," he claimed, "to interpose at such a crisis, and by an appeal to the spirit of our merciful religion, to deprecate all unjustifiable violence in dealing with the revolted States." For Boardman, the nation needed more "Peace-Makers" and fewer troublemakers.[51] In this milieu, some northern Presbyterians endeavored to reunite their sectionally fractured denomination, and in late April, a group of Ohio Presbyterians proclaimed that they were "cordially in favour of reunion of the two branches of the Presbyterian Church."[52] But Old School Presbyterians did not offer forgiveness free and clear. They demanded that if the northern and southern branches of the denomination were to reconcile, southern whites must repent of their wrongs. "[K]indness and a conciliatory spirit were recommended toward the erring," wrote Reverend Samuel Miller, but "[r]epentance neither the state nor political parties demanded, but the church never restored offenders without it, and was to be governed by a simple regard to right far more than to policy."[53]

Southern whites showed little inclination to ask for forgiveness. Neither Confederate defeat nor Lincoln's assassination nor the accusations by northern ministers persuaded them to shed their allegiance to southern society as they knew it. Although some southerners feared that northerners would take revenge upon the South for Lincoln's assassination, most refused to show any remorse for the deceased president. Ministers denied any Confederate responsibility for Booth's actions, and many churchgoers refused to attend memorial services for Lincoln. Although somewhat uncommon, direct defiance and rebelliousness did occur in some southern churches. A minister in Pendleton, South Carolina, for instance, assured his congregation that they "must not despair" over the Confederacy's surrender, for "they would not be conquered—the next generation would see the South *free* and independent."[54] Other southerners may have been less optimistic, but were equally bold. "Though conquered, they are as bitter, proud and arrogant as ever," one northerner in the South wrote. "As to the sentiments of White inhabitants," claimed another Yankee in Virginia, "while they acknowledge themselves whipped and profess future loyalty—all of their feelings are Confederate—Confederate Generals are their heroes—Confederate bravery, and endurance under difficulties, their pride and boast—Confederate dead their martyrs."[55]

Southern denominations were especially aggravated by the punitive and antagonistic attitude they perceived from northerners. The occupation of southern Methodist churches enraged their leaders. The first meeting of the southern Methodist bishops after the war, for instance, denounced "[t]he conduct of certain Northern Methodist bishops and preachers . . . to intrude themselves into several of our house of worship, and in continuing to hold these places." Southern Baptists likewise denied any wrongdoing for slaveholding or for waging a bloody rebellion. Ministers and editors defended the honor of Jefferson Davis, Robert E. Lee, Stonewall Jackson, and other Confederate leaders, while they asserted that they would accept "harmony and conciliation *in the Union*," but "shall ever regard it as a most sacred duty to guard the reputation and cherish the memory of those men who laid down their lives in the Confederate service." Commitments to the Confederacy did not die with the war's end. Clearly, an identity attached to the Confederacy maintained a tight grip on many southerners. A southern civil religion that honored the "ghosts of the Confederacy" was already emerging in the spring of 1865.[56]

The only northern Protestant denomination willing to overlook southern secession and warfare was the Episcopal Church, whose priests and bishops quickly resolved to reunite as one national body after the war. Unlike most northern denominations, the Episcopal Church was not dominated by Republicans. In fact, its leadership and rank-and-file members were far more likely to be members of the Democratic Party.[57] Although the Church had split at the start of the Civil War, many northern and southern Episcopalians sought reunion even during the conflict. In 1862, the northern general convention resolved "to shut no door of reconciliation which is still open, and to afford the best hope that they may be induced to reconsider and retrace their steps, and to renew their relations in Christian love and loyalty, to a common Church and a common country."[58] Even in the wartime environment of bloody mayhem, Episcopal leaders pledged to accept southerners as brethren.

After the collapse of the Confederacy, northern Episcopalians were well positioned to implement their longing for reunion. The leading northern bishop, John H. Hopkins of Vermont, had been a staunch supporter of peace at any cost—before, during, and after the military conflict. As sectional passions had heated up in 1860, members of the denomination had looked to him to quench the fires of discord. Northern Episcopalians hoped that if Hopkins would publish an essay defending slavery with biblical texts, northerners would cease opposing the peculiar institution and the crisis would be averted. As Hopkins's son, John Hopkins Jr. (author of the Christmas hymn "We Three Kings"), wrote later, "[H]is friends thought that the wide circulation of a cheap tract containing the substance of the Bible teaching [on slavery], might do much to cool down the fiery zeal for the abolition of Slavery as the one great Sin of the times, which was a leading element in the mixed cup of the country's dangers."[59] In his subsequent "cheap tract," *Bible View of Slavery,* Hopkins asserted that southerners not only had every religious and moral right to hold African Americans in bondage, but also had the political right to secede from the Union. If America's system of chattel slavery was ordained biblically, it followed that neither statesmen nor Christians should question it.[60] As a leading member of the "American Society for Promoting National Unity" during the Civil War, Hopkins repeatedly asserted that the obligation of the North was to show "brotherly kindness, patience, and an affectionate spirit of conciliation" to southern whites.[61]

At the war's end, Hopkins wanted nothing more than the reconciliation of the northern and southern wings of the Episcopal Church. Several weeks before the northern convention in October 1865, he wrote two circular letters to southern bishops imploring them to take their seats at the convention. Hopkins desired that the northern assemblage would become a national one. "I consider it a duty especially incumbent on me, as the Senior Bishop," he asserted, "to testify my affectionate attachment to those amongst my colleagues from whom I have been separated during those years of suffering and calamity; and to assure you personally of the cordial welcome which awaits you at our approaching General Convention."[62]

Other leading Episcopalians also encouraged southerners to attend the convention, especially by assuring them that they would not be expected to recant on slavery or secession. Unlike the northern Old School Presbyterians, the Episcopal Church leaders did not consider repentance necessary. Hopkins Jr. noted that in the months between the war and the general convention, "[P]rivate correspondence in various quarters between North and South . . . helped . . . to prepare men's hearts and minds" for reunion.[63] Union major general E. D. Townsend, a close friend of Lincoln's during the war, recounted a conversation he had with a southern Episcopalian in which the southerner worried about the "price of reunion." "[W]hat would be exacted . . . to secure a reunion?" he asked. Townsend promised that all southern brethren "would be received with open arms." He then drew attention to the many voices of sectional peace and fraternity coming from leaders in the

Episcopal Church as evidence that former Confederates would not have to apologize: "[I]n proof of my position, [I] instanced the many strong expressions I had heard from public men, . . . a desire that all the people of the South would with alacrity return to a cordial support, without coercion, or penalties of any sort." [64]

At the Episcopal general conference in Philadelphia in early October 1865, reunion was clearly the order of the day. Northern Episcopalians extended the right hand of fellowship to the representatives from the South. When Bishop Hopkins arrived, he immediately met with a bishop from North Carolina and "urg[ed] the Bishop . . . to return at once to his own place, and enter, robed, in the procession with his brethren." [65] Major-General Townsend remembered that at the convention, "[w]herever they [southerners] were recognized they were most cordially received. In the Upper House a bishop discovered one of his Southern brethren in a pew of the church. After a short, whispered conference with the few nearest him, he rose, went to the pew, seized his old friend by the hand, and insisted that he should accompany him back to his seat. There he was met by the entire body with unfeigned joy, and urged to take his seat as one of them." [66] Northern Episcopalians, in sum, were in no mood to seek revenge or punishment. After the convention, the northern and southern denominations reunited into one structural unit. [67]

Most southern white Episcopal leaders responded to northern calls for reunion and the reconciliation of the denomination with jubilation. In 1866, a number of southern dioceses invited Hopkins to visit them, and when he did so in the closing months of that year, his message of reconciliation was greeted with warm affection. As his son remembered, "In some cases, formal deputations waited upon him, with addressees of fervent feeling; in others, persons rushed into the railway car for the pleasure of taking him by the hand even for a moment." A bishop from Georgia wrote to Hopkins that he had done a great deal to "bring about the reunion of the children of God at the North and South. . . . The South can never forget your manly consistency and dignified self-reliance, . . . and future times will do full justice to your wisdom, and your Christian sympathy." [68]

Although the Episcopal Church had far fewer parishioners than the Presbyterian, Baptist, or Methodist churches, there were some in both sections that firmly maintained that the Episcopal reunion could improve national harmony and even serve as a catalyst for a broader national reconciliation. Before the general convention in 1865, a bishop from North Carolina predicted that religious fraternity would help bolster national solidarity. "It is then of cardinal importance to the peace and welfare of the country . . . that there should be a re-union of the different religious denominations which now have distinct organizations at the

North, and the South," he claimed. "[I]t must begin with the Episcopal Church, if that cannot, or will not, re-unite, none can or will." At the conclusion of his address, this bishop once more connected denominational and national reconciliation: "The advantages of such a re-union in spirit, as well as in fact, cannot be overestimated. The cause of religion, the prosperity and extension of the Church, and the political well-being of our country, are all materially involved in it."[69] A writer to the *New York Times* echoed this opinion. "[I]f the Episcopal Church . . . can re-unite," he suggested, "there is no good reason why other divided churches may not do the same." Indeed, "[n]o political scheme or policy for sectional concord can prosper unless they, too, choose to 'follow things that make for peace.'"[70]

As religious leaders debated the merits and potential effects of ecclesiastical reunion, some politicians and reformers employed religious rationales in their calls for national reconciliation. Former Democratic congressman and Illinois governor John Reynolds, who died only one month after Lincoln, begged Protestants to follow paths of forgiveness. "I appeal particularly to Church members, North and South, who profess to be pure, holy and converted Christians, to follow the principles you profess," he told one crowd. "You Christians have sworn before the altar of God to 'love those that hate you,' to 'love God with all thy heart and thy neighbor as thyself.' . . . The Savior was crucified, when he had the power to avoid it, but said, with his dying breath, 'Father forgive them, they know not what they do.' A man who has in his heart the shedding of his brother's blood is no Christian."[71] Leading abolitionist Gerrit Smith, who was left confused and emotionally unstable after John Brown's hopeless raid on Harpers Ferry failed in 1859, preached that northerners had no business judging southern whites harshly. The North, he maintained, was itself in need of redemption: "However important it may be for the North to be impressing herself with the great wickedness of those who are preeminently responsible for this war and for the starving and murdering of tens of thousands of prisoners, her more important duty, nevertheless, is to repent of her own sins."[72]

All of these calls for reunion did little to piece back together the fractured state of the denominations or the republic. In fact, northerners themselves formed no consensus on how to regard southern whites. Henry Ward Beecher and his entreaties for forgiveness, which filled both his Plymouth Church in Brooklyn and the pages of the *New York Independent*, were met by fierce resistance. In July, Reverend John Jenkins, a radical Republican, wrote to the *Independent* denouncing Beecher and other ministers of sectional goodwill. Upset with "an alarming and most reprehensible disposition . . . to tone down the severity of justice, and to demand clemency," he attacked pastors who preached "long homilies upon lenity and mercy in dealing with the great criminals of all time." Jenkins even went so far as to portray these clerics as allies of the "vanquished rebels."[73] Others also blasted Beecher as an exemplar of northern forgiveness. Claiming a divine mandate for Confederate executions, Methodist Bostwick Hawley chided, "[L]et the Plymouth Pulpit dissuade." Senator Charles Sumner, a leading radical Republican, lamented over Beecher's position. "I have read B's sermon with inexpressible pain, even to tears," he wrote in a private letter to the editor of the *Independent*. "It is a mistake to cry over. Freedom must have 'shrieked' at that fall. . . . It is sad— very sad."[74]

By the end of 1865, then, the religious milieu seethed with conflict, not consensus. The *Independent* grumbled that Protestants and northerners in general had formed no unified plan regarding the South. "What shall be the punishment?" it asked. Northern religious voices offered no clear answer: "The air is filled with various replies—confiscation, disfranchisement, exile, death. Other voices cry, pardon."[75] With no monolithic northern Protestant response to national reconciliation, ministers seemed just as divided as the politicians. Their battles presaged the tensions within the postwar Congress and the North as a whole from 1865 to 1868. Before the Thirty-Ninth Congress could gather in December 1865, the struggle to make sense of Lincoln's assassination had already been fought in the churches and in the newspapers. The North and the South stood as divided as ever, but the majority of northern Protestants seemed in no mood to accept Confederates as their national brethren.

III

While Yankee ministers debated the racial, political, social, and religious relationship between northern and southern whites, they also engaged in a parallel discussion over the position of African Americans within the national community. At the heart of the postwar struggle between the North and the South swirled the increasingly bitter battle over the status of African Americans. Several dozen prominent ministers joined their voices to those of radical Republican politicians and editors in seeking to use the trauma of Lincoln's assassination to advocate revolutionary changes in American racial thought and national identity. Religious arguments for social justice, interpretations of universal humanity, and diatribes against racism reflected a northern consciousness far more radical than many scholars have recognized.[76] To this vocal contingent, the abolition of slavery was not sufficient to create a new American nation. The country must now dismantle the white republic.

Loyalty to the nation and shared commitments to the American political system must become the defining features of national citizenship, they declared. Although southern whites refused to bend to religious arguments for restructuring American society, African Americans perceived that northern whites' racial and national imaginations had drastically changed. To them, a new North had emerged from the war, a North where a large group of influential political and religious leaders were seriously committed to extending citizenship to people of color. The Civil War's fracturing of the white republic provided an opportunity for the racial restructuring of the nation's citizenry, as northern Protestants repudiated the ethnic nationalism of the antebellum era and put their moral weight behind the full civic inclusion of those who had been most loyal to the nation—African Americans.

Of course, not all northern pastors desired equality for blacks. Scores, especially Democrats and some moderate Republicans, abhorred any form of racial egalitarianism and considered racial segregation the only way to stave off a war between the races.[77] During the Civil War, as the North had first considered the moral, political, and pragmatic ramifications of emancipation, several white Protestants continued to assert the sacredness of chattel slavery and excused it by claiming that people of color were inherently inferior to whites. As Bishop Hopkins of the Episcopal Church implored northern and southern whites to reconcile, his slew of pamphlets and letters justifying slavery demonstrated that many northern religious leaders were as committed as ever to keeping United States a "white man's country." Pointing to scriptural verses that acknowledged human bondage, Hopkins rationalized the exploitation of African Americans by asserting that blacks were mentally inferior to whites. "I know that there may be exceptions, now and then, to this intellectual inferiority of the negro race," he wrote, "though I believe it would be very difficult to find one, unless the intermixture of superior blood has operated to change the mental constitution of the individual." To Hopkins, blacks were preordained to slavery, while whites were preordained to mastery: "For every candid observer agrees that the negro is happier and better as a slave than as a free man, and no individual belonging to the Anglo-Saxon stock would acknowledge that the intellect of the negro is equal to his own."[78]

Yet assertions like Hopkins's were largely drowned out in the religious debates following Lincoln's death. After the assassination, a wide variety of radical evangelicals imagined a nation in which freedpeople would become full American citizens, and they tended to dominate the public discussions. In their sermons, these religious leaders attempted to determine the meaning of both Lincoln's death and the end of the war vis-à-vis the future social position of African Americans and the racial ideologies of whites. Pastors articulated their commitments to rights for blacks by lauding emancipation, by championing civil rights and suffrage, and by inventing a mythical Lincoln who stood as the epitome of racial egalitarianism. Most revolutionary of all, several ministers battled national prejudice and prevailing racist scientific theories and theologians with an antiracist egalitarianism rooted in their Christian beliefs. In 1865, white racism was suddenly no longer a given; it was under fire. These pastors advanced the doctrine of God's universal human creation and called for a color-blind society. In doing so, they epitomized the fluctuating nature of northern white racial and national imaginations during and after the Civil War, as commitments to civic nationalism rose above previous allegiances to ethnic nationalism. Their antiracist religious arguments even pervaded political radicalism in the spring and summer of 1865 and led many African Americans to believe that a new era had commenced in which racial prejudice would be exterminated.

While many northern Protestants had begun the Civil War perceiving it as a cosmic struggle for the Union, by the spring of 1865, some had fused abolition and Union as equally lofty and sacred.[79] In their post-assassination sermons, ministers hailed the Emancipation Proclamation as Lincoln's crowning achievement. Speaking to an overflowing Baptist congregation in Philadelphia, George Dana Boardman painted emancipation as the supreme moment of the war, "[I]t overtops all the other great events of this unparalleled epoch."[80] Connecticut's Henry Deming considered the Proclamation the very work of God: "I can almost see a mighty arm, stretching out of the unfathomable blue" to guide "the great liberator."[81] Ultimately, these ministers viewed the restoration of the Union and the emancipation of the slaves as equally significant and glorious. "Two stars flamed in the sky," declared Reverend James McCauley in Baltimore, "Union—liberty conserved for those already free; and Emancipation—liberty decreed for the millions hitherto enslaved."[82]

Likewise, several northern religious and political leaders recognized that emancipation did not end the battle for liberty. Contrary to religious historian James Moorhead's suggestion that most northern Protestants viewed Reconstruction as "one more mopping up project," several influential clerics believed that the nation was now undertaking a new struggle for racial equality and civil rights.[83] "We are beginning a new war," proclaimed Charles Robinson, "the weapons of which are not carnal."[84] While lamenting the death of Lincoln, Methodist and radical Republican Gilbert Haven encouraged his parishioners to push on for African American suffrage and other political rights: "His work is done. Ours is yet unfinished."[85] These public statements signified more than mere patriotic rhetoric. Congregationalist George Walker confided in his diary shortly after the war that "we have a new battle to wage for civil equality."[86] Major politicians made similar claims. "The battle for a perfect Union and impartial Freedom was not finished by the surrender of the rebel armies, but only assumed a new phase," claimed Republican governor John Andrew of Massachusetts. Similarly, arch-radical Thaddeus Stevens referred to the quest for African American rights as the "last and greatest battle of freedom!"[87] The vast majority of northerners may have begun the Civil War with the intent of only saving the Union, but now, to these ministers and radical Republicans, God seemed to demand the remaking of the entire nation, even beyond the achievement of emancipation. Only when African Americans enjoyed complete civil rights would this transformation reach fruition.

To wage this new war, radical ministers insisted that the federal government extend full civil rights to the freedpeople and redistribute rebel property. Pastors such as W. H. Benade believed that blacks deserved equal citizenship: only when the government offered freedpeople all the "duties of citizenship . . . will the great principle of humanity of labor, of the divine humanity of labor, stand fully vindicated before the world."[88] In Philadelphia, Universalist Richard Eddy claimed that God demanded "equality of all men before the law," and the *New York Independent* seconded this appraisal, suggesting that when "all enjoy equal civil rights," the Civil War would be completely over. Methodist J. P. Newman declared that "retributive and compensative justice demand that property in the South should change hands, and a just God will see to it that those who have been robbed of their earnings for generations shall not fail to obtain their share." Land reform and civil rights would usher in a radical revolution. "Everything is now drifting that way," he concluded, "and in the golden age coming the planters of the South will be black men." Reverend George Cheever put it best, praying that "the colored race might live as we lived."[89]

These pastors championed universal manhood suffrage as the key to social and civil equality. Preaching in Boston, Methodist Gilbert Haven maintained that the "enfranchisement of the negro alone can renew that land."[90] Religious periodicals such as the *Independent* and the *Christian Advocate and Journal* repeatedly called for black enfranchisement. "Negro suffrage," the *Independent* maintained, is the "prime duty of the hour."[91] In a letter to Charles Sumner in early May, abolitionist Wendell Phillips noted an almost universal ministerial acceptance of black suffrage in Boston: "[A]ll around to clergymen small & great & to rank & file here, literally *no dissent.*"[92] In the months following Lincoln's assassination, ministers did more than just preach about suffrage reform. They took the cause to the people and to the politicians. George Cheever circulated a petition for African American voting privileges in New York, while his brother Henry Cheever appealed to the Massachusetts legislature to endorse rights for African Americans in the North as well as the South. Protestants further contributed to the radical cause by aiding and encouraging Republican political leaders like Senator Charles Sumner and Congressman Thaddeus Stevens.[93]

Demonstrating their strong commitment to African American rights, these ministers broke with President Andrew Johnson in the summer of 1865 after he refused to offer federal protection to freedpeople and showed great leniency toward most former Confederates. After Lincoln's assassination, northern Protestants had welcomed the new president with open arms. Overlooking Johnson's drunkenness during his vice presidential inauguration, they now believed he would complete the social revolution that the war had launched. "Andrew Johnson," prophesied C. B. Crane to his Connecticut congregation, "will be used for the accomplishment of our deliverance."[94] But when Johnson refused to mandate rights for freedpeople in the months following his ascension, many pastors reversed their appraisals. Of the fourteen sermons that historian Paul Brownlow found discussing Johnson's policies from 1866 to 1868, all of them condemned the president.[95] Johnson's public silence on African American voting perplexed and annoyed Yankee Protestants. "On one point he seems quite reticent," the *Christian Advocate and Journal* complained, "and that we deem the most important element of the problem, namely, negro suffrage."[96] In his diary, George Walker fretted over Johnson's failure to bring suffrage. After Johnson's General Amnesty and North Carolina Reconstruction proclamations on May 29, 1865, which restored suffrage only to white southern loyalists who were eligible to vote before the war, Walker lamented that "this rules out the blacks."[97] As Johnson continued to ignore rights for African Americans, northern Protestants attacked him and in the late 1860s demanded his removal from office. When Congress impeached him in 1868, the Methodist Episcopal Church's general convention held a special hour of prayer that the nation might be saved from the "corrupt influences" that were trying to save the president.[98]

To justify their attacks on Johnson and their calls for civil rights and suffrage, radical ministers pointed both to the heroic deeds of African Americans during the Civil War and to the Bible. No force was more powerful in transforming northern whites' attitudes toward African Americans than the willingness of black men to fight and die for the cause of the Union. Their loyalty to the nation inspired many northern whites to rethink the tenets of America's national identity. At the raising of the Union flag at Fort Sumter in April 1865, even Henry Ward Beecher lauded the "capacity, moral and military, of the black race." "It is a revelation indeed," announced Beecher, "[t]hey were said to be lazy, lying, impudent, and cowardly wretches. . . . [But] after the government, honouring them as men, summoned them to the field, when once they were disciplined, and had learned the arts of war, they proved themselves to be not second to their white brethren in arms."[99] Some ministers also rooted their radical contentions in the teachings of Christ. Specifically, they invoked the Golden Rule. Regarding "the question whether Liberty was to be made universal, or to be confined to a class or a race," Richard Edwards of Illinois maintained that the North must now be "willing to adopt the Golden Rule—to do unto others as we would have them do to us."[100]

Perhaps even more radical than their calls for civil rights was the battle some pastors took up against prevailing theological and scientific notions of racial difference. These ministers preached in a society that had created a massive ideological bulwark to defend racism and slavery. Scientists such as Samuel Morton, Josiah Nott, and Louis Agassiz had constructed a sophisticated and diabolical rationale for African American bondage by suggesting that races constituted different species and must therefore have stemmed from multiple creations. "Polygenesis," as they had termed it, helped explain African American and Native American inferiority as deep and permanent. Accepting these racist doctrines, some antebellum Protestants had reinterpreted the book of Genesis to buttress racial hierarchy. They maintained that dark skin was the biblical "curse of Canaan" and "marked" African Americans as subordinate. As historians George Fredrickson, Reginald Horsman, and William Stanton have shown, nineteenth-century whites fused science and religion into a powerful defense of racism, slavery, and continental imperialism.[101]

White supremacist theologizing continued to influence racial thinking after emancipation, as some whites held fast to their claims that the Bible and science "proved" that Euro-Americans and people of color were inherently distinct. When visiting the United States in the 1860s, Reverend David Macrae of Great Britain encountered one southern white who, "[r]eferring to a book which he had been reading on the subject," claimed that this text made "it clear as day that though the nigger is called a man in the Bible, it don't mean a real man like you or me." White men were the true sons of God, he insisted. "When God came to make the real man, the white man, Adam, He said, 'Let us make man *in our own image*,' meaning that He had already made a kind of man—that is, a nigger—*not* in His own image, but with flat skull, thick lips, wooly head, flat nose, and no soul in him. Scripture calls the nigger a man, but it calls Adam *the* man, the white real man, the Son of God."[102]

When a number of postbellum northern ministers affirmed the belief in universal creation and the unity of humankind, they stood as the radical vanguard of opposition to scientific and theological theories of racial difference. They denied any biological definition of the "children of God" or the citizenry of the United States. Instead, these pastors rewarded loyalty to the Union as the key determinant in national brotherhood, which situated African Americans within the nation and rebellious southern whites outside of it. These preachers espoused a commitment to egalitarianism in a variety of ways, eulogizing Lincoln as a friend to all humanity, attacking prevailing racial theories, and rooting their beliefs in the biblical creation story. In their heroic war against national white prejudice, these ministers reflected the shifting conceptions of race and the future of the American nation.

Radical ministers envisioned a time when white Americans would look beyond race to a brotherhood of humanity, and they depicted Lincoln as an unprejudiced leader whom northerners should emulate. "It was not the white man, or the red man, or the black man, that [Lincoln] saw," lectured Wilbur F. Paddock. "It was humanity, suffering and needy."[103] Reverend Reuben Jeffrey of Philadelphia made a similar point when he commented, "In the narrow, technical sense of the word, [Lincoln] was not an abolitionist. He was not specially and exclusively a friend of the negro." Rather, Jeffrey continued, Lincoln "loved the human race. He believed in the brotherhood of man, and allowed no differences in constitution, color, culture or country, to commit him to unjust discriminations against the manhood of man."[104] Although modern historians have rightly questioned such portrayals of Lincoln and have shown that the president was far more moderate than radical in his racial views, northern ministers clearly described Lincoln in such ways in order to inculcate egalitarian beliefs into their audiences.

As they called for human brotherhood, some radical pastors directly confronted prevailing racist theologies and scientific theories. "Our assertion of the inferiority of the races is a lie," proclaimed Richard Eddy in Philadelphia. Inherent inferiority, he contended, was "condemned by all the inspired testimony of God." Other ministers echoed Eddy's statement. Henry Deming maintained that "of one blood all the children of men were made," while Charles Robinson concluded that "the truth of the Gospel . . . [shows] the indefeasible equality of all the creatures of God in natural conditions of existence, no matter what may be the color of their skin." Henry Fowler of Auburn, New York, further suggested that skin color did not determine character or capacity. "Shall you and I never learn to look below the skin?" he asked; even in the wake of the gloom following Lincoln's death, Fowler answered optimistically: "Yes, we shall!"[105] Such arguments continued throughout the summer, as ministers such as Elihu Holland proclaimed that "God did not write the unity of this race so blindly as to require the presence of sages to interpret it." [106]

While Holland saw universal humanity as self-evident, other radical ministers rooted their antiracist claims in biblical passages and the Genesis creation story. Quoting the biblical book of the Acts of the Apostles, ministers and abolitionists proclaimed that God "hath made of one blood all the nations of men." [107] This "of one blood" argument stood as a staple in the abolitionist war on slavery, and even Supreme Court Justice Curtis McLean used it in his dissenting opinion in the *Dred Scott* case of 1857, in which Chief Justice Roger Taney maintained that slaves had absolutely no federal citizenship rights. To McLean, Taney's assertion flouted true religion. "A slave is not a mere chattel," he contended. "He bears the impress of his Maker, and is amenable to the laws of God and man; and he is destined to an endless existence." [108] To Justice McLean and the radical ministers after Lincoln's assassination, all humans regardless of skin tone or other perceived physical differences were Adam's progeny. Reverend Joseph Seiss articulated this argument as he lauded Lincoln's egalitarianism: "[H]e regarded all men as of one blood, and entitled by their Maker to the same rights, and acted out to sublime distinction the golden rule." [109] In July, even the *Princeton Review*, which normally reflected the conservative positions of the Old School Presbyterians, endorsed limited African American suffrage, claiming that "all men are the children of Adam; made of one blood and possessing the same nature; and therefore are all entitled to be regarded and treated as men." [110]

One minister even theorized about history, philosophy, and racial distinctions in ways that leaned toward modern conceptions of race. Methodist Episcopal pastor Robert Yard of Newark, New Jersey, drew attention to the long and shifting history of racial classification, and he indicted Enlightenment thinkers such as Voltaire and Rousseau for their theories of racial categorization. Yard unmercifully assailed principles of racial inferiority based upon scientific or religious grounds. Whites had portrayed "Africans" as "not human," he claimed, in order to give themselves a "simple justification of their deeds of oppression." Racism emerged as a rationale for economic exploitation, not as a scientific or moral truth. But Christianity could undo prejudice and discrimination. Unlike race-defining Enlightenment views, he argued, Christianity contained a racially leveling ideology in which all people were made in "the likeness of God, whether inframed in *ebony or in ivory*." [111]

Radical pastors denounced all forms of racial distinction, whether in the North or in the South, and they looked to religious beliefs to transform whites' racial imaginations. Gilbert Haven expended a great deal of energy railing against both ecclesiastical and social discrimination. "We are persisting in recognizing a wicked spirit of caste," he wrote to the *Christian Advocate and Journal*, "which He [God] has always and everywhere in his word and his dealings with his Church declared to be against the whole letter and life of the Gospel." Defying northern prejudice, Haven asserted, "We presume to distinguish between His children on account of certain shades of complexion, or sources of distant origin." Only a "true" Christian worldview could "cure" this prejudice: "We should say, there and everywhere, a redeemed soul is our brother, one called of God . . . our equal and companion, and no act or thought of separation from him on account of these unrighteous distinctions should find the least place in our heart." Editors of the *Christian Advocate and Journal* endorsed Haven's call to egalitarianism: "We . . . entirely agree with Brother Haven as to the fact that the Church is grievously afflicted with a most absurd, and, we must also admit, a sinful prejudice against colored people."[112]

While backing African American civil rights and challenging conceptions of racial differences, northern ministers also exhorted their congregations to support freedpeople's education. Christian uplift, claimed J. G. Butler of Washington, D.C., is "to educate and elevate, so far as sanctified knowledge can elevate, the four millions of freedmen."[113] Lyman Abbott begged the North to give its funds and energies: "We only need the money to open at once hundreds of schools, where the lessons of Union, liberty, and Christian religion, shall be wholly taught, and you may be sure, gladly learned."[114] Throughout the spring of 1865, these ministers appealed to northerners to join their capital in venturing south. "We hear a providential voice . . . louder than ever," lectured Samuel Dutton to his New England congregation. The end of the war "calls for a large increase of laborers" in the South.[115] These ministers were joined by northern politicians who also hoped to generate concern for the social and educational needs of the freedpeople. After listening to Reverend James Freeman Clarke preach on the duty to aid the freedpeople, Governor John Andrew of Massachusetts called on all northerners: "We of the North . . . must intervene for the immediate preservation of the colored people of the South, powerless, for the moment, to save themselves, and by wise and prudent generosity help to float them over until a new crop can be made."[116]

These religious voices and arguments in favor of racial equality played a major role in political debates on the place of African Americans in the nation. In June 1865, for instance, *Harper's Weekly* combined religious arguments with the image of African American soldiers in combat to endorse black manhood suffrage: "[A]mid the fire and storm of battle we have acknowledged that God has made of one blood all the nations of the earth." [117] In August 1865, Iowa's Judge Chester C. Cole claimed that voting rights were a matter of "*God's law* of equality. . . . Providence has devolved upon us the duty of . . . making all men equal before the law, as they are before their Maker." [118]

For radical congressman Thaddeus Stevens, biblical narratives were central to his adamant support of universal civil rights and land reform for freedpeople. In December 1865, he proclaimed, "If we have not yet been sufficiently scourged for our national sin to teach us to do justice to all God's creatures, without distinction of race or color, we must expect the still more heavy vengeance of an offended Father, still increasing his inflictions as he increased the severity of the plagues of Egypt." For Stevens, the fear of a judging God who would evaluate the actions of all humans weighed heavily on his mind and heart. "I believe that we must all account hereafter for deeds done in the body, and that political deeds will be among those accounts," he told his colleagues in Congress. "I desire to take to the bar of that final settlement the record which I shall this day make on the great question of human rights. . . . Are there any who will venture to take the list, with their negative seal upon it, and will dare to unroll it before that stern Judge who is the Father of immortal beings whom they have been trampling under foot, and whose souls they have been crushing out?" Christian beliefs played a powerful role not only in the political language of politicians like Stevens, but also provided crucial images and ideologies to motivate actions.[119]

In turn, southern whites and northern Democrats attacked these radical arguments as perversions of biblical teachings, drawing upon the long history of white supremacist theology. One northern Democrat who had supported the war wrote to Andrew Johnson denouncing all calls for the inclusion of nonwhites in the national body. "I did not seek to uphold the American flag that ignorant Negroes may rule over white men," he fumed. To him, the United States was a "country of the white race, given by the Almighty on which to build a great white nation." Other Democrats opposed "the commingling of what God and nature had so unmistakably intended to preserve separate and distinct." Several southern white ministers denied that the "one blood" and other biblical arguments applied to race relations. "The plea that all men sprang from Adam, that 'God is no respecter of persons,' and that in Christ Jesus there is neither bond nor free," wrote the *New Orleans Christian Advocate,* could not "soften the wickedness of attempting to break down that social distinction between the white and black races which Nature, God, and the best interests of mankind have so preserved." In short, southern whites and their Democratic allies in the North refused to accept that God or the Bible called for racial justice. As a result, they held fast to their vision of the United States as a nation ordained by God to be a "white man's country." [120]

But the claims of northern religious and political radicals had a powerful impact on African Americans. Many people of color believed that a new and marvelous period of racial egalitarianism was already commencing. They recognized that northern whites' racial and national views were in a state of flux at the end of the Civil War. In August 1865, members of the Pennsylvania State Equal Rights' League praised God that public opinion was now on their side and that "[p]owerful advocates are pleading our cause in the pulpit, in the press, in the Legislative Halls and on the Stump." [121] The African Methodist Episcopal Church's *Christian Recorder* was even more effusive. "Old notions have been discarded," it reported, "and new ones inaugurated in their stead, comprehending the universal brotherhood of the human race." The notion of universal brotherhood, though, was a recent ideology and feeling in the United States: "Before the war little was known of him, except as a 'nigger,' to be degraded, outlawed, and spit upon." The Civil War had challenged whites to discard these prejudices: "But his very condition before, being the cause of the war, has brought him before the nation and world in a new light: 'He is a man and a brother,' brave in battle, humane in victory, and he has shown, that in his ignorance he possesses all the attributes of the enlightenment." [122] On another occasion, the *Christian Recorder* praised God for the waning of racism. "And we rejoice that the day of Christianity is dawning, yea, now we see the glorious sun of knowledge and understanding rising with healing in her wings, and the dark clouds of ignorance and prejudice are passing away." [123]

Other northern and southern blacks testified to their new experience of rising status in the nation. Speaking at a Fourth of July celebration that also served as the dedication of a monument for Lincoln, several African American leaders declared that the Civil War had brought hope to many blacks. Reverend D. W. Anderson of the Nineteenth Street Baptist Church in Washington, D.C., claimed that the "nation [had been] redeemed by the commingled blood of the Anglo-Saxon and the Anglo-African races, poured out like water upon many battle-fields." The war, in other words, had created an indivisible bond between whites and blacks as their blood mixed together on the well-known battlefields of honor. Later in the ceremony, William Howard Day, a young African American from New York, declared that the nation was about to be reconstructed on egalitarian grounds: "We come to the National Capital—our Capital—with new hopes, new prospects, new joys, in view of the future and past of the people." [124]

The belief among African Americans that they could now celebrate the United States as their nation contrasted starkly with the antebellum recognition of abolitionists that holidays like the Fourth of July were days for whites to rejoice and for blacks to mourn. In 1852, for example, Frederick Douglass had lamented that "[t]his Fourth of July is yours, not mine." For African Americans and to God, Douglass had further commented, "your celebration is a sham; your boasted liberty, an unholy license; . . . your sermons and thanksgivings, with all your religious parade and solemnity, are, to Him, mere bombast, fraud, deception, impiety, and hypocrisy."[125] Thirteen years later, though, African Americans were celebrating the Fourth of July in unison with northern whites. "Our future is sure," boasted William H. Grey at an African American convention in Little Rock, Arkansas. "God has marked it out with his own finger; . . . here, where we have been degraded, will we be exalted—AMERICANS IN AMERICA, ONE AND INDIVISIBLE." Unlike any other time in black America, the spring and summer of 1865 was a time of boundless confidence. They believed that white racism and exclusion from the nation's grace and bounty were things of the past. A new United States seemed to be emerging, one that privileged loyalty to the Union over skin color or racial classification. The white republic appeared to be crumbling, and people of color now felt that the United States was their country as much as anyone else's.[126]

These African American preachers, orators, and writers had their fingers on the nation's pulse. In the days and months following Lincoln's assassination, northern Protestantism was swept up in and helped nurture a revolutionary tide in which racial prejudice was in retreat and the postwar national status of white southerners was unclear. Yankee Protestants engaged in two parallel debates, both bearing directly on the nation's identity. With the exception of the Episcopal Church and the Democratic Party, most northerners demanded that southern whites at least admit that slavery and secession were sins. At the same time, northern Protestants engaged in a hotly contested ideological war over the rights and place of blacks in American society. Constructing Lincoln as a friend to all peoples, assailing racist scientific and theological teachings, and discussing the possibilities of human brotherhood, they maintained that the war for the Union should be refashioned into a war for racial egalitarianism.

The forces of racial justice did much more than merely discuss the merits of an integrated and equal nation. Hopes for remaking the South and the nation were made tangible in the form of thousands of missionaries and millions of dollars sent to aid the freedpeople. Northern Protestants sought to create nothing less than a Christian and Republican citizenry among southern blacks. Northern novelist Albion Tourgée remembered the Protestant responses to the end of the war as quite possibly the most magnificent moment in American history. "Perhaps there has been no grander thing in our history" than when "the civilization of the North in the very hour of victory threw aside the cartridge-box, and appealed at once to the contribution-box to heal the ravages of war," he wrote. "[I]t was the noblest spectacle that Christian civilization has ever witnessed."[127] Working and laughing together, praying and singing together, hoping and dreaming together, and crying and struggling together, freed African Americans and the northern missionaries embodied the purest kind of radicalism. They carried "the new and greatest battle of freedom" into the postbellum South. Armed with little more than school primers and Bibles, these northern "soldiers of light and love" met a fierce resistance from former Confederates. But dreams of an egalitarian nation and hopes for heaven on earth were more powerful than the demons of white supremacy— at least for a season under the sun.

2

ON THE VERGE OF HEAVEN

Religious Missions, Interracial Contact, and the Radicalism of Radical Reconstruction

After serving as a doctor among African American soldiers during the Civil War, Esther Hawks was teaching black children in Charleston, South Carolina, when news of Lincoln's assassination arrived. She agreed with the northern ministers who proposed a "fatalistic theory" of Lincoln's murder, believing that his "work was accomplished and he is removed." Even in her despair, Hawks was certain that "God has other men and means, to finish what is yet undone!" But missionaries like Hawks had much more to accomplish than to simply make theological sense of the president's assassination for themselves. They also had to break the news to their African American pupils. Confused, angered, and saddened, these northern whites and southern blacks grieved together. After she and the school's principal informed the students of the tragic event, "many of the older children cried aloud. . . . several of the large girls who are in classes. . . . came to me, weeping bitterly." The sadness of the freedpeople was almost too much to bear. "The colord [sic] people express their sorrow and sense of loss in many cases, with sobs and loud lamentations."[1]

Hawks was one of thousands of northern whites who traveled south during and after the war in a massive movement to aid the freedpeople, and emotional encounters similar to those she described helped further tie northern radicals and African Americans together. By the war's end, at least seventy "freedmen's aid societies" were collecting and distributing a host of goods to send to the South, while men and women from a variety of theological and racial backgrounds rallied to the cause. The American Missionary Association (AMA), principally led by Congregationalists, received the endorsement of the Dutch Reformed Church, the New School Presbyterians, the United Brethren, the Free Methodist Church, and even the Church of Scotland. Other denominations, including the African Methodist Episcopal Church, the African Methodist Episcopal Zion Church, the Methodist Episcopal Church, the United Presbyterians, the Northern Baptists, and the New and Old School Presbyterians, formed their own societies and sent their own missionaries.[2] Several associations eschewed particular denominational labels and allowed thousands of other northerners to contribute as well. These nonsectarian groups, principally composed of Quakers and Unitarians and misidentified by some historians as "secular," banded together after the war to form the American Freedmen's Union Commission (AFUC). Together, these organizations and their missionaries were the hands and feet of the radical northern Protestant quest to transform former slaves into Christian and Republican citizens.[3]

For the most part, historians have found much more to criticize than to compliment in the Reconstruction-education crusade and "radical" Reconstruction. While white scholars in the early twentieth century denounced the missionaries as blind fanatics who had little understanding of southern racial dynamics, historians in the late twentieth century have portrayed them as bourgeois moralists who merely wanted to inculcate notions of time-management and thrift into southern blacks so that they would become contented wage laborers. Even more sympathetic accounts of the crusaders, such as those by Jacqueline Jones and Joe Richardson, have maintained that while the teachers endeavored to help African Americans, they could never overcome their paternalistic and prejudicial attitudes. Their chauvinism created a cultural "chasm" between northern whites and southern blacks that could not be bridged.[4]

But the image of Esther Hawks and countless other white northerners weeping with southern freedpeople complicates these scholarly appraisals. There was something powerful and precious occurring during the 1860s and early 1870s as whites and blacks sought to work together in new ways and under new conditions. As W. E. B. Du Bois first recognized in his magisterial *The Souls of Black Folk* in 1903, interracial contact was one of the most critical aspects of post–Civil War Reconstruction. He considered the northerners who ventured south "saintly souls" who initiated "the finest thing in American history." He waxed poetic about them: "This was the gift of New England to the freed Negro, not alms, but a friend; not cash, but character. It was and is not money that these seething millions want, but love and sympathy. . . . In actual formal content their curriculum was doubtless old-fashioned, but in educational power it was supreme, for it was the contact of living souls."[5]

Taken from the perspective of white and black Americans in the 1860s, the Reconstruction-education crusade was a dramatic moment of interracial fraternity that had the power to alter southern and American society. It was part of a widespread effort among northern Protestants and radical Republicans to restructure the nature of national citizenship. In addition to the missions, Congress passed a number of bills, laws, and constitutional amendments that overturned much of the legislation that had previously upheld the white republic. The years of radical Reconstruction were loaded with revolutionary potential as politicians, religious leaders, and the relief associations envisioned a nation in which race and freed people's former status as slaves no longer determined citizenship and civil rights. Through their publishing, their reports to the federal government, their letters and diaries, and their actions, organizational leaders and missionaries imagined and endeavored to create an integrated nation where whites and blacks learned, worked, and lived together. Although they did not represent the attitudes of the majority of northern whites, the extremity and intensity of their radicalism suggests that the tenets of the white republic were being fully and systematically challenged.[6]

The educational crusade created unprecedented levels of interracial cooperation, and contact led some missionaries, especially those who remained in the South for several years and labored closely with people of color, to ascend to new heights of radicalism. Some of these teachers not only shed their paternalism and cultural chauvinism, but also launched a sustained assault against racism and exploitation. Several even blurred distinctions between "whiteness" and "blackness" by "forgetting" the skin color of southern blacks or by depicting themselves as full-fledged members of African American communities. Ultimately, these missionaries enacted their beliefs in an American civic nationalism in which citizenship had nothing to do with racial or ethnic affiliation. From this perspective, radical Reconstruction can be viewed not as a time of insurmountable friction between paternalistic northern whites and disappointed southern blacks, but as an innovative era of dynamic cultural exchange and social cooperation in which missionary-teachers put into action their goals to create a Protestant and Republican citizenry among the freedpeople.

The teachers who remained in the South and who became part of African American society were genuine "rebels." They were people who, as the existentialist theologian Albert Camus once wrote, refuse "to accept the absurd conditions of things but fight against them." Particularly those rebels who revolt on behalf of others experience new "feeling[s] of identification with other individuals." This new identification is not "a mere subterfuge by which the individual contrives to feel that it is he who has been oppressed." Instead, their rebellion constitutes "an identification of destinies and a choice of sides" with the oppressed.[7] Radical Reconstruction teachers who committed years of effort to the South and forged close relationships with people of color did exactly that. They identified with southern blacks and joined them in the battle for civil rights and brotherhood.

The missionaries produced a powerful effect on relationships among northerners, freedpeople, and southern whites during the mid- and late 1860s. Their crusade strengthened the alliance between the North and southern blacks that had been created during wartime Reconstruction. Radical efforts left an indelible mark on southern black society, creating the institutional basis from which a black middle class emerged later in the century. And many people of color considered the teachers trusted confidants and true friends. African Americans largely praised the efforts of northern educators and thanked them for their support and care. To southern whites, however, northern teachers represented a vile new invasion force dedicated to elevating people of color. Former Confederates mocked, threatened, and physically attacked the teachers and their pupils. In the eyes of white southerners, education and interracial social contact certainly had revolutionary potential, and they refused to stand for it. Vigilantism and counter-revolutionary violence became the tools to stave off a radical transformation. For their part, northern missionaries were often unkind toward southern whites, viewing them as villainous traitors who deserved national subordination. By describing the southern white reign of terror in reports to the North, the missionary-teachers helped stoke the fires of sectional distrust. With the white republic in shambles, in short, the crusaders of the mid-1860s battled to make a new America that transcended the discrimination of the past.

I

The drive to provide humanitarian relief and education to southern freedpeople was an interdenominational and interracial crusade that brought thousands of northerners into a common cause and generated massive amounts of concern for African American rights and privileges. Compassion for the physical and spiritual well-being of freedpeople was part of a long history of Protestant missionary involvement in conveying the gospel and bringing western-style education to peoples of various cultures. Although many historians have focused on single denominations or organizations, the crusade to aid southern blacks was a mass movement of northerners, especially Protestants. As one missionary recalled, "Almost every Church in the North has contributed to educational purposes in the South." Another claimed that "freedman's aid societies were started in churches of all denominations. Members of families and neighbors joined themselves into independent clubs,—all to help on this great work amongst the negroes." Missionary Elizabeth Botome perhaps summed up the need for relief best when she claimed: "A common cause made all friends."[8]

While the relief associations united northerners from countless denominational and religious backgrounds, they also linked whites and blacks in a shared effort. Of course, as historian Clarence Walker has pointed out, interracial cooperation was not without its share of conflict. Northern African American religious leaders did not fully trust northern whites to give people of color a fair deal, while many whites held condescending views of African Americans.[9] Nonetheless, whites and blacks labored together to move into the South. Northern blacks sat on the AMA's executive council, for instance, and the AMA employed Reverend Sella Martin, an African American Presbyterian minister, as their leading spokesman to Europe. Black state conventions endorsed the plans of the missionary organizations, and the AMA supported several delegates to these conventions. Branches of the AFUC, the AMA, and the African Methodist Episcopal Church provided funds for several hundred northern blacks to travel south as missionaries and employed hundreds of former slaves as teachers. Of the 145 teachers supported by the New England branch of the AFUC in 1867 and 1868, twenty-four were African American. In schools formed in the South, moreover, blacks and whites served as trustees and African Americans held positions as presidents and principals in many of these institutions.[10]

The relief associations adamantly asserted that southern blacks were or would soon become full and equal citizens in the nation and that they should be treated as such. They envisioned a new America beyond the white republic, a country that transcended racial antagonism and exploitation. Railing against racial prejudice in the United States, these organizations sought to hire only individuals who shared similar convictions. "[B]elieving the feeling of prejudice, extensively existing in this country against the people of color, to be both wicked in itself and a great barrier in the way of their elevation," the AMA resolved in 1867 that "we renew the expression of the principle that has underlain the operations of this Association from the beginning, that no person who yields to that prejudice, or suffers himself to be influenced thereby, ought to be appointed or sustained among its officers, teachers, or agents."[11] Declarations against prejudice within the relief associations were part of a much larger mission to obliterate all notions of social, political, and economic caste inequalities in American society. The American Baptist Home Missionary Society claimed that their mission was to "lift up the millions of freemen to the exercise of all the rights and duties of citizenship and Christian brotherhood." In 1865, the American Freedmen's Union resolved that "the government should recognize no distinction among the people of the South but loyalty and disloyalty, and that the right of suffrage is not only due to the fidelity of the colored man, but is the only basis for a permanent, and righteous reconstruction of the

Union." In short, skin color or racial affiliation should cease to matter in the eyes of the government, the denominations, and the northern people in general.[12]

The benevolent associations continually lobbied for political changes that would extend civil rights and all other privileges to African Americans. Famous northern evangelicals, such as the revivalist and president of Oberlin College, Charles Grandison Finney, maintained that the government should grant land to southern blacks, while most of the organizations demanded civil rights legislation from Congress. They vigorously supported the Thirteenth, Fourteen, and Fifteenth Amendments to the Constitution and cheered that a "New Era" had arrived when southern blacks were elected to Congress.[13] The denominations and relief associations made it quite clear that they supported the radicals within the Republican Party. "The whole Methodist press," wrote the *Northwestern Christian Advocate* in October 1866, "is thoroughly radical for the restoration of the Southern States on the most uncompromised principles of universal rights and loyalty; the rebuke and legal punishment of treason, . . . the enfranchisement and elevation of our emancipated population; and the stern repression of every remnant of the rebellion."[14]

While the relief societies endeavored to influence national politics, the Republican-dominated federal government bestowed its blessing on the educational crusade by providing funds and support via the Bureau of Refugees, Freedmen, and Abandoned Lands, usually referred to simply as "The Freedmen's Bureau." Before Congress phased out the Bureau in the late 1860s and early 1870s, it had funneled millions of dollars to the cause and had provided land, buildings, and protection to the relief organizations and missionaries. The leader of the Bureau, General Oliver Otis Howard, had close friendships with leaders in the AMA, and the chief superintendent of the Bureau's educational branch, John W. Alvord, was himself a Congregational minister and a devout proponent of missions to the freedpeople.[15]

Many in the benevolent organizations hoped to create an egalitarian nation, and they expressed this desire in the tracts, pamphlets, and books they produced specifically for freedpeople's education. Propaganda specialists such as the American Tract Society sent thousands of Bibles, school primers, and advice-literature to southern blacks.[16] Some of these works exuded paternalism. Both Helen Brown's *John Freeman and His Family* and Reverend Isaac Brinckerhoff's *Advice to Freedmen*, to cite two examples, directed African Americans to maintain clean homes, to show respect for southern whites, and to abstain from lying, cheating, and marital infidelity. If African Americans followed these simple rules, the advice literature asserted, then they would truly experience freedom.[17] But other texts were far less interested in inculcating bourgeois values into southern blacks or convincing them to treat their former masters with respect. Some authors were committed to creating an integrated nation—at least on paper. Lydia Marie Child's *The Freedmen's Book* not only contained articles on black historical figures who had demonstrated unique gifts and talents, including Benjamin Banneker, Phillis Wheatley, and Touissant L'Ouverture, but also printed articles written by white and black authors. Poems by African American author Frances E. W. Harper and white author Lydia H. Sigourney graced the pages, while the words of Frederick Douglass sat only paragraphs away from those of Charles Sumner.[18]

In other works for freedpeople, northern whites specifically constructed Abraham Lincoln as the representative and advocate of all the people—white and black. Similar to the radical ministers after Lincoln's assassination, tract authors and editors highlighted his alleged egalitarianism by focusing on his interactions with African Americans. A monthly journal published by Boston's American Tract Society, the *Freedman*, ran a story on Lincoln's meeting with a group of prominent African Americans on the day he signed the Emancipation Proclamation. The journal predicted that in the near future, scenes like this one would be so common that they would no longer be noteworthy. "Several colored men called to pay their respects to President Lincoln on New Year's day, and were received by him precisely as were his other visitors," the *Freedman* reported. "How strange it will one day seem, that this simple, yet significant act, of a truly republican President, should have been accounted a noticeable thing!"[19]

These publications emphasized the actions of African Americans in national politics and freedpeople's education. The *Freedman* regularly reported on the activities of black soldiers both in the Civil War and earlier during the American Revolutionary War. The freedpeople's literature also carried stories on southern blacks' forming and running their own schools, fully recognizing that African Americans were the chief agents in their own educational uplift. "The colored people in Nashville, Tenn., carry on eight schools of their own, which are attended regularly by six hundred pupils," wrote a correspondent to the *Freedman* in the January 1864 issue. "The teachers, trustees, and all concerned are blacks. The Nashville Union calls them 'highly respectable schools.'"[20] Several books and journals lauded Frederick Douglass in particular and unabashedly deemed him a wise political leader. One lesson on Douglass in *The Freedman's Third Reader* ended by pointing out that he "still lives in Rochester; and often, now, his voice is heard advocating the claims of his brethren of the South. He is a true orator." After commenting favorably on one of Douglass's speeches, the *Freedman* concluded that he "was right: Douglass is usually right."[21]

Unlike white supremacist theologians, these tract authors considered a person's character, not the color of his or her skin, to be the determining factor of an individual's worth in the eyes of God. As Lydia Sigourney wrote in Child's *The Freedmen's Book*:

> 'Tis the hue of *deeds* and *thoughts*
> He traces in his book
> 'Tis the complexion of the *heart*
> On which He designs to look.
>
> Not by the tinted cheek,
> That fades away so fast,
> But by the color of the *soul*,
> We shall be judged at last.[22]

Another poet similarly stated:

> Black or white, 'tis all the same,
> For the world the Saviour came;
> He who died upon the tree
> Died alike for you and me.[23]

Primers written for black schoolchildren firmly emphasized human brotherhood and friendship, claiming that God was the father of all humankind. One article in *The Freedman's Third Reader*, "All Mankind of One Blood," claimed that this biblical teaching proved that all people were "brethren." Thus, all people had an obligation to love one another. "Our first duty, then, toward every human being, is to love them," the lesson instructed. "No one, however far away from us, however different in customs or features, though poorer, or more unfortunate, or more sinful, than we are, must be denied our kind regard, as bound to us by this tie of universal brotherhood."[24]

As was the case after Lincoln's assassination, the biblical passage from the Acts of the Apostles that all men were created "of one blood" served as an especially authoritative argument, and it underscored a radical commitment to creating a new national community. The one blood argument constituted perhaps the most powerful justification for the racial restructuring of the American republic. "[T]hough these people differ in the color of their skin," editorialized the *Freedman* in reference to southern blacks, "God says that he has made them all of one blood, and that they are equal in his sight. He loves and cares for all of them the same, and has sent his dear Son into the world to die for all." In 1867, the superintendent of education for the Freedmen's Bureau, John W. Alvord, asserted that the northern commitment to freedpeople's education and their determination to obtain schools provided "increasing evidence that 'God hath made of one blood all the nations of men.'" Then two years later, he once again maintained, "[W]hat has been actually accomplished, show[s] beyond a doubt that the 'one blood' of which God 'hath made all nations of men' is susceptible of, and about to receive, a common culture." [25]

Northerners and southern freedpeople demonstrated their commitments to transforming southern society and the nation's identity by donating an impressive amount of capital and goods to racial uplift. By the end of the war, northern organizations had sent over thirty thousand books and pamphlets, ninety thousand garments, and fifty-eight hundred yards of cloth to the South. In 1866, the AMA alone garnered over $250,000 in cash donations, a five-fold increase from the amount it had received in 1862. The federal government and southern blacks also chipped in large amounts. In 1869, the Freedmen's Bureau reported over $500,000 in expenditures on southern education, while freedpeople supplied roughly $180,000 for their schools during that year. Donations continued to pour in throughout the late 1860s. In 1870, the AMA's receipts had risen to over $430,000. Northern Presbyterians gave $77,000 to aid the freedpeople in 1871. All in all, between 1861 and 1889 northerners contributed an estimated $20 million in cash to the relief associations. Compared to spending on political campaigns during the same years, the donation amounts were remarkable. For the presidential campaign of 1868, for instance, the Republican Party spent only around $200,000. [26]

Radical Reconstruction, in sum, was a moment when northerners were willing to spend much more on humanitarian relief than on partisan politicking. Whether through funds or books, lobbying Congress, or asserting the unity of mankind, these relief associations lent assistance to the hopes of radical Republicans in the North to remake the South and the nation. They endeavored to create a new American nation where loyal whites and blacks had equal claims, rights, and responsibilities. The missionary associations clearly reflected radical Republican Thaddeus Stevens's belief that African Americans were now *Fellow Citizens* and "joint rulers of a mighty nation nearly free." [27]

II

Money, supplies, and books were not the heart and soul of this crusade, however. The thousands of missionaries who flocked to the South served as the lifeblood of the movement. They embodied radicalism, endeavoring to put ideas of equal citizenship into practice. As W. E. B. Du Bois noted at the turn of the century, contact was more powerful than capital; handshakes were more meaningful than handouts. From 1862 to 1870, more than eight thousand northerners—men and women, black and white—streamed into the South to work with the freedpeople. These missionaries believed they were holy crusaders whom God had chosen to redeem the South and the nation. Although many began their ventures holding disparaging stereotypes of African Americans, some of the teachers shed their racism as they labored and lived among southern blacks. The letters, diaries, and reminiscences of several missionary-teachers, especially those who remained among African Americans for more than two years, demonstrate the amazing power of interracial contact. Initial prejudices and stereotypes were dissolved; distance and reticence gave way to closeness and affection; religious chauvinism dwindled and appreciation took its place; otherness, in short, became oneness.

Most historians have failed to differentiate between the experiences of missionaries who lived in the South for several years and those who stayed only a short time. But there are good sociological reasons to distinguish between the two. In studies of interracial contact in twentieth-century housing and educational programs, numerous social theorists have shown that interracial interaction can have dramatic effects on racial attitudes and beliefs. Sociologists have found that certain forms of contact in specific social milieus are more likely to have a positive influence on racial opinions than others. "Contact theory" proposes that attitudes are most susceptible to improvement when contact occurs outside of competitive contexts, is personal, informal, approved of by authorities, takes place where both parties enjoy generally equal status, and is sustained.[28]

Not surprisingly, then, Reconstruction teachers who worked in the South for only several months or those who remained in the South but withdrew from personal and informal contact did not change their attitudes as much as those who remained for several years and had direct, personal contact. Moreover, since personal contact was crucial, female missionaries were more likely to ascend to new heights of radicalism than their male counterparts. While male missionaries typically held supervisory or other administrative positions that distanced them from personal interaction with freedpeople, female missionaries more often taught in classrooms and interacted socially with people of color.[29] The letters, diaries, and memoirs of over a dozen missionaries who spent several years in the South show that the missionary experience had the power to transform the racial and social imaginations of the teachers.

Northern missionary teachers went south for a variety of reasons—from the thirst for adventure to the desire to flee overbearing fathers and mothers. Yet the overriding motivation was religious. They and their supporters conceived of the effort as a spiritual crusade destined to transform the nation. The task of the teachers, asserted Methodist minister Gilbert Haven, was nothing less than to destroy all religious justifications of racial difference. "What then is the service to which the Master calls us?" he asked and then answered, "This, and only this: to abolish from the national action and the arising from color or origin all thought and feeling that such distinctions are divinely intended to separate members of the same human family, who are and must ever be one in blood and in destiny, in sin and in salvation, in Adam and in Christ."[30] "They came in the name and in the spirit of Jesus," recalled missionary Linda Slaughter several years afterward. An inspector for the Freedmen's Bureau likewise considered the teachers "a band of missionaries who have come from the Christian homes of the land—following the example of their Divine Master—going about doing good." Some teachers even put their spiritual feelings to verse, as Marie Waterbury did regarding her journey to the South:

> No more talks about our Lord
> No more searching for his word
> No more longings for his grace
> She hath seen him face to face.[31]

Despite their religious zeal, most of these missionaries displayed a great deal of cultural and racial chauvinism when they first arrived in the South. Most believed that northern middle-class society was ordained in heaven, and they generally scorned African American customs and social mores. When many southern blacks did not rigorously obey the dictates of the clock, but rather followed agrarian time rhythms, the teachers viewed them as "lazy" or "idle." Even some black missionaries of the African Methodist Episcopal Church felt this way.[32] For some teachers, their initial impressions of freedpeople led to the belief that southern blacks lacked the virtues necessary to wield American citizenship. In Lynchburg, Virginia, for instance, Jacob Yoder proclaimed that freedpeople "must learn a great many things before they are what the country wants them to be. They are not reliable enough. They lack independence and energy."[33]

Missionaries regularly commented that they thought all African Americans looked the same and were members of a weak, effeminate, ignorant, juvenile, and uncharitable race. "All these children were black as ink and as shy as wild animals," Elizabeth Botome remembered of her first days with southern blacks. "[T]hey all looked alike to me."[34] "They are simple, childlike people," wrote E. S. Philbrick in March 1862. Cornelia Hancock claimed when she first arrived in 1864, "I never could have known that people could keep body and soul together and be so ignorant as these people if I had not been an eye witness to it."[35] Regarding the possibility of enlisting black soldiers in the Union army, E. S. Philbrick wrote, "I don't regard the blacks as of any account in a military light, for they are not a military race, and have not sufficient intelligence to act in concert in any way where firmness of purpose is required."[36] To physician and teacher Esther Hawks, African American freedpeople "are like ignorant unformed children, and the difficulty of reasoning them out of an opinion or ideas when it once takes possession of them, can never be known 'till tried.'" Working in a hospital primarily for African American civilians and black soldiers, she was especially critical of the lack of charitableness she initially perceived: "They are not thoughtful for each others' comforts, and I never cease wondering at their indifference to the death of their comrads [sic] and even of near friends."[37]

White and black missionaries from the North were shocked by the freedpeople's religious beliefs and practices. "At one of their prayer-meetings, which we attended, last night," wrote Lucy Chase to her parents, "we saw a painful exhibition of their barbarism. Their religious feeling is purely emotional; void of principle, and of no practical utility."[38] Esther Hawks concurred: "They have little or no, idea of *practical religion*. They have certain notions in regard to religion which is quite detrimental to their moral character."[39] In Richmond, Virginia, Cornelia Hancock considered blacks' church services "rude and enthusiastic."[40] These missionaries voiced particular contempt for the "ring shout," a ceremony with West African religious roots in which participants gathered and rotated in a circle as they sang, danced, and clapped. It "seems to me certainly the remains of some old idol worship," claimed Laura Towne after observing such an event on the Sea Islands of South Carolina. "I never saw anything so savage. They call it a religious ceremony, but it seems more like a frolic to me." Charlotte Forten, an African American teacher from Philadelphia, felt similarly. Upon first arriving in the South, she described the shout as "wild and strange."[41]

Several missionary-teachers expressed great reluctance to participate in black society when they first arrived. In April 1862, Laura Towne described how she and other white missionaries observed a ring shout from afar: "Miss Walker and I . . . were there—a little white crowd at the door looking at such a wild firelight scene."[42] Likewise, Lucy and Sarah Chase characterized themselves as "door-way visitors" at a ball, while in West Virginia, Sarah Jane Foster recorded in a letter to a friend that she largely abstained from conversations with locals: "I have not talked much as yet with the people." But when Foster later approached people of color, she felt sickened and prayed that "God will give me grace not to feel contempt for their emotional extravagance."[43] Some other teachers refused not only to share meals with African Americans, but even to shake hands with them. The African Methodist Episcopal Church's *Christian Recorder* rightly complained that some teachers "who, while in the North make loud pretension to Abolition, when they get South partake so largely of that contemptible prejudice that they are ashamed to be seen in company with colored men."[44]

Persistent interracial contact, however, had the power to melt some whites' stereotypes and prejudices. It also offered a moment when these missionaries sharpened cultural tools or forged new ones in order to challenge the chief tenets of white supremacy. The longer a northern teacher remained in the South and the more often that teacher interacted socially with people of color, the stronger the effect the missionary experience had on her imagination and life. From the classroom to the church room, from the lecture hall to the lunch table, and from baptismal fonts to birthday parties, these missionary-teachers took part in an unprecedented amount of interracial cooperation and social contact. They began to view African Americans as individuals, not just as a group. The missionaries increasingly battled for freedpeople's political rights and fought against the infamous "black codes" and other laws that curtailed the liberties of African Americans. Moreover, the teachers attacked whites' racial stereotypes and prejudices. Some of the missionaries even blurred racial lines between "whiteness" and "blackness." In small hamlets throughout the South, these northern Protestants and southern blacks lived out the dream of an integrated nation of fraternity and compassion. They helped create havens of interracial solidarity amid a white-dominated nation marred by a long history of racial hatred and exploitation.

Among the missionaries and the leaders of relief organizations, there was no consensus regarding the merits of social contact between white teachers and African Americans. The Pennsylvania Freedmen's Association mandated that its teachers do all they could "to interest themselves in the moral, religious and social improvement of the families of their pupils; to visit them in their homes; to instruct the women and girls in sewing and domestic economy; to encourage and take part in religious meetings and Sunday Schools."[45] Some leaders, however, discouraged social contact. It "gives me great pleasure to say," wrote the superintendent of education in Mississippi for the Freedmen's Bureau, "that no body of young people whom I have ever known has shown conduct more exemplary and discret [sic]. I have not known a single case of association with the colored people on the ground of social equality."[46]

But regardless of what Freedmen's Bureau leaders wanted or what the relief organizations advised, interracial interaction was almost unavoidable for many of the teachers, especially the female missionaries. Some of them went to great lengths to interact with African Americans, believing that only by ingratiating themselves with the people could they be of service. Social contact reached extraordinary limits during radical Reconstruction. The teachers spent countless hours pouring over spellers and Bibles alongside black children and adults in day schools, night schools, and Sabbath schools. Integrated worship services and other religious ceremonies allowed whites and blacks to enjoy spiritual communion together. The missionaries also joined people of color in sports, parties, meals, and political meetings, while these teachers and southern blacks shared newspapers and magazines, wrote letters for and to one another, and celebrated national and religious holidays collectively. All together, the varieties of social contact did a great deal to tighten the bonds between Protestant missionaries and southern freedpeople.

The belief that all African Americans looked, acted, and felt the same was one of the first stereotypes to be cast aside by white missionaries. "It is a misconception of the African race," wrote one teacher, "which many Anglo-Saxons cherish, *that all the negroes are alike.*" This was patently untrue. "There is as much *individuality*—as much variety of intellectual and moral temperament," he continued, "among the negroes as there is among persons of any other race."[47] "My Northern friends need not think that I have any difficulty in recognizing my flock," wrote Sarah Jane Foster to *Zion's Advocate,* a Freewill Baptist Church periodical. "There is as much individuality among them as among white people."[48] A Quaker teacher in Clarkesville, Tennessee, similarly assured her northern friends that after "a little acquaintance," her students "were [as] distinguishable as our students at home."[49] "I notice as much individuality in the faces of Negroes as I do in those of the whites," affirmed Lucy Chase in a letter to her family.[50]

As they spent more time with local blacks in classrooms and Sabbath schools, the missionaries were amazed by the intelligence of the freedpeople and their earnest desire for education. Before, during, and after the Civil War, southern blacks went to extraordinary lengths to learn to read and write, and teachers recognized and applauded these strivings. Laura Haviland, for instance, marveled at one African American woman "who had taught a midnight school for years" before the war. "It was opened at eleven or twelve o'clock at night, and closed at two o'clock A. M. Every window and door was carefully closed to prevent discovery. In that little school hundreds of slaves learned to read and write a legible hand. After toiling all day for their masters they crept stealthily into this back alley, each with a bundle of pitch-pine splinters for lights."[51] Upon talking with Will Capers, a local black who had received an education before the war, Laura Towne recorded, "He is very intelligent and self-respecting. He is in hopes he will be paid for teaching." In a later entry, she referred to him as "a fine fellow in every respect."[52]

Countless missionary-teachers wrote to their supporters in the North that African American children learned just as quickly as white students and were equally capable. The reports of the teachers influenced broader northern opinions. According to John W. Alvord, the general superintendent of education for the Freedmen's Bureau, the teachers' findings thoroughly destroyed the "charge that the negro is 'too stupid too learn.'" This stereotype, he concluded, "has passed away."[53]

Along with the classroom experiences, Christian worship services provided numerous moments for northern missionaries and southern blacks to interact with one another spiritually and to experience new feelings of community. Although most religious historians have focused on why southern African Americans left white churches en masse after the Civil War and further solidified the segregation of the churches, these scholars have overlooked the scores of examples of integrated religious services during radical Reconstruction. Moreover, few historians have recognized the importance of integrated worship on the minds and spirits of nineteenth-century whites.[54] Missionary accounts were filled with descriptions of black worship services, prayers, and sermons. During church meetings northerners sang and prayed alongside blacks, and several missionary-teachers preached to these congregations. Some were even invited to "secret" church services like those African Americans had held during the antebellum period in order to worship outside of their masters' or mistresses' gaze.[55]

Church services, along with weddings, baptisms, and funerals, provided powerful moments of interracial socializing and had a marked effect on several missionaries. Some recorded being emotionally and spiritually moved by the prayers of freedpeople. Lucy Chase was struck when one freedman "prayed for black and white, for rich and poor, for bond and free."[56] "A prayer-meeting" of fifty African Americans deeply stirred Marie Waterbury. Some of the participants, she recalled, "were stolen from Africa when they were infants; some whose mothers had been sold and run off to the sugar plantations, before they were a year old. Ah! how such had learned to pray."[57] Laura Towne was equally touched when a local elder "prayed that 'the little white sisters who came to give learning to the children might be blessed.'"[58] A missionary in Mississippi probably put the impact of interracial worship most poignantly. "As I walked home in the beautiful moonlight" from attending and preaching at a worship service with local blacks, "I could but think that perhaps God was as well pleased with that lowly group in the humble cabin, as with many a gilded throng in splendid cathedrals."[59]

Death often brought together northern whites and southern blacks in common feelings of grief and led to integrated rituals of bereavement. As the pioneering sociologist of religion Emile Durkheim and his followers have shown, rituals have integrative social functions that bind members of society into a unit. In the context of radical Reconstruction, racially integrated rituals fostered strong ties between white missionaries and southern blacks.[60] After attending a funeral for an African American on the Sea Islands, in which local black children sang hymns and read from their school primers, William Gannett penned a poem describing the beautiful scene:

> 'Twas at set of sun; a tattered troop
>   Of children circled a little grave,
> Chanting an anthem rich in its peace
>   As ever pealed in cathedral-nave,—
>
> . . . .
>
> The holiest hymn that the children knew!
>   'Twas dreams come real, and heaven come near;
> 'Twas light, and liberty, and joy,
>   And "white folks' sense,"—and God right here.
>
> . . . .
>
> Children, too, and the mysteries last!
>   We are but comrades with them *there*,—
> Stammering over a meaning vast,
>   Crooning our guesses of how and where.[61]

When a white missionary, Martha Johnson, died in 1871 in South Carolina, local blacks and whites collectively mourned over their loss. Several African American ministers offered eulogies, and, as another northern missionary wrote, "then, white and colored friends shared in the privilege of filling up the grave." When performing these rituals, feelings of comradeship and friendship emerged. Whether grieving together, praising "new life" found in baptism, or merely worshiping the Lord, scores of missionary-teachers and southern blacks forged new and powerful friendships during religious services.[62]

Several teachers expressed a new respect for African American religious practices as they spent more spiritual time with freedpeople. After speaking with an elderly black woman and her family, Reverend W. J. Richardson wrote from South Carolina, "Such interviews, even in the *lowly cabin—seem quite on the verge of Heaven*." "This aged mother cannot read a word," he continued, "and yet she seemed to possess the life experience of a mature Christian."[63] In July 1862,

Towne described one local minister as "looking like Jupiter himself, grave, power-ful, and awfully dignified." Historian Kurt Wolfe has shown that with time Towne stopped using words like "superstitious" or "backward" to describe black religion in her diary. Even more, she began to seek out African American elders to learn about African customs. "I went to-day to see Maum Katie, an old African woman, who remembers worshipping her own gods in Africa," Towne wrote in her jour-nal. She was deeply impressed by Katie: "She is very bright and talkative, and is a great 'spiritual mother,' a fortune-teller, or rather prophetess, and a woman of tremendous influence." Katie so captivated Towne, in fact, that she determined to "cultivate her acquaintance."[64] African American religious services thoroughly enthralled one missionary in Mississippi. "The religion of these people is not a cold abstraction," she asserted. "Its life giving influence lightens the eye, quickens the step, gives tone and vigor to the whole man."[65] Several teachers expressed sin-cere fondness for the slave spirituals. The Chase sisters lauded African American hymns and songs as "poetic and picturesque." Elizabeth Botome concurred, writ-ing years later, "One who has not heard these spirituals under such circumstances cannot understand their power and pathos. I can never hear them, even at this date, without emotion."[66]

Even the ring shout was seen in a new light. Several missionaries who had ini-tially viewed this ritual as a barbaric relic of ancient African traditions soon showed appreciation for it. After Charlotte Forten had been working among the Sea Islanders for nine months, she began to enjoy the shouts. "The whole thing was quite inspiring," she wrote on April 26, 1863. A couple of days later, she once again noted, "I enjoy these 'shouts' very much."[67] Several years among the freed-people in West Virginia led Sarah Jane Foster to reverse her original disdain for the ceremonies, and she now considered them "very beautiful."[68] The new enjoyment for the ring shout reflected a much broader transformation. While these mission-aries had at first disdained blacks' religious and cultural customs, months and years of contact and interaction led them to find beauty, joy, and communion with the sacred among African American communities.

Many hours spent cooking, cleaning, and visiting with southern blacks proved just as powerful in altering teachers' attitudes. In particular, the art and discipline of listening was central to transforming their imaginations. These missionaries lived what twentieth-century black liberationist theologian James Cone has vigor-ously asserted was necessary for whites to cast off their paternalism. "If whites were really serious about their radicalism," he wrote in 1970, "they would keep silent and take instructions from black people."[69] That was precisely what several missionaries did during radical Reconstruction. Laura Towne and Laura Haviland specifically asked black women to share their stories of slavery. The tales wrenched their hearts. Towne noted repeatedly in her diary that slaves disclosed their memories of being "licked," "whipped," and "shot." Towne heard about the scars of slavery and saw them as well. On several occasions, African Americans revealed their bruised and lacerated bodies. "Loretta of this place showed me her back and arms to-day," Towne wrote in May 1862. "In many places there were ridges as high and long as my little finger, and she said she had had four babies killed within her by whipping." [70] After listening to similar "sad recitals," Haviland closed one meeting "with prayer. . . . A solemn season it was, to mingle our tears and voices with those who had passed through such scenes of suffering and were now praising the Lord for freedom." [71] Sarah Jane Foster made it a point to pay attention to the tales of local blacks. "I keep still and listen," she recorded in her diary. [72] When black men and women recounted stories of slavery and freedom to the Chase sisters, they commiserated deeply, especially with the African American women. "Heart-broken, too, some of them are!" wrote Lucy. "Husbands are with the army, they know not where. They are alone, with no one to comfort them." [73] Esther Hawks noted in her diary that she desired every opportunity to make "myself as thoroughly conversant with their inner lives as I could." [74]

Encountering and spending time with African American soldiers propelled some teachers to express unexpected admiration for them. In early 1864, Esther Hawks traveled with several regiments of the U.S. Colored Troops to Florida, where she tended to their medical needs, wrote letters for them, and taught school. She felt enormous pride in the fighting prowess of these soldiers: "The men especially the colored troops fought like demons." She also articulated a newfound emotional attachment to them. "Strange how much I miss them," she wrote after the men had been away for several days on a mission, "especially when I remember that I had hardly a speaking acquaintance with a single officer or man in the Regt. but they were so quiet and gentlemanly that I felt a sort of protection in their nearness which I now miss!" [75] African Americans' willingness to fight and to give their lives led missionaries such as Hawks to a new appreciation for black "manhood." One teacher in Tennessee put it this way: African American soldiers "are men who ask no *title* of nobility, but whose whole bearing tells the story of a princely heart and a manhood that puts doubt to shame." [76]

African Americans also convinced Hawks that she had been wrong in her initial opinion of them as uncharitable. After the soldiers of the Massachusetts 54th Regiment made their ill-fated assault on South Carolina's Battery Wagner, local freedpeople rallied to help care for the hundreds of wounded soldiers. Their compassion and generosity amazed Hawks. "We had no beds, and no means even of building a fire," she wrote in her diary, "but the colored people come promptly to our aid and almost before we knew what we needed they brought us buckets full of nice broth and gruels, pitchers of lemonade, fruits, cakes, vegetables indeed everything needed for the immediate wants of the men was furnished—not for one day but for many." On another occasion she expressed surprise when an injured African American encouraged his doctor to operate on a more badly wounded man. "While the Surgeon Dr. H. [J. M. Hawks] was dressing the wounds of one of the men—another man came up with his arm badly shattered—when the first man stepped back saying 'fix him first, boss he's worse than I is.'" To Hawks, this was truly a noble act: "How few are the men of any color who could have been more unselfish!"[77]

Ultimately, interracial interaction transformed the ways in which missionaries viewed themselves and their relationships to the black community. When most northerners first ventured south, they tended to characterize blacks as "they" and "them." But as these teachers attended worship services, cooked dinners, and taught schools alongside freedpeople, the pronouns "we" and "us" slowly crept into their writings. Martha Johnson was a case in point. In her initial letters home from Port Royal, she regularly referred to local African Americans as "they" or "them." But with time, her viewpoint shifted. "If I do my duty by my school and visit among my people I have very little time or strength for household work," she wrote to her sisters in Vermont.[78] Likewise, when leaving Virginia's Fort Magruder for the summer, Margaret Newbold Thorpe recalled that "[i]t was very painful to leave our people." When Thorpe returned to the school in the early fall, she recorded that "[o]ur people are now taking up letter writing."[79] Lucy Chase recognized that something new was happening to her. "I can truly say," she wrote in March 1863, "white-man though I am, that I have, with the Negro, 'a feeling sense' of this state of transition. Lo! an episode! Every hour of my life here is strange; it is not the past; it is not the future, and, with all the chances and changes of war it does not seem to be the present either." By 1866, Lucy's sister Sarah had cast off identification as a "white-man." She now characterized herself as part of the African American community. "*If* I live, I must work *among* my people again," she wrote.[80] In a study of missionary letters, one modern historian has found that northern missionaries so often employed idioms like "my people" in reference to African Americans that "one could be easily led astray by thinking that the writer who used such phrases. . . . was black."[81]

Indeed, the racial self-images of some teachers seemed to be melting in the crucible of radical Reconstruction. Several missionaries collapsed distinctions between whites and blacks either by claiming that they ceased viewing their African American friends as "black," or by characterizing themselves as people of color. Shifting racial views seemed to occur specifically during moments of interracial contact. "I never think of their black skins when I am with them," Martha Johnson wrote home. On another occasion, she claimed that "I am very much interested [in] my work and never think of these black faces when I am with them." [82] "I suppose it would seem strange to you to sit down with two colored people," Laura Towne wrote to northern friends on Christmas Day, 1864, "but to us it is the most natural thing in the world. I actually forget these people are black, and it is only when I see them at a distance and cannot recognize their features that I remember it." [83]

While Towne and Johnson claimed to "forget" the alleged racial differences between whites and blacks, several other missionary-teachers characterized themselves as full-fledged members of African American society. One teacher wrote to a northern friend, "I declare, I never think but I am black too when I am with my scholars." [84] In 1865, Esther Hawks situated herself within black society when describing celebrations of the end of the war. "The great day for us 'colored' people" has come, she wrote: "[T]he day most jubilant and the longest to be remembered by us." [85] Similarly, some African Americans viewed missionary-teachers as not white. Referring to the Euro-American teachers at Towne's school in South Carolina, one black student maintained that she and her classmates "never think of *you* as *white*." [86]

Surprisingly, at least one missionary even sought to pass as black so that southern whites would leave her alone. In West Virginia, Sarah Jane Foster forged close relationships with several African American men, and they regularly escorted her home in the evenings. Her interactions with these black men led some local whites to wonder about her race. "Out there it has been told that I was part colored and was *married to Geo. Brown*," Foster noted in February 1866. One neighbor even asked if Foster was "half nigger." These assertions and queries, which would have infuriated most other northern whites, did not enrage Foster. Instead, she actually preferred that local whites consider her "part black" so that she could work with the freedpeople without interference. "I hope they will believe it," Foster wrote to *Zion's Advocate*, "for then surely they could not complain of my teaching the people of my own race." To Foster, becoming "part colored" was an effective strategy to continue her great work.[87]

Social contact, emerging friendships, and the blurring of racial lines reinforced a larger political and social radicalism enacted by these missionary teachers. Their personal encounters generated larger social and political awareness. Many became staunch and life-long advocates of political and civil rights for people of color, striving for a new American republic that would look beyond race as the key determinant of civic inclusion. Not only did they express a hope that blacks would obtain equal rights, but they also actively championed that cause. Methodist teachers in New Orleans, for example, asserted that "[t]he question . . . of equal rights . . . among men, irrespective of . . . race, is not one to be argued, but accepted by those who believe in the Bible."[88] Sounding much like Thaddeus Stevens when he repeatedly called on the federal government to give confiscated lands to freedpeople, Cornelia Hancock thought that "the best plan would be to put all the secesh in the poor house and let the negroes have the land."[89] Connecting her experiences with African American soldiers at church to her growing feeling that God demanded universal manhood suffrage, a missionary in Baltimore professed, "As I watched their coming into church on their crutches, as I saw their earnest and devout attention, the intelligence manifested in their engaging in the different parts of worship, . . . I thought, can there be found a man who would dare deny these men the right of suffrage or any other privilege which freemen have? If so, God will by some *other* judgment teach us *His* will." Linda Slaughter clearly expressed the belief that American citizenship and identity should not be premised upon racial categories when she referred to freedpeople as America's "true home-born sons."[90]

From her initial venture to the South Carolina Sea Islands in 1862 to her death there four decades later, Laura Towne remained an unfailing supporter of social and political rights for African Americans. In 1863 she rejoiced when the Union government decreed that local blacks would receive titles to property on the Sea Islands. "Hurrah! Jubilee!" she cheered, "Lands are to be set apart for the people so that they cannot be oppressed, or driven to work for speculators, or ejected from their homesteads." Towne spent countless hours with freedpeople discussing the best ways for them to purchase and develop property. In 1864, she wrote a letter to President Abraham Lincoln on behalf of an elderly Sea Islander who did not want to lose his land.[91] Then in the 1870s, she befriended Robert Smalls, an African American who had gained fame and freedom during the Civil War when he piloted a Confederate steamer into the hands of the Union navy in a daring effort to liberate himself and several other black families. Smalls went on to become one of the first African American congressmen. When he fell on hard times in the late 1870s after white Democrats had him arrested on a trumped up charge of accepting a bribe, Towne offered him advice. They even debated the possibilities of moving all blacks from the Sea Islands to Arizona.[92]

Towne vigorously attacked white supremacy. She assailed former Confederates for seeking to return African Americans to state-imposed bondage under convict-lease systems and apprenticeship programs aimed at black youth. To her, the abuses of the criminal justice system were alarming: "Men are there chained with their necks in an iron collar and joined to ankle chains. They never take these off." Tales of young black men psychologically, spiritually, and physically destroyed by the system deeply saddened and enraged her: "A young boy of fourteen, sentenced to five years for only *being* in a whiskey shop where a man was killed, wears hand-cuffs, and the poor fellow says he prays night and day that God will let him die. The irons have cut into his wrists. The beds are rotten straw, full of vermin." [93]

In addition to advocating civil rights for people of color, these teachers launched a full-scale offensive against racial stereotypes of all sorts. Reports of African Americans traveling great distances and braving great odds to attend schools subverted racist arguments of blacks' laziness. "How few of those who call the Freedmen 'lazy niggers' would walk five and six miles after working hard all day, for the sake of learning to read?" asked one missionary. [94] Quaker teacher Alida Clarke chastised her northern Quaker brethren for harboring racial stereotypes. To her, the chasm separating white Friends from southern blacks was not the fault of the freedpeople. The separation resulted from whites' sins. "Many *good* people profess to believe that the *colored people* are too emotional and impressible ever to become Friends," she wrote. But a "thorough and deep work of grace is just the same in the heart, no matter the color of the skin. . . . Let us examine ourselves and see if there is not a prejudice and jealousy (cruel as the grave) against color that is hindering our ultimate success, in doing all the good we desire among them, profiting the present generation, and reaching down to posterity." [95]

Traveling north with a group of black scholars during the summer of 1867, Sarah Jane Foster found northern white racism abhorrent. Old family friends now appalled her with their disparaging "remarks about the 'niggers.'" She realized that her own sympathies had grown since she had begun her mission to the freedpeople, and Foster celebrated her personal transformation in her journal. "I thank God that I have a broader interest in humanity," she wrote in her diary. "God forgive me that I ever lacked it at all. Now I shall do all that I can henceforth to help the colored people rise." A year later she further reflected upon the importance of persistent contact, maintaining, "The longer I know them the more my soul revolts at the tyranny which would fain deny them the right to all human feelings and passions." [96]

Back in the South in 1868, Foster challenged a number of racist myths held by whites in a letter to *Zion's Advocate*. Her own experiences with people of color provided the ammunition to assail prominent stereotypes. "Are these the people who in freedom were to relapse into barbarism?" she asked and answered: "Things do not look like it here." African Americans were not dull or unintelligent, she contended, and they did not wish to rule over whites. "[W]e hear a great deal of cant about 'negro domination' and 'negro insolence,'" she acknowledged, "but I am bold to say that I am very pleasantly situated on a black man's farm, with no white neighbors, and rarely seeing a white face, and I was never better treated." She derided the notion that blacks were lazy. "[P]eople tell us that 'negroes won't work,'" she wrote, "however, these Gatson's are black," and they ran one of the finest farms in the area. "I do not find them exceptions to the general rule of conduct."[97]

Some missionary-teachers and their northern advocates even challenged whites' phobias surrounding interracial marriage and sexuality. In the North, prominent abolitionist and Christian reformer Lewis Tappan, one of the vice presidents of the AMA, claimed that since the Bible made no declaration against interracial marriage, then humans ought not to either. There were, moreover, several instances of interracial marriages among those who took part in the education crusade, and some missionaries adamantly defended the rights of whites and blacks to marry whomever they wished.[98] In 1869, Gilbert Haven predicted that interracial marriage would become the norm in the near future. "The hour is not far off when the white hued husband shall boast of the dusky beauty of his wife," he claimed, "and the Caucasian wife shall admire the sun-kissed countenance of her husband as deeply and as unconsciously of the present ruling abhorrence as is his admiration for her lighter tint."[99] When a chaplain in Florida refused to wed a black soldier and his white fiancée, a southern woman who had formerly owned him, Esther Hawks vigorously disputed his decision. "I took the ground that he had no right to refuse to perform the ceremony *simply* on account of color," she wrote in her journal: "If a white woman *chooses* to marry a black man who can say her nay. . . . The discussion grew quite animated but I do not think we made the Chaplin see the *foolishness* of his position."[100]

Hawks went far beyond accepting social interaction and equality between whites and blacks. She helped foster it. In July 1865, she threw a party for African American members of the Massachusetts 54th Regiment and white Yankee schoolteachers and nurses. The party was a smashing success in Hawks's estimation, because it overcame notions of racial difference if only for the moment. She wrote triumphantly: "[F]or *one* evening, at least, a company of ladies and gentlemen treated each other as such without regard to *color*." To Hawks, "the most observing critic could not have noticed the least prejudice—or unpleasant feeling of any kind towards each other." She considered these soldiers "gentlemen" regardless of their skin color, and she saw no reason for northern women not to enjoy their company.[101]

The acceptance and even facilitation of intimate socializing between black men and white women clashed directly with one of the most powerful aspects of nineteenth-century white Negrophobia—the fear of interracial sexuality. In the second half of the century, beginning most blatantly during the Civil War, white supremacists asserted that greater rights for African Americans would invariably lead to interracial sex. In an effort to undermine Abraham Lincoln's presidential campaign of 1864, Democrats played upon the fears that many northern whites held regarding interracial relationships. If victorious, Democrats claimed, Lincoln and his Republican cohorts would bring social equality, which would lead to "detestable" scenes of black men courting white women and dancing with them.[102] By and large, northern Republicans responded to these attacks by rejecting all notions of interracial sexuality and social equality. At a political meeting in Springfield, Illinois, in 1857, Lincoln had acknowledged such abhorrence among northern whites. "There is a natural disgust," he announced, "in the minds of nearly all white people, to the idea of an indiscriminate amalgamation of the white and black races." The Republican Party was not interested in overcoming or rejecting this "natural disgust." [103]

But Hawks and Haven refused to bend to whites' racial and sexual phobias. To them, the sight of African American men socializing with and even marrying white women was not abhorrent. On the contrary, it was glorious. Hawks's desire to promote such opportunities for black men and white women demonstrated a willingness to advocate levels of social equality far in advance of nearly all her contemporaries. Her praise for social interactions between men and women, blacks and whites, showed how severely whites' imaginations could change in the 1860s. For her, interracial sexuality was no longer taboo. Marriage was a personal matter between two individuals. Racial differences were irrelevant.

Although parties like the one Hawks organized were doubtless uncommon throughout the South, regular holiday celebrations were occasions for whites and blacks to reflect upon and enact changes in their racial and national imaginations. Northern missionaries regularly observed Christmas, Thanksgiving, New Year's Day, and the Fourth of July with southern blacks, often commenting that these interracial celebrations seemed to prove that a new and integrated nation was being forged.[104] On New Year's Day, 1863—the day Lincoln signed the Emancipation Proclamation—a massive celebration took place on the Sea Islands of

South Carolina. Thousands of whites and blacks prayed, sang, and cheered to-gether. Charlotte Forten penned a powerful description of the event, which was later published in the *Atlantic Monthly* and reprinted in Lydia Marie Child's *The Freedmen's Book*. "New-Year's Day, Emancipation Day, was a glorious one to us," she claimed. It was "[t]he greatest day in the nation's history." Local blacks be-lieved that emancipation had made the country their own. After Colonel Thomas Wentworth Higginson, the white leader of the 2nd Regiment of the U.S. Colored Troops, had finished speaking, "some of the colored people, of their own accord, began to sing, 'My country 'tis of thee/Sweet land of liberty,/Of thee we sing.'" Forten and the local freedpeople were ecstatic. "'Forever free! forever free!'— those magical words in the President's Proclamation were constantly singing themselves in my soul."[105]

Other missionary-teachers made similar observations. William Gannett of Port Royal recognized that when whites and blacks celebrated the Fourth of July together, something completely new was happening in the nation. "It was strange and moving down here on South Carolina ground, with the old flag waving above us, to tell a thousand slaves that they were freemen, that the flag was theirs, that our country now meant their country," he wrote.[106] On New Year's Day in 1866, Laura Haviland attended a huge interracial parade in Richmond, Virginia, where banners proclaimed "Peace, Liberty, and Freedom with all Mankind."[107] On that same day, Elizabeth Botome took part in an "Emancipation Jubilee," in which she and other whites sang with local blacks. Truly, she believed, they had found the "New Jerusalem."[108]

While many modern historians have much more readily pointed out the missionary-teachers' racial prejudice than their progress, African Americans dur-ing and after the Civil War were much more likely to praise these northerners. People of color could distinguish their allies from their enemies. Even historian Leon Litwack, who castigated the white missionaries for their paternalism in his Pulitzer Prize–winning *Been in the Storm So Long*, has acknowledged that "nearly every postwar black convention and newspaper praised the white benevolent so-cieties for their efforts."[109] In June 1868, one southern black wrote to an AMA field secretary, "We know that you all is the only friend we have save god."[110] Two of Lucy and Sarah Chase's former black students affirmed this sense of friendship in letters to their teachers. "Miss G received A letter from you and was glad to hear from you," wrote one student. "Miss Gayle say she would like to see you so would I." Another wrote, "I often wish you were here to teach. I trust I will have the pleasure of seeing you once more. Should we not meet on earth may we meet in heaven where parting is no more."[111] A bishop of the African Methodist Episcopal Church astutely recognized that "[m]any thousands of our white friends are doing all they can to atone for the past."[112]

One freed man defied anyone to denounce the northern white teachers, writing, "If you say the yankee is no friend how is it that the ladies from the north have left their homes and came down here? Why are they laboring day and night to elevate the collord people?" To this southern black, the educational crusade was a gift from heaven, and African Americans must take advantage of it: "I'm going to school now to try to learn some things which I hope will enable me to be of some use to my race. These few lines will show that I am a new beginner. I will try, and do better. . . . Thank God I have a book now. The Lord has sent us books and teachers. We must not hesitate a moment, but go on and learn all we can." Education was a crucial aspect of the road to genuine liberation. "Leaving learning to your children was better than leaving them a fortune," commented one Louisiana farmer. Another claimed, "I shall give my children a chance to go to school, for I considers education next best ting [sic] to liberty."[113]

III

While these northern whites and southern blacks gained new appreciations for one another and worked together to bring full citizenship rights to freedpeople, their efforts greatly antagonized most southern whites and kept the sections in opposition to one another. Former Confederates almost universally despised the invasion of the "Yankee schoolmarm," because educational advancement would further liberate African Americans from the control of southern whites. Although some southern whites supported schools for freedpeople, most felt insulted by the crusade. They lashed out in anger and frustration. Southern terrorist organizations, such as the Ku Klux Klan and the Knights of the White Camellia, battled against radical Reconstruction in all of its forms—religious, political, and social. The struggle for the South transformed from one of large, organized armies into a guerrilla war that pitted largely defenseless teachers and freedpeople against white vigilantes hell-bent on using any amount of force to preserve the prewar order.

Northern missionaries often exacerbated this animosity since they regularly described southerners as poor, uneducated, and uncivilized traitors who did not deserve equal citizenship in the nation. "I have never seen, in all my life, a more destitute section," wrote one missionary. "It is absolutely distressing to think of it. No intelligence—no refinement, and as stupid as ignorance can make them."[114] Some northerners—white and black—were especially critical of poor southern whites. "These Fla. Crackers are much less human than the negroes, more igno-rant, dirty and lifeless," claimed Esther Hawks. "[M]any of them look as if they had already been buried for months—their hair and skin and dirty, faded butter-nut clothes, look all of a piece. Even the negro's have great contempt for them."[115] One African Methodist Episcopal minister likewise claimed that poor whites were "the most miserable specimens of humanity he had ever seen."[116] Another teacher de-picted white southerners as thoroughly unrepentant and unwilling to join the na-tion in good faith. "It is my opinion that the spirit [of] '61 is rife today as it was then," asserted Reverend H. C. Vogell, "and like burning lava, is only waiting an outlet to deluge the country with contention and strife."[117] At various times, Char-lotte Forten referred to the South as a "barbarous place," while another teacher claimed that living in the South was like living in the land of the "uncircumcised Philistine." "I cannot treat a Rebel with the cordiality of an acquaintance," wrote Martha Smedley to a friend in the North. "No! No!"[118]

Former Confederates reacted to the crusade for racial uplift with intense dis-pleasure. Many southern whites refused to board or sell food to northern visitors, while some snubbed missionaries on railroad coaches. Northern teachers often ex-perienced social ostracism for the first time when attending church services with former Confederates. Margaret Thorpe reported that "when the [church] services were concluded they [the southern whites] quietly withdrew, no one speaking to them [the missionaries], nor did I ever hear of any member of the church making them a visit."[119] Novelist Albion Tourgée claimed that when southern whites sought to "expel" Yankee missionaries, the first step involved rejection from the church. "We do not often go to church now," lamented one northerner in Tourgée's semi-autobiographical *A Fool's Errand.* "[T]here is constant coldness, which says, plainer than words can, that we are not wanted." Tourgée recounted other complaints about religious ostracism. One man was "dropped from the church-roll" after he had defended black manhood suffrage, while others "were ex-cluded from the Lord's Communion for establishing Sabbath schools for colored people."[120]

Northern missionaries regularly commented on the "coldness" they encoun-tered in the South. A Quaker teacher in Clarkesville, Tennessee, believed that local whites "would have been glad of the opportunity to have poisoned us. No white person spoke to us, and the town people never moved an inch on the walk for us."[121] From North Carolina, Margaret Thorpe wrote to one of her friends in the North, "You can't imagine how strange it seems never to speak to a white person, and have absolutely no social life, not one visitor. The Southern women will not notice us at all."[122] "We never see anyone except ourselves and two or three northern gentlemen who have plantations near here," noted Cornelia Hancock in a letter to her mother in April 1866. "Everyone hates us with a bitter hatred here. They would be glad if a consuming fire would come over the land and annihilate both the contrabands and their teachers."[123] One northern teacher put it most simply: "we are shut out from white society."[124]

Southern religious leaders often did their best to engender anger toward northern missionaries. While most southern denominations at least tacitly encouraged education for freedpeople, they adamantly refused to join northerners in the effort. Historian J. Wayne Flynt has shown that Alabama Baptists felt that too much blood had been spilled during the war for amicable relations between the North and the South. The northern emphasis on African American citizenship and equal civil rights was also extremely disturbing. Southern Baptists wanted nothing to do with any mission that mixed religion and politics. Likewise, some southern Methodists proclaimed, "The churchmen of the Presbyterian and Methodist Churches in the North are largely identified with this attempt of violent revolution." They denounced any camaraderie with them. "Preachers, white or black, imported from the North, infected with extreme notions, and burning with fanatical ardor, would inflict incurable damage upon" their churches.[125]

Some southerners took to openly denouncing and threatening the teachers, sometimes rhetorically associating the missionaries with demonic forces. A writer for the *Norfolk Virginian* described the teachers as "a lot of ignorant, narrow-minded, bigoted fanatics."[126] The epithet "nigger teacher" became widely employed. "From one set of students, whose boarding-house I was compelled constantly to pass, I habitually received the polite salutation of 'damned Yankee bitch of a nigger teacher,' with the occasional admonition to take up my abode in the infernal regions," said one missionary. Another teacher heard local whites proclaiming, "Here comes Hell," every time she came near.[127] Lucy and Sarah Chase recounted similar episodes. "One of our main-land neighbors," Lucy wrote in March 1863, "is disgusted at the very thought that any-body could be found so silly as to come out here to teach the negroes! 'I'd poison a Yankee in a moment, if I could get a chance,' she says." Another southern woman told one of Lucy's friends, "I wish I had a pistol, and I would shoot you." At least one opponent of the teachers explicitly denounced them for defying the chief tenets of the white republic. "The Radicals are flail of Deity," a white supremacist theologian asserted, "they have turned traitors to their race, their religion and their God."[128]

But verbal barbs and church ostracism were perhaps the least of northern-ers' worries. During Reconstruction the symbols of blacks' empowerment and interracial fraternity—schools, churches, teachers, and politicians—became ob-jects of such hatred that former Confederates often resorted to violence. Guns, ar-son, and intimidation became the chief tools of opposition to the new nation that the radicals envisioned.[129] Examples of violence committed against teachers and African Americans littered John Alvord's reports for the Freedmen's Bureau. The Bureau superintendent in Louisiana, for instance, wrote in 1866, "The hostility to colored schools was so great that many acts of violence and insult were commit-ted on the teachers; school-houses were burned, and pupils beaten and fright-ened."[130] Scores of churches and schools were set ablaze, while white and black teachers were brutalized. The tale of Alonzo B. Corliss, a partially crippled teacher at a Quaker-sponsored school, revealed the extent to which southern whites would go to rid their land of northern missionaries. On November 26, 1869, sev-eral disguised men dragged Corliss from his house and gave him about thirty lashes with a rawhide and hickory sticks, shaved one side of his head, painted it black, and warned him to leave. Corliss eventually did vacate the South, but only after his landlord forced him out. Local authorities did nothing to arrest or prosecute the attackers.[131]

Former Confederates became especially enraged when they perceived that northern whites regarded people of color as social equals. Alonzo Corliss was attacked for "teaching niggers and making them like white men."[132] Southern Baptists denounced the northern missionaries for teaching "politics rather than religion" and "equal suffrage rather than repentance."[133] Southern Methodists complained that "we must express, with regret, our apprehension that a large pro-portion, if not a majority of Northern Methodists have become incurably radical. They teach for doctrine the commandments of men. They preach another Gospel. They have incorporated social dogmas and political tests into their Church creeds."[134] One native Georgian made it very clear that southerners despised social interactions between northerners and southern blacks. He found mis-sionaries' assertions that blacks were equal to whites particularly obnoxious. "For a white Northern lady here to kiss a colored child is very *imprudent* to say the least of it," he insisted, "and, in replying to an insulting remark made by a white person, to say that the negroes are as good as that white person, is *entirely unnecessary.*"[135] A teacher in Macon, Georgia, believed that she and her mis-sionary colleagues were disliked because "our workers recognize respectable colored men & women *socially.*"[136] James G. Southall of the *Charlottesville Chronicle* indicated that this missionary's claim was accurate. Southern whites tolerated northern schoolteachers who taught basic reading and writing, but when the missionary-teachers chose to "communicate to the colored people ideas of social equality with whites," the former Confederates had no choice but to fight back.[137]

Violence induced great fear among northern missionaries. Often writing about and discussing violence committed against their brethren, some northern teachers were in an almost constant state of terror. One missionary in Americus, Georgia, wrote, "I sometimes feel so utterly helpless and alone and have so many severe and bitter [experiences] to bear that I yell at times. I cannot bear it. My life is in danger every hour."[138] Jacob Yoder recorded in his diary of having "terrible" dreams that he "had fallen into the hands of murderous party."[139] "I can hardly tell whether I have really been in much danger or not," asserted a missionary in Savannah, Georgia, "but I truly believe myself to be, and I know that nothing but my being a lady, and utterly without protection, saved me."[140] Another put it most poignantly: "Bands of armed and masked men are prowling around nights whipping some, and murdering others. Politicians, at a public meeting, have threatened our schools, and being isolated from every human protection, we are in great fear and peril."[141] The stress of impending danger made this missionary's life remarkably difficult. "I have devoted the nights to watching, for the protection of life, and to guard our buildings against fire. To be for weeks in constant expectation of being murdered or burned out, and without losing faith in God, is something of a strain on the nerves." In short, education for freedpeople was not the "easy panacea" that historian Ronald Butchart has claimed it was. Missions to southern blacks were full of danger and often led to physical and psychological violence committed against the northern teachers.[142]

While southern terrorism made many missionaries tremble, it also led to stronger ties between some teachers and black communities. As Harriet Jacobs, author of one of the most compelling slave narratives, wrote, "There are no bonds so strong as those which are formed by suffering together."[143] This was especially true of Sarah Jane Foster's experience. When local whites fired their guns at a meeting of local blacks she attended in January 1866, she quickly grabbed the hand of an African American man for comfort. Later, she confided in her diary that because of the attack, she "never felt so much like staying here as now."[144] She did remain among freedpeople, until her death in 1868, probably of yellow fever. Another teacher, Edward Payson Hall, resolved that he would willingly face death for the cause. "It was better to die at our posts than to flee from duty," he maintained, "Many a time . . . I dreaded the bullet or poison of the assassin—but never has that fear overcome my care for the friendless."[145]

During the 1860s and early 1870s, these northern missionaries helped publicize to a national audience the viciousness of southern society and the militant unwillingness of former Confederates to change their ways. Letters from the teachers and their visits to the North kept northerners informed of events in the South, making it virtually impossible for northerners to accept that peace had come to the South. Some relief organizations mandated that the teachers write letters about their experiences. The New England Freedmen's Aid Society, for example, instructed its members that "it is the duty of the adopted teacher to correspond with the branch society, which assumes her support, giving them all the interesting information in her power."[146] Northern newspapers and magazines, including the *Congregationalist,* the *New York Tribune,* the *New York Times,* the *American Missionary,* the *New York Independent,* and the *North American Review,* were filled with stories of "white terror," and northern radical Republicans regularly invoked the news as evidence of the need for a stronger federal presence in the South.[147]

Reports of violence against schools, churches, and teachers were so pervasive that when Congress commissioned an inquiry about the Ku Klux Klan, federal investigators repeatedly asked defendants: "Has there been in your county or your part of the State any disturbances of your schools?" The answers were horrifying, since teachers and pupils had been whipped, burned, and murdered. The Klan hearings shored up the claims of countless missionaries that the South was a lawless land. The Civil War's violent struggle had shifted to a chaotic battle between southern vigilantes and largely unarmed schoolteachers and their pupils.[148]

Observing and reading about southern violence led several missionaries and their northern friends to reject any calls for national reconciliation with the South. "There is one thing certain, the Rebels are violent rebels yet and no compromises with them will have beneficial results," wrote Cornelia Hancock.[149] In a letter to another missionary in February 1866, Sarah Chase heaped scorn on any notion that the sections could or should be reunited: "Union! I can more easily conceive of the Lion and the Lambs lying down together, than of a union of the North and the South." Northern friends of the Chase sisters seconded this appraisal. "Magnanimity to the South may be very good in its place," wrote Hannah Stevenson of Boston to Lucy and Sarah, "but I regard it as clear bosh; and we will see how many of the Union white schools admit black children."[150] As early as February 1865,

Laura Towne fumed over some northerners' willingness to reunite with southern whites: "I am astonished at the gammon still prevailing at the North about our Southern brethren, and their softened feelings and longings to come back, etc., etc." "Nobody seems to remember that the South is only half-civilized," she wrote a decade later, referring to former Confederates, "and that the negroes are . . . more loyal than the whites."[151] Violence in the South over freedpeople's education proved that southern whites were not prepared for a new United States that rejected racial affiliation or previous status as a prerequisite for citizenship. To radical northerners, thus, it was southern whites—not southern blacks—that should have been barred from full national inclusion.

IV

For all of the violence and mayhem, southern whites could not obliterate the dramatic changes that the educational crusade imposed upon southern society. Nor could white supremacists destroy the commitments of the teachers who remained in the South. Klan members could burn schoolhouses, but they could never get to all of the books, primers, and Bibles. Southern whites could whip northern teachers, but they could not drive out the friendships forged between white teachers and black students. African Americans could be terrorized, but that would not stop them from seeking to provide a better future for their children. The Reconstruction-education crusade drastically and radically altered the landscape of southern society and the lives of African Americans. It provided the funds, schools, and teachers that led to one of the most remarkable increases in literacy in the modern world and the creation of an African American middle class that would continue to battle for social and civil rights long after Reconstruction ended. The missions also offered a historical legacy of white radicalism and friendship that African Americans drew upon for courage and hope. In short, the mission of the northern schoolteacher had a powerful and long-lasting influence that white terror could rage against with all of its might, but never fully defeat.

Missionary groups and southern blacks created a host of schools, colleges, and universities for the educational advancement of African Americans that proved critical to the fight against white supremacy in the late nineteenth and twentieth centuries. Atlanta University, Fisk University, Clark University, Morehouse College, Scotia Seminary, Howard University, and Lincoln University were only the most prominent. By 1892, there were more than twenty-five thousand schools for African Americans in the South, with more than twenty thousand southern blacks teaching in them. Thirteen thousand of these teachers had themselves been educated in schools created during radical Reconstruction. Over 2 million southern blacks had learned to read by the early 1890s, and many of them could write as well. These schools, moreover, did not collapse when southern whites put an end to Reconstruction. Schools for southern blacks continued to persevere throughout the nineteenth and twentieth centuries. The educational crusade also provided theological seminaries for African American religious leaders and fuel for the rise of the African American press. By the early 1890s, there were more than 150 newspapers edited in the South by African Americans, several of which were published at black colleges. This black press was crucial in creating a counter public sphere in which African Americans could resist the derogatory reports of their lives and qualities that permeated the white press. Furthermore, the press provided opportunities for African Americans to hone their literary skills and their arguments against racial exploitation.[152]

The growth of black schools and newspapers was matched by an amazing rise in African American literacy, which the Reconstruction-education crusade had helped to bring about. As of 1865, less than 10 percent of southern blacks were literate. By 1870, that percentage had only advanced to 18.6 percent, but only two decades later it was more than 55 percent. By 1940, African American literacy stood at 89 percent.[153] Put in international perspective, this increase was particularly impressive. African American educational improvements far outstripped similar gains in other nations. In post-emancipation societies, including Trinidad, Haiti, and British Guiana, literacy rates of freedpeople and their descendants remained well behind those in the United States. As late as the 1930s, Haiti's Afro-Caribbean literacy rate stood under 20 percent, while literacy in Trinidad was under 60 percent. But even compared to more economically sound European nations , such as Spain and Italy, the advance of African American education was astonishing. In 1860 about 25 percent of Spain's citizens were literate. By 1900, that rate had increased only to 37 percent. Furthermore, in Italy, literacy rates stood at about 31 percent in 1871. By 1901, they had increased to 52 percent. The improvement in African American literacy was nothing short of remarkable. It stood as a testament to the desire of people of color within the United States to obtain educational advancement and to the commitment of northern relief organizations and missionaries.[154]

Schools, rising literacy, and a prodigious black press provided black men and women with a sense of "collective empowerment," to use historian Evelyn Brooks-Higginbotham's phrase, that allowed them to continue the fight for civil rights into the late nineteenth and twentieth centuries. As the secretary of the

AMA pointed out in 1892, "In 1865 there were two negro attorneys; there are now 250. Twenty seven years ago there were three colored physicians; now there are 749."[155] Modern scholars like Brooks-Higginbotham, Clarence Walker, Glenda Gilmore, and Stephanie Shaw have shown that a powerful African American middle class emerged from the Reconstruction schools, and this new "black bourgeois" was dedicated to fighting for black men's and women's political and social rights. Black reformers testified to the importance of these schools in the formation of their social justice consciousness. One African American reformer during this time, for instance, remembered that her instructors at Scotia Seminary, an institution that continued to employ a biracial faculty, taught that "the color of a person's skin has nothing to do with his brains, and that color, caste, or class distinctions are an evil thing." A graduate of Richmond Theological Seminary, who became the pastor of Pilgrim Baptist Church in St. Paul, Minnesota, claimed that his education instilled into him a quest for racial uplift. "My course of study," he wrote, "has caused me to yearn for their up-building, intellectually, financially, morally, and spiritually, as never before."[156]

But perhaps just as important as the organizational legacy of the education crusade was the heritage of memories it left for civil rights advocates. As historian Rayford Logan put it in 1954, the Reconstruction schools "ignited a spark which burst into flame in the twentieth century."[157] In the years following Reconstruction, the efforts of the missionary-teachers provided African Americans with images and memories of heroic whites who linked arms with people of color to attack white supremacy. Throughout his long career, W. E. B. Du Bois continually looked back to the missionary-teachers for encouragement and even characterized himself as a part of their legacy. He referred to their mission as a "Ninth Crusade" and the female missionaries as "women who dared." "The crusade of the New England schoolmarm was in full swing," Du Bois remembered of his years as an undergraduate at Fisk University. "The freed slaves, if properly led, had a great future. Temporarily deprived of their full voting privileges, this was but a passing set-back. Black folk were bound in time to dominate the South. They needed trained leadership. I was sent to help furnish it." Du Bois even concluded one chapter of *Black Reconstruction in America* by recalling that "through it all has gone a thread of brave and splendid friendship from those few and rare men and women of white skins, North and South, who have dared to know and help and love black folk."[158]

In praising the schoolteachers as harbingers of a new America, Du Bois was not alone. Referring to the AMA, one African American claimed, "[O]f all organizations that have been working among us as a race, your great Association has shown most of the spirit of what I call true, genuine Christianity."[159] Henry Hugh Proctor, a graduate of Fisk University and Yale's Divinity School, professed that the Reconstruction crusade was "without exception . . . the very finest thing in American history."[160] Even Booker T. Washington, who in the 1890s encouraged African Americans to abandon the fight for social and political equality in favor of economic improvement, asserted that "[w]henever it was written—and I hope it will be—the part that the Yankee teachers played in the education of the Negroes immediately after the war will make one of the most thrilling parts of the history of this country."[161] To these and countless other African Americans, the "crusade of the Yankee schoolmarm" held symbolic power that should not be repudiated or forgotten. They had left a legacy of friendship, contact, and brotherhood—a legacy that white supremacists could twist and turn, but could never efface.

During the high-water mark of radical Reconstruction, a young African American scholar at Trinity School in Athens, Alabama, asked a poignant question in a letter to the white students of a northern Sunday school class: "[W]ould you speak to a black boy?"[162] During and after the Civil War, thousands of northerners answered this rhetorical question by traveling south, working on behalf of African American education, and joining black men and women in a struggle for racial uplift. Although cultural chauvinism and deep-seated prejudices marred many of their missions, some schoolteachers had their racial views altered. Their opinions and beliefs about race were not static, but dynamic, and contact led them to new planes of human brotherhood and solidarity. These teachers stood as the arm of the post–Civil War Protestant and radical plan for a new American republic constructed around loyalty to the Union, rather than racial classification. They sought nothing less than to dismantle the chief bulwarks of the white republic and construct in their place a new country of brotherhood and fraternity.

Lucy Chase was right to describe her work and experiences with southern freedpeople as "not the past" and "not the future," because the endeavors of these schoolteachers were truly revolutionary. Nothing like it on such a massive scale had been attempted before in the United States. On thousands of occasions, whites and blacks dined, worshipped, laughed, and celebrated together. They suffered together, too, as southern whites rose up to attack them. To many historians, these missionaries were naive fools for believing that they could radically alter southern and American society. But as novelist Albion Tourgée put it, "the fool" is never far from genius: "[The Fool] may run after a will-o'-the-wisp, while the Wise deride; but to him it is a veritable star of hope. He differs from his fellow-mortals chiefly in this, that he sees or believes what they do not, and consequently undertakes what they never attempt. If he succeed in his endeavor, the world stops laughing, and calls him a Genius: if he fail, it laughs the more, and derides his undertaking as A Fool's Errand."[163] Whether described as a "fool's errand" or as "the finest thing in American history," these missions held enormous potential. The "contact of living souls" had the power to change racial imaginations. As abolitionist and poet John Greenleaf Whittier put it when he paraphrased the response of a black student to the leader of the Freedmen's Bureau: "They are rising,—all are rising,/The black and white together!"[164]

These missionaries sought to create the "beloved community" of which Martin Luther King Jr. would so passionately preach during the modern Civil Rights movement—America's "second Reconstruction." But the path of the post–Civil War "rebel" was taken only by some. Hopes for an integrated and egalitarian American republic were attacked and betrayed, not only by white supremacists of the South, but also by northern Protestants who abandoned the crusade. While radical Protestants labored in the South and helped to construct the institutional basis from which the twentieth-century struggle for civil rights would continue, a moral battle raged in the North between the apostles of sectional forgiveness who hoped to rebuild the white republic and the prophets of racial justice who desired to continue the process of restructuring the racial composition of the nation's citizenry. From the mid-1860s to the turn of the century, northern whites' interest in racial liberation waned considerably as a vocal group of religious leaders, revivalists, reformers, politicians, businessmen, and authors shifted the North's moral imperative away from racial liberation and toward sectional reunion. In these years, religious idioms and ideologies came to pervade a broad northern culture of conciliation that prized white solidarity and accepted black exploitation. The northern retreat from radical Reconstruction was not "inevitable," as one historian has recently suggested.[165] It was authorized and even sanctified by northern religious leaders and ideologies. The forces of reconciliation did not spread their gospel uncontested, though. African Americans and their white supporters continually rose up to meet them with their own religious appeals. As black ministers, writers, and politicians characterized civil rights as a sacred cause, they endeavored to cast Reconstruction as a spiritual endavor that could incorporate people of color into the national body as full citizens. But they would lose this battle, for the conflation of whiteness, Protestant Christianity, and American nationalism once again ascended and refashioned a new white republic as the minions of white supremacy dressed themselves as angels of national unity.

3

THE APOSTLES OF FORGIVENESS

Religion and National Reunion in Northern Society, Popular
Culture, and National Politics, 1865–1875

For many missionaries to the South, northern newspapers and monthly magazines
were highly coveted commodities. They provided social sustenance for the teachers and kept them in touch with trends and opinions in the North. As the principal of a school for freedpeople in Virginia, Jacob Yoder found that his most cherished sources of information were newspapers. He subscribed to *Harper's Weekly*,
the *New York Star*, and the *New York Baptist Register*, yet the paper he and several
other missionary-teachers prized most was the *New York Independent*, edited by
Theodore Tilton. "The welcome Independent was read with its usual interest," he
confided in his diary on December 27, 1866. "Who can do without such a visitor?"
In January 1866, Charlotte Forten similarly recorded in her personal journal that
she "[s]pent the evening alone, reading the 'Independent,'—an exceedingly interesting number,—as usual." Yoder especially enjoyed poring over the sermons and
editorials of Henry Ward Beecher, the North's most popular preacher. Yoder
looked to Beecher's words in the *Independent* for spiritual and religious guidance.
After absorbing one sermon in September 1866, he wrote, "Read choice extracts
of H. W. Beechers. They are choice too. Oh! Valuable is such literature."[1]

Although Yoder and his fellow colleagues found moral nourishment and direc-
tions in the *Independent*, Beecher and the authors of editorials in the weekly ironically represented two distinct and opposing strands in postwar Protestantism and
postwar northern society in general. Beecher and the editorialists disagreed
sharply on how northern whites should treat and regard former Confederates and
freedpeople. After the Civil War, several writers for the *Independent* continued to
advance the radical Republicans' arguments that God demanded a stern punishment of Confederates and that the North should dominate the South completely.
In this, they echoed the convictions of Thaddeus Stevens. "There is one, and only
one, sure and safe policy for the immediate future," asserted an editorial in May
1865. "[T]*he North must remain the absolute Dictator of the Republic until the spirit of*

the North shall become the spirit of the whole country."[2] Many *Independent* writers also advocated civil rights for African Americans, calling for universal manhood suffrage and denouncing prejudice in the North and South. One editorial put the attack upon the tenets of the white republic most succinctly, "The color of a man's skin must completely vanish from the public feeling as the color of his eyes."[3]

Beecher's positions on sectional and racial relations diametrically opposed those of the more radical writers to the *Independent*. For Beecher, southern whites were his national brethren and his Christianity called for immediate sectional forgiveness. "[M]y heart goes out toward my whole country," he lectured. "I mourn for those outcast States. The bitterness of their destruction; the wrath that has come upon them; their desolation—you know nothing of these."[4] He specifically encouraged northerners to overlook the reports of southern mistreatment of freedpeople coming from all over the South. "You must not be disappointed or startled because you see in the newspapers accounts of shocking barbarities committed upon these people [freedpeople]," Beecher continued. Racial violence was to be expected, he explained, for southern whites were merely adjusting to the new order. Only time would heal these wounds. "[A]bove all," he claimed, northerners needed to have "patience with Southern men as they are, and patience with Southern opinions as they have been, until the great normal, industrial, and moral laws shall work such gradual changes as shall enable them to pass from the old to the new."[5]

The conflicting viewpoints of Beecher and the editorials in the *Independent* reflected an important clash in the postwar North. From 1865 to 1875, a religious, social, and political battle engulfed northern society, as advocates of sectional punishment and racial justice squared off against proponents of sectional harmony and racial oppression. The decade witnessed an amazing amount of political change. In only five years the states ratified three new constitutional amendments: the Thirteenth Amendment forbade slavery; the Fourteenth Amendment assured the national and state citizenship of all persons born or naturalized in the United States; and the Fifteenth Amendment outlawed the use of race or previous condition of servitude to determine suffrage eligibility. Together, the Reconstruction Amendments and a series of civil rights bills passed by Congress destroyed slavery, protected the legal rights of African Americans, and mandated universal manhood suffrage. At the same time, the vast majority of former Confederates received pardons and all but three of the southern states were readmitted to full status in the nation by 1875. In many locations, southern white planters quickly reestablished their economic and political power. Although radicalism was in its ascendance in the months and years immediately following Lincoln's assassination, the forces of national reunion quickly grew in power and might. A host of political and economic factors led northern whites to seek to abandon their commitments to transforming the South, including a rising number of northern businessmen who beseeched their politicians to bring order and harmony to ensure economic prosperity, and the deaths or retirements of several radical Republican leaders.[6]

But the repudiation of radicalism required more than the demands of business interests and the loss of individual leaders. Radical Reconstruction had been built in large part upon religious convictions, and new profoundly different religious imperatives were necessary to undermine it. To turn away from the moral necessity of civil rights for freedpeople, a group of northern religious leaders created a counter morality, one that prized national solidarity among whites at the expense of equal inclusion of people of color. These Protestants believed that God mandated the reforging of the white republic, while the protection of equal rights and citizenship for African Americans came to be seen as inferior or even antithetical to true Christianity.

Throughout postwar Reconstruction, a coterie of white Protestant leaders joined together to authorize and sanctify the northern embrace of southern whites. Following the lead of those who had endorsed national harmony in the days and weeks following Lincoln's assassination, a growing majority of Protestants increasingly favored denominational and national reconciliation. Through a variety of media, including sermons, novels, short stories, denominational meetings, and political cartoons, these apostles of forgiveness lobbied for national reunion at all costs. In response, a significant number of northern whites came to accept former Confederates as national brethren. With more regularity, Protestant Yankees wished to forget and forgive southern whites for the war. Southern white Protestants responded to appeals for reconciliation by agreeing that the North and the South should constitute one nation-state and by accepting fraternal brotherhood with the northern denominations. But these former Confederates stopped short of organic denominational reunion. They could reluctantly stomach the military defeat of their southern nation, but they steadfastly refused to give up their commitments to a distinctively southern white identity.[7]

Northern Protestant leaders, however, were not the only ones enlisting religious ideologies and metaphors to the service of reconciliation. Religion suffused a broader culture of sectional reunion, because Christian ideologies of forgiveness, sacrifice, and atonement functioned as supposedly disinterested arguments for resolidifying American nationalism. From postwar poetry and novels to congressional speeches and the propaganda of the presidential campaign of 1872, religious rhetoric saturated pleas for the remaking of the white republic. Indeed, appealing to religious sentiments constituted an effective strategy in a society that spoke and thought in Christian themes and tropes. Casting sectional issues as religious ones, politicians and writers echoed the voices of most northern Protestants. They chastised sectional divisiveness as un-Christian and sanctified national white solidarity as a spiritual imperative.[8]

Central to the project of diminishing sectional antagonism was a retreat from the radicals' commitments to civic nationalism. Racial discrimination and prejudice had been immensely powerful social forces in the North during the antebellum era, and the use of racist tropes by religious figures in the postwar era resonated with the previous northern commitments to white supremacy.[9] Furthermore, rejecting the civic nationalism of the radicals served as an appeal to southern whites for national reunion. In order for northerners to prove that their desire for reconciliation among whites was genuine, northern white Protestants largely abandoned the freedpeople in the early 1870s. The generous financial support and missionary zeal of the 1860s dwindled, and a growing number of white Protestants came to rationalize second-class citizenship for blacks as divinely sanctioned. In part, northern Protestants broke their alliance with African Americans because they believed the mission of racial uplift was completed with the ratification of the Fifteenth Amendment in 1870.[10] But even when Protestants realized that suffrage had not brought racial peace and justice, they pressed for national reconciliation nonetheless. White religious leaders justified the retreat from Reconstruction by asserting that southern whites were the most adequate caretakers of African Americans and by depicting blacks as animal-like children who best served the nation as a permanent laboring caste. These northern Protestants not only capitulated to second-class citizenship for African Americans, they also sanctified that status as essential to the rebuilding of the white republic.

Yet the forces of reconciliation and abandonment did not go unchallenged throughout the decade. Many leading African Americans and their white supporters recognized that religious arguments were being used to undermine racial justice. The biracial coalition dedicated to bringing about a new, integrated nation continued to persevere and to craft biblical and spiritual arguments that demanded sustained federal protection and religiously inspired support for the freedpeople. Proponents of civil rights rejected the claim that Christianity dictated full forgiveness for southern whites. Frederick Douglass, Frances E. W. Harper, and an assortment of other blacks and whites maintained that northerners should only forgive former Confederates after they had repented of their sins.

Only when southerners had completely turned away from slavery and racial oppression should the nation be reforged. Such appeals for civil rights kept the apostles of forgiveness from suddenly and completely carrying the day. But the advocates of civil rights recognized that they were losing ground and that fewer and fewer northern whites were interested in remaking the American republic. The ethnic nationalism that focused on the shared racial affiliation of whites that had been so powerful in the antebellum era was quickly supplanting the civic nationalism of the radicals that had been so vibrant in the mid-1860s and early 1870s.[11]

I

Throughout the late 1860s, some northern Protestants persisted in advocating vengeance upon the South. At a Thanksgiving service in San Francisco, for instance, Reverend Joseph N. McGiffert endorsed punishment for traitors and demanded equality for freedpeople. "For the protection of the country," he preached, "treason should be judicially declared a crime and properly punished." He warned his parishioners, "*The nation runs a fearful risk in letting such men go unpunished.*" At the same time, the North had to maintain its alliance with and support for African Americans. "We must accord to the negro *equal political rights,*" McGiffert concluded. "The equality of all men, by creation and redemption, is the 'Magna Charta' of the race in its demand for liberty and equal rights."[12]

But during the decade following the war, recriminations and calls for racial justice were met by an intensifying chorus of Protestant voices committed to sectional reconciliation. Although only a few Protestant leaders, most notably Henry Ward Beecher and Harriet Beecher Stowe, actively encouraged sectional and ecclesiastical reunion in the mid-1860s, religious support for reunion grew much stronger in the late 1860s and early 1870s. Indeed, by 1875, the largest northern denominations had come out decidedly for sectional reconciliation over rights for African Americans. In roughly a decade, a host of northern white Protestants shifted their moral imperative from supporting equality for freedpeople to desiring peace at the direct expense of African Americans.

The son of the famous preacher Lyman Beecher and brother of Harriet Beecher Stowe, perhaps the most well-known author of the mid-nineteenth century, Henry Ward Beecher was himself a force to be reckoned with during the mid-nineteenth century. He was the North's most popular minister and spent much of his postwar career entreating northern Protestants to forgive southern whites and to receive them quickly back into the national fold. Beecher repeatedly endorsed sectional harmony with his sermons, speeches, and writings. In addition, he explicitly rejected ideas of equality for African Americans by depicting people of color as "overgrown children" or as "marmots" who had no place in society except as obedient laborers. In the early Reconstruction period, Beecher stood as the most prominent northern religious figure to advocate reunion, and a commitment to white solidarity and second-class citizenship for blacks clearly marked his national imagination.

With his sermons preached at the prestigious Plymouth Congregational Church of Brooklyn and his writings that were widely published in northern newspapers, pamphlets, and northern periodicals, Beecher had a massive following. "He was far more than a pastor of a well-to-do suburban church," religious historian William McLoughlin has written of him. "He was for much of his life an editor and weekly columnist of religious and secular newspapers with hundreds of thousands of readers."[13] Beecher's contemporaries recognized that his religious and political opinions were extremely influential. A writer for the Congregationalist *New Englander and Yale Review* claimed that Beecher "is preeminently a popular preacher. . . . [He] is a man of genius and cannot be imitated. . . . He is a 'king of men' in moral and spiritual things. . . . He takes hold of all classes. Old men read his sermons when they can read nothing else out of the Bible. In the log-house of the pioneer the 'Plymouth pulpit' is preaching. Young men in the Universities go to his discourses as to fresh springs."[14] *Putnam's Monthly* further suggested that "Mr. Beecher is one of a half-dozen men who belong to the whole country; . . . whose opinions are looked for with interest on every occasion, when the public mind is stirred by important questions, involving the morals of politics." British visitor Reverend David Macrae probably put it best, "In America, Beecher is an independent power."[15]

In the months and years following the Civil War, Beecher vigorously promoted sectional forgiveness and assailed radical Republicans as devilish evildoers who only wanted to stir up trouble. He denounced northern calls for the executions of top-ranking Confederate leaders as inhumane and anti-Christian.[16] In a letter to the *New York Independent*, appropriately titled "Love to Enemies," Beecher maintained that northern affection for southern whites was a religious imperative. "[B]enignity, compassion, [and] tender sorrow for them," he claimed, were of "Christ's spirit"[17] In Beecher's view, those who perpetuated sectional hostility constituted forces of darkness. In a sermon in Brooklyn in 1866, he denounced Thaddeus Stevens and his appeals for the disfranchisement of former Confederates and southern land redistribution as "doctrines of Belial, leading to destruction." Beecher passionately desired that his listeners and readers would apply biblical teachings of forgiveness to their social and political worlds. "Be not overcome of evil, but overcome evil with good," he preached. "There, go: *vote that*. You have been talking it long enough: *do it*. You have been praying it long enough: *try it*." [18]

Beecher's repeated calls for good will led others interested in national reconciliation to seek out his services. In 1866, the executive committee for a "National Convention of Soldiers and Sailors" to be held in Cleveland, Ohio, requested that he offer the introductory prayer for their meeting. They specifically requested Beecher because he had committed himself to national solidarity. They lauded him for using his "eloquence and the just weight of [his] name . . . to enforce upon the country a generous and magnanimous policy toward the people of the lately rebellious States." To them, Beecher was the voice of "the new order of things," a new American nation built upon "Christian brotherhood." [19] Although illness kept Beecher from attending the convention, he nonetheless endorsed its desires. In a letter to the executive committee, he suggested that "[e]very month we delay [recognizing southern representatives to the federal government] complicates the case. The excluded population, enough unsettled before, grow more irritable; . . . the Government at Washington is called to interfere in one and another difficulty, and this will be done inaptly, and sometimes with great injustice." Beecher claimed that the North's chief responsibility was national reconciliation: "[T]he first demand of our time is entire reunion!" [20]

Beecher also opposed the use of the federal government to protect African Americans in the South. In his "Cleveland letter" he contended that southern home rule was the only possible means to improve life for African Americans. He attacked the widely held belief "that the restoration of the South to her full independence will be detrimental to the freedmen." Instead, Beecher argued that keeping the South out of the Union hampered African American uplift. "The negro is part and parcel of Southern society," he maintained. "He cannot be prosperous while it is unprospered. Its evils will rebound upon him. Its happiness and reinvigoration cannot be kept from his participation. The restoration of the South . . . [will] rebound to the freedmen's benefit." Beecher's essential endorsement of second-class citizenship for African Americans became so notorious that a rumor circulated that he had actually authored the white supremacist theological tract *The Negro: What is His Ethnological Status?*, in which the author "Ariel" unequivocally asserted that "the negro has no soul." [21]

At the same time, Beecher cast his lot with President Andrew Johnson, who likewise urged a swift reunion by rallying conservatives from the Republican and Democratic parties into a new "Union Party" that would restore southern whites to the Union without advancing social rights or political privileges to the freed-people. Although Johnson's efforts failed badly and actually propelled many moderate Republicans to side with the radical Republicans, Beecher backed him nonetheless. When Johnson vetoed a bill to extend the life of the Freedmen's Bureau in early 1866, Beecher lauded the decision. To him, the benefits reaped by the millions of dollars the federal government had poured into education for freed-people via the Bureau were not worth the costs of further antagonizing southern whites. Like Johnson, Beecher hoped that the elimination of the Bureau would pacify southern whites. He vigorously maintained that the North should steer clear of southern racial issues.[22]

At least one influential northern Protestant minister voiced agreement with Beecher. "I have read with great delight Mr. Beecher's unanswerable letter," Episcopal minister Stephen Higginson Tyng of New York City wrote to the head of the Cleveland convention. "It will be a glorious result if the people of the land unite with them in the universal determination that Union, liberty, and generous interpretation and action shall end all controversies of the day in which we live." To Tyng, Protestantism dictated that the North be a "generous victor."[23] Some northern editors recognized that although Tyng and Beecher held opinions that were in the minority, they and their views were extremely powerful. "It is a matter of no trivial significance and importance when two such men" defend the same ideas, observed the *Springfield Republican,* for they were two of the most influential religious leaders in the land.[24]

Northerners who promoted rights for freedpeople and advocated a stern chastising of former Confederates knew that Beecher was a powerful social and political force, and they sternly opposed him. They could not allow his sermons and writings to go unanswered. By trusting southern whites to govern justly over blacks, Beecher left himself vulnerable to enormous criticism. Many northerners found his faith in southern whites appallingly naive. Members of his Brooklyn congregation demanded that he retract or explain his Cleveland letter, while his brother Edward Beecher, a theologian and pastor in Galesburg, Illinois, denounced Henry's views. "You rely, in fact, on those white aristocracies," Edward mocked. "[Y]ou rely on pleasing, quieting, prospering them, giving them all political power, and then trusting in them to educate, elevate, enfranchise the freedmen." Edward then suggested that his brother failed to balance biblical imperatives for forgiveness with divine mandates for justice. "The truths that are thus one-sided and unbalanced in your mind, as it seems to me, are the duties of forgiveness, confidence in evil-doers, magnanimity, and overcoming evil with good," he wrote in the *Independent*. "On these you were speaking when you denounced the policy of Thaddeus Stevens as satanic."[25]

Other northerners also attacked Beecher for abandoning the freedpeople. For his part, Thaddeus Stevens referred to Beecher sarcastically in a speech before Congress as "that eloquent divine who so lately has slaughtered whole herds of fatted calves." Stevens even assailed a fellow member of the House of Representatives who advocated immediate reunion as a tool of Beecher's. In a pamphlet responding to Beecher's Cleveland letter, John Reese declared him a traitor more vile than "Judas Iscariot" and "Benedict Arnold." "Your remarks on the condition of the Freedmen are insults to men of common sence [*sic*]," Reese maintained, "and an impeachment of the intelligence of the community. You want us to believe that it will be all right with the Freedmen when all power of government will be restored unto their late masters. But all the evidence and facts gives the lie to your assertion"[26]

Frederick Douglass found Beecher's positions especially confusing and troubling. When Douglass denounced President Johnson's "wholesale pardoning" of former Confederates and "contrasted Presidential clemency with Rebel cruelty and hate" in a speech in September 1866, one member of the audience asked, "'How about Beecher?'" Douglass was unsure of how to respond. In the past Beecher had been an advocate of emancipation and of fundamentally transforming the South, even supporting John Brown's battle against proslavery forces in Kansas in the 1850s. But now Beecher had turned away from racial justice. "I have been often asked the question, 'How do you account for Henry Ward Beecher's position?'" Douglass admitted, but "I have never been able to answer it satisfactorily to myself." He could only claim that he did not know what to make of the Brooklyn preacher and poked a little fun at him: "I answer it about as he answered a question put to him on one occasion by a pert, inquisitive lady who said, 'Mr. Beecher can you tell in what condition Paul was when he was elevated up to the third heavens?' 'I am sure,' said Mr. Beecher, 'if Paul didn't know himself, I don't see how I should.' And that is my answer to that question."[27]

In other speeches, however, Douglass was not as equivocal or lighthearted. He recognized that Beecher's stance undermined northern commitments to rights for freedpeople. "[O]f this gospel of forgiveness there is a new advocate," Douglass warned a crowd in Boston in October 1865. "I thought President Johnson stood alone high above the New Testament. But lately there has sprung up another preacher in Brooklyn who seems to be equally in the forgiving and forgetting mood." To Douglass, reunion should only occur after southern whites had acknowledged their wrongdoing: "I demand that the man that shall receive forgiveness at my hands shall repent of the crime of which he asks for forgiveness."[28]

Beecher's insistence that southern blacks were best served by the pacification of southern whites enraged Douglass. In another address he denounced Beecher for valuing magnanimity to former slaveholders instead of rights for freedpeople. Douglass recounted that before the war, Beecher had said "that, if he could abolish slavery on the instant, or, by waiting twenty-five years, could have it so abolished that its overthrow would redound to the glory of the Christian Church, he would prefer the latter." Douglass thought this policy absurd. "[I]f I were a Maryland slaveholder," he concluded, "and Mr. Beecher were my slave, and I had a rawhide, I could take this opinion out of him in less than half an hour." Perhaps Beecher needed to feel the rawhide now. If he had, as Douglass and other slaves had, he would know that the only "glory" was universal equality.[29]

Yet Beecher did not back down from these critics. Throughout the 1860s and the 1870s, he continued to seek national harmony over racial justice. In 1868 Beecher put his conciliatory beliefs into action and won the applause of many in the South. Along with Gerrit Smith and Horace Greeley, Beecher spoke at a fundraising event for Virginia's Washington University, which had recently hired General Robert E. Lee as its president.[30] Likewise, in *Norwood* (1868), his novel about life in a small New England town, Beecher endorsed national reconciliation and expressed his conviction that African Americans would never be more than second-class citizens in the nation. He painted the leading southern white character of the novel, Tom Heywood, as honorable and noble, while he depicted the singular African American character, Pete Sawmill, as childlike and bestial. When Beecher introduced Heywood midway through the novel, he heaped praise upon his "southern" aristocratic qualities. Heywood had "peculiarly winning manners, uniting a certain lofty air to a genial familiarity." He was, Beecher claimed, a "brilliant young Southerner." Sawmill, however, was anything but brilliant. He was a "great, black, clumsy-moving fellow." Unlike virtuous, hardworking Yankees, Sawmill was lazy and indolent. "He had no purpose in life," Beecher wrote. He "had no trade or calling. He was an idle fellow." Sawmill was, in fact, nothing more than "an overgrown child." In short, this black character was not fully a man because he lacked what sociologist Max Weber identified as the Protestant work ethic.[31] Beecher even explicitly compared Sawmill to animals. On one occasion, he wrote, "Rex, a Newfoundland dog, . . . seemed to be another Pete running on all fours." Ultimately, although Sawmill lived *in* Norwood, he was not *of* Norwood: "Pete was one of those peculiar natures that can never be organized into society, but live, as marmots do, by burrowing, in the neighborhood of men, without living among them." [32]

In the conclusion of the novel, Beecher constructed a mythical northern response to the end of the Civil War in which Yankees performed the roles of the magnanimous victors that he had hoped they would have in 1865. "In every generous bosom rose the thought," Beecher wrote of Norwood's residents, "[t]hese are not another nation, but our citizens." Beecher then claimed that northerners fully forgave Confederates and honored their bravery and military prowess: "Their mistakes, their evil cause, belonged to the system under which they were reared, but their military skill and heroic bravery belong to the nation, that will never cease to mourn that such valor had not been expended in a better cause." [33] In Beecher's national and racial imagination, Norwood (and the United States) was a place for whites, regardless of their sectional backgrounds. Blacks could reside there, but only as "marmots."

Literary reviews of Norwood demonstrated that Beecher's sectional and racial depictions resonated with many northern white audiences. Writing in the Atlantic Monthly, William Dean Howells considered Pete Sawmill the epitome of northern blacks, "the vagabond half-wit, whom no well-regulated village is without." A reviewer for the New York Times thought Beecher's representation of blacks far superior to those of other northern novelists, perhaps even surpassing the black characters in his sister's Uncle Tom's Cabin. "Pete Sawmill is also an important character in the story," this reviewer noted. "Unlike most negroes, as we find them in New-England novels, he is a genuine 'nigger,' not a saint in charcoal, nor a paragon of virtue. A faithful, warmly attached servant, he has his little human failings, and has a great weakness for whiskey. It is really pleasant to meet with a darkey in a New-England novel, who isn't a living reproach to all white men." The Times writer also lauded Beecher for his celebratory characterizations of southern characters and hoped that Norwood would help reunite the North and South. "The largeness of Mr. Beecher's mind, and his superiority over sectional prejudice, are shown in his general treatment of the Southern people in his novel," asserted the Times writer. "He makes one of his New England girls—Barton's own beautiful sister—fall in love with a Southern gentleman, who attains high rank in the rebel service without losing her love; and he does full justice to their bravery on the field, and to the motives that led them into secession." [34] Beecher and his reviewers appeared to share a similar understanding of the United States. They evinced an ethnic nationalism, in which whiteness—rather than loyalty to the Union—served as the crucial arbiter of inclusion and equality.

But Beecher was not the only prominent northern writer and religious figure to back sectional reunion above racial justice. He was not the only one to press for a reunited white republic built upon racial hierarchies. During the late 1860s, northern proponents of sectional harmony got an enormous boost when his sister, one of the North's most acclaimed writers, took up their cause. Best remembered as "the little lady who made this big war" with her best-selling novel, *Uncle Tom's Cabin,* Harriet Beecher Stowe became an apostle of reconciliation in the years following the war. Stowe defended her brother against his critics; she purchased a winter home in Florida and wrote a flurry of letters to northerners, in which she depicted the South as a heaven on earth; she published a book on her adventures in Florida that helped make the state a magnet for northern tourists; and like Henry, she came to value accord among whites as vastly more important than equality for African Americans. Her allegiance to the white republic drew upon both the long history of northern racial prejudice and the rising hopes in the North for reconciliation with southern whites.[35]

Harriet Beecher Stowe had not endorsed sectional reconciliation or the northern retreat from Reconstruction immediately following the war, however. After Lincoln's death, she echoed the calls of countless northern ministers for stern punishments of southern whites and for justice for emancipated blacks. She was swept up in the radicalism of the mid-1860s, seeming to earnestly believe that a new, color-blind nation could be born. In an article for the *Atlantic Monthly* in August 1865, she drew attention to the wartime mistreatment of Union prisoners in order to rally northerners against a quick forgiveness. Stowe recounted several stories of young, God-fearing Union soldiers physically and spiritually demoralized in Confederate prisons. "And is there to be no retribution for a cruelty so vast, so aggravated, so cowardly and base?" she asked. Surely this could not be so. "These are crimes against God," she concluded. In direct opposition to her brother Henry's preaching, she hoped that northerners would grieve over fallen Union soldiers, not defeated southerners: "Oh, man or woman, if you have pity to spare, spend it not on Lee or Davis, spend it on their victims, on the thousands of living hearts which these men of sin have doomed."[36]

Like other radical Protestants, Stowe also championed political and social rights for African Americans. In a short story for the *Atlantic Monthly* published in January 1866, one of her characters, Jennie, placed her faith in the federal government and in God to support the freedpeople. "There never has been a time in our history when so many honest and just men held power in our land as now," Jennie told a pessimistic friend who had lamented that people of color would be quickly

relegated to second-class status. "There never was instance of a powerful government showing more tenderness in the protection of a weak and defence-less race
than ours has shown in the care of the freedmen hitherto." Jennie then claimed
that God had the power to alter the prejudices of whites: "[I]n general, human nature is selfish, callous, unfeeling. . . . Nevertheless, thanks to God's teaching and
fatherly care, the world has worked along to the point of a great nation founded on
the principles of strict equality." In short, this was a time for Christian faith in justice. The federal government and the Protestant God were working together to
make a new American nation of benevolence and equality.[37]

Stowe outlined her early hopes for Reconstruction in a letter to her brother
Henry in October 1866. Although she had read his "Cleveland letter" and had appreciated it as "the outcome of the noblest and purest feelings, a tribute honestly
given to a great problem," she dissented from his opinions. She believed that
Beecher had a skewed vision of the South and agreed with her brother Edward's
critique: "It has been rather my impression that you have received your impression
of the South and its needs from the former aristocracy, the men who have hereto-
fore governed her and want to govern her again." Stowe thought it was time
for other southerners, "the *common people*," to lead the South. To her, only through
integrated schools could the rise and rule of the middling class be achieved.
For this reason, she characterized the missionary teachers from the North as harbingers of a new day of racial uplift and fraternity. "They are women baptised [*sic*]
from above and the Holy Ghost is with them," she wrote. "[T]he teachers at
Richmond . . . of colored and white are working in one body and spirit and helping each other." Stowe implored Beecher to help the crusade for southern education by enlisting his congregation to send funds, supplies, and teachers.[38]

Yet Stowe abandoned her anger toward the South as well as her commitments
to uplift for freedpeople in the late 1860s and early 1870s. As Henry came under
attack in the North for advocating the very "mercy and magnanimity" Stowe had
railed against, she rose to his defense. She asserted that her brother's actions were
rooted in a genuine Christian spirit. Writing to the Duchess of Argyll, Stowe
claimed, "Henry has been called a back-slider because of the lenity of his counsels,
but I cannot but think it is the Spirit of Christ that influences him."[39] Stowe also
attempted to shield her brother from accusations in public. In a lengthy book, *Men
of Our Times; or Leading Patriots of the Day*, which contained biographical chapters
on Horace Greeley, Abraham Lincoln, and Wendell Phillips among others, she
wrote that Henry's appeals for national harmony emerged from his Christian "instinct to defend the weaker side." His "strong impulse to *forgive*," she claimed,

"was from that source in his higher nature whence have come all the best inspirations of his life."[40]

Like Henry, Harriet became a strong advocate of white reconciliation and a racially hierarchical society. In 1867, she traveled to Florida to purchase land for her son Fred, who had turned to alcohol because of the physical and emotional trauma he had experienced during the war.[41] Stowe also sought to do her part for the newly emancipated. She intended on setting up a school for African Americans, writing, "My heart is with that poor people whose course in words I have tried to plead, and who now, ignorant and docile, are just in that formative stage in which whoever seizes them has them."[42] Like many other northern white missionaries to the South, she initially exuded paternalism by assuming that freedpeople were immature and largely uncivilized. After she arrived in Florida, Stowe put her desires into action by teaching at a school for black and white children.

Stowe quickly fell in love with Florida and escaped from the North to spend most of her winters there from 1867 to 1896. Over this period, she spent increasingly less time advocating rights for African Americans and expended more energy forming friendships with southern whites. In letters to friends in the North, she gloried in her new surroundings and encouraged them to view Florida and the South as an "enchanted country."[43] To her, Florida was everything that the industrializing and urbanizing North was not: warm, relaxed, peaceful, slow, and full of beautiful flowers, trees, and colors. "When I get here I enter another life," she wrote to British author George Eliot. "The world recedes; I am out of it; it ceases to influence; its bustle and noise die away in the far distance; and here is no winter." In another letter to Eliot, Stowe claimed, "It is the place to forget the outside world, and live in one's self."[44] Stowe even compared Florida to the peaceful island where the apostle John had written the Book of Revelation. "I hate to leave my calm isle of Patmos—where the world is not & I have such quiet long hours for writing."[45] Indeed, for Stowe, Florida was a spiritual retreat from a rapidly changing and bewildering world.

In the late 1860s and 1870s, Stowe penned a series of articles on Florida for the *Christian Union*, a new religious journal edited by Henry, and the *Atlantic Monthly*, in which she chronicled her activities in Florida so that northerners could decide to visit and set up winter homes. Her *Christian Union* letters, collected and published as a book titled *Palmetto Leaves* (1873), revealed that Stowe's publicly presented views of the South and of African Americans had changed substantially from her end-of-the-war utterances. She depicted former Confederates as friendly and African Americans as pleasant laborers. Well before it became all the rage for wealthy northern whites to travel to southern vacation spots like White Springs, Virginia, and fall in love with a South of old, gorgeous plantations and servile African Americans, Stowe constructed a Florida that would suit northerners' fancies for antebellum luxury. To her, God had created people of color to toil happily in the South so that whites could relax and enjoy prosperity. A new and ideal United States would be one in which northern and southern whites ruled benevolently and former slaves worked cheerfully in a naturally subservient status.[46]

Part travelogue, part tourist guide, *Palmetto Leaves* described Florida as an idyllic land where God revealed himself through nature. Northern whites, she maintained, needed to experience the beauty for themselves. On one occasion she responded to northerners who sent her letters of inquiry about Florida. "Come down here once," she wrote, "and use your own eyes, and you will know more than we can teach you." In one chapter, aptly titled "The Grand Tour Up River," Stowe described the best time for northerners to visit Florida and partake in "the season" of tourism. Stowe believed that her writings had an enormous impact on tourism to Florida. In a letter to a friend, she claimed that her articles and book were responsible for leading more than fourteen thousand northerners to visit Florida in 1873.[47]

Stowe painted southern society in ways that would appeal to northern white audiences who held prejudicial racial views and desperately wanted to believe that economic progress and racial harmony were possible in the South. Since 1865, northern whites had read account after account of racial exploitation and planter intransigency from the former Confederate states. Now Stowe offered them a South much more to their liking, a place that needed no more reconstructing. She characterized southern whites as amicable and African Americans as passive and docile laborers. She referred to local whites as "friends and neighbors" and expressed deep admiration for the ways Confederates accepted defeat. One former colonel, she wrote, was "miserably poor" at the end of the war, but "brave and undiscouraged, he retained his former slaves as free laborers." He was, in Stowe's estimation, a model middle-class white man, a southern Horatio-Alger figure who by luck and by pluck had elevated himself.[48] African Americans, Stowe further suggested, experienced freedom with propriety and had no interest in radically altering a society rightfully dominated by whites. "Those who formerly were their slaves settled peaceably around them as free laborers," she claimed, "still looking up to them [the whites] for advice, depending on them for aid, and rendering to them the willing, well-paid services of freemen." Stowe regularly claimed that local blacks were happy, carefree workers: "Never was harder work done in a more jolly spirit." The transition from masters and slaves to employers and employees had been a peaceful one in Stowe's world. Emancipation had changed society very little. The free labor society was not all that different from the slave society. Those who once had been masters had become paternal employers; those who once had been chattel slaves had become contented wage earners. The white republic of racial hierarchy remained pleasantly intact in Stowe's imagination.[49]

Her depictions of African Americans in Florida demonstrated that Stowe had backed away from ideas of political equality for African Americans. Now she characterized people of color as subhuman animals who best served the nation as a permanent labor force. In one case, she likened African American bodies to those of alligators. "The fore leg and paw of the alligator has a pitiful and rather shocking resemblance to a black human hand," she wrote. On another occasion she drew upon new scientific theories of evolution and natural selection to describe African Americans as a subhuman species. One local black, she wrote, "was black as night itself; . . . he might have been taken for a big baboon,—the missing link of Darwin." Environmental factors, Stowe claimed, made these "big baboons" perfectly suited to work under the scorching Florida sun. "The negro is the natural laborer of tropical regions," she asserted. "The sun awakens all their vigor and all their boundless jollity. When the nooning time comes, they sit down, not in the shade, but in some good hot place in the sand, and eat their lunch, and then stretch out, hot and comfortable, to take their noon siesta with the full glare of the sun upon them."[50]

Postwar Florida, of course, was not a utopia of benevolent whites and carefree, sunbathing blacks, and Stowe knew it. For people of color, the scorching sun was the least of their worries. As in other places throughout the postwar South, racial violence abounded in Florida. Missionary Esther Hawks reported several incidents of murder while stationed in Florida. "We are hearing reports, every week of the shooting of negroes by infuriated white men," she recorded in her diary.[51] In 1866, a reporter for the *New York Times* in Fernandina wrote, "There is a terrible state of feeling in this city between the whites and blacks."[52] One year later a group of white "Regulators" dragged an African American man into a swamp and whipped him to death. Throughout the late 1860s and 1870s, moreover, white supremacist groups, such as the Ku Klux Klan, continually terrorized Florida's blacks.[53]

Stowe herself privately acknowledged that Florida was not a safe haven for freedpeople, but this did not stop her from publicly affirming otherwise. White residents would become violent if black children received an education and not their own children. "Teaching the whites is the only way of protecting the blacks," she claimed. In letters to friends in Britain, she wrote that local whites absolutely refused to have their children educated in the same schools as African Americans: "Although the school should be of the very best kind and freely offered, no inducement would ever persuade parents to let their children come to them—they would greatly prefer that they should grow up without any education at all."[54] Stowe purposefully kept this information from her northern reading public, though, specifically requesting that her British friends not publish her letters or share the information about racial antagonism. "[I]t would be sure to get over here and set the country all in a flame," she penned, and would potentially damage her appeals to the North. Stowe, in short, was fully cognizant that her construction of a racially idyllic Florida was more fantasy than reality.

Between 1865 and 1875, then, Stowe's public voice altered dramatically. In the early years of Reconstruction she had assailed southern whites for their mistreatment of Union soldiers and defended the rights of African Americans. In fact, she traveled to Florida hoping to help the "poor people whose course in words I have tried to plead." But her own racial prejudices stymied her venture. She quickly took up the banners of sectional reconciliation and abandoned calls for racial justice. Although she disagreed with her brother Henry in 1866, she had come to share the bulk of his views by the 1870s. She appealed to northern whites to travel to and invest in the South by describing Florida as an Edenic land where southern whites and southern blacks lived in a world of racial peace and mutually accepted racial and class hierarchy. The mythic Florida that Stowe propagated to northerners was a perfect new society, one where whites relaxed and happy blacks served them in an imaginary society that looked eerily similar to that desired by plantation masters before the war and by white supremacists after it.[55]

Although Stowe and Beecher vigorously advocated the reforging of the white republic in the years following Lee's surrender at Appomattox, neither of them garnered unanimous acclaim in the North or the South. Some former Confederates still bristled at the sound of their names. Stowe's *Uncle Tom's Cabin* continued to be much maligned and hated, while Beecher's prewar diatribes against slavery and his open support for John Brown aggravated many southern whites even after the war. One southern white told David Macrae, a British traveler in the United States during the early 1870s, that he had never "read more than a few pages of *Uncle Tom's Cabin*, but I've read enough of it to condemn it." "That book and old John Brown's raid," he fumed, "may be said to have brought on the war." Toward Beecher, southern whites were a bit more kind. Macrae found that some former Confederates appreciated Beecher's postwar calls for reconciliation, and they humorously cherished "a desperate hope that, after a few thousand years of purgatorial fire, he might find a way of approach on his knees to the heaven of redeemed planters."[56] Beecher and Stowe alone were not powerful enough to unify the people, but they were merely the beginning of a much larger movement among northern Protestants for national reconciliation with southern whites.

II

In the late 1860s, a rising chorus of northern Protestant voices joined Stowe and Beecher in calling for sectional reconciliation. "Fraternity" became the watchword for many white Protestants. Like Stowe and Beecher, they resurrected white supremacist rhetoric from the antebellum era and backed away from commitments to blacks. These Protestants repudiated any notion of a nationalism built upon shared commitments to democracy, liberty, and loyalty to the federal Union. Believing they had done enough for African Americans with the Thirteenth, Fourteenth, and Fifteenth Amendments, northern Protestants reduced their funding to African Americans in the South and paid less attention to issues of racial justice. The decade following the war witnessed a great reversal in northern religious opinion as the apostles of forgiveness convinced northern whites to abandon the freedpeople and embrace former Confederates.

Over these years a growing number of Methodist and Presbyterian leaders endeavored to create stronger fraternal relations between northern and southern whites. They did so primarily by seeking to reunite their denominations, which had split along sectional lines before the Civil War. In 1868 and 1869, numerous northern Methodist ministers wanted to reopen friendly dialogues with southern Methodists. After the 1868 Methodist general assembly meeting, the *New York Herald* reported that "the proceedings of the Chicago Conference are noteworthy at this time as evincing a desire on the part of the Church North to reunite with the Church South—on its own terms."[57] Two years later the northern general conference sent Bishop Edmund Janes and Reverend C. R. Harris to meet with the southern conference, and during the convention Bishop Janes made it clear that his hope was for solidarity and goodwill. "I do believe that the prayer of Christ will be heard," he lectured, "and that the time will come when his people will be one. Any thing to hasten that end should be done."[58] A writer to the *Milwaukee Index* clearly observed that by 1870 "[t]he Methodist Episcopal Church of these United States has been of decidedly wooing tendencies for the last two or three years. She has *gone* for *Union* strong."[59] Throughout the early 1870s northern and southern Methodists continued to send "fraternal" delegations to one another's meetings, and in 1876 representatives from both denominations convened in Cape May,

New Jersey, for a "Joint Commission on Fraternal Relations." The delegates spent a week discussing how cooperation would help both groups. By the end of the convention all were committed to sectional peace and solidarity. They closed the convention singing:

> Blest be the tie that binds
> Our hearts in Christian love;
> The fellowship of kindred minds
> Is like to that above.[60]

Many northern Presbyterians also wanted to strengthen the "ties that bind." In 1869, Old School Presbyterians conveyed their "Christian salutations" to the southern general assembly, and in 1870 the newly reunited northern Old School and New School Presbyterians expressed desires for "fraternal" relations with their southern counterparts. At the northern general convention, the Presbyterians committed themselves to "the speedy establishment of cordial fraternal relations with the body known as the 'Southern Presbyterian Church,' on terms of mutual confidence, respect, Christian honor and love."[61] At that same general assembly the northern publishing committee consented to eliminate any text that contained negative statements regarding the South or secession "in order that no remaining ground of prejudice to the great work of denominational charity may exist." Indeed, they were willing to obliterate parts of their history to appease former Confederates.[62] Some Presbyterians, furthermore, justified their hopes for harmony by pointing to the reconciliatory actions and tones of other denominations. "The Episcopalians were reunited at once," Reverend John Leyburn wrote to the *Central Presbyterian* in 1873. "[T]he Baptists North and South have met in a Missionary reunion; the Methodist papers speak more kindly, and delegates have visited their conferences." To Leyburn, the lesson was clear. Presbyterians should follow the lead of other denominations and tender the "olive branch," for reunion would beget reunion.[63]

Northern Protestants, especially leaders in the Baptist Church, hoped that the formation of a national Sunday school movement would usher in a new era of sectional solidarity. One American Bible Society agent, for instance, professed, "Thank God the American Bible Society is doing all it can to unite Northern and southern Christians"[64] At the 1869 National Baptist Sunday-School Convention, furthermore, a committee resolved "that this Convention and Institute most earnestly desire and seek to promote the unity and co-operation of our entire American Baptist brotherhood in our Sunday-school work." Convention attendees hoped that Sunday school work would provide a "blending of our hearts in holy brotherhood."[65]

White southern Protestant leaders became more amenable to fraternal relations in the decades following the Civil War, but they continued to oppose any immediate denominational reunion. Wounds of the past and of the present were still too sore, and former Confederate divines believed that distinctive southern traits made them the most prepared men to shepherd flocks below the Mason-Dixon Line. "It is well enough for citizens to fraternize," wrote the editor of the *Atlanta Constitution* in 1877, but the churches must retain their sectional identities. To this editor, northern religious leaders were nothing more than "imposters who brought the country to grief, and who were most appropriately named the 'hell-hounds of Zion.'" Throughout the 1870s and the 1880s, southern Presbyterian leader Robert Lewis Dabney of Virginia's Union Theological Seminary agreed with the *Atlanta Constitution* editor. Dabney continually opposed denominational reunion, principally because he associated the northern churches with racial egalitarianism and interracial sexuality. Presbyterian reunion, he claimed in 1882, was a "step which would seal the moral and doctrinal corruption of our church in the South, and be a direct step towards that final perdition of southern society, domestic amalgamation."[66]

Most southern religious leaders were not as vehemently opposed to denominational fraternity as Dabney, yet they nonetheless remained committed to separate denominational organizations. While southern Baptists and Methodists accepted the exchange of "fraternal delegates" with their respective northern counterparts, both adamantly refused to fold the denominations back together. In 1869 the southern Methodist convention declared that "the true interests of the Church of Christ require and demand the maintenance of our separate and distinct organizations." In a study of the rise of the Sunday school movement in the South, Sally McMillen has recently shown that southern whites viewed the creation of their own Sabbath classes and curriculums as ways to inculcate specifically southern ways of being Christian. All in all, the northern and southern denominations did not formally reunite during the nineteenth century, but members and leaders from each section extolled the virtues of national political reunion in the 1870s. Religious "fraternity" was one way that southern whites could reenter the national body while remaining distinctively southern.[67]

In order to further demonstrate the genuineness of their desires for national reunion, northern Protestants retreated in great numbers from supporting social justice for African Americans. The American Freedmen's Union Commission disbanded in 1870, while northern denominations curbed spending on missions to freedpeople and sent fewer missionaries in the early 1870s. The American Baptist

Home Mission Society, for instance, which sent an average of between sixty and one hundred missionaries to the South in the 1860s, never had more than fifty after 1872, and the majority of those were in "Indian territories."[68] As historian Ralph Morrow has shown in a study of northern Methodists during Reconstruction, their missionary society drastically reduced its spending in the South after 1870. The Freedmen's Aid Society of the Methodist Church collected $92,190 over a twelve-month period in 1868 and 1869. Three years later, in 1872, the society collected only $45,024.[69] The drop in financial giving by the Methodists was mirrored by the northern Presbyterians. In 1871, they sent $77,000 to the South; in 1872, $65,000; in 1873, $63,000. By 1873, of the 4,730 New School churches in the North, only 1,535 contributed to funds for freedpeople.[70]

Although religious historians have attributed this Protestant retrenchment to the financial panic that paralyzed Wall Street in 1873 and the six years of economic depression that followed, the Methodist and Presbyterian examples showed that spending had started to decline well before 1873.[71] Hard times were neither the sole cause nor the main reason for the retreat. In part, white Protestants curbed their donations to the South because the humanitarian crisis during and shortly after the war no longer seemed as alarming. There were no longer thousands of homeless black refugees displaced by raging armies, and African American churches had grown in size and stature. The Great Chicago Fire of 1871 and the Boston Earthquake of 1872, moreover, helped direct funds away from those suffering in the South to those recovering in the North.[72] But some northern whites also viewed their abandonment of missions to African Americans as a way to prove to southern white Christians their earnest hopes for reunion. In 1871 northern Presbyterian leaders made this connection, explicitly claiming that they pulled out of missionary efforts to freedpeople to avoid "all unpleasant collisions with the Southern churches."[73]

Even many within the educational and missionary movement to the freedpeople repudiated their previous radicalism. In 1879, the faculty at Atlanta University voted to cease using the terms "young gentlemen" and "young ladies" when speaking with their students. Instead, the teachers would now call their pupils "young men" and "young women," because the faculty did not want to enrage local whites by showing too much respect to people of color.[74] The northern Methodist general assembly, which had held firm to the hopes of having integrated churches in the South, permitted local congregations to decide upon racial matters in 1876. This policy, as the denominational leaders well knew it would, quickly resulted in the segregation of their churches throughout the South. Even the American

Missionary Association turned away from its commitment to full integration and civil rights. One of its pamphlets in 1876 insisted that "the alienation between the North and the South" was now the nation's most pressing issue, not racial uplift and civil rights. In fact, this article contended that the AMA had never fully endorsed the idea that the races were genuinely equal. It had merely asserted that "all men shall be regarded as equal before God and the law."[75]

Realizing that sectional reconciliation was gaining support, African American religious leaders refused to allow white Protestants like Stowe, Beecher, and other denominational spokesmen to dominate completely the public debates over national reunion and race relations. Together with Frederick Douglass, they assailed the apostles of forgiveness and entreated the North to remain faithful to the vision of a nation defined by wartime loyalty, not by skin color. For many people of color, the Protestant retreat was part of a much larger betrayal they sensed from northern whites, one that led some blacks, such as Reverend Alexander Crummell, to wonder if they would ever be accepted as national brethren in the United States.

During the late 1860s and the 1870s, the North slowly but surely pulled back from radical Reconstruction. Presidents Johnson and Ulysses S. Grant reduced the number of federal troops in the South, who had offered at least some physical protection to blacks, and pardoned thousands of former Confederates, even Ku Klux Klan members. Northern Republicans refused to offer aid to embattled Republican leaders in Virginia and North Carolina who were being illegally driven from office, and they phased out the Freedmen's Bureau. By the mid-1870s, African Americans realized that the ranks of their friends were growing thinner with every passing year.[76]

Many northern people of color viewed the Yankee repudiation of radical Reconstruction as a moral travesty that could only be averted with God's help. In 1872, leaders of the African Methodist Episcopal Zion Church (AMEZ) voiced their displeasure with the growing desire of northern white Methodists for national reunion and pointed to continued northern racism. In a letter to the northern general conference, they claimed that the recent "unfortunate developments" of sectional fraternity and "the prejudice of caste that still exists in the mother church" made it impossible for them to pursue closer connections with northern Methodists. In short, the AMEZ wanted nothing to do with white Methodists who sought national reconciliation while maintaining racial prejudice.[77] At the same time, writers to the *New York Independent* repeatedly lamented that northern Protestants were losing interest in racial justice, even while "the cries of the murdered ones are in our ears."[78]

African American poet, novelist, newspaper correspondent, and social reformer Frances E. W. Harper regularly called on white northerners to fulfill their
commitments to freedpeople and to reject the teachings of the apostles of forgiveness. In several poems published in 1871, most notably "An Appeal to the American People" and "Words for the Hour," she implored northern whites not to squan-
der the rights African American troops and their white allies had won in battle:

> But to-day the traitor stands
> With crimson on his hands,
> Scowling 'neath his brow of hate,
> On our weak and desolate,
> With the blood-rust on the knife
> Aimed at the nation's life.
>
> . . . .
>
> Asking you to weakly yield
> All we won upon the field,
> To ignore, on land and flood,
> All the offerings of our blood,
> And to write above our slain
> "They have fought and died in vain." [79]

To Harper, the North must not forgive and forget, since violence against African
Americans had not ended in the South. Northern whites must continue to battle
for racial justice:

> The minions of a baffled wrong
>   Are marshalling their clan,
> Rise up, rise up, enchanted North!
>   And strike for God and man. [80]

As Harper, AMEZ ministers, writers to the *Independent,* and Douglass assailed the northern retreat from Reconstruction, they expressed an awareness
that the legions of reconciliation were growing during the late 1860s and 1870s.
Missionary Laura Towne wrote despondently in 1873, "The need of education
here seems to me greater than ever—the means less; friends are fewer." [81] Sounding strikingly similar to Frederick Douglass and Thaddeus Stevens, missionary
Margaret Newbold Thorpe lamented the growing inclination of northerners and
the federal government to absolve former Confederates. "[T]he great forgiveness
and forbearance of our Government," she complained, "or its new version of 'The
Prodigal Son' returning to his Father's house not asking to be received as one of
the servants because of his unworthiness to occupy a higher position, but saying,

'Here I am conquered in flesh but not in spirit, take me again in to thy household and let me occupy my former high position, for by nature I am fitted to rule and cannot serve.'" Thorpe indicted her northern brethren for accepting southerners who had yet to repent. "And the North has opened its arms to welcome him, and for the fatted calf has killed the trust of the loyal people, and has sold its honor to purchase the gold chain for the Southern neck." [82]

To Reverend Alexander Crummell, one of the most prominent African American ministers of the nineteenth century, whom W. E. B. Du Bois looked to as a great "spiritual father figure," the betrayal of radical Reconstruction was proof that blacks had no place in the United States and that their national destiny was not inextricably linked with whites. In his annual Thanksgiving Day sermon in 1875, he unequivocally asserted that people of color were strangers in the nation and they would be better off leaving it. "We are living in this country, a part of its population, and yet, in diverse respects, we are as foreign to its inhabitants as though we were living in the Sandwich Islands," he contended. Racial alienation was so high, in fact, that African Americans constituted a "nation within a nation" in the United States. Ultimately, Crummell trusted that true Christianity would one day destroy white supremacy, but before that time blacks must remember that they were a pariah peoples. "The Gospel is sure to work out all the issues and results of brotherhood," he maintained, "but, until that day arrives, we are a nation, set apart, in this country." [83]

African American religious leaders continued to assail discussions of denominational reunion among whites during the 1880s. Presbyterian minister Francis Grimké, the husband of the northern missionary to the South Charlotte Forten, thoroughly denounced northern white Presbyterians for encouraging and entertaining discussions of reunion with southern white Presbyterians. He and Charlotte found it reprehensible that northern Presbyterians could overlook the violence and mayhem that plagued southern society. "I must confess I have been quite disgusted with the *cringing* spirit manifested by the Northern churches," Charlotte confided in her diary. "They are so anxious for union that they are willing to purchase it at any sacrifice of their colored brethren which will gratify the prejudices of the South. The latter, however, are in no such hurry, & both sides have decided to wait until another year. But our Gen. Assembly has plainly showed its spirit toward the colored brother, & that spirit is not a Christian one." [84]

These proponents of racial justice and integration found themselves increasingly on the defensive, and their efforts to drive northerners back to the radicalism they had evinced in the mid-1860s largely failed. Most Protestant Yankees eventually followed the lead of the Episcopal Church, Henry Ward Beecher, and Harriet Beecher Stowe in seeking fraternity and goodwill with southern whites at the expense of support for African Americans. By 1875, leaders in the major northern denominations had not only expressed deep desires to reconcile with southern white Protestants, but also had shown diminished interest in African Americans by withdrawing funds. The Protestant forces of sectional reunion and racial subjugation clearly had the advantage by the mid-1870s. The commitment to civic nationalism, which had flashed so brilliantly during and immediately following the Civil War, was now fading rapidly.

III

The religious influence on postwar reconciliation and on the northern rejection of radical Reconstruction, however, was not limited to Protestant spokespersons and leaders. Christian idioms and ideas suffused appeals for reconciliation at the level of popular culture and national politics as well. In everything from postwar literature to political cartoons during the presidential election of 1872, advocates of national harmony employed biblical narratives and Christian teachings to further their cause. Religious imagery provided a way for northern whites to sanctify the massive amounts of death during the Civil War and to call for national harmony. The use of biblical tropes sanctified pleas for reconciliation in ways that other political and economic rationales could not, for religious rhetoric served as an ideal medium by which northern whites could legitimate reunion as sacred and holy. African Americans and their friends recognized the influence of religious rhetoric and responded in kind, crafting opposing biblical readings that mandated justice before forgiveness. Their appeals, however, found fewer listeners and produced even fewer converts in the 1870s.[85]

Spiritual and religious themes allowed some postwar poets to attempt to come to grips with the appalling amount of carnage and mayhem that had accompanied the Civil War. Although historian and literary critic Alice Fahs has shown how elaborate mourning rituals in popular fiction helped unify northerners in support of the war effort, she did not point out that the narratives of soldiers' deaths changed substantially after the war. Now the war's casualties became emotional tools in the service of national reunion.[86] In December 1865, for instance, *Harper's New Monthly Magazine* carried a poem by Caroline Seymour in which Death brought harmony:

> O Death, the great Peace-Maker!
> If enmity have come between

> There's naught like death to heal it;
> And if we love priceless pain,
> O bitter-sweet when love is vain!
> There's naught like death to seal it.[87]

As Christ's crucifixion reconciled Christians to God, death in the wake of the Civil War could bring peace. Although Seymour's poem did not explicitly connect death and national reconciliation, Frances Miles Finch's immensely popular poem "The Blue and the Gray" did. After reading a story of how white women in Columbus, Mississippi, decorated the graves of Confederate and Union soldiers with flowers, Fitch reflected upon the spiritual meanings of their actions and the fact that these soldiers shared a common burial ground. He lauded the women for their kindness and claimed that their actions eased the pain of northerners:

> No more shall the war cry sever,
> Or the winding rivers be red
> They banish our anger forever
> When they laurel the graves of our dead!

To Fitch, the fallen soldiers made the burial ground a holy place. Underneath the soil, they rested and awaited the return of their Lord:

> Under the sod and dew,
> Waiting the judgment-day;
> Under the one, the Blue,
> Under the other, the Gray.[88]

By conceiving of death as a means of spiritual and mystical national reunion for the former foes, these writers attempted to redeem the destructiveness of the war. The blood of the fallen soldiers had somehow purified the land, and in death they and the nation were now made fellow Americans.

Religious imagery was also apparent in some postwar fiction about reconciliation. In June 1868, *Putnam's Monthly Magazine* printed a short story by S. M. Alcott in which the Christ-like actions of a Union soldier eased the sectional hatred of one Confederate private. After a skirmish, a wounded Confederate and a Union soldier were brought to a Union hospital for aid. As their nurse, the aptly named "Miss Mercy," cared for them, she observed the influence that religious forgiveness and sacrificial death could have on sectional reconciliation. She learned that Clay, the Confederate soldier, had shot Murry, the wounded Union soldier. While in the hospital, Clay attempted to finish off Murry by putting poison in his glass of water. But even this heinous act did not stop Murry from seeking to reconcile with Clay. "I knew he was the man who shot me, when he came, I forgive him," Murry told Miss Mercy one night. Amazed by Murry's generosity, she asked, "Can you really pardon him?" Murry responded, "I can. . . . He will be sorry one day, perhaps; at any rate, he did what he thought his duty; and war makes brutes of all sometimes, I fear." As Murry died, he drew on the words of Christ to reinforce the righteousness of forgiveness, whispering (with Clay listening from the next bed), "It should be so—love our enemies; we should be brothers." With this last breath, Murry "stretched his hand toward the man who had murdered him" in fraternal kindness. Murry's words and actions had a remarkable effect on Clay. He repented of his anger toward northerners and bequeathed an immense sum of money to Murry's widow. Murry's death and his invocation of Christ's teaching to "love our enemies" served as the catalyst for Clay's reconciliation with the Union.[89]

Religious rationales for national reunion and endorsements of white supremacy also figured prominently in Horace Greeley's bid to unseat Ulysses Grant in the presidential election of 1872. The popular editor of the *New York Tribune*, Greeley had been an abolitionist during the Civil War, but he quickly switched his emphasis to sectional reunion when the war ended.[90] Many scholars have pointed out that national reconciliation was one of the most crucial issues of this presidential race and that Greeley did a great deal to encourage sectional peace. Historian Paul Buck, for example, has suggested that the 1872 election signified the first time that a large number of Republicans softened their attitudes toward Democrats and the South.[91] Yet historians have overlooked the ways in which religious idioms and rhetoric influenced the campaign. Both camps regularly employed biblical texts and metaphors. While Greeley and his supporters cast their drive for national solidarity in religious terms, positing Greeley as America's "Christian candidate," his Republican rivals countered with religious allusions of their own. They asserted that southerners had yet to repent and should therefore not be trusted. Ultimately, these politicians recognized the power of religious themes and invoked them for their own benefit.

From 1868 to 1872, a number of factors led Greeley and other former Republicans to despise Grant and oppose him in 1872. Many long-time Republicans, most notably Carl Schurz, George Julian, Lyman Trumbull, Charles Sumner, and Salmon Chase, became frustrated with Grant for his patronage decisions, his corruption-riddled administration, his ill-fated plans to annex Santo Domingo, and the enactment of a new tariff.[92] In addition, they were wearied and vexed by continued sectional hostilities. In 1872, self-titled "Liberal Republicans" met in Cincinnati and formed their own political party to challenge Grant in the upcoming presidential contest. Dedicating themselves to universal amnesty, civil service reform, and acceptance of the Thirteenth, Fourteenth, and Fifteenth Amendments to the Constitution, the delegates decided to nominate Greeley for president. Several weeks later, the Democrats cast their lot with the Liberal Republicans and endorsed Greeley as well. He made it clear from the very beginning that sectional reunion would constitute the hallmark of his campaign. "I accept your nomination," Greeley wrote to the Liberal Republican committee, "in the confident trust that the masses of our countrymen North and South are eager to clasp hands across the bloody chasm which has too long divided them, forgetting that they have been enemies in the joyous consciousness that they are, and must henceforth remain, brethren." [93]

For several years Greeley and his supporters had repeatedly spoken of national reconciliation in spiritual terms. Writing to Greeley in 1867, John C. Underwood of Richmond, Virginia, asserted that only when members of both sections followed the teachings of Christ would the nation be reunited. "May we learn to return good for their evil," he wrote, "blessings for their cursing & try to imitate the glorious example of our divine Lord & Saviour." [94] Greeley likewise adopted religious examples to foster national solidarity. He often portrayed himself in the image of an Old Testament prophet who voiced the words of God to the people. Before a congregation of whites and blacks in Richmond, Virginia, in 1867, he began his address referencing "a Hebrew prophet." "SHALL THE SWORD DEVOUR FOREVER?" he asked. Greeley answered in a prophetic tongue: "[I] shall speak in the spirit of that prophet, asking you whether the time has not fully come when all the differences, all the heart-burnings, all the feuds and the hatreds . . . should be abandoned forever?" [95]

Five years later, during the presidential race, the Greeley campaign continued to invoke Old Testament teachings. "I felt that there had been bloodshed enough," he told a group in Harrisburg, Pennsylvania, affirming his conviction that the sections needed to forgive one another. "Remember that dying injunction of the great King David, that vengeance should be brought on his chief officer, Joab, because he had shed the blood of war in peace." On another occasion, he declared, "I trust the day is not distant wherein, putting behind us the things that concern the past, we shall remember that grand old injunction of the Bible: 'Speak to the children of Israel that they go forward.'" [96] As Greeley used his speeches to position himself as America's prophet of reconciliation, political cartoonist and designer of racy burlesque shows Matt Morgan depicted him as fulfilling biblical prophecies. In Morgan's print, Grant watched in the background as Greeley and his running mate, Benjamin Gratz Brown, enacted the predictions of the biblical writer Isaiah: "They shall beat their swords into plowshares, and their spears into pruning-hooks: nation shall not lift up sword against nation, neither shall they learn war any more." (See figure 7.)

Much like Beecher, Greeley described northerners whom he perceived to be stirring up sectional hostility as villainous evildoers who corrupted the teachings of Christ. After visiting Texas in 1871 and decrying "Carpetbagger Rule" as odious to many white Texans, he characterized northerners in the South as demonic forces who defiled biblical teachings. Claiming that carpetbaggers were worse than Ku Klux Klan members, he told a New York audience that "these fellows—many of them long-faced and with eyes rolled up—are greatly concerned for the education of the blacks and for the salvation of their souls . . . 'Let us pray,' they say. But they spell pray with an *e*, and, thus spelled, they obey the apostolic injunction to 'prey without ceasing.'"[97]

Greeley's supporters routinely employed religious rhetoric and metaphors to strengthen his appeal. Even the former president of Oberlin College, a religious institution in Ohio that was the nation's first college to accept women and people of color, Asa Mahan, claimed that Greeley stood as America's "Christian candidate." To Mahan, Greeley's policies were "godlike and Christian," and he told a convention in Chicago that Greeley "represent[ed] the angel of amnesty, peace, and national brotherhood."[98] Arch-radical Senator Charles Sumner, who joined the Liberal Republican–Democrat camp because he disdained President Grant and his administration, went even further. Calling sectional reconciliation "the most important issue ever presented to the American people," he claimed that God had inspired Greeley's presidential candidacy. "It is the spirit of the Lord, and is irresistible," Sumner said of Greeley's nomination. "[T]o my mind it is Providential." In addition, he asserted that the Republican Party had cast off Christianity when it inflamed sectional passions: "[T]he Sermon on the Mount is forgotten, . . . the Beatitudes are put aside." To Sumner, Greeley's election and national reunion would bring God's glory: "So will the Republic be elevated to new heights of moral grandeur, and our people will manifest that virtue, 'greatest of all,' which is found in charity."[99] Along with Sumner and Mahan, Theodore Tilton, a Congregationalist and former editor of the radical *New York Independent,* regularly described Greeley as America's "Christian candidate." In fact, as historian James McPherson has shown, Tilton and his new paper, the *Golden Age,* were extremely influential in garnering Greeley the Liberal Republican nomiation.[100]

While Liberal Republicans and Greeley called for sectional peace as a religious imperative, Greeley rejected the idea that African Americans needed any more support from the federal government. He held the freedpeople to blame for their continued impoverishment. While touring Texas in 1871, he sounded very much like Henry Ward Beecher when he professed that former Confederates were more adequately suited to lead the South than African Americans or northern whites. "By their experience and knowledge," he claimed, "they were better fitted for the conduct of public affairs than the emancipated blacks." At a rally in Cleveland, Ohio, he told a crowd that "we desire that the rubbish and debris of the old controversy be swept out of sight. There is no longer reason for contention concerning the rights of the black man. They are secured by the Constitution." [101] Greeley even questioned the merits of emancipation. "I was, in the days of slavery, an enemy of slavery, because I thought slavery inconsistent with the rights, the dignity, the highest well-being of free labor," he announced while in Indiana. "That might have been a mistake." [102]

To Greeley, the key to explaining African Americans' impoverishment was their sinfulness. "Had [Negroes] saved the money they have since 1865 spent in drink, tobacco, balls, gambling, and other dissipations," Greeley wrote in the *Tribune*, "they might have bought therewith at least Ten Million acres of soil in their respective states." [103] Blacks' immorality, he argued, was responsible for their inability to improve themselves. In Greeley's hands, the moral imperatives of the Civil War era had been turned on their head. The Christian God now seemed to demand that northern whites forgive southern whites, but that same God no longer insisted on rights for freedpeople. For Greeley, Beecher, and the other apostles of forgiveness, a reforged white republic now stood as the Lord's will.

The connections among religion, race, and the 1872 presidential race found graphic expression in a campaign print by New York artist Svobodin Merinsky. Using the Old Testament story of David and Goliath, Merinsky depicted Greely as God's chosen candidate and Grant as his evil opponent. In the print, Greeley stood as the young and virtuous Israelite David, Grant as a huge Goliath. Like the biblical shepherd boy, Greeley would defeat his menacing enemy with deceptively powerful tools, a quill, an inkwell, and several copies of the *New York Tribune*. Just as God was on the side of the Israelites, he was now on the side of the Liberal Republicans. Yet Greeley would not only defeat Grant. He would also end Grant's protection of the black soldier hiding behind him—the southern freedman. Clearly, Merinsky fused religious, racial, and national imagery to depict Greeley as God's chosen instrument who would overthrow Grant, end "negro rule" in the South, and bring a new American promised land built upon white solidarity. (See figure 8.)

Greeley's political opponents, in turn, forged their own religious interpretations that continued to prize justice over reunion. To Wendell Phillips and

Frederick Douglass, religious teachings were on the side of racial justice, not national white solidarity. Phillips told a crowd in Boston, "We do forgive. We have forgiven. But duty to the dead and to the negro forbids us to trust power to any hands without undoubted, indubitable certainty that such hands are trustworthy."[104] Douglass attacked the attempts of Greeley and the Liberal Republicans to claim themselves as the party of true religion. The Democrats and Liberal Republicans have "become very Scriptural and preach the doctrine of forgiveness," Douglass, tongue in cheek, told a crowd at Faneuil Hall in Boston. But he was not ready to accept them as spiritual brothers: "I don't know but that I am prepared to act on the principle inculcated by the parable of the Prodigal Son." Southerners had yet to repent as the Prodigal Son had, and therefore it was inappropriate for the North to invite southern whites back into the nation.[105] Douglass once again turned the tale of the Prodigal Son against the South. To him, only when former Confederates followed the example of the Prodigal by prostrating themselves and by expressing willingness to be servants should they be reinstated as true Americans.

When the ballots were counted, Grant and the Republican Party carried the day, and the Democrats remained banished from the White House for another twelve years. But Reconstruction was clearly losing support in the North. Although Greeley received only 43 percent of the popular vote and died shortly after the election, his followers continued to claim him as God's prophet of peace. Performing Greeley's funeral at the Church of the Divine Paternity in New York, Reverend E. H. Chapin proclaimed that Greeley's Christianity "was no holiday faith, worn for a time-serving purpose. It was not put on him; it grew out of him, the earliest ingrained conviction of his youth and his after life." A rumor circulated widely that with his dying words Greeley echoed the biblical character Job experiencing devastating trials and suffering: "I know that my redeemer liveth." Other preachers likewise associated Greeley's hopes for national reconciliation with his religious faith. Chapin believed that "this country will never forget the fact that Horace Greeley longed to be President that he might put the balm of Gilead into the troubled bosom of this country."[106] Upon hearing of Greeley's death, Pennsylvania poet Bayard Taylor composed his own eulogy, in which he described Greeley as a true man of peace and righteousness. To Taylor, Greeley "[e]mbodied Love" and "incarnate Charity":

> There is no threshold but his feet
> Might cross, a messenger of counsel sweet,
> Of peace and patience and forgiving love,
> Of Toil that bends and Faith that looks above![107]

For many white Americans, Greeley was more than an editor or a political candidate. He was a beloved prophet who had spoken and lived the dictates of the Protestant God.

From the mid-1860s and into the 1870s, a diverse crowd of northern whites used religious narratives, ideas, and metaphors to justify sectional reconciliation and racial discrimination in a variety of popular media. In poems, short stories, and political speeches, even former abolitionists like Greeley, Sumner, and Fitch wove religious themes into their calls for national reunion. Christian narratives served as one of the primary rhetorical vehicles to inspire feelings of national forgiveness and solidarity among whites. These arguments paralleled those of leading Protestant denominational leaders who in the 1870s authorized the northern abandonment of African Americans in favor of fraternity with southern whites. Northern Protestantism and religious metaphors were powerful tools in the struggle for national reconciliation among northern and southern whites. At the same time, religious and political leaders sanctified the repudiation of civil rights and helped turn northern whites away from their religious and political alliance with African Americans. By the mid-1870s, nearly all northern Republicans had given up on Reconstruction.

But the apostles of forgiveness did not preach their message uncontested. Over the decade and throughout the rest of the century, African Americans and some whites challenged them at every turn. Black denominational leaders refused to accept white solidarity as long as the South practiced violent racism. Journals like the *New York Independent* repeatedly called northern Protestants to remember the war and the righteousness of justice for African Americans. Spokesmen such as Frederick Douglass assailed claims that biblical teachings endorsed blind conciliation toward southern whites. In fact, even after Greeley's death, one white minister claimed that Greeley's affection for the white South revealed a perverted type of Christian faith. This pastor blamed Greeley's "sympathy with the Rebels of the South" on "his defective Christian faith, or his paganized belief which would indiscriminately pardon all rebellious souls." Forgiveness, in short, should only be offered to the repentant.[108] Proponents of civil rights and protection for southern blacks persistently advocated a social gospel of racial justice, a goal that would be achieved only if northern whites honored their commitments to freedpeople. They remained devoted to a radical civic nationalism that rewarded loyalty to the Union over racial affiliation as the mark of citizenship.

Although African Americans struggled intrepidly to keep the rising tide of Protestant reconciliationists from overwhelming them, one of their greatest challenges came from a former shoe salesman–turned–evangelist. In the mid-1870s and 1880s, Dwight Lyman Moody led one of the most spectacular religious revival campaigns in American history. Dubbed the harbinger of a "Great Awakening," Moody preached a gospel of reconciliation to northern whites deeply desiring an end to the "southern problem." Moody offered precisely what these northern whites sought. As he rallied northern and southern whites together, he repudiated radical Reconstruction and called for the rejection of the civic nationalist imagination. Moody denounced religious involvement in politics and accepted racial segregation. The result was a large constituency of southern whites who adored him as much as northerners did. An assortment of African American religious leaders rose to combat him, but they could not quench the revival fires of sectional reconciliation and racial oppression. Dreams of an integrated, egalitarian nation were not dead, but they were certainly faltering and fading.

4

INVENTOR OF LEGENDS MIRACULOUS

National Reconciliation and Racial Segregation during
America's Third Great Awakening

During the tumultuous spring of 1865, when the war had ended but the fate of the nation remained undetermined, an interdenominational body of Protestant leaders in Missouri decided to hold their annual meeting in St. Louis. Reflecting the bitterness of much of the country, the city was rife with sectional antagonism. It "was divided between the friends of the Union and the friends of the late Confederacy," noted one contemporary, "and every prominent religious man in the State was known as a partisan on one side or the other." "This dangerous combination of fire and gunpowder," observed one delegate, threatened to explode any chance of Christian cooperation. For religious unity, these men needed a presiding officer who could quickly quell any tensions. They needed a leader who would take their focus off of sectional hatreds. They needed an individual who would honor Christian solidarity above all other considerations.[1]

For these reasons, the delegates looked to Dwight Lyman Moody, a rising star in American Protestantism. They hoped that he could navigate them through the dangerous waters of sectional division. And he did not disappoint. While ministers throughout the North vigorously debated the national status of southern whites and freedpeople, Moody did everything in his power to raise the Cross above the flags of the Union and the Confederacy. When disputes arose and tempers flared, he tactfully changed the subject or had the members pray or sing hymns. This strategy was extremely successful, according to one of his first biographers, and "Mr. Moody seemed to hold the Union men by one hand and the ex-Confederates by the other, thus constituting himself a tie of Christian brotherhood between them."[2] For Moody, this Missouri convention was the first time he would help assuage sectional animosity and reconcile northern and southern whites. Indeed, this 1865 convention presaged what Moody would accomplish on a national scale in the mid-1870s—when he would unite Union men and former Confederates all over the nation.

Born in 1837, Dwight Moody spent most of his childhood in a small town outside of Boston. After his father died early in Dwight's youth, his mother found solace in the local Unitarian church and had Dwight baptized there at the age of five. She later enrolled him in the Northfield Academy for boys, but his academic abilities and interests proved limited. In 1854, he moved to Boston, where his uncle helped him get a job selling shoes. The footwear industry held great economic possibilities for young men like Moody. It was a booming part of the business sector, and, as his son later remembered, it was Moody's ambition "to be worth $100,000—a fortune in those days." [3]

When not peddling shoes, Moody came under the influence of Congregational minister and revivalist Edward N. Kirk. Moody joined Kirk's Mount Vernon Church and "gave himself and his life to Christ." He even exhibited some political awareness, siding with the forces of abolitionism. In May 1854, a runaway slave from Virginia, Anthony Burns, was caught and imprisoned in Boston. The city exploded with anger. While some Bostonians were dedicated to the cause of antislavery and desperately wanted to free Burns, many other whites were much more agitated by the new federal Fugitive Slave Act that compelled them to aid slave catchers in the apprehension of runaways. Along with hundreds of others, Moody attended public meetings to oppose the imminent return of Burns to his master. At one gathering, Moody recalled, "Wendell Phillips had spoken, and quite a number of others," and they inflamed the audience with a passion to liberate Burns. When news came that some Bostonians were already breaking into the jail that held Burns, Moody was swept up with the crowd. They rushed to join the liberators. Alas, he lamented, "all of us couldn't liberate that poor captive." Federal marshals escorted Burns in chains back to his master's southern plantation. [4]

Moody then went west in search of greater economic opportunity in Chicago. When he arrived in 1856, he had little idea that he would be transformed from a religiously tepid salesman into an evangelical firebrand. But the revivals of 1857–1858, which quickly became known as the "businessmen's revivals," led him to forsake the selling of shoes for the kingdom of souls. During the revivals, Moody participated in lunchtime prayer meetings, attended the Young Men's Christian Association (YMCA), and heard revival preachers regularly. As historian Kathryn Long has shown, in an atmosphere of intense economic and national turmoil, revival leaders consciously sought to keep political and social issues separated from spiritual ones. They refused to entertain discussions of sectional politicking or slavery, and they impressed upon Moody a belief that "worldly" affairs and spiritual revivals should be detached from one another. [5]

By the start of the Civil War, Moody had given up his business aspirations and had committed himself to religious ministry. Whether teaching Sunday school or riding a horse through the slums of Chicago to attract young people to the YMCA, "Crazy Moody" (as the locals contemptuously dubbed him) immersed himself in the Lord's service. He later reminisced fondly about "the time I was sleeping and living in the Young Men's Christian Association rooms, where I was then president, secretary, janitor, and everything else." He became so popular in Chicago that president-elect Abraham Lincoln visited Moody's Sunday school class on his way to the capital. Reportedly, Lincoln gave his first and only Sabbath school lecture during that visit.[6] (See figure 9.)

When the Civil War erupted, Moody joined the Civil War Christian Commission as a chaplain, made nine frontline trips, spent a considerable amount of time with General Ulysses S. Grant's regiments, ministered to captured Confederates in Illinois, and befriended the future leader of the Freedmen's Bureau, General Oliver Otis Howard. Moody carried with him an overriding focus on spiritual redemption at the expense of temporal issues, but in this he was not terribly popular in the 1860s, when political radicalism was in its heyday. As he traveled to the front lines with a company of missionaries during the Civil War, Moody found himself in the middle of a spirited discussion on whether chaplains should concentrate their energies on helping wounded men or on saving the souls of those about to die. One of Moody's friends recounted, "Mr. Moody, full of the idea of saving souls, urged that the very first business in every case was to find out whether the sick or dying man were a child of God." If the wounded combatant already had faith, Moody maintained, then the chaplain should continue searching for soldiers who needed salvation. Robert Collyer, a Unitarian minister, thought Moody's position despicable. He contended that the chaplain should administer physical comfort to the men to "help keep them alive, rather than begin by trying to prepare them for death." One listener attempted to settle the dispute by postulating a middle ground. He argued that a chaplain should do all he could to assist injured soldiers, but if a combatant seemed close to death, then a chaplain should "offer him a short and swift salvation, by telling him the story of the thief on the cross." Collyer would make no such compromise: "What! Are we to tell our dying heroes, who have gone forth to fight our battles and save our flag, while we stay comfortably at home,—are we to talk to them about thieves?" The crowd of missionaries exploded with a "storm of applause." Collyer had won the debate, and Moody's otherworldly emphasis seemed to have been out of step with the national religious temper of the 1860s.[7]

When the war ended, Moody returned to work in Chicago, where he built the Illinois Street Church, a monumental structure with seating for over fifteen hundred people. After the Great Chicago Fire of 1871 rampaged through the city, destroying thousands of buildings, including Moody's church, he decided to travel to Great Britain with a new associate, the singer and songwriter Ira Sankey. From 1873 to 1875, Moody and Sankey led massive revival meetings throughout Great Britain. From the hills of Scotland to the streets of London, they were beloved. Even Queen Victoria and Friedrich Engels commented, albeit critically, on Moody and Sankey's visit. The American evangelists returned to the United States in 1875 and proceeded to set the people of the United States "religiously crazy," as poet Walt Whitman put it.[8]

Much of Moody's acculturation in evangelicalism and northern society before the 1870s served to define his career and prepared him to be the most famous and powerful evangelical leader in the United States. Socially and economically, he ascribed to and defended the middle-class values of thrift, self-reliance, individualism, and hard work. Religiously, he was devoted to evangelical Protestantism and to interdenominational cooperation. Politically, he was a moderate Republican who opposed slavery, but he felt no motivation to battle racism or even address social issues, such as racial injustice. In fact, his inclination was to attempt to separate political issues from religious ones.

Although Moody endeavored to be apolitical in his ministry, his amazing American revivals in the mid-1870s had a profound political effect. They played a crucial role in reuniting the North and the South while religiously legitimating the northern retreat from radical Reconstruction. As awakening leaders had done during the businessmen's revivals and as he himself had done at the Missouri Christian convention in 1865, Moody encouraged Americans to set aside social and political issues in order to focus on spiritual conversions and personal piety. In so doing, Moody successfully brought together northern and southern whites who had long been divided. Like Beecher, Stowe, and the other apostles of reunion, Moody implored northern whites to forgive and forget wartime disagreements. His sermons promoted a depoliticized and distanced version of the Civil War, with stories in which white soldiers from both sections were considered equally valiant; he crafted biblical typologies that legitimated the northern desire to retreat from radical Reconstruction; he denounced religious involvement in politics and entreated his followers to abandon partisan issues amid the sectionally and racially charged political atmosphere of the 1870s; and he employed prominent southern ministers to great advantage in his northern evangelistic crusades. Moreover, when preaching in the South, Moody garnered white support by praying for the Confederate dead, by paying homage to the Lost Cause, and by condoning racial segregation.

Commitments to civil rights and justice for freedpeople fell by the wayside in Moody's calls for white evangelicals to reunite, and African Americans sternly criticized him for building his national revivals upon racial separation. As they had opposed Beecher and Greeley, black religious leaders, especially Ida B. Wells, now blasted Moody for providing segregation with religious sanction. Many people of color boycotted Moody's meetings and expressed bitterness over the advent of Jim Crow. They recognized that the revivals helped undermine the religious motivations behind radical Reconstruction. Highlighting social consensus at the expense of social reform, Moody's revivals contributed to the repudiation of commitments to civic nationalism, while they offered spiritual justification to an ethnic nationalism centered upon whiteness. This was a reversal of great importance, for northern and southern whites were coming to believe that God desired peace among whites far more than justice for all citizens.

I

When Moody returned to the United States in 1875 from his triumphant revival tour in Great Britain, he encountered a nation gripped in social and political turmoil. In the fall of 1873, a panic on Wall Street paralyzed the economy and plunged the country into six years of depression. The New York Stock Exchange closed for ten days, while thousands of businesses were forced into bankruptcy. One financial group reported that the total number of bankruptcies across the nation doubled from 5,183 in 1873 to 10,478 in 1878. Within two years of the panic, almost half of the nation's iron furnaces had ceased operating, and railroad stocks declined almost 60 percent. Laborers and the working class suffered the worst. Hard economic times led to bitter and violent class conflict. In Chicago and New York City, mass meetings of the unemployed sparked great fear among middle- and upper-class Americans. As the panic turned into depression, and as textile workers and coal miners in Pennsylvania opposed wage reductions and layoffs with strikes that bordered on violence, members of the "better" classes worried that the United States might end up like Paris in 1871. In that year, Parisian workers had taken control of their city only to be crushed by Napoleon III's forces. Bourgeois Americans, who had consumed stories about the rise and fall of the Paris Commune, now agonized over a possible revolution in the United States.[9]

While financial distress and class conflict created intense anxiety among many northerners, "the southern problem" continued to generate a great deal of frustration. Racial violence in the South kept southern concerns in the northern purview, for belligerence knew few bounds in the post–Civil War South. In the countryside and in the cities, Democrats, Republicans, whites, and blacks took up arms against one another. Rioting, kidnapping, and violence forced northerners to attend to events below the Mason-Dixon Line. Along with letters and reports from missionaries in the South, northern newspapers and weeklies, including the *New York Tribune,* the *Springfield Republican,* the *Chicago Tribune,* and the *New York Independent,* often carried stories about turmoil in the South. Many northern whites continued to view the South as a bastion of disloyalty. Republican politicians contributed to sectional divisions by vigorously "waving the bloody shirt" in Congress and during election campaigns, making sure that anyone within earshot knew which candidate had supported the Union and which candidate had not. As one clerk in the White House commented in 1872, "I cannot get over a distrust I have had always of the southern states."[10]

But an increasing majority of northern whites found the federal government's use of force to uphold southern Reconstruction more appalling than southern whites' attacks upon the freedpeople and white Republicans. In part, the general northern frustration with the federal government stemmed from the highly publicized corruption in President Ulysses S. Grant's administration, but events in the South were crucial.[11] Especially after the "de Trobriand affair" in Louisiana in early 1875, exasperation with the continuing problems in the South reached a fevered pitch. In the Bayou State, Democrats and Republicans had been battling for months over the election of state legislators. After a melee of kidnappings, shootings, and verbal assaults, two rival governments set themselves up in New Orleans. The episode climaxed when Colonel Philippe R. de Trobriand entered the legislative chamber with federal troops and expelled five Democratic members. Trobriand's actions, coupled with General Philip Sheridan's recommendation that some southerners be "exterminated," outraged northern whites. They had had enough of reports of chaos and mayhem. On January 11, 1875, New York politicians and merchants, "without distinction of party," staged an "Indignation Meeting" to oppose the federal government's role in Reconstruction. Even in Boston, once the domain of the most rabid abolitionists, citizens doubted whether the government should continue to prop up Republican regimes in the South. The *New York Times* rightly pointed out that radicals such as "Wendell Phillips and William Lloyd Garrison . . . represent ideas in regard to the South which the majority of the Republican party have outgrown." Ulysses S. Grant's secretary of state, Hamilton Fish, probably summed up the situation best when he wrote, "The country wants peace, quiet, and harmony between all the sections."[12]

Social and political chaos in Louisiana and throughout the South prompted many northern whites to become more open to appeals for sectional harmony at the expense of people of color. Northern Republicans steadily shifted the blame for southern problems from whites' refusal to accept blacks' citizenship rights to the alleged inabilities of African Americans to govern properly. Books like Charles Nordhoff's *The Cotton States*, Edward King's *The Great South*, and James S. Pike's *The Prostrate State*—all of which were first serialized in northern papers before being published in book form—characterized the South as a place where black suffrage and civil rights were destroying public stability. In Nordhoff's, King's, and Pike's estimations, although the majority of southern whites wanted reconciliation with northern whites, it was impossible as long as "negro rule" dominated. The "Africanization" of the South, which meant that African Americans voted and served in state legislatures, was too much for southern whites to bear, and national reunion could not take place until southern whites had been granted home rule.[13]

These new views of the South, coupled with the seemingly interminable racial hostility, led many northern whites to seek an escape from southern traumas, to embrace southern whites, and to wash their hands of civil liberties and justice for African Americans. The editor of the *Nation*, E. L. Godkin, for instance, denounced the radical Republicans for "the insane task of making newly-emancipated field hands, led by barbers and barkeepers, fancy they knew as much about government and were as capable of administering it, as the whites." To Godkin, suffrage for blacks was "a silly attempt." When southern whites slaughtered thirty blacks in Hinds County, Mississippi, in September 1875, northern presses largely ignored the atrocity. Even the leading Republican paper in the South commented that "there was little use in even calling attention to those outrages, for almost no one seemed to care." Future president James Garfield perceived, "I have for some time had the impression that there is a general apathy among the people concerning the War and the Negro. The public seems to have tired of the subject."[14]

II

It was at this precise moment that Dwight Moody returned to the United States from Great Britain. While religious historians Sidney Mead, James Findlay, William McLoughlin, Martin Marty, and Sidney Ahlstrom have shown that Moody's revivals strongly appealed to middle-class Americans who felt distressed by urbanization and industrialization, these scholars and others have failed to connect the American awakening to the repudiation of radical Reconstruction and the post–Civil War healing of the white republic.[15] Moody preached both to a nation struggling through an industrial transformation and to one seeking an escape from sectional and class divisions. The revivals were not just expressions of bourgeois fears; they were also part of the drive to reforge a sense of American nationalism after decades of internecine conflict. Moody's disdain for Christian social and political activism, his emphasis on reconciliation and reunion, his biblical typologies that emphasized peace, his sentimentalized Civil War stories, his promotion of southern religious leaders, and his own widely popular tour in the South made his revivals a powerful force in reconciling northern and southern whites. Although most northern and southern denominations were unable to reunite institutionally, Moody's campaigns provided powerful moments of interdenominational and intersectional cooperation and care that helped former opponents overlook their past animosities.

During the final quarter of the nineteenth century, Moody ranked as the most popular religious figure in the nation. In fact, as Henry Ward Beecher's reputation languished in the mid-1870s because of his scandalous, and perhaps adulterous, relationship with Elizabeth Tilton, wife of editor Theodore Tilton, Moody supplanted Beecher in fame.[16] Often preaching three times a day, Moody addressed millions in Brooklyn, Philadelphia, New York City, Chicago, and Boston. Revival audiences comprised a who's who of nineteenth-century American society, including President Ulysses S. Grant, members of the U.S. Supreme Court, railroad mogul Tom Scott, poets Walt Whitman and John Greenleaf Whittier, and historian and statesman George Bancroft. Some notables even lent the evangelist a hand. International banker J. Pierpont Morgan presided as treasurer of revival finances, while New York's "merchant prince" William E. Dodge filled the campaign coffers. John Wanamaker purchased the spacious Pennsylvania Railroad depot to house Moody's meetings in Philadelphia and proceeded to refurbish the depot into a department store after the revivals. Henry Ward Beecher and the rector of Harvard College, Phillips Brooks, preached in Moody's place when he was sick or simply exhausted. Even Charles Guiteau, the future assassin of President James Garfield, led one of Moody's prayer meetings.[17]

While thousands of northerners attended his daily meetings, Moody's words were also printed widely in secular newspapers, magazines, and books. As historian Bruce Evensen has shown, Moody and the nineteenth-century press enjoyed a mutually beneficial relationship. Editors found that the evangelist's escapades made great copy and helped increase sales during the economic depression, and Moody used the power of the press to advertise and create his revivals. The *New York Herald, Boston Evening Transcript, Chicago Herald,* and *Boston Daily Globe* were just a few of the papers that reported on the revivals daily. The nationally popular *Harper's Weekly* featured a large cover illustration and a major article on Moody in 1876.[18] These publications did a great deal to announce that Moody's ministry had indeed created a mass national revival. The *Cleveland Leader,* for instance, insisted that "the United States is now in the midst of the throes of the third of [its] great Religious Awakening[s]."[19] (See figure 10.)

Moody and his colossal revivals left an indelible mark on northern society. For decades afterward, northerners remembered the evangelist's influence and the religious energy he created. In the wake of Moody's death in 1899, Presbyterian and department store magnate John Wanamaker boldly asserted that "it would be [as] impossible to replace D. L. Moody as it would be to replace Abraham Lincoln . . . the great characters of the century."[20] Thirty years later, Gaius Glenn Atkins, a leading religious writer, recalled that Moody was "better known throughout the English-speaking world than any other religious leader. . . . [He had] a passion for souls, a flame-like faith, a sovereignty of speech and wisdom and an ascendancy of purpose which made him the master of any situation in which he was involved."[21] Even in the midst of the darkest days of the Great Depression, Americans still looked back to Moody and his revivals. In 1938, octogenarian Frederick Savage, a poor "Old Yankee" from New England, told a worker with the New Deal Federal Writers' Project, "What the world needs is more thought of God. I was born in Northfield, the same town as Dwight Moody. I heard him preach when I was seventeen. He said it was good for a man to walk with God and I've always remembered it."[22]

To those desiring an escape from the "southern problem" and the political corruption of the 1870s, Moody's revivals offered great assurance. In stark contrast to the northern ministers after Lincoln's assassination, the evangelist found little meaning in political affairs. In fact, he encouraged his parishioners to put away such concerns. "If the President should die to-night," he preached to a Philadelphia audience, "that would make an outcry here. But perhaps even so great an event would not be mentioned in heaven at all."[23] Extending this logic, Moody railed against Christian involvement in secular affairs. He especially denounced political and social activism: "I have noticed that when a Christian man goes into the world to get an influence over the world, he suffers more than the world does." On another occasion he explained, "Don't flatter yourselves that the world is going to get any better. . . . [T]he world is on the rocks."[24] True to his pre-millennial theological convictions, which supposed that the apocalypse could occur at any moment and that the world would get increasingly evil before Christ's return, Moody energetically sought to save individual souls rather than radically transform society.[25] In the context of the mid-1870s, however, this general abandonment of politics had a specific meaning. It invariably meant a rejection of radical Reconstruction and its emphasis on black civil rights and civic nationalism.

Along with championing a retreat from secular affairs, Moody preached a message centered on forgiveness and reconciliation rather than one on social justice. "Let me tell everyone in this hall tonight that I bring good news . . . it is the Gospel of Reconciliation," he proclaimed in Chicago. Moody did not merely want to break down barriers between God and man; he also set out to destroy the walls separating man from man. Most important, he attacked sectarianism and denominational conflict. He insisted that his revivals were obliterating the evil force of sectarian prejudice. "And there was a time—but, thank God, we are getting over it," he told his audience in Chicago, "when a Methodist would not touch a Baptist . . . or a Presbyterian a Congregationalist." The congregants liked what they heard and responded with a resounding "Amen."[26]

Moody's coterie of coworkers and supporters reflected his hope for interdenominational unity. While William E. Dodge maintained a membership in the Old School Presbyterian Church throughout the 1860s, Frances Willard grew up among abolitionist Methodists and ultimately became a Methodist deaconess. John Wanamaker attended a New School Presbyterian Church in Philadelphia, and John D. Rockefeller was a lifelong Baptist. Phillips Brooks and J. P. Morgan were Episcopalians, while Henry Ward Beecher led a Congregational church in Brooklyn. Moody's constituency and his leaders came from diverse theological and denominational backgrounds within Protestantism, and amid the revivals sectarian particularities were diminished in favor of broad evangelical appeals.[27]

Interdenominationalism not only unified northerners; it also had the power to transcend sectional animosities and boundaries. While Moody directed his messages of peace toward warring denominations, he embraced national reconciliation as well. "I think if I know my own heart," he proudly announced to well over ten thousand New Yorkers, "I love the South as well as I do the North." Statements like this from Henry Ward Beecher in the mid-1860s had been decidedly unpopular and a host of individuals had arisen to denounce. By 1875, the northern mood had changed. Moody's audiences willingly accepted his approval for the land of southern cavaliers.[28] His conciliatory attitudes and comments about the South, moreover, were not feigned or merely rhetorical. Throughout the 1870s and 1880s, he often expressed sincere admiration for the South and sought to appreciate its citizens. The evangelist even demonstrated his respect for southern opinions in his personal life. In 1885, for instance, he sent his son Willie several pictures from the Civil War and historical accounts about the era. "The books will interest you," he wrote Willie, "for they will tell you all about the war of 1861–65 from the Southern view of it." [29]

Moody's affinity for the southern version of the Civil War and his purchasing of books that highlighted the Civil War experiences of southerners were part of a much larger culture of national conciliation, a public mood in which northerners expressed greater acceptance for southern society in general and for former Confederate soldiers in particular. In 1874 and 1875, officers in the U.S. Army who were still in the South joined southern white women in decorating the graves of fallen Confederates, while former Union soldiers in the North participated in ceremonies to honor both Union and Confederate troops who perished during the conflict. Crowds in Boston and New York City in 1875, moreover, gave great cheers to Confederate veterans who paraded through the city streets. At the same time, southern writers and poets, such as Paul Hamilton Hayne and Sidney Lanier, gained a wide following among northern readers, and in the early 1880s, *Century Magazine* published a series of highly popular articles on Civil War battles and tactics that purposefully downplayed the larger social and political issues of the Civil War. The articles proved so popular that they were compiled into the four-volume set titled *Battles and Leaders of the Civil War*, which is still in print today. From soldiers to citizens, from poets to preachers, a growing constituency of northerners seemed to agree that the South had been barred from national fraternity long enough and that the time for brotherhood was long overdue. [30]

That sectional reconciliation was one of Moody's principal objectives pleased many of his contemporaries. The *New York Times, New York Tribune,* and *Chicago Tribune* all commended him and his revivals for their unifying effects. In a preface to a published collection of Moody's sermons, the editors of the *New York Tribune* rejoiced, "Denominational differences are forgotten, and Christian people, long separated by church barriers are coming together, and are thinking less of Creed and more of Christ." [31] Writing twenty years after the revivals, Moody's Scottish friend Henry Drummond boldly commented, "No other living man has done so much to unite man with man . . . bringing into united worship and harmonious cooperation men of diverse views and dispositions." [32]

Some southern editors eagerly welcomed Moody's nonsectarianism and rallied to his side. Even excessively pro-southern journalist Albert Taylor Bledsoe agreed with the appraisals of the northern papers. A southern Methodist minister and founder of the *Southern Review*, Bledsoe hailed Moody and his meetings as "the most wonderful phenomenon of the nineteenth century." Moody's revivals had ushered in a *"truce to all sectarianism,"* Bledsoe boasted. His endorsement of the revivals demonstrated a clear and mutual connection between the diminishment of denominational antagonisms and the amelioration of sectional animosities. No lover of Yankees, Bledsoe spent most of his career denouncing the North. As historian Charles Reagan Wilson has shown in his study of the southern Lost Cause, Bledsoe stood as "one of the most anguished and embittered Lost Cause ministers." He regularly defended Jefferson Davis, attacked northern material greed, and despised Yankee ideas in general. Bledsoe's *Southern Review*, Wilson further commented, was an "important forum for diehard defenders of the confederacy." Bledsoe was not just voicing the feelings of embittered former Confederates from the Deep South. Published in Baltimore, the *Southern Review* reached across the upper South, the border states, and the North. In the midst of national revivals, sectional divisiveness and denominational particularities seem to have been nearly forgotten.[33]

Unlike the deeply divided and politically charged atmosphere of Protestantism during the 1860s, Moody's ambivalence toward social reform and his interdenominational emphasis made his evangelistic campaigns public events where ecclesiastical and sectional bickering could be ignored. In the process, the awakenings became acceptable to a variety of Americans—northerners and southerners, Republicans and Democrats, Presbyterians, Baptists, and Methodists. In this way, Moody's revivals did not just unify denominations, they became a genuinely national phenomenon that glorified a solidly white American republic.

Along with highlighting reconciliation in a variety of forms, Moody constructed biblical typologies that reflected and sanctified the northern impulse to retreat from radical Reconstruction and to forget the intense bitterness of the previous decade. Often while preaching in the North, he compared contemporary events in the United States with the biblical account of Noah and the flood. Moody argued that during the antediluvian period, God offered mankind an opportunity for mercy through Noah's Ark. Most, however, rejected God's benevolence and perished under the judgment of water. After God's wrath subsided and Noah and his family left the Ark, peace and harmony swept over the world. Placing the current state of the nation within this framework, Moody expounded, "In 1857 there was the great revival, in which there was a tide of salvation that swept over this land and brought many people into the Church of God. Right after that came our terrible war, and we were baptized in blood. Now we are again living in a glorious day. . . . Is not to-day a day of mercy and grace?"[34]

A time of mercy and grace followed neither the flood nor the war. Moody's theological and historical observations overlooked both the scathing curse Noah placed on his grandson Canaan—a story which had been used by countless white Americans to explain and justify slavery since African Americans were said to be descendants of Canaan, who had been cursed by Noah to be "a servant of servants . . . to his brethren"—and the atrocities committed against black freedpeople and northern whites in the South. By interpreting both the decade of Reconstruction and the period after the biblical flood as eras of "good feeling," Moody displayed an historical amnesia that mirrored and theologically justified the northern impulse to step away from radical Reconstruction. Such forgetfulness glossed over the decade of horrible sectional and racial violence. He preached as if the countless letters from northern missionaries in the South, which detailed episodes of vigilante violence, had never been written. He lectured as if hundreds of African Americans and their white friends had not faced continual terror whenever they tried to vote, to attend schools, and to worship at church. In Moody's ministry, desires for religious and national unity clearly trumped all other considerations, even biblical and historical accuracy.

III

Moody's mass appeal, however, did not hinge on his theological skill. As northern editor E. L. Godkin wrote in the *Nation*, very "little dogmatic theology or biblical exegesis" actually appeared in Moody's sermons. Although no scholar, Moody was the nation's best teller of tales, and he played an important role in transforming American sermons from discursive arguments and biblical expositions to sentimental storytelling. *Scribner's Monthly* suggested that his compelling stories wielded a "power over the popular mind" that few other public figures could achieve. The *Boston Sunday Times* considered "the story" Moody's primary method of suasion: "On an average, [Moody] relates four anecdotes in every address, and three addresses per day—that's about six dozen first-class stories a week." The evangelist's fame and his ability to spin yarns caused Walt Whitman to describe him as the "magnet of religion, inventor of legends miraculous and mythical, the boss story-teller of this year 101 of the States."[35]

With his tales, especially those about the Civil War, Moody enthralled his revival audiences. He preached a depoliticized, sentimentalized, and distanced version of the struggle that diminished differences between the warring sections. Similar to the feminized Civil War literature described by literary critic Alice Fahs, which positioned white women as central players in the conflict, Moody's stories were much more likely to focus on the power of a person's faith than on racial justice or liberation.[36] In one story, Moody described a "young man" from New York who volunteered for the war when Lincoln called for troops, although he was engaged to be married. The young lovers regularly sent letters to one another, but the woman received no correspondence from him in the weeks following the Battle of the Wilderness. Then one day a letter "came [written] in a strange hand. She opened it with trembling fingers, and read these words: 'We have fought a terrible battle. I have been wounded so awfully that I shall never be able to support you more. A friend writes this for me. I love you more tenderly than ever, but I release you from your promise. I will not ask you to join your life with the maimed life of mine.'" The woman refused to abandon her fiancé, however. "The next train that left the young lady was on it," Moody continued. "She went to his hospital. She found out the number of his cot and she went down the aisle, between the long rows of wounded men. At last she saw the number; she threw her arms around his neck and said: 'I'll not desert you. I'll take care of you.' . . . They were married, and there is no happier couple than this one." Although set in the Civil War, this story has nothing to do with the sectional crisis. The Civil War was mere window dressing for Moody to moralize about the importance of steadfast love. The woman, like Christ and God, would never leave her beloved.[37]

Similarly, Moody recounted a time "[w]hen I was in Nashville during our late war, a great strong man come up to me, trembling from head to foot. He took a letter out of his pocket and wanted to have me read it. It was from his sister." The letter profoundly affected this soldier: "The sister stated in that letter that every night as the sun went down she went down on her knees to pray for him. The sister was six hundred miles away, and said the soldier, 'I never thought about my soul until last night. I have stood before the cannon's mouth and it never made me tremble, but, Sir, I haven't slept a wink since I got that letter.'" In this anecdote, the sectional loyalty of the combatant is completely irrelevant and even unknown. He could have been from the North or from the South. Like the previous story, this tale underscored the ways women's faith and commitments could bring even "great strong" men to their knees. What these Civil War heroes had fought for, what they had been willing to die for, and what the Union army had achieved remained unspoken by Moody. The crucial issues of the war were effaced, only to be replaced by moralistic tales of familial love and devotion.[38]

In other stories, Moody focused upon direct similarities between Yankees and Confederates. Preaching in Chicago on the "integrity of commitment," he asked,

"How was it during our war with the men who lived on the borders?" Answering his own question, he criticized the people of the Border States who refused to chose one side or the other. "When a Union soldier came along," he fumed, "they were Union men and when a Southern soldier came to them, 'Oh, we are Southern people; we believe in the Confederacy,' and they would run up the Confederate flag." "What was the result?" Moody again asked rhetorically, and answered: "Both the Southern and Union men had a contempt for those fellows."[39] In short, such waffling, not rebellion or slaveholding, represented the most heinous sin. True Americans had shared the common bond of steadfast allegiance. It did not matter which side one supported as long as one stuck to that conviction. Moody obscured the fact that the war had been a bitter and bloody sectional struggle and that it had involved the enslavement of millions of African Americans.

Several of Moody's religious contemporaries in the North, including novelists and poets, adopted the same style. Even some of the revival's "Gospel Hymns" reflected a shameless sentimentalization of the Civil War. The most popular of these songs, "Hold the Fort," which was supposedly based on an order from General William Tecumseh Sherman to a band of Union soldiers protecting rations near Atlanta, was little more than a domesticated and bloodless version of the war. The song neither held the South responsible for any wrongdoing nor specifically mentioned sectional conflict:

"Hold the fort, for I am coming,"
Jesus signals still;
Wave the answer back to heaven,
"By Thy grace we will."

Unlike Julia Ward Howe's popular "Battle Hymn of the Republic," which explicitly urged northerners during the Civil War to take up arms and strike a blow against slavery and "die to make men free," "Hold the Fort" encouraged religious passivity. According to "Hold the Fort," Christians must only wait patiently for Jesus to arrive, not march out and defeat an evil world.[40]

Some northerners even rewrote "Hold the Fort" to mock the evangelist or to use the song's popularity for their own political advantage. Spending several months lampooning Moody for not appealing to Boston's working class, the editor of the *Boston Sunday Times* jeered, "Every night I hear some new version of 'Hold the Fort' shouted by the enterprising gamins [poor children] of the gutter. This is one of the latest":

Hold the forks, the knives are coming,
The plates are on the way.

> Shouting the chorus to your neighbor,
> Sling the hash this way.[41]

During the election of 1876 this tune was even reworked into a Republican campaign song titled "Hold the Fort for Hayes and Wheeler."[42] The hymn's connection to the Civil War clearly inspired little awe or reverence. In story and song, the cataclysmic struggle was reduced to a metaphor to inspire religious feeling, mock the evangelist, or inspire political lightheartedness.

Moody's stories and revival hymns obfuscated the fact that the conflict had actually been a battle over the fate of the Union and the entire country's future. Unlike the radical missionaries to the South who referred to southern whites as "they" and "them," Moody honored the struggle in which "*we* had to give up *our* young men, both North and South, to death." To make sure that no one would interpret his stories as nationally divisive, Moody prefaced them with conciliatory remarks. "I hope if there are any Southern people here they will not think, in this allusion, I am trying to wound their feelings," he stated. Foreshadowing Civil War tales like Steven Crane's *The Red Badge of Courage* (1895), which implicitly minimized sectional differences by emphasizing the shared emotions of common soldiers, Moody's stories and hymns sentimentalized the war in ways that downplayed sectional distinctions.[43]

In his diminishing of sectional differences, Moody also ignored pertinent racial issues in the North during the war. As Beecher had created a mythic northern response to the war's end in *Norwood*, Moody constructed a mythic memory of the North's response to the call to arms. "All Abraham Lincoln had to do, was to call for men, and how speedily they came," Moody proclaimed. "When he called for 600,000 men how quick they sprang up all over the nation. Are not souls worth more than this republic?" When Moody told this particular story, the *New York Tribune* reported, "the attention of the audience was very close." This may have been the history New Yorkers wanted to believe. It might have been one that stroked their egos. But it was hardly accurate. After Lincoln's call for troops, many northerners "sprang up" not to defend the Union, but to resist enlistment and often to assault African Americans. Moody conveniently ignored the New York Draft Riots of 1863, which saw large mobs of New York's white working class murder more than a hundred blacks and destroy an orphanage for African American children, and a host of other such embarrassing episodes. Handily, racial antagonism and northern divisions became invisible in Moody's sermons. He refused to condemn northern whites for failing to treat people of color with dignity and respect. Instead, he constructed a fraudulent history of unified allegiance to the Union that allowed northerners to think well of themselves as they continued to neglect rights for African Americans.[44]

Moody distorted the realties of sectional and racial hostilities in other revival tales as well. He often portrayed southern freedpeople as "unclean" or as resigned to their lack of political power in the United States. On several occasions he quoted one former missionary to the South, Quaker Sarah F. Smiley, who repeatedly associated African Americans with filth. "[E]verything [was] covered with dirt," she recalled of her encounters with blacks. "The tables were dirty, dishes dirty, and the beds dirty." Rather than include heroic stories of freedpeople striving to rise from slavery or tales of cash-poor African Americans donating much of their income and time for the education of their children, Moody, like Smiley, merely drew attention to their poverty. Moreover, as cultural anthropologist Mary Douglas has suggested, referring to someone or something as "unclean" or "impure" is a way of claiming that that person or object is "matter out of place." Soil, for instance, is "dirty" and out of place when on a dinner table, but not when it is in a field. Thus, by repeatedly drawing attention to the dirtiness of African Americans in the South, Moody and the missionary he quoted seemed to consider freedpeople "out of place" in the United States, much like Henry Ward Beecher's fictional Pete Sawmill.[45]

In another story, one that Moody repeated in each city, he clearly implied that the thought of universal equal rights was unimaginable, even to people of color. "Two young men went from Yale College down to Natchez to teach," Moody preached. "As they went along a road one day, a venerable colored man was coming toward them." These Yale students decided to have some fun "with the old Sambo." A sign alongside the road read, "Forty miles to Liberty," and when the old man approached them, they asked, "Can you read, uncle?" "No; can't read; black men ain't 'lowed to read," he replied. Pointing to the sign, one of young men further inquired, "Why don't you go and get liberty, it's only forty miles?" "Ah, massa," responded the former slave, "it points down that road to Liberty, but it's all a sham; but if it pointed up there it would point to Christ, and it would be true."[46] In other words, blacks would never have "liberty" in the United States. In this story, Moody's white friends and the "old darkey" all accepted this "reality." The implication was clear. Moody's audience need not bother with defending civil rights for blacks. Heaven, not the United States, was the appropriate place for equality. By downplaying both racial equality and sectional issues, Moody's stories justified forgiveness and exalted the white nation. Responding bitterly to Moody's tales, Walt Whitman raged, "I do not believe in him. Nor his God . . . nor his stories which sound like lies."[47]

Biographers and newspaper publishers reinforced themes of sectional reconciliation when they narrated stories of Moody's own Civil War and Reconstruction experiences as a Union chaplain. Most extolled him for his ministry to imprisoned Confederates and praised him for treating them "as brethren of Christ." The editors of one collection of Moody's revival sermons wrote that during the war his "labors were greatly blessed, not only to the soldiers of the northern army, but also the rebel prisoners at Camp Douglas." Reverend E. J. Goodspeed similarly praised Moody for "visit[ing] them with all the tender love of a brother." Another account even applauded the evangelist for deceiving Union officials so that he could preach to captured Confederates at Camp Douglas.[48]

Between 1875 and 1877 a revival of national pomp, reconciliation, and reunion squared well with the domestic mood, especially as northerners became entranced with honoring America's centennial. Celebrating the anniversary of the Revolutionary War provided an excellent emotional outlet for Americans mired in the economic depression of the 1870s and disenchanted with sectional hostilities. The celebration in Philadelphia, with its massive Corliss Engine supplying power to all of the buildings, extolled commercial progress and prosperity. Memories of the American victory over Great Britain during the Revolutionary War, which northerners and southerners had shared, engendered feelings of national pride and sectional reconciliation. *Scribner's Monthly,* for instance, hoped that the "Spirit of '76" was one that would "heal all the old wounds, [and] reconcile all the old differences." Moody's revivals occurred at precisely the right moment to aid in this process. Along with the work of Beecher, Stowe, Greeley, the Episcopal Church, and other apostles of forgiveness, Moody's meetings helped religiously invigorate this spirit of friendship and feelings of patriotic unity.[49]

National reconciliation, in fact, played a part in Moody's own centennial celebration service in Philadelphia on New Year's Eve, 1875. On that evening the evangelist invited Presbyterian minister William Plumer of South Carolina to share the stage with him. Moody proceeded to "interview" Plumer, using him as an exemplar of the Christian faith. As the service neared midnight, Moody and Plumer closed the meeting by wishing all a "Happy New Year." It was, in the words of one witness, "a most impressive service."[50] Moody once again "interviewed" Plumer during his revival meetings in New York, and after listening to the exchange, a reporter commented, "It was a scene never to be forgotten either here or in eternity, and was one of the most dramatic as it was one of the most interesting features of Mr. Moody's work in this city." Their dialogue was so popular that Anson D. F. Randolf's New York publishing house decided to print it as a pamphlet.[51]

Plumer's participation at the revival was a clear mark of sectional reconciliation, for this Presbyterian minister epitomized the transition from religious and national division to religious and national reunion. Born in western Pennsylvania in 1802, Plumer graduated from Washington College in Virginia and then studied at the Princeton Theological Seminary in the mid-1820s. From the late 1820s to the 1840s, he organized churches and preached in North Carolina, Virginia, and Maryland. In 1855, he accepted a position in Alleghany, Pennsylvania, and served as professor of didactic and pastoral theology at Western Theological Seminary. In the years before the Civil War, Plumer was anything but a national reconciler. In the 1830s, he stood as a critical player in the Old School–New School Presbyterian schism, serving as one of the Old School leaders. He defended slavery with biblical texts and refused to accept any denominational proscription against it. Plumer did not view slavery as God's foreordained plan for people of African descent, but he did consider the peculiar institution a benefit to them. He acknowledged that the slave trade and slavery were "both cruel and bloody," yet he believed that God had used them to bring African peoples out of heathenism and to expose them to Christianity.[52]

Plumer wanted nothing to do with anyone who proclaimed slavery a sin. At the Presbyterian general assembly meeting in 1837, he contended that "should the [Presbyterian] Assembly . . . legislate and decide that slaveholding is a sin . . . Then nothing is left [but to] rend the star-spangled banner in twain." National disunion, Plumer thundered, would invariably follow ecclesiastical disunion. As historians C. C. Goen and Mitchell Snay have suggested, southern ministers like Plumer offered arguments and rhetoric for disunion that northern and southern politicians readily drew upon during the antebellum period. When the denomination did split between the New and Old Schools, the conservative and primarily southern Old School branch rewarded Plumer for his efforts by electing him the denomination's first moderator.[53]

Accepting slavery and advocating national separation, Plumer was thoroughly disdained by northern audiences during the 1860s. When the nation divided in 1861, he found himself on the wrong side of both the Mason-Dixon Line and the domestic temper. The mass of northerners during and immediately following the war rejected preachers who had defended slavery or who would not offer unreserved allegiance to the Union cause. Several ministers, including Plumer, found themselves under the scrutiny of their denominations and state officials when they did not back the federal government. After Plumer refused to pray publicly for the Union flag, members of his Presbyterian church in Allegheny, Pennsylvania, dismissed him. Public scorn continued to follow Plumer even after he left this post. Later, during revival meetings in New England where Plumer was set to preach, some locals avoided the meeting specifically because of his dubious patriotic allegiance. During the mid-1860s, neither Plumer nor Moody seemed in touch with the sentiments of the northern people.[54]

But public rejection turned into widely heralded appreciation in the 1870s for these men, as northern white Protestants became far more interested in national reunion. In the early 1870s, Plumer fled the North and took a position at Columbia Seminary in South Carolina. When Protestant hopes for national and denominational reunion rose in the mid-1870s, he joined the growing chorus of voices urging national solidarity. Although general histories of American Presbyterians often neglect Plumer, according to one Mississippi newspaper, he was "the most notable and distinguished member" of the southern Presbyterian general assembly.[55] At the 1874 general assembly meeting, he responded to northern appeals for denominational reunion by begging his fellow southerners to extend the right hand of fellowship to their northern brethren. Then in 1875, when visiting friends in Chicago, he was invited to attend the northern Presbyterian general assembly. As he entered the gathering, intense emotions of forgiveness and love flowed freely. One newspaper correspondent vividly described the touching scene. When Plumer came through a door in the back, "a little gentle clapping of hands [began] in that direction" and a group of ministers surrounded him. "Slowly the group separated, and through a friendly breach thus formed strolled a majestic figure." As the rest of the crowd recognized Plumer, they went wild with jubilation: "As the grand vision dawned upon the upturned faces . . . generous impulse overcame the heat of prejudice, and courtesy paid voluntary tribute to the highest type of manliness. . . . The applause rose and swelled and waned again, then waxed higher and more fervent as the royal form went on down the aisle. . . . [L]adies and gentlemen rose en masse and cheered again, while the pent-up emotion of the scene found vent here and there in unchecked tears."[56]

When Plumer addressed the assembly, he invoked fraternity, brotherhood, and unity in ways that contrasted sharply with his antebellum and wartime proclamations. Now he preached love and acceptance, rather than enmity and disunion. "One hour of brotherly love is worth a whole eternity of strife and bitterness," he declared. One Presbyterian fully recognized Plumer's transformation, commenting, "Thus the son of thunder of the 1837 Assembly, like the Apostle John, another son of thunder, became in his old age the Apostle of Love." An assembly member made a similar comment in a letter to Plumer's daughter: "Dr. Plumer never was more honored than today—by our Assembly North or South." In the 1870s, Plumer not only encouraged national reunion, but also came to symbolize reconciliation when he stood side by side with Moody at the Philadelphia centennial celebration. Moody and Plumer rode the wave of popular support for national reconciliation and in many ways embodied the shift from sectional disdain to national white fraternity.[57]

While Moody embraced prominent southern leaders such as Plumer, described African Americans as resigned to second-class status, diminished sectional differences in his stories, and preached unity, he also acted as a national unifier during a trip to the South in 1876. Ostensibly, Moody ventured south for a vacation between his New York City and Chicago revivals. But while there, he led several meetings that were immensely popular. Not all southern whites appreciated his brand of revivalism. Some Alabama Baptists criticized him for failing to identify with any particular denomination, but the critics were in the minority.[58] Thousands of southerners flocked to his evangelistic crusades. In Augusta, Georgia, for example, Moody held revival meetings for two weeks and regularly had more than three thousand in the audience. Preaching on the "beautiful lawn" of the local Presbyterian church, Moody captivated these southerners. Democratic newspapers such as the *Augusta Constitutionalist* celebrated Moody's efforts by printing news about the revival meetings and his sermons *verbatim*. At the end of the evangelist's two-week stay, the *Constitutionalist* congratulated him for his authority, tenderness, zeal, and efficiency. "Not since the days of Mahomet (if the Pagan can be mentioned)," editorialized the *Constitutionalist*, "can we call to mind one who has acquired such fame and influence as the obscure orphan who on a New England farm developed [such] powers of strength and endurance which were afterwards to do such service for God." Another Georgian, writing to the *Atlanta Constitution*, agreed, "[T]here was never a time before now where religious feeling was stronger, deeper or more general."[59] Most white American Protestants—whether in the South or North—were now in agreement on who was the nation's chief evangelist.

Moody's southern popularity hinged on his refusal to engage political and social issues and on his genuine desire for national fraternity. A Georgian, in fact, warned that Moody would be unsuccessful if he preached social and racial reform. "If Mr. Moody has come south for the purpose of endeavoring to change" southern racial mores, "his visit will be utterly unavailing, while it will at the same time bring down upon him the contempt and abhorrence of the people." This writer had very little to worry about, though, because Moody had no intention of disrupting the status quo. His southern messages consisted of entreaties for reunion and denunciations of social reform. On a "Decoration Day" for memorializing dead Confederate soldiers, the evangelist prayed for "broken-hearted ones, both North and South . . . who were mourning for friends lost in the late war." Later, Moody commented that he "wished especially to say that he had no sympathy at all with men in any section of the country who were continually seeking to stir up strife and embitter the people against each other." Writing in 1876, one of Moody's friends summed up the evangelist's position on politics by assuring northerners and southerners that Moody had absolutely no "interest in Northern radicals."[60]

His intense emphasis on reconciliation and reunion had disastrous consequences for any hopes for racial inclusiveness. Unlike the northern missionaries of radical Reconstruction who prized interracial worship and braved social ostracism because of their religious commitments to civil rights, Moody craved unity among whites at all costs. In the North, although African Americans had not attended the revivals in droves, they had not been separated from whites at the evangelical meetings. Blacks and whites sat together in the crowds, and northern people of color did not accuse the evangelist of discrimination. They did, however, have mixed reviews of the revivals. The editor of the *Christian Recorder* appreciated Moody's ability to encourage religious enthusiasm, but worried that no social good would come from it.[61] In the South, however, local whites forced Moody to choose between racial integration and public popularity—Moody chose popularity. In Augusta, some whites became enraged at the sight of African Americans mingling with other whites, and they constructed a wooden "dividing fence" to segregate the races. Moody seemed surprised and expressed faint disapproval over the separation to one of the local pastors. Moody was almost naively unaware that racial prejudice existed. The southern minister promptly retorted, "I am proud of my rebellious feelings, and will rebel until the day I die." Internally, Moody may have disliked racial separation at revivals, but his desire for unity trumped any impulse for equality. He acquiesced to the demands. The "matter was dropped," and the meetings continued—segregated. Racial inclusiveness had been dealt a powerful blow, since revival meetings were one of the last bastions of interracial Christian worship. From this meeting until the mid-1890s, blacks and whites were separated during Moody's crusades. It would not be until the mid-twentieth century under Billy Graham that large-scale, national revival meetings would once again be integrated. With Moody, southern whites had everything they wanted, a northern religious leader who capitulated to southern racial etiquette, who refused to chastise them for slavery, and who railed against northern radicalism just as they had.[62]

IV

In the 1880s, sectional and racial issues once again flared up when Moody held meetings in the South. He continued to spin stories from the Civil War that highlighted the shared experiences of northerners and southerners during the titanic conflict.[63] Moody further expressed his admiration for the South during a revival campaign in Richmond, Virginia, in 1885. Possibly upset by the attempts of some African Americans to attend the revival, one local newspaper accused Moody of preaching against the South during the Civil War. This writer claimed that Moody, most egregiously, had allegedly denounced Generals Robert E. Lee and Thomas J. "Stonewall" Jackson—a misstep tantamount to blasphemy in the South. The evangelist quickly defended himself to the public, asserting that he had never said any such thing. Southern papers such as the *Washington Post* rallied to his side. Moody commented to a *Post* reporter that he had always "entertained the highest respect for Gens. Lee and Jackson. They lived and died Christian gentlemen, and were friends of mine." Moody became further vindicated when Mrs. Stonewall Jackson, widow of the powerful symbol of the Lost Cause and a regular participant in commemorations to honor the men of the Confederacy, made several publicized visits to Moody's revival meetings. Southern whites knew that Moody was not an enemy, and, as the *Post* noted, "[I]mmense crowds . . . often waited lunch in hand to get sitting or even standing room."[64]

In addition to associating himself with the heroes and heroines of the Lost Cause, Moody continued to segregate his revivals. This led to denunciations by many African American leaders. When Moody held racially separated meetings in Chattanooga, Tennessee, and Louisville, Kentucky, people of color either ignored him or boycotted his meetings. One pastor commented, "[I]t is doubtful if Mr. Moody could successfully reach his people, owing . . . to the color-line having been drawn." A delegate to the African Methodist Episcopal Church's annual conference further blasted the evangelist: "His conduct toward the Negroes during his Southern tour has been shameless, and I would not have him preach in a barroom, let alone a church. In Charleston he refused to give the Negro churches representation at his evangelical meetings." Moody, this minister fumed, had "placed caste above Christianity."[65]

Voicing the combination of dejection and fury felt by many African Americans toward Moody and his followers, Frederick Douglass contrasted Moody's meetings with those of the religious infidel Robert Ingersoll. "Infidel though Mr. Ingersoll may be called," Douglass asserted, "he never turned his back upon his colored brothers, as did the evangelical Christians of this city [Philadelphia] on the occasion of the late visit of Mr. Moody." Douglass continued by singling out religious segregation as one of the most pernicious forms of separation. "Of all the forms of negro hate in this world," he proclaimed, "save me from that one which clothes itself with the name of the loving Jesus." To Douglass, the hypocrisy of Moody's revivals was galling: "The negro can go into the circus, the theatre, and can be admitted to the lectures of Mr. Ingersoll, but he cannot go into an evangelical Christian meeting."[66]

During the 1890s, Ida B. Wells, the outspoken black female critic of lynching and devout proponent of civil rights, continued the attack on Moody. She recognized that his acceptance of Jim Crow and his unwillingness to speak out against racial injustice severely handicapped the crusade for equality. While speaking in England on a tour dedicated to raising funds for her anti-lynching crusade, Wells denounced him for his Jim Crow revivalism. "I remember very clearly," she observed, "that when Rev. Moody had come to the South with his revival sermons the notices printed said that the Negroes who wished to attend his meetings would have to go into the gallery or that a special service would be set aside for colored people only." To Wells, religious segregation was abhorrent, and Moody authorized religious and spiritual exclusion at large. "Mr. Moody has encouraged the drawing of the color line in the churches by consenting to preach on separate days and in separate churches to the colored people," she further claimed. To Wells, Douglass, and other African American religious leaders, Moody's revivals constituted despicable events.[67]

After almost twenty years of capitulating to Jim Crow, Moody took an unexpected turn in his stance toward racial segregation in his revival meetings in the mid-1890s. As racial violence and legalized Jim Crow rose to new heights in the final decade of the century, the evangelist actually reversed his policies on segregation.[68] While Moody had followed southern whites' desires from the late 1870s to the early 1890s, he had nonetheless still attempted to reach out to African Americans. He had spoken at religious services in several black colleges in the South, including Fisk University, where W. E. B. Du Bois sat in one of the audiences. Moody had also traveled to black churches throughout the South and performed revival meetings. After he visited several African American congregations in Savannah, Georgia, one African Methodist Episcopal Church minister wrote to him that "the Negroes of Savannah, thank you more than language can express . . . for the service you gave us at our churches."[69] In a bold move only four years before his death, during revival meetings in Texas in 1895, Moody openly defied Jim Crow and racial discrimination. He became outraged when he saw physical barriers separating blacks from whites. Like Samson, one of his biblical heroes, Moody thrust his

270-pound frame against the wooden railings. Although exerting all of his force, he could not pull them down. Perhaps Moody had always hated racial segregation. Perhaps he never felt right about dividing his meetings. Although he did not offer a reason for his actions, his message was loud and clear. The next day, the dividing structure was removed. Blacks and whites would no longer have separate seating arrangements at Moody's revival.[70]

It was a marvelous turn of events. The most noteworthy evangelical of the late nineteenth century took a clear stand against racial segregation. Tragically, it was too late. Moody no longer wielded the public power he once had, and this action garnered almost no attention from the press. By this time his influence had waned considerably. He no longer drew massive public attention, and he had lost most of the stamina that had allowed him to preach for nights on end. In the 1890s, in fact, the southern evangelist Reverend Sam Jones, a Methodist preacher whose popularity in the South brought him the title of "the Moody of the South," supplanted him. Far more overtly racist than Moody, Jones openly appealed to white supremacists and had taken part in vigilante violence in the late 1860s. He sometimes even boosted that he had "stuffed a few ballot boxes" during Reconstruction. At Jones's meetings in Texas after Moody departed, Ku Klux Klan members were offered safe haven. In one particularly disturbing example, Jones embraced the leader of a lynch mob that had brutally murdered Henry Smith, a mentally retarded former slave, only two years earlier. Smith's execution had been amazingly disturbing. The incensed crowd had poked his eyes out, set him on fire, and prodded him with hot irons. Then, after Smith was dead, a wild scramble for his clothing, teeth, and other remains had ensued. Although Moody never would have condoned such behavior, he had done much to sever the cords between social justice and evangelical revivalism. In the process, he had offered vital spiritual nourishment to both national reconciliation and racial segregation.[71]

At the height of his public power in the 1870s, Moody had not challenged the racial status quo. He had kept quiet; he had prized unity among whites over human brotherhood. In the years that white Americans flocked to hear him and sat riveted by his stories, he had refused to stand against the tide of racial prejudice and segregation. In fact, he had brought the force of his own spiritual authority to propel those waters. When Moody did rise against segregation in the 1890s, Jim Crow was too firmly entrenched in American society. Segregation *de jure*, expressly condoned by the Supreme Court's *Plessy v. Ferguson* decision in 1896, coupled with disenfranchisement of black voters throughout the South, had effectively stripped people of color of the last vestiges of rights and privileges they had achieved during radical Reconstruction. In Moody's moment of power and persuasiveness, he had helped to rebuild the white republic by sanctifying reconciliation and repudiating the civic nationalist imagination that had been so powerful in the mid-1860s and early 1870s.

With Moody's gigantic revivals in the 1870s and his smaller ones in the 1880s, a gospel of reconciliation and reunion further triumphed over biblical interpretations of divine judgment and religious activism. By preaching against social reform, advocating interdenominationalism, depoliticizing the Civil War in his stories, characterizing African Americans as outsiders in the national community, and reaching out to southern whites, Moody acted as a bridge between the white North and the white South. Reunion was forged at the expense of racial reform and African American rights, and people of color tried to resist it. But in the years following Moody's campaigns in the 1870s, the forces of white solidarity and racial oppression continued to grow and multiply. The white republic continued to ascend in power.

The year 1878 proved an especially crucial moment for reuniting northern and southern whites at the expense of African Americans. As Moody rested from his almost four years of continual trans-Atlantic revivalism, a yellow fever epidemic swept across the South. Amid the terror and trauma of the outbreak, northern whites demonstrated just how far they had come in embracing southern whites by offering enormous economic and emotional assistance. For their part, former Confederates claimed a new allegiance to the American republic as long as it meant that northerners would supply them with support, while also leaving the region alone to determine racial matters. Southern African Americans cried out for help as well during this horrific year, but their appeals fell on deaf ears. Northern whites had largely cast aside hopes to create an integrated and egalitarian nation. Their retreat from radicalism had been spiritually facilitated by apostles of reunion, such as Beecher and Moody, and it would have deadly consequences for people of color when the fever struck.

5

THE WHITE FLAG WAVES

Spiritual Reunion and Genocidal Visions during the
Yellow Fever Epidemic of 1878

Few southern whites were more passionate about or dedicated to the Confederacy and the Lost Cause than Father Abram J. Ryan, a Catholic priest and poet in New Orleans and other southern cities. During the Civil War he served as a chaplain in the Confederate army and exhorted his southern brethren to drive back their northern invaders. Like most southern whites, he refused to be reconstructed when the smoke cleared. He immortalized Confederate soldiers with dozens of poems that grieved over their deaths and generally lauded southern virtue. "Our heroes in Gray" will never be forgotten, Ryan wrote in one of his most famous poems, "C.S.A.": "Their memories e'er shall remain for us." In another poem, he lionized Robert E. Lee for "[s]hielding the feeble, smiting the strong,/Guarding the right, avenging the wrong." Ryan's glorification of the South brought him enormous fame. By the mid-1870s he was acclaimed as the "poet-priest" of the Lost Cause, and Ryan's book-length collection of poems went through twelve editions between 1880 and 1892.[1]

But Ryan's feelings toward northerners and toward the Union changed dramatically in the late 1870s. It was neither Dwight Moody's revivals nor Henry Ward Beecher's preaching, however, that convinced him to offer his heart to the North and the American nation. Only after a devastating yellow fever outbreak ravaged the South in 1878 and was met by a massive relief effort on the part of northern whites did Ryan embrace national reunion. In the summer and fall following America's Third Great Awakening, the pestilence claimed more than 20,000 lives and infected roughly 120,000 southerners. Northerners rushed to help the suffering South by sending letters, funds, goods, telegraph operators, nurses, and doctors. In response, Ryan claimed that the nation had been metaphysically reconciled. In the aftermath of the epidemic, he put these emotions to verse in his aptly titled "Reunited":

> For at the touch of Mercy's hand
> The North and South stood side by side:
> The Bride of Snow, the Bride of Sun,
> In Charity's espousals are made one.

"Reunited" was nothing less than a requital for the bitterness of war:

> "Thou givest back my sons again,"
> The Southland to the Northland cries;
> "For all my dead, on battle plain,
> Thou biddest my dying now uprise:
> I still my sobs, I cease my tears,
> And thou has recompensed my anguished years.["][2]

In seeking to save the South, rather than ignore it, the North had brought about a spiritual reunification that political Reconstruction had not. The traumatic months of 1878 had eased the anguish that filled Ryan's memories of the Civil War and had provided him with an opportunity to claim national fidelity.

Although left out of most studies of Reconstruction, the outbreak stood as a pivotal moment in postwar national reconciliation and the marginalization of African Americans. The epidemic was a devastating event, but it also helped northern and southern whites rediscover their commitments to one another. The widespread nature of fear caused by the outbreak created common convictions and shared experiences for whites. Yellow fever evoked sympathy from thousands of northerners, and as they donated money and prayed for southern whites, northerners collectively expressed feelings of reunion. Northern whites consciously effaced memories of southerners as belligerent evildoers seeking to destroy the Union. Instead, southerners were reconceived as stricken, yet honorable, brothers in need. At the same time, southern whites re-conceptualized northerners and their relationship to the nation. Rather than regarding Yankees as infidel invaders bent on destroying southern civilization, former Confederates now praised them as heroic and Christian compatriots. In effect, the fever opened a way for southerners to accept national unity without rejecting their love for the South or admitting wrong over slavery, secession, and war. Through newspapers, personal diaries and letters, poems, cartoons, sermons, medical pamphlets, speeches, relief agency records, and mass meetings, countless northern and southern whites asserted that the epidemic led them to put away their sectional bitterness and mistrust. The trauma supplied Yankees and former Confederates a pretext to proclaim a spiritual reconciliation of the nation that Protestants such as Moody, Beecher, and Stowe had long advocated. The fractured white republic was pieced back together, in part, through benevolence and sympathy during the terrible pestilence.[3]

Religious ideas and leaders played central roles in making 1878 a crucial year in the reforging of the white republic. Northern churches enthusiastically rallied to support southern whites with funds and prayers, while white southern Protestants responded with deep appreciation. Bitter sectional partisans, such as Presbyterian

Benjamin Morgan Palmer of New Orleans, were transformed into champions of national unity. Several southern poets and northern religious writers came to view the epidemic as God's way of closing the bloody chasm of the Civil War. They sought to transform the death and destruction of the outbreak into a sacred and metaphysical national rebirth. Much like Moody's revivals, the epidemic provided a moment when denominational strife and divisions were minimized in favor of intersectional and interdenominational compassion. Although the major denominations remained institutionally separated, northern and southern Protestants found avenues to work together and build networks of sympathy amid the devastation.

While northern and southern whites reveled in their newfound solidarity, they also joined together to neglect the medical needs of southern blacks. In stark contrast to northern relief efforts immediately following the Civil War, northern aid did not flow in abundance to southern people of color in 1878. Instead, it was directed almost exclusively to southern whites. Northern and southern whites demonstrated throughout the epidemic that they cared very little for the lives of blacks. In at least one instance, whites so disregarded African American health that they placed a hospital for sick whites in an area largely populated by African Americans. For some whites the outbreak evoked genocidal visions of an American nation, in which there would be no more people of color in the United States. In response, blacks across the nation were forced to rely upon one another for help. Ultimately, the actions of whites and blacks during the epidemic showed that the biracial civic nationalism of the era of radical Reconstruction had almost completely evaporated, and two "nations" were rapidly and painfully developing within the United States: one white, one black.

What people remember and what they forget during and after traumatic experiences is largely determined by their social, cultural, historical, and political contexts. Modern psychological and anthropological theorists have recently shown that disasters such as massive medical epidemics and earthquakes have the power to create, erase, and transform memories and perceptions. As psychologist Craig C. Piers has asserted, "Remembering is an active and reconstructive process . . . what we remember is influenced by a number of factors, both at the time of the experience and at the time of recalling it."[4] Cultural anthropologists have also observed that "acts of remembering often take on performative meaning within a charged field of contested moral and political claims."[5] The yellow fever epidemic of 1878 constituted just such a traumatic national experience. Painful memories of sectional antagonism were dampened and hopeful memories of spiritual and national solidarity were championed. This revival of a white American nation and patriotic memory, however, was shared by whites and denied to blacks.

I

Prior to the yellow fever epidemic, during the years Moody's urban revivals helped diminish northern religious commitment to radical Reconstruction, the United States experienced one of its most divisive and complicated presidential elections. The political events of 1876 and 1877 did a great deal to exacerbate the sectional and political animosities that Moody had sought to dampen. The campaign pitted Republican Rutherford B. Hayes, a brevet major general during the Civil War and former congressman and governor of Ohio, against Democrat Samuel J. Tilden, a vigorous opponent of radical Reconstruction and governor of New York. Because of the depression, economic issues were far more prominent than they had been in the previous fifteen years. But sectionalism and partisan loyalties remained decisive factors. Republican Party leaders vacillated between a campaign of waving the bloody shirt and one of appealing to white economic conservatives in the South. Democrats and Republicans fought bitterly, and the election was amazingly close. The victor remained unclear even after all of the ballots had been cast. The balance hung in South Carolina, Florida, and Louisiana—states that Republicans and Democrats alike claimed to have carried. After both parties leveled denunciations at one another for vote stealing, they struck up a compromise. Hayes was awarded the presidency, and in return, he pledged that the federal government would cease interfering in the South.[6]

Hayes's election ushered in a shift in Republican policy, a "great departure from the principles, traditions, and wishes of the Republican party," as the new president referred to it. The Republicans altered their southern policy from appealing to black voters and seeking to uphold their voting privileges to one that centered on southern whites. A policy of noninterference and sectional reconciliation marked Hayes's administration. He pursued a strategy of national unity, in which he sought to win the support of former Whigs in the South, who endorsed high tariffs like most northern Republicans. Hayes ordered the federal troops protecting Republican governors in Louisiana and South Carolina to return to their barracks, thereby ceding the state governments to the Democrats. He appointed Democrats to several state and national posts, including the position of postmaster general, and he largely neglected African American political aspirants. In addition, he made two separate trips to the South, pleading for sectional harmony. Hayes repeatedly referred to southern whites as "friends, my Confederate friends." The

Nation judged that the "Compromise of 1877" and the new Republican strategy meant that the African American "will disappear from the field of national politics. Henceforth, the nation, as a nation, will have nothing to do with him."[7]

The compromise of 1877 and Hayes's blatant pandering to southern whites thoroughly enraged many African Americans and their white friends who remained committed to upholding civil rights for people of color. A body of northern white Methodists protested "earnestly against the action of the new Administration," while the African Methodist Episcopal minister Henry Turner offered a mock eulogy for the now deceased radical Republican Party. "It is with unusual pain, we are compelled to chronicle the sad news," he wrote, "that the great Republican Party, hero of many battles and author of National Sovereignty, American Freedom, Civil and Political rights and many other world renowned and heaven approved words, was slaughtered in the house of his friends, April 24, 1877." "Too many false friends had gotten hold of the party," Turner continued. The Republican "had been indisposed for some years, being seriously afflicted by Negro haters, office seekers, dough faces, weathercocks, time servers, and large numbers of political hypocrites, false pretenders, and unprincipled vagabonds. Such a number of wounds and diseases all preying upon his system at once was too much to be resisted, and the political giant of the 19th century had to succumb to the inevitable." Some people of color lost all hope for an integrated American nation with the Compromise of 1877. In contrast to the ways African Americans celebrated national holidays during the mid-1860s and with great similarity to Frederick Douglass's take on the Fourth of July before the Civil War, many African Americans now once again viewed the Fourth of July as a day "for white folks."[8]

For all of Hayes's efforts, however, he was not fully successful in reuniting northern and southern whites. Many in both sections maintained their sectional bitterness. In June 1878, for instance, the *Washington National Republican* claimed that in the South, "the spirit of rebellion still lives and is liable at any moment to be again entrenched in arms."[9] Southern whites, likewise, continued to harbor ill feelings toward the North. Recounting the years before 1878, Father Ryan wrote, "No hand might clasp across the tears/And blood and anguish of four deathless years."[10] In short, while African Americans felt a deep sense of betrayal from the Compromise of 1877, northern and southern whites had yet fully to close ranks. National divisions continued to plague the country.

When yellow fever struck in 1878 and enveloped much of the South, however, sectional animosities almost disappeared as thousands of northerners and southerners experienced, performed, and articulated reconciliation. There had

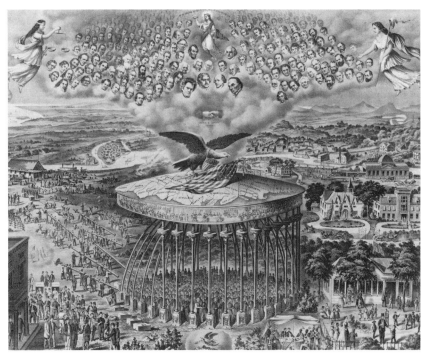

Fig. 1. J. L. Giles, "Reconstruction" (New York: n.p., 1867). Courtesy of the Library of Congress, Washington, D.C., LC-USZ62-10395.

Fig. 2. J. L. Magee, "Satan Tempting Booth to the Murder of the President" (n.p., 1865). Courtesy of the Lincoln Museum, Fort Wayne, Indiana (1691). In this lithograph, the artist clearly depicted evil spiritual forces inspiring Booth. Satan prods Booth to take Lincoln's life by pointing to the derringer with his right hand and to Lincoln with his left.

Fig. 3. "A Proper Family Re-Union" (Cincinnati: Opera House, 1865). Courtesy of the Library of Congress, Washington, D.C., LC-USZ62-40505.

Fig. 4. "Jeff Arming for the Final Struggle," in *Frank Leslie's Illustrated Newspaper* 20, no. 505 (June 3, 1865): 176.

Fig. 5. "Southern Women Feeling the Effects of the Rebellion and Creating Bread Riots," in *Frank Leslie's Illustrated Newspaper* 16, no. 399 (May 23, 1863): 141.

Fig. 6. "Reception of the 'Brute Butler' by the Ladies of the North," in *Harper's Weekly* 12, no. 317 (January 24, 1863): 64. Courtesy of the Armstrong Browning Library, Baylor University, Waco, Texas.

Fig. 7. "1868–1872," in *Frank Leslie's Illustrated Newspaper* 34, no. 869 (May 25, 1872): 161. Caption reads: " 'They shall beat their swords into plowshares, and their spears into pruning hooks: nation shall not lift up sword against nation, neither shall they learn war any more.'—Isaiah II, 4."

Fig. 8. Svobodin Merinsky, "David and Goliath" (New York: n.p., 1872). Courtesy of the Library of Congress, Washington, D.C., LC-USZ62-89735.

Fig. 9. "Lincoln Visiting Moody's Sunday School as President Elect," Moody Bible Institute, Special Collections Archive, Chicago, Illinois, Drawer 69, "DLM—Sunday School."

Fig. 10. "The Great Revival," in *Harper's Weekly* 20, no. 1002 (March 11, 1876): 201. Courtesy of the Armstrong Browning Library, Baylor University, Waco, Texas.

Fig. 11. "Ferry Passengers Depositing Money in the Yellow-Fever Box at Fulton Ferry," in *Frank Leslie's Illustrated Newspaper* 47, no. 1200 (September 28, 1878): 49.

Fig. 12. "Agonizing Appeal of Women and Children, In Memphis, To An Overworked Physician, To Hasten To Their Homes," in *Frank Leslie's Illustrated Newspaper* 47, no. 1200 (September 28, 1878): 57.

Fig. 13. "Another 'federal interference.' The struggle between Athena Hygeia and Yellow Jack," in *Harper's Weekly* 23, no. 1164 (April 19, 1879): 308–9.

Fig. 14. "Procession Five Hundred Strong," in [Eliza Daniel] Mother Stewart, *Memories of the Crusade* (Columbus, Ohio: W. G. Hubbard, 1888), 304.

Fig. 15. "The New Temptation on the Mount," *Literary Digest* 18, no. 13 (April 1, 1899): 364. In this image, the devil "imperialism" tempts Columbia to take a "world-wide empire."

been yellow fever epidemics and national traumas before, but none had done much to encourage national solidarity. Before the Civil War, major epidemics like cholera and yellow fever were generally isolated to specific locations, especially cities, principally because infected human carriers were unable to travel extensively to other regions. Even the Chicago Fire of 1871, which drew the attention of Americans throughout the entire country, did not engender feelings of national compassion everywhere. Although a host of northerners asserted that the United States reunited in order to aid the thousands of displaced Chicagoans, southern whites showed remarkably little interest in the catastrophe. In his research on the Chicago Fire, historian John J. Pauly found no record of supplies donated from Alabama, Florida, Mississippi, Arkansas, Virginia, or South Carolina. A newspaper in Austin, Texas, even claimed that the fire in Chicago and one in Boston were divine punishments for the Civil War. "Chicago and Boston were the hot beds of diabolism that led to the late war between the two sections," it editorialized, and now "the tables have been turned."[11]

But the relationship between catastrophe and sectional relations changed considerably in 1878. None of the previous medical epidemics was as devastating as the one that began in New Orleans in late May 1878 with the arrival of a sailor infected in Havana. The disease spread slowly in and around New Orleans during June, and then victims began to multiply in late July. Cities were hit the hardest. Memphis lost over five thousand of its roughly thirty thousand residents, and about forty-six hundred died in New Orleans. By December, yellow fever, also known as "yellow jack" and "the saffron scourge," struck large parts of Mississippi, Louisiana, Tennessee, Kentucky, Georgia, Ohio, and Missouri.[12] After traveling from New Orleans to New York City in September, a dry goods merchant recounted that "the country between Louisville, Kentucky and New Orleans is one entire scene of desolation and woe."[13]

Yellow fever was a horrible disease. In mild cases, the infected felt muscular pain, likely vomited for several days, and swung from intense chills to high fevers. In severe cases, the skin turned yellow as the disease incapacitated the liver, kidneys, and heart. The victims then vomited digested blood that had turned black. Finally, they became delirious, convulsed, shook, and perished. Usually death occurred seven to twelve days after the onset of symptoms.[14] One survivor detailed his horrific experience in a letter to the *Detroit Evening News*. Headache and intense muscular pain, he remembered, were followed by "an overpowering nausea in my stomach, and my mouth filled. My nurse said not a word but turned deadly pale. As I saw an inky substance before me in the basin I said lightly: 'This is the black vomit isn't it.'" It was an "indescribable torture." "My stomach and bowels have a burning heat, as though scalded by boiling water or scorched by coals of fire." He eventually collapsed after witnessing his bloodshot eyes and swollen lips in a mirror and uttering, "[T]his is the face of a demon!"[15]

The outbreak quickly took the lives of thousands of southerners, especially along the Mississippi River Basin. As the fever spread, businesses closed, people fled from major cities, and dread descended on the populace. Illness and mass exoduses put many who remained out of work. Countless southerners found it impossible to obtain life's basic necessities. The *Washington Post* reported, "The unprecedented spread and fatality of the yellow fever, causing an entire suspension of business has left several thousand poor people in this city who are destitute of means of subsistence and unable to procure work."[16] One woman who had fled from Vicksburg, Mississippi, poignantly detailed the travails of many southerners. "[F]ood was painfully scarce," she cried. "For over a week I had eaten only bread."[17] The *North American Review* also commented on the widespread ramifications of the epidemic: "The paralysis of commercial interests in that vast region is felt far and wide."[18] By January 1879, some businessmen and economists observed that the total amount of loss due from the fever totaled "hundred millions of dollars"—a substantial blow given that the federal treasury expended less than $237 million in 1878.[19]

Illness and poverty led to intense anxiety throughout the South. When word came to the small town of Holly Springs, Mississippi, that yellow fever infections were on the rise, "the very air, which seemed so health giving, was filled with a solemn awe, and dread and un-named fears possessed every heart."[20] One Mississippi reporter observed that townspeople could not stop discussing the disease: "Whenever you see two or three of our citizens talking on the street you may bet your bottom dollar they are discussing either the quarantine or yellow fever."[21] Amid the terror, residents of Jackson, Tennessee, placed detectives and armed guards on incoming roads to turn away anyone attempting to enter.[22] Towns in Texas refused trains, mail, and people from New Orleans or Memphis lest they be tainted with the fever.[23] "Shot-gun quarantines," the *Memphis Appeal* reported, "were by this time (the 26th of August) established at nearly all points" in the Mississippi Valley.[24] As the *McMinnville New Era* of Tennessee simply put it, "Our experience is one we will never forget, and it is a common one."[25]

Southern whites commented in their diaries and letters on the horror brought about by the fever. A Memphis physician who ultimately sacrificed his life fighting the pestilence wrote regularly to his wife about the city's depression. "The outlook grows more gloomy each day," he reported on August 24. "Some of the bodies," he lamented, "lie . . . three and four days unburied and produce horrid smells in the locality."[26] In Jackson, Tennessee, a sixty-three-year-old teacher expressed his concern over the epidemic in his diary. "The yellow fever is still on the increase," he wrote in late August: "How dreadful the scourge! and what sufferings are induced! Lord our God pity those cities and stay the ravages of the disease." Throughout September and October he continued to record the progress of the out-break and called on God for help: "The *fever* still rages on. . . . O Lord my God have mercy upon us and save us."[27] A Presbyterian minister in North Carolina, Reverend Samuel Agnew, recorded news about the outbreak and commented on the "country's" moods in his diary. Every new case of the fever, he observed, led to "quite a panic." In several entries Agnew acknowledged his own deep sadness and fear regarding the pestilence: "[E]ach day it gets worse. . . . Memphis is about depopulated. Vicksburg is suffering terrible. Oh, it is fearful! fearful."[28]

Many southern whites cried out to God in their anguish. In one poem written after the outbreak, a southern man who lost his wife and child due to the fever despaired that God no longer heard his pleas:

> I called on God, He did not hear;
> I prayed for death, it came not near;
> I wept, I shrieked, I tore my hair,
> For I was wild with fell despair.[29]

This poetic example became all too real for the former president of the Confederate States of America, Jefferson Davis. When his son, Jefferson Davis Jr., fell ill with the fever, Davis prayed fervently that God would spare him. "May God shield him and our other two children is my constant prayer," the elder Davis wrote to a friend in October. Alas, his prayers did not save his son. "The last of my four sons has left me," the former president lamented, "I presume not God to scorn, but the many and humble prayers offered before my boy was taken from me, are hushed in the despair of my bereavement."[30]

Terror of the epidemic knew no sectional bounds, for fear was felt across the nation. From New York to California, Maine to Florida, Americans fretted over the possibility of infection in their region. "We are thinking a great deal about the poor fever-stricken cities of the South," Oliver Wendell Holmes Sr. wrote to southern poet Paul Hamilton Hayne. "Every morning as the paper comes, the first question is 'What is the last account from Memphis, Grenada, and New Orleans.'"[31] On August 17, the *Washington Post* reported that northerners were anxious about the disease spreading to their region: "Considerable alarm has been felt in some of the more Northern cities along the Atlantic seaboard, lest the pestilence now raging in the South should be brought among them."[32] In San Francisco, residents quarantined a ship that supposedly carried the disease.[33] There were numerous reports— some true, some false—of yellow fever cases in New York City, Pittsburgh, Cairo, Illinois, and other northern locations. The *New York Times* summed up the national concern best when it claimed, "No one feels safe."[34]

Contemporaries were correct in their belief that this yellow fever outbreak constituted one of the worst epidemics and medical catastrophes in American history. "The disease from the first moved with a celerity and violence never known before," observed *Frank Leslie's Illustrated* of New York.[35] A Tennessee physician concurred: "Surely the United States never witnessed such a thing before." *Harper's New Monthly Magazine* grieved, "The pestilence of yellow fever which has desolated the Southern cities this year will be known as one of the most fearful in their annals."[36] The epidemic was so powerful that it even appeared to alter time. "Every day seemed a week, every week a month, and every month a year," recalled J. L. Power of Jackson, Mississippi. "Verily, we knew not what a day might bring forth."[37]

II

In such a trying context, sectional hatred was quickly forgotten. While the pestilence evoked common feelings of terror throughout the United States, it also offered white Americans an occasion to sympathize with one another and to work together in unprecedented ways. As the disease spread, poorly funded southern relief associations recognized that they would not be able to combat the outbreak alone. They quickly sought help from northerners, and their requests were amply met. Thousands of northerners responded with compassion and relief, and denominational divisions were set aside as they had been during Dwight Moody's revivals. Suspending sectional animosity, northerners contributed money and goods, prayed and wrote letters, and sent scores of doctors, nurses, and telegraph operators southward. While seeking to help southern whites, northerners also expressed new views of their former adversaries. Memories of southern whites as intractable and uncivilized rebels were explicitly effaced, and visions of southerners as honorable, God-fearing citizens took priority. Many northern whites became more intent on regarding southerners as brethren, rather than as enemies. The chaotic year helped to reforge the white republic in ways that political rhetoric and appointments could never accomplish.

In the early stages of the disease a number of organizations in the South formed relief committees to handle the outbreak and ensuing poverty. Masons, Odd

Fellows, Young Men's Christian Associations, and a host of "special" committees worked to ease the hardship. The largest and most prepared society was the group of charitable organizations known collectively as the "Howards." Named after English philanthropist John Howard, who had spent several decades tending to the needs of the sick and suffering, the first Howard organization formed in 1832. Composed of young doctors and businessmen, the Howards dedicated themselves to care for one another and their families in times of distress. They specifically agreed to pool their resources if a disease like yellow fever or cholera struck. Throughout the 1840s and the 1850s the organization grew and included chapters in New Orleans, Memphis, and Atlanta. In times of widespread need, the Howards divided their cities into districts and appointed members to care for the people of specific locations. The epidemic of 1878, however, proved far too great for the Howards and other local southern relief organizations.[38]

In late August these relief societies began pleading for northern assistance. One Memphis committee issued a general call to northern newspapers. "We need your sympathy," it stated, "and God alone knows how soon your aid."[39] The Howards also cried out for help: "We appeal to the charitable and the good; we appeal to the ministers of God for their influence and to their congregations. . . . In the name of a common country and a kindred humanity we invoke for our stricken dying and starving people."[40] As one Memphis editor later recalled, "The cry for food, for clothing, for money, for doctors, for as many as a thousand coffins, went out by telegraph to the ends of the earth, and a prompt and generous response came back."[41]

As this editor rightly observed, many northerners answered with great energy. Southern requests for aid supplied northern newspaper editors and religious figures with an opportunity not only to encourage the North to show compassion for the South, but also to describe southern whites as full–fledged members of the nation. "[L]et no man . . . withhold his cash sympathies from the South," the *Cincinnati Star* proclaimed.[42] *Frank Leslie's Illustrated* urged that sympathy must be made tangible with direct relief: "[T]hese horrors should at least inspire a genuine sympathy with the suffering, and induce on the part of all of us generous contributions . . . for the relief." To withhold aid even for a moment was a heinous sin, "a reproach upon our humanity."[43]

Nineteenth-century Americans generally assumed that the federal government would do little in times of medical epidemics, thus benevolence and aid needed to come primarily from private sources. Thousands of northerners joined together to assist the South, and their giving cut across class and religious lines.

New York City's Chamber of Commerce, led by banker J. P. Morgan, raised tens of thousands of dollars in relief.[44] Schools in Pittsburgh held special days for children to donate nickels and pennies. Coal miners and ironworkers also gave several hundred dollars. "Teachers and pupils of [the] Iowa College for the Blind" contributed twenty-one dollars to the cause.[45]

Northerners showed impressive innovation in their fund-raising and sent an amazing amount of money to the South. A gospel choir in Wheeling, West Virginia, donated its concert proceeds, while actors in Philadelphia held special performances and sent the ticket sales to the South.[46] Two baseball teams in Kalamazoo, Michigan, offered their earnings from a game, and in Crete, Illinois, a group of "little girls" formed a club, "The Milton Busy Bees," to solicit and send contributions.[47] The Howards of Memphis reported that they alone received over twenty-two hundred financial donations from individuals or organizations during the crisis. In sum, total monetary donations to yellow fever relief societies exceeded $4.5 million.[48] In an era when national political party committees rarely raised over $300,000 for presidential campaigns and when average annual incomes for nonagricultural families hovered around $380, the amount raised in only a few months was truly remarkable.[49]

Donations to the South included goods along with funds, and northerners regularly commented on the conciliatory significance of their gifts. In New York, a clothing drive raised over 4,500 cubic feet of "blankets, bedding, mattresses, worsted shawls, clothing, shoes, boots, felt hats, straw hats, high hats, and low hats."[50] Ice merchants in Gardiner, Maine, transported 1,000 tons of ice to the fever sufferers, while citizens of Peoria, Illinois, sent 161 bushels of potatoes, 132 bushels of onions, 475 sacks of flour, and 240 sacks of meal.[51] Other northerners sent an assortment of goods, including crackers, chickens, tea, underwear, wine, clothing, canned fruits, ginger ale, soap, deodorizer, and mustard.[52] Northern benevolence reached such heights that by the end of September the Citizen's Relief Committee of Memphis claimed that the "generous contributions . . . and what is now on the way to us, has placed us beyond the reach of immediate or probable want in the future. We have enough, not only for our own needs, but to enable us to assist the people of our country, and of the villages of this and the adjoining states."[53] Several newspapers asserted that the broad coalition of contributors made the relief drive an extraordinary national event. "The Republic," commented one Memphis editor, "to its remotest confines, was moved." The people of the North, he concluded, "have filled our sacks to overflowing, many, many times, and yet they are not done." As *Frank Leslie's Illustrated* observed, "The whole country is responding with royal unanimity and generosity to the appeals from the fever-smitten South."[54] Individual contributions, in short, were subsumed under the rubric of "national" benevolence.

Church groups and leaders did a great deal to contribute to the benevolence campaign. Northern ministers announced southern calls for aid from their pulpits and encouraged their parishioners to give liberally, while religious editors used their press offices as clearinghouses for relief funds and goods.[55] Protestant papers that had supported the radical crusade of the 1860s now implored northern whites to help the stricken South. The *New York Independent* instructed its readers that "now is the time for compassion and help," and the *Christian Advocate* rejoiced that the northern public showed such compassion for the South. In stark contrast to the 1860s, these journals now described southern whites as "brethren" and "friends."[56] Even President Hayes joined the religious crusade on behalf of the South when he auctioned off the Bible of a Union soldier at a fund-raiser for the relief fund. This soldiers' family hoped that the money could be used to ameliorate sectional animosities, and it specifically requested that "the proceeds [be] given to a family, or families, of Southern Confederate soldiers suffering from yellow fever."[57] And northerners from a variety of religious groups did indeed support the South. Several hundred Catholic nuns traveled to southern cities to care for the sick and needy, while northern churches and religious individuals contributed an inestimable amount of money to the relief campaign.[58]

While thousands of northerners donated money and goods, others either traveled or offered to travel south to alleviate the pain. Dozens of northern physicians ventured into infected regions to care for the sick. Seventeen doctors from northern states journeyed to Memphis to relieve the hardship, and some of them lost their lives in the fight. New York's Dr. M. T. Keating, for instance, achieved notoriety in the city for his brave commitment to battling the plague. "Not one of all the volunteer physicians more endeared himself to the people of Memphis," observed a local newspaper after Keating fell victim to the scourge, "and his untimely death cast a shadow over a community bowed down with the weight of woe."[59] Northern nurses offered help as well. On August 27, the *New York Times* reported that "during the day a number of women called at the rooms of the Chamber [of Commerce], desiring to be sent South in the capacity of nurses." On the next day, the *Times* further commented, "The Chamber of Commerce was overrun yesterday with persons desirous to be sent to the south as nurses." Although any volunteer who had not previously had the disease was barred from entering infected regions, several who had lived through previous infections traveled south.[60] In Memphis, more than forty nurses from northern cities offered aid to the sufferers, and some of them died in the effort.[61]

Northerners who volunteered as telegraph operators in southern cities played particularly important roles in raising local morale by keeping residents connected with the outside world. "At the height of the epidemic, on a call for volunteers for the telegraphic service in the fever districts, three young men of this city tendered their services," reported the Pittsburgh Relief Committee. All three "died of fever while faithfully performing their duties." Several young Philadelphia men also perished while working in the South. Southerners deeply appreciated these telegraph operators. "They stood to their posts like men," reported the *Memphis Appeal*, "and did their duty like heroes indeed, in whom was united the broadest humanity and the tenderest sentiments of love for their fellow-men."[62]

In the process of gift giving and sacrifice, northerners collectively voiced appreciation for former Confederates through prayers and letters. Many northerners beseeched their God on behalf of the suffering South. In Ohio, for example, Governor Richard Bishop called on "all Christian people in the State of Ohio [to] assemble in their respective houses of worship and offer up their united prayers to God to check the dreadful plague . . . and that He in His infinite goodness will restore health, ease, and prosperity to the houses and homes which have been called upon to mourn the loss of friends and relatives."[63] On September 10, the *New York Times* reported that "prayers are now being sent up in all the churches imploring the mercy of God."[64] A resident of Muscatine, Iowa, testified to this in a letter to a white Mississippian: "There is a wide-spread feeling of sympathy [in the] North for your suffering, and prayers are ascending that the term of the pestilence may be shortened."[65]

Group prayer helped create a northern consciousness during the epidemic that centered minds and hearts on caring for those in the South. Prayer linked northerners in a common crusade, and observers hoped that group supplications to the Lord would lead to a new sense of national brotherhood. When "fellow countrymen and brothers united in a common prayer," the *Memphis Appeal* asserted, they dampened "all sectional and party lines and [swept] away all prejudices and jealousy." In a letter to the New York City Chamber of Commerce, the old abolitionist poet John Greenleaf Whittier underscored the ways prayer drew the people together in a new brotherhood. "The great sorrow effaces all sectional and party lines and sweeps away all [sectional] prejudices and jealousy," he wrote. "Under its solemn shadow we are one people, fellow countrymen and brothers united in a common prayer."[66]

Through their benevolence northern whites exhibited collective expressions of care, concern, and national reunion. All over the country, secular and religious newspapers, along with relief agencies, listed the names of contributors and their donations.[67] Donation areas served as physical proof of northern generosity—to southerners as well as northerners. *Frank Leslie's Illustrated* and *Harper's Weekly* regularly carried pictures of northern benevolence, allowing people to see themselves and others giving. A popular illustration titled "Ferry Passengers Depositing Money in the Yellow-Fever Box at Fulton Ferry" in *Frank Leslie's Illustrated* not only showed a donation box situated in a conspicuous public area, but also highlighted how benevolence cut across class as "respectable ladies" and shoeless children joined in the cause. The print revealed several layers of "watching." While newspaper readers witnessed donations, characters within the picture watched one another. Donating and witnessing donations in newspapers served to reinforce and promote compassion and reconciliation. (See figure 11.)

Communication between northerners and southerners in the context of the epidemic also provided a vehicle for Yankees to express feelings of national community. The Pittsburgh Relief Committee specifically drew attention to the importance of intersectional communication in its summary of its efforts during the fever. Financial aid, it reported, was always sent with "[r]egular correspondence by mail and telegraph."[68] One newspaper editor in Mississippi, J. L. Power, actually collected dozens of communications and published excerpts from them in his history, *The Epidemic of 1878*. Most letters expressed sincere care for the many ill, impoverished, and frightened southerners. A Grand Rapids, Michigan, resident encouraged a white Mississippian: "I assure you [that] our hearts beat in unison with you and yours in your hour of trial." "Our hearts bleed with you," wrote a Helena, Montana, man, "and we pray devotedly that the delivering angel may come to replace the destroying angel." In their letters, northerners and southerners regularly referred to one another as "brethren" and expressed collective feelings with phrases like "we pray," "our hearts," and "our Union."[69] The use of "our Union" revealed a substantial rhetorical shift from the 1860s. Rather than refer to southern whites as *them* or *they*, as some Protestant missionaries had done during radical Reconstruction, northerners now chose first-person pronouns, such as *us* and *we*, to express common ties. In the national and group imaginations of these letter writers, southern and northern whites were again one nation united spiritually by pain and perseverance.

As southerners battled against the disease, northerners depicted and described them much more positively than they had before. A small number of northern whites interpreted the epidemic as a sign of God's judgment on the South. A writer for the *New York Advocate*, for example, described the outbreak as yet another "plague" that the Lord had leveled against the South because of slavery and racism. Then "came the yellow fever," he wrote, "till the whole South moaned like a sick baby, and whimpered for help."[70] This opinion, however, was a minority one. Instead of portraying southerners as unrepentant barbarians or indolent ne'er do wells, most northern whites now characterized southern whites as noble warriors and heroic martyrs. In one pictorial print in *Frank Leslie's Illustrated*, southern women agonized, but they did so with honor. Gone were the Civil War images of knife-wielding, uncivilized, repulsive southern women. Now southern ladies maintained orderliness even though they were in desperate trouble. Their faces were smooth and their demeanors respectable. Even the kneeling woman supplicated with dignity, for her upright posture evinced pride. Images of southern whites during the epidemic, in short, were remarkably different than depictions only thirteen years earlier. (See figure 12.)

Northern newspapers also offered positive assessments of southern whites during the outbreak. Writers for the *New York Independent*, who had denounced southerners as untrustworthy "rebels" before the outbreak, now praised southerners as noble. In one 1878 article, the editor declared, "Heroes, indeed, are the Howards and others who have left their homes and their friends—some of them forever—to go amid the pestilence and give Christian care to the suffering and dying."[71]

Northerners even expressed admiration for southern Protestant ministers who had previously lent their moral and intellectual support to the Confederacy. This was nowhere more evident than in descriptions of Benjamin Morgan Palmer, a leading southern Old School Presbyterian. In the 1860s and early 1870s, Palmer had been one of the most vigorous anti-northern clerics in the South, and he had few friends north of the Mason-Dixon Line. Like many of his ministerial colleagues during the Civil War, he had charged the North as having a *"malignant and vindictive spirit."* Palmer had led his presbytery to secede from the Old School faction of the Presbyterian Church and had served as the first moderator of the Presbyterian Church of the Confederate States of America. In the years following the war, Palmer had refused to admit that the Confederacy had committed any wrong, and he remained a stern advocate of denominational separation between northern and southern churches.[72]

In the summer of 1878, though, after Palmer returned to New Orleans from his vacation in order to serve the ailing city, he was transformed in the northern press into an example of southern nobility. The *New York Times* highlighted Palmer, "the

Southern orator and theologian," as one of the heroes of the epidemic, while *Frank Leslie's Illustrated* wrote, "the eminent Presbyterian divine of New Orleans, has given a rare illustration of self-sacrifice." Palmer gained such notoriety in the North that more than one hundred northern churches directed their contributions to the South through him. Their contributions, in fact, totaled more than four thousand dollars.[73] Southerners such as Palmer had been transformed in the northern imagination from sinners into saints.

Ultimately, many northern whites hoped that their actions and the shared experience of trauma would wipe out memories of national division and create new feelings of American unity. The *New York Times* predicted that the pestilence would eradicate past animosities: "The North puts aside all irritating remembrances, and heeds only the cry of anguish for help which comes from the fever-stricken districts." "The truth is," the *Times* continued, "the experience which the two sections are now undergoing should uproot lingering animosities and demonstrate the depth and unselfishness of the feeling which regards their interests as identical."[74] Other writers made similar points. The ways northerners responded to the deadly disease, maintained a relief committee in Pittsburgh, "showed that our American brotherhood had a deeper meaning than we generally attribute it; that all distinction of section or party . . . were swept away by the universal distress and want, and the whole people were merged in the common humanity, benevolence, and sympathy."[75] *Frank Leslie's Illustrated* suggested that if "the spectacle of the children of the North pouring their gifts into the laps of the suffering South" did not "disarm sectional hate and point the way to a closer brotherhood," then nothing would.[76]

Harper's New Monthly Magazine best summed up the sentiments of many northerners by explicitly claiming that the emotions of national love felt amid the trauma of 1878 rose above all memories of sectional antagonism. When the yellow fever outbreak began, "[t]he whole community was stirred as in the bitter days of sixteen and seventeen years ago, but with what a different emotion!" this writer recognized. "This, at least, must be one of the great consolations of so melancholy a situation. It rebukes factitious fury and confronts us with realities. It alleviates that sectional hostility which is carefully fostered not for patriotic ends, and it tends to confirm the union of hearts, without which that of hands is fruitless."[77]

III

The trauma of 1878 was not merely a time for northern whites to reconceptualize the South. It also supplied southern whites with an occasion to recast their views of northerners and their relationship to the Union, but somewhat differently.

A host of southern whites indeed claimed that northern generosity alleviated their sectional grievances and somehow reunited the nation metaphysically. These southerners also held on to their southern identities tenaciously. Doctors, businessmen, relief leaders, poets, ministers, and politicians joined in praising northerners for their support. At meetings and conventions dedicated to thanking the North and through poems and proclamations, southerners cooperatively engaged in reunion. They extolled northern honor and claimed that their memories of the Civil War and civil strife had been eased. In the process, southern whites re-envisioned northern whites. Instead of describing Yankees as malicious intruders, they now considered them invited guests and Christian compatriots. To them, northern generosity created a spiritual rebirth of the American republic that once and for all destroyed sectional animosity. They believed that God had used the suffering and the benevolence to create a new brotherhood that transcended past divisions.

The epidemic proved an almost ideal occasion for southerners to proclaim allegiance to the United States without repudiating their sense of southern identity. It allowed southern whites to "surrender" to the nation—to "wave the white flag"— without acknowledging any past wrong or guilt. By claiming that northern generosity diminished sectional antagonisms, southern whites preserved their belief that they had not erred against God or man in fighting the Civil War. Disease and benevolence were their conquerors, not Union armies. Many southern whites retained their love for the South, while at the same time announcing appreciation for national fraternity. Affirmations of national affiliation, moreover, often met pragmatic purposes. Some southern politicians and businessmen employed claims of reconciliation to seek greater financial aid. The epidemic ultimately served as an occasion for a wide variety of southern whites to assert new memories of northerners, to participate in reunion, and to claim a new national solidarity without feeling any compulsion to reject their allegiance to the South or the Lost Cause.

Southern physicians were deeply thankful for northern support, especially northern doctors, and they announced their gratitude in a variety of settings. J. P. Dromgoole, a doctor from Kentucky, praised the "noble sons of the North" who traveled to the South. They were a "noble band of Hero Martyrs" who "plunge[d] into the great maelstrom of death to save a suffering brother." The epidemic had annihilated the hatreds of the past, and Dromgoole prayed that God would maintain the unity of the nation. "The hideous phantoms and weird ghosts of past differences and animosities are of the buried past," he proclaimed. The "*North and the South have shaken hands over the bloody chasm*; and may the God of heaven and earth decree that it be closed forever!"[78]

Likewise, in a speech before the Tri-State Medical Society in Springfield, Illinois, in November 1878, Dr. J. W. Singleton of Paducah, Kentucky, contended that when "heroic medical men from the North, South, East and West" bravely attacked the disease, they helped create a new national brotherhood. "Who were the principal actors in this melancholy drama?" he asked and answered. "Were they Southerners? No! Were they only Northerners? No! Were they American physicians? Yes, most gloriously yes!" Singleton, whose speech was later reprinted in the *St. Louis Medical and Surgical Journal* and as a pamphlet, went on to claim that a new national fraternity emerged from the war on yellow fever: "Never before has the spirit of our national brotherhood developed to such an extent as to make us feel and know that there is ever a chord in the American heart which needs only to be touched by the magic power of sympathy to cause it to yield the most precious fruits of benevolence and charity." A new republic had been formed, he concluded, "one in common fraternity and common solidarity of mutual interests, loving dependence and brotherly protection." The national implications of the epidemic were obvious. "American" doctors worked together to heal "Americans."[79]

Businessmen and southern relief organizers also expressed new emotions of national brotherhood during relief society meetings and in their annual reports. For many of these men, proclamations of national unity were part of an emerging "New South" rhetoric and ideology that highlighted sectional reconciliation as a means to remake and revitalize the southern economy.[80] When the first shipments of donations arrived in New Orleans from the North, "there was not a dry eye in the throng." The chairman of one local relief organization became so "completely overcome with emotion" that he exclaimed, "Let any man use the word 'Yankee' again in my presence and I will insult him. Were the people of the North our own flesh and blood they could not be more our brothers."[81] Other aid society leaders were quick to heap praise upon the North. Intersectional generosity, the Howards of New Orleans declared in their annual report, not only "brought solace and succor," but also created "a brotherhood wider than birthplace and a patriotic sympathy as ample as the bounds of our common country."[82] A Memphis merchant wrote to the *Washington Post* that the "assistance which the generous people of the North are pouring in upon us" alleviated many hard feelings.[83] In short, financial aid and relief of illness had the power to dampen sectional hostilities and provided an occasion to call for emotional and financial national reconciliation.

As physicians and relief organizers proclaimed their appreciation to the North and to the nation as a whole, southern newspaper editors joined in the chorus. To cite but one example, J. M. Keating, owner of the *Memphis Appeal*, praised northern doctors, nurses, and contributions for easing his city's sorrow. To him, northern benevolence was most impressive because it transcended regional, class, and social standing: "From far Oregon and Montana to Vermont, from villages, towns, and cities of all the busy northern States, from the miners' camp, the newsboys' home, from the banker and the farmer, the professor and the mechanic, from all classes of that section of the country" came "the light of an enduring brotherly love." "Blood is thicker than water" he continued, and northern compassion had obliterated all anger-filled memories. "[N]o memories of sectional divisions, of political animosi-ties, or of civil war, have been allowed to stay the steady flow of the bounteous stream that has brought us . . . the assurance that we are one people in fact as well as in name." "[B]eyond the froth and fuss of politics, and the deceits and dangers of demagogues," he concluded, "the popular heart is safe, yielding only of its fullness when challenged in the cause of humanity and brothers' lives are at stake." [84]

Southern poets similarly sought to immortalize the efforts of northerners in verse. The fever and the massive northern response, these bards suggested, had resurrected the South and the nation. Southern writers considered 1878 a mysti-cal and spiritual year in which the South—its living and its dead—returned to the nation in peace and harmony. They proclaimed that God had used the events to turn enmity and sorrow into fraternity and joy.[85] Yet their verses also demon-strated that the epidemic supplied an honorable means for southern whites to ac-cept national affiliation. In Mississippi, Judge J. F. Simmons claimed that while the South had not surrendered in 1865, it could now submit:

> The white flag waves! Our hearts are conquered now;
> The frown of hate has fled the Southron's brow;
> Our gratitude, unclaimed, is freely giv'n,
> Our vows of love are registered in Heav'n

He predicted that after 1878 the resurrected nation would continue to grow in affection in this world and the world beyond:

> And now reborn in her maturer life,
> Oblivion fling o'er bitterness and strife,—
> Cemented be in one unbroken chain,
> To stronger grow and ne'er abrade again;
> And may we ever be in deathless love
> One brotherhood on earth and one above.[86]

Another Mississippian, Emmett Ross, also announced that northern benevo-lence brought an end to hatreds lingering from the Civil War. But as he pledged na-tional fraternity, Ross refused to turn against the righteousness of the Confederate cause. In fact, even within his poem dedicated to national unity, he extolled Confederate southerners for their virtue:

The Southron's hand that erstwhile drew his saber from its sheath
And dipped its blade in brother's blood to win the patriot's wreath,
Now presses on a throbbing breast in pledge to self and God
That Peace and Love shall ever reign where hostile armies trod.[87]

Similarly, Paul Hamilton Hayne contrasted the sectional rancor of the Civil War years with the newfound national solidarity experienced during the epidemic. He considered God the primary force behind national reunion:

Whose voice? Whose hand? Oh, thanks, divinest Master,
Thanks for those grand emotions which impart
Grace to the North to feel the South's disaster,
The South to bow with touched and cordial heart!
Now, now at last the links which war had broken
Are welded fast, at mercy's charmed commands;
Now, now at last the magic words are spoken
Which blend in one two long-divided lands!
O North! you came with warrior strife and clangor;
You left our South one gory burial ground;
But love, more potent than your haughtiest anger,
Subdues the souls which hate could only wound![88]

In their poems on the epidemic, Ross, Simmons, and Hayne cherished both sectional loyalty and national identification. They could, in fact, have their region and their nation.

Mass meetings dedicated to thanking the North provided another type of forum for southern whites to enact reconciliation. Even some of the most belligerent, proslavery southerners used the occasions to articulate national solidarity. In New Orleans, the Presbyterian leader Benjamin Morgan Palmer, who had been lauded in the northern press, suspended his disdain for northerners. Offering the introductory prayer at a mass meeting in New Orleans held "to return thanks for the succor extended to the city during the epidemic of 1878," Palmer praised God for using the national "sorrow" to bring a new sense of nationalism. He concluded by asking God to reconcile the people: "And may it please Thee to cause those threads of sympathy woven across a continent to grow stronger and stronger—that this great Congress of States, bound together in harmony and peace, may be prepared for a blessed destiny in the generations yet to come." And Palmer was not the only southern religious leader to thank the North. The Southern Baptist Convention applauded the events of 1878 and proclaimed, "Surely the bloody chasm has rapidly closed."[89]

Appreciation for the North also found political expression in 1878 and 1879. Southern congressmen promised national reconciliation in order to acquire financial aid and commented widely on the influence of northern generosity on southern memories. In the midst of the outbreak, Louisiana congressman Joseph Acklen "utter[ed] the thanks of the South for Northern Benevolence" at a meeting of the New York City Chamber of Commerce. Generosity, he affirmed, would "finally close the breach that the late war made between the two sections." Northern gifts "shall have gained an undying gratitude of our suffering people." Predictions of national unity, Acklen hoped, would spur northern donations.[90] Other politicians contrasted memories of military defeat with new feelings of national fraternity engendered during the trauma. At a town meeting in Nashville, Democratic congressman and former Confederate soldier John House commented, "Grander than the victory of Appomattox is the victory won by the people of the North in their noble and generous contributions to the stricken and suffering South." While the South had surrendered militarily in 1865, it finally rejoined the Union after the plague: "Within the shadow of the dark wing of pestilence, beside the new-made graves of her heroic sons and daughters, with bowed head and tearful eyes, she extends her hand and surrenders her heart to the generous and magnanimous North." For House, the epidemic was not only a time of heroes from both the North and the South, but also a moment of cosmic significance. "God's own hand," he concluded, "has bridged the bloody chasm."[91]

Several top-ranking southern politicians even held a special meeting in Washington, D.C., to announce their gratitude and pledge their commitment to the Union. In December 1878, a group of southern senators and representatives, including Mississippi's L. Q. C. Lamar, Louisiana's E. John Ellis, Virginia's John Goode, Tennessee's I. G. Harris, and Arkansas's A. H. Garland, gathered to praise the "broad spirit of American patriotism." Claiming to represent "the whole southern people," the committee showered northern whites with praise and declared national solidarity an established fact. "Charity," they maintained, "has not only healed the sick, fed the hungry, clothed the naked, solaced the dying, gave hope and comfort to the widow and orphan and buried the dead. It has accomplished a work far higher and more important. It has healed the wounds of war." Benevolence, in short, had helped to reforge the republic: "[I]t has bound our hearts to theirs; it has cemented anew the bonds between them and us; it has renewed the aspirations of all our people toward the idea of an American Union based upon affection." Love and compassion had triumphed over violence and hate: "To-day, far above the victorious flag of Appomattox floats the banner of love and charity. Better, brighter and far more enduring are the victories of love and charity." Concluding, the committee pledged "the undying fealty of our hearts to the Constitution of our common country, and the perpetual Union of the States thereunder— not alone the physical, geographical and political Union, but a union of affection, of brotherhood, inspired by a common origin and a common destiny, ratified by the covenant of our fathers, and now cemented forever by their love and their charity to us and our people."[92]

These politicians echoed the sentiments of southern poets, editors, and businessmen when they joined northern whites in voicing reconciliation through pronouncements, meetings, poems, editorials, pamphlets, and lectures. Throughout, these southerners expressed new views of northern whites. Yankees were now much-needed Christian brethren, not condescending aggressors or vindictive, grasping conquerors. Southern whites, however, saw no need to reject their southern-ness or their devotion to deceased Confederates. There was no reason for them to do so. By "surrendering" during the epidemic, southern whites joined a new nation they perceived as seeking their betterment rather than their destruction. Predictions and proclamations of national unity, moreover, served as ideal ways to procure more benevolence from the North. In short, southerners had everything to gain from claims to national affiliation and nothing to lose. They could acquire funds and reconceptualize northerners without repudiating their beloved Lost Cause or admitting wrong. For southern whites, trauma allowed them moments to "forget" memories of sectional dissension and "remember" their common bonds as Americans. The nation, they professed, had been spiritually reborn amid death, trauma, and benevolence.

IV

The national reunion announced during the epidemic did not include all Americans, however. Alongside the paeans to national unity ran a darker current of racial alienation, one seen in Moody's southern revivals two years earlier. The outbreak was part of the racialized postwar reconciliation that excluded African Americans from full status in the nation, a process that had been and was being religiously legitimated by key Protestant figures. While northern and southern whites embraced one another during the plague, some severely criticized blacks, neglected the medical needs of African Americans, and actually exacerbated blacks' suffering. As southern blacks realized that they would not receive aid from whites, they sought assistance from African Americans throughout the nation. In these ways, the responses to the fever reflected and intensified a major trend in Reconstruction and post-Reconstruction America: the social and spiritual separation of the races amid the re-creation of the white republic. In this way, 1878 proved a crucial year in the rise of the postwar white republic, a nation built upon an ethnic nationalism that focused upon perceived similarities between northern and southern whites and perceived differences between whites and blacks.[93]

Several whites displaced their anxieties over the fever and their inability to control it onto blacks. Terror over sexual relations between black men and white women struck the South with new force during the crisis, and stories of rapes proliferated. The *Washington Post* carried an interview with a physician from Memphis who insisted that "he had been authentically informed that white women have to take negro men for nurses or go without, and that such negro men nurses have taken advantage of their helpless victims." A Memphis editor warned that local whites completely feared a rage of "wholesale rape[s] of white women by negro male nurses." Others denounced African Americans as lazy and cruel heathens who refused to work or assist in battling the fever. "It was a sad and sickening sight," wrote one resident of Memphis, "[a]ll over the Southland the fields are whitening with cotton ready for the picker, and yet these able-bodied, healthy men and women stand here in Memphis and draw free rations." In Grenada, Mississippi, one white complained that while "the negroes never fail to show up for their rations, [they] can not be found when a grave is to be dug or a corpse to be removed."[94]

At least one white conjured up genocidal visions in response to the epidemic. One Memphis man hoped that the fever could be harnessed to solve the South's racial problems by turning the disease and the ensuing poverty against local African Americans. State authorities, he wrote, should "establish martial law, build warehouses at points accessible to railroads, guard them [the blacks], remove all the provisions from the city, and then let starvation and disease do their legitimate work."[95] For this white writer, the fever evoked the possibilities of racial genocide, a chance to make the United States truly into a "white man's country." His disturbing plan may have reflected a radical racism far beyond that of most whites, but he was not the first, nor the last, white to recommend seriously the removal of African Americans from the nation.

Black unemployment in urban areas did not stem from innate laziness or disregard for the well-being of whites, however. Many blacks were jobless because thousands of whites had fled southern cities and most businesses in Memphis and New Orleans had shut down. Furthermore, although whites generally ignored them in their accounts of relief, thousands of African Americans participated valiantly in the battle against the plague, serving as nurses, gravediggers, and financial contributors. Cash-poor African American farmers in Fort Scott, Kansas, for instance, collected $275 during a benefit concert in September to send to the suffering. Their willingness to sacrifice was lost on most whites, who were more interested in condemning blacks than recognizing that people of color also perished from the disease and helped in the relief effort.[96]

Racism went well beyond criticism and threats of genocide. It led to tangible neglect and abuse of black sufferers that resulted in unnecessary deaths. Although southern agencies such as the Howards claimed that they supplied goods and aid without regard for race, evidence from missionary associations and newspapers belied these assertions. The organ of the American Missionary Association, the *American Missionary*, carried several letters from southern black leaders and white missionaries that described the discriminatory practices of the relief agencies. One black minister complained that the Memphis Howard Association made blacks go through rigorous and difficult procedures to obtain relief. "[T]he supplies in the hands of the Howards and Relief Committee are ample," he acknowledged, "but there is such a routine imposed upon the colored people that many of them get out of heart before they reach the end." Other writers lamented that many African American lives would have been saved if they had received the attention that whites had. "The death rate is very high among the colored people," wrote Hattie A. Milton, a white missionary to African Americans in Memphis, "in many cases, no doubt, resulting from want of proper attention." In another letter, Milton castigated local whites for ignoring the needs of blacks: "Although several thousand dollars were sent here to relieve yellow fever sufferers, many of the colored people received but little, some nothing." She condemned the rigorous rules and regulations of the relief agencies, which clearly privileged whites and penalized blacks: "It is very sad to hear of those who were so feeble that they could not stand in the ranks to await their turn at the relief office, but sat on the ground till night came, and then receiving no attention, went home to die!"[97]

One of the most egregious examples of whites' blatant disregard for African Americans occurred outside of Memphis in September. As the disease raged out of control in the city during late August and early September, several white relief leaders decided to set up a hospital camp five miles south of the city. They intended to transport the sick to the camp for treatment. The location of "Camp Joe Williams," as it came to be called, was in an area predominantly inhabited by African

Americans. Understandably, local blacks opposed the creation of the camp. Although unsure of the particular transmitter of the disease, blacks knew just as well as whites that close proximity to infected individuals heightened the prospect for contamination. When doctors first arrived to set up the compound, then, a group of African Americans drove them away. As *Frank Leslie's Illustrated* explained, local blacks "disliked the invasion by a possibly fever-bearing rabble." Backed by two military companies the next day, the physicians returned and constructed the camp without any further disruptions. By placing the camp near African American residents, these doctors showed a clear disregard for black safety and well-being.[98] Although there is no way to know exactly how many local African Americans contracted yellow fever because of the hospitalized whites, it is probable that many became infected. In fact, one doctor reported that the infected whites who traveled to Camp Joe Williams "gave" the disease to local blacks. "Colored families," he wrote, "living within a few hundred yards of our hospital who have not visited the infected district at all and kept aloof from our camps, have sickened and died."[99]

The mistreatment of African Americans in 1878 was not necessarily a new form of racism, but its post-Reconstruction context was pivotal. Disregard for the lives of African Americans had been widespread before 1878. "A thing that shocks me is the prevalent indifference to the negro's fate and life," Sidney Andrews had written in 1865 during his tour of the postwar South. "It is a sad, but solemn fact, that three fourths of the native whites consider him a nuisance, and would gladly be rid of his presence, even at the expense of his existence."[100] In many ways, responses to the outbreak of 1878 signified a turning point. In the 1860s and early 1870s, African Americans had been the principal beneficiaries of much northern aid and compassion. During radical Reconstruction, northern Protestants had sent millions of dollars to aid people of color, and the federal government had put its weight behind improving the lives of freedpeople. But in 1878 northern whites paid very little attention to the plight of African Americans and spent the vast majority of their time helping southern whites. Reunion among whites eclipsed humanitarian compassion. A white ethnic nationalism trumped any form of civic nationalism and universal concern. This was genuinely a great reversal from the radical 1860s, a reversal that had deadly consequences for people of color.

Medical neglect and mistreatment by whites led African Americans to look to one another for aid. In early September, for instance, Louisiana blacks solicited help from northern African Americans. "In the midst of suffering and death," they begged, "we appeal to the Christian charity of our brethren everywhere. . . . Organized bodies among our people will afford much needed aid and relieve great distress." Although not always explicitly stated, most African American calls for relief indicated that they needed it because white donations primarily went to whites. Reverend A. A. Dixon of Port Gibson, Mississippi, wrote to the *Christian Recorder*, "Will you not send us substantial aid, as the whites are doing to the sufferers of their color?" Many southern blacks, moreover, had to set up their own relief organizations because white ones so often neglected them. In Memphis, a group of black pastors formed a "Ministers' Aid Association" to seek relief for African Americans.[101] Indeed, the twin forces of disease and racism made African American suffering far worse than that of whites. Prejudice created a wall of racial division and propelled African Americans to seek national unity with one another.

Many African Americans also felt enraged, depressed, and alienated by the odes to reconciliation sung by northern and southern whites. Rather than viewing the epidemic as a cosmic moment of national reconciliation, some African Americans and their white supporters viewed it as a time of divine judgment upon the oppressive white nation. A writer for the *Christian Recorder* hoped that "the nation could be persuaded to see in this affliction the hand of the Almighty, and so humble itself in the dust." Reverend J. M. Cargill of Cumberland, Maryland, asserted that "the whole nation was cursed" because of slavery, and the epidemic of 1878 was but one example of God's vengeance. "In these days He has sent another destroying angel," Cargill wrote, "the yellow fever." Only when the nation repented of its sins would it find God's blessing.[102] A black sharecropper in Mississippi perhaps put this point most poignantly. He wrote the state's governor that God had brought the fever upon the United States because of whites' sin and racism. "The wrath of God is now let loose upon the South for all their wickedness," he fumed, "the southern people are whiskey-drinking, Tobacco-chewing, constant-spitting, Negro-hating, Negro-killing, red-handed, ignorant, uneducated, uncivilized set of devils."[103] Another African American bitterly resented the ways northern and southern whites reunited while they abused blacks. "The simple word of the Southerner is remembered, while his act is forgotten," raged an African Methodist Episcopal minister. Alas, he lamented, "Southerners have never repented," but northerners forgave them anyway.[104]

This minister astutely recognized one of the key effects of the yellow fever epidemic and accurately pinpointed one of the main themes of racial and sectional relations from the 1870s to the 1890s. Responses to the yellow fever crisis reflected and exacerbated broader postwar trends of sectional reunion and racial alienation. The sermons of preachers such as Beecher and Moody were upsetting enough, but northern neglect during the epidemic was devastating for people of color. At the level of human contact, northern nurses, doctors, telegraph operators, and gifts helped ameliorate past grievances between the white North and the white South. Yet as whites expressed a common national unity, most plugged their ears to the calls of African Americans and showed very little respect for suffering blacks. People of color had to contend with both pestilence and prejudice. Compassion transcended sectionalism, but it failed to rise above racism. Even the crucible of disease could not melt away the racial tensions, angers, and hatreds that were fast developing in post–Civil War America. On the contrary, such feelings grew.

Even after the fever subsided, northern and southern whites continued to invoke memories of the epidemic as powerful tools to call for "national" political aims over "local" ones. As historian John Ellis has chronicled, the magnitude of the outbreak created widespread support for a national health agency.[105] "The fearful spread of this pestilence," claimed President Rutherford B. Hayes in his annual message to Congress, "has awakened a very general public sentiment in favor of national sanitary administration, which shall not only control quarantine, but have sanitary supervision of internal commerce in times of epidemics."[106] Several prominent politicians and businessmen who had proclaimed that northern generosity had reunited the nation led the battle for national health legislation. In fact, during the Forty-Fifth Congress, James Eustis, L. Q. C. Lamar, and I. G. Harris offered several resolutions for the establishment of a national bureau of public health. Southern businessmen from New Orleans also lobbied for help from the federal government. One merchant justified the engagement of the national government in disease control by characterizing it as a natural extension of federal powers that had started during the Civil War: "As they [federal powers] have been expanded by the war there can be no doubt that any measure necessary for the general welfare of the Union would justify any legislation to carry into effect the grandest powers so constructed."[107]

Some northerners also continued to connect the epidemic with national issues, memories of the Civil War, and the notion that God's benevolent hand was in the forging of national solidarity. Writing to the *Christian Advocate* in late December 1878, A. B. Leonard maintained that sectionalism was the worst sin of the United States, because it made it impossible for northerners and southerners to battle collectively other national sins, such as intemperance, dishonesty, and political corruption. "The removal of this sectional bitterness," he asserted, "is of the first importance, and must precede any national advancement." But thankfully, the epidemic had done much to diminish sectional rancor. Northerners had offered the right hand of fellowship to the South. "The North has poured out its millions of money and sent forward physicians and nurses to relieve the suffering," Leonard continued, "while heaven has been supplicated from church and family altars for the removal of the plague." Southerners responded with love and affection. To Leonard, God had employed the outbreak in order to fashion a new and more holy United States. He concluded, "Let the good work of genuine reconciliation, thus begun in the presence of a great national affliction, go on until we shall know no North, no South, except as describing two geographical parts of a great, united, loving, and prosperous people!"[108]

During the spring of 1879, furthermore, a cartoon in *Harper's Weekly* depicted the "U.S." (emblazoned on the helmet, shield, and spear of "Athena Hygeia") ending the life of "State Rights" during the epidemic. The sword of "Pestilence," the print insisted, was no match for the spear of "National Quarantine." Ultimately, this cartoon suggested that northern whites hoped that the intensity of the 1878 fever had proved that the justification for rebellion—states' rights—was illegitimate and outdated. The North's response to yellow fever could be thanked for providing the occasion for national reunion. Northern and southern whites indeed waved "the white flag" throughout the nation, as southern whites surrendered to the American nation and northern whites surrendered to southern racism. (See figure 13.)

In the 1880s and 1890s, memories of the yellow fever outbreak receded as the nation dealt with a new set of issues and problems. During these years, national reconciliation and American nationalism took on increasing importance, especially because the composition of the United States changed dramatically as millions of "new immigrants" from southern and eastern Europe entered the nation. White Protestant Americans fretted over the increasing number of new immigrants, while African Americans continued to find themselves further stripped of their citizenship rights. Even the most phenomenal reform movement of the late nineteenth century—the Woman's Christian Temperance Union (WCTU)—failed to stand against nativism and racism. In fact, they played a large role in rebuilding the white republic at the expense of commitments to civic nationalism and racial reform. The WCTU and its crusade helped further cement the foundations of the white republic, a nation in which white Protestant reformers no longer advocated national inclusion for peoples of all colors and previous conditions, but instead lent their moral weight to racial restriction and exploitation.

6

NO NORTH, NO SOUTH, NO SECTIONALISM
IN POLITICS, NO SEX IN CITIZENSHIP
Race, Nationalism, and Gender Politics in the Rise of the
Woman's Christian Temperance Union

Like many other southern white women after the Civil War, Belle Kearney often felt depressed about the condition of Dixie. Born in 1863 to an affluent family near Vernon, Mississippi, she spent her childhood hearing stories about how the glorious "Old South" had been demolished by the war and radical Reconstruction. When yellow fever struck in 1878, terror again seized her people. "For the period of time it lasted its deadly ravages exceeded the destruction of the civil war," she recalled years later. "Thousands stood shuddering in 'The Valley of the Shadow.' Death, grim and awful, stalked through the land knowing no surfeit. It was the blackness of despair. The acme of desolation. . . . There was the thud of spades in the earth, driven by men digging grave after grave, but all else was silent—waiting, waiting, waiting."[1]

The outbreak was but one difficulty Kearney faced. Although yellow fever disrupted her life for several months, race relations proved a more perennial problem. The idea and reality of freed African Americans tormented her, and for this reason she considered emancipation a grave mistake. "With a few rare exceptions," she claimed, "the negroes defined freedom as the liberty to be idle." To her, African Americans were mired in infancy: "It should be remembered that a race, like an individual, has its period of youth. The African in America has not yet advanced beyond that age." She considered people of color debauched, writing, "The blacks leave their deadly, immoral trail wherever massed in large numbers." Ultimately, Kearney deemed racial equality impossible because of the heritage of slavery in the United States and the alleged barbarity of African Americans: "Nowhere on the earth have two races who bear or have borne the relation of master and slave existed together as social equals; nor do superior and inferior so co-exist anywhere until the superior is degraded to the level of the inferior."[2]

Before the 1880s, Kearney had few, if any, public or political avenues to address these types of social issues. She had spent her youth "waiting, waiting, waiting" for an opportunity to be a part of public debates, but nineteenth-century gender ide-ologies, which were especially strong in the South, prescribed that white women spend their lives caring for their families or perhaps teaching school.[3] Kearney wanted to do more than raise children and care for a husband, however. She desperately wanted to avoid what she considered a "useless" or "purposeless" life. Kearney desired to help southern white civilization rise anew. As a teenager, she became a schoolteacher in the hopes that service as an educator would provide a sense of importance. But her deep sense of meaninglessness lingered. "What is there for me to do?" she wrote in the 1870s. "Life is so empty, so unsatisfying! I wish I had never been born!"[4]

Her sense of helplessness and hopelessness vanished in the 1880s when a new and dynamic movement swept through the South: the Woman's Christian Temperance Union (WCTU). After hearing the national president of the WCTU, Frances Willard, speak in 1889 Kearney's entire outlook changed. It was, as she put it, "the moment of my destiny." "She came quietly into the pulpit, modestly at-tired," Kearney wrote of Willard. Yet the speech was anything but modest: "Miss Willard that night was a peerless orator, the gracious Christian, the marvelous reformer who shall stand forth in history 'until there shall be no more curse' and 'the kingdoms of this world are become the kingdoms of our Lord, and of His Christ.'" In Kearney's mind, Willard stood as a prophet of a new day dawning and the WCTU as a religious crusade that would unchain southern white womanhood. It was "the golden key that unlocked the prison doors of pent-up possibilities. It was the generous liberator, the joyous iconoclast, the discoverer, the developer of Southern women."[5]

Very little in Willard's childhood and early adulthood indicated that she would become a grand motivator of southern women. She had embraced a sense of north-ern nationalism as strongly as Kearney held on to her southern patriotism, because from Willard's youth through the 1880s, she had been a staunch regionalist. Born outside of Rochester, New York, in 1839, Willard spent most of her childhood in Oberlin, Ohio, attending the church of the famous revivalist Charles Grandison Finney. After moving to Wisconsin, Willard developed a deep love for humanity and for the American nation. After reading an abolitionist tract, "The Slave's Friend," she felt a keen "sense of brotherhood of all nations as really one, and of God as the equal Father of all races." At the same time, she learned to love the United States with an almost religious devotion. "Mother had talked to us so much about America that from earliest recollections," Willard wrote in her autobiogra-phy, "we had spelled nation with a capital N." Like many of her contemporaries, Willard conflated nationalism and religion. Patriotism, she asserted, "was the most

attractive form of religion that my reckless childhood knew," and she firmly believed that the United States was "GOD'S COUNTRY." In the mid-1850s, she became
a devout follower of the Republican Party and reveled in the nomination and election of Abraham Lincoln. When the war broke out, she joined other northern
whites in denouncing the South.[6]

During the 1860s and 1870s, Willard rose to prominence as an educator, a religious leader, an outspoken proponent of women's rights, and a temperance activist.
She attended the Northwestern Female College in Evanston, Illinois, and received
her degree in 1859. A month after the attack on Fort Sumter, as she recovered from
a bout with tuberculosis, Willard professed faith in God, was baptized, and joined
the Methodist Church. She then taught at a variety of schools—eleven in sixteen
years—eventually becoming dean of the Woman's College at Northwestern University, her alma mater. In 1874, the Illinois Republican Party nominated her for
state superintendent of public instruction, although she did not win the election.
In that same year, she became the corresponding secretary for the WCTU, which
had recently formed. Then, in 1876, Willard put her WCTU responsibilities
on hold in order to join forces with Dwight Moody's evangelical coalition at the
Boston revivals. She eventually broke with Moody because he attempted to cir-
cumscribe the roles of women in the ministry. Writing to Moody's wife, Willard
claimed that she had been "devoted to the advancement of women" for all her life
and maintained that female leaders were critical in religious enterprises. "I firmly
believe God has a work for them to do as evangelists," she argued, "as bearers of
Christ's message to the ungospeled, to the prayer meeting, to the church generally
and the world at large, such as most people have not dreamed." Willard returned
to full-time work with the WCTU and put all of her energies into temperance reform. In 1879, she was elected to the presidency of the WCTU, and by the time of
her death in 1898 was hailed as the most powerful temperance and women's rights
leader in the nation, if not the world.[7]

Willard's power extended throughout the United States. Her effect on Belle
Kearney was enormous. After hearing Willard speak in 1889, Kearney joined the
WCTU and began "her ministry" to form WCTU chapters for young women. She
read temperance pamphlets and other literature voraciously; she traveled throughout Mississippi giving speeches on the need for temperance; and in the following
years, she toured other southern states speaking to a variety of groups and organizations. The WCTU offered her and other southern women an entrance into public events by describing these debates as sacred obligations. "Its purpose," Kearney
wrote of the WCTU, "is to carry the philosophy of Jesus Christ into politics, to

make a practical application of the laws of God to those of men." In 1889 she represented Mississippi at the WCTU's national convention in Chicago, and this meeting constituted another watershed in her life. It was the first time she met with and worked alongside a large body of northern women. "That was my first attendance upon a *national* convention," she stressed. The WCTU was a marvel because it provided an institutional structure in which women from the North and South could unite, find courage, and battle for the Lord.[8]

Inspired by the organization and by her new sense of importance, Kearney gained the confidence to speak out on racial antagonism in the South. She considered the radical Republicans' attempt to create a system of integrated education imprudent. "[C]o-education of the races is not tolerated" in the South, she wrote, and "[i]t is an unwise friend of the negro who attempts to alter this custom. It is futile to advance a plea for the unreasonableness and unrighteousness of race prejudice." Instead, Kearney advocated the passage of educational requirements that would restrict voting to only the most learned immigrants and persons of color. Such a plan would go a long way to purify the ballot. "This system has worked admirably" in Mississippi and Louisiana, she claimed, "in substituting a rule of intelligence for that of ignorance; it is worth the serious consideration of all states that have a large foreign population." To her, the growing tide of immigrants from southern and eastern Europe to the North and the large numbers of African Americans in the South had no business voting since they were obviously inferior to "Anglo-Saxons."[9]

Kearney's tale was one example of the WCTU's and Frances Willard's impact during the late nineteenth century. As northern WCTU members reached out to the South, thousands of southern women responded as Kearney had. They enlisted in the WCTU and assumed new roles as lecturers, organizers, and political activists. Not only did the WCTU motivate southern white women to speak publicly, but it also created bonds of sisterhood between thousands of northern and southern women. In the 1880s, with chapters in every state and territory, the WCTU became the most influential American reform organization. With a dues-paying membership of nearly two hundred thousand during the 1890s and hundreds of thousands affiliated members, the WCTU was one of the largest organizations in the country. Willard and others in the WCTU drew a great deal of attention to their nationwide reach when pushing for women's political rights. Historian Ruth Bordin has contended that the WCTU was the "major vehicle for the women's movement" in the postbellum period, while Gaines Foster has recently highlighted its impact in the formation of a "Christian lobby" in Washington, D.C., that sought to influence the national government on "moral issues," such as alcohol use, birth control, censorship, and education.[10] American nationalism, in fact, served as a powerful tool for the WCTU.[11]

Historians have usually explained the WCTU's success by focusing on the ways its leaders employed concepts of "domesticity" and "disinterested morality" to characterize political debates such as temperance legislation and female suffrage as private matters. Barbara Epstein, Nina Silber, and Rebecca Edwards have suggested that the WCTU offered disenfranchised women a public voice by extending the "private sphere." By asserting that women would use their votes to protect their children and families, the WCTU sought to domesticate politics. In this way, the temperance movement had a long and close relationship with the broader "women's rights" crusade. Willard and Susan B. Anthony were close friends, and Willard and other WCTU members regularly took part in meetings of the National Woman Suffrage Association (NWSA). The conservative feminism of the WCTU proved especially important in bringing southern women into the organization. Recognizing that many southern whites were reluctant to accept women as public and political figures, northern temperance leaders presented their crusade as a natural extension of the "domestic sphere." Because nineteenth-century whites considered mothers the chief protectors of "home and hearth" and since alcoholic husbands terrorized their wives and children, women had every responsibility to battle against intemperance. In effect, they brought their venture into the public realm by focusing on the private ramifications of reforms and legislation.[12]

This gendered and unifying "rhetoric of domesticity," however, also had a racial component. As the WCTU created an institutional space and ideology that united northern and southern white women in pursuits of public power, it also offered them a podium from which they could comment upon and shape debates over racial issues. For the most part, whites in the WCTU echoed Kearney's arguments justifying racial segregation and disenfranchisement. Whites in the WCTU either ignored African Americans or used temperance as a tool to exercise social control over blacks and immigrants alike.[13] Like Kearney, many endorsed segregated schools and suffrage restrictions. Women in the WCTU also constructed their arguments for female suffrage by contrasting themselves with African Americans and immigrants, whom they deemed unfit for citizenship. The WCTU's allegiance to white supremacy appealed both to white northerners who were nervous about the influx of new immigrants to the nation and to white southerners who were concerned about maintaining their superiority over African Americans. From the late 1870s, when the organization made its first inroads into the South, to the 1890s, when it reached its apogee, the WCTU played a crucial role in creating a forum in which northern and southern whites could together sanctify racial segregation, disenfranchisement, and even violence.[14]

In addition to the rhetorics of domesticity and social benevolence, leaders in the WCTU employed narrative strategies that invoked images of and memories from the Civil War to galvanize northern and southern women. The Civil War provided analogies, metaphors, and a language for WCTU leaders to draw upon. They conceived of themselves as a new and holy army, a national "army of women," that would replace the old sectional forces of civil war and bitterness. Drunkenness and the saloon served as common enemies against which northern and southern white Christian women aligned. Through the use of military, domestic, and religious idioms and metaphors, leaders in the WCTU sought to form a national constituency of white women that would help ease sectional grievances and construct a stronger sense of white American nationalism. They firmly tied temperance and women's political rights to the re-ascendance of the white republic.

I

Throughout the nineteenth century, there had been sporadic moments of temperance agitation, but none could rival the one that launched the WCTU into being— "The Crusade" of 1873–1874. During the winter of these years, women throughout the North arose to attack "the saloon." It began in Fredonia, New York, a town of about twenty-six hundred residents. After a lecture by reformer Diocletian "Dio" Lewis on "The Duty of Christian Women in the Temperance Work" on December 14, 1873 (a speech he had given almost 340 times previously), local women decided to act. While men filled their church to pray the next day, women marched to local liquor stores. They sang hymns, prayed, and entreated the owners to cease dispensing liquor. In the weeks and months following the Fredonia Crusade, women from Maine to Iowa replicated it. Over six months, more than fifty thousand women marched in more than nine hundred locations. Often, women barged into saloons to shame vendors and drinkers publicly. As one reformer described it, the women would enter a bar and "offer up a special petition for him [the bartender]; he has to stand meekly there behind the bar, under the eyes of a great concourse of ladies who are better than he is and aware of it, and hear all the iniquities of his business divulged to the angels above, accompanied by a sharp sting of wishes for his regeneration. . . . If he holds out bravely, the crusaders hold out more bravely still."[15]

From the very beginning, some female reformers conceived of themselves as soldiers on a religious and military campaign. One such woman was Eliza Stewart.

Orphaned at twelve, she had become a schoolteacher in Ohio and had obtained the nickname "Mother" for her service during the Civil War in the U.S. Sanitary Commission. She firmly believed that in 1873 and 1874 a "spiritual baptism . . . came down upon the women." One of the most influential women in the crusade, Stewart plainly described her involvement as a religious calling. She believed that God told her that he "*will* hear and answer the cries of the people. . . . And to prove it beyond a peradventure, and for all generations to come, I will call forth my weakest instruments, my hand-maidens, and set them in battle arrayed against the most powerful enemy of mankind. . . . And it shall be unto them according to their faith. I will give the enemy into their hand."[16]

Although some temperance women played upon domestic themes, claiming that they were "meekly doing the will of the Father who pities his children," other supporters as well as their opponents readily employed martial rhetoric and took aggressive and sometimes violent action.[17] Female temperance reformers styled themselves as "crusaders," and their activities became known as "the Crusade." During the winter, women "marched" to saloons, and caricatures showed them in military-like formations. (See figure 14.)

Temperance women referred to their picketing and demonstrating at saloons as "sieges," and when vendors decided to cease selling alcohol, they labeled it "surrendering." In a clear mixture of the religious and the martial, Mother Stewart became both the "Deborah"—a biblical leader of Israel—and the "Philip Sheridan"—a northern Civil War general—of the campaign. The publishers of her memoirs recounted that "our author dashed along the lines of forces through Ohio from the lake to the river, and from the East to the West, everywhere, Sheridan-like, inspiring the forces by her presence, and firing the multitude with her speeches."[18] Temperance opponents responded to these "lines of forces" with their own physical force. They doused crusaders with dirty water or stale beer. In Plano, Illinois, "the contents of baser toilet-ware" rained down upon protesters from a window. In Ashland, Nebraska, paint covered several women. Crowds in Cincinnati threw stones and old boots at the women, while rotten eggs rained down upon organizers in Manchester, Iowa.[19]

In 1874, the scores of local women's temperance organizations that had formed in the winter banded together to create the "National Woman's Christian Temperance Union." Serving as president from 1874 to 1879, Annie Wittenmyer, a temperance organizer who had been a member of the Iowa State Sanitary Commission during the Civil War, directed the WCTU to focus primarily on the individual use of alcohol and to avoid demands for legal prohibition or political involvement. She preferred that WCTU members use "moral suasion" to bring change. Like the crusaders of 1873, they prayed, signed petitions, and tried to convince saloon owners to stop selling alcohol and drinkers to stop drinking it. Rarely did they actively seek political reform or demand female suffrage during these initial years.[20]

In 1879, when Frances Willard became the president of the WCTU, the organization became much more committed to radically redefining America's political and social landscape. Rather than only focus on moral suasion, Willard encouraged her followers to "Do Everything." Along with the temperance cause, she advocated female suffrage, women in church pulpits, and any other reform that would expand women's social and political power in the nation. Under her leadership, the WCTU experienced massive growth and a new vitality, even achieving a large constituency in the conservative South.[21] Willard's contemporaries recognized her as one of the nation's finest orators, organizers, and leaders. Belle Kearney asserted that "Mrs. Willard's leadership was incomparable. She had the great power of drawing more people to her, and of keeping them bound by the closest bonds of devotion, than any being that ever lived. . . . Miss Willard was a marvelous orator, organizer, author, statesman, [and] Christian." Another WCTU member rhapsodized that Willard was "one of God's best gifts to the American women of the nineteenth century, for she has done more to enlarge our sympathies, widen our outlook, and develop our gifts, than any man, or any other woman of her time."[22]

Willard and other northern WCTU leaders viewed their organization as a new and holy army in a war for human liberation. To them, religion and politics could not be separated. "The Bible is the most political of books," she told the WCTU national convention in Nashville, Tennessee, in 1887. The goal of the WCTU was to "recognize Christ as the great world-force for righteousness and purity, and enthrone him King of nations in faith, as He will one day be in fact, through Christian politics and laws, no less than Christian being."[23] The movement was not just holy. It was militant Christian reform, at least in rhetoric. Willard called the temperance cause "the new abolition war, in which Northern and Southern bayonets point the same way."[24] Mother Stewart referred to the women's actions as "temperance warfare" and asserted that saloon keepers and drugstore owners who sold liquor were "worse than southern slave-drivers."[25] Even Wittenmyer, who generally deemphasized political involvement, claimed in 1876 that "we have held the fort in defensive warfare long enough, and the time, in my opinion, has come for us to make a decided aggressive movement; and I know that many of our best workers are this hour awaiting your orders for an assault on the enemy's lines."[26] Unlike the hymns of Moody's revivals that encouraged social passivity, WCTU music was aggressive. In "Stand up for Prohibition," (an adaptation of "Stand up for Jesus") temperance women sang of themselves as "soldiers true and brave," and in the song "Fight for the Right," they constructed themselves as warriors:

> Fight on, fight on, your cause is just,
> And pebbles smooth will save,
> If only they are hurled aright,
> Thro' ribs of steel with armor bright,
> With lightning speed they'll wing away.[27]

Throughout the late nineteenth century, the WCTU maintained a cooperative, yet deeply strained, relationship with the northern churches and their denominational leaders. The WCTU embraced women from a variety of denominational backgrounds and made it a point to welcome members of evangelical and liberal churches. Many of the northern Protestant churches demonstrated earnest support for the WCTU, inviting its leaders to speak in their churches and opening their halls to the WCTU's local and national conventions. But northern denominational leaders did not unequivocally support the women of the WCTU. When Willard and other WCTU women sought to attend and participate in general denominational conferences, battles over "the woman question" ensued. Northern Methodists and Presbyterians, in particular, fought vigorously over whether to accept women as deaconesses and assembly members. In response to recurring rebuffs from denominational leaders and attacks upon women's public leadership in the church, Willard wrote *Woman in the Pulpit* (1888), a brilliant call for female ministers and theologians. It was principally within the WCTU, however, that most of its members found a place to follow their religious and social convictions.[28]

During the 1870s the WCTU grew in size and strength in the North, but had few enlistees in the South. Of the former Confederate States, only Arkansas and Louisiana had state unions as of 1880.[29] A variety of factors explaine why the WCTU failed to garner a mass following in the South in the 1870s. Before the Civil War, women's political activism had been associated with the abolitionist movement, and it understandably had few friends in the South.[30] Southern churches, moreover, were more reticent than their northern counterparts to encourage women to speak in public venues regarding any issue. In fact, they often opposed it.[31] One woman from Tennessee admitted that the deep-seated conservatism of southern society hindered the movement. "I can not hope to convey to your mind any idea of what uphill work it is to get our Christian women to realize that they are called upon, or in any wise able to do anything outside their own doors," she wrote to the WCTU national convention in 1876. "The prejudices of the Southern people are against women doing anything in public, and especially opposed to the Woman's Temperance Crusade. Particularly is this true of our ministers." Extensive poverty in the South and lack of formal organizing skills also made some southern white women unsure of whether or not they could form viable temperance organizations. In 1879, the Committee on Southern Work reported that "the Christian *women* of the South yet feel great timidity in the presence of the almost insuperable pecuniary and other difficulties in the way of organizing work to be done by themselves." [32]

At least one northern WCTU leader believed that sectional bitterness and animosity also played a role in keeping southern women out of the union. The hurts and pains of the Civil War continued to be felt, especially because Democratic and Republican politicians repeatedly invoked sectionalism to attack their opponents. "The sectional prejudices had in the past kept us apart and given each section erroneous and exaggerated ideas of the other, and the war had intensified these sentiments into bitter hate," asserted Mother Stewart in the late 1870s. Reconstruction further exacerbated tensions between the North and the South. "Then the political 'reconstruction,' and the forever harping on the 'bloody shirt' and 'lost cause,' in every political campaign, by unprincipled leaders, was serving to increase the hate and widen the breach,'" she further noted. In short, by 1880, "there was no unity or community of interests" in the United States, and this hindered female solidarity. [33]

Northern temperance women strongly desired to build a national constituency in order to increase their social and political might. Recognizing that southerners were largely "still 'out of the union'" as of 1877, Mrs. J. C. Johnson of Memphis suggested that the WCTU focus greater energy on the South in the following years. She recommended "that workers from a distance be induced to commence organizing in Tennessee" and other southern states. Northern leaders felt that without southern support they would have little chance at influencing political legislation. President Wittenmyer argued, "We can never gain a decided national victory till we secure the co-operation of the South." Frances Willard told delegates to the WCTU national convention in 1880 that "the Southern States, in which we have hardly gained a foothold, demand our next attention." [34]

During the late 1870s and early 1880s, WCTU leaders hoped that by reaching out to southern white women, the WCTU would help reunite the nation. Mother Stewart explicitly claimed that God directed her and the WCTU to help heal the wounds of the past. "The Lord showed me," she wrote, "that He had given into the hands of the Christian Temperance Women, with the watchword and battle cry, 'For God and Home and Native Land,' to reach out the olive branch of Christian sisterhood and to pour the oil of peace on the turbid and forever seething sea of political strife and sectional animosities."[35] In fact, both Stewart and Willard referred to WCTU work in the South as "our new national peace policy."[36] A writer to the *Christian Advocate* recognized that "I know that many of the good women [in the WCTU] hoped that such waving of the white ribbon (the Union's badge) over the South would awaken desires for national fraternity in other interests than temperance."[37]

Members of the WCTU did much more than merely discuss the importance of bringing southern women into the Union. They set out on energetic campaigns to enlist these sisters. In her presidential addresses at the WCTU national convention in 1878, Wittenmyer implored the delegates to consider traveling south. "To meet and win the conservative women of the South, the best consecrated talent we have, wielded with prudence, will be needed," she proclaimed. "Every advantage should be eagerly followed up till we win the women of the South as co-laborers." During a convention address the following year, Mother Stewart quoted a southern woman who implored northerners to head south and help build the movement: "We see the great need of Woman's Christian Temperance work among us, and are willing to engage in it; but we have no one who can lead the movement, and no means with which to begin the work."[38]

Several high-ranking leaders accepted the call to bring the South into the Union. President Wittenmyer, Mother Stewart, Judith Foster, and Frances Willard spent considerable time touring the South, speaking in churches, theaters, and temperance organizations, and helping in the organization of local and state WCTUs. During their trips these women sought to create a national "army of women" dedicated to warring against saloons, intemperance, and other sorts of immorality. But they also attempted to accomplish what American politicians had failed to do throughout the postwar era: bring a new sense of national cohesiveness to the United States.[39]

Although President Wittenmyer visited the South in 1876 and organized a few unions, Mother Stewart's tours in 1877 and 1880 were the first trips in which large numbers of southern women joined. Initially invited to Virginia by the Good Templars, Stewart anticipated hostility from southern white women. She believed that lingering sectional grievances would keep the women from her. Mother Stewart feared "that the dear women, remembering all they had suffered—and I could see too plainly everywhere what the terrible conflict had cost them—would not feel that they could co-operate with one whose people were responsible, as they claimed, for the ruin of their country." Her worries, however, were quickly allayed. As Stewart traveled and lectured throughout Virginia, southern whites treated her with kindness. They entertained her during meals and carriage rides through the countryside, and she captivated them with tales of the "crusade of 1873." As she told these women about "the wonderful baptism that came down upon the women" of 1873, she recalled, "tears would rain down their cheeks, and . . . they would beg, 'Oh, tell us more, tell us more.'" The decisions of former Confederate men and women to join her in a battle against liquor led Stewart to marvel at the possibilities of creating a new national coalition that would bring together the former antagonists. "These dear friends were on the Confederate side in the war," she wrote in her autobiography, "but ready to join now with might and influence with the Northern Crusader against our common enemy."[40]

Stewart formed only a handful of WCTU unions during her first trip, but she carried her concern for the South with her in the following years. She made it a point to convince northern women to put forth more effort into the South. The actions of the WCTU were crucial to forging a new solidarity among Americans, she told the delegates to the national convention of 1880. "So much depends upon our success—more than appears on the surface." She again lamented that internal discord racked the United States because of demagogic politicians: "The antagonisms of the past, instead of being permitted to remain in the grave of the past, are brought forth periodically and played upon and intensified by politicians more intent upon the success of their party than the welfare of the country." But now, God had commissioned the WCTU to reunite the United States. "I do believe if we had a tithe of the means that are now being spent to widen instead of heal the breach," Mother Stewart announced, "the Lord would not only enable the women to drive the nail into the temple of this Sisera, the scourge of North and South, but would, through the preaching of our blessed gospel of temperance, righteousness, and peace, give the land, a united country, into our hands."[41] In the years after her trip, Stewart's concern and prayers went out to the South. "Though busy in whatever phase of work I found to do," she reminisced, "I did not lose sight of the Southern field, to which my heart continually turned, and for which I still prayed the blessed Lord to give me an open door."[42]

Her prayers were answered in 1879 when she became chair of the WCTU Committee on Southern Work. The committee immediately sent a circular letter to a host of southern newspapers, in which it extended its hand to women of the South as "Christian sisters," entreating them to join their struggle. Stewart and the committee expressed a strong desire to create female bonds of affection that could transcend sectionalism. "Neither is there any sectarianism or sectionalism" in the WCTU, the letter claimed.[43] On the heels of the circular letter, Stewart made another venture into the South in 1880. Both the letter and Stewart were well received, and they spurred southern membership. During the trip, Stewart helped form chapters in Chattanooga, Tennessee, and in Atlanta, Griffith, Forsyth, and Macon, Georgia. Scores of women thanked Stewart for her kind words. One from Mississippi professed that they reinspired her to fight for temperance. "[W]hen I saw your circular in the Vicksburg *Herald*," this woman wrote, "I was so struck with the magnanimity of the Northern people that I was stimulated to make another effort in the temperance cause." Another woman from Arkansas believed that Stewart was a gift from God: "I can indeed say it is the Lord's doings." While she toured the South, ministers and politicians showed remarkable openness toward Stewart and her cause. In August she spoke at Democratic and Greenback Party barbecues. The Methodist Church, South, enthusiastically endorsed her trip, and one Methodist minister went so far as to say that Stewart and the WCTU were "just what he had been praying for."[44]

In the late 1880s, when Stewart wrote her "memories" of her involvement in the temperance cause, she congratulated herself for doing God's work in helping to bring southern women into the WCTU and reconciling the nation. "It was the beginning," she boasted. "I went by the call of the Master, carrying the olive branch of the W.C.T.U., and the people—women and men—gave me a warm welcome and cordially co-operated with me in planting it in that warm, Southern soil." Mother Stewart believed that her actions had helped usher southern women into a grand new army. "These, our Southern sisters, are pushing the battle to the gates of the enemy," she rejoiced, "and are, by their untiring zeal and practical methods, often giving us hints we would do well to act upon." Ultimately, the WCTU and its southern members had accomplished what they believed God intended and what male politicians had failed to achieve: the reforging of the American republic. "While thus working for their own beloved South land, they have gladly joined us in bridging the chasm of sectional hate. . . . And so we are once more a united people,— united through the loving missions of the Woman's Christian Temperance Union," Stewart insisted.[45]

Stewart, however, was not the key northern woman to usher southern women into the WCTU and make it a truly national organization. That role belonged to Willard, and she played it marvelously. More than any other leader in the WCTU, she drew together a southern white constituency and encouraged northern women to reconstruct their images of southern society. From 1881 to 1896, Willard made six highly publicized tours of the South and showed impressive acumen in rallying southern women to the temperance cause. In 1881, she spent fourteen weeks in the South and spoke in more than fifty cities. The next year she lectured in sixty-six cities and towns in fourteen southern states. In a whirlwind tour through Texas in 1882, for example, Willard visited sixteen of the most populous cities and towns in the state and spoke to record crowds at each venue. From the 1880s to the 1890s, Willard exerted an enormous amount of energy to make the WCTU a truly national union.[46]

Sectional reconciliation and the subtle political influence of women stood as central themes of Willard's tour. Perhaps her most famous temperance story, which she told in almost every southern venue, was of a "southern incident" first narrated to her by a "gentleman in Texas." A Kentuckian, "John," served as the central character in the tale. After many years of hard drinking, he decided to sober up. John had "got the flask out of his side pocket and the New Testament in there instead." On one Election Day, his wife implored him to cast a vote for temperance. "Dear John, you know I never said a word about your politics before," she told him, "but if I've been a comfort to you, do please go to-day and vote against the saloon for my sake and that of the little ones." John, the story went, "made no reply, but went straight out of the house and over to the polls." There, his friends encouraged him to cast his "regular regulation ballot." But this time John wanted nothing to do with them: "[A] temperance man stood by with earnest face and a bunch of different notes. 'See here, I reckon I'll sample your lot,' said John." After casting his ballot, he looked at his old buddies and commented, "Boys, I've always joined with you before, but, by the grace of God, here goes a vote *for Sallie and the children*."[47] This tale highlighted the virtue of southern men and women, and it became extremely popular within the WCTU. *"For Sallie and the children"* became an oft-repeated slogan.[48] Moreover, Willard even declared that this narrative had national conciliatory power, as northern men learned from and emulated John's example. She wrote, "It has been a great comfort to me to hear from different parts of the State of Northern men as noble as tis generous Southron, who said, as they cast in their ballots . . . in Iowa, 'Well, I do this just as John did, away down South, 'for Sallie and the children.'"[49] Northerners, in short, had much to learn from southern men and women like John and his wife.

With her tales about the Civil War, Willard echoed the grand evangelistic sermons of Dwight Moody in extolling the similarities of northern and southern combatants. In one of her stories, she spun about "one time during the war, the opposing armies lay idle, close beside each other, only the waters of the Rappa-hannock dividing them." The men, however, were more interested in playing with musical instruments than fighting with military arms: "[E]very time a Union band would strike up 'The Star Spangled Banner,' or other strain sweet to the boys in blue, a Confederate band would oppose it with 'Dixie' or some kindred sentiment. Tired of the contest, both would subside into quiet." On one night, however, an-other tune brought the men of both camps together:

> [O]ne evening a lone bugler sat musing on the scenes about the Northern fireside, where he knew they missed him. Instinctively he placed the bugle to his lips and piped alone the mellow strains of "Home Sweet Home." Yet only a moment did the dear boy play alone. His comrades picked up their instruments of music and shared his reverie of home. A moment more and hark! what note is it that comes over the swift waters! Not "Dixie" now, nor other discord, but the loved harmony of "Home, Sweet Home,"—that is al-ways the same all around the world. Then up and down each river-bank it spread till, if tradition says right, all bands of both armies were harmo-niously filling the fields with the blessed recollection that every man in all those ranks had a home he loved and would see happy.[50]

"Home" was the one place and feeling upon which northern and southern boys could agree.

Willard's trips to the South were a smashing success. Organizationally, she helped set up scores of chapters, energized those that had been exhausted, and helped form a dynamic band of leadership within the WCTU and southern politics. Willard was directly responsible for aiding in the formation of unions in Maryland, Virginia, North Carolina, South Carolina, Georgia, Florida, Alabama, Mississippi, Arkansas, Tennessee, and Kentucky.[51] Between Stewart's first visit in 1877 and Willard's final one in 1896, women in Alabama, South Carolina, North Carolina, Florida, Georgia, Missouri, Texas, and Virginia formed state WCTU chapters and sent delegates to the national conventions. By the mid-1890s, more than ten thou-sand southern women had joined the WCTU, and thousands of others were con-nected to it in one way or another.[52] Temperance women recognized the stunning growth of the WCTU in the South, one remarking at the national convention in 1883 that "[s]teadily during the year has the work in the South grown and strengthened."[53]

Southern men and women testified to Willard's brilliance in the South. In lavishing her with praise, they demonstrated a remarkable willingness to overlook previous sectional animosity. Dr. A. G. Haywood of Emory University, for instance, commented, "Few persons in our country have been more liberally endowed with natural gifts. Modest, self-poised, with masterful use of her resources, she gave us the best address I have heard on the subject of temperance."[54] Missouri's *Hannibal Morning Journal* likewise reported, "Miss Willard spoke for over an hour, and it must be confessed that hers was the greatest speech ever delivered by a lady in Hannibal. The effort was an oratorical gem, Miss Willard holding from first to last the undivided attention of the vast audience by the power of her eloquence."[55]

The most laudatory statements came from southern women, many of whom considered Willard's visit a watershed in their lives. They expressed a special kinship with her. Seeing and hearing a woman captivate and motivate public crowds inspired them. Many viewed Willard as a gift of God sent to liberate men from alcohol and southern women from silence. Belle Kearney remembered that after first hearing Willard in a meeting, she "lay awake all night for sheer gladness. It was such a wonderful revelation to me that a woman like Miss Willard could exist. I thanked God and took courage for humanity."[56] A thirteen-year-old student at the Female College in Columbia, South Carolina, recorded in her diary that Willard was "one of the greatest women in America." After attending two of Willard's lectures, this girl felt "just charmed with her! She is just perfectly lovely. . . . She came to the College one morning, and delivered a talk to the girls. . . . Lots of the girls cried when she went."[57] A woman from Arkansas wrote to Willard, "When I know your mission to our Sunny South is 'love and peace,' we wellcome [sic] you warmly and we feel that our hearts beat in unison with yours."[58] Southern temperance women admired Willard so deeply that they resolved to thank her on behalf of their section at the WCTU's national convention in 1881. "[I]n the name of the whole South," they proclaimed, "we return our heartfelt thanks for . . . Miss Frances E. Willard."[59]

Several southern men and women made direct connections between Willard's missions, memories of the Civil War, and hopes for national reconciliation. When a Methodist bishop who had supposedly fired the first shot against the Union at Fort Sumter in 1861 introduced Willard, he made it clear that her crusade was one of peace and reconciliation. "This woman, this Northern woman, this Northern temperance woman," professed P. F. Stevens of Charleston, South Carolina, "brings us the magic initials of the W.C.T.U. Shall we not interpret them in our case to mean, We come to unite the North and the South, and we come to upset the liquor traffic?"[60] After hearing a speech in which Willard quoted Frances Miles Finch's "The Blue and the Gray," a group of southern women sent her a basket of flowers with blue and gray ribbon tied around it. They attached a note to the gift expressing thanks for Willard's commitments to national solidarity and echoed her calls for reunion. "We feel so deeply grateful for your kind, brave words, in defense of that harmony we so earnestly desire." [61]

Suffragist and temperance leader Caroline Merrick asserted that the WCTU came at an ideal moment for white women in the South. Since they no longer had to manage their slaves, and since many of them felt disoriented during the postwar years by the massive social changes occurring around them, southern white women now needed something to occupy their time and give them hope. "There was a peculiar fitness in the time of Miss Willard's early visits to the South," Merrick remembered in 1901. "Women who had been fully occupied [with] . . . the responsibilities of a dependency of slaves, were now tossed to and fro amidst the exigencies and bewilderments of strange and for the most part painful circumstances." "Frances Willard gave to many of them a holy purpose," she continued, "directing [them] into broader fields of spiritual and philanthropic culture than they had ever known." [62] Another woman put it more simply when she noted that the WCTU "was the first ray of hope that had come into our lives since the war." [63] Like Willard and other northern WCTU leaders, some southern women trusted that the WCTU would bring a new sense of national unity. They explicitly constructed Willard as a "national" woman and not merely a "northern" one. Baltimore's Georgia McLeod quoted another southern woman as writing to the North, "*Your* Miss Willard is our Miss Willard as well; she belongs to the country, and we claim a share in her counsel and teachings." [64]

Not only did Willard want to bring southern women into the WCTU, but she also committed herself to convincing northern women to accept southern whites as sisters and brothers. She spent substantial time characterizing the South as a land of virtue and righteousness in order to appeal to her northern audiences. Willard's trips to the South thoroughly altered her perceptions of southern society. She admitted that, like many women in her audience, she had long suspected southern whites of harboring sectional bitterness. "I labored under the hallucination that the South secretly waited its opportunities to re-open the issues of the war." [65] But as she spent time with southerners and as they appreciated her work, Willard grew fond of them. In her autobiography, she recounted that southerners had become her "firmest friends." She felt ashamed for her earlier feelings of sectional disdain. Her trip to the South "was the most unique of all my history," Willard concluded. "It 'reconstructed' me." [66]

Willard sought to "reconstruct" other northern WCTU women by depicting southern women, men, and society as honorable. She told a reporter for the *Voice*, a temperance periodical based in New York, "I am a true lover of the Southern people. Have spoken and worked in perhaps 200 of their towns and cities, have been taken into their love and confidence at scores of hospitable firesides." [67] In her autobiography and two chronicles of women's temperance activities, *Woman and Temperance* (1883) and *Woman of the Century* (1893), Willard portrayed southern women in glowing terms. She lauded Baltimore's Georgia Hulse McLeod for her "pure womanliness and exalted piety" and considered Sallie Chapin of South Carolina "a great-hearted woman." Mrs. Jefferson Davis was "one of the best talkers imaginable, a queenly looking woman of cosmopolitan culture and broad progressive views." [68] Willard also extolled a variety of men of the South, especially its poets and novelists. The writings of Paul Hayne were "*par excellence*," while Father Abram Ryan was "umatched in fire and pathos by our Northern verse of that unequaled period." She thanked southerners for their cordiality, and unlike the missionaries to Dixie during Reconstruction who had denounced southern whites as barbaric and largely uneducated, Willard described the South as a land brimming with intellectual vigor: "The South is moving steadily toward its rightful place as one born of the purple of literary power." In the late 1880s she praised the southern temperance movement for its amazing growth in size and authority. At a Decoration Day service in 1888, where more than five hundred former Union and Confederate soldiers were present, she paid homage to the Confederacy and the Lost Cause by quoting Ryan's "The Sword of Lee" and then proceded to tell the men that "I never expected to speak with pride about the Solid South as such, but surely I may do this now that it is becoming solid for the 'dry ticket.'" To Willard, because northern and southern whites were of the same race, they could not remain angry with one another. They were "one Anglo-Saxon race," she proclaimed, and this "one heritage of a queenly language and a heroic history of hardships mutually borne" made it "hard for us to hate each other." [69]

Willard also sought to reconcile northern and southern white women by claiming that southerners had ceased fighting the Civil War in their hearts and souls. Her invented South appeared strikingly similar to the one in Harriet Beecher Stowe's *Palmetto Leaves*. In a host of interviews reported in northern newspapers, Willard described the South as a peaceful land of national pride and racial peace. Asked how she was treated in the South, Willard repeatedly commented, "Everywhere my welcome was cordial, spontaneous, fraternal, [and] beyond all my experience at the north even." [70] She also claimed that former Confederates wanted to forget past sectional disagreements, telling WCTU delegates that southerners had accepted "in good faith" the "issues of the war." [71] Now southerners wanted peace and goodwill. "Their widely prevailing spirit is for peace," she reported: "There is, I think, a much greater willingness on the part of Southern people to know us of the North and to fraternize with us than they usually have credit for." In addition, Willard depicted race relations in the South as harmonious. "I found the era of good feeling [between whites and blacks] had indeed set in," she recounted. "The real people there," she wrote, "the great middle-class of whites and the most intelligent class of blacks have emphatically gone to work. They have largely abandoned politics as a sectional trade; they do not encourage the few relics of the Confederacy who are forever disposed to warm over old feuds."[72]

In many ways, Willard's radiant portrayal of the South served to counteract negative depictions of the region still being voiced from those committed to including African Americans in the nation as full citizens, especially the politician and novelist Albion Tourgée. In his semi-autobiographical account of his life in North Carolina during Reconstruction, A Fool's Errand, and several other works, Tourgée blasted the South as a land of violence, hostility, and barbarism. He narrated tales of Ku Klux Klan members killing innocent blacks, of whites manipulating and exploiting freedpeople, and of African Americans and their true white friends bravely resisting white supremacy. Tourgée carried forward the radical Reconstruction vision of a nation remade according to civic nationalistic commitments, rather than one built around perceived racial similarities and differences. He described a white South unwilling to cooperate with northerners and in defiance of federal laws that protected the rights of African Americans. To him, the North and the South could never truly reconcile under these circumstances, for they were two utterly different societies: "The North and the South are simply convenient names for two distinct, hostile, and irreconcilable ideas,—two civilizations they are sometimes called, especially of the South." The two societies, he contended, were locked in a "contest between civilization and semi-barbarism."[73]

Several northern and southern whites, including Willard, recognized the vast differences between her portrayal of the South and Tourgée's. While Tourgée endeavored to stir up sectional rancor in order to alert northerners to the need for federal protection for African Americans and white Republicans in the South, Willard described the South as a place of racial harmony. Regarding her trips to the South, she juxtaposed her experiences in the South with Tourgée's. In a letter to the New York Independent, she wrote, "Many good and thoughtful people had predicted that this would prove 'a fool's errand' number two," but her encounters were quite different. One northern editor suggested that Willard's "story puts to shame the efforts of the Tourgée Class of pettifogging political agitators."[74] Although it is difficult, if not impossible, to assess how successful Willard was in transforming northern attitudes toward the South, she at least reflected the shift from negative to positive views. One southern newspaper writer did suggest that her words and actions were especially crucial. "She traveled throughout the South last winter," the *Mississippi Daily Clarion* reported, "and by letters, addresses, etc., in the North, has done much to bring that section to a better understanding of the Southern people."[75]

II

While Willard endeavored to bring an "era of good feeling" to northern and southern whites, rank-and-file temperance women forged ties that transcended sectional interests at WCTU national conventions. These meetings served as sites of national reunion and sisterhood. As thousands of women in the South and North convened, they interacted socially and befriended one another in personal and professional ways. These conventions provided spaces where WCTU women could proclaim and enact national solidarity. In speeches and poems, and on banners and posters, temperance women announced their commitments to national healing and female solidarity. National meetings served as moments when the reunion of heart and hand that Willard so desperately wanted could happen and when American nationalism could be turned into a powerful tool for advancing women's political rights. It was from these meetings and with national fraternity as her primary theme that Willard launched her effort to drive WCTU women out of the Republican and Democratic camps and into third-party politics.

While only a handful of southern women attended the first WCTU national conventions in the 1870s, their numbers grew substantially in the 1880s and 1890s. Willard made sure to invite southerners and to make them feel comfortable at the conventions. During her first visit to the South, for instance, she encouraged Jane Elizabeth Sibley, the newly elected president of the chapter in Augusta, Georgia, and Missouria Stokes, the corresponding secretary of the Atlanta Union, to attend the national convention.[76] At these meetings women spent countless hours speaking to one another, dining together, and participating in a host of other activities. They heard lectures, prayed, and sang hymns together as well.[77] The importance of such interaction did not escape WCTU members. At the national convention in Washington, D.C., in 1881, which constituted the first national meeting in which a large body of southern women attended, Mrs. Clara L. Roach, a representative from the D.C. chapter, specifically thanked southern women for attending. She contrasted this meeting with former times of bitterness. "And you of the Sunny South, many with us for the first time in national convention," she announced, "welcome, thrice welcome. There has been music in your coming. We listened once for your footsteps as those of an advancing enemy, but to-night we clasp hands lovingly—our cause, our country is one."[78]

Northern and southern women regularly commented on the importance of national reconciliation at WCTU national conventions. Of the national convention of 1881, Willard observed that "the most notable feature was the large attendance from the Southern states, a delegation of thirty or more from a majority of these states, being present, headed by Mrs. Sallie F. Chapin."[79] Regarding this same convention, Anna Gordon maintained that God used the WCTU to create a new national crusade of women. Not only did relatives of Stonewall Jackson and Robert E. Lee participate, but "Southern women for the first time sat side by side with their Northern sisters, saying to the beloved president of them all, 'We have enlisted with you to wage a peaceful war for God and Home and Native Land.'"[80] Baltimore's Georgia McLeod effusively wrote to the *Christian Advocate*, "Representatives from New England's sea-girt shore sat side by side with those whose homes were in the land of flowers—fair Florida. Delegations from North, East, South and West, Kansas, Colorado, and California—were all animated with one hope and prayer."[81]

At these meetings, women from the North and South regularly proclaimed their commitments to the rebuilding of the American republic with speeches, poems, and banners. They congratulated themselves for having a "national" organization. In 1881, the *Christian Statesman* applauded Willard because her "Temperance Union is now truly *National*."[82] Celebrating the tenth anniversary of the "crusade of 1873," Willard pronounced that the rise of the WCTU as a national body in only a decade was astounding. "The Woman's Christian Temperance Union was never weak, but it is a giant now," she told the delegates. "The Pacific Coast, the New Northwest, the South are all with us today. But yesterday, Mary A. Livermore of Massachusetts, sent to Sallie F. Chapin of South Carolina . . . this telegraphic message: 'If your heart is as our heart, give us thy hand.' Back came this message from our gifted southern leader: 'For God and Home and Native Land, we'll give you both our heart and hand.'" Willard concluded this section of her address by asserting that "we press forward to our grand destiny as a union of States, whose outlook embraces the Republic as a whole, and whose aims, methods and spirit are nothing less than *national*."[83] At the 1888 convention, temperance women echoed Willard's claims with a giant banner that stated in large, bold print: "NO NORTH, NO SOUTH, NO SECTIONALISM IN POLITICS, NO SEX IN CITIZENSHIP."[84]

Southern women played upon conciliatory themes just as frequently as northern women, because the WCTU and assertions of national allegiance provided avenues to public and political power—avenues that southern churches did not offer. In a speech at the 1881 meeting that Willard later called "brilliant," Sallie Chapin of Charleston, South Carolina, claimed that sectionalism perished in the WCTU:

No North, no South, no alien name,
Firm in one cause we stand;
Hearts melted in the sacred flame
For God and native land.

To Chapin, alcohol represented a shared enemy that women must unite against: "[A]ll are here, brought together by the threatening of a common peril, and all deeply, earnestly resolved that this war against our homes and dear ones *shall cease.*"[85] The next year, at the national convention in Louisville, she once again boasted that the WCTU and Christ had reunited the women. "Mason and Dixon's line," Chapin proclaimed, "no longer separates us but unites us, for we are one in Christ Jesus, and the great work He has given us to do."[86] As the superintendent of the young women's work in Mississippi, Belle Kearney looked forward to a time when the WCTU and national temperance legislation would bring together young women from all over the country: "[G]irls of the East and West and South will unite some day in glad rejoicing over the overthrow of old King Alcohol."[87] Some of these delegates reiterated Willard's claims that southern women wanted to put issues of the Civil War and past sectional strife behind them. In 1881, McLeod declared that although they would never forget their Confederate champions, southern women should band together with northerners to deliver their land from evil. "Grieving with you for fallen heroes, darkened homes, missing voices, I also rejoice that no stain rests upon the memory of our lost and loved. Far more sad are the records of today—the ravages of the foe destroying both body and soul—even the demon of drink. . . . It is women who suffer and weep; it is for them to work in faith and prayer that the rum traffic may be banished from the land."[88]

In 1889, delegates from southern states put into practice their hopes to end sectionalism by starting within the WCTU. They motioned to have the "Department of Southern Work" abolished, because its existence suggested that the South was somehow a foreign land outside of the nation. "The South is in no sense a missionary field," the delegates complained, and "each State supports its own work and pays money into the National Treasury." Southern delegates disliked having a specific regional department because it seemed to associate them with African Americans and immigrants. "It is painful to be reported as a missionary field," they argued, "as are the colored and Foreign Work." Ultimately, the existence of the Department on Southern Work appeared diametrically opposed to the new nationalism that the WCTU sought to forge. "The Southern Unions believe it is contrary to our platform 'No Sectionalism,' to make a special provision for the Southern work," the motion concluded. The executive committee accepted their arguments, and "the Southern Department" was disbanded. After 1889 "the South" no longer existed as a department within the WCTU.[89]

Amid proclamations of national solidarity at WCTU conventions, Willard sought to direct members' sentiments toward third-party politics. As part of this movement for political realignment, Willard viewed temperance reform and women's suffrage as means to redraw the political map. She regularly employed themes of national reconciliation in order to generate support for a new prohibition party that would also endorse women's suffrage. Recently several historians, especially Rebecca Edwards and Michael Goldberg, have examined the relations between women and Gilded Age political parties and have shown how women in the WCTU battled over whether or not to endorse Willard's Prohibition and Home Protection Party. Both Edwards and Goldberg concluded that previous partisan loyalties were usually so strong that large numbers of women did not flock to endorse third parties.[90]

But Willard battled valiantly for political realignment. In so doing, she joined a chorus of voices in the 1880s and 1890s that hoped for the restructuring of national political competition. During these decades, sectional disagreements were slowly displaced by other social matters, especially the economy. The national tariff and currency issues became increasingly important to thousands of northerners and southerners, and divisions no longer split neatly along sectional lines. For the most part, small farmers in the South and the Midwest had much to gain by supporting a low tariff and an elastic currency, while urbanites and manufacturers benefitted from maintaining high tariffs and keeping the United States on the rigid gold standard. Comprising perhaps the most democratic movement in American history, the Populists implored southern and northwestern farmers to cease "voting as they shot" and to start voting their collective interest, which would shift political divisions from sectional lines to economic lines.[91]

In this political atmosphere, Willard drew upon national reunion as a key argument to undermine women's prior political affiliations, and she repeatedly claimed that the main impetus for her move to a third party stemmed from her first visit to the South. In her autobiography, she recalled that she began to think that a "South 'Solid' for prohibition of the liquor traffic might be exchanged for the

South Solid against the North." Perhaps a new party "would put the temperance men of North and South in the same camp. Therefore it was borne in upon my spirit that I must declare in my next annual address, as President of the National Woman's Christian Temperance Union, the new faith that was within me." [92]

Willard hoped that a new prohibition party, with the women of the WCTU rallying to it, would finally put sectionalism to death and supply women with collective political authority. "I believe the South is ready for a party along the lines of longitude," she told WCTU delegates in 1881. She considered the Republican and Democratic parties morally unfit to lead the nation to unity. Both had too much invested in sectional identities. Neither would end sectional bickering, nor would the Republicans push vigorously for temperance legislation or women's rights. "[T]his new party cannot bear the name of Republican or Democrat," she declared, for "[n]either the victor nor vanquished would accept the old war-cry of a section; besides, 'the party of moral ideas' has ceased to have a distinctive policy." The Prohibition and Home Protection Party was now the party of godliness, "wherein dwelleth righteousness." This new organization constituted the "party that shall wipe Mason and Dixon's line out of the heart as well as off the map, weld the Anglo-Saxons of the New World into a royal family, and give us a really re-United States." She extolled the party's meetings as events in which men and women of the "North and South clasped hands in a union never to be broken." [93] Willard's vision for the Prohibition Party and for the WCTU now became clear. They would obliterate sectional divisions: "In its glowing crucible, the dross of sectional enmity is being rapidly dissolved." [94]

Willard maintained that the Prohibition and Home Protection Party stood as a new battalion that would supplant the sectional armies of the past, and in it, the women of the WCTU would achieve a new measure of political control. At the national convention in 1885, she asserted, "The blue and gray uniforms of the past are to be superseded by the pure white uniform of the new party 'for God, and Home, and Native Land,' which shall move forward in a brotherhood unequaled since the days of Washington." [95] On another occasion, she imagined the WCTU to be the one organization that could and would assemble the women of the Civil War by praising the virtue of women on both sides. "The women who uniformed their sons in gray and said, like the Spartan mothers of old, 'Come in victory or come no more,' are here beside those other women who belted Northern swords upon the boys in blue with words as pitiless and brave." But now women from the North and South "sit side by side to-day and wear the badge of peace above the hearts that hate no more, while we clasp hands in a compact never to be broken, and solemnly declare before high Heaven our mutual loyalty to 'God and Home and Native Land.'" The temperance crusade, she suggested, would finally allow the women to bury the trauma of the past: "The bloodless warfare of to-day, where women share the field with men, makes us forget the past." [96]

The Prohibition and Home Protection Party, however, never acquired the mass following that Willard hoped it would, and the party was never able to rival the Democrats or the Republicans at the national level. In fact, Willard's endorsement of women's suffrage and her calls for national political realignment led some southern church leaders to oppose her and the WCTU. In 1888, for example, the editor of the *Alabama Baptist* warned that southern Protestants could never align with the WCTU because it advocated votes for women and did not endorse the Democratic Party. [97]

But the desire of Willard and others within the WCTU to help reconcile the nation did not fail completely. Several individuals insisted that the WCTU did a great deal to reunite the nation. The *Christian Union* reported that "[t]he interchange of thought between the North and the South through such representatives as Miss Willard, whatever special direction it may take, will serve the good purpose of unifying the two sections." [98] In 1882, Colonel George Bain of Kentucky profoundly agreed: "I believe no one organization is doing so much to bury the past, break down sectional strife and restore harmony in this country as the Woman's Christian Temperance Union." He singled out the work of Willard and Chapin: "Miss Willard in the South and Mrs. Chapin in the North, have done more to bring together the divided sections, than all the politicians who have ever gone to Washington." [99] Likewise, Senator Henry Blair from New Hampshire spoke with even greater force. "The Union was restored," he rhapsodized, "when after the civil war the women of the North and those of the South assembled together as one, intermingled their tears and prayers over the sorrows of their common country, and, forgiving, if not forgetting the past, consecrated themselves to the new crusade. 'For God, and Home, and Native Land.'" [100]

III

But while the WCTU, the Prohibition and Home Protection Party, and Willard sought to ease hatreds between northern and southern whites by conceiving of national reunion as a sacred enterprise, they did very little to ameliorate racial tension. Rather, they advanced arguments for black suffrage restrictions and racial segregation, while contributing to the reemergence of anti-immigrant and anti-Catholic nativism during the Gilded Age. In the last two decades of the century, immigration patterns to the United States shifted dramatically, as "new immigrants" from southern and eastern Europe—who were more likely Catholic or Jewish than Protestant—arrived in greater numbers than the "old immigrants" from Britain, Germany, and other western European countries. In response, a variety of new nativists groups ascended, led by the American Protective Association. At the same time, class and racial hostilities rocked the nation and drenched it in blood. The Haymarket Tragedy, the Homestead Strike, and the Pullman Strike were but the three most spectacular episodes of class conflict amid thousands of strikes in the 1880s and 1890s.[101]

A dark cloud of racial brutality descended upon the South during these years. According to modern historians, white mobs lynched at least one thousand African Americans from 1889 to 1899. Ida B. Wells estimated that as many as ten thousand blacks had been lynched from the end of the Civil War to the turn of the century. Even assuming the more conservative number, roughly one hundred blacks per year were brutally murdered, often in horribly gruesome fashion. People of color were beaten, tortured, burned alive, and dismembered. Some had their genitals mutilated, while others were decapitated. In the late 1880s these events became public spectacles and rituals as whites joined to watch, photograph, and generally revel in the killings.[102]

Yet amid this racial terror, exploding class conflict, and rising anti-immigrant fervor, Willard's "Do Everything" policy offered little room for racial reform. The WCTU generally remained silent regarding racial violence, and it sanctified Jim Crow by permitting it within the organization. WCTU leaders nourished disfranchisement by actively arguing on its behalf, and they aided nativism with disparaging remarks aimed at immigrants and Catholics. While the WCTU thundered against drinking and domestic abuse, it generally remained mute when it came to unlawful public executions. When they did address the issue, WCTU leaders generally blamed African Americans themselves for the rise in lynching and suggested that only by limiting black suffrage would peace ever come to the South. Ultimately, the great reform crusade of the Gilded Age, which prided itself on reaching out to disempowered women, had little heart for the struggles of people of color or for immigrants.

Similar to Dwight L. Moody, white WCTU leaders minimized issues of racial oppression and liberation when discussing the past, especially the Civil War. They suggested that their battle for temperance and women's rights were far more important than the liberation of the slaves. Intemperance stood as a crime far worse than slavery, according to Mother Stewart: "And—so the curse, more fearful than southern slavery, has ever been steadily gaining upon us."[103] Chapin even contended that the North committed a grievous error by emancipating the slaves because it merely released them to alcoholism and madness. "'Before the war' any one selling liquor to a slave was punished, so drunkenness was never one of their faults," she asserted. "Now the poor creatures are not only made drunk, but actually maddened and destroyed with the vile decoction sold to them under the name 'liquor.'"[104] To Willard, there were only two positive gains from the Civil War, and freedom for African Americans was not one of them. First, northern whites experienced a new respect for the martial abilities of southern whites. The war, she claimed in her autobiography, taught northerners that they "had foemen worthy of our steel!" Second, the war "helped to individualize each woman's character; it taught the stern, but royal lesson of self-help." In short, the liberation of four million slaves was relatively unimportant compared with the ways it propelled white women to new jobs and political actions.[105]

WCTU spokeswomen often depicted African Americans, immigrants, and Catholics as aliens in the country who endangered the safety of the nation. Historian Beryl Satter has shown how women in the WCTU pushed for white women's suffrage by comparing their alleged "purity" with the supposed insanity, criminality, and poverty of African Americans and the new immigrants.[106] Temperance leaders regularly described people of color and immigrants in derogatory terms. One temperance hymn, "De Massa ob de Sheepfol,'" referred to people of color as "black an' thin . . . an' good for nuffin.'"[107] Testifying before Congress in 1885, the superintendent of the WCTU's educational department, Mary Hunt, argued that blacks were an "alien race" in America, and at the 1880 national convention, members of the Committee on Work Among the Indians, Chinese, and Colored People admitted that most WCTU women felt revulsion around African Americans and immigrants. Although white women wanted to "acknowledge kinship" with these people, it was too difficult: "[C]reeping over all generous feeling, stifling every kindly emotion is a nausea of the flesh, the baleful consciousness of the Negro skin."[108]

Other union members likened southern blacks to beasts. Sounding much worse than Harriet Beecher Stowe, Mother Stewart stated that African Americans were "ignorant, debased, half human, half animal beings, that must be a continual source of solicitude, a heavy tax, and a menace to the community and the State."[109] Regarding sectional relations, Willard suggested that the South would be a fruitful region for temperance activism principally because of the docility of African Americans and the small number of immigrants. "[T]he foreign element [is] so insignificant in influence and numbers," she claimed, "that temperance has an immense advantage at the South."[110]

Since WCTU leaders viewed African Americans and immigrants as deviants, temperance women strove for state and federal legislation that would control them. In her last address as the president of the WCTU, Willard called upon the U.S. Congress to restrict immigration. The nation needed "a stringent immigration law prohibiting the influx into our land of more of the scum of the Old World," she contended, "until we have educated those who are here."[111] African Americans also found themselves under attack from the WCTU. If left to vote as free citizens, WCTU leaders warned, African Americans would be manipulated by the liquor interests and cast their ballots for saloon keepers and other evil men. Chapin repeatedly made this argument in her speeches for temperance legislation. At the national convention of 1881, she told delegates that southern blacks and southern politics were in a horrible state of affairs because of alcohol. "Do you call them free?" she asked regarding southern blacks. "Ah, they are in far more abject slavery than we ever held them in." The government must do something to save them from themselves. "They are wards of the nation," she claimed, "[w]hat is the nation doing for them?" WCTU leaders such as Chapin described blacks and immigrants as mindless pawns of the liquor interests, and only educational requirements for voting could stop political manipulation. "We should have an educational qualification," Chapin charged the WCTU: "We need it, and we ought to have it."[112]

In 1890, Frances Willard echoed and even extended Chapin's arguments in an interview with *Voice*, a leading temperance journal. It asked her generally about race relations in the nation and specifically about the merits of Republican Henry Cabot Lodge's proposed Federal Elections Bill of 1890, dubbed the "Force Bill" by the Democrats. The bill was intended to protect the voting privileges of African Americans in the South by allowing federal courts to appoint commissioners to oversee federal elections and use federal troops to enforce laws if necessary.[113] Sounding similar to the Democratic opponents of the bill, Willard denounced it and proceeded to rail against the Fifteenth Amendment, which was supposed to protect voting rights. "I think we have wronged the South," she insisted, "we had irreparably wronged ourselves by putting no safeguard on the ballot-box at the North that would sift out alien illiterates. . . . It is not fair that they should vote, nor is it fair that a plantation Negro, who can neither read nor write, whose ideas are bound by the fence of his own field and the price of his own mule, should be entrusted with the ballot." Willard then asserted that "[w]e ought to have put an educational test upon that ballot from the first." She went on to suggest that whites and blacks were essentially different from one another and that people of color should emigrate to Africa. "If I were black and young, no steamer could revolve its wheels fast enough to convey me to the dark continent," she claimed, "I should go where my color was the correct thing, and leave these pale faces to work out their own destiny." To her, African Americans were destined to leave America and save Africa: "They are to be the leaders of their race. They are to bring America to all that Christianity and education can win for any race, and in Africa they are to build upa great republic, founded upon the love of God and humanity." [114]

Willard concluded her interview raging against blacks and the new immigrants, while lauding Anglo-Saxons. "Alien illiterates . . . rule our cities today," she lamented. "[T]he saloon is their palace, and the toddy stick their sceptre." In the end, virtuous whites would never stand for such social injustice. "The Anglo-Saxon race will never submit to be dominated by the Negro so long as his altitude reaches no higher than the personal liberty of the saloon, and the power of appreciating the amount of liquor that dollar will buy." [115]

Willard also took the side of southern whites regarding the rise of racial lynching. Although she deplored mob violence, Willard nonetheless sympathized with southern whites who claimed that the rapes of white women by black men stood as the primary reason for lynching. Southern women, she asserted, had every reason to be afraid: "The colored race multiplies like the locusts of Egypt. The grog shop is its centre of power. The safety of women, of childhood, of the home, is menaced in a thousand localities at this moment, so that men dare not go beyond the sight of their own roof-tree." [116] In her 1893 presidential address, she referred to African American men as "the devourers of women and children." Although southern whites should allow the legal system to handle these "devourers," the fact that white men took the law into their own hands was understandable, if not "manly." [117]

While pushing to limit suffrage and blaming African Americans for their own murders, Willard and other WCTU members accepted racial segregation within their organization. African American men and women had supported temperance societies throughout the antebellum and postbellum periods, and when the WCTU rose in the 1870s, they too sought to join. Throughout the South and the North, black women formed WCTU chapters, elected local leaders, and agitated for legislation against alcohol use. For the most part, however, white and black WCTU chapters remained independent of one another throughout the nation. Although there had been some integrated local chapters and statewide union meetings in the 1880s, these generally vanished in the 1890s, as the WCTU became an almost completely divided organization. Often, in fact, whites forced African American chapters to prefix their chapter names with the word "colored" in order to keep them clearly differentiated.[118]

Segregation in the WCTU deeply offended many African American women who were sympathetic to the temperance cause. In 1888, several of them wrote to the *American Missionary* denouncing Jim Crow in the WCTU. "We regret that the color-line is rigidly drawn . . . in the woman's work for temperance," the article began. While these writers acknowledged that some interracial interaction occurred among WCTU women, they noted that such contact was infrequent and on whites' terms. From Storrs School in Atlanta, for instance, one black woman wrote that "occasionally one or two ladies from the white W.C.T.U. will visit ours," but the white state union refused to recognize the black chapter. White unions completely excluded African Americans. "Our colored members would *not* be admitted," if they attempted to enter one, this writer lamented. Other African American women expressed outrage at the attempt of whites to change the name of their WCTU chapter, and they decided to leave the organization. In Louisville, Kentucky, "whites insisted that the name given them should be changed to *Colored W.C.T.U.*," but "the colored women refused, and the Union disbanded." Since then, it became impossible to rally local black women to the cause.[119]

While the women of Louisville decided to abandon the WCTU, some African American women battled the racism of the WCTU from within. One group refused to name their chapter "colored" and decided on "North Carolina, No. 2" instead. They would not replicate the racial prejudice of the WCTU's naming policies. "We cautiously avoided using the word *colored*," explained the president of North Carolina, No. 2., to the *Union Signal*, "for that would exclude any white sister who might wish to work with us; in other words, we wanted it distinctly understood that we had no race prejudice, for *we* believe *all* men are *equal*."[120] Elected chair of the Work Among Colored People committee in 1883, poet and novelist Frances E. W. Harper challenged white members to push for racial justice as well as temperance. Drawing a direct comparison between the experiences of African Americans and Jesus Christ, she sought to convince white women of the moral imperatives of helping people of color:

> And can any one despise the least of Christ's brethren without despising
> him? Is there any path that the slave once trod that Jesus did not tread before him, and leave luminous with the light of His steps? Was the Negro bought and sold? Christ was sold for thirty pieces of silver. Has he been poor? 'The birds had nests, the foxes had holes, but the Son of man no

where to lay His head.' Were they beaten in the house of bondage? They took Jesus and scourged Him. Have they occupied a low social position? 'He made himself of no reputation and was numbered with the transgressors.' Despised and trodden under foot? He was despised and rejected of men; spit upon by the rabble, crucified between thieves, and died as did Rome's meanest criminal slave.[121]

In her annual WCTU reports, moreover, Harper repeatedly indicted white women for not doing more to reach out to African Americans. "In conclusion, permit me to bespeak for this department, an increasing interest in the future," she told delegates in 1885. She warned them that neglect would cause further alienation, and she implored them to look beyond skin color: "What shall be your influence upon the future of this people? shall it be the influence of an extended Christly sympathy which will look with anointed vision through the darkened skin and shaded countenance, and see their souls all written over with the hand-marks of divinity[?]"[122]

During the 1880s and 1890s, many blacks refused to accept the WCTU's antipathy toward the cause of racial justice, and they sought to compel the organization to put its moral authority behind the fight for protecting civil rights for African Americans. The most vigilant critic of the WCTU's racial policies was the black reformer Ida B. Wells, who spearheaded her own anti-lynching campaign after a white mob in Memphis brutally lynched three black businessmen in 1892. A journalist, civil rights activist, and close friend of one of the lynched men, Wells set out to expose lynching for what it was—the illegal and despicable group murder of an individual without a fair trial. As historian Gail Bederman has shown, Wells inverted and subverted American Victorian understandings of masculinity, race, and civilization by describing white men as uncivilized and primal (as opposed to black men) and black men as the embodiment of civilized respectability (as opposed to white men).[123]

As part of her anti-lynching crusade, Wells called Willard to task for accepting segregation and demanded that the WCTU take a stand against racial lynching. Often her critiques of the WCTU were made in tandem with her denunciations of Dwight Moody's segregated revivals. While speaking during a tour in England on behalf of her anti-lynching crusade, she attacked Willard for being more harmful to African Americans than Moody. To her, "Miss Willard, the great temperance leader, went even further in putting her seal of her approval upon the Southerners' method of dealing with the Negro." Quoting Willard's interview with *Voice*, Wells condemned her for supporting racial violence. "Here we have Miss Willard's words in full," Wells complained, "condoning fraud, violence, murder, at the ballot box; rapine, shooting, hanging, and burning."[124] Willard's comments did not offend Wells as much as the WCTU's reticence to speak out against bloodshed. The WCTU's principal guilt lay in its sins of omission, not commission. Wells fumed in her 1895 anti-lynching pamphlet, *A Red Record,* "I said then and repeat now, that in all the ten terrible years of shooting, hanging and burning of men, women and children in America, the Women's Christian Temperance Union never suggested one plan or made one move to prevent those awful crimes."[125]

Although the WCTU's national convention did endorse a mild anti-lynching resolution in 1893, Willard continued to claim that interracial sexuality was the cause of lynching, not white racism. She embraced and propagated "that old-thread bare lie," as Wells often put it, that lynchings stemmed from the rapes of white women by black men, and she asserted that alcohol abuse made interracial sexuality possible. Willard argued that "the nameless outrages perpetrated upon white women and little girls were a cause of constant anxiety" for southern whites. But black men were not the only sexual fiends—white men were as well. She considered sexual relations between white men and black women a vile social and religious sin, for it created a "mixed" and powerless race: "[T]he immoralities of white men in their relations with colored women are the source of intolerable race prejudice and hatred, and that there is not a more withering curse upon the manhood of any nation than that which the eternal laws of nature visited upon those men and those homes in which the helpless bondwomen was made the victim of her master's base desire." Again, Willard blamed alcohol for leading to interracial sexuality. "An average colored man when sober is loyal to the purity of white women; but when under the influence of intoxicating liquors the tendency in all men is toward a loss of self-control, and the ignorant and vicious, whether white or black, are the most dangerous characters."[126]

Willard altered her original arguments on lynching by leveling blame at both white and black men, but she missed Wells's main points. To Wells, interracial sexuality was not necessarily immoral or the result of drunkenness; it was a choice made between whites and blacks that could be grounded in genuine love and affection. Furthermore, Wells exposed the fabrication that lynchings resulted from rapes of white women. As she showed in her investigation of murders of African Americans, economic rivalry constituted one of the main reasons for lynching. In short, the bugaboo of interracial sexuality was a falsehood constructed by whites to justify their murderous behavior. All of this, however, was lost on Willard. She could not conceive of whites and blacks desiring intimate contact with one another.

Other African Americans also railed against Willard for defending southern whites while ignoring the civil rights of people of color. The editors of the *Cleveland Gazette* denounced Willard as a leader who easily yielded to the whims of popular opinion. "The fact is," the editors complained, "Frances E. Willard is a *temporizer* as far as our people's interests are concerned. Her views on lynching and the color line in temperance work do not, as she thinks need further explanation, but they so need and badly, too, revision and change. They sap her plainly as a *temporizer,* pure and simple."[127]

Frederick Douglass criticized Willard, Daniel Chamberlain, former Republican governor of South Carolina, and Bishop Atticus Green Haygood, a southern Methodist leader who had published several books urging southern whites to support education for African Americans, as the white leaders most responsible for making segregation morally acceptable. To Douglass, the supposedly progressive attitudes of Willard, Chamberlain, and Haygood made their endorsements of Jim Crow particularly devastating. Although Chamberlain, Haygood, and Willard claimed to support racial uplift, they undercut racial integration and equality by supporting segregation and describing African Americans as "moral monsters." Douglass contended that blacks were not to blame for immorality in the nation; whites were. "We claim to be a highly-civilized and Christian country," he thundered, "yet I fearlessly affirm that there is nothing in the history of savages to surpass the blood-chilling horrors and fiendish excesses perpetrated against the coloured people of this country, by the so-called enlightened and Christian people of the South." He specifically accused Willard of seeking to protect whites while neglecting African Americans: "And now comes the sweet voice of a Northern woman, Miss Frances Willard . . . distinguished among her sisters for benevolence and Christian charity." But Willard was no better than other white supremacists. "She speaks in the same bitter tone and hurls the same blasting accusation," he asserted. Douglass then followed Wells in quoting Willard's interview with *Voice* and censured her for depicting blacks as beasts who were "ferociously invading the sacred rights of woman and endangering the home of the whites."[128]

To Douglass, Wells, and many other African Americans, racial lynching and the silence of the WCTU proved that the United States was a sinful nation in need of repentance and God's forgiveness. "Christianity is to be the test," Wells told a reporter for Britain's *Westminster Gazette,* and she was "prouder to belong to the dark race that is the most practically Christian known to history, than to the white race that in its dealings with us has for centuries shown every quality that is savage, treacherous, and unchristian."[129] Douglass felt the same. He concluded that racism would end only when white religious leaders and white Americans in general followed biblical teachings. Only when the moral leaders of the nation realized their divine destiny and took a stand against racial injustice would the sins of the United States be extirpated. "Let the great Northern press and pulpit proclaim the gospel of truth and justice against war now being made upon the negro. . . . Let them cease putting new wine into old bottles, and mending old garments with new cloth."[130]

In the 1880s and 1890s, however, white women in the WCTU were uninterested in creating a nation of freedom and equality for all individuals. Unlike the northern missionaries to the South during and immediately following the Civil War who had battled for a new nation of racial integration and equality, WCTU women hoped to create a land of peace and stability in which northern and southern whites could clasp hands and blacks would either emigrate or remain subordinate citizens. Willard, Mother Stewart, and other northern women viewed a strong southern white constituency as indispensable to their temperance crusade, and they employed national reconciliation as a rhetorical trope to lobby for increased political rights for white women. Traveling to the South, praising the virtue of southern white womanhood, and forming WCTU chapters throughout Dixie, northern temperance women reached out with hands of sisterhood to southern white women. In the 1880s, WCTU national conventions became crucial sites of conciliatory interaction and rhetoric. White women from the North and South joined an "army of women" that sought to bring temperance, reconciliation, and peace to the nation.

But gender and national solidarity did not have the power to rise above racial antagonism. The ethnic nationalism of whiteness pervaded the words and actions of the white WCTU women. The WCTU contributed to the rising anti-immigrant and anti-Catholic fervor in Gilded Age Protestantism, and it did little to stop the destruction of African Americans' political rights or the violence committed against them. At various times, the leaders of this reform organization either tacitly condoned or explicitly endorsed murdering African Americans and limiting their suffrage. Although African Americans like Wells, Douglass, and Harper challenged the racial prejudice of the WCTU, hoping that the organization would use its great might to aid people of color and the cause of human justice, they found few friends. The largest and perhaps most powerful women's organization in the nation had little sympathy for racial justice. Their banner said and left unsaid their ultimate goals: "No North, No South, No Sectionalism in Politics, No Sex in Citizenship." Alas, "no discrimination in the nation" would never fit on their banner.

In the 1880s and 1890s, white nationalism and racial exploitation took on a new and more virulent form as the WCTU and other Gilded Age Protestant organizations pushed beyond the boundaries of the United States. The new white nationalism they had helped create within the United States bred a new white American religious and political imperialism abroad. By the end of the century, the U.S. government engaged in military combat in Cuba, the Philippines, Guam, and Puerto Rico. This new overseas imperialism stood as the high-water mark of post–Civil War national reunion and racial oppression, and the War of 1898 served as the culmination of post–Civil War sectional reconciliation. It completed the remaking of the white republic, as whites throughout the country embraced an ethnic American nationalism centered on whiteness. But amid the swell of white nationalism, new voices of radicalism arose that would carry forward the civic nationalistic imagination into the twentieth century and continue to defy the conflation of whiteness, godliness, and American nationalism. These new opponents would make certain that this conflation was never as stable as white Protestant Americans believed it to be.

7

Global Missions, Religious Belief, and the Making
of the Imperial White Republic

On February 17, 1898, the United States lost its most powerful female leader. After battling anemia intermittently for several years and influenza for weeks,
Frances Willard died at her home in New York. Women and men from all over the
nation mourned. At her funeral in Brooklyn and at hundreds of memorial services
throughout the country, thousands gathered to honor Willard's life and lament her
death. Some hoped that she would rise from the dead like Christ. "[T]he angels
watched and waited," Anna Gordon wrote of the women who cared for Willard in
her last days. "Surely in more than one heart was heard a voice saying, 'She is not
here; she is risen.'"[1] Another woman depicted Willard's grieving compatriots as
"mournful and helpless, talking in low, awe-stricken tones of the one dearest in all
the world to them. . . . I thought of the little band of disciples in the long ago who
stood desolate, gazing, 'steadfastly toward heaven' after their departing Lord, and
the appearance of the angels in their midst."[2] Others compared the outpouring of
emotion wrought by her demise to that shown after President Lincoln's assassination thirty-three years previously. "The death of what private individual since
Abraham Lincoln's time has called forth a thousand memorial funeral services
upon the afternoon of one day?" asked Anna Gordon.[3]

As in her life, Willard served as a national reconciler in her death. When southern and northern white women lamented their loss, they engaged in cooperative
efforts of bereavement. Many WCTU women acknowledged that Willard's illness
and passing created "a common sorrow and a common joy."[4] Scores of southerners stood side by side with northern whites at the Brooklyn funeral, while those
who could not attend expressed their solidarity with Willard's followers. In South
Carolina, one woman wrote in her diary, "Miss Frances Willard died . . . and I feel
like I have lost a friend. I am so glad I entertained her when in our town two years
ago. . . . I have a lead pencil that was hers, and several letters she wrote, and a book
she sent me afterward, 'Do Everything.'"[5] Willard's death shook Belle Kearney's

entire spiritual existence. "On hearing of her death I felt that one of the foundations of my existence had slipped from under me and had drifted out to sea," she
recalled. "Miss Willard was like no other human being. There was a divineness
about her and a personal influence that no one else possessed. There will be many
leaders, and great ones, but the world will never see just such a 'chieftain' among
women as Frances E. Willard."[6] In summing up Willard's numerous contributions
to the world and to the nation, several eulogists drew attention to her ability to heal
the wounds of the Civil War for northern and southern white women. "If no other
work had been accomplished," observed Great Britain's Lady Henry Somerset,
"one of the greatest achievements of Frances Willard's life has been her mission of
reconciliation to the women of the South while yet the scars of war throbbed in
their breasts, and new-made graves stretched wide between sections that had
learned the misery of hated."[7]

Another Briton interpreted Willard and the WCTU as carrying even broader
significance than just helping to reunite the antagonistic sections of the United
States. To journalist and reformer William T. Stead, the woman's temperance crusade was one of the dynamic forces driving "the Americanization of the World."
While northern WCTU leaders succeeded in bringing southern women into the
crusade, their vision expanded to encompass lands and peoples across the globe.
In the 1880s, Willard and other leaders in the WCTU had formed the World's
Woman's Christian Temperance Union (WWCTU) to unify women's temperance
groups throughout the world. By 1902, the WWCTU had a worldwide membership
of more than half a million women in a host of nations, including the United States,
Great Britain, Australia, Bengal, Bulgaria, Canada, Denmark, France, Germany,
Iceland, and Hawaii. In Stead's opinion, the WWCTU was one of the key players in
transforming the United States into a global power. "The advent of the United
States of America as the greatest of world-Powers," he bellowed, "is the greatest
political, social, and commercial phenomenon of our times."[8]

The WCTU was one of many Protestant religious organizations propelling
citizens of the United States to assume new interests in global affairs. Sectional
reunion bred a new confidence in American nationalism that encouraged thousands of white American missionaries and millions of Protestant dollars to flow
into lands all over the world. From Asia to Africa, the Philippines to Puerto Rico,
American missionaries trekked all over the globe. Thousands went to China,
Japan, Korea, Chile, Africa, and a host of other locations in the second half of the
nineteenth century, while millions of Protestants within the United States read
accounts and narratives about these foreign lands in religious journals. As Stead

recognized, the missionary agenda was intimately connected to the rise of American economic and political involvement in these foreign lands. The American "advance . . . has been very rapid," he stated. "It began without any notion on the part of the American people of what was going to happen. The missionaries were as usual the pioneers first of trade and then of political dominion. The process was uniform."[9]

The growth in missionary activity was part of a broader rise in America's engagement with the world. Economic and political leaders within the United States took up a new and more aggressive role in world affairs during the Gilded Age. Industrial growth at home led to massive increases in exports, while businessmen and politicians paid much more attention to foreign markets, in part because of fears that overproduction and underconsumption led to boom-and-bust periods of economic instability within the United States. By the beginning of the twentieth century, only Great Britain outranked the United States in foreign trade. Concerned that the United States was falling behind European nations that had footholds in Asia, South America, and Africa, American politicians also became more interested in forming trade relationships with countries abroad. At the same time, members of the U.S. military hoped to establish coaling stations throughout the Pacific in order to fuel the navy that would be needed to protect America's expanding markets.[10]

The late nineteenth century was an imperial epoch throughout the world, and these were years marked by intense "confidence and fear" within the United States. Economic growth, new inventions, such as the telephone and phonograph, and territorial expansion led many Americans to evince profound pride in their national accomplishments. But a host of other factors engendered widespread concern. To many, the nation seemed to be falling apart. White middle- and upper-class Protestant Americans were perplexed by continued sectional animosities, racial violence, the Populist uprising in the South and West, the sense that the American "frontier" had closed, the influx of new immigrants from southern and eastern Europe, the unstable nature of industrial capitalism, class conflict and warfare, and gender anxieties wrought by the rise of consumer culture and "the new woman." All of these concerns were punctuated by a gruesome economic depression that began in 1893 and led to thousands of strikes and massive disenchantment with the nation. Middle-class white Americans worried that they and their nation were losing "vitality." Involvement in foreign affairs served psychologically and materially to assuage these fears. By exerting religious, economic, and political authority over foreign peoples, the United States would not only open up new commercial markets, and thereby allow for increased production and employment at home, but Americans would also prove their national unity, their manliness, and the racial supremacy of Anglo-Saxons.[11]

The religious leaders who helped create a new sense of American ethnic nationalism after the Civil War also did a great deal to push the United States outside of its borders. They justified economic and state expansion, in part, by disseminating derogatory and demeaning depictions of foreign peoples. Missionaries described peoples of Asia, South America, and Africa as ignorant children or subhuman demons who desperately needed American "civilization," which was shorthand for Protestant Christianity, consumer capitalism, and racial hierarchies. In heightening attention on foreign peoples and lands, these missionaries helped to diminish the last vestiges of northern white Protestant interest in racial issues within the United States. Their racialized remarks about foreign peoples further justified the subjugation of African Americans. In short, the remaking of the white republic after the Civil War and the rise of an American imperial empire had a dialectical relationship. The new, religiously inspired and highly racialized American nationalism on the home front supported boldness in extending America's economic, political, and religious power over foreign peoples, and imperialism in turn further bolstered the sense that the United States was God's chosen nation.

The zeal for missions and American involvement abroad took on a new force and energy in 1898, when the United States annexed the Hawaiian Islands and engaged in a series of wars against the Spanish Empire and insurgent natives in Cuba, the Philippines, Guam, and Puerto Rico. The War of 1898 brought northern and southern whites uniformly to support the federal government in military activity. Men from both sections swarmed to fight, while former Confederate officers were called upon to lead American soldiers. Although the War of 1898 initially began with the intent of ending the terrible atrocities committed in Cuba by the Spanish, it quickly embroiled the United States in combat across the globe. Admiral George Dewey's victory at Manila Bay in the Philippines helped transform the war into one for empire. With the defeat of Spain in early 1899, the United States was left to deal with "freedom fighters" in the Philippines. Throughout the numerous twists and turns of the conflicts, most white Protestants exuberantly supported the administration. Whether backing "Cuba libre" or the subjugation of the Filipinos, whether focusing on aiding their "little brown brothers" or on demonstrating America's manliness, they generally viewed the actions of the United States as ordained in heaven. They characterized the War of 1898 as a moral endeavor and applauded the new sense of nationalism that these battles forged. To many whites, the War of 1898 was God's means of finally ending sectional bitterness within the United States and fully restoring the white republic.[12]

Missionaries and their supporters provided political leaders and advocates of imperialism with religious idioms and images that were crucial to justifying global expansion. To several key statesmen and intellectuals, God had called the United States to intervene in the affairs of other nations, and they discerned a divine blessing in the ways the white North and the white South proclaimed national fidelity during the war. American leaders and writers, including President William McKinley, Senator Albert Beveridge, future president Theodore Roosevelt, and novelist Thomas Dixon Jr., cast the imperialist venture as a religious, racial, and nationalist mission in which God ordained the subjugation of foreign peoples. America's rise to global power and the War of 1898 served as the culmination of the post–Civil War remaking of the white republic, in which northern and southern whites linked arms with a profound sense of religious and racial superiority. Pervading the entire missionary and imperialistic venture was an ethnic nationalism, in which white Protestants and political leaders assumed the inseparability of whiteness, American-ness, and godliness.

Yet the jingoes and the imperialists were met by an energetic anti-imperialist crusade. Opponents of an American empire declared imperialism hypocritical, sinful, and a rejection of Christian teachings. They railed against religious rationalizations of martial aggressiveness and attacked the new gospel of "Bibles and Gatling guns." Ethnic nationalism, however, even suffused the anti-imperialist imagination. Many white opponents of imperialism argued from within an ethnic nationalism framework, suggesting that the United States should not incorporate these nations because of the perceived racial inferiority of foreigners. But one segment of the anti-imperialist campaign discerned clear connections among religious beliefs, national reconciliation, racial oppression, and global imperialism. For many African Americans, in particular, the cause of peoples of color abroad and at home was one and the same, and they assailed white American chauvinism. Vigorously protesting the ways northern and southern whites claimed national solidarity during the war while racial violence and injustice continued to plague the United States, black Americans recognized that a nation that allowed oppression at home could never offer egalitarianism abroad. Feeling betrayed by northern whites, they lashed out at American imperialism as anti-Christian and looked to God to rain down justice. Although northern whites generally ignored such appeals, and although the anti-imperialist movement crumbled after the presidential election of 1900, the United States that entered the twentieth century was clearly not one endorsed by its entire people. The War of 1898 served as the nineteenth century's last battle for America's soul, and white Protestants demonstrated that the ethnic nationalism of whiteness had pervaded their worldviews.

I

During the Gilded Age, interest in American foreign missionary work grew substantially. Shifting their missionary focus from the southern United States to the rest of the globe, thousands of white American Protestants ventured abroad to bring Christianity and the fruits of "western civilization" to the world. Millions of Protestants within the United States took part in the missionary efforts by supporting them financially, and they avidly read the missionaries' letters, tracts, books, and journals. These missionaries and their advocates continually characterized their crusades as military ventures and drew intimate connections between religious, commercial, and political expansion. They hoped that Christianity would infuse foreign peoples with a consumer ethic and transform them into avid purchasers of American commodities. The missionaries also encouraged American political involvement in these countries by calling for state intervention and by depicting native peoples as childlike barbarians who were in immediate need of American faith, goods, and uplift. In stark and disturbing contrast to the civic nationalism of the missionaries of the 1860s, Protestants in the 1880s and 1890s were far more likely to denigrate those in their mission field than to praise them. Unlike teachers in the South following the Civil War who labored in a social context that supported transformations in racial attitudes, late nineteenth-century missionaries rarely sought to ingratiate themselves as part of foreign communities. Missionaries' arguments and energy not only helped direct American religious interest away from the South and toward the world, but also helped legitimate white racism and pave the way for the War of 1898.

Although white Americans had shown concern for foreign missions from the inception of the republic, they did not focus their attention abroad in large numbers until the last two decades of the nineteenth century. In the last decade of the century, the number of missionaries to foreign lands skyrocketed. While only 513 American missionaries served in China in 1889, around thirteen hundred were there in 1905.[13] Overall, by 1900, the United States had just fewer than fifteen thousand missionaries abroad, and they formed over four thousand churches and seven thousand Sunday schools.[14] The rise in missionary numbers was matched by the remarkable growth of missionary societies to support them. At the start of the

nineteenth century, the United States had six Protestant missionary organizations; by the end, it had 537.[15] Religious historian Sidney Ahlstrom has observed
that the "closing two decades of the nineteenth century witnessed the climactic
phase of the foreign missions movement in American Protestantism."[16]

White women played crucial roles as missionaries and as supporters of global
evangelism, and their participation often led to a stronger sense of American nationalism. Between 1870 and 1900, the number of female Presbyterian missionary
auxiliaries rose from fewer than one hundred to more than ten thousand, while
over 150,000 Methodists were members of female missionary societies in 1895.
Committed to spreading both their faith and their ideas of middle-class domesticity, female missionaries sought to have a "blessed influence" on foreign societies.
They focused principally on working with women and girls, seeking to educate
them in Christianity and Victorian home management. Encounters with native
peoples and missionaries from other countries led some American missionaries to
express new feelings of national identity. For them, celebrating the Fourth of July
and prominently displaying American flags became increasingly important. One
female missionary in China, for example, requested that after her death her family should wrap her in the "dear stars and stripes."[17]

Perhaps the most dynamic missionary organization to emerge came from
American college students. Shifting his attention from revivalism to institution-
building and global missionary work, Dwight Moody helped galvanize the missionary movement by hosting annual summer conventions for college students to
discuss the state of Christianity in their schools, their nation, and the world. During one of these meetings in 1886, one hundred students pledged themselves to
foreign missions and vowed to encourage their peers to take an interest in global
evangelism. One year later, their ranks swelled to more than two thousand, and in
1888 the "Student Volunteer Movement for Foreign Missions" was officially organized.[18] By the time of their first national convention in 1891, more than six thousand students had joined, and more than five hundred attended the convention.
Four years later, well over one thousand students took part in the national convention.[19] Several contemporaries expressed amazement at the spectacular growth
and force of the Student Volunteer Movement. One reported that it had inaugurated "one of the greatest missionary revivals since the days of the apostles," while
the president of Amherst College declared it "of larger proportion than anything
of the kind in modern times." Moody, who many of these college students considered their spiritual father, labeled the Student Volunteer Movement "the greatest
Christian movement of the century."[20]

Although dominated by college students from the North, leaders of the Student Volunteer Movement sought to follow the WCTU's lead by creating a genuinely national organization. They actively sought and encouraged southern white Protestants to join the crusade. Participants at the 1891 national convention applauded themselves for having representatives from all over the nation in attendance. "Every State east of the Missouri River and north of the Gulf line of States, save one, was represented," their convention report boasted.[21] In 1894, John R. Mott, who would become the leader of the Student Volunteer Movement, serve as a special diplomat to Russia in 1917 under President Woodrow Wilson, and later win the Nobel Peace Prize, recommended that the movement exert even more energy working in the South. "The colleges of the South should receive special attention during the new future," he maintained. "The missionary record of certain southern institutions shows what splendid possibilities there are in this important section."[22] Southern whites greatly enjoyed their membership in the Student Volunteer Movement. After attending Moody's Northfield Conference in 1889, L. O. Dawson of the Southern Baptist Theological Seminary in Louisville, Kentucky, praised the rising fervor of college students for missions. "[F]ew can realize," he wrote in the *Seminary Magazine,* "the hold . . . the missionary spirit . . . has taken, and is taking, upon the young men of our colleges."[23]

The Student Volunteer Movement helped instill a sense of urgency in American foreign missions. Its watchword, first popularized by Moody's colleague Reverend Arthur T. Pierson and later taken up by countless other missionary proponents and organizations, proclaimed its institutional desire: "the evangelization of the world in this generation."[24] Certain that Christ would return to rule the Earth only after all peoples had gained access to the gospel message, these Protestants sought an active role in the coming of the kingdom of God. "Now or never!" thundered Pierson, as he called Americans to look abroad.[25] As Mott put it in 1898, "The Christians of today are the only ones to whom the heathens of this generation can look for the gospel. It is our duty to evangelize the world, because Christ has commanded it. His command to us applies to this, the one generation in all eternity for which we are responsible."[26] Gaius Atkins, a religious leader and author in the early twentieth century, recalled that the Student Volunteers "were on fire to win the world for Christ in their generation and victoriously complete the unfinished task of nineteen hundred years."[27]

In order to encourage white American Protestants to join the missionary crusade or to support it with prayers and donations, the Student Volunteer Movement and the other missionary organizations inundated the American public with information on missions and foreign peoples. The most popular and influential of these texts was Reverend Josiah Strong's *Our Country* (1885), an impassioned analysis of many late nineteenth-century social, religious, and economic "challenges" facing the United States. A Congregational minister and secretary of the Congregational Home Missionary Society, Strong became the most well-known proponent of American missions with *Our Country*. In it, he played upon a variety of fears held by white Protestants. Strong warned that there were seven great "perils" hovering over the United States: immigration; Catholicism; the precarious future of public schools; Mormonism; alcoholism; socialism; extreme disparities of individual wealth; and urbanization.

Indicative of much of the missionary literature, Strong's *Our Country* neglected the South as a national problem. Well before historian Frederick Jackson Turner proclaimed the "closing" of the frontier and drew attention to the West in American history, Strong redrew sectional issues within the nation from a North-South division to an East-West one. He believed that the seven perils were especially dangerous in the American West, for that is where the future of the nation and of civilization rested. "[I]t is the West," Strong prophesied, "not the South or the North, which holds the key to the nation's future." When Strong did discuss the South, he either praised its economic growth or characterized it as more like the "East" than the "West." "And mills are now being built in the South, which manufacture the cotton where it is grown," he reported. The lesson from Strong was apparent. American Protestants needed to focus their attention on the West and the rest of the world. The South was no longer a "problem," as it had been portrayed in missionary literature of the 1860s and 1870s. With economic growth, Dixie would be just fine.[28]

Strong most assuredly touched the public conscience. Other than the Bible, *Our Country* sold more copies than any other book following the Civil War. By 1900, more than 170,000 copies had circulated in the United States alone.[29] Missionaries especially loved it. At the 1891 Student Volunteer Movement national convention, Reverend George W. Chamberlain, who had been a missionary to Brazil, acknowledged both the fame and importance of Strong's work: "The author of 'Our Country,' a book which you have all read I trust, in the first chapter of the book says, that what has transpired in our country in the last century is without precedent and must remain without a parallel, because there are no new worlds to be discovered." Chamberlain even recounted a tale of meeting another Brazilian missionary in the rainforests who was busily reading *Our Country*.[30]

But Strong's complete neglect of racial problems in the South did not go unnoticed. Two writers to *American Missionary* complained about Strong's disregard of racial problems in the South. One reviewer admitted, "Among the recent issues of the press, none has been more effective and deservedly popular than the pamphlet entitled, *Our Country*. . . . It has aroused public attention in a remarkable degree, and has opened the way for a career of most promising usefulness to the author." Yet *Our Country* did not discuss the entire nation. "Our only regret," the reviewer continued, "has risen from the fact, that in its survey it leaves almost entirely out of account nearly one third part of our country, namely, the South." Important problems remained below the Mason-Dixon Line, because white supremacists were undermining the rights of African Americans through "intimidation, corruption, force and fraud."[31] Most reviewers, however, did not point out the absence of discussion of "the southern problem." The writers for *American Missionary* were like voices crying out in the wilderness. Late nineteenth-century white northern Protestants had become far more interested in urban and global problems than in southern ones.[32]

Our Country was merely one part of an explosion in Protestant publications on immigration and foreign lands. Many of these publications exuded an ethnic nationalism that assumed deep connections between God's will, whiteness, and American values, and they did a great deal to legitimate American racism at home and abroad. During the Gilded Age, American religious organizations started a host of monthlies and quarterlies to discuss global evangelism and to provide missionaries a venue to describe their work. By 1900, Protestant women published *Light and Life for Heathen Women, Heathen Woman's Friend,* and *Woman's Work for Woman,* while the Methodist Church printed *Gospel in All Lands,* which had a circulation of more than eighty-four thousand copies in 1896, and *World-Wide Missions,* which had a circulation of more than one hundred thousand copies in 1889.[33] Along with these journals, missionaries and their organizations produced hundreds of books and tracts on their adventures. The published proceedings of the 1891 Student Volunteer Movement national convention contained a list of "selected missionary books" that included more than one hundred texts.[34] Much of the missionary literature was published for use in colleges and seminaries, while other pieces were aimed at a much broader audience. Most texts were designed to spur interest in global missions. As a review of Reverend Charles Creegan and Josephine Goodnow's *Great Missionaries of the Church* maintained, "If these sketches help to deepen sympathy for missions, and to increase gifts to the cause, and if they may be the means of leading some of our young people to follow the example of these noble men, . . . they will have fully answered the purpose for which they are now sent forth."[35] And missionary texts begat missionary texts, as publishers advertised tract in missionary journals and other missionary books. So many books about missions had been published by 1898 that Reverend Frances E. Clark claimed that "a large library might be formed consisting entirely of the additions made by Protestant missionaries to the worlds' knowledge of geography, ethnology, philology, and history."[36]

While missionaries and their proponents sought to generate enthusiasm for foreign missions, their ideas and rhetoric provided religious support for American military, economic, and racial imperialism. In many ways, the missionaries were the most imperialistic of the imperialists, and they aided in the militarization of American culture in the 1880s and 1890s. They cast their mission in martial terms, and their tracts were full of masculine bravado. These missionaries were not ministers of peace bringing a gospel of forgiveness and harmony. They characterized themselves as God's army in the world, destined to vanquish the forces of evil. "This is a council of war," A. T. Pierson told representatives to the Student Volunteer Movement's first national convention. "In the tent of the Commander we are gathered, and the Commander-in-chief is here. Here are his subordinates, the heads of departments, the under captains, and here are the volunteers in the army. And the question for consideration is, How can the marching orders of this invisible captain be carried out promptly and energetically?"[37] At that same conference, a missionary who had recently returned from China asserted that American Christians must look at "missions as a war of conquest, and not as a mere wrecking expedition." By 1894, the movement had fully accepted this position, and the theme of its national convention was "The World's Conquest for Christ."[38] After discussing Africa in his series on missions, J. T. Gracey concluded, "Take it all in all, here is a new world thrown up for the conquest of christian civilization."[39]

This militancy was more than just rhetorical. Many Protestant ministers and missionaries depicted physical warfare as godly. Methodist minister Elbert S. Todd claimed in 1890 that war actually furthered the kingdom of Christ. "The issue of battle has in nearly every case been on the side of truth and progress," he asserted, "and in no case has it acted to cripple the civilizing forces of the world or re-enforce the powers of darkness." Wars were natural components of the perpetual conflict between good and evil, he further opined. "They have been rather the inevitable result of the contact of civilization and barbarism, light and darkness, which the expansion of the age has brought about." In fact, Todd claimed that Christians should pray for military conflict in heathen lands: "[O]n the score of humanity we might well pray that the sound of the cannon may ere long be heard in some regions which now enjoy peace."[40] As historian Stuart Creighton Miller has pointed out, missionaries to China repeatedly maintained that the Chinese only understood physical force and that diplomacy without weaponry would be fruitless. One suggested that "China must learn at whatever cost, that treaty obligations are to be observed, and the citizens of other nations residing in her empire respected and protected."[41] In 1893, when missionaries found themselves threatened by Chinese militants, President Benjamin Harrison responded to their calls for protection by having several gunboats constructed to patrol Chinese waters.[42]

Missionaries applauded European interventions in Africa and Asia as well. A. T. Pierson characterized the Berlin Africa Conference of 1884, in which European powers carved up Africa for colonization, as fundamentally Christian: "Perhaps no more wonderful occurrence has been recorded since Pentecost than the Berlin Conference, that, in the closing weeks of 1884, met to determine the Constitution of the Congo Free State." According to Pierson, God now brought the resources of Africa within the grasp of Europeans and Americans so that they might overwhelm and civilize the continent: "Well may all eyes turn to Africa. God is disclosing by His providence the great mineral, metallic, and vegetable resources of the interior."[43]

By the late 1890s, Protestantism in the United States had been thoroughly militarized. To refer "to the Christian religion as a religion of peace," a writer for *Century* recognized, "one is brought at once into an atmosphere of contradictions both historical and contemporaneous." Christ used violence, for instance, when he drove the money-changers out of the Temple in Jerusalem, and nineteenth-century "Christian nations" followed the example of this belligerent savior: "Christian wars have been frequent and popular throughout the centuries." War was a tool of God in the minds of late nineteenth-century Protestants, and belligerence had become a overriding force in the Anglo-Saxon psyche. "Christianity is a religion thoroughly identified with the warrior instincts of the race," this author concluded, "it is a psychological phenomenon of immense import that the military tone of the Old Testament has made an uneffaced impression upon all Christian nations . . . [and] has dominated the mind and habit of Christian civilization."[44]

As northern Protestants employed martial themes and justified the use of military force, they also connected their work with economic and commercial prosperity. They hoped that as foreign lands and peoples became more Christianized, they would become better markets for American goods. Protestant missionaries and many other American leaders supposed that expanding markets would allow increasing industrial production without lowering the prices of products. In *Our Country,* Josiah Strong asked and answered, "And what is the process of civilizing but *the creating of more and higher wants?* Commerce follows the missionary." At the turn of the century, Strong continued to point out that "[a]s our manufactures increase, we shall become increasingly dependent for our well-being on foreign markets," and missionaries were necessary to expand commercial circles.[45] Reverend John B. McGuffin echoed Strong's sentiments, writing that "missionary work is the best-paying financial enterprise in the world," for it inculcated the "expensive standard of Christian living." Another minister told his general missionary conference that "it is the missionary that is preparing the way for your cotton, . . . your lumber, . . . the output of your rolling mills, and to all those things that look to and await the development of Eastern Asia."[46]

American diplomats quickly recognized that commerce followed the cross, and missionaries, in turn, went to great lengths to lead the way. In a paper presented at the Peking Oriental Society, the American minister to China from 1885 to 1898, Charles Denby, claimed that "missionaries are the pioneers of trade and commerce. . . . The missionary, inspired by holy zeal, goes everywhere, and by degrees foreign commerce and trade follow."[47] The connection between missionaries and American business was nowhere more apparent than in Korea, where Dr. Horace N. Allen, a Presbyterian medical missionary, helped two American businessmen secure lucrative rights to gold mines. The Oriental Consolidated Mining Company, based out of West Virginia, held land and mineral titles from 1897 to 1938, although local Koreans continually protested the ways the company exploited local labor. The mines proved the best in Asia, and the company had extracted well over 9 million tons of ore by the time it left.[48]

Missionaries and their supporters coupled economic rationales with racial ones. To proponents of global evangelism, God had called Anglo-Saxon Protestants to hold dominion over the entire earth. He had also, they believed, created peoples of foreign lands as inherently inferior to whites. In both *Our Country* and *The New Era, or the Coming Kingdom,* Strong proclaimed that God had made Anglo-Saxons the great missionary race of the world. "[A]nother marked characteristic of the Anglo-Saxon," he insisted, "is what may be called an instinct or genius for colonizing. His unequaled energy, his indomitable perseverance, and his personal independence, made him a pioneer. He excels all others in pushing his way into new countries."[49] If other races failed to submit to Anglo-Saxon civilization, they would vanish. "Whether the extinction of inferior races before the advancing Anglo-Saxon seems to the reader sad or otherwise," he continued, it did not matter. "[I]t certainly appears probable."[50] Methodist minister John Robinson considered the American Anglo-Saxon "the most intelligent, practical, enterprising and powerful being on the planet," and a writer to the *World-Wide Missions* claimed that the race was "destined to dispossess the weaker [races], assimilate others, and mould the remainder."[51] Whites would soon rule the continent of Africa, prophesied J. T. Gracey. "All this [missionary and political work] aims to build up a great civilization [in Africa] which, if it is successful, . . . will make the white man the leader of the black man for the next hundred years."[52] Racial supremacy ultimately left American Protestants with a keen sense of religious and national obligation. A. T. Pierson, for instance, claimed that he heard "the imperative voice of *duty*" directing all Anglo-Saxons to support the evangelical crusade to the world.[53]

Notions of Anglo-Saxon superiority were central to justifications of global imperialism, and they contributed to a rising, more virulent form of white supremacy within the United States. As missionaries lauded Anglo-Saxon virtues, they also depicted foreign people as ignorant children, evil savages, or subhuman animals. Often they sought to prove the backwardness of these cultures by describing their gender relations as the antithesis of those prescribed by white middle-class domestic ideology. One missionary to British Guiana repeatedly referred to native men as children who mistreated their women. "These children of the forests," he wrote, "have never taken to civilized habits and they compel their women to till the ground, reserving for themselves the more exhilarating work of hunting." "They are children still," this missionary concluded, "they live for to-day, leaving to-morrow to care for itself."[54] Other white Protestants characterized foreign peoples as unusually debased, but easily controlled. A missionary to Hawaii referred to the locals as "vicious, shameless, yet tractable, slaves to their chiefs, and herding together like animals."[55] Lucy E. Guiness quoted one missionary to South America who maintained that when he first encountered the natives, he thought that he had found "Charles Darwin's missing link."[56] Reverend A. T. Pierson contended that "some of the unevangelized races seemed on too low a level to be lifted even by the lever of the gospel. . . . In some not only the image of God, but the image of man, was defaced, if not effaced; they were dumb beasts for shamelessness and wild beasts for brutality and ferocity, not only dehumanized but demonized."[57]

Like Pierson, several other missionary writers directly associated native peoples with spiritual evil. Reverend H. C. Tucker wrote of Brazilians as "savages. . . . Many of them have been very warlike, ferocious, vengeful and bloodthirsty. Some of them were known to be cannibals and ate their enemies with great ceremony."[58] To Reverend Elbert Todd, the Chinese were innately sinful: "A Chinaman is never so much in his element as when telling a barefaced falsehood." [59] The editor of the *Argonaut*, Frank M. Pixley, put this opinion even more forcefully: "[W]here one Chinese soul has been saved, a hundred white souls have been lost by contamination of their presence. . . . The Chinese are inferior to any race God ever made; they have got the perfection of crimes of 4,000 years; they have no souls to save, and if they have, they are not worth the saving." [60]

White Protestant missionaries suggested that foreign peoples possessed an inherent sinfulness that went deeper than the total depravity of all humans. Evil was viewed as a naturalized part of their souls and blood. "The kingdoms of heathenism," announced Henry Forman at the first Student Volunteer national convention, "are the kingdoms of Satan." [61] Another speaker compared Africa to hell: "I believe if Jesus Christ were here to-night, and could point to that picture [indicating the map of Africa], he would say there is only one place in this universe darker than that spot, and that is the land of the blackness of darkness forever." [62] Writing on Africans in Dutch Guiana, Professor J. Taylor Hamilton asserted that "immorality is the special weakness and curse of the African blood—here as elsewhere." [63] Sinfulness for these people was not merely a part of their humanness; it was central to their racial essence.

In a similar fashion some American theologians and religious leaders revived the antebellum debate regarding the origins and humanity of African Americans. With several pamphlets and books, author and minister Charles Carroll defied the idea that African Americans were human in any way. Rather, he maintained that "Negroes" were the biblical "beasts of the field" who were created by God to serve humankind. They had minds and bodies, but lacked souls. Only "pure-bred" whites were creatures made in the "image of God," Carroll insisted, and therefore they were the only "true humans." He considered emancipation a terrible mistake, because blacks were created by God to serve whites. The great sin of white humankind, moreover, was "amalgamation" between the "children of God" and the "beasts of the field." It had caused the downfall of the Israelites, and if white Americans were not careful, it would cause the downfall of the American republic. In opposition to thousands of years of biblical theology, Carroll defined the "children of God" not as those individuals who put their faith and trust in the Judeo-Christian God, but as biological entities. Echoing the missionary writers, Carroll viewed race, rather than action or belief, as the chief determinant of spiritual standing. White supremacists of the late nineteenth century were interested in denying people of color far more than civil rights or national citizenship. These theologians sought to deny their claims to having any eternal importance or connection to God. [64]

Related to this virulent white supremacy was a rabid form of anti-Catholicism. Rooted in anxieties generated by conflicts with Catholic missionaries and natives abroad and by the influx of millions of Catholic immigrants from southern and eastern Europe to the United States, many Protestants denounced Catholics as backward and dangerous. Prefacing their study of missions to South America, E. C. Millard and Lucy E. Guiness argued that Catholicism was "corrupt" at its core and only led to "indifference, sensuality, infidelity, and anarchy."[65] A missionary to Chile wrote that "Romanism can only flourish in *the soil of ignorance*," while Josiah Strong considered Catholicism one of America's chief "perils," because it was antagonistic to individual liberty and freedom. "Roman Catholic training," he contended, "from childhood up, is calculated to disqualify the mind for independent action, and renders it highly improbable that any considerable number of even moderate and liberal Romanists would, in the supposed event, forsake their allegiance to the Pope."[66]

Anti-Catholicism sometimes took a decidedly anti-Spanish form. In 1893, as Americans commemorated the four hundred-year anniversary of Christopher Columbus's first voyages to America, Reverend William Stevens Perry railed against any speakers who would associate Spain with the rise of the United States. To him, the Spanish had offered nothing to the New World other than religious oppression. Ignoring the exploitation of Native Americans and African Americans by Protestant Anglo-Americans, he maintained that "[t]he Christianizing of the natives by the Spaniards, dating back to the days of Columbus himself was the enslavement and extermination of these guileless children of nature. . . . The Latin race sought rather to gratify its greed for gold than to colonize commonwealths in the New World."[67] When the United States went to war with Spain in 1898, some ministers even depicted Spaniards as racially debased humans. "The Spaniards have become insane," preached Reverend Henry Frank in New York. "Ages of cruelty, barbarism, and bigotry have eaten into their breasts, until their native humanity has been transformed into the basest bestiality. And now, in the face of defeat, like the fabled scorpion, unable to slay her enemy, she threatens to thrust her own venomous fangs into her own bosom and tear asunder her tumultuous entrails."[68]

As missionaries and other northern white Protestants focused attention abroad and issued derogatory comments about foreign peoples of color, they contributed to diminishing public concern for racial issues in the South. By characterizing peoples of color in foreign lands as debased and their lives as dreadful, missionaries made racial inequality and exploitation within the United States appear far less vile. Contrasted with the deplorable conditions of Asians, Africans, and South Americans, the economic, political, and social disadvantages of African Americans seemed acceptable, even just and fair. In Brazil, wrote Reverend H. C. Tucker, slavery had failed to inculcate notions of "right" and "wrong" into those held in bondage. But in the United States, slaves had benefitted from paternal masters. "The teachings of rewards and punishments," he maintained, "which has had such a wholesome effect upon the North American negroes, has been lacking in this country." [69] As historian Matthew Frye Jacobson has noted, comparisons like these "redeemed blots on the United States' humanitarian record like the slave trade, Jim Crow, and even lynching." [70] By sending missionaries and funds abroad rather than "down South," by focusing on worldwide problems rather than national ones, and by depicting foreign peoples of color as more disadvantaged than African Americans, advocates of global missions helped justify the shift in northern white concern away from southern blacks and toward foreign peoples.

Missionary writings did a great deal to propel the United States to take an interest in foreign affairs and societies. Some contemporaries recognized, in fact, that missionary tracts and reports provided crucial information for scientists and the public about these lands and people. In a study of languages in Africa, Dr. Robert Cust maintained that missionaries to the "Dark Continent . . . have emitted bright sparks of linguistic light, which have rendered luminous a region previously shrouded in darkness, . . . and to them personally unknown, scholars, working in their studies in Vienna, Berlin, or some German university, scholars who, alas! cared little for the object of the missionaries' going forth, but rejoiced exceedingly at the wonderful, unexpected and epoch-making results of their quiet labors." [71] In his lecture and article, "Do Foreign Missions Pay?" Reverend Frances E. Clark fundamentally agreed with Cust. Quoting a host of secular and political leaders, he asserted that missions enhanced geographical and scientific knowledge. "What royal geographical society has such a record of discovery and exploration as have missionary societies of America and Great Britain?" he inquired and answered. "The two names of Livingstone and Moffat would never have appeared." Missionaries furnished scientists with crucial information. Professor Louis Agassiz recognized that "few are aware how much we owe them both for their intelligent observation of facts and for their collecting of specimens. We must look to them not a little for aid in our efforts to advance future science." [72]

Many native peoples perceived the cultural chauvinism and militarism of these missionaries, and they protested loudly and sometimes violently. The Boxer Rebellion of 1900, when legions of Chinese men and women rose against and killed thousands of Chinese converts to Christianity along with American, British, German, and French missionaries, was merely the most spectacular form of resistance.[73] In the two decades leading up to the Boxer uprising, several anti-Christian tracts had circulated widely in China. "The Christian religion is vulgar, shallow, and erroneous, and is an instance of the vileness of Barbarian customs," one proclaimed.[74] "We cannot wonder that the Chinese officials should hate the missionaries," contended Wen Ching in *The Chinese Crisis from Within* in 1901, because the church in China "is an *imperium in imperio*, propagating a strange faith and alienating the people from that of their ancestors."[75] By the late 1890s, a number of white Americans even recognized that white Protestantism had become a fighting faith. "It has long been apparent," wrote the editor of *The Call*, "that what is called the 'missionary spirit' in its dealings with China has been anything but justice and Christian ethics, and the Western powers have taken their cue from its savage aggressions."[76]

II

Largely anti-Catholic, anti-Spanish, racist, commercially minded, and militant, the vast majority of white American Protestants became exuberant when the United States embarked on a series of conflicts in 1898 that set Americans against Catholic Spain and insurgent natives in Cuba, the Philippines, Guam, and Puerto Rico. Decades of characterizing missionary work as duties to God and American civilization as divine led them to offer almost unwavering support. White Protestants believed that American military victories would open up new venues for Protestant missionaries and that they would also finally end any lingering sectional animosities. The Gilded Age history of American Protestant missionary work and the responses of churchgoers and religious leaders to the War of 1898 were central to the formation and sanctification of an American empire and a fully reunified and strengthened white republic.

The War of 1898 served as the high-water mark of post-Civil War national reunion. Throughout the country, northern and southern whites proclaimed the death of sectional antagonism and animosity as men from both sections flocked to join the war effort. One military commander observed that with the war, "we had a new Union, no Northerners, no Southerners, but Americans all." Northern troops in the South reveled in the ways southerners displayed the American flag with pride and supported the military. One Ohioan noted as he marched to Tampa, Florida, that "[a]t every station crowds of people poured out to bid us Godspeed on our way to war. Ovation after ovation was given to the boys in b[lue] once so hated in this sunny Dixie land." "Our grand 'Old Glory,'" he continued, "was prominently displayed at nearly every town, binding closer the link of affection of our North and South, now united in a common cause of national honor and national pride." Even northern children paid homage to national reunion, singing in their schoolyards, "They've named a cruiser *Dixie*—/that's what the papers say—/ An' I hears they're goin' to man her with/the boys that wore the gray." [77]

Northern white Protestants joined the celebration of the war as a grand moment of national reconciliation and were especially adamant in declaring it a religious crusade. Religious leaders enthusiastically pledged their fidelity to the nation during the conflict. One Methodist minister announced, "[O]ur cause will be just, and Methodism will be ready to do its full duty. Every Methodist preacher will be a recruiting officer." [78] Preaching at Madison Avenue Reformed Church in New York City, Reverend A. E. Kittredge told his congregation, "The present crisis of this Nation . . . is in harmony with Christian teachings. . . . This contest is a holy uprising in God's name for the uplifting of a wronged and downtrodden people." [79] One poet thanked God for military conflict:

> Almighty God! eternal source
> Of every arm we dare to wield,
> Be Thine the thanks, as Thine the force,
> On reeling deck or stricken field;
> The thunder of the battle hour
> Is but the whisper of Thy power. [80]

Others explicitly employed missionary idioms when describing the nation's call to arms. M. Pardee Adams compared the response of the United States to the Cuban crisis to that of the apostle Paul's to the man calling from Macedonia:

> From Cuba to the Philippines,
> A cry for rescue came;
> As Macedonia of old:
> "Come! Help in Jesus' name!"
> . . . .
> To these "the least" who need us,
> God calls, "My truth proclaim."
> Go! To the faint and fallen;
> Send peace through Jesus' name. [81]

As Protestants gloried in foreign war, they praised God for the impact international conflict would have on the home front. Several pastors believed that common enemies would solidify the new sense of American nationalism that had been growing in the years since the Civil War. Reverend Kittredge declared that the War of 1898 was a godsend, for it would reunite the nation: "We know no North, no South. Every State and the people everywhere are seeking only to uphold our President in fulfilling the destiny set before this Nation."[82] Reverend Samuel McComb of Rutgers Riverside Presbyterian Church echoed Kittredge's claim and asserted that the war would also draw the United States and Great Britain closer together as well. "The war is proof to the world that America is the foe of injustice and wrong," he lectured, and "the effect of the war will be to awaken a new sense of National consciousness, to unite the North and South, and to add an impetus to the growing friendship of England and America." Reverend R. A. Torrey, a close friend of Dwight Moody, told the students at the Northfield Conference in 1898 that "[e]very American ought to be grateful to God for the reunion between the North and South which has been brought by this war. The Civil War is over at last, and all its antagonisms are forgotten. In the South you see the stars and stripes floating everywhere. Every man, woman and child seems to wear them, and those Southerners are shouting for the American flag with an enthusiasm that I have not seen equaled in the North."[83]

Southern church leaders also offered proclamations of national reunion during the War of 1898. The *Christian Index* of Atlanta declared that the "greatest blessings" from the war "will come along the line of reuniting our country in the ties of nationalism," while Greenville, South Carolina's *Baptist Courier* declared that the "[m]en who stood face to face as enemies in the internecine war that threatened the way of life of the nation thirty-five years ago now stand shoulder to shoulder in defence of their country with an unsuspected valor and patriotism." It was pleased to announce that "[t]he last vestiges of bitter rancor and prejudice are rapidly disappearing."[84]

Even when the struggle evolved from a crusade for Cuban liberation into one of imperial expansion in the Philippines, most Protestants in the North and the South continued to defend the government's policies. Many staunchly advocated the formation of a religious and political empire. The editor of the Presbyterian *Interior* wrote that he could hear "the ringing of the bell of Divine Providence calling upon those who have the gospel of the world's salvation to see, and to seize this new, this august opportunity for preaching it in a world-empire that has so long been waiting for it."[85] One missionary secretary told a reporter for the *New York Times*, "We fight for the right. We fight for missions in Cuba. . . . The lesson which we as a nation are giving to the world is one that the world will never forget, and one that only a Christian nation could give."[86] In a poll of five occupational groups, the *Boston Herald* found that ministers were the strongest supporters of empire.[87] White Protestants, in sum, considered the time ripe for "evangelization of the world in this generation," and contributions to foreign missions soared throughout the war.[88]

Many white northern Protestants so steadfastly and passionately supported the American cause that they endorsed the use of torture and unrestrained violence to subdue the nation's opponents. In his article "The 'Water Cure' From a Missionary Point of View," Reverend Homer Stuntz went so far as to justify the "water cure," a cruel torture technique in which American soldiers in the Philippines pumped natives full of water, pressed down upon the victims' stomachs to forcibly remove the liquid, and then repeated the process until they divulged information or died. Stuntz claimed that "since the victim has it in his own power to stop the process, or prevent it altogether [by offering information] before the operation has gone far enough to seriously hurt him," is should not have been labeled "torture."[89] After the Boxer Rebellion of 1900, American missionaries called for swift and vicious justice against the Chinese. Reverend W. S. Ament, a member of the American Board of Foreign Missions, told a reporter for the *New York Sun*, "*The soft hand of the Americans is not as good as the mailed fist of the Germans*. If you deal with the Chinese with a soft hand they will take advantage of it."[90]

In the estimation of anti-imperialists, Protestants were the most jingoistic of American jingoes. Pointing out that most Filipinos were Catholic and did not need Christian missionaries, E. L. Godkin of *Nation* complained that "the fervent Methodists, at the beginning of the war, resolved that it was going to be a righteous and holy war because it would destroy 'Romish superstition' in the Spanish West Indies."[91] In 1900, Godkin continued his attack upon the Methodists, denouncing them as "the most powerful propagandists of the McKinley wars."[92] On another occasion, a writer for *Nation* noted, "I don't think I should be going too far in saying that it is the eager support of the clergy which has launched McKinley on his career of conquest."[93] At a minister's meeting in Boston, Congregationalist Reverend A. A. Berle recognized that "[i]t has been said and is commonly alleged that it was the Church and the clergy that hurried the nation into the Spanish war, urging the cry of suffering humanity demanded that the sword be drawn for the defence of the weak and the redress of grievous wrong."[94]

Perhaps the most popular writer to criticize missionary militarism and religious hypocrisy in imperialism was Mark Twain. In several letters and articles, he denounced the American "missionary spirit" as hypocritical and evil. "I bring you the stately matron called CHRISTENDOM, returning bedraggled, besmirched and dishonored by pirate raids in Kiaochow, Manchuria, South Africa, and the Philippines; with her soul full of meanness, her pocket full of boodle and her mouth full of pious hypocrisies," he wrote in an essay that editors refused to publish.[95] His essay "To the Person Sitting in Darkness" did make it into print in the *North American Review*, and it specifically indicted American Protestants for seeking to oppress foreign peoples. Attacking missionaries for advocating violence against natives and seeking to exploit them economically, Twain claimed that many Protestants were giving missions a dishonorable name. "Christendom has been playing it badly of late years," he observed, "and must certainly suffer by it, in my opinion." He quoted one correspondent in China who asserted that "the feeling here is that missionary organizations constitute a constant menace to peaceful international relations."[96] Business tycoon Andrew Carnegie, who opposed American involvement in the Philippines as Twain did, applauded "To the Person Sitting in Darkness" and referred to it jokingly as a new biblical text. "There's a new Gospel of Saint Mark," he wrote to Twain, "which I like better than anything I've read for many a day. I am willing to borrow a thousand dollars to distribute that sacred message in proper form."[97]

III

Gilded Age white American Protestants did much more than offer their support to the war effort and justify torture and exploitation. They also provided ready-made narratives, images, and ideologies for imperialist-minded politicians and writers to exploit. From President McKinley to novelist Thomas Dixon Jr., from Senator Albert Beveridge and future president Theodore Roosevelt to countless poets, proponents of expansion relished opportunities to cast the war in religious and racial terms. For them, not only had God ordained the Anglo-Saxon race to dominate, but he had also demonstrated his favor toward the United States in solidifying American reconciliation during the hostilities. National reunion was construed as proof of God's hand in their fight. As northern and southern whites joined together to support the war, as former Confederate generals, such as Joseph Wheeler and Fitzhugh Lee, led American troops, and as southern editors and politicians declared their fidelity to the American nation, it appeared that God was forging a new republic in which sectional bitterness had been thoroughly ameliorated and whites embraced each other as brethren.[98]

White missionary-minded Protestants could not have asked for a president more agreeable to their aims than William McKinley. Raised in the Methodist Church and remaining a churchgoer for his entire life, McKinley regularly expressed an interest in religious affairs. In 1896, his campaign biographer claimed that "William McKinley is not only a sincere and earnest man, but a religious man" as well. He often spoke to religious groups and even to missionary organizations.[99] In 1900, for example, the president told the Ecumenical Conference on Foreign Missions in New York City, "The story of the Christian missions is one of thrilling interest and marvelous results." Missionaries, he assured his audience, not only brought civilization to foreign lands, but they also provided examples for political leaders to follow. "They have been the pioneers of civilization," he lectured. "They have illumined the darkness of idolatry and superstition with the light of intelligence and truth. . . . They furnish us examples of forbearance and fortitude, of patience and unyielding purpose, and of a spirit which triumphs, not by force of might, but by the majesty of the right."[100] Even Ida McKinley, the president's wife, expended considerable energy thinking about and discussing religious missions. One visitor to the White House during the war found her talking incessantly about "converting the Igorrotes."[101]

Although McKinley at first sought to avoid conflict with Spain, when the USS *Maine* exploded outside of Havana in February 1898, and diplomacy failed, he led the nation to war. Before and during military battles, he often referred to the struggle as a moral war of duty and obligation. "I shall never get into a war until I am sure that God and man approve," he remarked at one point.[102] As historian Julius W. Pratt has pointed out, McKinley's wartime speeches were littered with references to "duty," "destiny," and the "hand of God." At the Trans-Mississippi Exposition in Omaha, Nebraska, for instance, he told the crowd that "[t]he faith of a Christian nation recognizes the hand of Almighty God in the ordeal through which we have passed. Divine favor seemed manifest everywhere. In fighting for humanity's sake we have been signally blessed."[103] Like most late nineteenth-century white Protestants, McKinley considered religion and patriotism close bedfellows and consciously conflated the two. "Piety and patriotism go well together," he announced while speaking in Ocean Grove, New Jersey. "Love of flag, love of country, are not inconsistent with our religious faith; and I think we have more love for our country and more people love our flag than ever before."[104] Stories even circulated that McKinley's decision to maintain America's hold on the Philippines after the Spanish surrender was religiously motivated. One Christian editor reported that as the president struggled with what to do regarding the Philippines, he paced the floor of the White House until midnight on several occasions. Finally, while praying on his knees, God spoke to him. "[T]here was nothing left for us to do but to take them all," McKinley presumably remembered, "and to educate the

Filipinos, and ulift and civilize them, and by God's grace do the very best we could by them as our fellow-men for whom Christ also died." [105]

Much of McKinley's presidency was dedicated to national reunion, and to him the war was doubly marvelous because it served as the final act in the divine drama of remaking the white republic after the Civil War. For him, God had his hand firmly on sectional reunion. During the presidential election of 1896, McKinley used calls for sectional reunion as an effective way to undermine William Jennings Bryan's campaign, and after being elected to the presidency, McKinley showed every indication that he favored solidarity among whites over and at the expense of civil rights for African Americans. He made no direct statements against lynching or the disenfranchisement of blacks, but he repeatedly assured whites that it was his "constant aim" to continue the project of national reconciliation. [106]

When the War of 1898 came, he made it clear that reunion was crucial to the effort. When imploring former Confederate Joseph Wheeler to accept the position as major general of the volunteers, McKinley declared, "There must be a high officer from the south. There must be a symbol that the old days are gone. You are needed." [107] In speech after speech the president praised northern and southern whites for rallying together to the flag. "No development of the war has been more gratifying and exalting than the complete unification of the nation," he told a crowd in Cedar Rapids, Iowa. "Sectional lines have been obliterated; party differences have been hushed in the great chorus of patriotism which has been heard from one end of the country to the other." [108] He characterized this national solidarity as a "holy alliance." "For the first time for more than half a century," he thundered at Tipton, Indiana, "North and South are united in a holy alliance, with one aim, with one purpose, and with one determination." [109] On another occasion, while speaking in Richmond, Virginia, he described national solidarity as a gift from God. "The voice which would kindle the flame of passion and prejudice is rarely heard," he acknowledged, and he continued by praising God for this development with a poem:

> Lord of the Universe,
> Shield us and guide us,
> Trusting thee always
> Through shadow and sun.
> Thou has united us,
> Who shall divide us?
> Keep us, oh, keep us,
> The "Many in One." [110]

McKinley was not the only American politician to view God's hand in the War of 1898. A young and outspoken United States senator from Indiana, Albert Beveridge, whose popularity rose enormously during the conflict, likewise connected religious missions, American empire, and Anglo-Saxon supremacy.[111] Known as the "golden orator" of expansion, Beveridge told his fellow congressmen during the debate over whether the United States should hold on to the Philippines that "[w]e will not renounce our part in the mission of the race, trustee, under God, of the civilization of the world. . . . He made us . . . the master organizers of the world to establish system where chaos reigns. . . . He has made us adepts in government that we may administer government among savages and servile peoples." In short, God had handpicked white Americans to serve as his torchbearers. "[O]f all our race, He has marked the American people as His chosen Nation to finally lead in the regeneration of the world," Beveridge announced. "This is the divine mission of America, and it holds for us all the profit, all the glory, all the happiness possible to man. . . . The judgment of the Master is upon us: 'Ye have been faithful over a few things; I will make you ruler over many things.'"[112] To determine the popular mood regarding whether the United States should maintain the Philippines as a colony or not, he invited his fellow congressmen to attend any white church. "If any one cherishes the delusion that the American government will ever be withdrawn from our possessions let him consult the religious convictions of the Christian people," he noted. "Let him find what the American pulpit thinks of such surrender to non-Christian powers of our duty and opportunity."[113]

Author and aspiring politician Theodore Roosevelt, as well as Connecticut senator Orville Platt, also praised the War of 1898 as sanctified in heaven and as a powerful means of reuniting the nation. Serving in the Senate from 1879 to 1904 and author of the bill that guaranteed at least a semblance of independence for Cuba in 1903, Platt was one of the most respected congressmen in the nation, and he clearly recognized the connection between American imperialism and Protestant missionary work. "Among Christian, thoughtful people," he told his colleagues, the desire to wage the war and retain control of the islands was "akin to that which has maintained the missionary work of the last century in foreign lands."[114] For Roosevelt, the war was both "righteous" and "advantageous." As he called on volunteers to join his "Rough Riders," he found that men from all over the nation were willing to join him. Roosevelt was remarkably pleased, moreover, when he and his troops encountered affection from southern whites, especially former Confederates. "Everywhere the people came out to greet us and cheer us," he wrote in his history of the Rough Riders. "We were traveling through a region where practically all the older men had served in the Confederate Army, and where the young men had all their lives long drunk in the endless tales told by their elders, at home, and at the cross-roads taverns, and in the court-house squares, about the cavalry of Forrest and Morgan and the infantry of Jackson and Hood." Support came from southern whites of all ages. "The blood of the old men stirred to the distant breath of battle; the blood of the young men leaped hot with eager desire to accompany us. . . . [T]he young girls drove down in bevies, arrayed in their finery, to wave flags in farewell to the troopers and to beg cartridges and buttons as mementos." The Americn flag was ubiquitous, he recalled. "Everywhere we saw the Stars and Stripes, and everywhere we were told, half-laughingly, by grizzled ex-Confederates that they had never dreamed in the bygone days of bitterness to greet the old flag as they now were greeting it, and to send their sons, as now they were sending them, to fight and die under it." [115]

Numerous poets echoed these politicians in depicting the war as a moment of national reconciliation forged by God. Rudyard Kipling's "The White Man's Burden" was merely the most popular of many poems to highlight the American quest as a religious, racial, and gendered crusade:

> Take up the White Man's burden—
>   Send forth the best ye breed—
> Go, bind your sons to exile
>   To serve your captives' need;
> To wait, in heavy harness,
>   On fluttered folk and wild—
> Your new-caught sullen peoples,
>   Half devil and half child. [116]

Other poets cast similar visions for the war. Louis Amonson, for instance, implored Columbia to follow God into combat:

> Then gird thy loins and draw thy sword,
>   The solemn hour of vengeance is at hand;
> Thus reads the mandate of the outraged Lord,
>   Thus roars the echo from thy anguished land. [117]

Another poet, John W. Fitzmaurice, described God as calling to the United States to take up arms against the Spanish:

> Through the land rings out the tocsin;
>   Calling loud: "To arms, to arms!"
> And each patriot's heart re-echoes,
>   To the voice of war's alarms.

"Up!"—it calls—'tis God is speaking:
　　"Hearts for right and hands on sword!"
Sea and land in concert meeting,
　　For their captain is the Lord!
'Tis the God of battles calling—
　　Shall his summons be in vain?
'Tis the tottering pillars falling,
　　Long supporting cruel Spain!
'Tis the cry of slaughtered millions—
　　From God's throne comes loudly down—
"From Spain's brows remove the diadem,"
　　"From her head take off the crown!"[118]

These authors praised the war as a moment when the Anglo-Saxon religious and racial domination of foreign peoples could unify the United States. In their national and international imaginations, whiteness, godliness, and sectional reconciliation were intimately connected. They lauded the War of 1898 as the final culmination of post–Civil War national solidarity. As one editor of a series of poems put it, "[S]uch unanimity of patriotic sentiment had never before been exhibited in our history. . . . Those who wore the blue and those who wore the gray during the great Civil War, now touched fraternal elbows as they fell into rank under the beautiful banner of their common country."[119] One northern poet wrote:

And now when danger threatens,
　　No North, no South, we know,
Once more we stand together
　　To fight the common foe.[120]

Some of these writers even described national reconciliation in terms of blood and faith, implying that amid the crucible of war, northerners and southerners had become racially and religiously unified. In "Chant of the New Union," Edmund Russel declared:

Blood of the North
　　To the Blood of the South—
　　　　Are we the same blood?
Now the same blood!
. . . .
Prayer of the North
　　To the Prayer of the South—

Breathe we the same prayer?

Yes—Now the same prayer.[121]

To Russel and poets like him, the War of 1898 stood as the culmination of America's religious and national reconciliation. Northern and southern whites were no longer divided; the mixing of prayers and blood had made them one in spirit and in body.

These poets were not alone among American writers in conceiving of the war as a time when God reforged American nationalism during the fires of battle. Thomas Dixon Jr., perhaps the most popular and influential novelist of the early twentieth century, considered the War of 1898 a glorious time when the Christian Lord brought national reconciliation through Anglo-Saxon domination of foreign lands. His works, which glorified the Ku Klux Klan and demonized African American men as sexual predators, were profoundly racist. Dixon regularly connected religious and scientific rationales for racial supremacy. "Racial purity is not prejudice," one his characters in *The Sins of the Father* announced, "but God's first law of life—the instinct of self-preservation."[122] His white supremacist vision brought him unimagined fame. Historian Joel Williamson has estimated that Dixon's novels, together with plays and movies based on them, were so popular that he "probably did more to shape the lives of modern Americans than have some Presidents." Dixon's novels, in fact, provided the storyline and the images for D. W. Griffith's *The Birth of a Nation* (1915), which helped solidify the popular perception of radical Reconstruction as an evil tragedy perpetuated by vindictive northerners and lustful freedpeople.[123] Understandably, African Americans denounced Dixon with righteous anger. Black intellectual Kelly Miller called him "the chief priest of those who worship at the shrine of race hatred and wrath."[124]

In *The Leopard's Spots: A Romance of the White Man's Burden, 1865–1900* (1902), which sold so many copies that contemporaries labeled it a "mob novel," Dixon directly connected religion and white supremacy at home with imperialism abroad. The "white man's burden" stood as the dual enterprise of subduing people of color in foreign lands and of controlling African Americans within the United States. He depicted the War of 1898 as an especially miraculous time when the Christian Lord brought national reconciliation through Anglo-Saxon domination of foreign lands.[125] No Anglo-Saxon, a southern politician in the novel proclaimed, could resist the "tide of the rising consciousness of Nationality and World-Missions. . . . We dream of the conquest of the globe." It was God who had instilled such visions in the minds and hearts of whites. "We believe that God has raised up our race, as he ordained Israel of old, in this world-crisis to establish and maintain for weaker races, as a trust for civilisation, the principles of civil and religious Liberty and the forms of Constitutional Government," this politician continued. The United States must not make the same mistake that it had during Reconstruction, he maintained, and bring "semi-barbaric black men" into the nation as equal citizens. "I believe in God's call to our race to do His work in history," he concluded, and God called the United States to subjugate and rule over foreigners for their own benefit. "The Anglo-Saxon race is united and has entered upon its world mission. It is the law of God."[126]

Regarding American expansion and imperialism, Dixon's southern white politician sounded very similar to Albert Beveridge, Theodore Roosevelt, William McKinley, and a host of northern white Protestants and poets. The white North and the white South were now one, and God had made it so through military conflict and imperialism. The language of religious mission and sacred racial domination frequently employed by Gilded Age missionaries and their organizations became a staple of the political and cultural justifications of the War of 1898 and American imperialism. The white republic had finally been restored, and whiteness, godliness, and American nationalism had become firmly locked together in the minds and hearts of countless white Americans. The flood of American jingoism completed the deluge that drowned out the civic nationalism of the 1860s, and it further instilled an ethnic nationalism of whiteness that religiously legitimated some of the most heinous crimes of the late nineteenth century.

IV

But Dixon, Beveridge, McKinley, and other promoters of imperialism and America's "world mission" did not go uncontested throughout the war years. The vast majority of Americans, white and black, supported the liberation of Cuba, but a tide of opposition rose against holding on to the former Spanish colonies.[127] In particular, anti-imperialists blasted the ways politicians, editors, writers, ministers, and missionaries conflated political and religious endeavors. But even the arguments of the opponents of empire demonstrated the pervasiveness of ethnic nationalism. Although they stood against the acquisition of foreign countries, many anti-imperialists did so by asserting that the supposed racial inferiority of foreign peoples made their inclusion in the national body dangerous. In contrast, African American anti-imperialists were far more likely to point out that expansion was undesirable, not because of the race of the Cubans or Filipinos, but because of the unjustness and prejudices of white Americans. They recognized that a nation that mistreated people of color in its own home population would not do much better toward people of color abroad.

Anti-imperialists, whether white or black, lost no time in pointing out the religious hypocrisy of the imperialists. Carl Schurz, an indefatigable anti-imperialist, claimed that casting the war as a holy crusade was blasphemous: "The American people may well pause before accepting a counsel which, in seeking to unload upon Providence the responsibility for schemes of reckless ambition involving a palpable breach of faith, falls little short of downright blasphemy."[128] Responding to one of Beveridge's speeches in the Senate, George F. Hoar compared the lust for imperialism to the temptation of Christ: "The Devil taketh him up into an extremely high mountain and showeth him all the kingdoms of this world and the glory of them and saith unto him 'All these things will be thine if thou wilt fall down and worship me.'" This biblical story was used by at least one anti-imperialist artist as well. (See figure 15.)[129]

Poet Bertrand Shadwell, moreover, parodied Kipling's "White Man's Burden" to ridicule religious justifications of imperial conquests:

> Take up the sword and rifle,
> Send forth your ships with speed,
> To join the nations' scramble,
> And vie with them in greed;
>
> . . . .
>
> Take up the sword and rifle
> Rob every savage race,
> Annex their lands and harbors,
> For this is Christian grace.[130]

Even some white American soldiers and Protestant ministers found the religious hypocrisy of the nation too much to bear. One general in the Philippines wrote to his wife about an incident when an "infantry came into this place the other night and literally destroyed it—looted, ransacked, and burned it—and we propose to civilize, Christianize, these people." He lamented, "We come as a Christian people to relieve them of the Spanish yoke and bear ourselves like barbarians. Well I have said enough."[131] But others had much more to say. Presbyterian minister Charles Spahr railed against the American public, especially Protestant Christians, for creating a new set of divine edicts that legitimated greed and hate. Americans, he raged, acted as if the Ten Commandments actually read: "Thou shalt have no other Gods before me and only gold above me. . . . Thou shalt not take the name of the Lord thy God in vain, but shalt use it profitably to sanctify thy greed. . . . Thou shalt not kill except to extend trade. . . . Thou shalt not covet but grab."[132]

While these anti-imperialists assailed the conflation of religion and political mission, many had little difficulty employing racism in their attacks upon imperialism. In fact, racist ideologies were central to the crusade against empire. Historian Christopher Lasch has pointed out that many anti-imperialist arguments revolved around notions that foreign peoples were innately incapable of wielding American citizenship appropriately.[133] Politicians and ministers, such as South Carolina's Senator Benjamin Tillman and New York's Reverend Theodore Cuyler argued that the United States should not annex the Philippines, Cuba, or any other land because such policies might entitle millions of "inferior" peoples to citizenship. The nation, they insisted, must remain racially pure, and it already had enough difficulties with African Americans in the South and immigrants from Europe. Cuyler repeatedly assailed imperialism, but did so by depicting Cubans and Filipinos as incapable of maintaining the virtue of the Republic. The Philippine Islands, he asserted, "with their mongrel hordes of half-civilized and barbarians," could never become a part of the American nation. The ethnic nationalism of the white anti-imperialists appeared just as deeply rooted as that of their imperialist-minded opponents.[134]

White leaders in the WCTU echoed the racist anti-imperialism of ministers like Cuyler. Although they and many other Protestant women denounced American military imperialism and strongly endorsed international arbitration, temperance women repeatedly characterized foreign peoples of color as barbarians who would pollute the nation. To Hannah Bailey, the superintendent of the WCTU's "Peace and Arbitration Department," "[T]he social plane of the people [Filipinos] . . . is at the lowest [level]. Their only wants realized by themselves consist of shelter, food, and enough clothing to partially cover themselves, and perhaps ornamental decorations for their almost nude bodies. Their moral status is unmistakable when we remember that the custom of cannibalism still prevails in many of the islands."[135] For the women of the WCTU, foreign peoples—whether immigrating to the United States or achieving a measure of citizenship as conquered people—had no business becoming part of the American nation.

The racism of the anti-imperialists reflected the rising tidal wave of virulent white supremacy sweeping across the United States in the 1890s, which revealed itself forcefully against Cubans, Filipinos, Puerto Ricans, and African Americans. In many ways, the descriptions of foreigners by U.S. military men sounded eerily similar to the descriptions of them by Protestant missionaries in the 1880s and

1890s. One soldier in Cuba, for instance, described the typical local as "a treacherous, lying, cowardly, thieving, worthless, half-breed mongrel; born of a mongrel spawn of Europe, crossed upon the fetiches of darkest Africa and aboriginal America. He is no more capable of self-government than the Hottentots that roam the wilds of Africa or the Bushmen of Australia. He can not be trusted like the Indian, will not work like a negro, and will not fight like a Spaniard." Another soldier in Puerto Rico claimed that the islands' inhabitants were "ignorant, filthy, untruthful, lazy, treacherous, murderous, brutal, and black."[136]

There were direct connections, moreover, between religiously based racism abroad and racism at home. In 1900, Josiah Strong declared that all people of color, whether within the United States or not, were "many centuries behind the Anglo-Saxon in development [and] seem as incapable of operating complicated machinery as they are of adopting and successfully administering representative government." Unlike Protestants immediately following Lincoln's assassination who had believed that racial differences could be overcome with education, Christianity, and national citizenship, Strong now contended that "[t]he difference between races and civilizations is not simply one of time and of degree, but one of kind" and that all an African American could do was accept his subordination and learn "to adjust himself to them [whites] in a passive spirit."[137] The link between racism in foreign lands and the United States went beyond mere words, though. After an African American editor in Wilmington, North Carolina, denounced Rebecca Felton, a prominent leader in the WCTU, for defending lynching, the city exploded in a gruesome race riot. Over four hundred whites—some of whom appropriated the name of Theodore Roosevelt's regiment, the "Rough Riders"—marched into the black section of town and inflicted a reign of terror. Thousands of African Americans fled the city, never to return. The riot effectively destroyed black political rights in North Carolina for more than a decade.[138]

One strain of anti-imperialism, however, was also anti-racist and deeply committed to egalitarianism. For many African Americans, who fully understood the power and violence of white supremacy, American imperialism was hypocritical, sinful, and unholy. They considered religiously justified racism abroad and at home to be parts of the same American project of violence and hate. They despised the ways that northern and southern whites proclaimed a new sense of national fraternity while people of color were being disfranchised, segregated, and brutalized at the turn of the century. From 1898 to 1900, racial violence continued to plague the country, punctuated by the lynching of Sam Hose in Georgia, where more than two thousand whites showed up to revel in the torturous murder. Even the more than ten thousand blacks who patriotically volunteered to serve in the War of 1898 became objects of scorn and contempt.[139]

Some African Americans expressed a strong sense of fraternity with the oppressed Cubans and Filipinos, and they likened racism within the United States to the vile treatment of the Cubans by the Spanish. Regularly, black editors referred to Cubans and Filipinos as "kinsmen" and "our colored brothers."[140] In a pamphlet for the Anti-Imperial League, Kelly Miller directly connected imperialism and racism. "The welfare of the negro race," he asserted, "is involved in the impending policy of imperialism," because how the American government treated people of color abroad reflected how they treated and planned to treat people of color at home. And things did not look promising. The Republican Party had turned its back on racial justice, while the southern Democratic Party had become increasingly aggressive. Miller lamented that the African American's "friends have grown cold as his enemies have become hot."[141] In a letter to the *Cleveland Gazette*, one African American chaplain directly compared the United States to the Spanish Empire: "Is America any better than Spain? Has she not subjects in her very midst who are murdered daily without a trial of judge or jury? Has she not subjects in her own boarders whose children are half-fed and half-clothed, because their father's skin is black."[142] After linking racism within the United States to that overseas, another black minister declared, "I would rather take a gun and kill an American citizen than to aid the Americans in a war with Spain."[143]

Many black Americans expressed outrage when President McKinley and other northern white politicians and religious leaders declared the War of 1898 to be the completion of national reconciliation and solidarity. To them, national harmony was preposterous when people of color remained disadvantaged. In December 1898, one black soldier lamented that "[t]here are dirty, low, white brutes down here that the devil wouldn't have for a precious gift and it is to these also the president has tendered 'the olive branch.' My God!" This same soldier later wrote to the *Cleveland Gazette* that "[t]he statement that the North and South are 'bound by ties of a united nation, with common interest to all,' etc. is not a reality. It is a myth with only symptoms of reality for the sake of aggrandizement. Should Providence bless us with a new allotment of Joshua E. Giddings, Lovejoys and Charles Sumners to cause all God-fearing people in all parts of the country to lend their ears, hearts and wills to the cause of the down-trodden and despised Afro-Americans . . . the feeling that is now dormant would be dominant."[144] African Americans knew that sectional reconciliation and reunion among whites spelled disaster, and they blasted white Christians for allowing this to occur. "His former friends are silent and indifferent," a writer to the *Savannah Tribune* lamented. "His enemies have grown bolder and more defiant. It looks as though annihilation is what is desired, and the Christian public fold their arms and say, 'Let him die' he is not Anglo-Saxon."[145]

Segregation during the war was especially aggravating to African Americans. When northern evangelists, including Dwight Moody, who worked with troops shortly before his death in 1899, held segregated camp meetings for soldiers stationed in Florida, African Americans censured them. Even though Moody had integrated his revival meetings in Paris, Texas, in 1894, he had become synonymous with religious Jim Crow by the end of the century. "Dwight Moody is here galore," wrote one black soldier, "but the colored boys care nothing for his color prejudiced religion."[146] Segregation in southern churches was also thoroughly enraging. Writing to the *Christian Recorder*, Chaplain George W. Prioleau described his encounter at a white church. "[W]hen an officer of the United States Army, a Negro chaplain . . . goes on Sunday to the M.E. Church (White) to worship god, he is given three propositions to consider, take the extreme back seat, go up in the gallery or go out," Prioleau contended. He and his compatriots chose the last option, "as we were not a back seat or gallery Christian, we preferred going out." But they refused to let the matter die, and "inform[ed] them on the next day that the act was heinous, uncivilized, un-christian, [and] un-American."[147] Racism and violence were now so prevalent within the nation, in fact, that one black editor proposed that the thousands of white missionaries abroad immediately return home to civilize white Americans. "With the government acquiescing in the oppression and butchery of a dark race in this country and the enslaving and slaughtering of a dark race in the Philippines," he suggested that "we think it time to call all missionaries home and have them work on our own people."[148]

Feeling betrayed by northern whites who had offered civil liberties and protection to freedpeople only to show little interest when they were stolen, black Americans scoffed openly at the idea of a "white man's burden." The burden bearers in the United States were not white, they protested, but black. In a poem in *Colored American*, the author drew attention to the enormous weight black men had to shoulder:

> To h—— with the "White Man's Burden!"
> To h– with Kipling's verse!
> The Black Man demands our attention:
> His condition is getting worse.
> Why lose sleep over his burden?
> All mortals have their share,

> The black man's growing hardships
> Are more than he can bear.[149]

Other African Americans parodied Kipling to claim that God would ultimately judge whites for racial injustice:

> Pile on the Black Man's burden,
>   At length 'twill heaven pierce;
> Then on you or your children
>   Will reign God's judgment fierce.
> Your battleships and armies
>   May weaker one appall,
> But God Almighty's justice
>   They'll not disturb at all.[150]

Indeed, the anti-imperialism of African Americans stemmed from a deep understanding of what white political control meant: violence, hypocrisy, and exploitation. The hopefulness of African Americans immediately following the Civil War had faded. Three and a half decades of betrayal, disfranchisement, and terror had led to a thorough disenchantment with the United States. They recognized that race problems within the United States and the world were far from being resolved. It was in this milieu that, during an address at the first Pan-African conference in 1900, W. E. B. Du Bois claimed, "the problem of the Twentieth Century is the problem of the color-line." Sadly, the events of the new century proved Du Bois an accurate prophet.[151]

These anti-imperialist, anti-racist arguments, however, generally fell on deaf ears at the turn of the century. When McKinley and his popular running mate, Theodore Roosevelt, soundly defeated William Jennings Bryan in the presidential election of 1900, the anti-imperialist movement quickly disintegrated.[152] American whites had embarked on a new war to free Cuba and to dominate foreign peoples, and this new battle solidified the white republic. The mission of the apostles of forgiveness was finally completed. As the twentieth century began, whites of the North and whites of the South clasped hands as brethren. An ethnic nationalism centered on whiteness had prevailed over the radical civic nationalism of the 1860s. White Protestant Americans believed that their God now smiled down upon them and had inaugurated a grand new era of American nationalism. The religious, political, and economic mission to the world was the final piece in the reforging of the white republic. Although scores of African Americans and other anti-imperialists railed against empire and called the nation to respect the rights and humanity of peoples of color, the vast majority of white Protestants refused to hear or to see.

Dreaming of the White Republic, Defending the
Souls of Black Folk

Amid the public debate over American imperialism in 1899, the former vice con-
sul-general to Haiti, Arthur Bird, mused about how the United States and the
world would change over the next hundred years. Playing off Edward Bellamy's
enormously popular utopian novel, *Looking Backward, 2000–1887*, Bird penned his
own prediction for the future, *Looking Forward: A Dream of the United States of
America in 1999*. His vision of what the future held demonstrated how radically
northern whites' religious, national, and racial imaginations had altered since the
mid-1860s. An ethnic nationalism of whiteness, underpinned by Protestantism,
had penetrated and had come to dominate the American psyche. *Looking Forward*
showed that whiteness, Protestantism, American nationalism, and imperialism
were bound tightly together in the moral conception of whites by the turn of the
century. African Americans, especially W. E. B. Du Bois, continued to attack the
tenets of the white republic and armed themselves for a long battle. They held fast
to the belief that racial status or affiliation should not be considered in determining the national citizenry, but they lost the battle for America's identity. They
stepped into the new century ready for war, but with far less hope than they had
a generation earlier.

In Bird's *Looking Forward*, the world was drastically transformed during the
twentieth century. These hundred years were marked by the ascendance and control of whiteness and Protestant Christianity. Germany gobbled up France; the
Spanish and Turkish nations were wiped off the map; Central and South Americans
rushed to link arms with the United States after the War of 1898; and the United
States dominated the entire Western Hemisphere. The American capital was
moved to Mexico, a land of "perpetual sunshine and flowers," and Admiral Dewey,
"the idol of America," became President Dewey. Sectional grievances within the
original United States were completely obliterated. "[T]hat little strip of territory
lying between Mason and Dixon's line and the gulf of Mexico was no longer known

or recognized as the South," Bird wrote. While the end of the twentieth century witnessed hemispheric control by the United States, it also entailed the global supremacy of Protestant Christianity and the Anglo-Saxon race. Great Britain triumphed victoriously throughout the globe, maintaining its control over India and ruling the entire continent of Africa. "The power and stamina of the Anglo-Saxon race," Bird claimed, "dominated the world in 1999 through the vast Republic of the Americas and the world-wide British empire." Religious faith was especially crucial to Anglo-Saxon authority, and missionaries marched across the Earth leaving schools and churches along the way. "At the close of the twentieth century indications point to a general christianizing of all peoples on the globe." "America," he concluded, "is destined to become the Light of the World."[1]

Racial antagonism and alienation continued to flourish in Bird's twentieth century, as the blood of whites and blacks drenched the land. To Bird, the reason for the violence was simple: "the troublesome Ethiopians" refused to accept second-class citizenship passively. And whites became increasingly frustrated with these black ne'er do wells. "The fact cannot be denied," Bird professed, "that the presence of the negro in North America is undesirable." He imagined that by 1960 an enormous mass movement would form to push people of color out of the original United States: "People commenced to realize that the negro was an utterly alien race; that when they landed here America gained nothing," he prophesied. "The proposition to transfer the negro population to the Central and Southern American States was agitated in that year." Congress followed the will of the people, and African Americans were removed to several provinces in Venezuela. There, they farmed and lived on horse meat. In 1975, "[e]ven Boston," the hub of opposition to African American removal, "applauded the movement as being a philanthropic one, calculated to increase the well being of the negro. The brainy men of Boston argued that reservations had been frequently purchased for the use of Indians, and there was no good reason why one should not be purchased for the use of the American negro." The United States would finally become a "white man's country" in name and in reality.[2]

Bird's predictions regarding race relations in this future world were dark and disturbing, but they were not far from mainstream public opinions. His forecast of racial segregation paralleled that of author and reformer Edward Bellamy, whose *Looking Backward* was undoubtedly the most popular utopian novel of the nineteenth century. It sold sixty thousand copies in its first full year of distribution, and more than one hundred thousand in 1889. His novel was so popular, in fact, that it led thousands of northerners to form "Nationalist Clubs" to discuss how Bellamy's vision could be realized in the United States. In *Looking Backward*, Bellamy presented a United States that would become a socialistic utopia during the twentieth century where all men and women would reach their full potential. In the America of 2000 there would be no more hunger and no more social animosity. There would be neither greed nor envy. Private property would be abolished and lawyers would be as extinct as dinosaurs. Sectional divisions would also be relics of the past, and the new American nationalism would lead to a new and profound sense of human brotherhood.[3]

But even for Bellamy, this was a racialized nation and brotherhood. In the sequel to *Looking Backward*, ironically titled *Equality: A Novel*, the United States of the twentieth century was a thoroughly segregated nation. As one of the main characters maintained, the American utopia "related entirely to economic organization, and had nothing to do with them than it has now with social relations. Even for industrial purposes the new system involved no more commingling of the races than the old one had done. It was perfectly consistent with any degree of race separation in industry which the most bigoted local prejudices might demand." While Bellamy was willing to challenge so many cardinal "American" values, even the sanctity of private property, he could not consider a racially integrated nation. Neither Bellamy nor Bird was able to fathom or cast a vision for a nation of interracial fraternity.[4]

Although hideous, Bird's and Bellamy's imagined futures for African Americans were not the most shocking ones advocated in the United States at the turn of the century. Atlanta's John Temple Graves, the editor of the *Georgian*, suggested that branding and castration should once again be legalized throughout the South in order to stop black crimes and racial lynchings. To him, removing the genitalia of black men and "unsexing" black women stood as the only humanitarian means to handle race relations in the South. The castration of black men, moreover, became a staple of lynchings as white crowds viciously raped and murdered the black men they accused of raping white women.[5]

Northerners' tacit acceptance of lynching and Bird's global, national, religious, and racial predictions showed how completely the radical dreams and civic nationalism of 1860s northern white Protestants had evaporated. The United States imagined by J. L. Giles in his 1867 print, "Reconstruction," in which whites and blacks resided in an integrated and egalitarian American republic, was a nation completely foreign to Arthur Bird and most other turn-of-the-century whites. When General Robert E. Lee had surrendered at Appomattox and John Wilkes Booth had assassinated Abraham Lincoln in the spring of 1865, the identity of the

United States had been anything but clear. Profoundly angered and confused by President Lincoln's assassination, a host of white Protestant ministers had pushed for a radical reformulation of the American republic. Protestants had focused on loyalty to the Union, rather than perceived racial differences, as the chief determiners of national citizenship. They had set out to topple the white republic and to build a new nation of racial justice, egalitarianism, and brotherhood in its place. A civic nationalism that prized loyalty to the principles of union, democracy, and freedom had been a powerful force in the 1860s. Ministers and many of the missionaries who ventured south after the war had believed that a color-blind, integrated world was not only desirable, but also imminently possible. They had railed against white prejudice and racism as anti-Christian and they had poured their capital and energies into making a new South and a new America. Many missionary-teachers, in fact, believed they were experiencing a glimpse of heaven. It appeared that God was creating a new world and that he was smiling at his handiwork.

But this world was betrayed. An ethnic nationalism that prized whiteness quickly replaced the civic nationalism of the 1860s. While a wide variety of white businessmen and politicians pressed for national reconciliation at the direct expense of racial justice, northern white Protestant leaders helped lead the charge for reunion. As Henry Ward Beecher implored his audiences to forgive the white South and as his sister Harriet Beecher Stowe invited northerners to view Florida as a land of idyllic race relations, they encouraged northern whites to re-envision white Confederates and the South. Then, in the mid-1870s, Dwight Moody's gigantic urban revival crusade turned the attention of northern Protestants away from racial justice and toward regional forgiveness. The yellow fever epidemic of 1878 provided northerners an opportunity to show their care for the white South, and for former Confederates to respond with affirmations of new patriotic bonds between the North and the South. In the 1880s, with a common crusade against alcohol, the women of the WCTU built bridges between northern and southern white women, and in the 1890s, America's religious, economic, political, and military expansion benighted the nation's post–Civil War reunion. As the new century dawned, northern white Protestants could congratulate themselves for helping to reforge the white republic once and for all.

Although the white republic was thoroughly reestablished by the end of the century, a new generation of African Americans continued to fight against racial injustice and exploitation. For African Americans, the joy of the 1860s had turned into the sorrow of the 1890s. People of color recognized that they had lost many battles since the Civil War, but they refused to admit that the war was over. Some blacks became so enraged by violence committed against their people that they denounced whites as demons. After the lynching of George White in 1906, African Methodist Episcopal Church minister Montrose Thornton lambasted white America: "The white man, in the face of his boasted civilization, stands before my eyes tonight the demon of the world's races, a monster incarnate. . . . The white is a heathen, a fiend, a monstrosity before God."[6]

Other blacks held fast to the conviction that they would one day achieve full inclusion in the nation and government. In January 1901, when the last black congressmen of the Reconstruction era, George H. White of North Carolina, left office, he prophesied that although largely disfranchised, African Americans would make their way back to positions of leadership. "This, Mr. Chairman, is perhaps the Negroes' temporary farewell to the American Congress," he announced, "but let me say, Phoenix-like he will rise up some day and come again. These parting words are in behalf of an outraged, heart-broken, bruised and bleeding, but God-fearing people, faithful, industrious, loyal, rising people—full of potential force."[7]

The black leader most committed to defying the conflation of whiteness, Protestant Christianity, and American nationalism at the end of the nineteenth century and into the twentieth was W. E. B. Du Bois. At the same time that white supremacist theologian Charles Carroll published discourses that depicted "Negroes" as subhuman, Du Bois proclaimed that black folk owned exactly what whites sought to deny them: souls. In his collection of essays *The Souls of Black Folk* (1903), Du Bois continued the legacy of black resistance to the notion that white Americans were divinely ordained to dominate people of color. He sought to demonstrate that African Americans had contributed significantly to the making of the United States. Their love for freedom and independence made African Americans the truest "exponents of the pure human spirit of the Declaration of Independence," he declared, while the "sorrow songs" of the slaves were "the most beautiful expression of human experience born this side of the seas." Furthermore, Du Bois held northern whites just as responsible as southern whites for the exploitation and marginalization of African Americans, referring to the North as the South's "co-partner in guilt." To Du Bois, Reconstruction had brought neither atonement for the evils of the white republic nor the genuine liberation of African Americans. "The Nation has not yet found peace from its sins," he lamented. "[T]he freedman has not yet found in freedom his promised land."[8]

During the early twentieth century, Du Bois continued to assail whites for believing that their racist and imperialistic country could be considered a "Christian nation." "[I]t is absurd to call the practical religion of this nation Christian," he lectured to the students and faculty at the Philadelphia Divinity School in 1907. As a nation, the United States defied each lesson of what Du Bois considered the heart of Christianity, the Sermon on the Mount. "We are not humble, we are impudently proud," Du Bois contended. "[W]e are not peaceful nor peacefully inclined as our armies and battle-ships declare; . . . we do not seek continuously, and prayerfully inculcate, love and justice for our fellow men, but on the contrary the treatment of the poor, the unfortunate, and the black within our borders is almost a national crime."[9]

But Du Bois remained hopeful that a truly Christian United States could be built that would include all individuals and groups. He refused to believe that the biblical Christ would endorse materialism, discrimination, and imperialism. Instead he clung tightly to a social gospel understanding of the faith. Before Christmas in 1910 or 1911, he prayed with his students at Atlanta University that "[o]ut of the depths of selfishness and languor and envy, let spring the spirit of humility and poverty, of gentleness and sacrifice—the eternal dawn of Peace, good-will toward men. Let the birth-bells of God call our vain imaginings back from pomp and glory and wealth—back from the wasteful warships searching the seas—back to the lowly barn-yard and the homely cradle of a yellow and despised Jew, whom the world has not yet learned to call Wonderful, Counsellor, the Mighty God, the Everlasting Father, and the Prince of Peace. Amen." Du Bois maintained faith that the power of the spirit of Christ could fundamentally re-create the United States.[10]

Du Bois's prayers, along with those of Frederick Douglass, Ida B. Wells, Frances E. W. Harper, and many other African Americans, were beautiful, but in the end unable to stem the national descent into violence, disfranchisement, and hatred. A new, religiously inspired American ethnic nationalism had been forged. It was a national and religious identity suffused with racism and alienation. As the United States barged into the twentieth century, the supremacy of whiteness, the supremacy of the United States, and the supremacy of Christ had again become viewed as one in the same. Giles's radical vision of an integrated and egalitarian nation existed now in the minds and hearts of only a few. The reforging of the white republic was complete. And perhaps, as Du Bois once wrote, God wept.

Notes

INTRODUCTION

1. Quoted in Eric Foner, *Reconstruction: America's Unfinished Revolution, 1863–1877* (New York: Harper and Row, Publishers, 1988), 26–7.

2. Philip Dray, *At the Hands of Persons Unknown: The Lynching of Black America* (New York: Modern Library, 2003), 190–215; Michael Paul Rogin, *Ronald Reagan, the Movie, and Other Episodes in Political Demonology* (Berkeley: Univ. of California Press, 1987), 190–235; Lary May, *Screening out the Past: The Birth of Mass Culture and the Motion Picture Industry* (New York: Oxford Univ. Press, 1980), 19–67; D. W. Griffith, producer and director, *The Birth of a Nation* (film) (1915; Los Angeles: Republic Pictures Home Video, 1991).

3. W. E. B. Du Bois, *Black Reconstruction in America* (1935; reprint, New York: Atheneum Books, 1992), 707.

4. Throughout this study, I refer to the wars between the United States and the Spanish, Cubans, and Filipinos beginning 1898 as the "War of 1898." Other names, such as "Spanish-American War" and the "Spanish-American-Cuban-Filipino War," are either nationally biased or overly cumbersome. For a discussion of what to call these wars, see Thomas G. Patterson, "United States Intervention in Cuba, 1898: Interpretations of the Spanish-American-Cuban-Filipino War," *The History Teacher* 29, no. 3 (May 1996): 341–61.

5. Reginald Horsman, *Race and Manifest Destiny: The Origins of American Racial Anglo-Saxonism* (Cambridge, Mass.: Harvard Univ. Press, 1981), 22; Martin Marty, *Righteous Empire: The Protestant Experience in America* (New York: Dial Press, 1970); Ernest Lee Tuveson, *Redeemer Nation: The Idea of America's Millennial Role* (Chicago: Univ. of Chicago Press, 1968); David R. Roediger, *The Wages of Whiteness: Race and the Making of the American Working Class* (London: Verso, 1991); Noel Ignatiev, *How the Irish Became White* (New York: Routledge, 1995); Alexander Saxton, *The Rise and Fall of the White Republic: Class Politics and Mass Culture in Nineteenth-Century America* (London: Verso, 1990); Matthew Frye Jacobson, *Whiteness of a Different Color: European Immigrants and the Alchemy of Race* (Cambridge, Mass.: Harvard Univ. Press, 1998); Leon F. Litwack, *North of Slavery: The Negro in the Free States, 1790–1860* (Chicago: Univ. of Chicago Press, 1961); Joanne Pope Melish, *Disowning Slavery: Gradual Emancipation and "Race" in New England, 1780–1860* (Ithaca: Cornell Univ. Press, 1998).

6. Palmer, quoted in Stephen R. Haynes, *Noah's Curse: The Biblical Justification of American Slavery* (New York: Oxford Univ. Press, 2002), 131; James M. McPherson, *Is Blood Thicker Than Water? Crises of Nationalism in the Modern World* (New York: Vintage Books, 1998), 55; William Robert Taylor, *Cavalier and Yankee: The Old South and American National Character* (1961; reprint, Cambridge, Mass.: Harvard Univ. Press, 1979); Susan-Mary Grant, *North Over South: Northern Nationalism and American Identity in the Antebellum Era* (Lawrence: Univ. Press of Kansas, 2000); Chester F. Dunham, *The Attitude of Northern Clergy toward the South* (Toledo, Ohio: Gray, 1942); Randall C. Jimerson, *The Private*

Civil War: Popular Thought during the Sectional Conflict (Baton Rouge: Louisiana State Univ. Press, 1988), 124; Drew Gilpin Faust, *The Creation of Confederate Nationalism: Ideology and Identity in the Civil War South* (Baton Rouge: Louisiana State Univ. Press, 1988).

7. Faust, *The Creation of Confederate Nationalism*, 30–58; James H. Moorhead, *American Apocalypse: Yankee Protestants and the Civil War, 1860–1869* (New Haven, Conn.: Yale Univ. Press, 1978); Peter J. Parish, "From Necessary Evil to National Blessing: The Northern Protestant Clergy Interpret the Civil War," in *An Uncommon Time: The Civil War and the Northern Home Front*, edited by Paul A. Cimbala and Randall M. Miller (New York: Fordham Univ. Press, 2002), 61–89; Phillip P. Paludan, "Religion and the American Civil War," in Randall M. Miller, Harry S. Stout, and Charles Reagan Wilson, eds., *Religion and the American Civil War* (New York: Oxford Univ. Press, 1998), 21–42.

8. James M. McPherson, *The Struggle for Equality: Abolitionists and the Negro in the Civil War and Reconstruction* (Princeton, N.J.: Princeton Univ. Press, 1964); Bruce Levine, *Half Slave and Half Free: The Roots of Civil War* (New York: Hill and Wang, 1992); Foner, *Reconstruction*, 24–8; Don E. Fehrenbacher, "Only his Stepchildren: Lincoln and the Negro," in *A Nation Divided: Problems and Issues of the Civil War and Reconstruction*, edited by George M. Fredrickson (Minneapolis: Burgess Publishing Company, 1975), 35–56.

9. Quoted in R. J. M. Blackett, *Beating Against the Barriers: The Lives of Six Nineteenth-Century Afro-Americans* (Ithaca: Cornell Univ. Press, 1986), 192.

10. Roediger, *The Wages of Whiteness*; Ignatiev, *How the Irish Became White*; Saxton, *The Rise and Fall of the White Republic*; Jacobson, *Whiteness of a Different Color*; Grace Elizabeth Hale, *Making Whiteness: The Culture of Segregation in the South, 1890–1940* (New York: Pantheon Books, 1998); Michael Omi and Howard Winant, *Racial Formation in the United States: From the 1960s to the 1980s* (New York: Routledge and Kegan Paul, 1986), 61.

11. The distinction between "ethnic nationalism" and "civic nationalism" is discussed by Michael Ignatieff, *Blood and Belonging: Journeys into the New Nationalism* (New York: Farrar, Straus, and Giroux, 1993), and McPherson, *Is Blood Thicker Than Water?*

12. Moorhead, *American Apocalypse*; Parish, "From Necessary Evil to National Blessing"; George M. Fredrickson, *The Inner Civil War: Northern Intellectuals and the Crisis of the Union* (New York, Harper and Row, 1965).

13. William Archibald Dunning, *Essays on the Civil War and Reconstruction and Related Topics* (New York: P. Smith, 1931); Eric L. McKitrick, *Andrew Johnson and Reconstruction* (New York: Oxford Univ. Press, 1960); John Hope Franklin, *Reconstruction: After the Civil War* (Chicago: Univ. of Chicago Press, 1961); Kenneth M. Stampp, *The Era of Reconstruction, 1865–1877* (New York: Alfred A. Knopf, 1965); Foner, *Reconstruction*; James M. McPherson, *Ordeal by Fire: The Civil War and Reconstruction* (New York: McGraw-Hill, 1982); Laura F. Edwards, *Gendered Strife and Confusion: The Political Culture of Reconstruction* (Urbana: Univ. of Illinois Press, 1997); Heather Cox Richardson, *The Death of Reconstruction: Race, Labor, and Politics in the Post–Civil War North, 1865–1901* (Cambridge, Mass.: Harvard Univ. Press, 2001).

14. Charles Reagan Wilson, *Baptized in Blood: The Religion of the Lost Cause, 1865–1920* (Athens: Univ. of Georgia Press, 1980); Gaines M. Foster, *Ghosts of the Confederacy: Defeat, the Lost Cause, and the Emergence of the New South, 1865 to 1913* (New York: Oxford Univ. Press, 1987); W. Scott Poole, "Religion, Gender, and the Lost Cause in South Carolina's 1876 Governor's Race: 'Hampton or Hell!'" *Journal of Southern History* 68, no. 3 (2002): 573–95; W. Scott Poole, *Never Surrender: Confederate*

Memory and Conservatism in the South Carolina Upcountry (Athens: Univ. of Georgia Press, 2003); Daniel W. Stowell, *Rebuilding Zion: The Religious Reconstruction of the South, 1863–1877* (New York: Oxford Univ. Press, 1998); Gaines M. Foster, *Moral Reconstruction: Christian Lobbyists and the Federal Legislation of Morality, 1865–1920* (Chapel Hill: Univ. of North Carolina Press, 2002).

15. Paul H. Buck, *The Road to Reunion, 1865–1900* (Boston: Little, Brown and Company, 1937); C. Vann Woodward, *Origins of the New South, 1877–1913* (1951; reprint, Baton Rouge: Louisiana State Univ. Press, 1971), 43–50; Mark W. Summers, *The Gilded Age, or, The Hazard of New Functions* (Upper Saddle River, N.J.: Prentice Hall, 1997), 75–89; Nina Silber, *The Romance of Reunion: Northerners and the South, 1865–1900* (Chapel Hill: Univ. of North Carolina Press, 1993); Cecilia Elizabeth O'Leary, *To Die For: The Paradox of American Patriotism* (Princeton, N.J.: Princeton Univ. Press, 1999); David W. Blight, *Race and Reunion: The Civil War in American Memory* (Cambridge, Mass.: Harvard Univ. Press, 2001).

16. Arthur Meier Schlesinger Sr., *A Critical Period in American Religion, 1875–1900* (Philadelphia: Fortress Press, 1967). Schlesinger's study was first published in *Massachusetts Historical Society Proceedings* (October 1930–June 1932): 523–46. Henry F. May, *Protestant Churches and Industrial America* (New York: Harper and Brothers, 1949); Sidney E. Mead, *The Lively Experiment: The Shaping of Christianity in America* (New York: Harper and Row, 1963), 134–89; Marty, *Righteous Empire*; Paul A. Carter, *The Spiritual Crisis of the Gilded Age* (DeKalb: Northern Illinois Univ. Press, 1971); Sidney E. Ahlstrom, *A Religious History of the American People* (New Haven, Conn.: Yale Univ. Press, 1972), 733. Bruce Kuklick was one of the first dissenters to the "reaction thesis"; in *Churchmen and Philosophers: From Jonathan Edwards to John Dewey* (New Haven, Conn.: Yale Univ. Press, 1985), he suggested that the New England theology of Jonathan Edwards and Nathaniel Taylor stood as the most sustained intellectual tradition in the United States throughout the nineteenth century. Protestant theology, especially revisions made by social gospelers in the late nineteenth century, played a critical role in shaping intellectual traditions during the Gilded Age and Progressive Era and fundamentally shaped the thought of John Dewey.

17. For more on religion and politics in the antebellum era, see Daniel Walker Howe, "The Evangelical Movement and Political Culture in the North during the Second Party System," *Journal of American History* 77, no. 4 (March 1991): 1216–39; Richard J. Carwardine, *Evangelicals and Politics in Antebellum America* (New Haven, Conn.: Yale Univ. Press, 1993).

18. Anthony Trollope, *North America* (New York: Harper and Brothers Publishers, 1862), 274, 278; Ernest Duvergier de Hauranne, *A Frenchman in Lincoln's America,* vol. 2 (1866; reprint, Chicago: R. R. Donnelley and Sons, 1974), 163, 437; James Bryce, *Social Institutions of the United States* (New York: Chautauqua Press, 1891), 100. On Tocqueville and religion, see Norman A. Graebner, "Christianity and Democracy: Tocqueville's Views of Religion in America," *Journal of Religion* 56 (1976): 263–73.

19. Trollope, *North America,* 278; de Hauranne, *A Frenchman in Lincoln's America,* 167; *Church of the Holy Trinity v. United States,* 143 U.S. 457; 12 S. Ct. 511; 36 L. Ed. 226 (1892). Brewer extended these arguments in David J. Brewer, *The United States as a Christian Nation* (Philadelphia: John C. Winston, 1905).

20. J. Franklin Jameson, "The American Acta Sanctorum," *American Historical Review* 13, no. 2 (January 1908): 286–302.

21. Benedict R. Anderson, *Imagined Communities: Reflections on the Origin and Spread of Nationalism* (1983; rev. ed., London: Verso, 1991), 7. For other works on nationalism and national identity,

see Ernest Gellner, *Nationalism* (Washington Square, N.Y.: New York Univ. Press, 1997); Anthony D. Smith, *National Identity* (Reno: Univ. of Nevada Press, 1991); Anthony D. Smith, *Nationalism and Modernism: A Critical Survey of Recent Theories of Nations and Nationalism* (New York: Routledge, 1998); Linda Colley, *Britons: Forging the Nation, 1707–1837* (New Haven, Conn.: Yale Univ. Press, 1992); Eric Hobsbawm, *Nations and Nationalism since 1780: Programme, Myth, Reality* (Cambridge, U.K.: Cambridge Univ. Press, 1990); Liah Greenfeld, *Nationalism: Five Roads to Modernity* (Cambridge, Mass.: Harvard Univ. Press, 1992).

22. Booker T. Washington and W. E. B. Du Bois, *The Negro in the South: His Economic Progress in Relation to His Moral and Religious Development* (Philadelphia: George W. Jacobs and Company, 1907), 185.

23. For an analysis of post–Civil War African American religion as a "shield," see William E. Montgomery, *Under Their Own Vine and Fig Tree: The African-American Church in the South, 1865–1900* (Baton Rouge: Louisiana State Univ. Press, 1993). For a discussion of the ways religious beliefs led African American women to attack racism and patriarchy, see Evelyn Brooks Higginbotham, *Righteous Discontent: The Women's Movement in the Black Baptist Church, 1880–1920* (Cambridge, Mass.: Harvard Univ. Press, 1993).

24. Rudyard Kipling, "The White Man's Burden," *McClure's Magazine* 12, no. 4 (February 1899): 290–1; "Opinions of W. D. Howells," *Sun* (New York), April 30, 1899, p. 5.

1. THE LAST AND GREATEST BATTLE OF FREEDOM

1. Jim Bishop, *The Day Lincoln Was Shot* (1955; reprint, New York: Scholastic Book Services, 1973), 299–301.

2. Herman Melville, *Poems Containing Battle-Pieces, John Marr and Other Sailors, Timoleon, and Miscellaneous Poems* (New York: Harper and Brothers, 1866), 141–2.

3. Rupert Sargent Holland, ed., *Letters and Diary of Laura M. Towne Written from the Sea Islands of South Carolina, 1862–1884* (1912; reprint, New York: Negro Univs. Press, 1969), 162.

4. "The Ohio Conference," *Christian Recorder,* April 29, 1865, p. 65.

5. "In Memoriam: Written On Hearing of the Death of President Lincoln," *Christian Recorder,* April 22, 1865, p. 61.

6. Frederick Douglass, "Our Martyred President: An Address Delivered in Rochester, New York, on 15 April 1865," in *The Frederick Douglass Papers: Series One: Speeches, Debates, and Interviews,* vol. 4, *1864–1880,* edited by John W. Blassingame and John R. McKivigan (New Haven, Conn.: Yale Univ. Press, 1991), 75–9. Douglass spent much of his post–Civil War career on this theme. See David W. Blight, "'For Something beyond the Battlefield': Frederick Douglass and the Struggle for the Memory of the Civil War," *Journal of American History* 75, no. 4 (March 1989): 1156–78.

7. Joel H. Silbey, *A Respectable Minority: The Democratic Party in the Civil War Era, 1860–1868* (New York: Norton, 1977); Edward L. Gambill, *Conservative Ordeal: Northern Democrats and Reconstruction, 1865–1868* (Ames: Iowa State Univ. Press, 1981).

8. Michael Les Benedict, *A Compromise of Principle: Congressional Republicans and Reconstruction, 1863–1869* (New York: Norton, 1974), 22–5.

9. Paul Laurence Dunbar, *The Fanatics* (1901; reprint, New York: Negro Univs. Press, 1969), 90.

10. Allan Nevins and Milton Halsey Thomas, eds., *The Diary of George Templeton Strong: The Civil War, 1860–1865* (1952; reprint, New York: Octagon Books, 1974), 585; see also, "Sermons by Our Leading Clergy," *New York Herald,* April 20, 1865, p. 2.

11. "In the Churches," *Cincinnati Gazette,* April 17, 1865, p. 2.

12. For information on Troy, see *A Tribute of Respect by the Citizens of Troy, to the Memory of Abraham Lincoln* (Troy, N.Y.: Young and Benson, 1865); George Walker Diary, April 20, 1865, George Leon Walker and Williston Walker Papers, Yale Divinity School Special Collections, box 1, vol. 3.

13. Barry Schwartz, *Abraham Lincoln and the Forge of National Memory* (Chicago: Univ. of Chicago Press, 2000).

14. "The Scene in New York," *Independent,* April 17, 1865, pp. 4–5.

15. See Cheslyn Jones, Geoffrey Wainwright, Edward Yarnold, eds., *The Study of Liturgy* (New York: Oxford Univ. Press, 1992).

16. For more on "the sermon," see Donald M. Scott, *From Office to Profession: The New England Ministry, 1750–1850* (Philadelphia: Univ. of Pennsylvania Press, 1978), 138–47; F. R. Webber, *A History of Preaching in Britain and America: Including the Biographies of Many Princes of the Pulpit and the Men who Influenced Them, Part Three* (Milwaukee: Northwestern Publishing House, 1957); Russel Hirst, "The Sermon as Public Discourse: Austin Phelps and the Conservative Homiletic Tradition in Nineteenth-Century America," in *Oratorical Culture in the Nineteenth-Century: Transformations in the Theory and Practice of Rhetoric,* edited by Gregory Clark and S. Michael Halloran (Carbondale: Southern Illinois Univ. Press, 1993), 78–109.

17. Daniel P. Kidder, *A Treatise on Homiletics: Designed to Illustrate the True Theory and Practice of Preaching the Gospel,* rev. ed. (New York: Nelson and Phillips, 1864), 111, 411–2.

18. Phelps quoted in Hirst, "The Sermon as Public Discourse," 88; for similar arguments by ministers and professors, see John A. Broadus, *A Treatise on the Preparation and Delivery of Sermons* (1870; reprint, New York: A. C. Armstrong and Sons, 1895), 18; and Henry Ward Beecher, *Yale Lectures on Preaching* (New York: J. B. Ford and Company, 1872), 2.

19. Richard D. Brown, *The Strength of a People: The Idea of an Informed Citizenry in America, 1650–1870* (Chapel Hill: Univ. of North Carolina Press, 1996), especially 121–4; R. Laurence Moore, *Selling God: American Religion in the Marketplace of Culture* (New York: Oxford Univ. Press, 1994), 12–39; Colleen McDaniel, *Material Christianity: Religion and Popular Culture in America* (New Haven, Conn.: Yale Univ. Press, 1995), 67–102. For more on secular newspapers publishing sermons and other religious news, see Kathryn Teresa Long, *The Revival of 1857–58: Interpreting an American Religious Awakening* (New York: Oxford Univ. Press, 1998), 26–45.

20. Rev. Robert F. Sample, *The Curtained Throne* (Philadelphia: James S. Claxton, 1865), 29.

21. Rev. C. B. Crane, *Sermon on the Occasion of the Death of President Lincoln* (Hartford, Conn.: Press of Case, Lockwood and Company, 1865), 3.

22. Edwin B. Webb, *Memorial Sermons* (Boston: Press of Geo. C. Rand and Avery, 1865), 3. The vast majority of sermons I analyzed were published upon request of local congregants.

23. *Our Martyr President, Abraham Lincoln. Voices from the Pulpit of New York and Brooklyn* (New York: Tibbals and Whiting, 1865), viii.

24. Other historians have also shown the ways churches in the nineteenth century served as crucial sites of political and social debate; see especially Nancy Isenberg, *Sex and Citizenship in Antebellum America* (Chapel Hill: Univ. of North Carolina Press, 1998), chapter 4.

25. "The Blood-thirsty Preachers," *Easton-Sentinel* (Pennsylvania), June 22, 1865, p. 2.

26. Samuel T. Spear, *The Punishment of Treason* (Brooklyn: The Union Steam Presses, 1865), 20.

27. Joel F. Bingham, *National Disappointment. A Discourse Occasioned by the Assassination of President Lincoln* (Buffalo, N.Y.: Breed, Butler and Company, 1865), 11–7. Historian Thomas Turner maintains that such belligerent rhetoric sanctified mob violence against northern Democrats; see Thomas Reed Turner, *Beware the People Weeping: Public Opinion and the Assassination of Abraham Lincoln* (Baton Rouge: Louisiana State Univ. Press, 1982), 77–89; David B. Chesebrough, *"No Sorrow Like Our Sorrow": Northern Protestant Ministers and the Assassination of Lincoln* (Kent, Ohio: Kent State Univ. Press, 1994), 41–52.

28. Isaac Eddy Carey, *Abraham Lincoln, the Value to the Nation of his Exalted Character* (Freeport, Ill.: n.p., 1865), 2.

29. See Chesebrough, *"No Sorrow Like Our Sorrow,"* 53–65.

30. Nevins and Thomas, eds., *The Diary of George Templeton Strong: The Civil War,* 586–7.

31. Historian James McPherson argues that when northerners referred to southerners as a different race, they really meant "ethnicity." See McPherson, *Is Blood Thicker Than Water?,* 43. This claim, however, supposes that nineteenth-century Americans recognized a distinction between ethnicities and races, which they largely did not. For more on the multitude of "racial" differences in the nineteenth century, see Jacobson, *Whiteness of a Different Color.*

32. Charles S. Robinson, *The Martyred President: A Sermon Preached in the First Presbyterian Church, Brooklyn, N.Y.* (New York: John F. Trow, Printer, 1865), 16–7.

33. Examples abound of both northern and southern whites referring to each other as different "races." See Faust, *The Creation of Confederate Nationalism,* 10–1; C. Vann Woodward, ed., *Mary Chesnut's Civil War* (New Haven, Conn.: Yale Univ. Press, 1981), 600.

34. See Silber, *Romance of Reunion,* 13–38.

35. L. Perry Curtis, *Apes and Angels: The Irishman in Victorian Caricature* (Washington, D.C.: Smithsonian Institution Press, 1971).

36. Sidney Andrews, *The South Since the War As Shown by Fourteen Weeks of Travel and Observation in Georgia and the Carolinas* (1866; reprint, Boston: Houghton Mifflin, 1971), 40, 183; for other similar reports, see Whitelaw Reid, *After the War: A Southern Tour* (Cincinnati: Wilstach and Baldwin, 1866); and J. T. Trowbridge, *The South: A Tour of Its Battle-fields and Ruined Cities* (Hartford, Conn.: L. Stebbins, 1866). For more on these types of racial and gendered tropes, see George M. Fredrickson, *The Black Image in the White Mind: The Debate on Afro-American Character and Destiny, 1817–1914* (New York: Harper and Row, 1971), 53–8, 275–82; and Cynthia Eagle Russett, *Sexual Science: The Victorian Construction of Womanhood* (Cambridge, Mass.: Harvard Univ. Press, 1989), 16–7, 35–9.

37. Virginia Ingraham Burr, ed., *The Secret Eye: The Journal of Ella Gertrude Clanton Thomas, 1848–1889* (Chapel Hill: Univ. of North Carolina Press, 1990), 292; Henry Watterson, *The Compromises of Life and Other Lectures and Addresses Including Some Observations on Certain Downward Tendencies of Modern Society* (New York: Duffield and Company, 1906), 293.

38. Quoted in "Punishment of the Rebel Leaders," *Independent,* July 20, 1865, p. 1.

39. J. G. Butler, *The Martyr President* (Washington, D.C.: McGill and Witherow, Printers and Stereotypers, 1865), 13.

40. John McClintock, *Discourse Delivered on the Day of the Funeral of President Lincoln* (New York: J. M. Bradstreet and Son, 1865), 28.

41. Quoted in *A Tribute of Respect*, 46.

42. Silbey, *A Respectable Minority*, 190.

43. Thomas Laurie, *Three Discourses* (Dedham, Mass.: John Cox Jr., 1865), 33; for a discussion of the ways in which Protestants blamed "the theatre" for the assassination, see Chesebrough, *"No Sorrow Like Our Sorrow,"* 103. For more on Protestants' relationship with the theatre, see Moore, *Selling God*, 40–65.

44. Robinson, *The Martyred President*, 4; Sample, *The Curtained Throne*, 16. See also Thomas Tousey, *Discourse on the Death of Abraham Lincoln* (Rochester, N.Y.: C. D. Tracy and Co., Printers, Evening Express Office, 1865), 10.

45. "Meeting in Berea Baptist Church," *New York Times*, April 28, 1865, p. 8.

46. Hunter Dickinson Farish, *The Circuit Rider Dismounts: A Social History of Southern Methodism, 1865–1900* (1938; reprint, New York: Da Capo Press, 1969); William Warren Sweet, *Methodism in American History* (1953; reprint, Nashville: Abingdon Press, 1961); C. C. Goen, *Broken Churches, Broken Nation: Denominational Schisms and the Coming of the Civil War* (Macon, Ga.: Mercer Univ. Press, 1985).

47. "Death of Lincoln," *Christian Advocate and Journal*, April 20, 1865, p. 124.

48. "The End of the War: Our Troubles Not Ended in the South," *Christian Advocate and Journal*, June 1, 1865, p. 169.

49. "Dangers of Reconstruction," *Independent*, August 17, 1865, p. 4.

50. George M. Marsden, *The Evangelical Mind and the New School Presbyterian Experience: A Case Study of Thought and Theology in Nineteenth-Century America* (New York: Oxford Univ. Press, 1970); Goen, *Broken Churches, Broken Nation*; *Presbyterian Reunion Memorial Volume: 1837–1871* (New York: De-Witt C. Lent and Company, 1870), 2–47.

51. Quoted in "The Peace We Need," *Presbyterian*, June 24, 1865, p. 2.

52. "Presbytery of Findlay," *Presbyterian*, May 6, 1865, p. 4.

53. *Presbyterian Reunion Memorial Volume*, 2–47.

54. Carolyn L. Harrell, *When the Bells Tolled for Lincoln: Southern Reaction to the Assassination* (Macon, Ga.: Mercer Univ. Press, 1997), 60.

55. Harrell, *When the Bells Tolled for Lincoln*; Ralph E. Morrow, *Northern Methodism and Reconstruction* (East Lansing: Michigan State Univ. Press, 1956), 97–8; Joshua W. Sharp to Thaddeus Stevens, January 17, 1866, in *The Selected Papers of Thaddeus Stevens*, vol. 2, *April 1865—August 1868*, edited by Beverly Wilson Palmer (Pittsburgh: Univ. of Pittsburgh Press, 1998), 65.

56. Rufus B. Spain, *At Ease in Zion: A Social History of Southern Baptists, 1865–1900* (Nashville: Vanderbilt Univ. Press, 1961), 19–21; Farish, *The Circuit Rider Dismounts*, 22–60; Sweet, *Methodism in American History*; 305; Wilson, *Baptized in Blood*; Foster, *Ghosts of the Confederacy*, 11–78.

57. Paul Kleppner, *The Cross of Culture: A Social Analysis of Midwestern Politics, 1850–1900* (New York: Free Press, 1970).

58. Quoted in Mark Mohler, "The Episcopal Church and National Reconciliation, 1865," *Political Science Quarterly* 41, no. 4 (December 1926): 573. For more on the Episcopal Church in the nineteenth century, see Diane H. Butler, *Standing against the Whirlwind: Evangelical Episcopalians in Nineteenth-Century America* (New York: Oxford Univ. Press, 1995).

59. John H. Hopkins Jr., *The Life of the Late Right Reverend John Henry Hopkins, First Bishop of Vermont and Seventh Presiding Bishop By One of His Sons* (New York: F. J. Huntington, 1873), 320.

60. John Henry Hopkins, *Bible View of Slavery* (New York: Society for the Diffusion of Political Knowledge, 1863). Rather than calm the nation, this work sparked an enormous debate among northern religious leaders on the morality of slaveholding and secession; for the arguments of some of Hopkins's opponents, see Henry Drisler, *"Bible View of Slavery" by John H. Hopkins, D.D., Bishop of the Dioceses of Vermont, Examined* (New York: C. S. Westcott and Co., 1863); Stephen M. Vail, ed., *The Bible Against Slavery, With Replies to the "Bible View of Slavery," by John H. Hopkins, Bishop of the Diocese of Vermont* (Concord: Fogg, Hadley and Co., Printers, 1864); Richard Henry Lee, *Letter from Richard Henry Lee, of Washington, Pa., One of the Signers of the Clerical Protest Against Bishop Hopkins' Bible View of Slavery* (Philadelphia: Philadelphia Age, 1864).

61. Hopkins Jr., *The Life of the Late Right Reverend John Henry Hopkins*, 324.

62. Ibid., 347–8.

63. Ibid., 348.

64. Brevet Major General E. D. Townsend, *Anecdotes of the Civil War in the United States* (New York: D. Appleton and Company, 1884), 98–100.

65. Hopkins Jr., *The Life of the Late Right Reverend John Henry Hopkins*, 348.

66. Townsend, *Anecdotes of the Civil War in the United States*, 98–100.

67. See Mohler, "The Episcopal Church and National Reconciliation," 567–95.

68. Hopkins Jr., *The Life of the Late Right Reverend John Henry Hopkins*, 353, 355.

69. *Journal of the Forty Ninth Annual Council of the Protestant Episcopal Church in the State of North Carolina* (Raleigh, N.C.: J. C. Gorman's Book and Job Printing Office, 1865), 19, 31–2.

70. "The Episcopal Convention and Sectional Reconciliation," *New York Times,* September 29, 1865, p. 4. A writer for the *Daily Missouri Republican* made a similar assertion in August 1865: "This desirable event is certain, and will probably take place at the meeting of the Triennial Convention in Philadelphia on the 4th of October. . . . Such a noble example will have a happy effect on the whole country, and greatly aid in calming down the violence of passion, by promoting a speedy return to Christian and brotherly confidence and co-operation among those who for a season have been alienated from each other" ("Reunion of the Protestant Episcopal Church," *Daily Missouri Republican* [St. Louis], August 27, 1865, p. 2).

71. "Ex-Gov. Reynolds of Illinois on the Restoration of the Union," *Daily Missouri Republican* (St. Louis), May 5, 1865, p. 3.

72. "Gerrit Smith's Views. His Sermon on the Necessity of Mercy to the Leading Rebels," *Daily Missouri Republican* (St. Louis), June 8, 1865, p. 2. For more on Smith, see John Stauffer, *The Black Hearts of Men: Radical Abolitionists and the Transformation of Race* (Cambridge, Mass.: Harvard Univ. Press, 2002).

73. Quoted in "Retribution," *Independent,* July 20, 1865, p. 1. Though Jenkins never specifically mentions Beecher, he denounces, point by point, the exact arguments made by Beecher for forgiveness in his Plymouth Church sermon; see "Punishment of the Rebel Leaders," *Independent,* July 20, 1865, p. 1.

74. Charles Sumner to Theodore Tilton, November 2, 1865, in *The Selected Letters of Charles Sumner,* vol. 2, edited by Beverly Wilson Palmer (Boston: Northeastern Univ. Press, 1990), 340–34; Bostwick Hawley, *Truth and Righteousness Triumphant: A Discourse Commemorative of the Death of President Lincoln* (Albany, N.Y.: J. Munsell, 1865), 23.

75. "The Programme for the Future," *Independent*, May 4, 1865, p. 4. Methodists made similar observations. See "Reconstruction," *Christian Advocate and Journal*, June 15, 1865, p. 188.

76. Victor B. Howard, *Religion and the Radical Republican Movement, 1860–1870* (Lexington: Univ. Press of Kentucky, 1990), 1–6.

77. Ena L. Farley, "Methodists and Baptists on the Issue of Black Equality in New York: 1865 to 1868," *Journal of Negro History* 61, no. 4 (October 1976): 374–92.

78. Hopkins, *Bible View of Slavery*, 12–3; Parish, "From Necessary Evil to National Blessing," 61–89.

79. Some historians suggest that even after Lincoln's assassination, northern white ministers continued to view the Union as the most important aspect of the war and that the clergy cared very little about abolition. See Stowell, *Rebuilding Zion*, 7; Schwartz, *Abraham Lincoln and the Forge of National Memory*, 48–9.

80. Rev. George Dana Boardman, *An Address in Commemoration of Abraham Lincoln* (Philadelphia: Sherman and Co., 1865), 55; see also Tousey, *Discourse on the Death of Abraham Lincoln*, 15.

81. Henry Champion Deming, *Eulogy of Abraham Lincoln* (Hartford, Conn.: A. N. Clark and Co., 1865), 47.

82. Rev. Jas. A. McCauley, *Character and Services of Abraham Lincoln* (Baltimore: John D. Toy, Printer, 1865), 14.

83. Moorhead, *American Apocalypse*, 178.

84. Robinson, *The Martyred President*, 2.

85. Gilbert Haven, *The Uniter and Liberator of America* (Boston: James P. Magee, 1865), 31; *Services Held by the Maryland Union Commission, in Charles Street M. E. Church, On the Evening of June 1st, 1865* (Baltimore: Sherwood and Co., 1865), 11. In the same fashion, John Egar encouraged his Leavenworth congregation to press on, "the work, brethren, is not yet ended." See John H. Egar, *The Martyr-President: A Sermon Preached in the Church of St. Paul, Leavenworth* (Leavenworth, Kans.: Bulletin Job Printer Establishment, 1865), 15.

86. Walker Diary, June 6, 1865, Walker and Walker Papers, box 1, vol. 3.

87. Ronald E. Butchart, *Northern Schools, Southern Blacks, and Reconstruction: Freedmen's Education, 1862–1875* (Westport, Conn.: Greenwood Press, 1980), 25; Palmer, ed., *Selected Papers of Thaddeus Stevens*, 2:25.

88. W. H. Benade, *The Death of Abraham Lincoln; What it Represents* (Pittsburgh: W. G. Johnston and Co., Printers and Stationers, 1865), 27.

89. Richard Eddy, *The Martyr to Liberty* (Philadelphia: Horace W. Smith, 1865), 25; for Cheever's prayer, see "Our Grief: The Services in the City Churches," *New York Herald*, April 17, 1865, pp. 2, 8; Farish, *The Circuit Rider Dismounts*, 172; "Social Possibilities," *Independent*, May 25, 1865, p. 4.

90. Haven, *The Uniter and Liberator of America*, 23.

91. "The Programme for the Future," *Independent*, May 4, 1865, p. 4; see also, "Reconstruction— The Black Man," *Christian Advocate and Journal*, May 18, 1865, p. 156.

92. Quoted in Benedict, *A Compromise of Principle*, 103.

93. Howard, *Religion and the Radical Republican Movement*, 146–50; Theodore Tilton to Thaddeus Stevens, December 6, 1865, in Palmer, ed., *Selected Papers of Thaddeus Stevens*, 2:43.

94. Crane, *Sermon on the Occasion of the Death of President Lincoln*, 24; Butler, *The Martyr President*, 12–3.

95. Paul Clyde Brownlow, "The Northern Protestant Pulpit on Reconstruction, 1865–1877" (Ph.D. diss., Purdue University, 1970), 151–9.

96. "Reconstruction—The Black Man," *Christian Advocate and Journal*, May 18, 1865, p. 156.

97. Walker Diary, June 30, 1865, Walker and Walker Papers, box 1, vol. 3.

98. See Howard, *Religion and the Radical Republican Movement*, 155–64; Sweet, *Methodism in American History*, 320.

99. Henry Ward Beecher, *Oration at the Raising of "The Old Flag" at Sumter; and Sermon on the Death of Abraham Lincoln, President of the United States* (Manchester, U.K.: Alexander Ireland and Co., Pall Mall Court, 1865), 29–30.

100. Richard Edwards, *Life and Character of Abraham Lincoln: An Address* (Peoria, Ill.: N. C. Nason, Printer, 1865), 16; for another example, see "Proceedings of the New School Presbyterian General Assembly," *Independent*, May 25, 1865, p. 4.

101. Fredrickson, *The Black Image in the White Mind*, 85–7; Horsman, *Race and Manifest Destiny*; for another discussion, see McPherson, *The Struggle for Equality*, 136; see also William Stanton, *The Leopard's Spots: Scientific Attitudes toward Race in America, 1815–1859* (Chicago: Univ. of Chicago Press, 1960); David N. Livingston, "The Moral Discourse of Climate: Historical Considerations on Race, Place and Virtue," *Journal of Historical Geography* 17, no. 4 (October 1991): 413–34; Haynes, *Noah's Curse*.

102. David Macrae, *The Americans at Home* (1871; reprint, New York: E. P. Dutton, 1952), 301. See also John David Smith, *Religion and 'The Negro Problem' Part I, Volume Five: The 'Ariel' Controversy* (New York: Garland Publishing, 1993).

103. Wilbur F. Paddock, *A Great Man Fallen!* (Philadelphia: Sherman and Co., Printers, 1865), 12.

104. Reuben Jeffrey, *The Mission of Abraham Lincoln* (Philadelphia: Bryson and Son, Printers and Stationers, 1865), 24.

105. Eddy, *The Martyr to Liberty*, 26; Deming, *Eulogy of Abraham Lincoln*, 57; Robinson, *The Martyred President*, 29; Henry Fowler, *Character and Death of Abraham Lincoln* (Auburn, N.Y.: Wm. J. Moses' Steam Press Establishment, 1865), 15–6.

106. Quoted in "The Unity of the Human Race," *Independent*, June 15, 1865, p. 5.

107. Acts 17:26.

108. *Dred Scott v. John F. A. Sandford*, 60 U.S. 393; 15 L. Ed. 691 (1856).

109. Joseph A. Seiss, *The Assassinated President* (Philadelphia: Joseph A. Seiss, D.D., 1865), 41.

110. "President Lincoln," *Princeton Review*, July 3, 1865, p. 456–7; for an analysis of "one blood" arguments and the influence of African Americans upon antebellum abolitionists, see Paul Goodman, *Of One Blood: Abolitionism and the Origins of Racial Equality* (Berkeley: Univ. of California Press, 1998).

111. Robert B. Yard, *The Providential Significance of the Death of Abraham Lincoln* (Newark, N.J.: H. Harris, 1865), 14. For a discussion of competing race theories, see Kenan Malik, *The Meaning of Race: Race, History and Culture in Western Society* (Washington Square, N.Y.: New York Univ. Press, 1996), 38–70. Unlike Yard, Malik maintains that though these Enlightenment thinkers toyed with human categories, they did not create the rigid racial categories that would emerge during the eighteenth and nineteenth centuries. Furthermore, Malik draws a distinction between Rousseau's writings on race and Voltaire's. While Voltaire viewed skin color and racial difference as inherent, Malik contends, Rousseau recognized that skin color or racial categories did not equate to permanent or inherent differences. See Malik, *The Meaning of Race*, 50.

112. "Reconstruction," *Christian Advocate and Journal,* May 25, 1865, p. 164.

113. Butler, *The Martyr President,* 13.

114. *Services Held by the Maryland Union Commission,* 17.

115. "Home Missions," sermon in Samuel Dutton Papers, Yale Divinity School Special Collections, box 127; see also "Letter from Richmond," *Presbyterian,* May 6, 1865, p. 2–3.

116. Quoted in Elizabeth Hyde Botome, *First Days Amongst the Contrabands* (1893; reprint, New York: Arno Press and the New York Times, 1968), 199.

117. "The Blacks and the Ballot," *Harper's Weekly* 9, no. 438 (May 20, 1865): 306. Methodists agreed with this argument and quoted *Harper's* in their journal; see "The Blacks and the Ballot," *Christian Advocate and Journal,* June 1, 1865, p. 170.

118. Quoted in Robert R. Dykstra, *Bright Radical Star: Black Freedom and White Supremacy on the Hawkeye Frontier* (Cambridge, Mass.: Harvard Univ. Press, 1993), 209; for another analysis of the malleability of white thought on African Americans during the Civil War, see William W. Freehling, *The South vs. the South: How Anti-Confederate Southerners Shaped the Course of the Civil War* (New York: Oxford Univ. Press, 2001), 85–176.

119. Palmer, ed., *The Selected Papers of Thaddeus Stevens,* 2:178–179, 70–4; Carwadine, *Evangelicals and Politics in Antebellum America,* xvii.

120. Silbey, *A Respectable Minority,* 190–2; Farish, *The Circuit Rider Dismounts,* 219–20.

121. "Preamble and Constitution of the Pennsylvania State Equal Rights' League, Acting Under the Jurisdiction of the National Equal Rights' League of the United States of America," in *Proceedings of the Black National and State Conventions, 1865–1900,* vol. 1, edited by Philip S. Foner and George E. Walker (Philadelphia: Temple Univ. Press, 1986), 160.

122. "The New Condition," *Christian Recorder,* April 15, 1865, p. 58.

123. "The Times," *Christian Recorder,* April 29, 1865, p. 65. See also Clarence E. Walker, *A Rock in a Weary Land: The African Methodist Episcopal Church during the Civil War and Reconstruction* (Baton Rouge: Louisiana State Univ. Press, 1982), 30–1.

124. *Celebration by the Colored People's Educational Monument Association in Memory of Abraham Lincoln* (Washington, D.C.: McGill and Witherow, Printers and Stereotypers, 1865), 1, 10.

125. Frederick Douglass, "What to the Slave Is the Fourth of July?" in *The Frederick Douglass Papers: Series One: Speeches, Debates, and Interviews,* vol. 2, *1847–54,* edited by John W. Blassingame (New Haven, Conn.: Yale Univ. Press, 1982), 359–87.

126. "Proceedings of the Convention of Colored Citizens of the State of Arkansas, Held in Little Rock, Thursday, Friday and Saturday, Nov. 30, Dec. 1 and 2, 1865," in *Proceedings of the Black National and State Conventions, 1865–1900,* 1:191. See also Reginald F. Hildebrand, *The Times Were Strange and Stirring: Methodist Preachers and the Crisis of Emancipation* (Durham: Duke Univ. Press, 1995), 32, 37, 50, 69.

127. Albion Tourgée, *Bricks Without Straw* (1880; reprint, Ridgewood, N.J.: Gregg Press, 1967), 133.

2. ON THE VERGE OF HEAVEN

1. Gerald Schwartz, ed. *A Woman Doctor's Civil War: Esther Hill Hawks' Diary* (Columbia: Univ. of South Carolina Press, 1994), 133–4.

2. Luther P. Jackson, "The Educational Efforts of the Freedmen's Bureau and Freedmen's Aid Societies in South Carolina, 1862–1872," *Journal of Negro History* 8, no. 1 (January 1923): 1–40; Richard Bryant Drake, "The American Missionary Association and the Southern Negro, 1861–1888," (Ph.D. diss., Emory University, 1957), 26–7, 35; Patricia C. Click, *Time Full of Trial: The Roanoke Island Freedmen's Colony, 1862–1867* (Chapel Hill: Univ. of North Carolina Press, 2001), 64; Clara Merritt De Boer, "The Role of Afro-Americans in the Origin and Work of the American Missionary Association, 1839–1877," (Ph.D. diss., Rutgers University, 1973), 315, 337; Hildebrand, *The Times were Strange and Stirring*; John Lee Eighmy, *Churches in Cultural Captivity: A History of the Social Attitudes of Southern Baptists* (1972; reprint, Knoxville: Univ. of Tennessee Press, 1987), 32–4; J. Wayne Flynt, *Alabama Baptists: Southern Baptists in the Heart of Dixie* (Tuscaloosa: Univ. of Alabama Press, 1998), 134–41; H. Peers Brewer, "The Protestant Episcopal Freedmen's Commission, 1865–1878," *Historical Magazine of the Protestant Episcopal Church* 26 (1967): 361–81; Amory D. Mayo, *The Work of Certain Northern Churches in the Education of the Negro, 1862–1900* (Washington, D.C.: Government Printing Office, 1902); Vernon Lane Wharton, *The Negro in Mississippi, 1865–1890* (1947, reprint; New York: Harper and Row, 1965), 243, 256–65.

3. Allis Wolfe, "Women Who Dared: Northern Teachers of the Southern Freedmen, 1862–1872" (Ph.D. diss., City University of New York, 1982), 8; Robert C. Morris, *Reading, 'Riting, and Reconstruction: The Education of Freedmen in the South, 1861–1870* (Chicago: Univ. of Chicago Press, 1981); Ira V. Brown, "Lyman Abbott and Freedmen's Aid, 1865–1869," *Journal of Southern History* 15, no. 1 (February 1949): 22–38.

4. The historical literature on the missionary crusade is voluminous, and the following list merely touches the tip of the iceberg. Henry Lee Swint, *The Northern Teacher in the South, 1862–1870* (Nashville: Vanderbilt Univ. Press, 1941); George R. Bentley, *A History of the Freedmen's Bureau* (Philadelphia: Univ. of Pennsylvania Press, 1955); Wilbur J. Cash, *The Mind of the South* (New York: Knopf, 1941), 140–1; Jacqueline Jones, *Soldiers of Light and Love: Northern Teachers and Georgia Blacks, 1865–1873* (Chapel Hill: Univ. of North Carolina Press, 1980); Butchart, *Northern Schools, Southern Blacks, and Reconstruction*; James D. Anderson, *The Education of Blacks in the South, 1860–1935* (Chapel Hill: Univ. of North Carolina Press, 1988). See also William S. McFeely, *Yankee Stepfather: General O. O. Howard and the Freedmen* (New Haven, Conn.: Yale Univ. Press, 1968); Morris, *Reading, 'Riting, and Reconstruction*; Sandra E. Small, "The Yankee Schoolmarm in Freedmen's Schools: An Analysis of Attitudes," *Journal of Southern History* 45, no. 2 (August 1979): 381–402; Joe M. Richardson, *Christian Reconstruction: The American Missionary Association and Southern Blacks, 1861–1890* (Athens: Univ. of Georgia Press, 1986); Ronald E. Butchart, "'Outthinking and Outflanking the Owners of the World': A Historiography of the African American Struggle for Education," *History of Education Quarterly* (autumn 1988): 333–66. For several positive accounts of the missionaries, which principally came from historians in the 1960s, see John Hope Franklin, *Reconstruction: After the Civil War* (Chicago: Univ. of Chicago Press, 1961); LaWanda Cox and John H. Cox, *Politics, Principle, and Prejudice, 1865–1866: Dilemma of Reconstruction America* (New York: Free Press of Glence, 1963); Hans L. Trefousse, *The Radical Republicans: Lincoln's Vanguard for Racial Justice* (New York: Knopf, 1969); James M. McPherson, *The Abolitionist Legacy: From Reconstruction to the NAACP* (1975; reprint, Princeton, N.J.: Princeton Univ. Press, 1995), especially chapters 9–11.

5. W. E. B. Du Bois, *The Souls of Black Folk* (1903; reprint, New York: Norton, 1999), 69. Du Bois maintained these positive sentiments toward Yankee teachers even into the 1960s, when he wrote his

final autobiography. See W. E. B. Du Bois, *The Autobiography of W. E. B. Du Bois: A Soliloquy on Viewing My Life from the Last Decade of Its First Century* (New York: International Publishers, 1968), 106. Recently, a few historians have searched for moments of genuine interracial fraternity in the nineteenth century, but none have focused on radical Reconstruction. See Goodman, *Of One Blood*; Stauffer, *The Black Hearts of Men*; Jane Dailey, *Before Jim Crow: The Politics of Race in Postemancipation Virginia* (Chapel Hill: Univ. of North Carolina Press, 2000); Stanley Harrold, *Subversives: Antislavery Community in Washington, D.C., 1828–1865* (Baton Rouge: Louisiana State Univ. Press, 2003). Du Bois, *Black Reconstruction in America*, 708.

6. Roger M. Smith, *Civic Ideals: Conflicting Visions of Citizenship in U.S. History* (New Haven, Conn.: Yale Univ. Press, 1997), 286–323.

7. Albert Camus, *The Rebel*, trans. Anthony Bower (New York: Knopf, 1954), 22–3.

8. Botome, *First Days Amongst the Contrabands*, 19, 25; Laura S. Haviland, *A Woman's Life-Work: Labors and Experiences* (1881, reprint; Salem, N.H.: Ayer, 1984), 516. See also J. W. Alvord, *First Semi-Annual Report on Schools and Finances of Freedmen, January 1, 1866* (Washington, D.C.: Government Printing Office, 1868), 14; J. W. Alvord, *Sixth Semi-Annual Report on Schools for Freedmen, July 1, 1868* (Washington, D.C.: Government Printing Office, 1868), 68; Charles H. Corey, *A History of the Richmond Theological Seminary, with Reminiscences of Thirty Years' Work among the Colored People of the South* (Richmond, Va.: J. W. Randolph Company, 1895), 51–2. See also Harriet Beecher Stowe, "The Education of Freedmen," *North American Review* 128, no. 271 (June 1879): 605–16.

9. Walker, *A Rock in a Weary Land*, 48–50.

10. De Boer, "The Role of Afro-Americans," 384–413, 441; Jackson, "The Educational Efforts," 37; Richardson, *Christian Reconstruction*, 25; Farah Jasmine Griffin, ed., *Beloved Sisters and Loving Friends: Letters from Rebecca Primus of Royal Oak, Maryland, and Addie Brown of Hartford, Connecticut, 1854–1868* (New York: Knopf, 1999); Brenda Stevenson, ed., *The Journals of Charlotte Forten Grimké* (New York: Oxford Univ. Press, 1988); Wolfe, "Women Who Dared," 34. Blackett, *Beating against the Barriers*, 186–247.

11. *Twenty-First Annual Report of the American Missionary Association* (New York: American Missionary Association, 1867), 4.

12. Baptists quoted in Eighmy, *Churches in Cultural Captivity*, 34. "Intelligence," *Freedman* 2, no. 8 (August 1865): 32. See also Farish, *The Circuit Rider Dismounts*, 106–7.

13. Swint, *The Northern Teacher in the South*, 51, 59; Richardson, *Christian Reconstruction*, 12, 18–9; Butchart, *Northern Schools, Southern Blacks, and Reconstruction*, 68–9; Drake, "The American Missionary Association and the Southern Negro," 220; Morris, *Reading, 'Riting, and Reconstruction*, 219–24; Jones, *Soldiers of Light and Love*, 26–7.

14. Quoted in Farish, *The Circuit Rider Dismounts*, 117.

15. Swint, *The Northern Teacher in the South*, 5; Richardson, *Christian Reconstruction*, 75–8; J. W. Alvord, *Third Semi-Annual Report on Schools for Freedmen, January 1, 1867* (Washington, D.C.: Government Printing Office, 1867), 19; Donald G. Nieman, ed., *The Freedmen's Bureau and Black Freedom* (New York: Garland Publishing, 1994).

16. Morris, *Reading, 'Riting, and Reconstruction*, especially chapter 6.

17. Mrs. H. E. Brown, *John Freeman and His Family* (Boston: American Tract Society, 1864); Rev. I. W. Brinckerhoff, *Advice to Freedmen* (New York: American Tract Society, 1864).

18. L. Maria Child, *The Freedmen's Book* (Boston: Ticknor and Fields, 1865).

19. *Freedman* 1, no. 2 (February 1864): 8. See also *The Freedman's Third Reader* (Boston: American Tract Society, 1865), 221–2.

20. "Intelligence," *Freedman* 1, no. 6 (June 1864): 24; "The Colored Soldiers," *Freedman* 1, no. 8 (August 1864): 29–30; "Intelligence," *Freedman* 1, no. 1 (January 1864): 4. Literary critic Alice Fahs found that the secular press also discussed the new position of African Americans in society, but very rarely endorsed anything approaching full civic equality for blacks. The Protestant periodicals seem to have been far more radical in their hopes for the improved status of freedpeople. See Alice Fahs, *The Imagined Civil War: Popular Literature of the North and South, 1861–1865* (Chapel Hill: Univ. of North Carolina Press, 2001), chapter 5.

21. "Good Advice," *Freedman* 2, no. 3 (April 1865): 16; "Intelligence," *The Freedman* 2, no. 7 (July 1865): 28; *The Freedman's Third Reader*, 206–9; Child, *The Freedmen's Book*, 93, 167–74.

22. Lydia Sigourney, "Prejudice Reproved," in Child, *The Freedmen's Book*, 13.

23. "Black or White," *Freedman* 2, no. 3 (April 1865): 14.

24. *The Freedman's Third Reader*, 46–7.

25. "About the World," *Freedman* 1, no. 3 (March 1864): 12; J. W. Alvord, *Fourth Semi-Annual Report on Schools for Freedmen, July 1, 1867* (Washington, D.C.: Government Printing Office, 1867), 4; see also Child, *The Freedmen's Book*, 12.

26. Jackson, "The Educational Efforts," 9; J. W. Alvord, *Ninth Semi-Annual Report on Schools for Freedmen, January 1, 1870* (Washington, D.C.: Government Printing Office, 1870), 10; Swint, *The Northern Teacher in the South*, 3, 12; Drake, "The American Missionary Association and the Southern Negro," 98, 274–80; James P. Brawley, *Two Centuries of Methodist Concern: Bondage, Freedom and Education of Black People* (New York: Vantage Press, 1974), 515; Jones, *Soldiers of Light and Love*, 93; Willard Range, *The Rise and Progress of Negro Colleges in Georgia, 1865–1949* (Athens: Univ. of Georgia Press, 1951), 12; Lewis G. Vander Velde, *The Presbyterian Churches and the Federal Union, 1861–1869* (Cambridge, Mass.: Harvard Univ. Press, 1932), 450.

27. Thaddeus Stevens, "Address to Colored Delegation," in Palmer, ed., *The Selected Papers of Thaddeus Stevens*, 2:238–239.

28. Gordon Allport, *The Nature of Prejudice* (Cambridge, Mass.: Addison-Wesley, 1954); Morton Deutsch and Mary Collins, *Interracial Housing* (Minneapolis: Univ. of Minnesota Press, 1951); Mary R. Jackman and Marie Crane, " 'Some of My Best Friends Are Black . . . ': Interracial Friendship and Whites' Racial Attitudes," *Public Opinion Quarterly* 50, no. 4 (winter 1986): 459–86; Daniel A. Powers and Christopher G. Ellison, "Interracial Contact and Black Racial Attitudes: The Contact Hypothesis and Selectivity Bias," *Social Forces* 74, no. 1 (September 1995): 205–26; Jerry W. Robinson Jr. and James D. Preston, "Equal-Status Contact and Modification of Racial Prejudice: A Reexamination of the Contact Hypothesis," *Social Forces* 54, no. 4 (June 1976): 911–24; Michael O. Emerson and Christian Smith, *Divided by Faith: Evangelical Religion and the Problem of Race in America* (New York: Oxford Univ. Press, 2000), 74–91.

29. Jacqueline Jones found that over 78 percent of the missionaries to Georgia were female, that over 65 percent spent fewer than three years in the South, and that women made up 85 percent of the teachers. Male missionaries comprised 100 percent of the superintendents and principals. See Jones, *Soldiers of Light and Love*, 210–23. See also Wolfe, "Women Who Dared," 35.

30. *Methodist Quarterly Review* 47 (1865), 286, 272.

31. Linda Warfel Slaughter, *The Freedmen of the South* (1869; reprint, New York: Kraus Reprint Co., 1969), 110; Swint, *Northern Teachers in the South*, 43; M. Waterbury, *Seven Years Among the Freedmen* (Chicago: T. B. Arnold, 1891). See also Corey, *A History of the Richmond Theological Seminary*, 72.

32. Jones, *Soldiers of Light and Love*; Walker, *A Rock in a Weary Land*, 54–5.

33. Samuel L. Horst, ed., *The Fire of Liberty in Their Hearts: The Diary of Jacob E. Yoder of the Freedmen's Bureau School, Lynchburg, Virginia, 1866–1870* (Richmond, Va.: Library of Virginia, 1996), 47.

34. Botome, *First Days Amongst the Contrabands*, 43.

35. Elizabeth Ward Pearson, ed., *Letters from Port Royal, 1862–1868* (1906, reprint; New York: Arno Press, 1969), 15; Henrietta Stratton Jaquette, ed., *South after Gettysburg: Letters of Cornelia Hancock, 1863–1868* (New York: Crowell, 1956), 40.

36. Pearson, ed., *Letters from Port Royal*, 64.

37. Schwartz, ed. *A Woman Doctor's Civil War*, 49.

38. Henry L. Swint, ed., *Dear Ones at Home: Letters from Contraband Camps* (Nashville: Vanderbilt Univ. Press, 1966), 21–2; Flynt, *Alabama Baptists*, 135–7; James M. Washington, *Frustrated Fellowship: The Baptist Quest for Social Power* (Macon, Ga.: Mercer Univ. Press, 1986).

39. Schwartz, ed. *A Woman Doctor's Civil War*, 37.

40. Jacquette, ed., *South after Gettysburg*, 166.

41. Holland, ed., *Letters and Diary of Laura M. Towne*, 20; see also Laura M. Towne Diary, Penn School Papers, Manuscripts Department, University of North Carolina at Chapel Hill, box 32, vol. 1: 10.1862. Stevenson, ed., *The Journals of Charlotte Forten Grimké*, 402; Walker, *A Rock in a Weary Land*, 62. For more on the "shout," see Sylvia R. Frey and Betty Wood, *Come Shouting to Zion: African American Protestantism in the American South and British Caribbean to 1830* (Chapel Hill: Univ. of North Carolina Press, 1998), 48; Albert J. Raboteau, *Slave Religion: The "Invisible Institution" in the Antebellum South* (New York: Oxford Univ. Press, 1978), 66–73; and Sterling Stuckey, *Slave Culture: Nationalist Theory and the Foundations of Black America* (New York: Oxford Univ. Press, 1987), 12, 24, 36, 43, 53, 57, 62–4, 83–5, 138, 330.

42. Towne Diary, April 28, 1862, Penn School Papers, Manuscripts Department, University of North Carolina at Chapel Hill, box 32, vol. 1.

43. Swint, ed., *Dear Ones at Home*, 35; Wayne E. Reilly, ed., *Sarah Jane Foster: Teacher of the Freedmen, A Diary and Letters* (Charlottesville: Univ. Press of Virginia, 1990), 36–7, 55.

44. Quoted in Click, *Time Full of Trial*, 110.

45. Quoted in Jackson, "The Educational Efforts," 29.

46. Quoted in J. W. Alvord, *Second Semi-Annual Report on Schools and Finances of Freedmen, July 1, 1866* (Washington, D.C.: Government Printing Office, 1868), 7.

47. Quoted in Corey, *A History of the Richmond Theological Seminary*, 195.

48. Reilly, ed., *Sarah Jane Foster*, 35.

49. Quoted in Linda B. Selleck, *Gentle Invaders: Quaker Women Educators and Racial Issues during the Civil War and Reconstruction* (Richmond, Va.: Friends United Press, 1995), 96.

50. Swint, ed., *Dear Ones at Home*, 95.

51. Haviland, *A Woman's Life-Work*, 300. See also Martha Johnson to Sisters, April 11, 1863, Johnson Family Papers, Vermont Historical Society, 4; Click, *Time Full of Trial*, 115.

52. Holland, ed., *Letters and Diary of Laura M. Towne*, 27, 32.

53. Alvord, *Third Semi-Annual Report*, 35.

54. See especially Katharine L. Dvorak, *An African-American Exodus: The Segregation of the Southern Churches* (New York: Carlson Publishing, 1991); Harrold, *Subversives*, 41–3. Recently, scholars have become much more interested in integrated churches, but that focus has come more from sociologists than historians. See Curtis Paul DeYoung, Michael O. Emerson, George Yancey, Karen Chai Kim, *United by Faith: The Multiracial Congregation as an Answer to the Problem of Race* (New York: Oxford Univ. Press, 2003).

55. Haviland, *A Woman's Life-Work*, 397; Corey, *A History of the Richmond Theological Seminary*, 26–7.

56. Swint, ed., *Dear Ones at Home*, 35.

57. Waterbury, *Seven Years Among the Freedmen*, 43.

58. Holland, ed., *Letters and Diary of Laura M. Towne*, 135.

59. Slaughter, *The Freedmen of the South*, 123. See also Click, *Time Full of Trial*, 118.

60. Emile Durkheim, *The Elementary Forms of Religious Life* (1915; reprint, New York: Simon and Schuster, 1995).

61. Pearson, ed., *Letters from Port Royal*, 65–7.

62. "Life of Martha Johnson by Sister Clarissa Johnson Clark, 1871," Johnson Family Papers, Vermont Historical Society, 24; M. H. Clary to Mr. Johnson, January 27, 1872, Johnson Family Papers, Vermont Historical Society, 25–6; Mattie H. Clary to Friends, December 26, 1871, Johnson Family Papers, Vermont Historical Society, 27.

63. Reverend W. J. Richardson to Reverend George Whipple, South Carolina, July 3, 1863, American Missionary Association Archives, Amistad Research Center, New Orleans, Louisiana, Microfilm Edition, roll 1.

64. Holland, ed., *Letters and Diary of Laura M. Towne*, 79, 145–6, 178; Kurt J. Wolf, "Laura M. Towne and the Freed People of South Carolina, 1862–1901," *South Carolina Historical Magazine* 94, no. 4 (1997): 375–405.

65. Slaughter, *The Freedmen of the South*, 142.

66. Swint, ed., *Dear Ones at Home*, 125; Botome, *First Days Amongst the Contrabands*, 136.

67. Stevenson, ed., *The Journals of Charlotte Forten Grimké*, 480, 483.

68. Reilly, ed., *Sarah Jane Foster*, 177.

69. James H. Cone, *Liberation: A Black Theology of Liberation* (Philadelphia: J. B. Lippincott, 1970), 119.

70. Holland, ed., *Letters and Diary of Laura M. Towne*, 28–9, 58. See also Laura M. Towne Diary, Penn School Papers, Manuscripts Department, The University of North Carolina at Chapel Hill, box 32, vol. 1: 29.1862. At least one historian has suggested that encounters with the violence of slavery led many whites to embrace the abolitionist cause in the antebellum period. See James L. Huston, "The Experiential Basis of the Northern Antislavery Impulse," *Journal of Southern History* 56, no. 4 (November 1990): 609–40; Harrold, *Subversives*, 177–9.

71. Haviland, *A Woman's Life-Work*, 311–2.

72. Reilly, ed., *Sarah Jane Foster*, 113.

73. Swint, ed., *Dear Ones at Home*, 59.

74. Schwartz, ed. *A Woman Doctor's Civil War*, 49.

75. Ibid., 63–4.

76. Slaughter, *The Freedmen of the South*, 145.

77. Schwartz, ed., *A Woman Doctor's Civil War*, 40–1, 50. Laura Towne also acknowledged the massive amount of aid given to injured soldiers by freedpeople on the Sea Islands. See Laura M. Towne Diary, July 27, 1863, Penn School Papers, Manuscripts Department, The University of North Carolina at Chapel Hill, box 32, vol. 1: 152 : 1862.

78. Martha Johnson to Sisters, April 11, 1863, Johnson Family Papers, Vermont Historical Society, 3–5; Martha Johnson to Unknown, piece of a letter, 1863, Johnson Family Papers, Vermont Historical Society, 12.

79. Richard L. Morton, ed., "Life in Virginia, by a 'Yankee Teacher,' Margaret Newbold Thorpe," *Virginia Magazine of History and Biography* 64, no. 2 (April 1956): 189.

80. Swint, ed., *Dear Ones at Home*, 58, 210.

81. De Boer, "The Role of Afro-Americans," ix.

82. Martha Johnson to Sisters, April 11, 1863, Johnson Family Papers, Vermont Historical Society, 3–5; Martha Johnson to Brother and Sister, April 25, 1863, Johnson Family Papers, Vermont Historical Society, 6.

83. Holland, ed., *Letters and Diary of Laura M. Towne*, 146.

84. Nellie F. Stearns to "Lizzie," Nellie F. Stearns Letter, William R. Perkins Library, Duke University.

85. Schwartz, ed. *A Woman Doctor's Civil War*, 131.

86. Mrs. William R. Wister, "Recollections of Southern Plantation and School," Penn School Papers, Manuscripts Department, University of North Carolina at Chapel Hill, box 34, folder 343. For more on the malleability of whiteness and blackness during the nineteenth century, see Stauffer, *The Black Hearts of Men*; Jacobson, *Whiteness of a Different Color*; Ignatiev, *How the Irish Became White*; Saxton, *The Rise and Fall of the White Republic*; Roediger, *The Wages of Whiteness*.

87. Reilly, ed., *Sarah Jane Foster*, 35, 50, 62, 68.

88. Quoted in Morrow, *Northern Methodism and Reconstruction*, 191.

89. Jaquette, ed., *South after Gettysburg*, 198.

90. Slaughter, *The Freedmen of the South*, 124, 201.

91. Holland, ed., *Letters and Diary of Laura M. Towne*, 103. Laura Towne to Abraham Lincoln, May 29, 1864, The Abraham Lincoln Papers at the Library of Congress: Series 1, General Correspondence, 1833–1916, http://memory.loc.gov/ammem/alhtml/malhome.html (March 11, 2003). For more on issues of land allotment on the Sea Islands, see Willie Lee Rose, *Rehearsal for Reconstruction: The Port Royal Experiment* (Indianapolis: Bobbs-Merrill, 1964), 202–16, 272–300.

92. For more on Robert Smalls, see Okon Edet Uya, *From Slavery to Public Service: Robert Smalls, 1839–1915* (New York: Oxford Univ. Press, 1971), 108–11; Dorothy Sterling, *Captain of the Planter: The Story of Robert Smalls* (Garden City, N.Y.: Doubleday, 1958), 206–7.

93. Holland, ed., *Letters and Diary of Laura M. Towne*, 302.

94. Slaughter, *The Freedmen of the South*, 138.

95. Quoted in Selleck, *Gentle Invaders*, 191.

96. Reilly, ed., *Sarah Jane Foster*, 155; 178.

97. Ibid., 171–4.

98. Richardson, *Christian Reconstruction*, 21; Perry Chang, "'Angels of Peace in a Smitten Land': The Northern Teachers' Crusade in the Reconstruction South Reconsidered" *Southern Historian* 16

(spring 1995): 26–45; Judith Weisenfeld, " 'Who Is Sufficient for These Things?' Sara G. Stanley and the American Missionary Association, 1864–1868," *Church History* 60, no. 4 (December 1991): 493–507.

99. Quoted in Farish, *The Circuit Rider Dismounts*, 213.

100. Schwartz, ed., *A Woman Doctor's Civil War*, 189.

101. Ibid., 158.

102. Forrest G. Wood, *Black Scare: The Racist Response to Emancipation and Reconstruction* (Berkeley: Univ. of California Press, 1968), 55–79.

103. Roy P. Basler, ed., *The Collected Works of Abraham Lincoln*, vol. 2 (New Brunswick, N.J.: Rutgers Univ. Press, 1953), 405. For more on the ways northern Republicans distanced themselves from issues of social equality, see Litwack, *North of Slavery*, 268–77.

104. Click, *Time Full of Trial*, 147.

105. Stevenson, ed., *The Journals of Charlotte Forten Grimké*, 428–34; Charlotte Forten, "Life on the Atlantic Sea Islands," *Atlantic Monthly* 13, no. 80 (June 1864): 666–76; Child, *The Freedmen's Book*, 251–7; Thomas Wentworth Higginson, *Army Life in a Black Regiment* (1869; reprint; New York: Norton, 1984), 58–61.

106. Pearson, ed., *Letters from Port Royal*, 69–70.

107. Haviland, *A Woman's Life-Work*, 401–2.

108. Botome, *First Days Amongst the Contrabands*, 204–7.

109. Litwack, *Been in the Storm So Long: The Aftermath of Slavery* (New York: Vintage Books, 1979), 463.

110. Quoted in Jones, *Soldiers of Light and Love*, 135.

111. Swint, ed., *Dear Ones at Home*, 231, 237.

112. Quoted in Sally G. McMillen, *To Raise Up the South: Sunday Schools in Black and White Churches, 1865–1915* (Baton Rouge: Louisiana State Univ. Press, 2001), 47. See also Corey, *A History of the Richmond Theological Seminary*, 109.

113. Litwack, *Been in the Storm So Long*, 472–3. See also Hildebrand, *The Times Were Strange and Stirring*, 95; Griffin, ed., *Beloved Sisters and Loving Friends*, 203.

114. Quoted in McMillen, *To Raise Up the South*, 35.

115. Schwartz, ed. *A Woman Doctor's Civil War*, 108–9.

116. Walker, *A Rock in a Weary Land*, 53.

117. Quoted in Michael Goldhaber, "A Mission Unfulfilled: Freedmen's Education in North Carolina, 1865–1870," *Journal of Negro History* (autumn 1992), 199–210.

118. Stevenson, ed., *The Journals of Charlotte Forten Grimké*, 387, 443; Click, *Time Full of Trial*, 83; Katherine Smedley, *Martha Schofield and the Re-Education of the South, 1839–1916* (Lewiston/Queenston: Edwin Mellen Press, 1987), 82.

119. Richard L. Morton, ed., "A 'Yankee Teacher' in North Carolina, by Margaret Newbold Thorpe," *North Carolina Historical Review* 30, no. 4 (October 1953): 566.

120. Albion W. Tourgée, *A Fool's Errand: A Novel of the South* (1879; reprint, New York: Harper Torchbooks, 1961), 104, 107, 142.

121. Selleck, *Gentle Invaders*, 95.

122. Morton, ed., "A 'Yankee Teacher' in North Carolina," 570.

123. Jaquette, ed., *South after Gettysburg*, 234.

124. Quoted in McPherson, *The Abolitionist Legacy*, 172.

125. Flynt, *Alabama Baptists,* 133; Farish, *The Circuit Rider Dismounts,* 154.

126. Quoted in *American Missionary* (July 1867): 151–2.

127. Swint, *The Northern Teacher in the South,* 95–6, 98.

128. Swint, ed., *Dear Ones at Home,* 68–71; Prospero [pseud.], *Caliban: A Sequel to 'Ariel'* (New York: Published for the Proprietor, 1868), 30.

129. De Boer, "The Role of Afro-Americans," 328; Hildebrand, *The Times Were Strange and Stirring,* 47; Slaughter, *The Freedmen of the South,* 120; Dvorak, *An African-American Exodus,* 145–50.

130. Alvord, *Third Semi-Annual Report,* 22.

131. Foner, *Reconstruction,* 428; Walter Whitaker, *Centennial History of Alamance County, 1849–1949* (Charlotte: Dowd Press, 1949), 127; see also Flynt, *Alabama Baptists,* 140–1; Allen W. Trelease, *White Terror: The Ku Klux Klan Conspiracy and Southern Reconstruction* (1971; reprint, Baton Rouge: Louisiana State Univ. Press, 1995), 89, 124, 294.

132. Foner, *Reconstruction,* 428.

133. Quoted in Eighmy, *Churches in Cultural Captivity,* 33.

134. Farish, *The Circuit Rider Dismounts,* 55 (see also 145, 154, 165).

135. Morris, *Reading, 'Riting, and Reconstruction,* 41.

136. McPherson, *The Abolitionist Legacy,* 172.

137. Morris, *Reading, 'Riting, and Reconstruction,* 177–8. See also Swint, ed., *Dear Ones at Home,* 78; Ted Tunnell, *Edge of the Sword: The Ordeal of Carpetbagger Marshall H. Twitchell in the Civil War and Reconstruction* (Baton Rouge: Louisiana State Univ. Press, 2001), 108; Horst, ed., *The Fire of Liberty in Their Hearts,* 18; Smedley, *Martha Schofield and the Re-Education of the South,* 106–7.

138. Chang, "'Angels of Peace in a Smitten Land,'" 26.

139. Horst, ed., *The Fire of Liberty in Their Hearts,* 38.

140. Slaughter, *The Freedmen of the South,* 121.

141. Quoted in Range, *The Rise and Progress of Negro Colleges in Georgia,* 39.

142. Ibid.; Butchart, *Northern Schools, Southern Blacks, and Reconstruction.*

143. Harriet Brent Jacobs [Linda Brent, pseud.], *Incidents in the Life of a Slave* Girl (Boston: Boston Eleotype Foundry, 1861), 257.

144. Reilly, ed., *Sarah Jane Foster,* 51.

145. Goldhaber, "A Mission Unfulfilled," 205.

146. Wolfe, "Women Who Dared," 41.

147. Swint, *Northern Teacher in the South,* 99; Smedley, *Martha Schofield and the Re-Education of the South,* 146; Jackson, "The Educational Efforts," 1–40; Click, *Time Full of Trial,* 168. Thaddeus Stevens, "Speech on the Military Government of the South," in Palmer, ed., *The Selected Papers of Thaddeus Stevens,* 2:248.

148. U.S. Congress, *Report of the Joint Select Committee Appointed to Inquire into the Condition of Affairs in the Late Insurrectionary States,* vol. 4 (Washington, D.C.: Government Printing Office, 1872), 10. See also Farish, *The Circuit Rider Dismounts,* 128–30, 139.

149. Jaquette, ed., *South after Gettysburg,* 196,

150. Swint, ed., *Dear Ones at Home,* 194–195.

151. Holland, ed., *Letters and Diary of Laura M. Towne,* 155, 261.

152. Swint, *The Northern Teacher in the South,* 12; Brawley, *Two Centuries of Methodist Concern,* 82–5; Range, *The Rise and Progress of Negro Colleges in Georgia;* James M. McPherson, "White

Liberals and Black Power in Negro Education, 1865–1915," *American Historical Review* (June 1970): 1257–1386; Corey, *A History of the Richmond Theological Seminary,* 205; I. G. Penn, *Afro-American Press and its Editors* (Springfield, Mass.: Willey and Company Publishers, 1891); Dray, *At the Hands of Persons Unknown,* 35, 57.

153. For statistics, see Botome, *First Days Amongst the Contrabands,* 286. Rayford W. Logan, *The Negro in American Life and Thought: The Nadir, 1877–1901* (New York: Dial Press, 1954), 328.

154. For illiteracy in the Caribbean, see Eric Williams, *The Negro in the Caribbean* (Washington, D.C.: Associates in Negro Folk Education, 1942), 71–3. For information on literacy rates in other nations, see Antonio Viñao Frago, "The History of Literacy in Spain: Evolution, Traits, and Questions," *History of Education Quarterly* 30, no. 4 (winter 1990): 586; Harvey J. Gruff, *The Legacies of Literacy: Continuities and Contradictions in Western Culture and Society* (Bloomington: Indiana Univ. Press, 1987), 299, 361–6.

155. Botome, *First Days Amongst the Contrabands,* 286.

156. Quoted in Corey, *A History of the Richmond Theological Seminary,* 162.

157. Quoted in Glenda Elizabeth Gilmore, *Gender and Jim Crow: Women and the Politics of White Supremacy in North Carolina, 1896–1920* (Chapel Hill: Univ. of North Carolina Press, 1996), 11; Stephanie J. Shaw, *What a Woman Ought to Be and Do: Black Professional Women Workers during the Jim Crow Era* (Chicago: Univ. of Chicago Press, 1996); Higginbotham, *Righteous Discontent,* 20. Education also served as an important stepping-stone to economic and class advancement in other post-emancipation societies. See Walter Rodney, *A History of the Guyanese Working People, 1881–1905* (Baltimore: Johns Hopkins Univ. Press, 1981), 115–7; and Robert Conrad, *The Destruction of Brazilian Slavery, 1850–1888* (Berkeley: Univ. of California Press, 1972), 158.

158. W. E. B. Du Bois, *Dusk of Dawn: An Essay toward an Autobiography of a Race Concept* (1940; reprint, New York: Schocken Books, 1969), 24; Du Bois, *Black Reconstruction in America,* 708.

159. Quoted in Augustus Field Beard, *A Crusade of Brotherhood* (Boston: Pilgrim Press, 1909), 321–2.

160. Quoted in De Boer, "The Role of Afro-Americans," 565. See also Logan, *The Negro in American Life and Thought,* 328.

161. Booker T. Washington, *Up From Slavery: An Autobiography* (1900; reprint, Garden City, N.Y.: Doubleday, 1948), 62.

162. Slaughter, *The Freedmen of the South,* 193–5.

163. Tourgée, *A Fool's Errand,* 5.

164. J. G. Whittier, "Howard at Atlanta," *Atlantic Monthly* 23, no. 137 (March 1869): 367–8.

165. Dray, *At the Hands of Persons Unknown,* 52.

3. THE APOSTLES OF FORGIVENESS

1. Horst, ed., *The Fire of Liberty in Their Hearts,* 41, 94, 113; Stevenson, ed., *The Journals of Charlotte Forten Grimké,* 527.

2. "The Programme for the Future," *Independent,* May 4, 1865, p. 3. See also John Hay, "God's Vengeance," *Independent,* June 1, 1865, p. 1.

3. "The Church and the South," *Independent*, July 27, 1865, p. 4.

4. William C. Beecher and Rev. Samuel Scoville, *A Biography of Rev. Henry Ward Beecher* (New York: Charles L. Webster and Company, 1888), 460.

5. Henry Ward Beecher, "Reconstruction," *Independent*, July 6, 1865, p. 8.

6. Foner, *Reconstruction*; Michael Perman, *Emancipation and Reconstruction, 1862–1879* (Arlington Heights, Ill.: Harlan Davidson, 1987); William Gillette, *The Retreat from Reconstruction, 1869–1879* (Baton Rouge: Louisiana State Univ. Press, 1979).

7. The few religious histories that examine the North from 1865 to 1875 pay most of their attention to the ways in which an assortment of issues, especially rising class conflict, immigration, urbanization, and the women's rights movement, propelled northern Protestants to pay less attention to the South; see Moorhead, *American Apocalypse*, 218–44; Howard, *Religion and the Radical Republican Movement*, 212–4.

8. For business hopes for reconciliation, see Howard K. Beale, *The Critical Year: A Study of Andrew Johnson and Reconstruction* (New York: Harcourt, Brace and Company, 1930); C. Vann Woodward, *Reunion and Reaction: The Compromise of 1877 and the End of Reconstruction* (Boston: Little, Brown, 1966); and Stanley P. Hirshson, *Farewell to the Bloody Shirt* (Bloomington: Indiana Univ. Press, 1962).

9. Litwack, *North of Slavery*; Melish, *Disowning Slavery*; Leslie M. Harris, *In the Shadow of Slavery: African Americans in New York City, 1626–1863* (Chicago: Univ. of Chicago Press, 2003).

10. McPherson, *The Struggle for Equality*, 426–9; Howard, *Religion and the Radical Republican Movement*, 212–4.

11. For more on the ways some African American leaders cast their calls for civil equality and justice in religious tones, see David Howard-Pitney, "The Enduring Black Jeremiad: The American Jeremiad and Black Protest Rhetoric, from Frederick Douglass to W. E. B. Du Bois, 1841–1919," *American Quarterly* 38, no. 3 (1986): 481–92; David Howard-Pitney, *Afro-American Jeremiad: Appeals for Justice in America* (Philadelphia: Temple Univ. Press, 1993).

12. Joseph N. McGiffert, *God's Work and the Nation's Duty: A Thanksgiving Sermon, Delivered in the Presbyterian Church, Ashtabula, Ohio, November 29, 1866* (Cleveland, Ohio: G. S. Newcombe and Co., Printers, 1866), 11–6.

13. William G. McLoughlin, *The Meaning of Henry Ward Beecher: An Essay on the Shifting Values of Mid-Victorian America, 1840–1870* (New York: Knopf, 1970), x. For another biography of Beecher, see Clifford E. Clark, *Henry Ward Beecher: Spokesman for a Middle-Class America* (Urbana: Univ. of Illinois Press, 1978).

14. Prof. James M. Hoppin, "Henry Ward Beecher," *New Englander and Yale Review* 29, no. 12 (July 1870): 421–41; see also James Parton, "Henry Ward Beecher's Church," *Atlantic Monthly* 19, no. 111 (January 1867): 38–51.

15. Clarence Cook, "Rev. H. Ward Beecher," *Putnam's Monthly Magazine of American Literature, Science and Art* 11, no. 4 (April 1868): 504–5; Macrae, *The Americans at Home*, 61.

16. Henry Ward Beecher, "Punishment of the Rebel Leader," *Independent*, July 20, 1865, p. 1.

17. Henry Ward Beecher, "Love to Enemies," *Independent*, January 14, 1866, p. 2.

18. "Local Intelligence: Henry Ward Beecher on the Situation—Christian Treatment of Enemies," *New York Times*, June 11, 1866, p. 2.

19. Quoted in Beecher and Scoville, *A Biography of Rev. Henry Ward Beecher*, 461–2.

20. *Letters of Henry Ward Beecher and Dr. Tyng* (New York: National Union Executive Committee, 1866), 2; "Henry Ward Beecher on Reconstruction," *Independent*, September 6, 1866, p. 8.

21. *Letters of Henry Ward Beecher and Dr. Tyng*; Robert E. Young, *The Negro: A Reply to Ariel* (Nashville: J. W. M'Ferrin and Co., Booksellers and Stationers, 1867), 25–6.

22. McKitrick, *Andrew Johnson and Reconstruction*; "Henry Ward Beecher on Reconstruction," *Independent*, September 6, 1866, p. 8; McLoughlin, *The Meaning of Henry Ward Beecher*, 226. New York diarist George Templeton Strong, who denounced Beecher as a tool of the Democracy, agreed with the minister's position on the Freedmen's Bureau: "H. W. Beecher says in the course of a long lecture or address defending it and the President's general policy, that an executive officer declining power and patronage so immense as Congress offered Johnson by this bill is something new under the sun. It's quite true." Allan Nevins and Milton Halsey Thomas, eds., *The Diary of George Templeton Strong: Post-War Years, 1865–1875* (1952; reprint, New York: Octagon Books, 1974), 70.

23. *Letters of Henry Ward Beecher and Dr. Tyng*, 5.

24. Reprinted in "Dr. Tyng with Henry Ward Beecher," *New York Times*, September 16, 1866, p. 1. Tyng was one of the North's most prominent preachers, and even Beecher claimed that Tyng was his only rival in pulpit eloquence and authority. "He is the one man that I am afraid of," Beecher commented: "When he speaks first I do not care to follow him." Quoted in Theodore Cuyler, *Recollections of a Long Life* (New York: The Baker and Taylor, Co., 1902), 200.

25. "The Reply of Dr. Edward Beecher to Rev. Henry Ward Beecher," *Independent*, October 4, 1866, p. 2; "Reconstruction: Letter from Rev. Dr. Edward Beecher to Rev. Henry Ward Beecher, in Relation to Public Affairs," *New York Times*, September 28, 1866, p. 5.

26. "Speech on the Fourteenth Amendment," May 10, 1866, in Palmer, ed., *The Selected Papers of Thaddeus Stevens*, 2:138–139; John Reese, *Shall We Have Liberty or Slavery? Letter to Rev. Henry Ward Beecher* (Washington, D.C.: n.p., 1866), 2–3. For more on the Protestant debate over Beecher's Cleveland letter, see Howard, *Religion and the Radical Republican Movement*, 138–9.

27. "We Are Here And Want the Ballot-Box: An Address Delivered in Philadelphia, Pennsylvania, on 4 September 1866," in *The Frederick Douglass Papers: Series One: Speeches, Debates, and Interviews*, vol. 4, *1864–1880*, edited by John W. Blassingame and John R. McKivigan (New Haven, Conn.: Yale Univ. Press, 1991), 129–34.

28. Frederick Douglass, "The Assassination and Its Lessons," *Commonwealth*, October 28, 1865, p. 2.

29. "Application of the Rawhide," *New York Times*, February 2, 1866, p. 4. Pro-Beecher and anti–African American rights, the *Times* considered Douglass's speech abhorrent and claimed that Douglass would have a difficult time subduing a man like Beecher. They also suggested that Douglass's speech should teach a biblical lesson to northern white Protestants about Douglass and other African Americans: "Cast not your pearls before swine, lest they turn again and rend you."

30. "Henry Ward Beecher, Horace Greeley, and Gerritt Smith," *Cincinnati Commercial*, March 11, 1868; Macrae, *Americans at Home*, 62.

31. Beecher's claim that Sawmill had "no calling" is particularly interesting in light of Max Weber's claim that the Protestant Reformation created a social mood that facilitated the rise of capitalism by sanctifying work as a religious "calling." See Max Weber, *The Protestant Ethic and the Spirit of Capitalism* (1930; reprint, Los Angeles: Roxbury, 1996), 79–94.

32. Henry Ward Beecher, *Norwood: Or, Village Life in New England* (New York: Charles Scribner and Company, 1868), 279; 295; 20; 86; 89; 90; 83. For a similar evaluation of race and region in *Norwood*, see McLoughlin, *The Meaning of Henry Ward Beecher*, 213–4, 227–8. For more on depictions of African Americans as children and as animals, see Fredrickson, *The Black Image in the White Mind*, 52–8, 102–15, 121–8, 163–72, 275–82.

33. Beecher, *Norwood*, 540.

34. William Dean Howells, "Reviews and Literary Notices," *Atlantic Monthly* 21, no. 128 (June 1868): 761–4; "Reviews, Rev. H. W. Beecher, Norwood," *New York Times,* March 29, 1868, pp. 10–1. A British reviewer claimed, regarding the novel's Civil War moments, "our author's fairness is one of his great charms." See "Village Life in New England: An English Review of Henry Ward Beecher's Norwood," *New York Times,* January 5, 1868, p. 6. For more on romances between northern and southern whites in postwar literature, see Silber, *The Romance of Reunion,* 63–5.

35. For the most part, biographies of Stowe focus less attention on issues of Reconstruction and more on those of rights for women. See Joan D. Hedrick, *Harriet Beecher Stowe: A Life* (New York: Oxford Univ. Press, 1994), 325–83; Forrest Wilson, *Crusader in Crinoline: The Life of Harriet Beecher Stowe* (Philadelphia: J. B. Lippincott, 1941), 525–84.

36. Mrs. H. B. Stowe, "The Chimney-Corner," *Atlantic Monthly* 16, no. 94 (August 1865): 232–7.

37. Mrs. H. B. Stowe, "The Chimney Corner for 1866. I. Being a Family-Talk on Reconstruction," *Atlantic Monthly* 17, no. 99 (January 1866): 88–100.

38. HBS to HWB, October 8, 1866, Harriet Beecher Stowe Letters, Yale University Library, Microfilm Edition, reel 1. For Stowe supporting other efforts for the education of African Americans, see Harrold, *Subversives,* 188.

39. HBS to Elizabeth Argyll (Duchess of Argyll), February 19, 1866, in *Life of Harriet Beecher Stowe Compiled from her Letters and Journals,* edited by Charles Edward Stowe, (Boston: Houghton, Mifflin and Company, 1889), 398.

40. Harriet Beecher Stowe, *Men of Our Times; or Leading Patriots of the Day* (Hartford, Conn.: Hartford Publishing Co., 1868), 567.

41. For more on Stowe in Florida, see Susan A. Eacker, "Gender in Paradise: Harriet Beecher Stowe and Postbellum Prose on Florida," *Journal of Southern History* 64, no. 3 (August 1998): 495–512; John T. Foster Jr. and Sarah Whitmer Foster, *Beechers, Stowes, and Yankee Strangers: The Transformation of Florida* (Gainesville: Univ. Press of Florida, 1999); and Anne Rowe, *The Enchanted Country: Northern Writers in the South, 1865–1910* (Baton Rouge: Louisiana State Univ. Press, 1978), 1–19.

42. Quoted in *Life and Letters of Harriet Beecher Stowe,* edited by Annie Fields (Boston: Houghton, Mifflin and Company, 1897), 302.

43. Rowe, *Enchanted Country,* 1–19.

44. HBS to George Eliot, February 8, 1872, and HBS to George Eliot, May 11, 1872, in Charles Edward Stowe, ed., *Life of Harriet Beecher Stowe,* 463, 479.

45. Quoted in Hedrick, *Harriet Beecher Stowe,* 383.

46. Harriet Beecher Stowe, *Palmetto Leaves* (1873; reprint, Gainesville: Univ. Press of Florida, 1999). Comparing Stowe's writings from Florida with her antebellum works, especially *Uncle Tom's Cabin,* Anne Rowe has suggested that Stowe maintained a romantic view of southern white society and a condescending view of African Americans. See Rowe, *Enchanted Country,* 1–19. But considering her writings at the end of the Civil War and the drastically different historical context in the 1870s,

her attention to sectional reconciliation and African American marginalization was remarkably different than her antebellum prose. For more on northerners vacationing in the South, see Silber, *The Romance of Reunion*, 66–92.

47. Stowe, *Palmetto Leaves*, 14–5, 25, xv. Numerous historians of Florida have also claimed that Stowe was largely responsible for generating massive northern interest in visiting the state. See Foster Jr. and Foster, *Beechers, Stowes, and Yankee Strangers*, xvii.

48. In a letter to the *New York Daily Tribune*, Stowe described southern whites as "remarkably quiet, peaceable, and honest set of people, who believe in the apostolic injunction, 'Study to be quiet and mind your own business.' " "Life in Florida," *New York Daily Tribune*, February 17, 1877, p. 3.

49. Stowe, *Palmetto Leaves*, 183, 178–9, 230–1, 283. In a letter to the *Atlantic Monthly*, Stowe actually likened daily operations on her estate to those of plantations in slavery: "The old plantation *régime* was adopted, because they were accustomed to working in that way, and in no other. . . . They were divided into gangs, with a leader to each gang, and went directly into the field, putting in three hours of good work." Harriet Beecher Stowe, "Our Florida Plantation," *Atlantic Monthly* 43, no. 259 (May 1879): 648. In many ways, Stowe's vision of African Americans as content wage earners paralleled the hopes of many northerner writers that the transition to free labor would be painless. See Richardson, *The Death of Reconstruction*, 6–40.

50. Stowe, *Palmetto Leaves*, 75, 269, 280; for another time that Stowe suggested that environmental factors made blacks ideal laborers in the South, see Harriet Beecher Stowe, "What Is to Be Done with Them?" *Independent*, August 21, 1862, p. 1. For a discussion of this article, see Lyde Cullen Sizer, *The Political Work of Northern Women Writers and the Civil War, 1850–1872* (Chapel Hill: Univ. of North Carolina Press, 2000), 149–50.

51. Schwartz, ed. *A Woman Doctor's Civil War*, 243.

52. Quoted in, Joe M. Richardson, *The Negro in the Reconstruction of Florida, 1865–1877* (Tallahassee: Florida State Univ. Press, 1965), 163.

53. For violence committed against African Americans in Reconstruction Florida, see Richardson, *The Negro in the Reconstruction of Florida*, 164; Charlton W. Tebeau, *A History of Florida* (Coral Gables, Fla.: Univ. of Miami Press, 1971), 252–3.

54. Quoted in Alex L. Murray, "Harriet Beecher Stowe on Racial Segregation in the Schools," *American Quarterly* 12, no. 4 (winter 1960): 518–9.

55. For northern praise for the plantation South before the war, see Taylor, *Cavalier and Yankee*. For an analysis of the creation of the plantation myth after the war, see Hale, *Making Whiteness*, 48–93.

56. Macrae, *The Americans at Home*, 62, 546.

57. "Southern Religious Reconstruction—In Part," *New York Herald*, May 14, 1868, p. 6.

58. "The Reunion Deputation in Memphis—Action of the Southern General Conference," *Christian Advocate*, May 19, 1870, p. 156.

59. Reprinted as "Methodist Wooing," *Christian Advocate*, June 16, 1870, p. 185.

60. *Formal Fraternity: Proceedings of the General Conferences of the Methodist Episcopal Church and of the Methodist Episcopal Church, South, in 1872, 1874, and 1876, and of the Joint Commission of the Two Churches on Fraternal Relations, at Cape May, New Jersey, August 16–23, 1876*, (New York: Nelson and Phillips, 1876), 68. For more on northern Methodist desires for sectional reconciliation, see Dow Kirkpatrick, "Early Efforts at Reunion," in *The History of American Methodism in Three Volumes*, edited

by Emory Stevens Bucke (New York: Abingdon Press, 1964), 2:660–683; Morrow, *Northern Methodism and Reconstruction*, 77–87.

61. Quoted in Mohler, "The Episcopal Church and National Reconciliation, 1865," 576.

62. "Church Unification—North and South," *Christian Advocate*, May 12, 1870, p. 148.

63. Quoted in Ernest Trice Thompson, *Presbyterians in the South*, vol. 2, *1861–1890* (Richmond, Va.: John Knox Press, 1973), 231. For more on Presbyterian reconciliation, see Lefferts A. Loetscher, *A Brief History of the Presbyterians* (Philadelphia: Westminster Press, 1983), 123–4.

64. Quoted in McMillen, *To Raise Up the South*, 53.

65. *American Baptist Year-Book, 1870* (Philadelphia: American Baptist Publication Society, 1870), 34.

66. Farish, *The Circuit Rider Dismounts*, 90–1; Dabney quoted in Sean Michael Lewis, "'Old Times Are Not Forgotten': Robert Lewis Dabney's Public Theology for a Reconstructed South," *Journal of Presbyterian History* 81, no. 3 (fall 2003): 163–77.

67. McMillen, *To Raise Up the South*; Spain, *At Ease in Zion*, 25–30; Farish, *The Circuit Rider Dismounts*, 45–75 Flynt, *Alabama Baptists*, 112–55; Ella Lonn, "Reconciliation between the North and the South," *Journal of Southern History* 13, no. 1 (February 1947): 3–26; Stowell, *Rebuidling Zion*, 170–2.

68. Stowell, *Rebuilding Zion*, 142.

69. Morrow, *Northern Methodism and Reconstruction*, 167–77; Brawley, *Two Centuries of Methodist Concern*, 515.

70. Vander Velde, *The Presbyterian Churches and the Federal Union, 1861–1869*, 540.

71. Richard B. Drake, "Freedmen's Aid Societies and Sectional Compromise," *Journal of Southern History* 29, no. 2 (May 1963): 175–86.

72. De Boer, "The Role of Afro-Americans," 324; Carl S. Smith, *Urban Disorder and the Shape of Belief: The Great Chicago Fire, the Haymarket Bomb, and the Model Town of Pullman* (Chicago: Univ. of Chicago Press, 1995); John J. Pauly, "The Great Chicago Fire as a National Event," *American Quarterly* 35, no. 5 (winter 1984): 668–83.

73. *Minutes of the General Assembly of the Presbyterian Church in the United States of America* (New York: Presbyterian Board of Publication, 1871), 510; Stowell, *Rebuilding Zion*, 143.

74. "Minutes of the Faculty of Atlanta University," April 1, 1879, p. 154.

75. Hildebrand, *The Times Were Strange and Stirring*, 114–7; Drake, "Freedmen's Aid Societies and Sectional Compromise," 175–86; Theodore Dwight Woolsey, *The Nation Still in Danger; or, Ten Years After the War* (New York: American Missionary Association, 1875), 3.

76. Gillette, *The Retreat from Reconstruction*, 34–5, 82, 90. For more on the Bureau see the articles in Nieman, ed., *The Freedmen's Bureau and Black Freedom*, and Cimbala and Miller, eds., *The Freedmen's Bureau and Reconstruction*.

77. For more on the AMEZ response, see Kirkpatrick, "Early Efforts at Reunion," in Burke, ed., *The History of American Methodism in Three Volumes*, 2:677–679.

78. "The Republican Party," *Independent*, February 23, 1871, p. 4.

79. Frances Harper, "An Appeal to the American People," in *Complete Poems of Frances E. W. Harper*, edited by Maryemma Graham (New York: Oxford Univ. Press, 1988), 82.

80. Frances Harper, "Words for the Hour" in ibid., 102–3.

81. Laura M. Towne to F. R. Cope, April 9, 1873, Penn School Papers, Manuscripts Department, University of North Carolina at Chapel Hill, box 1, folder 1-A.

82. Morton, ed., "Life in Virginia, by a 'Yankee Teacher,' Margaret Newbold Thorpe," 195. Several other northerners recognized the growing northern apathy for issues of civil rights. See McPherson, *Abolitionist Legacy*, 143–4; Horst, ed., *The Fire of Liberty in Their Hearts*, 171; Brown, "Lyman Abbott and Freedmen's Aid, 1865–1869," 29.

83. Alexander Crummell, "The Social Principle among a People and its Bearing on their Progress and Development," in *Civilization and Black Progress: Selected Writings of Alexander Crummell on the South*, edited by J. R. Oldfield (Charlottesville: Univ. Press of Virginia, 1995), 30–41.

84. Henry J. Ferry, "Racism and Reunion: A Black Protest by Francis James Grimké," *Journal of Presbyterian History* 50 (1972): 77–88; Stevenson, ed., *The Journals of Charlotte Forten Grimké*, 533.

85. For studies of reconciliation in popular culture, see Silber, *Romance of Reunion*, 93–123.

86. Fahs, *The Imagined Civil War*, 87.

87. Caroline Seymour, "Death," *Harper's New Monthly Magazine* 32, no. 187 (December 1865): 85–6.

88. "The Blue and the Gray," *Atlantic Monthly* 20, no. 119 (September 1867): 369–70. For a similar interpretation of "The Blue and the Gray," see Gardiner H. Shattuck Jr., *A Shield and Hiding Place: The Religious Life of the Civil War Armies* (Macon, Ga.: Mercer Univ. Press, 1987), 127–36.

89. S. M. Alcott, "Blue and the Gray," *Putnam's Monthly Magazine of American Literature, Science and Art* 11, no. 6 (June 1868): 737–54; for more on the Civil War in literature, see Fahs, *The Imagined Civil War*.

90. Fahs, *The Imagined Civil War*, 297–9.

91. Buck, *The Road to Reunion*, 91; Blight, *Race and Reunion*, 122–8.

92. For historigraphical debates on the 1872 election, see James M. McPherson, "Grant or Greeley? The Abolitionist Dilemma in the Election of 1872," *American Historical Review* 71, no. 1 (October 1965): 43–61; Gillette, *Retreat from Reconstruction*, 56–75; Richard Allan Gerber, "The Liberal Republicans of 1872 in Historiographical Perspective," *Journal of American History* 62, no. 1 (June 1975): 40–73; Mark Wahlgren Summers, *The Era of Good Stealings* (New York: Oxford Univ. Press, 1993).

93. Quoted in Lurton D. Ingersoll, *The Life of Horace Greeley* (1873; reprint, New York: Beekman Publishers, 1974), 550.

94. John C. Underwood to Horace Greeley, November 27, 1867, Horace Greeley Papers, New York Public Library, Microfilm Edition, reel 2, frame 0911.

95. Ingersoll, *The Life of Horace Greeley*, 637.

96. Ibid., 528.

97. Ibid., 525.

98. In another letter, Mahan asserted: "As a Christian, I desire it [national unity] as not only such a good, but an immutable condition of the highest influence of 'the Gospel of peace.'" Mahan's letters were reprinted in *The True Issues of the Presidential Campaign: Speeches of Horace Greeley during his Western Trip and at Portland, Maine. Also, Ex-President Mahan's Letters* (New York: n.p., 1872), 31, 32.

99. Hon. George Frisbie Hoar, ed., *Charles Sumner: His Complete Works* (Boston: Lee and Shepard, 1883), 191, 228, 254. At least one Republican ridiculed Sumner for his use of religious imagery to advocate Greeley's cause, calling him the "great high priest and confessor" of the Democratic–Liberal Republican Party. See "Political Speech, 1872," Horace Greeley Papers, New York Public Library, Microfilm Edition, reel 4, frame 0588.

100. For a discussion of Tilton's support of Greeley, see McPherson, "Grant or Greeley?" 43–61.

101. Ingersoll, *The Life of Horace Greeley*, 520, 657.

102. *The True Issues of the Presidential Campaign*, 12.

103. Quoted in Patrick W. Riddleberger, "The Radicals' Abandonment of the Negro during Reconstruction," *Journal of Negro History* 45, no. 2 (April 1960): 88–102.

104. *Grant or Greeley—which? Facts and arguments for the consideration of the colored citizens of the United States: being extracts from letters, speeches, and editorials by colored men and their best friends. Sumner's mistakes, Greeley's surrender, and Grant's faithfulness. Opinions in brief of Wm. Lloyd Garrison, Wendell Phillips, Prof. J. Mercer Langston, R. H. Dana, Jr., Judge Hoar, Fred. Douglass, Speaker Blaine, Wm. D. Forten, Prof. Wm. Howard Day* (Washington, D.C.: National Congressional Committee, 1872), 4.

105. "My Reasons For Opposing Horace Greeley: Addresses Delivered in Boston, Massachusetts, on 5 September 1872," in *The Frederick Douglass Papers: Series One: Speeches, Debates, and Interviews*, vol. 4, *1864–1880*, edited by John W. Blassingame and John R. McKivigan (New Haven, Conn.: Yale Univ. Press, 1991), 327–8; for other times Douglass used religious rhetoric and metaphors during campaign speeches, see ibid., 336–7.

106. Newspaper clipping, Horace Greeley Papers, New York Public Library, Microfilm Edition, reel 4, frame 0436; for another article regarding Greeley's religious faith and national reconciliation, see "Horace Greeley's Faith," newspaper clipping, Horace Greeley Papers, New York Public Library, Microfilm Edition, reel 4, frames 0276–0277; for more on Greeley's funeral, see Ingersoll, *The Life of Horace Greeley*, 578; and Don C. Seitz, *Horace Greeley: Founder of the New York Tribune* (Indianapolis: The Bobbs-Merrill Company, 1926), 402–3.

107. Bayard Taylor, "A Pure and Faithful Soul," in Ingersoll, *The Life of Horace Greeley*, 676.

108. See "Horace Greeley's Faith," newspaper clipping, Horace Greeley Papers, New York Public Library, Microfilm Edition, reel 4, frame 0276.

4. INVENTOR OF LEGENDS MIRACULOUS

1. Rev. W. H. Daniels, *D. L. Moody and His Work* (Hartford, Conn.: American Publishing Company, 1876), 171–2. For a slightly different version of this chapter, see Edward J. Blum, "Gilded Crosses: Postbellum Revivalism and the Reforging of American Nationalism," *Journal of Presbyterian History* 79, no. 4 (winter 2001): 277–92.

2. Daniels, *D. L. Moody and His Work*, 171–2.

3. For the best scholarly biography of Moody, see James F. Findlay Jr., *Dwight L. Moody: American Evangelist, 1837–1899* (Chicago: Univ. of Chicago Press, 1969); William R. Moody, *The Life of Dwight L. Moody: The Official Authorized Edition* (New York: Revell Publishers, 1900), 48. For more on the shoe industry, see Hazard E. Blanche, *The Organization of the Boot and Shoe Industry in Massachusetts Before 1875* (Cambridge, Mass.: Harvard Univ. Press, 1921), chapters 3–5.

4. Richard K. Curtis, *They Called Him Mister Moody* (Grand Rapids, Mich.: Eerdmans, 1962), 47–52; J. C. Pollock, *Moody: A Biographical Portrait of the Pacesetter in Modern Mass Evangelism* (New York: MacMillan, 1963), 13; Lyle W. Dorsett, *A Passion for Souls: The Life of D. L. Moody* (Chicago: Moody Press, 1997), 39–52; William R. Moody, *The Life of Dwight L. Moody*, 30; Albert J. Von Frank, *The Trials of Anthony Burns: Freedom and Slavery in Emerson's Boston* (Cambridge, Mass.: Harvard Univ. Press, 1999).

5. Long, *The Revival of 1857–58*, 127–36.

6. August J. Fry, *D. L. Moody: The Chicago Years, 1856–1871* (Amsterdam: Free Univ. Press, 1984), 16–8.

7. Daniels, *D. L. Moody and His Work*, 94; Lemuel Moss, *Annals of the United States Christian Commission* (Philadelphia: J. B. Lippincott, 1868), 73, 309.

8. Findlay Jr., *Dwight L. Moody*, 92–135; William G. McLoughlin, *Modern Revivalism: Charles Grandison Finney to Billy Graham* (New York: Ronald Press, 1959), 177–98; I. A. M. Cumming [pseud.], *Tabernacle Sketches* (Boston: The Times Publishing Company, 1877), 33–4.

9. Nell Irvin Painter, *Standing at Armageddon: The United States, 1877–1919* (New York: Norton, 1987); Foner, *Reconstruction*, 512–23; Rendigs Fels, *American Business Cycles, 1865–1897* (Chapel Hill: Univ. of North Carolina Press, 1959), 99–107; Samuel Rezneck, "Distress, Relief, and Discontent in the United States during the Depression of 1873–78," *Journal of Political Economy* 58, no. 6 (December 1950): 495–7.

10. Gillette, *Retreat from Reconstruction*, 69; Buck, *The Road to Reunion*, chapters 3 and 4; Vincent P. De Santis, *Republicans Face the Southern Question: The New Departure Years, 1877–1897* (Baltimore: Johns Hopkins Univ. Press, 1959); Hirshson, *Farewell to the Bloody Shirt*.

11. Summers, *The Era of Good Stealings*.

12. Gillette, *Retreat from Reconstruction*, 121–33; Foner, *Reconstruction*, 554; "The Protest," *New York Herald*, January 12, 1875, p. 1; Hirshson, *Farewell to the Bloody Shirt*, 30.

13. Charles Nordhoff, *The Cotton States in the Spring and Summer of 1875* (New York: D. Appleton and Company, 1876); James S. Pike, *The Prostrate State: South Carolina Under Negro Government* (1873; reprint, New York: Loring and Mussey, 1935); Edward King, *The Great South* (Hartford, Conn.: American Publishing Co., 1875); Gillette, *Retreat from Reconstruction*, 131, 155.

14. De Santis, *Republicans Face the Southern Question*, 45; Gillette, *Retreat from Reconstruction*, 131.

15. McLoughlin, *Modern Revivalism*, 167; Marty, *Righteous Empire*, 162–3; Ahlstrom, *A Religious History of the American People*, 743–6; Mead, *The Lively Experiment*, 134–89. Some religious historians have attempted to connect Moody to the political issues of the day. Tamar Frankiel [Sandra S. Sizer], for example, suggests that Moody's revivals were dominated by Republicans and therefore bolstered their sense of political solidarity, see Tamar Frankiel [Sandra S. Sizer], "Politics and Apolitical Religion: The Great Urban Revivalism of the Late Nineteenth Century," *Church History* 48, no. 1 (1979): 81–98.

16. See Richard Wightman Fox, *Trials of Intimacy: Love and Loss in the Beecher-Tilton Scandal* (Chicago: Univ. of Chicago Press, 1999); Altina L. Waller, *Reverend Beecher and Mrs. Tilton: Sex and Class in Victorian America* (Amherst: Univ. of Massachusetts Press, 1982); Edmund B. Fairfield, *Wickedness in High Places: A Review of the Beecher Case* (Mansfield, O. L. D. Myers and Brother, Printers, 1874).

17. Findlay Jr., *Dwight Moody*, 192–226.

18. For more on the relationships between Moody and popular newspapers, see Bruce Evensen, "It Is a Marvel to Many People: Dwight L. Moody, Mass Media, and the New England Revival of 1877," *New England Quarterly* 72, no. 2 (June 1999): 251–74; and Bruce J. Evensen, *God's Man for the Gilded Age: D. L. Moody and the Rise of Modern Evangelism* (New York: Oxford Univ. Press, 2003).

19. Dwight Lyman Moody, *The Great Redemption; or, Gospel Light, Under the Labors of Moody and Sankey* (Cleveland: C. C. Wick and Co., 1880), 9.

20. Quoted in Henry Davenport Northrop, *Life and Labors of Dwight L. Moody: The Great Evangelist* (New Haven, Conn.: Butler and Alger, 1899), 160.

21. Gaius Glenn Atkins, *Religion in Our Times* (New York: Round Table Press, 1932), 1.

22. Frederick Savage, interviewed by Christabel Kidder, December 22, 1938, American Life Histories: Manuscripts from the Federal Writers' Project, 1936–1940, http://memory.loc.gov/ammem/wpaintro/wpahome.html (February 10, 2003).

23. Quoted in Robert Boyd, *The Wonderful Career of Moody and Sankey in Great Britain and America Together With The Trials and Triumphs of Faith* (New York: Henry S. Goodspeed and Company, 1875), 581.

24. See Dwight L. Moody, *To All People: Comprising Sermons, Bible Readings, Temperance Addresses and Prayer-Meeting Talks, Delivered in the Boston Tabernacle* (Boston: The Globe Publishing Company, 1877), 137. Books with Moody as the author are collections of his sermons as recorded by the local press during the revival campaigns.

25. For more on Moody's premillennialism, see Dorsett, *A Passion for Souls*, 135, 168, 251, 335, 365, 409; and Findlay, *Dwight L. Moody*, 125–6, 249–55, 276–7.

26. For these two quotes, see Dwight Lyman Moody, *New Sermons, Addresses and Prayers* (Chicago: J. W. Goodspeed, Publisher, 1877), 370, 40.

27. For Dodge, see Richard Lowitt, *A Merchant Prince of the Nineteenth Century, William E. Dodge* (New York: Columbia Univ. Press, 1952); for Wanamaker, see William Leach, *Land of Desire: Merchants, Power, and the Rise of a New American Culture* (New York: Vintage Books, 1993), 51, 91; for Willard, see Nancy A. Hardesty, *Women Called to Witness: Evangelical Feminism in the 19th Century* (Nashville: Abingdon Press, 1984), 13–25; for Rockefeller, see Ron Chernow, *Titan: The Life of John D. Rockefeller, Sr.* (New York: Knopf, 1999).

28. Moody, *Glad Tidings*, 335.

29. Dwight Moody to William Moody, January 21, 1885, Dwight Lyman Moody Papers, Yale Divinity School Special Collections, box 1, folder 22.

30. Silber, *The Romance of Reunion*, 39–123; Buck, *The Road to Reunion*, 115–43, 170–247; O'Leary, *To Die For*, 110–49; Blight, *Race and Reunion*, 98–254; R. U. Johnson and C. C. Buel, eds., *Battles and Leaders of the Civil War*, 4 vols. (New York: Century, 1887–1888).

31. See Moody, *Glad Tidings*, x; "Churches and Ministers," *New York Times*, January 21, 1877, p. 10; "The Revival," *The Inter Ocean* (Chicago) October 3, 1876, p. 1; "The Religious Press on Revival," *New York Herald*, October 24, 1875, p. 8.

32. Henry Drummond, "Mr. Moody: Some Impressions and Facts," *McClure's Magazine* 4 (1894–1895): 192.

33. Wilson, *Baptized in Blood*, 84; Michael Davis, *The Image of Lincoln in the South* (Knoxville: Univ. of Tennessee Press, 1971), 113–7; "Moody and Sankey," *Southern Review* (Baltimore), January 1876, pp. 181–205; Foster, *Ghosts of the Confederacy*, 49–51; H. Shelton Smith, *In His Image, But . . . Racism in Southern Religion, 1780–1910* (Durham: Duke Univ. Press, 1972), 214–5.

34. Moody, *Glad Tidings*, 351; for a similar typology, see Moody, *New Sermons*, 240.

35. "Moody and Sankey," *Nation* 22, no. 558 (March 9, 1876): 156–7; "Topics of the Time," *Scribner's Monthly* 10, no. 2 (June 1875): 239; Cumming, *Tabernacle Sketches*, 33–4; David S. Reynolds, "From Doctrine to Narrative: The Rise of Pulpit Storytelling in America," *American Quarterly* 32, no. 5 (winter 1980): 479–98.

36. Fahs, *The Imagined Civil War*, 121–48; Alice Fahs, "The Feminized Civil War: Gender, Northern Popular Literature, and the Memory of the Civil War, 1861–1900," *The Journal of American History* 85, no. 4 (March 1999): 1461–94.

37. Moody, *Glad Tidings*, 27.

38. Moody, *New Sermons*, 36.

39. Ibid., 321.

40. Tamar Frankiel [Sandra S. Sizer], *Gospel Hymns and Social Religion: The Rhetoric of Nineteenth-Century Revivalism* (Philadelphia: Temple Univ. Press, 1978), 41–3; Ira D. Sankey, *My Life and the Story of the Gospel Hymns* (Philadelphia: Sunday School Times Company, 1907), 152–5.

41. Cumming, *Tabernacle Sketches*, 18.

42. Findlay, *Dwight L. Moody*, 216.

43. Moody, *New Sermons*, 365, 485 (emphasis added). For a discussion of the ways in which novels about Civil War combat diminished the differences between the regions, see Summers, *The Gilded Age*, 53–4.

44. See Iver Bernstein, *The New York City Draft Riots: Their Significance for American Society and Politics in the Age of the Civil War* (New York: Oxford Univ. Press, 1990); Foner, *Reconstruction*, 32–3.

45. Moody, *New Sermons*, 281; Mary Douglas, *Purity and Danger: An Analysis of Concepts of Pollution and Taboo* (Harmondworth, U.K.: Penguin, 1970).

46. Moody, *New Sermons*, 28; Moody, *Glad Tidings*, 279.

47. Moody, *Glad Tidings*, 38; "Progress of Revival Work," *New York Tribune*, February 10, 1876, pp. 1, 5; for Whitman's poem, see Cumming, *Tabernacle Sketches*, 34.

48. Dwight Lyman Moody, *Moody and Sankey in Hartford* (Hartford, Conn.: W. H. Goodrich, 1878), x–xi; for other examples of this, see Rev. E. J. Goodspeed, *A Full History of the Wonderful Career of Moody and Sankey in Great Britain and America* (St. Louis: N. D. Thompson and Co., Publishers, 1876), 29; Daniels, *D. L. Moody and His Work*, 99–100.

49. See Buck, *The Road to Reunion*, 134–6; Blight, *Race and Reunion*, 132–4; Woodward, *Reunion and Reaction*, 232; for more on Moody and the centennial, see Dee Brown, *The Year of the Century: 1876* (New York: Scribner, 1966), 26–49.

50. Goodspeed, *A Full History of the Wonderful Career of Moody and Sankey*, 351–7.

51. For newspaper reports, see "William Swan Plumer Scrapbook," William Swan Plumer Manuscript Collection, Princeton Theological Seminary, box 6; D. L. Moody and Wm. S. Plumer, *Great Questions Answered: Two Colloquies* (New York: Anson D. F. Randolf and Company, 1876).

52. "William Swan Plumer," in *Appleton's Cyclopedia of American Biography*, edited by James Grant Wilson and John Fiske (New York: D. Appleton and Company, 1887–1889); William S. Plumer, *Thoughts on the Religious Instruction of the Negroes in this Country* (Savannah, Ga.: E. J. Purse, 1848), 1. "William Swan Plumer," *Dictionary of American Biography*, vol. 8 (New York: Charles Scribner's Sons, 1963), 13–4.

53. For Plumer's statements, see Goen, *Broken Churches, Broken Nation*, 70, 74; Mitchell Snay, *Gospel of Disunion: Religion and Separatism in the Antebellum South* (New York: Cambridge Univ. Press, 1993).

54. For Plumer and his northern activities in the 1860s, see Board of Trustees to W. S. Plumer, November 12, 1861, William Swan Plumer Manuscript Collection, Princeton Theological Seminary, box 3, folder 17; for Plumer's response, see W. S. Plumer, "My Fidelity to the Government," Plumer Collection, box 3, folder 17; for information on the New England rejection of Plumer, see Henry Hoyt

to WSP, January 31, 1865, Plumer Collection, box 3, folder 20. For more on northerners' disdain for Democratic ministers, see Byron C. Andreasen, "'As Good a Right to Pray': Copperhead Christians on the Northern Civil War Home Front" (Ph.D. diss., University of Illinois at Urbana-Champaign, 1998).

55. Plumer generally has been left out of Presbyterian histories. For example, see Randall Balmer and John R. Fitzmier, *The Presbyterians* (Westport, Conn.: Greenwood Press, 1993); for the statement regarding Plumer's importance, see "Rev. Wm. S. Plumer, D.D. L.L.D.," newspaper clipping, William Swan Plumer Manuscript Collection, Princeton Theological Seminary, box 10, folder 1.

56. For a description of the event, see Walter L. Lingle, "Talks on Timely Topics," *Christian Observer*, March 18, 1936, pp. 3–4; for the letter to Plumer's daughter, see R. Irvine to Mrs. Douglass, 1876, William Swan Plumer Manuscript Collection, Princeton Theological Seminary, box 11, folder 9.

57. Lingle, "Talks on Timely Topics," 3–4.

58. Flynt, *Alabama Baptists*, 189–90.

59. "Moody's Power," *Augusta Constitutionalist*, May 7, 1876, p. 4; "One Augusta Letter," *Atlanta Constitution*, May 4, 1876, p. 1.

60. Goodspeed, *A Full History of the Wonderful Career of Moody and Sankey*, 615–9.

61. See "How Can We Help on this Work?" *Christian Recorder*, October 26, 1875, p. 4; "Moody in Philadelphia," *Christian Recorder*, January 20, 1876, p. 8.

62. "One Augusta Letter," *Atlanta Constitution*, May 4, 1876, p. 1; "A Revival Incident," *New York Times*, May 10, 1876, p. 2. For Moody's internal battle regarding segregation, see Dorsett, *A Passion for Souls*, 245–6. For more on revival segregation in the early twentieth century, see William Martin, *A Prophet with Honor: The Billy Graham Story* (New York: Morrow, 1991), 168–72.

63. James Lutzweiler, ed., *The Revivals of Dwight L. Moody in North Carolina: Charlotte, NC—March 8–17, 1893; Wilmington, NC—March 18–25, 1893* (Greensboro, N.C.: Schnappsburg Univ. Press, 1993); "Moody's revivals in Louisville, KY, Dec. 13, 1887–Feb. 13, 1888," Moody Bible Institute, Special Collections Archive, Chicago, Illinois.

64. "A Talk with Moody," *Washington Post*, January 16, 1885, p. 1; "Original and Otherwise," *Washington Post*, January 6, 1885, p. 2. For another description of a Moody revival in the South in the 1880s, see George W. Bothwell, "The South: Revival at New Orleans, La." *American Missionary*, 40, no. 3 (April 1886): 103–4.

65. "Do Not Want Moody," *Louisville Courier-Journal*, February 13, 1888, p. 7; "Evangelist Moody Criticized," *New York Times*, June 11, 1887, p. 8; Findlay, *Dwight L. Moody*, 280.

66. "Oration of Frederick Douglass," *American Missionary* 39, no. 6 (June 1885): 164. The son of a Presbyterian minister, Robert Green Ingersoll was a prominent agnostic during the second half of the nineteenth century. He toured the United States popularizing Darwinian evolution theory, and he was often referred to as "the great infidel." See Orvin Prentiss Larson, *American Infidel: Robert G. Ingersall, A Biography* (New York: Citadel Press, 1962).

67. Alfreda M. Duster, ed., *Crusade for Justice: The Autobiography of Ida B. Wells* (Chicago: Univ. of Chicago Press, 1970), 111–2, 151.

68. For more on the rise in virulent racism in the 1890s, see Logan, *The Negro in American Life and Thought*.

69. Herbert Aptheker, ed., *The Correspondence of W. E. B. Du Bois*, vol. 3, *Selections, 1944–1963* (Amherst: Univ. of Massachusetts Press, 1978), 19–20; L. H. Smith to D. L. Moody, March 19, 1896, Dwight Lyman Moody Papers, Yale Divinity School Special Collections, box 1, folder 28.

70. "Race Prejudice—Is it Waning?" *American Missionary* 49, no. 7 (July 1895): 220–1.

71. W. Scott Poole, "Confederate Apocalypse: Theology and Violence in the White Reconstruction South," in *Vale of Tears: New Essays in Religion and Reconstruction*, edited by Edward J. Blum and W. Scott Poole (Macon, Ga.: Mercer Univ. Press, 2005); McLoughlin, *Modern Revivalism*; Dray, *At the Hands of Persons Unknown*, 77.

5. THE WHITE FLAG WAVES

1. Abram J. Ryan, *Poems: Patriotic, Religious, Miscellaneous* (1880; reprint, Baltimore: John Murphy and Co., 1892), 328–9, 63–4. For more on Ryan, see Foster, *Ghosts of the Confederacy*, 36–7, and Charles C. Boldrick, "Father Abram J. Ryan, 'The Poet-Priest of the Confederacy,'" *Filson Club History Quarterly* 46, no. 3 (1972): 201–18. Another version of this chapter has been published as Edward J. Blum, "The Crucible of Disease: Trauma, Memory, and National Reconciliation during the Yellow Fever Epidemic of 1878," *Journal of Southern History* 69, no. 4 (November 2003): 791–820.

2. Ryan, *Poems: Patriotic, Religious, Miscellaneous*, 78–9.

3. For the most part, studies of the fever have focused on its importance with regards to medical issues and federal health legislation. See John H. Ellis, *Yellow Fever and Public Health in the New South* (Lexington: Univ. Press of Kentucky, 1992); Khaled J. Bloom, *The Mississippi Valley's Great Yellow Fever Epidemic of 1878* (Baton Rouge: Louisiana State Univ. Press, 1993); Margaret Humphreys, *Yellow Fever and the South* (Baltimore: Johns Hopkins Univ. Press, 1992); and Gerald M. Capers Jr. "Yellow Fever in Memphis in the 1870's," *Mississippi Valley Historical Review* 24, no. 4 (March 1938): 483–502.

4. Craig C. Piers, "Remembering Trauma: A Characterological Perspective," in *Trauma and Memory*, edited by Linda M. Williams and Victoria L. Banyard (London: Sage Publications, 1999), 61.

5. Paul Antze and Michael Lambek, *Tense Past: Cultural Essays in Trauma and Memory* (New York: Routledge, 1996), vii.

6. For more on the election and aftermath of the 1876 presidential election, see Woodward, *Reunion and Reaction*; Keith Ian Polakoff, *The Politics of Inertia: The Election of 1876 and the End of Reconstruction* (Baton Rouge: Lousiana State Univ. Press, 1973); Foner, *Reconstruction*, 564–601.

7. De Santis, *Republicans Face the Southern Question*, 1–103; Logan, *The Negro in American Life and Thought*, 12–35; Hirshson, *Farewell to the Bloody Shirt*, 21–44; Foner, *Reconstruction*, 582.

8. Logan, *The Negro in American Life and Thought*, 20; Walker, *A Rock in a Weary Land*, 138; O'Leary, *To Die For*, 141.

9. Quoted in Woodward, *Origins of the New South*, 48.

10. Ryan, *Poems: Patriotic, Religious, Miscellaneous*, 78.

11. Charles E. Rosenberg, *The Cholera Years: The United States in 1832, 1849, and 1866* (Chicago: Univ. of Chicago Press, 1962); Pauly, "The Great Chicago Fire as a National Event," 668–83; Smith, *Urban Disorder and the Shape of Belief*, 29–33.

12. See Ellis, *Yellow Fever and Public Health*, 53; Bloom, *The Mississippi Valley's Great Yellow Fever Epidemic of 1878*, 141.

13. Quoted in Ellis, *Yellow Fever and Public Health*, 53.

14. For further descriptions of symptoms, see Bloom, *The Mississippi Valley's Great Yellow Fever Epidemic of 1878*, 4; Jo Ann Carrigan, "Yellow Fever: Scourge of the South," in *Disease and*

Distinctiveness in the American South, edited by Todd L. Savitt and James Harvey Young (Knoxville: Univ. of Tennessee Press, 1988), 58.

15. This report was reprinted in "Personal Experience of Yellow Fever," *Hickman Courier* (Kentucky), September 13, 1878, p. 1.

16. "Agonizing Appeals," *Washington Post,* August 31, 1878, p. 1.

17. "The Southern Scourge," *Frank Leslie's Illustrated,* September 18, 1878, p. 18.

18. "The Public Health," *North American Review* 127, no. 265 (November-December 1878), 444.

19. For estimates of the financial loss, see James D. Richardson, ed., *A Compilation of the Messages and Papers of the Presidents, 1789–1897,* vol. 7 (New York: Bureau of National Literature and Art, 1900), 492–507.

20. *A Chapter in the History of the Epidemic of 1878 from Private Memoranda* (Holly Springs, Miss.: McComb City Weekly Intelligencer, 1879), 4.

21. Quoted in Deanne Love Stephens Nuwer, "The 1878 Yellow Fever Epidemic in Mississippi" (Ph.D. diss., University of Southern Mississippi, 1996), 101.

22. "News of the Week," *Independent,* August 29, 1878, p. 9; Larry A. Bohn, "'An Oasis in a Desert of Woe': The Yellow Fever Epidemic in Jackson, Madison County, Tennessee," *West Tennessee Historical Society Papers* 50 (December 1996): 105–14.

23. "The Scourge of the South," *New York Times,* August 5, 1878, p. 1.

24. J. M. Keating, *A History of the Yellow Fever Epidemic of 1878, in Memphis, Tenn.* (Memphis: Printed for the Howard Association, 1879), 109.

25. "Laughing Absentees: A Heart-Rendering Statement of the Situation in Memphis," *McMinniville New Era* (Tennessee), September 19, 1878, p. 2; for another example, see Keating, *A History of the Yellow Fever Epidemic of 1878,* 130; see also "The Awful Epidemic," *Washington Post,* August 14, 1878, p. 1; James Randall, "Lines on the Yellow Fever Plague: Written for the Bazaar at Douglastown" (n.p., 1878).

26. Quoted in Marshall Wingfield, ed., "The Life and Letters of Dr. William J. Armstrong," *West Tennessee Historical Society Papers* 4 (1950): 109.

27. Reverend Amos W. Jones Diary, August 25, 1878, 132 (first), and October 16, 1878, 136 (second), Amos W. Jones Papers, Lambuth University Special Collections, Lambuth University, Lambuth, Tennessee.

28. Samuel Andrew Agnew Diary, August 31, 1878, 346 (first), and September 2, 1878, 357 (second), Samuel Andrew Agnew Papers, Southern Historical Collection, Wilson Library, University of North Carolina at Chapel Hill, microfilm, reel 14.

29. Julia Knapp Chandler, *Broken Hearted: An O'er True Tale of the Fever* (New Orleans: T. H. Thomason, Printer, 1878), 16.

30. Davis quoted in Hudson Strode, ed., *Jefferson Davis: Private Letters, 1823–1889* (New York: Harcourt, Brace and World, 1966), 487–93.

31. Quoted in Paul Hamilton Hayne, *Poems of Paul Hamilton Hayne* (Boston: D. Lothrop and Company, 1882), 299.

32. "Death's Awful March," *Washington Post,* August 17, 1878, p. 1. Several doctors warned that the epidemic would likely travel north; see "Some Peculiarities of Yellow Jack," *Harper's New Monthly Magazine* 58, no. 343 (December 1878): 128; "A Physician's Experience," *Chicago Tribune,* August 3, 1878, p. 2.

33. For one example, see "The Fatal Yellow Fever," *New York Times*, August 27, 1878, p. 1.

34. "Desolation in the South," *New York Times*, September 5, 1878, p. 1. A New York writer claimed that yellow fever was "the one all-absorbing topic in this city." See "Our New York Letter," *Christian Recorder*, September 9, 1878, p. 2. See also "New-York City—Yellow Fever; a False Alarm" *New York Times*, September 6, 1878, p. 2.

35. "Plague-Smitten Grenada," *Frank Leslie's Illustrated*, September 7, 1878, pp. 2–3. For another example, see *Report of the Special Relief Committee of Memphis, Tennessee, Containing Accurate Accounts of Funds on Hand, Received and Disbursed, during the Yellow Fever Epidemic of 1878* (Memphis: C. A. Beehn, Book and Job Printer, 1879), 7. This death toll has only been surpassed by the 1918 influenza epidemic, which took roughly a half million American lives. Alfred W. Crosby, *America's Forgotten Pandemic: The Influenza of 1918* (New York: Cambridge Univ. Press, 1989).

36. Quoted in Wingfield, ed., "The Life and Letters of Dr. William J. Armstrong," 107.

37. J. L. Power, *The Epidemic of 1878, in Mississippi: Report of the Yellow Fever Relief Work* (Jackson, Miss.: Clarion Steam Publishing House, 1879), 3.

38. Ellis, *Yellow Fever and Public Health in the New South*, 32–5; *Report of the Howard Association, of New Orleans, of Receipts, Expenditures, and their Work in the Epidemic of 1878, With Names of Contributors, Etc.* (New Orleans, La.: A. W. Hyatt, Stationer and Printer, 1878), 6.

39. Quoted in *Report of the Special Relief Committee of Memphis, Tennessee*, 7.

40. Quoted in Ellis, *Yellow Fever and Public Health in the New South*, 51–2; for another example, see "The Panic at Jackson," *New York Times*, August 25, 1878, p. 2.

41. Keating, *A History of the Yellow Fever Epidemic of 1878*, 115.

42. Quoted in Nuwer, "The 1878 Yellow Fever Epidemic in Mississippi," 94.

43. "Plague-Smitten Grenada," *Frank Leslie's Illustrated*, September 7, 1878, pp. 2–3; see also "The Yellow Fever," *Washington Post*, August 20, 1878, p. 2.

44. "New York Subscriptions," *New York Times*, August 25, 1878, p. 2.

45. *Report of the Pittsburgh Relief Committee, Having in Charge the Collection and Distribution of Funds, Provisions, and Other Supplies, For the Sufferers by Yellow Fever, in the South-Western States in the Summer and Fall of 1878* (Pittsburgh: Myers, Schoyer and Co., Printers, Corner of Wood Street and Virgin Alley, 1879), 17; *Report of the Relief Work of the Young Men's Christian Association of New Orleans in the Yellow Fever Epidemic of 1878* (New Orleans: A. H. Nelson, Print, 1879), 21.

46. *Concert for the Benefit of Yellow Fever Sufferers, at the M.E. Church* (Martinsburg, W.Va., 1878), broadside from the Virginia Historical Society; "The Actors and the Fever Fund," *New York Times*, September 9, 1878, p. 2.

47. "More Hopeful," *Chicago Tribune*, September 17, 1878, p. 1; "Louisiana: Straight University and the Central Church—A Week of Prayer and Work of Grace—Revival Incidents," *American Missionary* 33, no. 3 (March 1879): 83.

48. Keating, *A History of the Yellow Fever Epidemic of 1878*, 337–59, 363.

49. For expenditures on presidential campaigns, see Robert D. Marcus, *Grand Old Party: Political Structure in the Gilded Age, 1880–1896* (New York: Oxford Univ. Press, 1971), 25; for the average wage, see *Historical Statistics of the United States, Colonial Times to 1970: Part 1* (Washington, D.C.: U.S. Bureau of the Census, 1975), 165.

50. "The Yellow Fever Sufferers: The National Relief Boat on the Mississippi," *Frank Leslie's Illustrated*, October 26, 1878, p. 134.

51. "Aid from Abroad," *Daily Picayune* (Louisiana), September 15, 1878, p. 1; Keating, *A History of the Yellow Fever Epidemic of 1878*, 361.

52. *Report of the Howard Association, of New Orleans*, 56–7.

53. Keating, *A History of the Yellow Fever Epidemic of 1878*, 115, 178, 391.

54. *Frank Leslie's Illustrated*, September 28, 1878, p. 51.

55. See "Editor's Easy Chair," *Harper's New Monthly Magazine* 57, no. 342 (November 1878): 936; "Death and Dismay," *Washington Post*, September 3, 1878, p. 1; "The Sickly South," *Chicago Tribune*, September 3, 1878, p. 2; "Help for the Southern Sufferers," *Christian Advocate*, September 12, 1878, p. 580–4.

56. "Editorial Notes," *Independent*, September 12, 1878, p. 17; "Yellow Fever," *Christian Advocate*, August 29, 1878, p. 552.

57. "The Traveling Statesmen: President Hayes in the West," *New York Times*, September 9, 1878, p. 2.

58. For a discussion of Catholic nurses in Memphis, see Randal L. Hall, "Southern Conservatism at Work: Women, Nurses, and the 1878 Yellow Fever Epidemic in Memphis," *Tennessee Historical Quarterly* 56, no. 4 (winter 1997): 241–61. For lists of donations that included donations from northern churches, see *Report of the Philadelphia Yellow Fever Committee* (Philadelphia: Printed By Order of the Committee, 1879); *Report of the Relief Work of the Young Men's Christian Association of New Orleans in the Yellow Fever Epidemic of 1878*; *Report of the Pittsburgh Relief Committee*; *Report of the Howard Association, of New Orleans*.

59. "The Epidemic," *Hickman Courier* (Kentucky), September 13, 1878, p. 3; Keating, *A History of the Yellow Fever Epidemic of 1878*, 117–8, 181–2, 371.

60. "New York Subscriptions," *New York Times*, August 27, 1878, p. 2; "The Fever Relief Fund," *New York Times*, August 28, 1878, p. 2; "Mississippi's Stricken Cities," *New York Times*, September 7, 1878, p. 2.

61. "Mississippi's Stricken Cities," *New York Times*, September 7, 1878, p. 2.

62. *Report of the Pittsburgh Relief Committee*, 18; J. P. Dromgoole, M.D., *Yellow Fever: Heroes, Honors, and Horrors of 1878* (Louisville: John P. Morton and Company, 1879), 171; Keating, *A History of the Yellow Fever Epidemic of 1878*, 431.

63. "Measures of Relief," *New York Times*, September 9, 1878, p. 2.

64. "The Pest-Scourged South," *New York Times*, September 10, 1878, p. 1.

65. Power, *The Epidemic of 1878*, 80.

66. The *Memphis Appeal* and Whittier quoted in Peter William Bruton, "The National Board of Health" (Ph.D. diss., University of Maryland, 1974), 109.

67. See, for instance, "Relief for the South," *Christian Advocate*, October 17, 1878, p. 661.

68. *Report of the Pittsburgh Relief Committee*, 14.

69. Power, *The Epidemic of 1878*, 84.

70. Quoted in Farish, *The Circuit Rider Dismounts*, 131. A few northerners believed that the disease proved southern social backwardness, and that the North must merely protect itself from the South. See Ellis, *Yellow Fever and Public Health in the New South*, 60.

71. "Editorial Notes," *Independent*, August 29, 1878, p. 18; for southerners as rebels, see "The Coming Presidential Election," *Independent*, January 4, 1872, p. 1.

72. For information of Palmer and his importance in the South, see Thomas Cary Johnson, *The Life and Letters of Benjamin Morgan Palmer* (Richmond, Va.: Presbyterian Committee of Publications, 1906); Haynes, *Noah's Curse*, 125–76.

73. "The Struggle with Death," *New York Times*, September 11, 1878, p. 1; *Frank Leslie's Illustrated*, August 24, 1878, p. 423; *Report of the Relief Work of the Young Men's Christian Association of New Orleans*, 19–23.

74. "North and South," *New York Times*, September 10, 1878, p. 4.

75. *Report of the Pittsburgh Relief Committee*, 10.

76. *Frank Leslie's Illustrated*, September 28, 1878, p. 51.

77. "Editor's Easy Chair," *Harper's New Monthly Magazine* 57, no. 342 (November 1878): 936.

78. Dromgoole, *Yellow Fever*, 7.

79. J. W. Singleton, *Medical Heroism of 1878* (Geo. O. Rumbold and Co.: St. Louis, 1879), 3, 8–9.

80. For more on proponents of the New South, see Paul M. Gaston, *The New South Creed: A Study in Southern Mythmaking* (New York: Knopf, 1970).

81. Dromgoole, *Yellow Fever*, 99.

82. *Report of the Howard Association, of New Orleans*, 13; for other examples, see Power, *The Epidemic of 1878*, 75; and Nuwer, "The 1878 Yellow Fever Epidemic in Mississippi," 151.

83. "Thank God for Frost!" *Washington Post*, October 21, 1878, p. 1.

84. Keating, *A History of the Yellow Fever Epidemic of 1878*, 177–8; see also "Our Lesson," *Daily Picayune* (Louisiana), September 4, 1878, p. 4; "The Southern Relief Fund," *New York Times*, August 27, 1878, p. 2.

85. My analysis of themes of national rebirth in these poems is strongly influenced by Jay Winter's work on poetry during World War I; see Jay Winter, *Sites of Memory, Sites of Mourning: The Great War in European Cultural History* (Cambridge, U.K.: Cambridge Univ. Press, 1995), 204–22.

86. Judge J. F. Simmons, *The Welded Link: And Other Poems* (Philadelphia: J. B. Lippincott and Co., 1881), 33.

87. Power, *The Epidemic of 1878*, 116.

88. "The Stricken South to the North," in Hayne, *Poems of Paul Hamilton Hayne*, 299.

89. *Proceedings of a Mass Meeting Held in New Orleans, December 6, To Return Thanks for the Succor Extended to the City During the Epidemic of 1878* (New Orleans: A. W. Hyatt, Stationer and Printer, 1878), 5–6. For the Baptists, see Spain, *At Ease in Zion*, 30. See also Stowell, *Rebuilding Zion*, 173.

90. "Southern Congressmen Utter the Thanks of the South for Northern Benevolence," *New York Times*, August 30, 1878, p. 2.

91. *Frank Leslie's Illustrated*, November 9, 1878, p. 155.

92. *Report of the Pittsburgh Relief Committee*, 20–1.

93. Although the rest of this chapter will examine whites' neglect and mistreatment of African Americans during the outbreak, there were cases in which the chaos wrought by the fever actually enabled African Americans to achieve higher levels of employment. As historian Dennis Rousey has shown in a study of the fever in Memphis, the city hired several black men for their police force in order to handle social disorder. Rather than causing racial separation, the outbreak led to racial

integration of the police. In the years following the fever, however, city officials phased out African American police officers, and by 1895, none remained in Memphis. Indeed, the integration of the Memphis police force was borne of necessity, not egalitarianism. Dennis C. Rousey, "Yellow Fever and Black Policemen in Memphis: A Post-Reconstruction Anomaly," *Journal of Southern History* 51, no. 3 (August 1985): 357–74.

94. Dromgoole, *Yellow Fever*, 63, 76; Keating, *A History of the Yellow Fever Epidemic of 1878*, 113; Power, *The Epidemic of 1878*, 164.

95. Dromgoole, *Yellow Fever*, 71–2.

96. For nurses, see Hall, "Southern Conservatism at Work," 241–61; for donations, see "Deaths in Vicksburg and Delhi," *New York Times*, September 6, 1878, p. 2; "Measures of Relief," *New York Times*, September 6, 1878, p. 2; "Town and Country," *Colored Citizen*, September 6, 1878, p. 2.

97. "A Memphis Letter," *American Missionary* 32, no. 11 (November 1878): 322. "Woman's Work—Relief Fund—Health Matters—Cottage Meetings—Northern Helpers," *American Missionary* 33, no. 3 (March 1879): 84; "Tennessee: Material and Spiritual Value of the Yellow Fever Fund," *American Missionary* 33, no. 5 (May 1879): 149.

98. "Incidents of the Scourge at the South," *Frank Leslie's Illustrated*, September 21, 1878, p. 39.

99. Dromgoole, *Yellow Fever*, 69.

100. Andrews, *The South Since the War*, 27–8; see also Reid, *After the War*, 326.

101. "Appeal of the Colored People," *Washington Post*, September 4 1878, p. 1; "A Cry from South," *Christian Recorder*, September 26, 1878, p. 4; "Memphis, Tenn.," *Christian Recorder*, October 24, 1878, p. 4.

102. "The Pestilence," *Christian Recorder*, September 26, 1878, p. 2; Rev. J. M. Cargill, "The Nation's Curse," *Christian Recorder*, October 10, 1878, p. 1.

103. Quoted in Nuwer, "The 1878 Yellow Fever Epidemic in Mississippi," epilogue, 161–70.

104. *Christian Recorder*, October 31, 1878, p. 2.

105. See Ellis, *Yellow Fever and Public Health*, 60–82.

106. Richardson, ed., *A Compilation of the Messages and Papers of the Presidents, 1789–1897*, 7:492–507.

107. See Ellis, *Yellow Fever and Public Health*, 60–82.

108. A. B. Leonard, "The Plague," *Christian Advocate*, December 26, 1878, p. 828.

6. NO NORTH, NO SOUTH, NO SECTIONALISM IN POLITICS, NO SEX IN CITIZENSHIP

1. Belle Kearney, *A Slaveholder's Daughter* (New York: The Abbey Press Publishers, 1900), 49–52; for more on Kearney, see Clement Eaton, "Breaking a Path for the Liberation of Women in the South," *Georgia Review* 28, no. 2 (1974): 187–99.

2. Kearney, *A Slaveholder's Daughter*, 18, 64–5, 92.

3. For more on gender ideologies in the nineteenth-century South, see Jean E. Friedman, *The Enclosed Garden: Women and Community in the Evangelical South, 1830–1900* (Chapel Hill: Univ. of North Carolina Press, 1985); Virginia Bernhard, Elizabeth Fox-Genovese, Theda Perdue, and

Elizabeth Hayes Turner, eds., *Hidden Histories of Women in the New South* (Columbia: Univ. of Missouri Press, 1994); Anne Firor Scott, *The Southern Lady: From Pedestal to Politics, 1830–1930* (Chicago: Univ. of Chicago Press, 1970); Drew Gilpin Faust, *Mothers of Invention: Women of the Slaveholding South in the American Civil War* (Chapel Hill: Univ. of North Carolina Press, 1996); Edwards, *Gendered Strife and Confusion*; LeeAnn Whites, *The Civil War as a Crisis in Gender: Augusta, Georgia, 1860–1890* (Athens: Univ. of Georgia Press, 1995).

4. Kearney, *A Slaveholder's Daughter*, 69.

5. Ibid., 135, 118.

6. For quotes, see Frances E. Willard, *Glimpses of Fifty Years: The Autobiography of an American Woman* (Chicago: Woman's Temperance Publication Association, 1889), 7–8, 309, 651.

7. Ibid., 359–60; "A Lady Candidate," *New York Times*, June 28, 1874, p. 1. For more on Willard, see Ruth Bordin, "'A Baptism of Power and Liberty': The Women's Crusade of 1873–1874," *Ohio History* 87, no. 4 (autumn 1978): 393–404; Ruth Bordin, *Frances Willard: A Biography* (Chapel Hill: Univ. of North Carolina Press, 1986); Ruth Bordin, *Woman and Temperance: The Quest for Power and Liberty, 1873–1900* (Philadelphia: Temple Univ. Press, 1981); and Foster, *Moral Reconstruction*. For earlier studies of the WCTU, see Ray Strachey, *Frances Willard: Her Life and Work* (New York: Fleming H. Revell Company, 1913); and Mary Earhard, *Frances Willard: From Prayers to Politics* (Chicago: Univ. of Chicago Press, 1944).

8. Kearney, *A Slaveholder's Daughter*, 164–5.

9. Ibid., 91, 99.

10. Bordin, *Woman and Temperance*; Foster, *Moral Reconstruction*.

11. See Friedman, *The Enclosed Garden*, 118–24; and Scott, *The Southern Lady*, 144–56.

12. Barbara Leslie Epstein, *The Politics of Domesticity: Women, Evangelism, and Temperance in Nineteenth-Century America* (Middletown, Conn.: Wesleyan Univ. Press, 1981); Rebecca Edwards, *Angels in the Machinery: Gender in American Party Politics from the Civil War to the Progressive Era* (New York: Oxford Univ. Press, 1997), 42–55; and Silber, *The Romance of Reunion*, 102–5.

13. See Edwards, *Angels in the Machinery*, 143; Foster, *Moral Reconstruction*, 80–1; Bordin, *Woman and Temperance*, 82–3; and Friedman, *The Enclosed Garden*, 124.

14. Marjorie Spruill Wheeler, *New Women of the New South: The Leaders of the Woman Suffrage Movement in the Southern States* (New York: Oxford Univ. Press, 1993), xvi; Beryl Satter, *Each Mind a Kingdom: American Women, Sexual Purity, and the New Thought Movement, 1875–1920* (Berkeley: Univ. of California Press, 1999), 21–56; and Kathi Kern, *Mrs. Stanton's Bible* (Ithaca: Cornell Univ. Press, 2001), 121–9. Recently, historian Glenda Gilmore has endeavored to complicate this depiction by asserting that the WCTU in North Carolina actually provided a location and ideology of racial integration where white and black women could work together for the same cause: "Under the heat of temperance, racial boundaries 'melted' ever so slightly." Gilmore went as far as to claim that "in starting the WCTU [in North Carolina], white women recognized gender as a binding force that mitigated racial difficulties." Gilmore, *Gender and Jim Crow*, 45–59; quotes come from Glenda Gilmore, "'A Melting Time': Black Women, White Women, and the WCTU in North Carolina, 1880–1900," in Bernhard, Fox-Genovese, Perdue, and Turner, eds., *Hidden Histories*, 155.

15. For quote, see Bordin, "'A Baptism of Power,'" 395. For more on the crusade of 1873–1874, see Jack S. Blocker Jr., *"Give to the Winds Thy Fears": The Women's Temperance Crusade, 1873–1874* (Westport, Conn.: Greenwood Press, 1985).

16. [Eliza Daniel] Mother Stewart, *Memories of the Crusade* (1888; reprint, New York: Arno Press, 1972), 31, 90–1.

17. For quote, see Jack S. Blocker Jr., "'It Is Easy Enough to Conquer a Man, If You Only Know How': A Personal Account of the Women's Temperance Crusade," *Old Northwest* 15 (spring/summer 1990): 58.

18. For "crusaders," "siege," and "surrender," see Stewart, *Memories of the Crusade,* 9, 171, and 152, respectively; for Mother Stewart compared to Deborah and Sheridan, see the "publisher's note" in Stewart, *Memories of the Crusade,* 10.

19. For violent responses, see Blocker, *"Give to the Winds Thy Fears,"* 42–76.

20. See Epstein, *The Politics of Domesticity,* 115–20.

21. See Bordin, *Frances Willard*; Bordin, *Woman and Temperance*; and Epstein, *The Politics of Domesticity,* 120–46.

22. Kearney, *A Slaveholder's Daughter,* 266; Hannah Whitall Smith in Willard, *Glimpses of Fifty Years,* v.

23. *Minutes of the National Woman's Christian Temperance Union, at the Fourteenth Annual Meeting in Nashville, Tenn., November 16 to 21, 1887,* Woman's Christian Temperance Union National Headquarters Historical Files, Joint Ohio Historical-Michigan Historical Collections, Microfilm Edition (hereafter cited as WCTU microfilm), roll 2, frames 443–4; and Edwards, *Angels in the Machinery,* 44. Leaders in the WCTU were so committed to their Christian identity that they refused to omit the word "Christian" from their organizational name. See Willard, *Glimpses of Fifty Years,* 350.

24. Willard, *Glimpses of Fifty Years,* 375.

25. Stewart, *Memories of the Crusade,* 29, 251.

26. *Minutes of the Fourth Convention of the National Woman's Christian Temperance Union. Held in Chicago, Ill. October 24, 25, 26, and 27, 1877,* WCTU microfilm, reel 1, frames 75–6.

27. Flora Hamilton Cassel, ed., *White Ribbon Vibrations* (Hastings, Nebr.: The W.C.T.U. Song Book Publishing Association, 1890), nos. 104 and 63.

28. Bordin, *Frances Willard,* 155–70; Frances E. Willard, *Woman in the Pulpit* (Boston: D. Lothrop Company, 1888).

29. For a list of dates when state unions were formed, see *Minutes of the National Woman's Christian Temperance Union at the Nineteenth Annual Meeting Denver, Col., October 28th to November 2d, 1892,* WCTU microfilm, reel 3, frame 761.

30. See Scott, *The Southern Lady,* 1–102.

31. See Friedman, *The Enclosed Garden,* 12–7.

32. Quoted in *Minutes of the Third Convention of the National Woman's Christian Temperance Union. Held in Newark, N. J. October 25, 26, 27 and 28, 1876,* WCTU microfilm, reel 1, frame 50; and *Minutes of the Woman's National Christian Temperance Union, at the Sixth Annual Meeting, in Indianapolis, October 29th to November 3rd, 1879,* WCTU microfilm, reel 1, frame 251.

33. Stewart, *Memories of the Crusade,* 486.

34. *Minutes of the Fourth Convention of the National Woman's Christian Temperance Union. Held in Chicago, Ill. October 24, 25, 26, and 27, 1877,* WCTU microfilm, reel 1, frame 104; *Minutes of the Woman's National Christian Temperance Union, at the Annual Meeting, Held in Baltimore, Nov. 6–11th, 1878,* WCTU microfilm, reel 1, frame 125; and *Minutes of the Woman's National Christian Temperance Union, at the Seventh Annual Meeting, in Boston, October 27th to 30th, 1880,* WCTU microfilm, reel 1, frame 270.

35. Stewart, *Memories of the Crusade*, 486.

36. Stewart quoted in *Minutes of the Woman's National Christian Temperance Union, at the Seventh Annual Meeting, in Boston, October 27th to 30th, 1880*, WCTU microfilm, reel 1, frame 271.

37. "A Northern Woman South," *Christian Advocate*, June 16, 1881, newspaper clipping, WCTU microfilm, reel 30, frame 287.

38. *Minutes of the Woman's National Christian Temperance Union, at the Annual Meeting, Held in Baltimore, Nov. 6–11th, 1878*, WCTU microfilm, reel 1, frame 125; and *Minutes of the Woman's National Christian Temperance Union, at the Sixth Annual Meeting, in Indianapolis, October 29th to November 3rd, 1879*, WCTU microfilm, reel 1, frame 251.

39. For other examinations of the trips south, see Bordin, *Woman and Temperance*, 76–83; Bordin, *Frances Willard*, 112–5; and Scott, *The Southern Lady*, 144–56.

40. Stewart, *Memories of the Crusade*, 103, 489. For more on Stewart's trip, see Nancy A. Hardesty, "'The Best Temperance Organization in the Land': Southern Methodists and the W.C.T.U. in Georgia," *Methodist History* 28, no. 3 (April 1990): 187–94.

41. *Woman's National Christian Temperance Union, at the Seventh Annual Meeting, in Boston, October 27th to 30th, 1880*, WCTU microfilm, reel 1, frames 317–9.

42. Stewart, *Memories of the Crusade*, 497.

43. *Minutes of the Woman's National Christian Temperance Union, at the Seventh Annual Meeting, in Boston, October 27th to 30th, 1880*, WCTU microfilm, reel 1, frame 317–9; and Stewart, *Memories of the Crusade*, 497–508.

44. *Minutes of the Woman's National Christian Temperance Union, at the Seventh Annual Meeting, in Boston, October 27th to 30th, 1880*, WCTU microfilm, reel 1, frames 317–9. For formation of unions, see Stewart, *Memories of the Crusade*, 512–33; and Frances E. Willard, *Woman and Temperance; Or, the Work and Workers of the Woman's Christian Temperance Union* (1883; reprint, Hartford, Conn.: Park Publishing Co., 1884), 80–6.

45. Stewart, *Memories of the Crusade*, 531–3.

46. For other studies that discuss Willard in the South, see Scott, *The Southern Lady*, 144; Bordin, *Frances Willard*, 112–5; James D. Ivy, "'The Lone Star State Surrenders to a Lone Woman': Frances Willard's Forgotten 1882 Texas Temperance Tour," *Southwestern Historical Quarterly* 102, no. 1 (July 1998): 45–62; Hardesty, "'The Best Temperance Organization in the Land,'" 187–94; Anastasia Sims, "'The Sword of the Spirit': The WCTU and Moral Reform in North Carolina, 1883–1933," *North Carolina Historical Review* 64, no. 4 (October 1987): 394–415; Foster, *Moral Reconstruction*, 86.

47. Willard, *Woman and Temperance*, 410–1.

48. See Edwards, *Angels in the Machinery*, 44.

49. Willard, *Woman and Temperance*, 411.

50. "The Southern People," *National Liberator*, August 28, 1881, newspaper clipping, WCTU microfilm, reel 30, frame 340.

51. Willard, *Woman and Temperance*, 35–6.

52. For membership numbers and dates of state union formations, see *Minutes of the National Woman's Christian Temperance Union at the Nineteenth Annual Meeting Denver, Col., October 28th to November 2d, 1892*, WCTU microfilm, reel 3, frame 761.

53. *Minutes of the National Woman's Christian Temperance Union, at the Tenth Annual Meeting, in Detroit, Michigan, October 31st to November 3d, 1883*, WCTU microfilm, reel 1, frame 592.

54. Quoted in Earhart, *Frances Willard*, 180.

55. *Hannibal Morning Journal*, April 27, 1882, newspaper clipping, WCTU microfilm, reel 30, frame 418; see also Ivy, "'The Lone Star State Surrenders to a Lone Woman,'" 49–51. The WCTU papers, in fact, contain dozens of articles from southern newspapers that laud Willard's trip. See WCTU microfilm, reel 30, frames 287–429.

56. Quoted in Anna A. Gordon, *The Life of Frances Willard* (Evanston, Ill.: National Woman's Christian Temperance Union, 1912), 147.

57. Mamie Boozer's diary quoted in Florence Adams Mims, *Recorded History of South Carolina Woman's Christian Temperance Union from 1881–1901* (Edgefield, S.C.: n.p., 1950), 42.

58. Letter of Mrs. Erwin [last name unknown] to Frances Willard, February 8, 1882, WCTU microfilm, roll 32, frame 045.

59. *Minutes of the Woman's National Christian Temperance Union, at the Eighth Annual Meeting, in Washington, D.C., October 26th to 29th, 1881*, WCTU microfilm, reel 1, frame 367. Southern women even discussed Willard's movements and words in their personal letters. See L. E. Sibley to Missouria Stokes, February 28, 1882, Missouria H. Stokes Papers, Duke University, Special Collections Library, box 1, folder 1.

60. This story was often repeated in WCTU circles; see *Minutes of the Woman's National Christian Temperance Union, at the Eighth Annual Meeting, in Washington, D.C., October 26th to 29th, 1881*, WCTU microfilm, reel 1, frame 391; Anna A. Gordon, *The Beautiful Life of Frances E. Willard, A Memorial Volume* (Chicago: Woman's Temperance Publishing Association, 1898), 107–8; and Mims, *Recorded History of South Carolina Woman's Christian Temperance Union*, 23.

61. "Southern Ladies and Miss Willard," *Signal*, August 13, 1881, newspaper clipping, WCTU microfilm, reel 30, frame 298.

62. Caroline E. Merrick, *Old Times in Dixie Land: A Southern Matron's Memories* (New York: Grafton Press, 1901), 172–3.

63. Quoted in Gordon, *The Beautiful Life*, 107.

64. *Minutes of the Woman's National Christian Temperance Union, at the Eighth Annual Meeting, in Washington, D.C., October 26th to 29th, 1881*, WCTU microfilm, reel 1, frame 390.

65. *Minutes of the Woman's National Christian Temperance Union, at the Eighth Annual Meeting, in Washington, D.C., October 26th to 29th, 1881*, WCTU microfilm, reel 1, frame 412.

66. Willard, *Glimpses of Fifty Years*, 373–4. Willard even admitted that she was ashamed of her prior feelings of sectional animosity (162).

67. Quoted in Ida B. Wells, "Mr. Moody and Miss Willard," *Fraternity* (May 1894): 16–7.

68. For McLeod, see Willard, *Woman and Temperance*, 556; for Chapin, see Willard, *Woman and Temperance*, 546, and Frances E. Willard and Mary A. Livermore, eds., *A Woman of the Century: Fourteen Hundred-Seventy Biographical Sketches Accompanied by Portraits of Leading American Women in All Walks of Life* (Buffalo: Charles Wells Moulton, 1893), 168; for Davis, see Willard, *Glimpses of Fifty Years*, 566.

69. For Hayne, Ryan, and southern literature, see Willard, *Glimpses of Fifty Years*, 564–8; for the Decoration Day service, see Willard, *Glimpses of Fifty Years*, 441–51.

70. "An Honest Woman," *Republican*, newspaper clipping, WCTU microfilm, reel 30, frame 290.

71. *Minutes of the Woman's National Christian Temperance Union, at the Eighth Annual Meeting, in Washington, D.C., October 26th to 29th, 1881*, WCTU microfilm, reel 1, frame 412.

72. "The Southern People," *National Liberator,* August 28, 1881, newspaper clipping, WCTU microfilm, reel 30, frame 340.

73. Tourgée, *A Fool's Errand,* 381, 390; see also Albion W. Tourgée, *An Appeal to Cæsar* (New York: Fords, Howard, and Hulbert, 1884), 23–30.

74. *The Independent,* May 5, 1881, newspaper clipping, WCTU microfilm, reel 32, frame 441; "An Honest Woman," *Republican,* newspaper clipping, WCTU microfilm, reel 30, frame 290 (second).

75. *Mississippi Daily Clarion,* January 17, 1881, newspaper clipping, WCTU microfilm, reel 30, frame 409.

76. Hardesty, "'The Best Temperance Organization in the Land,'" 187–94.

77. For more on activities at conventions, see Ian Tyrrell, *Woman's World, Woman's Empire: The Woman's Christian Temperance Union in International Perspective, 1880–1930* (Chapel Hill: Univ. of North Carolina Press, 1991), 46–8.

78. *Minutes of the Woman's National Christian Temperance Union, at the Eighth Annual Meeting, in Washington, D.C., October 26th to 29th, 1881,* WCTU microfilm, reel 1, frame 355.

79. Willard, *Glimpses of Fifty Years,* 380.

80. Gordon, *The Beautiful Life,* 108.

81. Georgia McLeod, "Southern Woman's Work," *Christian Advocate,* newspaper clipping, WCTU microfilm, reel 32, frame 419.

82. "Good Sentiments South," *Christian Statesman,* June 9, 1881, newspaper clipping, WCTU microfilm, reel 32, frame 446.

83. *Minutes of the National Woman's Christian Temperance Union, at the Tenth Annual Meeting, in Detroit, Michigan, October 31st to November 3d, 1883,* WCTU microfilm, reel 1, frame 569.

84. See Edwards, *Angels in the Machinery,* 47.

85. *Minutes of the Woman's National Christian Temperance Union, at the Eighth Annual Meeting, in Washington, D.C., October 26th to 29th, 1881,* WCTU microfilm, reel 1, frame 358–9; for Willard's comment, see Willard and Livermore, eds., *A Woman of the Century,* 168.

86. *Minutes of the National Woman's Christian Temperance Union at the Annual Meeting in Louisville, KY., October 25th to 28th, 1882,* WCTU microfilm, reel 1, frames 465–6.

87. *Minutes of the National Woman's Christian Temperance Union at the Eighteenth Annual Meeting, Boston, Mass., November 13th to 18th, 1891,* WCTU microfilm, reel 3, frame 491.

88. *Minutes of the National Woman's Christian Temperance Union, at the Eighth Annual Meeting, in Washington, D.C., October 26th to 29th, 1881,* WCTU microfilm, reel 1, frames 390–1.

89. *Minutes of the National Woman's Christian Temperance Union, Sixteenth Annual Meeting, Chicago, Illinois, November 8 to 13, 1889,* WCTU microfilm, reel 3, frame 028.

90. See Edwards, *Angels in the Machinery,* 47–8; Michael L. Goldberg, *An Army of Women: Gender and Politics in Gilded Age Kansas* (Baltimore: Johns Hopkins Univ. Press, 1997). For more on the Prohibition Party, see John Kobler, *Ardent Spirits: The Rise and Fall of Prohibition* (New York: Putnam, 1973); and Jack S. Blocker Jr., *Retreat from Reform: The Prohibition Movement in the United States, 1890–1913* (Westport, Conn.: Greenwood Press, 1976).

91. Lawrence Goodwyn, *The Populist Moment: A Short History of the Agrarian Revolt in America* (New York: Oxford Univ. Press, 1978); Edwards, *Angels in the Machinery;* Summers, *The Gilded Age.*

92. Willard, *Glimpses of Fifty Years,* 374; see also Willard, *Woman and Temperance,* 35–7; and *Minutes of the Woman's National Christian Temperance Union, at the Eighth Annual Meeting, in Washington, D.C., October 26th to 29th, 1881,* WCTU microfilm, reel 1, frame 412.

93. *Minutes of the Woman's National Christian Temperance Union, at the Eighth Annual Meeting, in Washington, D.C., October 26th to 29th, 1881*, in WCTU microfilm, reel 1, frames 412–4.

94. *Minutes of the National Woman's Christian Temperance Union at the Twelfth Annual Meeting in Philadelphia, PA., October 30th, 31st and November 2nd and 3d*, WCTU microfilm, reel 2, frame 034.

95. *Minutes of the National Woman's Christian Temperance Union at the Twelfth Annual Meeting in Philadelphia, PA., October 30th, 31st and November 2nd and 3d*, WCTU microfilm, reel 2, frame 045.

96. *Minutes of the National Woman's Christian Temperance Union, at the Fourteenth Annual Meeting in Nashville, Tenn., November 16 to 21, 1887*, WCTU microfilm, reel 2, frame 453.

97. Flynt, *Alabama Baptists*, 215.

98. *Christian Union*, April 6, 1881, newspaper clipping, WCTU microfilm, reel 32, frame 436.

99. *Minutes of the National Woman's Christian Temperance Union at the Annual Meeting in Louisville, KY., October 25th to 28th, 1882*, WCTU microfilm, reel 1, frame 465.

100. Quoted in "Rise and Progress of the Woman's Christian Temperance Union," Hannah Johnston Bailey Papers, Swarthmore College Peace Collection, Microfilm Publications, Swarthmore College, Swarthmore, Pennsylvania, box 1, folder 8.

101. For more on nativism during these decades, see John Higham, *Strangers in the Land: Patterns of American Nativism, 1860–1925* (New Brunswick, N.J.: Rutgers Univ. Press, 1955); Donald L. Kinzer, *An Episode in Anti-Catholicism: The American Protective Association* (Seattle: Univ. of Washington Press, 1964); Wallace, *The Rhetoric of Anti-Catholicism*; Matthew Frye Jacobson, *Barbarian Virtues: The United States Encounters Foreign Peoples at Home and Abroad, 1876–1917* (New York: Hill and Wang, 2000); Satter, *Each Mind a Kingdom*, 1–20; Painter, *Standing at Armageddon*, 298–9, 303–4.

102. For the extensive literature on the rise of segregation, see C. Vann Woodward, *The Strange Career of Jim Crow* (1955; reprint, New York: Oxford Univ. Press, 1974); Howard Rabinowitz, *Race Relations in the Urban South, 1865–1890* (New York: Oxford Univ. Press, 1978); John W. Cell, *The Highest Stage of White Supremacy: The Origins of Segregation in South Africa and the American South* (Cambridge, U.K.: Cambridge Univ. Press, 1982); Joel Williamson, *The Crucible of Race: Black/White Relations in the American South since Emancipation* (New York: Oxford Univ. Press, 1984); Hale, *Making Whiteness*; Leon F. Litwack, *Trouble in Mind: Black Southerners in the Age of Jim Crow* (New York: Knopf, 1998). On lynching, see Edward L. Ayers, *Promise of the New South: Life after Reconstruction* (New York: Oxford Univ. Press, 1992), 156–9, 495–7 nn. 69, 70; Dray, *At the Hands of Persons Unknown*, xi; Logan, *The Negro in American Thought and Life*, 76; O'Leary, *To Die For*, 50; W. Fitzhugh Brundage, *Lynching in the New South: Georgia and Virginia, 1880–1930* (Urbana: Univ. of Illinois Press, 1993).

103. Stewart, *Memories of the Crusade*, 27.

104. Sallie Chapin, "Our Southern Letter," *Union Signal*, April 26, 1883, p. 4.

105. *Independent*, May 5, 1881, newspaper clipping, WCTU microfilm, reel 32, frame 441; Willard, *Glimpses of Fifty Years*, 162.

106. Satter, *Each Mind a Kingdom*, 1–20; see also Kern, *Mrs. Stanton's Bible*, 113.

107. Cassel, ed., *White Ribbon Vibrations*, no. 14.

108. Hunt quoted in Foster, *Moral Reconstruction*, 42; *Minutes of the Woman's National Christian Temperance Union, at the Seventh Annual Meeting, in Boston, October 27th to 30th, 1880*, WCTU microfilm, reel 1, frame 295.

109. Stewart, *Memories of the Crusade*, 524.

110. Willard, *Glimpses of Fifty Years*, 328–9; Dray, *At the Hands of Persons Unknown*, 106; Bordin, *Women and Temperance*; Higham, *Strangers in the Land*, 41.

111. Quoted in Bordin, *Woman and Temperance*, 87.

112. *Minutes of the Woman's National Christian Temperance Union, at the Eighth Annual Meeting, in Washington, D.C., October 26th to 29th, 1881*, WCTU microfilm, reel 1, frames 358–9.

113. Summers, *The Gilded Age*, 38, 214.

114. "The Race Problem: Miss Willard on the Political Puzzle of the South," *Voice*, October 23, 1890, p. 8.

115. Ibid.

116. Ibid.

117. *Minutes of the National Woman's Christian Temperance Union, at the Twentieth Annual Meeting*, WCTU microfilm, reel 4, frames 030–1.

118. Bordin, *Woman and Temperance*, 82–5; and Friedman, *The Enclosed Garden*, 124.

119. "Woman's Temperance Work in the South," *American Missionary* 42, no. 7 (July 1888): 198–9. For a similar struggle within the Women's Relief Corps, see O'Leary, *To Die For*, 83.

120. M. J. O'Connell, "North Carolina No. 2," *Union Signal*, December 10, 1891, p. 10.

121. Quoted in Melba Joyce Boyd, *Discarded Legacy: Politics and Poetics in the Life of Frances E. W. Harper, 1825–1911* (Detroit: Wayne State Univ. Press, 1994), 207.

122. *Minutes of the National Woman's Christian Temperance Union at the Twelfth Annual Meeting in Philadelphia, PA., October 30th, 31st and November 2nd and 3d*, WCTU microfilm, reel 2, frame 121.

123. Gail Bederman, *Manliness and Civilization: A Cultural History of Gender and Race in the United States, 1880–1917* (Chicago: Univ. of Chicago Press, 1995), 45–76. For more on Wells, see Duster, ed., *Crusade for Justice*; Patricia A. Schechter, *Ida B. Wells-Barnett and American Reform, 1880–1930* (Chapel Hill: Univ. of North Carolina Press, 2001); Linda O. McMurry, *To Keep the Waters Troubled: The Life of Ida B. Wells* (New York: Oxford Univ. Press, 1998).

124. Ida B. Wells, "Mr. Moody and Miss Willard," *Fraternity*, May 1894, pp. 16–7.

125. Ida B. Wells, *A Red Record* (Chicago: Donohue and Henneberry, 1895), 86.

126. *Minutes of the National Woman's Christian Temperance Union, at the Twenty-First Annual Meeting*, WCTU microfilm, reel 4, frames 303–4.

127. "Frances: A Temporizer," *Cleveland Gazette*, November 24, 1894, p. 2.

128. Frederick Douglass, *The Lesson of the Hour* (Baltimore: Press of Thomas and Evans, 1894), 27–33.

129. "The Bitter Cry of Black America," *Westminster Gazette*, May 10, 1894, pp. 1–2.

130. Douglass, *The Lesson of the Hour*, 27–33.

7. TO THE PERSON SITTING IN DARKNESS

1. Gordon, *The Beautiful Life of Frances E. Willard*, 324. For more on Willard's death, see Gordon, *The Beautiful Life of Frances E. Willard*, 294–387; Bordin, *Woman and Temperance*, 141–2; and Earhart, *Frances Willard: From Prayers to Politics*, 369.

2. Kearney, *A Slaveholder's Daughter*, 264.

3. Gordon, *The Beautiful Life of Frances E. Willard*, 364.

4. Kearney, *A Slaveholder's Daughter*, 265.

5. Quoted in Mims, *Recorded History of South Carolina Woman's Christian Temperance Union*, 79–80.

6. Kearney, *A Slaveholder's Daughter*, 268.

7. Quoted in Gordon, *The Beautiful Life of Frances E. Willard*, 221–2; for similar claims made by Willard's eulogists, see Gordon, *The Beautiful Life of Frances E. Willard*, 295.

8. William T. Stead, *The Americanization of the World: Or, The Trend of the Twentieth Century*, with a new introduction by Sandi E. Cooper (1902; reprint, New York: Garland Publishing, 1972), 103–4; for more on the WWCTU, see Tyrrell, *Woman's World, Woman's Empire*.

9. Stead, *The Americanization of the World*, 77–8.

10. From 1860 to 1897, overall American exports rose from $316,242,000 to $1,032,008,000. Cotton exports to China alone, for instance, increased from $1,741,942 in 1895 to $7,489,141 in 1897. Walter LaFeber, *The New Empire: An Interpretation of American Expansion, 1860–1898* (Ithaca: Cornell Univ. Press, 1963), 18; Ronald T. Takaki, *Iron Cages: Race and Culture in Nineteenth-Century America* (New York: Knopf, 1979), 251–89.

11. Silber, *Romance of Reunion*, 178–85; Buck, *The Road to Reunion*, 306–7; Richard Hofstadter, "Manifest Destiny and the Philippines," in *America in Crisis: Fourteen Crucial Episodes in American History*, edited by Daniel Aaron (New York: Knopf, 1952), 173–202; Takaki, *Iron Cages*, 251–89; LaFeber, *The New Empire*; Kristin L. Hoganson, *Fighting for American Manhood: How Gender Politics Provoked the Spanish-American and Philippine-American Wars* (New Haven, Conn.: Yale Univ. Press, 1998); Robert Dallek, "National Mood and American Foreign Policy: A Suggestive Essay," *American Quarterly* 34, no. 4 (autumn 1982): 339–61; Jacobson, *Barbarian Virtues*; David Axeen, "'Heroes of the Engine Room': American 'Civilization' and the War with Spain," *American Quarterly* 36, no. 4 (autumn 1984): 481–502; Summers, *The Gilded Age*, 263–79; Rubin Frances Weston, *Racism in U.S. Imperialism: The Influence of Racial Assumptions on American Foreign Policy, 1893–1946*, with a foreword by Nelson M. Blake (Columbia: Univ. of South Carolina Press, 1972); Painter, *Standing at Armageddon*, 141–69; David Healy, *U.S. Expansionism: The Imperialist Urge in the 1890s* (Madison: Univ. of Wisconsin Press, 1970); for a recent evaluation of the historiography, see John Offner, "United States Politics and the 1898 War over Cuba," in *The Crisis of 1898: Colonial Redistribution and Nationalist Mobilization*, edited by Angel Smith and Emma Dávila-Cox (New York: St. Martin's Press, 1999), 18–30.

12. For the best comprehensive overview of the War of 1898, see David F. Trask, *The War with Spain in 1898* (New York: Macmillan, 1981). For works that connect religious missions and American expansion, see Arthur Schlesinger Jr., "The Missionary Enterprise and Theories of Imperialism," in *The Missionary Enterprise in China and America*, edited by John K. Fairbank (Cambridge, Mass.: Harvard Univ. Press, 1974), 336–73; Fred Harvey Harrington, *God, Mammon, and the Japanese: Dr. Horace N. Allen and Korean-American Relations, 1884–1905* (Madison: Univ. of Wisconsin Press, 1944); Jane Hunter, *The Gospel of Gentility: American Women Missionaries in Turn-of-the-Century China* (New Haven, Conn.: Yale Univ. Press, 1984); Louise Michele Newman, *White Women's Rights: The Racial Origins of Feminism in the United States* (New York: Oxford Univ. Press, 1999), 22–52; Kenneth M. MacKenzie, *The Robe and the Sword: The Methodist Church and the Rise of American Imperialism* (Washington, D.C.: Public Affairs Press, 1961); Stuart Creighton Miller, *"Benevolent Assimilation": The American Conquest of the Philippines, 1899–1903* (New Haven, Conn.: Yale Univ. Press, 1982); Julius W. Pratt, *Expansionists of 1898: The Acquisition of Hawaii and the Spanish Islands* (1936; reprint, Gloucester, Mass.: Peter Smith, 1959), 279–316; Paul A. Varg, *Missionaries, Chinese,*

and Diplomats: The American Protestant Missionary Movement in China, 1890–1952 (Princeton, N.J., Princeton Univ. Press, 1958).

13. Hunter, *The Gospel of Gentility*, 5.

14. John R. Mott, *The Evangelization of the World in This Generation* (Nashville: Student Volunteer Movement for Foreign Missions, 1900), 121; Stead, *The Americanization of the World*, 77–8.

15. Mott, *The Evangelization of the World in This Generation*, 121.

16. Ahlstrom, *Religious History of the American People*, 864.

17. Hunter, *The Gospel of Gentility*, 148; Newman, *White Women's Rights*, 34–6; Joan Jacobs Brumberg, "Zenanas and Girlless Villages: The Ethnology of American Evangelical Women, 1870–1910," *Journal of American History* 69, no. 2 (September 1982): 347–71; Leslie A. Fleming, "A New Humanity: American Missionaries' Ideals for Women in North India, 1870–1930," in *Western Women and Imperialism: Complicity and Resistance*, edited by Nupur Chaudhuri and Margaret Strobel (Bloomington: Indiana Univ. Press, 1992), 192–202; Offner, "United States Politics and the 1898 War over Cuba," in Smith and Dávila-Cox, eds., *The Crisis of 1898*, 22.

18. For more on the rise of the Student Volunteer Movement, see Clifton J. Phillips, "The Student Volunteer Movement and Its Role in China Missions, 1886–1920," in Fairbank, ed., *The Missionary Enterprise in China and America*, 91–109; C. Howard Hopkins, *John R. Mott, 1865–1955: A Biography* (Grand Rapids: Eerdmans, 1979); C. Howard Hopkins, *History of the Y.M.C.A. in North America* (New York: Association Press, 1951), 271–305; Clarence P. Shedd, *Two Centuries of Student Christian Movements: Their Origin and Intercollegiate Life* (New York: Association Press, 1934), 187–214, 229–38, 263–76; Dorsett, *A Passion for Souls*, 352–5. Findlay, *Dwight L. Moody*, 339–46.

19. Max Wood Moorhead, ed., *The Student Missionary Enterprise. Addresses and Discussions of the Second International Convention of the Student Volunteer Movement for Foreign Missions, Held at Detroit, Michigan, February 28 and March 1, 2, 3, and 4, 1894* (Boston: T. O. Metcalf and Co., 1894), vii.

20. For these quotes, see Hopkins, *History of the Y.M.C.A. in North America*, 279, 298–9. Healy, *U.S. Expansionism*, 130.

21. *Report of the First International Convention of the Student Volunteer Movement for Foreign Missions, Held At Cleveland, Ohio, U.S.A., February 26, 27, 28, and March 1, 1891* (Boston: T. O. Metcalf and Co., 1891), 3.

22. Moorhead, ed., *The Student Missionary Enterprise*, 72.

23. Quoted in Dorsett, *A Passion for Souls*, 355.

24. For more on this phrase, see Mott, *The Evangelization of the World in This Generation*; Hopkins, *History of the Y.M.C.A. in North America*, 297; and Delavan Leonard Pierson, *Arthur T. Pierson: A Spiritual Warrior, Mighty in the Scriptures; A Leader in the Modern Missionary Crusade* (New York: Fleming H. Revell Company, 1912), 185–203.

25. Quoted in Phillips, "The Student Volunteer Movement," in Fairbank, ed., *The Missionary Enterprise in China and America*, 94.

26. Hopkins, *John R. Mott*, 232.

27. Atkins, *Religion in Our Times*, 158.

28. Rev. Josiah Strong, *Our Country: Its Possible Future and Its Present Crisis* (1885; rev. ed., New York: The Baker and Taylor Company, 1891), 26, 202; Summers, *The Gilded Age*, 56–74; Frederick Jackson Turner, "The Significance of the Frontier in American History," in *Frontier and Section: Selected Essays of Frederick Jackson Turner* (Englewood Cliffs, N.J.: Prentice Hall, 1961), 37–62. Price

Collier (*America and the Americans* [New York: Charles Scribner's Sons, 1897], 104–5) recognized the shift from North-South to East-West. Proponents of the emerging "Social Gospel" also tended to neglect racial issues, although Ralph Luker has shown that there was some concern. Logan, *The Negro in American Life and Thought*, 165; Ralph E. Luker, *The Social Gospel in Black and White: American Racial Reform, 1885–1912* (Chapel Hill: Univ. of North Carolina Press, 1991).

29. For more on Strong and the popularity of *Our Country*, see LaFeber, *The New Empire*, 72–9; Takaki, *Iron Cages*, 260–3; Pratt, *The Expansionists of 1898*, 5, 18; Martin E. Marty, *Pilgrims in Their Own Land: 500 Years of Religion in America* (Boston: Little, Brown, 1984), 338–40; Dorothea R. Miller, "Josiah Strong and American Nationalism: A Reevaluation," *Journal of American History* 53, no. 3 (December 1966): 487–503; Mead, *The Lively Experiment*, 150–3; and John Edwin Smylie, "Protestant Clergymen and America's World Role, 1865–1900: A Study of Christianity, Nationality, and International Relations" (Th.D. diss., Princeton Theological Seminary, 1959), 155–6.

30. *Report of the First International Convention of the Student Volunteer Movement for Foreign Missions*, 128.

31. See "Our Country," *American Missionary* 40, no. 5 (May 1886): 122–5; and "Our Whole Country," *American Missionary* 42, no. 6 (June 1888): 155.

32. For a discussion of reviews of Strong's *Our Country*, see Miller, "Josiah Strong and American Nationalism: A Reevaluation," 487–503.

33. Hunter, *The Gospel of Gentility*, 13; and MacKenzie, *The Robe and the Sword*, 11.

34. *Report of the First International Convention of the Student Volunteer Movement for Foreign Missions*, 207–17.

35. Quoted in Rev. Charles C. Creegan and Mrs. Josephine A. B. Goodnow, *Great Missionaries of the Church*, with an introduction by Rev. Frances E. Clark (Boston: Thomas Y. Crowell and Company, 1895), vii.

36. Frances E. Clark, "Do Foreign Missions Pay?" *North American Review* 166, no. 496 (March 1898): 271.

37. *Report of the First International Convention of the Student Volunteer Movement for Foreign Missions*, 81.

38. Quoted in Phillips, "The Student Volunteer Movement," in Fairbank, ed., *The Missionary Enterprise in China and America*, 102.

39. J. T. Gracey, *Open Doors: Hints About Opportunities for Christian Work in Africa, Japan, India, Burmah, China, Mexico, South America, the Turkish Empire, Korea, and the Islands of the Sea* (Rochester, N.Y.: J. T. Gracey, 1891), 9.

40. Rev. Elbert S. Todd, *Christian Missions in the Nineteenth Century* (New York: Hunt and Eaton, 1890), 80–6.

41. Stuart Creighton Miller, "Ends and Means: Missionary Justifications of Force in Nineteenth Century China," in Fairbank, ed., *The Missionary Enterprise in China and America*, 273.

42. Hunter, *The Gospel of Gentility*, 7.

43. Rev. Arthur T. Pierson, *The Crisis of Missions: Or, The Voice Out of the Cloud* (New York: Robert Carter and Brothers, 1886), 131; for more on the Berlin Conference, see Stig Forster, Wolfgang J. Mommsen, and Ronald Robinson, eds., *Bismarck, Europe, and Africa: The Berlin Africa Conference 1884–1885 and the Onset of Partition* (Oxford: Oxford Univ. Press, 1996).

44. "Christianity and War," *Century* 58, no. 3 (July 1899): 481.

45. Strong, *Our Country*, 28; Rev. Josiah Strong, *Expansion under New World-Conditions* (New York: The Baker and Taylor Company, 1900), 72.

46. For these quotes, see MacKenzie, *The Robe and the Sword*, 14–5. See also Margherita Arlina Hamm, "The Secular Value of Foreign Missions," *Independent* 52 (April 26, 1900): 1000–3; Charles Denby, "The Influence of Mission Work on Commerce," *Independent* 53 (December 12, 1901): 2960–2.

47. Quoted in Schlesinger Jr., "The Missionary Enterprise and Theories of Imperialism," in Fairbank, ed., *The Missionary Enterprise in China and America*, 345; see also Rev. John Liggins, *The Great Value and Success of Foreign Missions. Proved By Distinguished Witnesses* (New York: The Baker and Taylor Company, 1888), 61; Healy, *U.S. Expansionism*, 186.

48. Harrington, *God, Mammon, and the Japanese*, 125–67.

49. Strong, *Our Country*, 221; see also Rev. Josiah Strong, *The New Era or the Coming Kingdom* (New York: The Baker and Taylor Company, 1893), 55–6.

50. Strong, *Our Country*, 224.

51. Quoted in MacKenzie, *The Robe and the Sword*, 31–2.

52. Gracey, *Open Doors*, 7.

53. Pierson, *The Crisis of Missions*, 12.

54. Harlan P. Beach, F. A. G. S., Canon F. O. L. Josa, Professor J. Taylor Hamilton, Rev. H. C. Tucker, Rev. C. W. Drees, Rev. I. H. La Fetra, Rev. T. B. Wood, and Mrs. T. S. Pond, *Protestant Missions in South America* (New York: Student Volunteer Movement for Foreign Missions, 1900), 39.

55. Creegan and Goodnow, *Great Missionaries of the Church*, 19.

56. E. C. Millard and Lucy E. Guinness, *South America: The Neglected Continent* (New York: Fleming H. Revell Company, 1894), 149.

57. Pierson, *The Crisis of Missions*, 31–2.

58. Beach et al., *Protestant Missions in South America*, 66.

59. Todd, *Christian Missions in the Nineteenth Century*, 57.

60. Quoted in Weston, *Racism in U.S. Imperialism*, 60.

61. *Report of the First International Convention of the Student Volunteer Movement for Foreign Missions*, 155.

62. Ibid., 177.

63. Beach et al., *Protestant Missions in South America*, 47.

64. Charles Carroll, *The Tempter of Eve, or The Criminality of Man's Social, Political, and Religious Equality with the Negro, and the Amalgamation to which these Crimes Inevitably Lead* (St. Louis: Adamic Publishing Co., 1902); Charles Carroll, *The Negro, A Beast* (St. Louis: American Book and Bible House, 1900).

65. Millard and Guinness, *South America*, 5.

66. Beach et al., *Protestant Missions in South America*, 135; Strong, *Our Country*, 85.

67. William Stevens Perry, *America, The Study of Nations: Her Religious Destiny* (Davenport, Iowa: Edward Dorcherdt, Printer, 1893), 8.

68. "The Rev. Henry Frank Says: 'O, Mock Tears That Now Weep for Spilled Spanish Blood!'" *New York Times*, April 24, 1898, 13. Religious, political, and intellectual condescension toward Catholics and the Spanish was not new in the Gilded Age; see Richard L. Kagan, "Prescott's Paradigm: American Historical Scholarship and the Decline of Spain," in *The American Historical Review* 101,

no. 2 (April 1996): 423–46; Tyler Anbinder, *Nativism and Slavery: The Northern Know Nothings and the Politics of the 1850s* (New York: Oxford Univ. Press, 1992).

69. Beach et al., *South America*, 65.

70. Jacobson, *Barbarian Virtues*, 121.

71. Liggins, *The Great Value and Success of Foreign Missions*, 23.

72. Clark, "Do Foreign Missions Pay?" *North American Review*, 268–81. Missionary tracts have continued to serve as a source of information on foreign lands for scholars throughout the twentieth century. In 1970, Columbia University's Myron L. Cohen claimed that Arthur H. Smith's *Village Life in China* "is one of the vital sources for data on Chinese society during the late nineteenth century." See Arthur H. Smith, *Village Life in China* (1899; reprint, Boston: Little, Brown, 1970), ix.

73. Diana Preston, *The Boxer Rebellion: The Dramatic Story of China's War on Foreigners that Shook the World in the Summer of 1900* (New York: Berkley Books, 2000).

74. Quoted in Harrington, *God, Mammon, and the Japanese*, 110.

75. Quoted in Schlesinger Jr., "The Missionary Enterprise and Theories of Imperialism," in Fairbank, ed., *The Missionary Enterprise in China and America*, 366; Wen Ching [pseud.], *The Chinese Crisis from Within* (London: G. Richards, 1901).

76. Miller, "Ends and Means: Missionary Justifications of Force in Nineteenth Century China," in Fairbank, ed., *The Missionary Enterprise in China and America*, 280.

77. O'Leary, *To Die For*, 140–6; Trask, *The War with Spain in 1898*, 181–2.

78. Pratt, *Expansionists of 1898*, 282.

79. "The Duty of Christians," *New York Times*, April 24, 1898, 13.

80. James Henry Brownlee, ed., *War-Time Echoes: Patriotic Poems, Heroic and Pathetic, Humorous and Dialectic, of the Spanish-American War* (New York: The Werner Company, 1898), 206.

81. Sidney A. Witherbee, ed., *Spanish-American War Songs: A Complete Collection of Newspaper Verse During the Recent War with Spain* (Detroit: Sidney A. Witherbee, Publisher, 1898), 43.

82. "The Duty of Christians," *New York Times*, April 24, 1898, 13.

83. "America's Action Justified," *New York Times*, April 24, 1898, 13; Rev. R. A. Torrey, "Some Blessings of War," in *Northfield Echoes*, vol. 5, *Northfield Conference Addresses for 1898*, edited by Delavan L. Pierson (East Northfield, Mass.: Northfield Echoes, 1898), 192–203.

84. Spain, *At Ease in Zion*, 31–43.

85. Pratt, *Expansionists of 1898*, 281.

86. MacKenzie, *The Sword and the Robe*, 67.

87. See Schlesinger, Jr., "The Missionary Enterprise and Theories of Imperialism," in Fairbank, ed., *The Missionary Enterprise in China and America*, 356.

88. See Hunter, *The Gospel of Gentility*, 8.

89. Quoted in Miller, *"Benevolent Assimilation,"* 188.

90. Quoted in Jim Zwick, ed., *Mark Twain's Weapons of Satire: Anti-Imperialist Writings on the Philippine-American War* (Syracuse: Syracuse Univ. Press, 1992), 25–7.

91. "The Religious Problem in the Philippines," *Nation* 67, no. 1728 (August 11, 1898): 104–5.

92. MacKenzie, *The Robe and the Sword*, 66.

93. "The Clergy and War," *Nation* 71, no. 1840 (October 4, 1900): 266.

94. E. Winchester Donald, ed., *Ministers' Meeting of Protest Against the Atrocities in the Philippines* (Boston: n.p., 1902).

95. Zwick, ed., *Mark Twain's Weapons of Satire*, 12–3.

96. Ibid., 22–39.

97. Quoted in Robert L. Beisner, *Twelve Against Empire: The Anti-Imperialists, 1898–1900* (New York: McGraw-Hill, 1968), 180–1.

98. For more on reconciliation during the war, see Richard E. Wood, "The South and Reunion, 1898," *Historian* 31, no. 3 (May 1969): 415–30; Silber, *Romance of Reunion*, 178–85; Buck, *The Road to Reunion*, 306–7; John Oldfield, "Remembering the *Maine*: The United States, 1898 and Sectional Reconciliation," in Smith and Dávila-Cox, eds., *The Crisis of 1898*, 45–64.

99. Robert P. Porter, *Life of William McKinley: Soldier, Lawyer, Statesman* (Cleveland: N. G. Hamilton Publishing Co., 1896), 362–8.

100. *Speeches and Addresses of William McKinley from March 1, 1897 to May 30, 1900* (New York: Doubleday and McClure Co., 1900), 367.

101. Pratt, *Expansionists of 1898*, 316.

102. Trask, *The War with Spain in 1898*, 53, 58.

103. *Speeches and Addresses of William McKinley*, 105.

104. Ibid., 210.

105. Pratt, *Expansionists of 1898*, 316.

106. Logan, *The Negro in America Life and Thought*, 81–95; Patrick J. Kelly, "The Election of 1896 and the Restructuring of Civil War Memory," *Civil War History* 49, no. 3 (September 2003): 254–80.

107. Trask, *The War with Spain in 1898*, 219.

108. *Speeches and Addresses of William McKinley*, 88.

109. Ibid., 141.

110. Ibid., 353.

111. For more on Beveridge, see Claude G. Bowers, *Beveridge and the Progressive Era* (New York: The Literary Guild, 1932); John Braeman, *Albert J. Beveridge: American Nationalist* (Chicago: Univ. of Chicago Press, 1971); Weston, *Racism in U.S. Imperialism*, 45–50.

112. Quoted in Mead, *The Lively Experiment*, 153–4.

113. Quoted in Weston, *Racism in U.S. Imperialism*, 48.

114. Healy, *U.S. Expansionism*, 131.

115. Theodore Roosevelt, *The Rough Riders* (New York: P. F. Collier and Son Publishers, 1899), 9, 22, 53–4.

116. Rudyard Kipling, "The White Man's Burden," *The Annals of America*, vol. 12, *1895–1904* (Chicago: Encyclopedia Britannica, 1968), 246–7.

117. Witherbee, ed., *Spanish-American War Songs*, 56.

118. Ibid., 362.

119. Brownlee, ed., *War-Time Echoes*, ix.

120. Ibid., 71.

121. Ibid., 77–9.

122. Thomas Dixon Jr., *The Sins of the Father: A Romance of the South*. New York: Grosset and Dunlap, Publishers, 1912), 401.

123. See Williamson, *The Crucible of Race*, 141; for more on Dixon, see Maxwell Bloomfield, "Dixon's 'The Leopard's Spots': A Study in Popular Racism," *American Quarterly* 16, no. 3 (autumn 1964): 387–401; F. Gavin Davenport Jr., "Thomas Dixon's Mythology of Southern History," *Journal of*

Southern History 36, no. 3 (August 1970): 350–67; Raymond A. Cook, *Thomas Dixon* (New York: Twayne Publishers, 1974).

124. Kelly Miller, *As To the Leopard's Spots: An Open Letter to Thomas Dixon, Jr.* (Washington, D.C.: Hayworth Publishing House, 1905), 3–4.

125. Bloomfield, "Dixon's 'The Leopard's Spots,'" 399.

126. Thomas Dixon Jr., *The Leopard's Spots: A Romance of the White Man's Burden, 1865–1900.* (1902; reprint, Ridgewood, N.J.: Gregg Press, 1967), 409–12.

127. For more on the anti-imperialist movement, see Beisner, *Twelve Against Empire*; Richard E. Welch Jr., *Response to Imperialism: The United States and the Philippine-American War, 1899–1902* (Chapel Hill: Univ. of North Carolina Press, 1979); and Daniel B. Schirmer, *Republic or Empire: American Resistance to the Philippine War* (Cambridge, Mass.: Schenkman, 1972).

128. Carl Schurz, "Thoughts on American Imperialism," *Century* 56, no. 5 (September 1898): 781–8.

129. Quoted in Mead, *The Lively Experiment*, 154.

130. Bertrand Shadwell, "The Gospel of Force," in *Republic or Empire?: The Philippine Question*, edited by William Jennings Bryan et al. (Chicago: The Independence Company, 1899), 713–4.

131. Quoted in Miller, *"Benevolent Assimilation,"* 183.

132. Charles B. Spahr, "The Imperialist Religion," *Public* 3 (May 5, 1900): 60.

133. Christopher Lasch, "The Anti-Imperialists, the Philippines, and the Inequality of Man," *Journal of Southern History* 24, no. 3 (August 1958): 319–31.

134. Theodore Cuyler, "Americanism Versus Imperialism," newspaper clipping in Theodore Cuyler Papers, Princeton Theological Seminary Library, box 3, scrapbook 16; Healy, *U.S. Expansion*, 61; Stephen Kantrowitz, *Ben Tillman and the Reconstruction of White Supremacy* (Chapel Hill: Univ. of North Carolina Press, 2000), 262.

135. See Tyrell, *Woman's World, Woman's Empire*, 183–5.

136. Trask, *The War with Spain in 1898*, 210, 366.

137. Strong, *Expansion under New World-Conditions*, 36–7.

138. Dray, *At the Hands of Persons Unknown*, 123–5; Gilmore, *Gender and Jim Crow*, 92–117; David S. Cecelski and Timothy Tyson, eds., *Democracy Betrayed: The Wilmington Race Riot of 1898 and Its Legacy* (Chapel Hill: Univ. of North Carolina Press, 1998).

139. Dray, *At the Hands of Persons Unknown*, 3–16; Willard B. Gatewood Jr., *Black Americans and the White Man's Burden, 1898–1903* (Urbana: Univ. of Illinois Press, 1975); for more on African American anti-imperialism, see Jacobson, *Barbarian Virtues*, 248–59; Perry E. Gianakos, "The Spanish-American War and the Double Paradox of the Negro American," *Phylon* 26 (spring 1965): 34–49.

140. See Willard B. Gatewood Jr., ed.,*"Smoked Yankees" and the Struggle for Empire: Letters from Negro Soldiers, 1898–1902* (Urbana: Univ. of Illinois Press, 1972), 13.

141. Kelly Miller, "The Effect of Imperialism Upon the Negro Race," *Anti-Imperialist Broadside*, No. 11 (Boston: New England Anti-Imperialist League, 1900).

142. Quoted in Gatewood Jr., ed., *"Smoked Yankees,"* 28.

143. Quoted in Gatewood Jr., *Black Americans and the White Man's Burden*, 29.

144. Quoted in Gatewood Jr., ed., *"Smoked Yankees,"* 165, 167.

145. Gatewood, Jr., *Black Americans and the White Man's Burden*, 197.

146. Ibid., 50-1.

147. Quoted in Gatewood, Jr., *"Smoked Yankees,"* 74.

148. Quoted in Gatewood, Jr., *Black Americans and the White Man's Burden,* 185.

149. "Charity Begins at Home," *Colored American* (Washington, D.C.), March 18, 1899, p. 4.

150. H. T. Johnson, "The Black Man's Burden," *Christian Recorder,* reprinted in *Voice of Missions* 7 (April 1, 1899): 4.

151. W. E. B. Du Bois, *The Souls of Black Folk* (1903; reprint, New York: Norton, 1999), 5.

152. Beisner, *Twelve Against Empire,* 215-39; Schirmer, *Republic or Empire,* 205-60.

EPILOGUE

1. Arthur Bird, *Looking Forward: A Dream of the United States of America in 1999* (1899; reprint, New York: Arno Press, 1971), 105, 29, 15, 79, 201.

2. Ibid., 231.

3. Edward Bellamy, *Looking Backward: 2000–1887* (1888; reprint, Boston: Bedford/St. Martin's, 1995); Painter, *Standing at Armageddon,* 65–7; John L. Thomas, *Alternative America: Henry George, Edward Bellamy, Henry Demarest Lloyd and the Adversary Tradition* (Cambridge, Mass.: Belknap Press of Harvard Univ. Press, 1983); Jean Pfaelzer, *The Utopian Novel in America, 1886–1896: The Politics of Form* (Pittsburgh: Univ. of Pittsburgh Press, 1989).

4. Edward Bellamy, *Equality: A Novel* (1897; reprint, New York: D. Appleton-Century Company, Incorporated, 1934), 364–5.

5. Dray, *At the Hands of Persons Unknown,* 144–5.

6. Quoted in Orlando Patterson, *Rituals of Blood: Consequences of Slavery in Two American Centuries* (Washington, D.C.: Civitas Counterpoint, 1998), 226.

7. George H. White, *Speech of Hon. George H. White, of North Carolina, in the House of Representatives, January 29, 1901* (Washington, D.C.: National Government Publication, 1901), 14.

8. Du Bois, *The Souls of Black Folk,* 12, 16, 155.

9. Washington and Du Bois, *The Negro in the South,* 186.

10. For more on Du Bois and religion, see Edward J. Blum, "The Soul of W. E. B. Du Bois," *Philosophia Africana* 7, no. 2 (August 2004): 1–15.

Bibliography

PRIMARY SOURCES

Archives and Manuscript Collections

Samuel Andrew Agnew Papers, Southern Historical Collection, Wilson Library, University of North Carolina at Chapel Hill.

American Missionary Association Archives, Amistad Research Center, New Orleans, Louisiana, Microfilm Edition.

Hannah Johnston Bailey Papers, 1887–1923, Swarthmore College Peace Collection Microfilm Publications, Swarthmore College, Swarthmore, Pennsylvania.

Miscellaneous Personal Papers Collection, Henry Baldwin, Yale Divinity School Special Collections, New Haven, Connecticut.

Theodore Cuyler Manuscript Collection, Princeton Theological Seminary Library, Princeton, New Jersey.

Samuel Dutton Papers, Yale Divinity School Special Collections, New Haven, Connecticut.

Ellis Family Papers, South Caroliniana Library, Columbia, South Carolina.

Louise Gilman Papers, William L. Clements Library, University of Michigan, Ann Arbor, Michigan.

Horace Greeley Papers, New York Public Library, Microfilm Edition.

Milton and Esther Hawks Papers, Library of Congress, Washington, D.C., Microfilm Edition.

Johnson Family Papers, Vermont Historical Society, Montpelier, Vermont.

Amos W. Jones Papers, Lambuth University Special Collections, Lambuth University, Lambuth, Tennessee.

The Lincoln Museum, Fort Wayne, Indiana.

Robert O. Linster Papers, Special Collections Library, Duke University, Durham, North Carolina.

Dwight Lyman Moody Papers, Yale Divinity School Special Collections, New Haven, Connecticut.

Moody Bible Institute, Special Collections Archive, Chicago, Illinois.

Penn School Papers, Manuscripts Department, University of North Carolina at Chapel Hill

William S. Plumer Manuscript Collection, Princeton Theological Seminary Library, Princeton, New Jersey.

Savage, Frederick. Interviewed by Christabel Kidder. December 22, 1938. American Life Histories: Manuscripts from the Federal Writers' Project, 1936–1940. http://memory.loc.gov/ammem/wpaintro/wpahome.html (February 10, 2003).

Robert Speer Manuscript Collection, Princeton Theological Seminary Library, Princeton, New Jersey.

Nellie F. Stearns Letter, William R. Perkins Library, Duke University, Durham, North Carolina.

Missouria H. Stokes Papers, Special Collections Library, Duke University, Durham, North Carolina.

Harriet Beecher Stowe Letters, Yale University Library, New Haven, Connecticut, Microfilm Edition.

George Leon Walker and Williston Walker Papers, Yale Divinity School Special Collections, New Haven, Connecticut.

Woman's Christian Temperance Union National Headquarters Historical Files, Joint Ohio Historical–Michigan Historical Collections, Microfilm Edition, Columbus, Ohio.

Government Documents

The Abraham Lincoln Papers at the Library of Congress: Series 1, General Correspondence, 1833–1916, http://memory.loc.gov/ammem/alhtml/malhome.html.

American Political Prints, 1766–1876: A Catalog of the Collections in the Library of Congress. Edited by Bernard F. Reilly Jr. Boston: Hall, 1991.

Church of the Holy Trinity v. United States, 143 U.S. 457; 12 S. Ct. 511; 36 L. Ed. 226 (1892).

Congressional Globe, Thirty-Ninth Congress, Second Session.

Dred Scott v. John F. A. Sandford, 60 U.S. 393; 15 L. Ed. 691 (1856).

Historical Statistics of the United States, Colonial Times to 1970: Part 1. Washington, D.C.: U.S. Bureau of the Census, 1975.

Richardson, James D., ed. *A Compilation of the Messages and Papers of the Presidents, 1789–1897*, vol. 7. New York: Bureau of National Literature and Art, 1900.

U.S. Congress. *Report of the Joint Select Committee Appointed to Inquire into the Condition of Affairs in the Late Insurrectionary States.* Washington, D.C.: Government Printing Office, 1872.

Newspapers and Serials

American Missionary (1867–1895)

Appletons' Journal: A Magazine of General Literature (1869–1881)

Atlanta Constitution (1876–1877)

Atlantic Monthly (1861–1901)

Augusta Constitutionalist (1876)

Boston Daily Globe (1875–1878)

Boston Evening Transcript (1875–1878)

Century (1881–1899)

Chicago Tribune (1865–1898)

Christian Advocate and Journal (1865)

Christian Observer (1936)

Christian Recorder (New York) (1865–1899)

Cincinnati Commercial (1868)

Cincinnati Gazette (1865)

Cleveland Gazette (1894)

Colored American (1899)

Colored Citizen (1878)

Commonwealth (Boston) (1865)

Daily Missouri Republican (St. Louis) (1865)

Daily Picayune (New Orleans) (1878)

Easton-Sentinel (Pennsylvania) (1865)

Frank Leslie's Illustrated Newspaper (New York) (1865–1878)

Fraternity (1894)

Freedman (1864–1865)

Galaxy (1866–1878)

Harper's New Monthly Magazine (1865–1899)

Harper's Weekly (1865–1879)

Hickman Courier (Kentucky) (1878)

Independent (New York) (1862–1900)

Inter Ocean (Chicago) (1876)

Lousiville Courier-Journal (1888)

McClure's Magazine (1894–1899)

McMinniville New Era (Tennessee) (1878)

Methodist Quarterly Review (1865)

Nation (1865–1900)

New Englander and Yale Review (1865–1892)

New York Herald (1865–1898)

New York Times (1865–1901)

New York Tribune (1865–1898)

North American Review (1865–1900)

Old Guard (1863–1867)

Presbyterian (1865)

Princeton Review (1865–1882)

Public (1900)

Putnam's Monthly Magazine of American Literature, Science and Art (1865–1870)

Scribner's Magazine (1887–1896)

Scribner's Monthly (1870–1881)

Southern Review (Baltimore) (1876)

Sun (New York) (1899)

Union Signal (1883–1891)

Voice (1890)

Voice of Missions (1899)

Washington Post (1878–1885)

Westminster Gazette (1894)

Other Primary Sources

Alvord, J. W. *First Semi-Annual Report on Schools and Finances of Freedmen, January 1, 1866.* Washington, D.C.: Government Printing Office, 1868.

———. *Fourth Semi-Annual Report on Schools for Freedmen, July 1, 1867.* Washington, D.C.: Government Printing Office, 1867.

———. *Ninth Semi-Annual Report on Schools for Freedmen, January 1, 1870* (Washington, D.C.: Government Printing Office, 1870.

———. *Second Semi-Annual Report on Schools and Finances of Freedmen, July 1, 1866.* Washington, D.C.: Government Printing Office, 1868.

———. *Sixth Semi-Annual Report on Schools for Freedmen, July 1, 1868.* Washington, D.C.: Government Printing Office, 1868.

———. *Third Semi-Annual Report on Schools for Freedmen, January 1, 1867.* Washington, D.C.: Government Printing Office, 1867.

American Baptist Year-Book, 1870. Philadelphia: American Baptist Publication Society, 1870.

Andrews, Sidney. *The South Since the War As Shown by Fourteen Weeks of Travel and Observation in Georgia and the Carolinas.* 1866. Reprint, Boston: Houghton Mifflin, 1971.

Aptheker, Herbert, ed. *The Correspondence of W. E. B. Du Bois.* Vol. 3. *Selections, 1944–1963.* Amherst: Univ. of Massachusetts Press, 1978.

A Tribute of Respect by the Citizens of Troy, to the Memory of Abraham Lincoln. Troy, N.Y.: Young and Benson, 1865.

Badger, Rev. Henry C. *The Humble Conqueror: A Discourse Commemorative of the Life and Services of Abraham Lincoln.* Boston: William V. Spencer, 1865.

Bain, J. W. *National Lessons from the Life and Death of President Lincoln.* Pittsburgh: W. S. Haven, 1865.

Baker, Ray Stannard, *Following the Color Line: An Account of Negro Citizenship in the American Democracy.* New York, Doubleday, Page and Company, 1908.

Basler, Roy P., ed. *The Collected Works of Abraham Lincoln: The Abraham Lincoln Association, Springfield, Illinois,* vol. 2. New Brunswick, N.J.: Rutgers Univ. Press, 1953.

Beach, Harlan P., F. A. G. S., Canon F. O. L. Josa, Professor J. Taylor Hamilton, Rev. H. C. Tucker, Rev. C. W. Drees, Rev. I. H. La Fetra, Rev. T. B. Wood, and Mrs. T. S. Pond.

Protestant Missions in South America. New York: Student Volunteer Movement for Foreign Missions, 1900.

Beard, Augustus Field. *A Crusade of Brotherhood.* Boston: The Pilgrim Press, 1909.

Beecher, Henry Ward. *Norwood: Or, Village Life in New England.* New York: Charles Scribner and Company, 1868.

———. *Oration at the Raising of "The Old Flag" at Sumter; and Sermon on the Death of Abraham Lincoln, President of the United States.* Manchester: Alexander Ireland and Co., Pall Mall Court, 1865.

———. "Woman's Duty to Vote," in *Speeches by George W. Curtis and Henry Ward Beecher.* New York: The National American Woman Suffrage Association, 1898.

———. *Yale Lectures on Preaching.* New York: J. B. Ford and Company, 1872.

Beecher, William C., and Rev. Samuel Scoville. *A Biography of Rev. Henry Ward Beecher.* New York: Charles L. Webster, 1888.

Bellamy, Edward. *Equality: A Novel.* 1897. Reprint, New York: D. Appleton-Century Company, Incorporated, 1934.

———. *Looking Backward: 2000–1887.* 1888. Reprint, Boston: Bedford/St. Martin's Press, 1995.

Benade, W. H. *The Death of Abraham Lincoln; What it Represents.* Pittsburgh: W. G. Johnston and Co., Printers and Stationers, 1865.

Benedict, A. D. *Our Nation's Sorrow: An Address.* Racine, Ill.: Journal Print, 1865.

Beveridge, Albert Jeremiah, *The Bible As Good Reading.* Philadelphia: H. Altemus Company, 1907.

Bingham, Joel F. *National Disappointment. A Discourse Occasioned by the Assassination of President Lincoln.* Buffalo, N.Y.: Breed, Butler and Company, 1865.

Bird, Arthur. *Looking Forward: A Dream of the United States of America in 1999.* 1899. Reprint, New York: Arno Press, 1971.

Blake, John Falkner. *A Sermon on the Services and Death of Abraham Lincoln.* New York: John F. Trow, 1865.

Blassingame, John W., ed. *The Frederick Douglass Papers: Series One: Speeches, Debates, and Interviews.* Vol. 2, *1847–54.* New Haven, Conn.: Yale Univ. Press, 1991.

Blassingame, John W., and John R. McKivigan, eds. *The Frederick Douglass Papers: Series One: Speeches, Debates, and Interviews.* Vol. 4, *1864–1880.* New Haven, Conn.: Yale Univ. Press, 1991.

Boardman, George Dana. *An Address in Commemoration of Abraham Lincoln.* Philadelphia: Sherman and Co., 1865.

———. *An Address in Commemoration of the Re-Establishment of the National Flag at Fort Sumter.* New York: Sherman and Co., 1865.

———. *Death, the Law of Life.* Philadelphia: Sherman and Co., Printers, 1865.

Booth, Robert Russell. *Personal Forgiveness and Public Justice.* New York: Anson D. F. Randolf, 1865.

Botome, Elizabeth Hyde. *First Days Amongst the Contrabands*. 1893. Reprint, New York: Arno Press and the New York Times, 1968.

Boyd, Robert. *The Wonderful Career of Moody and Sankey in Great Britain and America Together With The Trials and Triumphs of Faith*. New York: Henry S. Goodspeed and Company, 1875.

Brewer, David J. *The United States as a Christian Nation*. Philadelphia: John C. Winston, 1905.

Brinckerhoff, Rev. I. W. *Advice to Freedmen*. New York: American Tract Society, 1864.

Broadus, John A. *A Treatise on the Preparation and Delivery of Sermons*. 1870. Reprint, New York: A. C. Armstrong and Sons, 1895.

Brown, Mrs. H. E. *John Freeman and His Family*. Boston: American Tract Society, 1864.

Brownlee, James Henry, ed. *War-Time Echoes: Patriotic Poems, Heroic and Pathetic, Humorous and Dialectic, of the Spanish-American War*. New York: The Werner Company, 1898.

Bryan, William Jennings, et al., eds. *Republic or Empire?: The Philippine Question*. Chicago: The Independence Company, 1899.

Bryce, James. *Social Institutions of the United States*. New York: Chautauqua Press, 1891.

Bullock, Alex H. *Abraham Lincoln: The Just Magistrate, the Representative Statesman, the Practical Philanthropist*. Worcester, Mass.: Charles Hamilton, Palladium Office, 1865.

Burr, Virginia Ingraham, ed. *The Secret Eye: The Journal of Ella Gertrude Clanton Thomas, 1848–1889*. Chapel Hill: Univ. of North Carolina Press, 1990.

Butler, J. G. *The Martyr President*. Washington, D.C.: McGill and Witherow, Printers and Stereotypers, 1865.

Carey, Isaac Eddy. *Abraham Lincoln, the Value to the Nation of his Exalted Character*. Freeport, Ill.: n.p., 1865.

Carroll, Charles. *The Negro, A Beast* (St. Louis: American Book and Bible House, 1900.

———. *The Tempter of Eve, or The Criminality of Man's Social, Political, and Religious Equality with the Negro, and the Amalgamation to which these Crimes Inevitably Lead*. St. Louis: Adamic Publishing Co., 1902.

Cassel, Flora Hamilton, ed. *White Ribbon Vibrations*. Hastings, Nebr.: The W.C.T.U. Song Book Publishing Association, 1890.

Celebration by the Colored People's Educational Monument Association in Memory of Abraham Lincoln. Washington, D.C.: McGill and Witherow, Printers and Stereotypers, 1865.

Chamberlain, N. H. *The Assassination of President Lincoln*. New York: G. W. Carleton, 1865.

Chandler, Julia Knapp. *Broken Hearted: An O'er True Tale of the Fever*. New Orleans: T. H. Thomason, Printer, 1878.

A Chapter in the History of the Epidemic of 1878 from Private Memoranda. Holly Springs, Miss.: McComb City Weekly Intelligencer, 1879.

Child, L. Maria. *The Freedmen's Book*. Boston: Ticknor and Fields, 1865.

Ching, Wen [pseud.]. *The Chinese Crisis from Within*. London: G. Richards, 1901.

———. *A Romance of the Republic*. 1867. Reprint, Lexington: Univ. Press of Kentucky, 1997.

Clemenceau, Georges. *American Reconstruction: 1865–1870*. 1928. Reprint, New York: Da Capo Press, 1969.

Collier, Price. *America and the Americans*. New York: Charles Scribner's Sons, 1897.

Concert for the Benefit of Yellow Fever Sufferers, at the M.E. Church. Martinsburg, W.Va., 1878.

Corey, Charles H. *A History of the Richmond Theological Seminary, with Reminiscences of Thirty Years' Work among the Colored People of the South*. Richmond, Va.: J. W. Randolph Company, 1895.

Crane, Rev. C. B. *Sermon on the Occasion of the Death of President Lincoln*. Hartford, Conn.: Press of Case, Lockwood and Company, 1865.

Creegan, Rev. Charles C., and Mrs. Josephine A. B. Goodnow. *Great Missionaries of the Church*. Boston: Thomas Y. Crowell and Company, 1895.

Cumming, I. A. M. [pseud.]. *Tabernacle Sketches*. Boston: The Times Publishing Company, 1877.

Cuyler, Theodore. *Recollections of a Long Life*. New York: The Baker and Taylor, Co., 1902.

Daggett, O. E. *A Sermon on the Death of Abraham Lincoln, April 15th, 1865*. Canadaigua, N.Y.: N. J. Milliken, Printer-Ontario County Times Office, 1865.

Daniels, Rev. W. H. *D. L. Moody and His Work*. Hartford, Conn.: American Publishing Company, 1876.

————, ed. *Moody: His Words, Works, and Workers. Compromising His Bible Portraits; His Outline of Doctrine, As Given in his Most Popular and Effective Sermons, Bible Readings, and Addresses in Edinburgh, Dublin, London, Philadelphia, New York, Chicago, and Boston*. New York: Nelson and Phillips Publishing, 1877.

Day, P. D. *A Memorial Discourse on the Character of Abraham Lincoln*. Concord, N.H.: McFarland and Jenks, 1865.

de Hauranne, Ernest Duvergier. *A Frenchman in Lincoln's America*. 2 vols. 1866. Reprint, Chicago: R. R. Donnelley and Sons Company, 1974.

Deming, Henry Champion. *Eulogy of Abraham Lincoln*. Hartford, Conn.: A. N. Clark and Co., 1865.

De Normandie, James. *The Lord Reigneth*. Portsmouth, N.H.: n.p., 1865.

Dixon, Thomas, Jr. *The Clansman: An Historical Romance of the Ku Klux Klan*. New York: Grosset and Dunlap, Publishers, 1905.

————. *The Leopard's Spots: A Romance of the White Man's Burden—1865–1900*. 1902. Reprint, Ridgewood, N.J.: The Gregg Press, 1967.

————. *The Sins of the Father: A Romance of the South*. New York: Grosset and Dunlap, Publishers, 1912.

Donald, E. Winchester, ed. *Ministers' Meeting of Protest Against the Atrocities in the Philippines*. Boston: n.p., 1902.

Douglass, Frederick. *The Lesson of the Hour*. Baltimore: Press of Thomas and Evans, 1894.

Drisler, Henry. *"Bible View of Slavery" by John H. Hopkins, D.D., Bishop of the Dioceses of Vermont, Examined*. New York: C. S. Westcott and Co., 1863.

Dromgoole, J. P., M.D. *Yellow Fever: Heroes, Honors, and Horrors of 1878*. Louisville: John P. Morton and Company, 1879.

Du Bois, W. E. B. *The Autobiography of W. E. B. Du Bois: A Soliloquy on Viewing My Life from the Last Decade of Its First Century*. New York: International Publishers, 1968.

———. *Dusk of Dawn: An Essay toward an Autobiography of a Race Concept*. 1940. Reprint, New York: Schocken Books, 1969.

———. *The Souls of Black Folk*. 1903. Reprint, New York: Norton, 1999.

Dunbar, Paul Laurence. *The Fanatics*. 1901. Reprint, New York: Negro Univs. Press, 1969.

Dunn, James B., ed. *Moody's Talks on Temperance, With Anecdotes and Incidents in Connection with the Tabernacle Temperance Work in Boston*. New York: National Temperance Society and Publication House, 1877.

Duster, Alfreda M., ed. *Crusade for Justice: The Autobiography of Ida B. Wells*. Chicago: Univ. of Chicago Press, 1970.

Eddy, Richard. *The Martyr to Liberty*. Philadelphia: Horace W. Smith, 1865.

Edwards, Richard. *Life and Character of Abraham Lincoln: An Address*. Peoria, Ill.: N. C. Nason, Printer, 1865.

Egar, John H. *The Martyr-President: A Sermon Preached in the Church of St. Paul, Leavenworth*. Leavenworth, Kans.: Bulletin Job Printer Establishment, 1865.

"Esther Hill Hawks, M.D." *Lynn Historical Society Register* (1906–1907): 40.

Fairfield, Edmund B. *Wickedness in High Places: A Review of the Beecher Case*. Mansfield: O. L. D. Myers and Brother, Printers, 1874.

Fields, Annie, ed. *Life and Letters of Harriet Beecher Stowe*. Boston: Houghton, Mifflin and Company, 1897.

Foner, Philip S., and George E. Walker, eds. *Proceedings of the Black National and State Conventions, 1865–1900*, vol. 1. Philadelphia: Temple Univ. Press, 1986.

Formal Fraternity: Proceedings of the General Conferences of the Methodist Episcopal Church and of the Methodist Episcopal Church, South, in 1872, 1874, and 1876, and of the Joint Commission of the Two Churches on Fraternal Relations, at Cape May, New Jersey, August 16–23, 1876. New York: Nelson and Phillips, 1876.

Fowler, Henry. *Character and Death of Abraham Lincoln*. Auburn, N.Y.: Wm. J. Moses' Steam Press Establishment, 1865.

The Freedman's Third Reader. Boston: The American Tract Society, 1865.

Garrison, J. F. *The Teachings of the Crisis*. Camden, N.J.: West Jersey Press, 1865.

Gatewood, Willard B., Jr., ed. *"Smoked Yankees" and the Struggle for Empire: Letters from Negro Soldiers, 1898–1902*. Urbana: Univ. of Illinois Press, 1972.

Gillette, A. D. *God Seen Above All National Calamities*. Washington, D.C.: McGill and Witherow, Printers and Stereotypers, 1865.

Goodspeed, Rev. E. J. *A Full History of the Wonderful Careers of Moody and Sankey in Great Britain and America*. St. Louis: N. D. Thompson and Co., Publishers, 1876.

Gordon, Anna A. *The Beautiful Life of Frances E. Willard, A Memorial Volume*. Chicago: Woman's Temperance Publishing Association, 1898.

——. *The Life of Frances Willard.* Evanston, Ill.: National Woman's Christian Temperance Union, 1912.

Gordon, W. R. *The Sin of Reviling, and Its Work.* New York: John A. Gray and Green, Printers, 1865.

Gracey, J. T. *Open Doors: Hints About Opportunities for Christian Work in Africa, Japan, India, Burmah, China, Mexico, South America, the Turkish Empire, Korea, and the Islands of the Sea.* Rochester, N.Y.: J. T. Gracey, 1891.

Graham, Maryemma, ed. *Complete Poems of Frances E. W. Harper.* New York: Oxford Univ. Press, 1988.

Grant or Greeley—which? Facts and arguments for the consideration of the colored citizens of the United States: being extracts from letters, speeches, and editorials by colored men and their best friends. *Sumner's mistakes, Greeley's surrender, and Grant's faithfulness. Opinions in brief of Wm. Lloyd Garrison, Wendell Phillips, Prof. J. Mercer Langston, R. H. Dana, Jr., Judge Hoar, Fred. Douglass, Speaker Blaine, Wm. D. Forten, Prof. Wm. Howard Day.* Washington, D.C.: National Congressional Committee, 1872.

Griffin, Farah Jasmine, ed. *Beloved Sisters and Loving Friends: Letters from Rebecca Primus of Royal Oak, Maryland, and Addie Brown of Hartford, Connecticut, 1854–1868.* New York: Knopf, 1999.

Griffith, D. W., producer and director. *The Birth of a Nation* (film). 1915. Los Angeles: Republic Pictures Home Video, 1991.

Hall, Gordon. *President Lincoln's Death: Its Voice to the People.* Northampton, Mass.: Trumbull and Gere Printers, 1865.

Hardinge, Emma. *The Great Funeral Oration on Abraham Lincoln.* New York: American News Company, 1865.

Hathaway, Warren. *A Discourse Occasioned by the Death of Abraham Lincoln.* Albany: J. Munsell, 1865.

Haven, Gilbert. *The Uniter and Liberator of America.* Boston: James P. Magee, 1865.

Haviland, Laura S. *A Woman's Life-Work: Labors and Experiences.* 1881. Reprint; Salem, N.H.: Ayer, 1984.

Hawley, Bostick. *Truth and Righteousness Triumphant: A Discourse Commemorative of the Death of President Lincoln.* Albany, N.Y.: J. Munsell, 1865.

Hayne, Paul Hamilton. *Poems of Paul Hamilton Hayne.* Boston: D. Lothrop and Company, 1882.

Higginson, Thomas Wentworth. *Army Life in a Black Regiment.* 1869. Reprint, New York: Norton, 1984.

Hoar, Hon. George Frisbie, ed. *Charles Sumner: His Complete Works.* Boston: Lee and Shepard, 1883.

Hoge, Moses D. *Portraiture of Four Pastors.* Richmond, Va.: Presbyterian Committee of Publication, 1892.

Holland, Rupert Sargent, ed. *Letters and Diary of Laura M. Towne Written from the Sea Islands of South Carolina, 1862–1884.* 1912. Reprint, New York: Negro Univs. Press, 1969.

Hopkins, John Henry. *Bible View of Slavery.* New York: The Society for the Diffusion of Political Knowledge, 1863.

Hopkins, John H., Jr. *The Life of the Late Right Reverend John Henry Hopkins, First Bishop of Vermont and Seventh Presiding Bishop By One of His Sons.* New York: F. J. Huntington, 1873.

Horst, Samuel L., ed. *The Fire of Liberty in Their Hearts: The Diary of Jacob E. Yoder of the Freedmen's Bureau School, Lynchburg, Virginia, 1866–1870.* Richmond, Va.: Library of Virginia, 1996.

Howells, W. D. *Through the Eye of the Needle: A Romance With an Introduction.* New York: Harper and Brothers Publishers, 1907.

Ingersoll, Lurton D. *The Life of Horace Greeley.* 1873. Reprint, New York: Beekman, 1974.

Jacobs, Harriet Brent [Linda Brent, pseud.]. *Incidents in the Life of a Slave Girl.* Boston: Boston Eleotype Foundry, 1861.

Jaquette, Henrietta Stratton, ed. *South after Gettysburg: Letters of Cornelia Hancock, 1863–1868.* New York: Crowell Company, 1956.

Jeffrey, Reuben. *The Mission of Abraham Lincoln.* Philadelphia: Bryson and Son, Printers and Stationers, 1865.

Johnson, Herrick. *God's Ways Unsearchable.* Pittsburgh, Pa.: W. G. Johnston and Co., 1865.

Johnson, R. U., and C. C. Buel, eds. *Battles and Leaders of the Civil War.* 4 vols. New York: Century, 1887–1888.

Johnson, Thomas Cary. *The Life and Letters of Benjamin Morgan Palmer.* Richmond, Va.: Presbyterian Committee of Publications, 1906.

Journal of the Forty Ninth Annual Council of the Protestant Episcopal Church in the State of North Carolina. Raleigh, N.C.: J. C. Gorman's Book and Job Printing Office, 1865.

Kearney, Belle. *A Slaveholder's Daughter.* New York: The Abbey Press Publishers, 1900.

Keating, J. M. *A History of the Yellow Fever Epidemic of 1878, in Memphis, Tenn.* Memphis, Tenn.: Printed for the Howard Association, 1879.

Kidder, Daniel P. *A Treatise on Homiletics: Designed to Illustrate the True Theory and Practice of Preaching the Gospel,* rev. ed. New York: Nelson and Phillips, 1864.

King, Edward. *The Great South.* Hartford, Conn.: American Publishing Co., 1875.

King, W. Nephew, *The Story of the Spanish-American War and the Revolt in the Philippines.* New York: Peter Fenelon Collier, 1898.

Kipling, Rudyard. "The White Man's Burden." *McClure's Magazine* 12, no. 4 (February 1899): 290–1.

Laurie, Thomas. *Three Discourses.* Dedham, Mass.: John Cox Jr., 1865.

Lee, Richard Henry. *Letter from Richard Henry Lee, of Washington, Pa., One of the Signers of the Clerical Protest Against Bishop Hopkins' Bible View of Slavery.* Philadelphia: Philadelphia Age, 1864.

Leffingwell, C. S. *Strength in Sorrow.* Canandaigua, N.Y.: C. Jobson's Office, 1865.

Letters of Henry Ward Beecher and Dr. Tyng. New York: National Union Executive Committee, 1866.

Liggins, Rev. John. *The Great Value and Success of Foreign Missions. Proved By Distinguished Witnesses.* New York: The Baker and Taylor Company, 1888.

Lowe, Charles. *Death of President Lincoln.* Boston: American Unitarian Association, 1865.

Lutzweiler, James, ed. *The Revivals of Dwight L. Moody in North Carolina: Charlotte, NC— March 8–17, 1893; Wilmington, NC—March 18–25, 1893.* Greensboro, N.C.: Schnappsburg Univ. Press, 1993.

Macrae, David. *The Americans at Home.* 1871. Reprint, New York: E. P. Dutton, 1952.

Mayo, Amory D. *The Nation's Sacrifice.* Cincinnati: Robert Clarke and Co., 1865.

———. *The Work of Certain Northern Churches in the Education of the Negro, 1862–1900.* Washington, D.C.: Government Printing Office, 1902.

McCauley, Rev. Jas. A. *Character and Services of Abraham Lincoln.* Baltimore: John D. Toy, Printer, 1865.

McClintock, John. *Discourse Delivered on the Day of the Funeral of President Lincoln.* New York: J. M. Bradstreet and Son, 1865.

McGiffert, Joseph N. *God's Work and the Nation's Duty: A Thanksgiving Sermon, Delivered in the Presbyterian Church, Ashtabula, Ohio, November 29, 1866.* Cleveland, Ohio: G. S. Newcombe and Co., Printers, 1866.

Melville, Herman. *Poems Containing Battle-Pieces, John Marr and Other Sailors, Timoleon, and Miscellaneous Poems.* New York: Harper and Brothers, 1866.

Merrick, Caroline E. *Old Times in Dixie Land: A Southern Matron's Memories.* New York: The Grafton Press, 1901.

Millard, E. C., and Lucy E. Guinness, *South America: The Neglected Continent.* New York: Fleming H. Revell Company, 1894.

Miller, Kelly. *As To the Leopard's Spots: An Open Letter to Thomas Dixon, Jr.* Washington, D.C.: Hayworth Publishing House, 1905.

———. "The Effect of Imperialism Upon the Negro Race," *Anti-Imperialist Broadside,* No. 11. Boston: New England Anti-Imperialist League, 1900.

Mims, Florence Adams. *Recorded History of South Carolina Woman's Christian Temperance Union from 1881–1901.* Edgefield, S.C.: n.p., 1950.

"Minutes of the Faculty of Atlanta University," April 1, 1879.

Minutes of the General Assembly of the Presbyterian Church in the United States of America. New York: Presbyterian Board of Publication, 1871.

Moody and Sankey in Hartford. Hartford: W. H. Goodrich, 1878.

Moody, Dwight Lyman. *Glad Tidings: Comprising Sermons and Prayer-Meeting Talks, Delivered at the N.Y. Hippodrome.* New York: E. B. Treat, 1876.

———. *The Great Redemption; or, Gospel Light, Under the Labors of Moody and Sankey.* Cleveland: C. C. Wich and Co., 1880.

———. *Moody and Sankey in Hartford.* Hartford, Conn.: W. H. Goodrich, 1878.

———. *New Sermons, Addresses and Prayers.* Chicago: J. W. Goodspeed, Publisher, 1877.

———. *To All People: Compromising Sermons, Bible Readings, Temperance Addresses and Prayer-Meeting Talks, Delivered in the Boston Tabernacle.* Boston: The Globe Publishing Company, 1877.

Moody, D. L., and Wm. S. Plumer, *Great Questions Answered: Two Colloquies.* New York: Anson D. F. Randolf and Company, 1876.

Moorhead, Max Wood, ed. *The Student Missionary Enterprise. Addresses and Discussions of the Second International Convention of the Student Volunteer Movement for Foreign Missions, Held at Detroit, Michigan, February 28 and March 1, 2, 3, and 4, 1894.* Boston: T. O. Metcalf and Co., 1894.

Morton, Richard L., ed. "Life in Virginia, by a 'Yankee Teacher,' Margaret Newbold Thorpe," *Virginia Magazine of History and Biography* 64, no. 2 (April 1956): 180–207.

———. "A 'Yankee Teacher' in North Carolina, by Margaret Newbold Thorpe," *North Carolina Historical Review* 30, no. 4 (October 1953): 564–82.

Moss, Lemuel. *Annals of the United States Christian Commission.* Philadelphia: J. B. Lippincott, 1868.

Mott, John R. *The Evangelization of the World in This Generation.* Nashville: Student Volunteer Movement for Foreign Missions, 1900.

Nelan, Charles. *Cartoons of Our War with Spain.* New York: Stokes, 1898.

Nevins, Allan, and Milton Halsey Thomas, eds. *The Diary of George Templeton Strong: The Civil War, 1860–1865.* 1952. Reprint, New York: Octagon Books, 1974.

———. *The Diary of George Templeton Strong: Post-War Years, 1865–1875.* 1952. Reprint, New York: Octagon Books, 1974.

Nordhoff, Charles. *The Cotton States in the Spring and Summer of 1875.* New York: D. Appleton and Company, 1876.

Northrop, Henry Davenport. *Life and Labors of Dwight L. Moody: The Great Evangelist.* New Haven, Conn.: Butler and Alger, 1899.

Oldfield, J. R., ed. *Civilization and Black Progress: Selected Writings of Alexander Crummell on the South.* Charlottesville: Univ. Press of Virginia, 1995.

Our Martyr President, Abraham Lincoln. Voices from the Pulpit of New York and Brooklyn. New York: Tibbals and Whiting, 1865.

Paddock, Wilbur F. *A Great Man Fallen!* Philadelphia: Sherman and Co., Printers, 1865.

Palmer, Beverly Wilson, ed. *The Selected Letters of Charles Sumner,* vol. 2. Boston: Northeastern Univ. Press, 1990.

———. *The Selected Papers of Thaddeus Stevens.* Vol. 2, *April 1865—August 1868.* Pittsburgh: Univ. of Pittsburgh Press, 1998.

Palmer, L. T., ed. *The Gospel Awakening.* Chicago: Fairbanks and Palmer Publishing Co., 1887.

Parker, Henry E. *Discourse the Day After the Reception of the Tidings of the Assassination of President Lincoln*. Concord, N.H.: McFarland and Jenks, 1865.

Pearson, Elizabeth Ward, ed. *Letters from Port Royal, 1862–1868*. 1906. Reprint; New York: Arno Press, 1969.

Penn, I. G. *Afro-American Press and its Editors*. Springfield, Mass.: Willey and Company Publishers, 1891.

Perry, William Stevens. *America, The Study of Nations: Her Religious Destiny*. Davenport, Iowa: Edward Dorcherdt, Printer, 1893.

Pierson, Rev. Arthur T. *The Crisis of Missions: Or, The Voice Out of the Cloud*. New York: Robert Carter and Brothers, 1886.

Pierson, Delavan Leonard. *Arthur T. Pierson: A Spiritual Warrior, Mighty in the Scriptures; A Leader in the Modern Missionary Crusade*. New York: Fleming H. Revell Company, 1912.

Pike, James S. *The Prostrate State: South Carolina Under Negro Government*. 1873. Reprint, New York: Loring and Mussey, 1935.

Plumer, William S. *Thoughts on the Religious Instruction of the Negroes in this Country*. Savannah, Ga.: E. J. Purse, 1848.

Porter, Robert P. *Life of William McKinley: Soldier, Lawyer, Statesman*. Cleveland, Ohio: The N. G. Hamilton Publishing Co., 1896.

Power, J. L. *The Epidemic of 1878, in Mississippi: Report of the Yellow Fever Relief Work*. Jackson, Miss.: Clarion Steam Publishing House, 1879.

Presbyterian Reunion Memorial Volume: 1837–1871. New York: De-Witt C. Lent and Company, 1870.

Proceedings of a Mass Meeting Held in New Orleans, December 6, To Return Thanks for the Succor Extended to the City During the Epidemic of 1878. New Orleans: A. W. Hyatt, Stationer and Printer, 1878.

Prospero [pseud.]. *Caliban: A Sequel to 'Ariel.'* New York: Published for the Proprietor, 1868.

Primus, Rebecca, and Farah Griffith, eds. *Beloved Sisters and Loving Friends: Letters from Rebecca Primus of Royal Oak, Maryland and Addie Brown of Hartford, Connecticut, 1854–1868*. New York: Knopf, 1999.

Randall, James. "Lines on the Yellow Fever Plague: Written for the Bazaar at Douglastown." N.p., 1878.

Rankin, J. E. *Moses and Joshua*. Boston: Dakin and Metcalf, 1865.

Reed, Villeroy Dibble. *The Conflict of Truth*. New Jersey: West Jersey Press, 1865.

Reese, John. *Shall We Have Liberty or Slavery? Letter to Rev. Henry Ward Beecher*. Washington, D.C.: n.p., 1866.

Reid, Whitelaw. *After the War: A Southern Tour*. Cincinnati: Wilstach and Baldwin, 1866.

Reilly, Wayne E., ed. *The Diaries of Sarah Jane and Emma Ann Foster: A Year in Maine During the Civil War*. Rockport, Maine: Picton Press, 2002.

———, ed. *Sarah Jane Foster: Teacher of the Freedmen, A Diary and Letters.* Charlottesville: Univ. Press of Virginia, 1990.

Report of the First International Convention of the Student Volunteer Movement for Foreign Missions, Held At Cleveland, Ohio, U.S.A., February 26, 27, 28, and March 1, 1891. Boston: T. O. Metcalf and Co., 1891.

Report of the Howard Association, of New Orleans, of Receipts, Expenditures, and their Work in the Epidemic of 1878, With Names of Contributors, Etc. New Orleans: A. W. Hyatt, Stationer and Printer, 1878.

Report of the Philadelphia Yellow Fever Committee. Philadelphia: Printed By Order of the Committee, 1879.

Report of the Pittsburgh Relief Committee, Having in Charge the Collection and Distribution of Funds, Provisions, and Other Supplies, For the Sufferers by Yellow Fever, in the South-Western States in the Summer and Fall of 1878. Pittsburgh, Pa.: Myers, Schoyer and Co., Printers, Corner of Wood Street and Virgin Alley, 1879.

Report of the Relief Work of the Young Men's Christian Association of New Orleans in the Yellow Fever Epidemic of 1878. New Orleans: A. H. Nelson, Print, 1879.

Report of the Special Relief Committee of Memphis, Tennessee, Containing Accurate Accounts of Funds on Hand, Received and Disbursed, during the Yellow Fever Epidemic of 1878. Memphis: C. A. Beehn, Book and Job Printer, 1879.

Rice, N. L. *Sermon on the Death of Abraham Lincoln, Late President of the United States. Preached on the Occasion of the National Funeral.* New York: Wm. C. Bryant and Co., Printers, 1865.

Robinson, Charles S. *The Martyred President: A Sermon Preached in the First Presbyterian Church, Brooklyn, N.Y.* New York: John F. Trow, Printer, 1865.

Roosevelt, Theodore. *The Rough Riders.* New York: P. F. Collier and Son Publishers, 1899.

Ryan, Abram J. *Poems: Patriotic, Religious, Miscellaneous.* 1880. Reprint, Baltimore: John Murphy and Co., 1892.

Sample, Rev. Robert F. *The Curtained Throne.* Philadelphia: James S. Claxton, 1865.

Sankey, Ira D. *My Life and the Story of the Gospel Hymns.* Philadelphia: The Sunday School Times Company, 1907.

Schwartz, Gerald, ed. *A Woman Doctor's Civil War: Esther Hill Hawks' Diary.* Columbia: Univ. of South Carolina Press, 1994.

Seiss, Joseph A. *The Assassinated President.* Philadelphia: Joseph A. Seiss, D.D., 1865.

Services Held by the Maryland Union Commission, in Charles Street M. E. Church, On the Evening of June 1st, 1865. Baltimore: Sherwood and Co., 1865.

Shedd, Clarence P. *Two Centuries of Student Christian Movements: Their Origin and Intercollegiate Life.* New York: Association Press, 1934.

Simmons, Judge J. F. *The Welded Link: And Other Poems.* Philadelphia: J. B. Lippincott and Co., 1881.

Simpson, Matthew. *Funeral Address Delivered at the Burial of President Lincoln*. New York: Carlton and Porter, 1865.

Singleton, J. W. *Medical Heroism of 1878*. Geo. O. Rumbold and Co.: St. Louis, 1879.

Slaughter, Linda Warfel. *The Freedmen of the South*. 1869. Reprint, New York: Kraus Reprint, 1969.

Smith, Arthur H. *Village Life in China*. 1899. Reprint. Boston: Little, Brown, 1970.

Smith, John David. *Religion and 'The Negro Problem' Part I, Volume Five: The 'Ariel' Controversy*. New York: Garland Publishing, 1993.

Spear, Samuel T. *The Punishment of Treason*. Brooklyn: The Union Steam Presses, 1865.

Speeches and Addresses of William McKinley from March 1, 1897 to May 30, 1900. New York: Doubleday and McClure Co., 1900.

Stead, William T. *The Americanization of the World: Or, The Trend of the Twentieth Century*. 1902. Reprint, New York: Garland Publishing, 1972.

Steele, Henry H. *Victory and Mourning*. New Brunswick, N.J.: Terhune and Van Anglen's Press, 1865.

Stevenson, Brenda, ed. *The Journals of Charlotte Forten Grimké*. New York: Oxford Univ. Press, 1988.

Stewart, [Eliza Daniel] Mother. *Memories of the Crusade*. 1888. Reprint, New York: Arno Press, 1972.

Stone, Andrew L. *A Discourse Occasioned by the Death of Abraham Lincoln*. Boston: J. K. Wiggin, 1865.

Stowe, Charles Edward, ed. *Life of Harriet Beecher Stowe Compiled from her Letters and Journals*. Boston: Houghton, Mifflin and Company, 1889.

Stowe, Harriet Beecher. *Men of Our Times; or Leading Patriots of the Day*. Hartford, Conn.: Hartford Publishing Co., 1868.

———. *Palmetto Leaves*. 1873. Reprint, Gainesville, Fla.: Univ. Press of Florida, 1999.

Strode, Hudson, ed. *Jefferson Davis: Private Letters, 1823–1889*. New York: Harcourt, Brace and World, 1966.

Strong, Rev. Josiah. *Expansion under New World-Conditions*. New York: The Baker and Taylor Company, 1900.

———. *The New Era or the Coming Kingdom*. New York: The Baker and Taylor Company, 1893.

———. *Our Country: Its Possible Future and Its Present Crisis*. 1885. Rev. ed., New York: The Baker and Taylor Company, 1891.

Sutphen, Morris C. *Discourse on the Occasion of the Death of Lincoln*. Philadelphia: Jas. B. Rodgers, Printers, 1865.

Sweetser, Seth. *A Commemorative Discourse on the Death of Abraham Lincoln*. Boston: Press of John Wilson and Son, 1865.

Swint, Henry L., ed. *Dear Ones at Home: Letters from Contraband Camps.* Nashville: Vanderbilt Univ. Press, 1966.

Thomas, A. G. *Our National Unity Perfected in the Martyrdom of our President.* Philadelphia: Smith, English, and Co., 1865.

Thompson, Joseph P. *Abraham Lincoln: His Life and Its Lessons.* New York: Loyal Publication Society, 1865.

Todd, Rev. Elbert S. *Christian Missions in the Nineteenth Century.* New York: Hunt and Eaton, 1890.

Torrey, Rev. R. A. "Some Blessings of War." In *Northfield Echoes.* Vol. 5, *Northfield Conference Addresses for 1898,* edited by Delavan L. Pierson. East Northfield, Mass.: Northfield Echoes, 1898.

Tourgée, Albion W. *An Appeal to Cæsar.* New York: Fords, Howard, and Hulbert, 1884.

———. *Bricks Without Straw.* 1880. Reprint, Ridgewood, N.J.: The Gregg Press, 1967.

———. *A Fool's Errand: A Novel of the South.* 1879. Reprint, New York: Harper Torchbooks, 1961.

Tousey, Thomas. *Discourse on the Death of Abraham Lincoln.* Rochester, N.Y.: C. D. Tracy and Co., Printers, Evening Express Office, 1865.

Townsend, Brevet Major-General E. D. *Anecdotes of the Civil War in the United States.* New York: D. Appleton and Company, 1884.

Trollope, Anthony. *North America.* New York: Harper and Brothers, Publishers, 1862.

Trowbridge, J. T. *The South: A Tour of Its Battle-fields and Ruined Cities.* Hartford, Conn.: L. Stebbins, 1866.

The True Issues of the Presidential Campaign: Speeches of Horace Greeley during his Western Trip and at Portland, Maine. Also, Ex-President Mahan's Letters. New York: n.p., 1872.

Tucker, J. T. *A Discourse in Memory of our Late President, Abraham Lincoln.* Holliston: Plimpton and Clark, 1865.

Tucker, Nathaniel Beverley, *Address of Beverley Tucker, Esq., to the People of the United States 1865.* Atlanta, Ga.: Library of Emory University, 1948.

Turner, Frederick Jackson. *Frontier and Section: Selected Essays of Frederick Jackson Turner.* Englewood Cliffs, N.J.: Prentice Hall, 1961.

Twain, Mark, and Charles Dudley Warner. *The Gilded Age—a Tale of To-day.* Hartford, Conn.: American Publishing Company, 1874.

Twenty-First Annual Report of the American Missionary Association. New York: The American Missionary Association, 1867.

Vail, Stephen M., ed. *The Bible Against Slavery, With Replies to the "Bible View of Slavery," by John H. Hopkins, Bishop of the Diocese of Vermont.* Concord: Fogg, Hadley and Co., Printers, 1864.

Vincent, Marvin R. *A Sermon on the Assassination of Abraham Lincoln.* Troy, N.Y.: A. W. Scribner, Book and Job Printer, 1865.

Washington, Booker T. *Up From Slavery: An Autobiography.* 1900. Reprint, Garden City, N.Y.: Doubleday, 1948.

Washington, Booker T., and W. E. B. Du Bois. *The Negro in the South: His Economic Progress in Relation to His Moral and Religious Development.* Philadelphia: George W. Jacobs and Company, 1907.

Waterbury, M. *Seven Years Among the Freedmen.* Chicago: T. B. Arnold, 1891.

Watterson, Henry. *The Compromises of Life and Other Lectures and Addresses Including Some Observations on Certain Downward Tendencies of Modern Society.* New York: Duffield and Company, 1906.

Webb, Edwin B. *Memorial Sermons.* Boston: Press of Geo. C. Rand and Avery, 1865.

Wells, Ida B. *A Red Record.* Chicago: Donohue and Henneberry, 1895.

White, George H. *Speech of Hon. George H. White, of North Carolina, in the House of Representatives, January 29, 1901.* Washington, D.C.: National Government Publication, 1901.

White, Pleny H. *A Sermon, Occasioned by the Assassination of Abraham Lincoln, President of the United States.* Battleboro, Vt.: The Vermont Record Office, 1865.

Willard, Frances E. *Glimpses of Fifty Years: The Autobiography of an American Woman.* Chicago: Woman's Temperance Publication Association, 1889.

———. *Woman and Temperance; Or, the Work and Workers of the Woman's Christian Temperance Union.* 1883. Reprint, Hartford, Conn.: Park Publishing Co., 1884.

———. *Woman in the Pulpit.* Boston: D. Lothrop Company, 1888.

Willard, Frances. E., and Mary A. Livermore, eds. *A Woman of the Century: Fourteen Hundred-Seventy Biographical Sketches Accompanied by Portraits of Leading American Women in All Walks of Life.* Buffalo: Charles Wells Moulton, 1893.

Wilson, James Grant, and John Fiske, eds. *Appleton's Cyclopedia of American Biography.* New York: D. Appleton and Company, 1887–1889.

Wingfield, Marshall, ed. "The Life and Letters of Dr. William J. Armstrong," *West Tennessee Historical Society Papers* 4 (1950): 97–144.

Witherbee, Sidney A., ed. *Spanish-American War Songs: A Complete Collection of Newspaper Verse During the Recent War with Spain.* Detroit: Sidney A. Witherbee, Publisher, 1898.

Woodward, C. Vann, ed. *Mary Chesnut's Civil War.* New Haven, Conn.: Yale Univ. Press, 1981.

Woolsey, Theodore Dwight. *The Nation Still in Danger; or, Ten Years After the War.* New York: American Missionary Association, 1875.

Wortman, Denis. *A Discourse on the Death of President Lincoln.* Albany: Weed, Parsons and Company, 1865.

Yard, Robert B. *The Providential Significance of the Death of Abraham Lincoln.* Newark, N.J.: H. Harris, 1865.

Young, Robert E. *The Negro: A Reply to Ariel.* Nashville: J. W. M'Ferrin and Co., Booksellers and Stationers, 1867.

Zwick, Jim, ed. *Mark Twain's Weapons of Satire: Anti-Imperialist Writings on the Philippine-American War.* Syracuse: Syracuse Univ. Press, 1992.

SECONDARY SOURCES

Articles

Axeen, David. "'Heroes of the Engine Room': American 'Civilization' and the War with Spain," *American Quarterly* 36, no. 4 (autumn 1984): 481–502.

Blight, David W. "'For Something beyond the Battlefield': Frederick Douglass and the Struggle for the Memory of the Civil War." *Journal of American History* 75, no. 4 (March 1989): 1156–78.

Blocker, Jack S., Jr. "'It Is Easy Enough to Conquer a Man, If You Only Know How': A Personal Account of the Women's Temperance Crusade." *Old Northwest* 15 (spring/summer 1990): 43–62.

Bloomfield, Maxwell. "Dixon's 'The Leopard's Spots': A Study in Popular Racism." *American Quarterly* 16, no. 3 (autumn 1964): 387–401.

Blum, Edward J. "'Beginning a New War': Religion, Race, and Reunion after Lincoln's Assassination." *Mid-America: An Historical Review* 84, nos. 1–3 (winter/summer/fall 2002): 27–54.

———. "The Crucible of Disease: Trauma, Memory, and National Reconciliation during the Yellow Fever Epidemic of 1878." *Journal of Southern History* 69, no. 4 (November 2003): 791–820.

———. "Gilded Crosses: Postbellum Revivalism and the Reforging of American Nationalism." *Journal of Presbyterian History* 79, no. 4 (winter 2001): 277–92.

——— "The Soul of W. E. B. Du Bois." *Philosophia Africana* 7, no 2 (August 2004): 1–15.

Bohn, Larry A. "'An Oasis in a Desert of Woe': The Yellow Fever Epidemic in Jackson, Madison County, Tennessee." *West Tennessee Historical Society Papers* 50 (December 1996): 105–14.

Boldrick, Charles C. "Father Abram J. Ryan, 'The Poet-Priest of the Confederacy.'" *Filson Club History Quarterly* 46, no. 3 (1972): 201–18.

Bonner, Robert E. "Roundheaded Cavaliers? The Context and Limits of a Confederate Racial Project." *Civil War History* 48, no. 1 (March 2002): 34–59.

Bordin, Ruth. "'A Baptism of Power and Liberty': The Women's Crusade of 1873–1874." *Ohio History* 87, no. 4 (autumn 1978): 393–404.

Brewer, H. Peers. "The Protestant Episcopal Freedmen's Commission, 1865–1878." *Historical Magazine of the Protestant Episcopal Church* 26 (1967): 361–81.

Brown, Ira V. "Lyman Abbott and Freedmen's Aid, 1865–1869." *Journal of Southern History* 15, no. 1 (February 1949): 22–38.

Brownlow, Paul C. "The Northern Protestant Pulpit and Andrew Johnson." *Southern Speech Communication Association* 39, no. 3 (spring 1974): 248–59.

Brumberg, Joan Jacobs. "Zenanas and Girlless Villages: The Ethnology of American Evangelical Women, 1870–1910." *Journal of American History* 69, no. 2 (September 1982): 347–71.

Butchart, Ronald E. "'Outthinking and Outflanking the Owners of the World': A Historiography of the African American Struggle for Education." *History of Education Quarterly* (autumn 1988): 333–66.

Butchart, Ronald E., and Amy F. Rolleri "Iowa Teachers among the Freedpeople of the South, 1862–1876" *Annals of Iowa* 62, no. 1 (winter 2003): 1–29.

Capers, Gerald M., Jr. "Yellow Fever in Memphis in the 1870's." *Mississippi Valley Historical Review* 24, no. 4 (March 1938): 483–502.

Chang, Perry. "'Angels of Peace in a Smitten Land': The Northern Teachers' Crusade in the Reconstruction South Reconsidered." *Southern Historian* 16 (spring 1995): 26–45.

Coben, Stanley. "Northeastern Business and Radical Reconstruction: A Re-Examination." *Mississippi Valley Historical Review* 46, no. 1 (June 1959): 67–90.

Dallek, Robert. "National Mood and American Foreign Policy: A Suggestive Essay." *American Quarterly* 34, no. 4 (autumn 1982): 339–61.

Davenport, F. Gavin, Jr. "Thomas Dixon's Mythology of Southern History." *Journal of Southern History* 36, no. 3 (August 1970): 350–67.

Drake, Richard B. "Freedmen's Aid Societies and Sectional Compromise." *Journal of Southern History* 29, no. 2 (May 1963): 175–86.

Eacker, Susan A. "Gender in Paradise: Harriet Beecher Stowe and Postbellum Prose on Florida." *Journal of Southern History* 64, no. 3 (August 1998): 495–512.

Eaton, Clement. "Breaking a Path for the Liberation of Women in the South." *Georgia Review* 28, no. 2 (1974): 187–99.

Evensen, Bruce. "It Is a Marvel to Many People: Dwight L. Moody, Mass Media, and the New England Revival of 1877." *New England Quarterly* 72, no. 2 (June 1999): 251–74.

Fahs, Alice. "The Feminized Civil War: Gender, Northern Popular Literature, and the Memory of the Civil War, 1861–1900." *Journal of American History* 85, no. 4 (March 1999): 1461–94.

Farley, Ena L. "Methodists and Baptists on the Issue of Black Equality in New York: 1865 to 1868." *Journal of Negro History* 61, no. 4 (October 1976): 374–92.

Ferry, Henry J. "Racism and Reunion: A Black Protest by Francis James Grimké." *Journal of Presbyterian History* 50 (1972): 77–88.

Foner, Eric. "The New View of Reconstruction." *American Heritage* (October/November 1983): 10–5.

———. "Reconstruction Revisited." *Reviews in American History* 10, no. 4 (December 1982): 82–100.

Frago, Antonio Viñao. "The History of Literacy in Spain: Evolution, Traits, and Questions." *History of Education Quarterly* 30, no. 4 (winter 1990): 573–99.

Frankiel, Tamar [Sandra S. Sizer]. "Politics and Apolitical Religion: The Great Urban Revivalism of the Late Nineteenth Century." *Church History* 48, no. 1 (1979): 81–98.

Franklin, John Hope. "Mirror for Americans: A Century of Reconstruction History." *American Historical Review* 85, no. 1 (February 1980): 1–14.

Gerber, Richard Allan. "The Liberal Republicans of 1872 in Historiographical Perspective." *Journal of American History* 62, no. 1 (June 1975): 40–73.

Gianakos, Perry E. "The Spanish-American War and the Double Paradox of the Negro American." *Phylon* 26 (spring 1965): 34–49.

Goldhaber, Michael. "A Mission Unfulfilled: Freedmen's Education in North Carolina, 1865–1870." *Journal of Negro History* (autumn 1992), 199–210.

Graebner, Norman A. "Christianity and Democracy: Tocqueville's Views of Religion in America." *Journal of Religion* 56 (1976): 263–73.

Hall, Randal L. "Southern Conservatism at Work: Women, Nurses, and the 1878 Yellow Fever Epidemic in Memphis." *Tennessee Historical Quarterly* 56, no. 4 (winter 1997): 241–61.

Hardesty, Nancy A. "'The Best Temperance Organization in the Land': Southern Methodists and the W.C.T.U. in Georgia." *Methodist History* 28, no. 3 (April 1990): 187–94.

Howard-Pitney, David. "The Enduring Black Jeremiad: The American Jeremiad and Black Protest Rhetoric, from Frederick Douglass to W. E. B. Du Bois, 1841–1919." *American Quarterly* 38, no. 3 (1986): 481–92.

Howe, Daniel Walker. "The Evangelical Movement and Political Culture in the North during the Second Party System," *Journal of American History* 77, no. 4 (March 1991): 1216–39.

Huston, James L. "The Experiential Basis of the Northern Antislavery Impulse." *Journal of Southern History* 56, no. 4 (November 1990): 609–40.

Ivy, James D. "'The Lone Star State Surrenders to a Lone Woman': Frances Willard's Forgotten 1882 Texas Temperance Tour." *Southwestern Historical Quarterly* 102, no. 1 (July 1998): 45–62.

Jackman, Mary R., and Marie Crane. "'Some of My Best Friends Are Black . . .': Interracial Friendship and Whites' Racial Attitudes." *Public Opinion Quarterly* 50, no. 4 (winter 1986): 459–86.

Jackson, Luther P. "The Educational Efforts of the Freedmen's Bureau and Freedmen's Aid Societies in South Carolina, 1862–1872." *Journal of Negro History* 8, no. 1 (January 1923): 1–40.

Jameson, J. Franklin. "The American Acta Sanctorum." *American Historical Review* 13, no. 2 (January 1908): 286–302.

Kagan, Richard L. "Prescott's Paradigm: American Historical Scholarship and the Decline of Spain." *American Historical Review* 101, no. 2. (April 1996): 423–46.

Kelly, Patrick J. "The Election of 1896 and the Restructuring of Civil War Memory." *Civil War History* 49, no. 3 (2003): 254–80.

Kerber, Linda K. "Separate Spheres, Female Worlds, Woman's Place: The Rhetoric of Women's History." *Journal of American History* 75, no. 1. (June 1988): 9–39.

Lasch, Christopher. "The Anti-Imperialists, the Philippines, and the Inequality of Man." *Journal of Southern History* 24, no. 3 (August 1958): 319–31.

Lensink, Judy Nolte. "Expanding the Boundaries of Criticism: The Diary as Female Autobiography." *Women's Studies* 14, no. 1 (1988): 39–53.

Lewis, Sean Michael. "'Old Times Are Not Forgotten': Robert Lewis Dabney's Public Theology for a Reconstructed South." *Journal of Presbyterian History* 81, no. 3 (fall 2003): 163–77.

Livingston, David N. "The Moral Discourse of Climate: Historical Considerations on Race, Place and Virtue." *Journal of Historical Geography* 17, no. 4 (October 1991): 413–34.

Lonn, Ella. "Reconciliation between the North and the South." *Journal of Southern History* 13, no. 1 (February 1947): 3–26.

McPherson, James M. "Grant or Greeley? The Abolitionist Dilemma in the Election of 1872." *American Historical Review* 71, no. 1 (October 1965): 43–61.

———. "White Liberals and Black Power in Negro Education, 1865–1915." *American Historical Review* 75, no. 5 (June 1970): 1257–1386.

Miller, Dorothea R. "Josiah Strong and American Nationalism: A Reevaluation." *Journal of American History* 53, no. 3 (December 1966): 487–503.

Mohler, Mark. "The Episcopal Church and National Reconciliation, 1865." *Political Science Quarterly* 41, no. 4 (December 1926): 567–95.

Murray, Alex L. "Harriet Beecher Stowe on Racial Segregation in the Schools." *American Quarterly* 12, no. 4 (winter 1960): 518–9.

Patterson, Thomas G. "United States Intervention in Cuba, 1898: Interpretations of the Spanish-American-Cuban-Filipino War." *History Teacher* 29, no. 3 (May 1996): 341–61.

Pauly, John J. "The Great Chicago Fire as a National Event." *American Quarterly* 35, no. 5 (winter 1984): 668–83.

Poole, W. Scott. "Religion, Gender, and the Lost Cause in South Carolina's 1876 Governor's Race: 'Hampton or Hell!'" *Journal of Southern History* 68, no. 3 (2002): 573–95.

Powers, Daniel A., and Christopher G. Ellison. "Interracial Contact and Black Racial Attitudes: The Contact Hypothesis and Selectivity Bias." *Social Forces* 74, no. 1 (September 1995): 205–26.

Price, Vinton M., Jr. "Will Women Turn the Tide?: Mississippi Women and the 1922 United States Senate Race." *Journal of Mississippi History* 42, no 3 (1980): 212–20.

Reynolds, David S. "From Doctrine to Narrative: The Rise of Pulpit Storytelling in America," *American Quarterly* 32, no. 5 (winter 1980): 479–98.

Rezneck, Samuel. "Distress, Relief, and Discontent in the United States during the Depression of 1873–78." *Journal of Political Economy* 58, no. 6 (December 1950): 495–7.

Riddleberger, Patrick W. "The Radicals' Abandonment of the Negro During Reconstruction," *Journal of Negro History* 45, no. 2 (April 1960): 88–102.

Robinson, Jerry W., Jr., and James D. Preston. "Equal-Status Contact and Modification of Racial Prejudice: A Reexamination of the Contact Hypothesis." *Social Forces* 54, no. 4 (June 1976): 911–24.

Rogers, Evelyna Keadle. "Famous Georgia Women: Rebecca Latimer Felton." *Georgia Life* 5, no. 1 (1978): 34–5.

Rousey, Dennis C. "Yellow Fever and Black Policemen in Memphis: A Post-Reconstruction Anomaly." *Journal of Southern History* 51, no. 3 (August 1985): 357–74.

Schwartz, Gerald. "An Integrated Free School in Civil War Florida." *Florida Historical Quarterly* 61, no. 2 (1982): 155–61.

Sims, Anastasia. "'The Sword of the Spirit': The WCTU and Moral Reform in North Carolina, 1883–1933." *North Carolina Historical Review* 64, no. 4 (October 1987): 394–415.

Small, Sandra E. "The Yankee Schoolmarm in Freedmen's Schools: An Analysis of Attitudes." *Journal of Southern History* 45, no. 3 (August 1979): 381–402.

Stewart, Charles J. "Lincoln's Assassination and the Protestant Clergy of the North." *Journal of the Illinois State Historical Society* 54, no. 3 (autumn 1961): 268–93.

———. "The Pulpit and the Assassination of Lincoln." *Quarterly Journal of Speech* 50, no. 3 (October 1964): 299–307.

Weisenfeld, Judith. "'Who Is Sufficient for These Things?' Sara G. Stanley and the American Missionary Association, 1864–1868." *Church History* 60, no. 4 (December 1991): 493–507.

Whites, LeeAnn. "Rebecca Latimer Felton and the Wife's Farm: The Class and Racial Politics of Gender Reform." *Georgia Historical Quarterly* 76, no. 2 (summer 1992): 354–72.

Wolf, Kurt J. "Laura M. Towne and the Freed People of South Carolina, 1862–1901." *South Carolina Historical Magazine* 94, no. 4 (1997): 375–405.

Wood, Richard E. "The South and Reunion, 1898." *Historian* 31, no. 3 (May 1969): 415–30.

Unpublished Dissertations

Andreasen, Byron C. "'As Good a Right to Pray': Copperhead Christians on the Northern Civil War Home Front," Ph.D. diss., University of Illinois at Urbana-Champaign, 1998.

Brownlow, Paul C. "The Northern Protestant Pulpit on Reconstruction, 1865–1877." Ph.D. diss., Purdue University, 1970.

Bruton, Peter William. "The National Board of Health." Ph.D. diss., University of Maryland, 1974.

De Boer, Clara Merritt. "The Role of Afro-Americans in the Origin and Work of the American Missionary Association, 1839–1877." Ph.D. diss., Rutgers University, 1973.

Drake, Richard Bryant. "The American Missionary Association and the Southern Negro, 1861–1888." Ph.D. diss., Emory University, 1957.

Nuwer, Deanne Love Stephens. "The 1878 Yellow Fever Epidemic in Mississippi." Ph.D. diss., University of Southern Mississippi, 1996.

Smylie, John Edwin. "Protestant Clergymen and America's World Role, 1865–1900: A Study of Christianity, Nationality, and International Relations." Th.D. diss., Princeton Theological Seminary, 1959.

Stewart, Charles Joseph. "A Rhetorical Study of the Reaction of the Protestant Pulpit in the North to Lincoln's Assassination." Ph.D. diss., University of Illinois, 1963.

Wolfe, Allis. "Women Who Dared: Northern Teachers of the Southern Freedmen, 1862–1872." Ph.D. diss., City University of New York, 1982.

Books

Aaron, Daniel, ed. *America in Crisis: Fourteen Crucial Episodes in American History.* New York: Knopf, 1952.

Ahlstrom, Sidney E. *A Religious History of the American People.* New Haven, Conn.: Yale Univ. Press, 1972.

Allen, Theodore. *The Invention of the White Race*, vol. 1. New York: Verso, 1994.

Allport, Gordon. *The Nature of Prejudice.* Cambridge, Mass.: Addison-Wesley, 1954.

Anbinder, Tyler. *Nativism and Slavery: The Northern Know Nothings and the Politics of the 1850s.* New York: Oxford Univ. Press, 1992.

Anderson, Benedict R. *Imagined Communities: Reflections on the Origin and Spread of Nationalism.* 1983. Rev. ed., London: Verso, 1991.

Anderson, David L. *Imperialism and Idealism: American Diplomats in China, 1861–1898.* Bloomington: Indiana Univ. Press, 1985.

Anderson, James D. *The Education of Blacks in the South, 1860–1935.* Chapel Hill: Univ. of North Carolina Press, 1988.

Anderson, Stuart. *Race and Rapprochement: Anglo-Saxonism and Anglo-American Relations, 1895–1904.* London: Associated Univ. Presses, 1981.

Antze, Paul, and Michael Lambek. *Tense Past: Cultural Essays in Trauma and Memory.* New York: Routledge, 1996.

Atkins, Gaius Glenn. *Religion in Our Times.* New York: Round Table Press, Inc., 1932.

Ayers, Edward L. *Promise of the New South: Life after Reconstruction.* New York: Oxford Univ. Press, 1992.

Balmer, Randall, and John R. Fitzmier. *The Presbyterians.* Westport, Conn.: Greenwood Press, 1993.

Beale, Howard K. *The Critical Year: A Study of Andrew Johnson and Reconstruction.* New York: Harcourt, Brace and Company, 1930.

Bederman, Gail. *Manliness and Civilization: A Cultural History of Gender and Race in the United States, 1880–1917.* Chicago: Univ. of Chicago Press, 1995.

Beisner, Robert L. *From the Old Diplomacy to the New, 1865–1900.* Arlington Heights, Ill.: Harlan Davidson, 1975.

———. *Twelve Against Empire: The Anti-Imperialists, 1898–1900.* New York: McGraw-Hill, 1968.

Bell, Marion L. *Crusade in the City: Revivalism in Nineteenth-Century Philadelphia.* Lewisburg, Pa.: Bucknell Univ. Press, 1977.

Benedict, Michael Les. *A Compromise of Principle: Congressional Republicans and Reconstruction, 1863–1869.* New York: Norton, 1974.

Bennett, Adrian A. *Missionary Journalist in China: Young J. Allen and his Magazines, 1860–1883.* Athens: Univ. of Georgia Press, 1983.

Bensel, Richard F. *Sectionalism and American Political Development, 1880–1980.* Madison: Univ. of Wisconsin Press, 1984.

Bentley, George R. *A History of the Freedmen's Bureau.* Philadelphia: Univ. of Pennsylvania Press, 1955.

Bernhard, Virginia, Elizabeth Fox-Genovese, Theda Perdue, and Elizabeth Hayes Turner, eds. *Hidden Histories of Women in the New South.* Columbia: Univ. of Missouri Press, 1994.

Bernstein, Iver. *The New York City Draft Riots: Their Significance for American Society and Politics in the Age of the Civil War.* New York: Oxford Univ. Press, 1990.

Bishop, Jim. *The Day Lincoln Was Shot.* 1955. Reprint; New York: Scholastic Book Services, 1973.

Blackett, R. J. M. *Beating Against the Barriers: The Lives of Six Nineteenth-Century Afro-Americans.* Ithaca: Cornell Univ. Press, 1986.

Blanche, Hazard E. *The Organization of the Boot and Shoe Industry in Massachusetts Before 1875.* Cambridge, Mass.: Harvard Univ. Press, 1921.

Blight, David W. *Race and Reunion: The Civil War in American Memory.* Cambridge, Mass.: Harvard Univ. Press, 2001.

Blocker, Jack S., Jr. *"Give to the Winds Thy Fears": The Women's Temperance Crusade, 1873–1874.* Westport, Conn.: Greenwood Press, 1985.

———. *Retreat from Reform: The Prohibition Movement in the United States, 1890–1913.* Westport, Conn.: Greenwood Press, 1976.

Bloom, Khaled J. *The Mississippi Valley's Great Yellow Fever Epidemic of 1878.* Baton Rouge: Louisiana State Univ. Press, 1993.

Blum, Edward J., and W. Scott Poole, eds. *Vale of Tears: New Essays in Religion and Reconstruction.* Macon, Ga.: Mercer Univ. Press, 2005.

Bordin, Ruth. *Frances Willard: A Biography.* Chapel Hill: Univ. of North Carolina Press, 1986.

———. *Woman and Temperance: The Quest for Power and Liberty, 1873–1900.* Philadelphia: Temple Univ. Press, 1981.

Boyd, Melba Joyce. *Discarded Legacy: Politics and Poetics in the Life of Frances E. W. Harper, 1825–1911.* Detroit: Wayne State Univ. Press, 1994.

Bowers, Claude G. *Beveridge and the Progressive Era.* New York: The Literary Guild, 1932.

Braeman, John. *Albert J. Beveridge: American Nationalist.* Chicago: Univ. of Chicago Press, 1971.

Brands, H. W. *The Reckless Decade: America in the 1890s.* New York: St. Martin's Press, 1995.

Brawley, James P. *Two Centuries of Methodist Concern: Bondage, Freedom and Education of Black People.* New York: Vantage Press, 1974.

Brown, Charles Henry. *The Correspondents' War: Journalists in the Spanish-American War.* New York: Scribner, 1967.

Brown, Dee. *The Year of the Century: 1876.* New York: Scribner, 1966.

Brown, Richard D. *The Strength of a People: The Idea of an Informed Citizenry in America, 1650–1870.* Chapel Hill: Univ. of North Carolina Press, 1996.

Brundage, W. Fitzhugh. *Lynching in the New South: Georgia and Virginia, 1880–1930.* Urbana: Univ. of Illinois Press, 1993.

Buck, Paul. *The Road to Reunion, 1865–1900.* Boston: Little, Brown, and Co., 1937.

Bucke, Emory Stevens, ed. *The History of American Methodism in Three Volumes,* vol. 2. New York: Abingdon Press, 1964.

Bunkers, Suzanne L., and Cynthia Huff, eds. *Inscribing the Daily: Critical Essays on Women's Diaries.* Amherst: Univ. of Massachusetts Press, 1996.

Butchart, Ronald E. *Northern Schools, Southern Blacks, and Reconstruction: Freedmen's Education, 1862–1875.* Westport, Conn.: Greenwood Press, 1980.

Butler, Diane H. *Standing against the Whirlwind: Evangelical Episcopalians in Nineteenth-Century America.* New York: Oxford Univ. Press, 1995.

Campbell, Charles S. *The Transformation of American Foreign Relations, 1865–1900.* New York: Harper and Row, 1976.

Camus, Albert. *The Rebel.* Translated by Anthony Bower. New York: Knopf, 1954.

Carter, Paul A. *The Spiritual Crisis of the Gilded Age.* DeKalb: Northern Illinois Univ. Press, 1971.

Carwadine, Richard J. *Evangelicals and Politics in Antebellum America.* New Haven, Conn.: Yale Univ. Press, 1993.

Cash, Wilbur J. *The Mind of the South.* New York: Knopf, 1941.

Cecelski, David S., and Timothy Tyson, eds. *Democracy Betrayed: The Wilmington Race Riot of 1898 and Its Legacy.* Chapel Hill: Univ. of North Carolina Press, 1998.

Cell, John W. *The Highest Stage of White Supremacy: The Origins of Segregation in South Africa and the American South.* Cambridge, U.K.: Cambridge Univ. Press, 1982.

Chalmers, David M. *Hooded Americanism: The History of the Ku Klux Klan.* New York: New Viewpoints, 1976.

Chaudhuri, Nupur, and Margaret Strobel, eds. *Western Women and Imperialism: Complicity and Resistance.* Bloomington: Indiana Univ. Press, 1992.

Chernow, Ron. *Titan: The Life of John D. Rockefeller, Sr.* New York: Knopf, 1999.

Chesebrough, David B. *"No Sorrow Like Our Sorrow": Northern Protestant Ministers and the Assassination of Lincoln.* Kent, Ohio: Kent State Univ. Press, 1994.

Cimbala Paul A., and Randall M. Miller, eds. *The Freedmen's Bureau and Reconstruction.* New York: Fordham Univ. Press, 1999.

———. *An Uncommon Time: The Civil War and the Northern Home Front.* New York: Fordham Univ. Press, 2002.

Clark, Clifford E. *Henry Ward Beecher: Spokesman for a Middle-Class America.* Urbana: Univ. of Illinois Press, 1978.

Clark, Gregory, and S. Michael Halloran, eds. *Oratorical Culture in the Nineteenth-Century: Transformations in the Theory and Practice of Rhetoric.* Carbondale: Southern Illinois Univ. Press, 1993.

Clebsch, William A. *Christian Interpretations of the Civil War.* Philadelphia: Fortress Press, 1969.

———. *From Sacred to Profane America: The Role of Religion in American History.* New York: Harper and Row, 1968.

Click, Patricia C. *Time Full of Trial: The Roanoke Island Freedmen's Colony, 1862–1867.* Chapel Hill: Univ. of North Carolina Press, 2001.

Clymer, Kenton J. *Protestant Missionaries in the Philippines, 1898–1916: An Inquiry into the American Colonial Mentality.* Urbana: Univ. of Illinois Press, 1986.

Colley, Linda. *Britons: Forging the Nation, 1707–1837.* New Haven, Conn.: Yale Univ. Press, 1992.

Cone, James H. *Liberation: A Black Theology of Liberation.* Philadelphia: J. B. Lippincott, 1970.

Conrad, Robert. *The Destruction of Brazilian Slavery, 1850–1888.* Berkeley: Univ. of California Press, 1972.

Cook, Raymond A. *Thomas Dixon.* New York: Twayne Publishers, 1974.

Cox, LaWanda, and John H. Cox. *Politics, Principle, and Prejudice, 1865–1866: Dilemma of Reconstruction America.* New York: Free Press of Glencoe, 1963.

Creel, Margaret Washington. *A Peculiar People: Slave Religion and Community-Culture Among the Gullahs.* New York: New York Univ. Press, 1988.

Crosby, Alfred W. *America's Forgotten Pandemic: The Influenza of 1918.* New York: Cambridge Univ. Press, 1989.

Culley, Margo, ed. *A Day at a Time: The Diary Literature of American Women from 1764 to the Present.* New York: Feminist Press, 1985.

Current, Richard N. *Northernizing the South.* Athens: Univ. of Georgia Press, 1983.

Curtis, L. Perry. *Apes and Angels: The Irishman in Victorian Caricature.* Washington, D.C.: Smithsonian Institution Press, 1971.

Curtis, Richard K. *They Called Him Mister Moody.* Grand Rapids, Mich.: Eerdmans, 1962.

Dailey, Jane. *Before Jim Crow: The Politics of Race in Postemancipation Virginia*. Chapel Hill: Univ. of North Carolina Press, 2000.

Dailey, Jane, Glenda Gilmore, and Bryant Simon, eds. *Jumpin' Jim Crow: Southern Politics from Civil War to Civil Rights*. Princeton, N.J.: Princeton Univ. Press, 2000.

Davis, Michael. *The Image of Lincoln in the South*. Knoxville: Univ. of Tennessee Press, 1971.

De Santis, Vincent P. *Republicans Face the Southern Question: The New Departure Years, 1877–1897*. Baltimore: Johns Hopkins Univ. Press, 1959.

Deutsch, Morton, and Mary Collins, *Interracial Housing*. Minneapolis: Univ. of Minnesota Press, 1951.

DeYoung, Curtis Paul, Michael O. Emerson, George Yancey, Karen Chai Kim, *United by Faith: The Multiracial Congregation as an Answer to the Problem of Race*. New York: Oxford Univ. Press, 2003.

Dray, Philip. *At the Hands of Persons Unknown: The Lynching of Black America*. New York: Modern Library, 2003.

Donald, David. *Charles Sumner and the Rights of Man*. New York: Knopf, 1970.

Dorsett, Lyle W. *A Passion for Souls: The Life of D. L. Moody*. Chicago: Moody Press, 1997.

Douglas, Mary. *Purity and Danger: An Analysis of Concepts of Pollution and Taboo*. Harmondworth, U.K.: Penguin, 1970.

Du Bois, W. E. B. *Black Reconstruction in America*. 1935. Reprint, New York, Antheneum Books, 1992.

Duncan, Russell. *Where Death and Glory Meet: Colonel Robert Gould Shaw and the 54th Massachusetts Infantry*. Athens: Univ. of Georgia Press, 1999.

Dunham, Chester F. *The Attitude of Northern Clergy toward the South*. Toledo, Ohio: Gray, 1942.

Dunning, William Archibald. *Essays on the Civil War and Reconstruction and Related Topics*. New York: P. Smith, 1931.

Durkheim, Emile. *The Elementary Forms of Religious Life*. 1915. Reprint, New York: Simon and Schuster, 1995.

Dvorak, Katharine L. *An African-American Exodus: The Segregation of the Southern Churches*. New York: Carlson Publishing, 1991.

Dykstra, Robert R. *Bright Radical Star: Black Freedom and White Supremacy on the Hawkeye Frontier*. Cambridge, Mass.: Harvard Univ. Press, 1993.

Earhart, Mary. *Frances Willard: From Prayers to Politics*. Chicago: Univ. of Chicago Press, 1944.

Edwards, Laura F. *Gendered Strife and Confusion: The Political Culture of Reconstruction*. Urbana: Univ. of Illinois Press, 1997.

Edwards, Rebecca. *Angel in the Machinery: Gender in American Party Politics from the Civil War to the Progressive Era*. New York: Oxford Univ. Press, 1997.

Eighmy, John Lee. *Churches in Cultural Captivity: A History of the Social Attitudes of Southern Baptists*. 1972. Reprint, Knoxville: Univ. of Tennessee Press, 1987.

Ellis, John H. *Yellow Fever and Public Health in the New South.* Lexington: Univ. Press of Kentucky, 1992.

Emerson, Michael O., and Christian Smith. *Divided by Faith: Evangelical Religion and the Problem of Race in America.* New York: Oxford Univ. Press, 2000.

Epstein, Barbara Leslie. *The Politics of Domesticity: Women, Evangelism, and Temperance in Nineteenth-Century America.* Middletown, Conn.: Wesleyan Univ. Press, 1981.

Essig, James D. *The Bonds of Wickedness: American Evangelicals Against Slavery.* Philadelphia, Pa.: Temple Univ. Press, 1982.

Evensen, Bruce J. *God's Man for the Gilded Age: D. L. Moody and the Rise of Modern Evangelism.* New York: Oxford Univ. Press, 2003.

Fahs, Alice. *The Imagined Civil War: Popular Literature of the North and South, 1861–1865.* Chapel Hill: Univ. of North Carolina Press, 2001.

Fairbank John K., ed. *The Missionary Enterprise in China and America* Cambridge, Mass.: Harvard Univ. Press, 1974.

Farish, Hunter Dickinson. *The Circuit Rider Dismounts: A Social History of Southern Methodism, 1865–1900.* 1938. Reprint, New York: Da Capo Press, 1969.

Faust, Drew Gilpin. *The Creation of Confederate Nationalism: Ideology and Identity in the Civil War South.* Baton Rouge: Louisiana State Univ. Press, 1988.

———. *Mothers of Invention: Women of the Slaveholding South in the American Civil War.* Chapel Hill: Univ. of North Carolina Press, 1996.

Fels, Rendigs. *American Business Cycles, 1865–1897.* Chapel Hill: Univ. of North Carolina Press, 1959.

Findlay, James F. *Dwight L. Moody: American Evangelist 1837–1899.* Chicago: Univ. of Chicago Press, 1969.

Fitzgerald, Michael W. *The Union League Movement in the Deep South: Politics and Agricultural Change during Reconstruction.* Baton Rouge: Louisiana State Univ. Press, 1989.

Flynt, J. Wayne. *Alabama Baptists: Southern Baptists in the Heart of Dixie.* Tuscaloosa: Univ. of Alabama Press, 1998.

Foner, Eric. *Free Soil, Free Labor, Free Men: The Ideology of the Republican Party before the Civil War.* New York: Oxford Univ. Press, 1970.

———. *Reconstruction: America's Unfinished Revolution, 1863–1877.* New York: Harper and Row, 1988.

Foner, Philip Sheldon. *The Spanish-Cuban-American War and the Birth of American Imperialism, 1895–1902.* New York: Monthly Review Press, 1972.

Forster, Stig, Wolfgang J. Mommsen, and Ronald Robinson, eds., *Bismarck, Europe, and Africa: The Berlin Africa Conference 1884–1885 and the Onset of Partition.* Oxford: Oxford Univ. Press, 1996.

Foster, Gaines M. *Ghosts of the Confederacy: Defeat, the Lost Cause, and the Emergence of the New South, 1865 to 1913.* New York: Oxford Univ. Press, 1987.

————. *Moral Reconstruction: Christian Lobbyists and the Federal Legislation of Morality, 1865–1920*. Chapel Hill: Univ. of North Carolina Press, 2002.

Foster, John T., Jr., and Sarah Whitmer Foster. *Beechers, Stowes, and Yankee Strangers: The Transformation of Florida*. Gainesville: Univ. Press of Florida, 1999.

Fox, Richard Wightman. *Trials of Intimacy: Love and Loss in the Beecher-Tilton Scandal*. Chicago: Univ. of Chicago Press, 1999.

Frankiel, Tamar [Sandra S. Sizer]. *Gospel Hymns and Social Religion: The Rhetoric of Nineteenth-Century Revivalism*. Philadelphia: Temple Univ. Press, 1978.

Franklin, John Hope. *Reconstruction: After the Civil War*. Chicago: Univ. of Chicago Press, 1961.

Franklin, Penelope, ed. *Private Pages: Diaries of American Women, 1830s-1970s*. New York: Ballantine Books, 1986.

Frawley, Maria H. *A Wider Range: Travel Writing by Women in Victorian England*. London: Associated Univ. Presses, 1994.

Fredrickson, George M. *The Black Image in the White Mind: The Debate on Afro-American Character and Destiny, 1817–1914*. New York: Harper and Row, 1971.

————. *The Inner Civil War: Northern Intellectuals and the Crisis of the Union*. New York: Harper and Row, 1965.

————, ed. *A Nation Divided: Problems and Issues of the Civil War and Reconstruction*. Minneapolis: Burgess, 1975.

Freehling, William W. *The South vs. the South: How Anti-Confederate Southerners Shaped the Course of the Civil War*. New York: Oxford Univ. Press, 2001.

Frey, Sylvia R., and Betty Wood. *Come Shouting to Zion: African American Protestantism in the American South and British Caribbean to 1830*. Chapel Hill: Univ. of North Carolina Press, 1998.

Friedman, Jean E. *The Enclosed Garden: Women and Community in the Evangelical South, 1830–1900*. Chapel Hill: Univ. of North Carolina Press, 1985.

Fry, August J. *D. L. Moody: The Chicago Years, 1856–1871*. Amsterdam: Free Univ. Press, 1984.

Gambill, Edward L. *Conservative Ordeal: Northern Democrats and Reconstruction, 1865–1868*. Ames: Iowa State Univ. Press, 1981.

Gaston, Paul M. *The New South Creed: A Study in Southern Mythmaking*. New York: Knopf, 1970.

Gatewood, Willard B., Jr. *Black Americans and the White Man's Burden, 1898–1903*. Urbana: Univ. of Illinois Press, 1975.

Gellner, Ernest. *Nationalism*. Washington Square, N.Y.: New York Univ. Press, 1997.

Genovese Eugene D. *Roll, Jordan, Roll: The World the Slaves Made*. New York: Random House, Pantheon Books, 1974.

Gillette, William. *Retreat from Reconstruction, 1869–1879*. Baton Rouge: Louisiana State Univ. Press, 1979.

Gilmore, Glenda Elizabeth. *Gender and Jim Crow: Women and the Politics of White Supremacy in North Carolina, 1896–1920*. Chapel Hill: Univ. of North Carolina Press, 1996.

Goen, C. C. *Broken Churches, Broken Nation: Denominational Schisms and the Coming of the Civil War*. Macon, Ga.: Mercer Univ. Press, 1985.

Goldberg, Michael L. *An Army of Women: Gender and Politics in Gilded Age Kansas*. Baltimore: Johns Hopkins Univ. Press, 1997.

Goodman, Paul. *Of One Blood: Abolitionism and the Origins of Racial Equality*. Berkeley: Univ. of California Press, 1998.

Goodwyn, Lawrence. *The Populist Moment: A Short History of the Agrarian Revolt in America*. New York: Oxford Univ. Press, 1978.

Gossett, Thomas F. *Race: The History of an Idea in America*. Dallas: Southern Methodist Univ. Press, 1963.

Graff, Harvey J. *The Legacies of Literacy: Continuities and Contradictions in Western Culture and Society*. Bloomington: Indiana Univ. Press, 1987.

Grant, Susan-Mary. *North over South: Northern Nationalism and American Identity in the Antebellum Era*. Lawrence: Univ. Press of Kansas, 2000.

Grantham, Dewey. *The South in Modern America: A Region at Odds*. New York: Harper Collins Publishers, 1994.

Gravely, William. *Gilbert Haven; Methodist Abolitionist: A Study in Race, Religion, and Reform, 1850–1880*. Nashville: Abingdon Press, 1973.

Greenfeld, Liah. *Nationalism: Five Roads to Modernity*. Cambridge, Mass.: Harvard Univ. Press, 1992.

Gruff, Harvey J. *The Legacies of Literacy: Continuities and Contradictions in Western Culture and Society*. Bloomington: Indiana Univ. Press, 1987.

Hale, Grace Elizabeth. *Making Whiteness: The Culture of Segregation in the South, 1890–1940*. New York: Pantheon Books, 1998.

Haller, John S., Jr. *Outcasts from Evolution: Scientific Attitudes of Racial Inferiority, 1859–1900*. Urbana: Univ. of Illinois Press, 1971.

Handy, Robert T. *A Christian America: Protestant Hopes and Historical Realities*. New York: Oxford Univ. Press, 1971.

Hardesty, Nancy A. *Women Called to Witness: Evangelical Feminism in the 19th Century*. Nashville: Abingdon Press, 1984.

Harrell, Carolyn L. *When the Bells Tolled for Lincoln: Southern Reaction to the Assassination*. Macon, Ga: Mercer Univ. Press, 1997.

Harrington, Fred Harvey. *God, Mammon, and the Japanese: Dr. Horace N. Allen and Korean-American Relations, 1884–1905*. Madison: Univ. of Wisconsin Press, 1944.

Harris, Leslie M. *In the Shadow of Slavery: African Americans in New York City, 1626–1863*. Chicago: Univ. of Chicago Press, 2003.

Harrold, Stanley. *Subversives: Antislavery Community in Washington, D.C., 1828–1865*. Baton Rouge: Louisiana State Univ. Press, 2003.

Hastings, Adrian. *The Construction of Nationhood: Ethnicity, Religion, and Nationalism.* New York: Cambridge Univ. Press, 1997.

Haynes, Stephen R. *Noah's Curse: The Biblical Justification of American Slavery.* New York: Oxford Univ. Press, 2002.

Hays, Samuel P. *American Political History as Social Analysis.* Knoxville: Univ. of Tennessee Press, 1980.

Healy, David. *U.S. Expansionism: The Imperialist Urge in the 1890s.* Madison: Univ. of Wisconsin Press, 1970.

Hedrick, Joan D. *Harriet Beecher Stowe: A Life.* New York: Oxford Univ. Press, 1994.

Higginbotham, Evelyn Brooks. *Righteous Discontent: The Women's Movement in the Black Baptist Church, 1880–1920.* Cambridge, Mass.: Harvard Univ. Press, 1993.

Higham, John. *Strangers in the Land: Patterns of American Nativism, 1860–1925.* New Brunswick, N.J.: Rutgers Univ. Press, 1955.

Hildebrand, Reginald F. *The Times Were Strange and Stirring: Methodist Preachers and the Crisis of Emancipation.* Durham: Duke Univ. Press, 1995.

Hill, Samuel S. *The South and the North in American Religion.* Athens: Univ. of Georgia Press, 1980.

Hirshson, Stanley P. *Farewell to the Bloody Shirt.* Bloomington: Indiana Univ. Press, 1962.

Hobsbawm, Eric. *Nations and Nationalism since 1780: Programme, Myth, Reality.* Cambridge, U.K.: Cambridge Univ. Press, 1990.

Hoffman, Lenore, and Margo Culley, eds. *Women's Personal Narratives: Essays in Criticism and Pedagogy.* New York: Modern Language Association of America, 1985.

Hoganson, Kristin L. *Fighting for American Manhood: How Gender Politics Provoked the Spanish-American and Philippine-American Wars.* New Haven, Conn.: Yale Univ. Press, 1998.

Hopkins, C. Howard. *History of the Y.M.C.A. in North America.* New York: Association Press, 1951.

———. *John R. Mott, 1865–1955: A Biography.* Grand Rapids: Eerdmans, 1979.

Horsman, Reginald. *Race and Manifest Destiny: The Origins of American Racial Anglo-Saxonism.* Cambridge, Mass.: Harvard Univ. Press, 1981.

Howard, Victor B. *Religion and the Radical Republican Movement, 1860–1870.* Lexington: Univ. Press of Kentucky, 1990.

Howard-Pitney, David. *Afro-American Jeremiad: Appeals for Justice in America.* Philadelphia: Temple Univ. Press, 1993.

Humphreys, Margaret. *Yellow Fever and the South.* Baltimore: Johns Hopkins Univ. Press, 1992.

Hunter, Jane. *The Gospel of Gentility: American Women Missionaries in Turn-of-the-Century China.* New Haven, Conn.: Yale Univ. Press, 1984.

Hutchinson, William R. *The Modernist Impulse in American Protestantism.* Cambridge, Mass.: Harvard Univ. Press, 1976.

Ignatieff, Michael. *Blood and Belonging: Journeys into the New Nationalism.* New York: Farrar, Straus, and Giroux, 1993.

Ignatiev, Noel. *How the Irish Became White.* New York: Routledge, 1995.

Isenberg, Nancy. *Sex and Citizenship in Antebellum America.* Chapel Hill: Univ. of North Carolina Press, 1998.

Jacobson, Matthew Frye. *Barbarian Virtues: The United States Encounters Foreign Peoples at Home and Abroad, 1876–1917.* New York: Hill and Wang, 2000.

———. *Whiteness of a Different Color: European Immigrants and the Alchemy of Race.* Cambridge, Mass.: Harvard Univ. Press, 1998.

Jacoway, Elizabeth. *Yankee Missionaries in the South: The Penn School Experiment.* Baton Rouge: Louisiana State Univ. Press, 1980.

Jimerson, Randall C. *The Private Civil War: Popular Thought during the Sectional Conflict.* Baton Rouge: Louisiana State Univ. Press, 1988.

Jones, Cheslyn, Geoffrey Wainwright, Edward Yarnold, eds. *The Study of Liturgy.* New York: Oxford Univ. Press, 1992.

Jones, Jacqueline. *Soldiers of Light and Love: Northern Teachers and Georgia Blacks, 1865–1873.* Chapel Hill: Univ. of North Carolina Press, 1980.

Kantrowitz, Stephen. *Ben Tillman and the Reconstruction of White Supremacy.* Chapel Hill: Univ. of North Carolina Press, 2000.

Kern, Kathi. *Mrs. Stanton's Bible.* Ithaca: Cornell Univ. Press, 2001.

Kinzer, Donald L. *An Episode in Anti-Catholicism: The American Protective Association.* Seattle: Univ. of Washington Press, 1964.

Kleppner, Paul. *The Cross of Culture: A Social Analysis of Midwestern Politics, 1850–1900.* New York: Free Press, 1970.

———. *The Third Electoral System, 1853–1892: Parties, Voters, and Political Cultures.* Chapel Hill: Univ. of North Carolina Press, 1979.

Kobler, John. *Ardent Spirits: The Rise and Fall of Prohibition.* New York: Putnam, 1973.

Kuklick, Bruce. *Churchmen and Philosophers: From Jonathan Edwards to John Dewey.* New Haven, Conn.: Yale Univ. Press, 1985.

LaFeber, Walter. *The New Empire: An Interpretation of American Expansion, 1860–1898.* Ithaca: Cornell Univ. Press, 1963.

Larson, Orvin Prentiss. *American Infidel: Robert G. Ingersall, A Biography.* New York: Citadel Press, 1962.

Leach, William. *Land of Desire: Merchants, Power, and the Rise of a New American Culture.* New York: Vintage Books, 1993.

Levine, Bruce. *Half Slave and Half Free: The Roots of Civil War.* New York: Hill and Wang, 1992.

Lewis, Lloyd. *The Assassination of Lincoln: History and Myth.* 1929. Reprint, Lincoln: Univ. of Nebraska Press, 1994.

Linderman, Gerald F. *The Mirror of War: American Society and the Spanish-American War.* Ann Arbor: Univ. of Michigan Press, 1974.

Litwack, Leon F. *Been in the Storm So Long: The Aftermath of Slavery.* New York: Vintage Books, 1979.

———. *North of Slavery: The Negro in the Free States, 1790–1860.* Chicago: Univ. of Chicago Press, 1961.

———. *Trouble in Mind: Black Southerners in the Age of Jim Crow.* New York: Knopf, 1998.

Lively, Robert A. *Fiction Fights the Civil War: An Unfinished Chapter in the Literary History of the American People.* Chapel Hill: Univ. of North Carolina Press, 1957.

Loetscher, Lefferts A. *A Brief History of the Presbyterians.* Philadelphia: Westminster Press, 1983.

Logan, Rayford W. *The Betrayal of the Negro: From Rutherford B. Hayes to Woodrow Wilson.* New York: Collier Books, 1965.

———. *The Negro in American Life and Thought: The Nadir, 1877–1901.* New York: Dial Press, 1954.

Long, Kathryn Teresa. *The Revival of 1857–58: Interpreting an American Religious Awakening.* New York: Oxford Univ. Press, 1998.

Lowitt, Richard. *A Merchant Prince of the Nineteenth Century, William E. Dodge.* New York: Columbia Univ. Press, 1952.

Luker, Ralph E. *The Social Gospel in Black and White: American Racial Reform, 1885–1912.* Chapel Hill: Univ. of North Carolina Press, 1991.

MacKenzie, Kenneth M. *The Robe and the Sword: The Methodist Church and the Rise of American Imperialism.* Washington, D.C.: Public Affairs Press, 1961.

Malik, Kenan. *The Meaning of Race: Race, History and Culture in Western Society.* Washington Square, N.Y.: New York Univ. Press, 1996.

Marcus, Robert D. *Grand Old Party: Political Structure in the Gilded Age, 1880–1896.* New York: Oxford Univ. Press, 1971.

Marsden, George M. *The Evangelical Mind and the New School Presbyterian Experience: A Case Study of Thought and Theology in Nineteenth-Century America.* New York: Oxford Univ. Press, 1970.

———. *Fundamentalism and American Culture: The Shaping of Twentieth-Century Evangelicalism, 1870–1925.* New York: Oxford Univ. Press, 1980.

Martin, William. *A Prophet with Honor: The Billy Graham Story.* New York: Morrow, 1991.

Marty, Martin E. *Pilgrims in Their Own Land: 500 Years of Religion in America.* Boston: Little, Brown, 1984.

———. *Righteous Empire: The Protestant Experience in America.* New York: Dial Press, 1970.

Marty, Martin E., and R. Scott Appleby. *Religion, Ethnicity, and Self-Identity: Nations in Turmoil.* Hanover, N.H.: Univ. Press of New England, 1997.

May, Henry F. *Protestant Churches and Industrial America.* New York: Harper and Brothers, 1949.

May, Lary. *Screening out the Past: The Birth of Mass Culture and the Motion Picture Industry.* New York: Oxford Univ. Press, 1980.

McConnell, Stuart. *Glorious Contentment: The Grand Army of the Republic, 1865–1900.* Chapel Hill: Univ. of North Carolina Press, 1992.

McDaniel, Colleen. *Material Christianity: Religion and Popular Culture in America.* New Haven, Conn.: Yale Univ. Press, 1995.

McDougal, Walter A. *Promised Land, Crusader State: The American Encounter with the World since 1776.* Boston: Houghton Mifflin, 1997.

McFeely, William S. *Yankee Stepfather: General O. O. Howard and the Freedmen.* New Haven, Conn.: Yale Univ. Press, 1968.

McKitrick, Eric L., *Andrew Johnson and Reconstruction.* Chicago: Univ. of Chicago Press, 1960.

———, ed. *Andrew Johnson: A Profile.* New York: Hill and Wang, 1969.

McKivigan, John R. *The War against Proslavery Religion: Abolitionism and the Northern Churches, 1830–1865.* Ithaca: Cornell Univ. Press, 1984.

McLoughlin, William G. *The Meaning of Henry Ward Beecher: An Essay on the Shifting Values of Mid-Victorian America, 1840–1870.* New York: Knopf, 1970.

———. *Modern Revivalism: Charles Grandison Finney to Billy Graham.* New York: Ronald Press, 1959.

———. *Revivals, Awakenings, and Reform: An Essay on Religion and Social Change in America, 1607–1977.* Chicago: Univ. of Chicago Press, 1978.

McMillen, Sally G. *To Raise up the South: Sunday Schools in Black and White Churches, 1865–1915.* Baton Rouge: Louisiana State Univ. Press, 2001.

McMurry, Linda O. *To Keep the Waters Troubled: The Life of Ida B. Wells.* New York: Oxford Univ. Press, 1998.

McPherson, James M. *The Abolitionist Legacy: from Reconstruction to the NAACP.* 1975. Reprint, Princeton, N.J.: Princeton Univ. Press, 1995.

———. *Is Blood Thicker Than Water? Crises of Nationalism in the Modern World.* New York: Vintage Books, 1998.

———. *Ordeal by Fire: The Civil War and Reconstruction.* New York: McGraw-Hill, 1982.

———. *The Struggle for Equality: Abolitionists and the Negro in the Civil War and Reconstruction.* Princeton, N.J.: Princeton Univ. Press, 1964.

Mead, Sidney E. *The Lively Experiment: The Shaping of Christianity in America.* New York, Harper and Row, 1963.

———. *The Nation with the Soul of a Church.* New York: Harper and Row, 1975.

Melish, Joanne Pope. *Disowning Slavery: Gradual Emancipation and "Race" in New England, 1780–1860.* Ithaca: Cornell Univ. Press, 1998.

Miller, Randall M., Harry S. Stout, and Charles Reagan Wilson, eds. *Religion and the American Civil War.* New York: Oxford Univ. Press, 1998.

Miller, Stuart Creighton. "*Benevolent Assimilation*": *The American Conquest of the Philippines, 1899–1903*. New Haven, Conn.: Yale Univ. Press, 1982.

Mjagkij, Nina. *Light in the Darkness: African Americans and the YMCA, 1852–1946*. Lexington: Univ. Press of Kentucky, 1994.

Montgomery, William E. *Under Their Own Vine and Fig Tree: The African-American Church in the South, 1865–1900*. Baton Rouge: Louisiana State Univ. Press, 1993.

Moody, William R. *The Life of Dwight L. Moody: The Official Authorized Edition*. New York: Fleming H. Revell Company, 1900.

Moore, R. Laurence. *Selling God: American Religion in the Marketplace of Culture*. New York: Oxford Univ. Press, 1994,

Moorhead, James H. *American Apocalypse: Yankee Protestants and the Civil War, 1860–1869*. New Haven, Conn.: Yale Univ. Press, 1978.

Morris, Robert C. *Reading, 'Riting, and Reconstruction: The Education of Freedmen in the South, 1861–1870*. Chicago: Univ. of Chicago Press, 1981.

Morrow, Ralph E. *Northern Methodism and Reconstruction*. East Lansing: Michigan State Univ. Press, 1956.

Musicant, Ivan. *Empire by Default: The Spanish-American War and the Dawn of the American Century*. New York: H. Holt, 1998.

Nelson, Dana D. *National Manhood: Capitalist Citizenship and the Imagined Fraternity of White Men*. Durham: Duke Univ. Press, 1998.

Newman, Louise Michele. *White Women's Rights: The Racial Origins of Feminism in the United States*. New York: Oxford Univ. Press, 1999.

Nevins, Allan. *American Press Opinion: Washington to Coolidge: A Documentary Record of Editorial Leadership and Criticism, 1785–1927*, vol. 2. 1929. Reprint, Post Washington, N.Y.: Kennikat Press, 1969.

———. *War for the Union, 1864–1865: The Organized War to Victory*. New York: Konecky and Konecky, 1971.

Nicholson, Philip Yale. *Who Do We Think We Are?: Race and Nation in the Modern World*. Armonk, N.Y.: M. E. Sharpe, 1999.

Nieman, Donald G., ed. *The Freedmen's Bureau and Black Freedom* (New York: Garland Publishing, 1994.

Noll, Mark A. *A History of Christianity in the United States and Canada*. Grand Rapids, Michigan: Eerdmans, 1992.

O'Connor, Leo F. *Religion in the American Novel: The Search for Belief, 1860–1920*. New York: Univ. Press of America, 1984.

O'Leary, Cecilia Elizabeth. *To Die For: The Paradox of American Patriotism*. Princeton, N.J.: Princeton Univ. Press, 1999.

Olsen, Otto H. *Carpetbagger's Crusade: The Life of Albion Winegar Tourgée*. Baltimore: Johns Hopkins Univ. Press, 1965.

Omi, Michael, and Howard Winant. *Racial Formation in the United States: From the 1960s to the 1980s.* New York: Routledge and Kegan Paul, 1986.

Orsi, Robert A. *The Madonna of 115th Street: Faith and Community in Italian Harlem, 1880–1950.* New Haven, Conn.: Yale Univ. Press, 1985.

Painter, Nell Irvin. *Standing at Armageddon: The United States, 1877–1919.* New York: Norton, 1987.

Patterson, Orlando. *Rituals of Blood: Consequences of Slavery in Two American Centuries.* Washington, D.C.: Civitas Counterpoint, 1998.

Pérez, Louis A. *The War of 1898: The United States and Cuba in History and Historiography.* Chapel Hill: Univ. of North Carolina Press, 1998.

Perlmatter, Philip. *Divided We Fall: A History of Ethnic, Religious, and Racial Prejudice in America.* Ames: Iowa State Univ. Press, 1992.

Perman, Michael. *Emancipation and Reconstruction, 1862–1879.* Arlington Heights, Ill.: Harlan Davidson, 1987.

———. *Reunion without Compromise: The South and Reconstruction: 1865–1868.* Cambridge, U.K.: Cambridge Univ. Press, 1973.

———. *Road to Redemption: Southern Politics, 1869–1879.* Chapel Hill: Univ. of North Carolina Press, 1984.

———. *Struggle for Mastery: Disfranchisement in the South, 1888–1908.* Chapel Hill: Univ. of North Carolina Press, 2001.

Peterson, Merrill D. *Lincoln in the American Mind.* New York: Oxford Univ. Press, 1994.

Polakoff, Keith Ian. *The Politics of Inertia: The Election of 1876 and the End of Reconstruction.* Baton Rouge: Louisiana State Univ. Press, 1973.

Pollock, J. C. *Moody: A Biographical Portrait of the Pacesetter in Modern Mass Evangelism.* New York: Macmillan, 1963.

Poole, W. Scott. *Never Surrender: Confederate Memory and Conservatism in the South Carolina Upcountry.* Athens: Univ. of Georgia Press, 2003.

Pratt, Julius W. *Expansionists of 1898: The Acquisition of Hawaii and the Spanish Islands.* 1936. Reprint, Gloucester, Mass.: Peter Smith, 1959.

Pratt, Mary Louise. *Imperial Eyes: Travel Writing and Transculturation.* New York: Routledge, 1992.

Preston, Diana. *The Boxer Rebellion: The Dramatic Story of China's War on Foreigners that Shook the World in the Summer of 1900* (New York: Berkley Books, 2000).

Quill, Michael J. *Prelude to the Radicals: The North and Reconstruction During 1865.* Washington, D.C.: Univ. Press of America, 1980.

Rabe, Valentin H. *The Home Base of American China Missions, 1880–1920.* Cambridge, Mass.: Harvard Univ. Press, 1978.

Rabinowitz, Howard N. *Race Relations in the Urban South, 1865–1890.* New York: Oxford Univ. Press, 1978.

Rable, George C. *But There Was No Peace: The Role of Violence in the Politics of Reconstruction.* Athens: Univ. of Georgia Press, 1984.

Raboteau, Albert J. *Slave Religion: The "Invisible Institution" in the Antebellum South.* New York: Oxford Univ. Press, 1978.

Range, Willard. *The Rise and Progress of Negro Colleges in Georgia, 1865–1949.* Athens: Univ. of Georgia Press, 1951.

Reimes, David M. *White Protestantism and the Negro.* New York: Oxford Univ. Press, 1965.

Richardson, Heather Cox. *The Death of Reconstruction: Race, Labor, and Politics in the Post–Civil War North, 1865–1901.* Cambridge, Mass.: Harvard Univ. Press, 2001.

Richardson, Joe M. *Christian Reconstruction: The American Missionary Association and Southern Blacks, 1861–1890.* Athens: Univ. of Georgia Press, 1986.

———. *The Negro in the Reconstruction of Florida, 1865–1877.* Tallahassee: Florida State Univ. Press, 1965.

Riddleberger, Patrick W. *1866: The Critical Year Revisited.* Carbondale: Southern Illinois Univ. Press, 1979.

Robertson, Darrel M. *The Chicago Revival, 1876: Society and Revivalism in a Nineteenth-Century City.* Metuchen, N.J.: Scarecrow Press, 1989.

Rodney, Walter. *A History of the Guyanese Working People, 1881–1905.* Baltimore: Johns Hopkins Univ. Press, 1981.

Roediger, David R. *The Wages of Whiteness: Race and the Making of the American Working Class.* London: Verso, 1991.

Rogin, Michael Paul. *Ronald Reagan, the Movie, and Other Episodes in Political Demonology.* Berkeley: Univ. of California Press, 1987.

Rose, Willie Lee. *Rehearsal for Reconstruction: The Port Royal Experiment.* Indianapolis: Bobbs-Merrill, 1964.

Rosenberg, Charles E. *The Cholera Years: The United States in 1832, 1849, and 1866.* Chicago: Univ. of Chicago Press, 1962.

Rowe, Anne. *The Enchanted Country: Northern Writers in the South, 1865–1910.* Baton Rouge: Louisiana State Univ. Press, 1978.

Russett, Cynthia Eagle. *Sexual Science: The Victorian Construction of Womanhood.* Cambridge, Mass.: Harvard Univ. Press, 1989.

Satter, Beryl. *Each Mind a Kingdom: American Women, Sexual Purity, and the New Thought Movement, 1875–1920.* Berkeley: Univ. of California Press, 1999.

Savitt, Todd L., and James Harvey Young, eds. *Disease and Distinctiveness in the American South.* Knoxville: Univ. of Tennessee Press, 1988.

Sawrey, Robert D. *Dubious Victory: The Reconstruction Debate in Ohio.* Lexington: Univ. Press of Kentucky, 1992.

Saxton, Alexander. *The Rise and Fall of the White Republic: Class Politics and Mass Culture in Nineteenth-Century America.* London: Verso, 1990.

Schechter, Patricia A. *Ida B. Wells-Barnett and American Reform, 1880–1930.* Chapel Hill: Univ. of North Carolina Press, 2001.

Schirmer, Daniel B. *Republic or Empire: American Resistance to the Philippine War.* Cambridge, Mass.: Schenkman, 1972.

Schlesinger, Arthur M., Sr. *A Critical Period in American Religion, 1875–1900.* Philadelphia: Fortress Press, 1967.

Schwartz, Barry. *Abraham Lincoln and the Forge of National Memory.* Chicago: Univ. of Chicago Press, 2000.

Scott, Anne Firor. *The Southern Lady: From Pedestal to Politics, 1830–1930.* Chicago: Univ. of Chicago Press, 1970.

Scott, Donald M. *From Office to Profession: The New England Ministry, 1750–1850.* Philadelphia: Univ. of Pennsylvania Press, 1978.

Scott, Rebecca J. *Slave Emancipation in Cuba: The Transition to Free Labor, 1860–1899.* Princeton, N.J.: Princeton Univ. Press, 1985.

Scott, Rebecca J., Seymour Drescher, Hebe Maria Mattos De Castro, George Reid Andrews, Robert M. Levine, eds. *The Abolition of Slavery and the Aftermath of Emancipation in Brazil.* Durham: Duke Univ. Press, 1988.

Seitz, Don C. *Horace Greeley: Founder of the New York Tribune.* Indianapolis: The Bobbs-Merrill Company, 1926.

Selleck, Linda B. *Gentle Invaders: Quaker Women Educators and Racial Issues during the Civil War and Reconstruction.* Richmond, Va.: Friends United Press, 1995.

Shattuck, Gardiner H., Jr. *Episcopalians and Race: Civil War to Civil Rights.* Lexington: Univ. Press of Kentucky, 2000.

———. *A Shield and Hiding Place: The Religious Life of the Civil War Armies.* Macon, Ga.: Mercer Univ. Press, 1987.

Shaw, Stephanie J. *What a Woman Ought to Be and Do: Black Professional Women Workers during the Jim Crow Era.* Chicago: Univ. of Chicago Press, 1996.

Silber, Nina. *The Romance of Reunion: Northerners and the South, 1865–1900.* Chapel Hill: Univ. of North Carolina Press, 1993.

Silbey, Joel H. *A Respectable Minority: The Democratic Party in the Civil War Era, 1860–1868.* New York: Norton, 1977.

Sizer, Lyde Cullen. *The Political Work of Northern Women Writers and the Civil War, 1850–1872.* Chapel Hill: Univ. of North Carolina Press, 2000.

Smedley, Katherine. *Martha Schofield and the Re-Education of the South, 1839–1916.* Lewiston/Queenston: Edwin Mellen Press, 1987.

Smith, Angel, and Emma Dávila-Cox, eds. *The Crisis of 1898: Colonial Redistribution and Nationalist Mobilization.* New York: St. Martin's Press, 1999.

Smith, Anthony D. *National Identity.* Reno: Univ. of Nevada Press, 1991.

———. *Nationalism and Modernism: A Critical Survey of Recent Theories of Nations and Nationalism.* New York: Routledge, 1998.

Smith, Carl S. *Urban Disorder and the Shape of Belief: The Great Chicago Fire, the Haymarket Bomb, and the Model Town of Pullman.* Chicago: Univ. of Chicago Press, 1995.

Smith, H. Shelton. *In His Image, But . . . Racism in Southern Religion, 1780–1910.* Durham: Duke Univ. Press, 1972.

Smith, Page. *Trial by Fire: A People's History of the Civil War and Reconstruction.* New York: Penguin Books, 1990.

Smith, Roger M. *Civic Ideals: Conflicting Visions of Citizenship in U.S. History.* New Haven, Conn.: Yale Univ. Press, 1997.

Smith, Timothy L. *Revivalism and Social Reform: American Protestantism on the Eve of the Civil War.* 1957. Reprint, Baltimore: Johns Hopkins Univ. Press, 1980.

Snay, Mitchell. *Gospel of Disunion: Religion and Separatism in the Antebellum South.* New York: Cambridge Univ. Press, 1993.

Spain, Rufus B. *At Ease in Zion: A Social History of Southern Baptists, 1865–1900.* Nashville: Vanderbilt Univ. Press, 1961.

Stampp, Kenneth M. *The Era of Reconstruction, 1865–1877.* New York: Knopf, 1965.

Stanton, William. *The Leopard's Spots: Scientific Attitudes toward Race in America, 1815–1859.* Chicago: Univ. of Chicago Press, 1960.

Stauffer, John. *The Black Hearts of Men: Radical Abolitionists and the Transformation of Race.* Cambridge, Mass.: Harvard Univ. Press, 2002.

Sterling, Dorothy. *Captain of the Planter: The Story of Robert Smalls.* Garden City, N.Y.: Doubleday, 1958.

Stowell, Daniel W. *Rebuilding Zion: The Religious Reconstruction of the South, 1863–1877.* New York: Oxford Univ. Press, 1998.

Strachey, Ray. *Frances Willard: Her Life and Work.* New York: Fleming H. Revell Company, 1913.

Stuckey, Sterling. *Slave Culture: Nationalist Theory and the Foundations of Black America.* New York: Oxford Univ. Press, 1987.

Summers, Mark Wahlgren. *The Era of Good Stealings.* New York: Oxford Univ. Press, 1993.

———. *The Gilded Age, or, The Hazard of New Functions.* Upper Saddle River, N.J.: Prentice Hall, 1997.

———. *Railroads, Reconstruction, and the Gospel of Prosperity: Aid under the Radical Republicans, 1865–1877.* Princeton, N.J.: Princeton Univ. Press, 1984.

Sweet, William Warren. *Methodism in American History.* 1953. Reprint, Nashville: Abingdon Press, 1961.

Swierenga, Robert P., ed. *Beyond the Civil War Synthesis: Political Essays of the Civil War Era.* Westport, Conn.: Greenwood Press, 1975.

Swint, Henry Lee. *The Northern Teacher in the South, 1862–1870.* Nashville: Vanderbilt Univ. Press, 1941.

Takaki, Ronald T. *Iron Cages: Race and Culture in Nineteenth-Century America.* New York: Knopf, 1979.

Taylor, William Robert. *Cavalier and Yankee: The Old South and American National Character.* 1961. Reprint, Cambridge, Mass.: Harvard Univ. Press, 1979.

Tebeau, Charlton W. *A History of Florida.* Coral Gables, Fla.: Univ. of Miami Press, 1971.

Thomas, John L. *Alternative America: Henry George, Edward Bellamy, Henry Demarest Lloyd and the Adversary Tradition.* Cambridge, Mass.: Belknap Press of Harvard Univ. Press, 1983.

Thompson, Ernest Trice. *Presbyterians in the South.* Vol. 2, *1861–1890.* Richmond, Va.: John Knox Press, 1973.

Trask, David F. *The War with Spain in 1898.* New York: Collier Macmillan, 1981.

Traxel, David. *1898: The Birth of the American Century.* New York: Knopf, 1998.

Trefousse, Hans L. *Andrew Johnson: A Biography.* New York: Norton, 1989.

———. *The Radical Republicans: Lincoln's Vanguard for Racial Justice.* New York: Knopf, 1969.

Trelease, Allen W. *White Terror: The Ku Klux Klan Conspiracy and Southern Reconstruction.* 1971. Reprint, Baton Rouge: Louisiana State Univ. Press, 1995.

Tunnell, Ted. *Edge of the Sword: The Ordeal of Carpetbagger Marshall H. Twitchell in the Civil War and Reconstruction.* Baton Rouge: Louisiana State Univ. Press, 2001.

Turner, James. *Without God, Without Creed: The Origins of Unbelief in America.* Baltimore: Johns Hopkins Univ. Press, 1985.

Turner, Thomas Reed, *Beware the People Weeping: Public Opinion and the Assassination of Abraham Lincoln.* Baton Rouge: Louisiana State Univ. Press, 1982.

Tuveson, Ernest Lee. *Redeemer Nation: The Idea of America's Millennial Role.* Chicago: Univ. of Chicago Press, 1968.

Tyrrell, Ian. *Woman's World, Woman's Empire: The Woman's Christian Temperance Union in International Perspective, 1880–1930.* Chapel Hill: Univ. of North Carolina Press, 1991.

Uya, Okon Edet. *From Slavery to Public Service: Robert Smalls, 1839–1915.* New York, Oxford Univ. Press, 1971.

Vander Velde, Lewis G. *The Presbyterian Churches and the Federal Union, 1861–1869.* Cambridge, Mass.: Harvard Univ. Press, 1932.

Varg, Paul A. *Missionaries, Chinese, and Diplomats: The American Protestant Missionary Movement in China, 1890–1952.* Princeton, N.J.: Princeton Univ. Press, 1958.

Von Frank, Albert J. *The Trials of Anthony Burns: Freedom and Slavery in Emerson's Boston.* Cambridge, Mass.: Harvard Univ. Press, 1999.

Walker, Clarence E. *A Rock in a Weary Land: The African Methodist Episcopal Church during the Civil War and Reconstruction.* Baton Rouge: Louisiana State Univ. Press, 1982.

Wallace, Lew. *The Rhetoric of Anti-Catholicism: The American Protective Association, 1887–1911.* New York: Garland Publishing, 1990.

Waller, Altina L. *Reverend Beecher and Mrs. Tilton: Sex and Class in Victorian America.* Amherst: Univ. of Massachusetts Press, 1982.

Washington, James M. *Frustrated Fellowship: The Baptist Quest for Social Power.* Macon, Ga.: Mercer Univ. Press, 1986.

Webber, F. R. *A History of Preaching in Britain and America: Including the Biographies of Many Princes of the Pulpit and the Men Who Influenced Them, Part Three.* Milwaukee: Northwestern Publishing House, 1957.

Weber, Max. *The Protestant Ethic and the Spirit of Capitalism.* 1930. Reprint (with an introduction by Randall Collins), Los Angeles: Roxbury, 1996.

Weisberger, Bernard A. *They Gathered at the River; The Story of the Great Revivalists and their Impact upon Religion in America.* Boston: Little, Brown, 1958.

Welch, Richard E., Jr. *Response to Imperialism: The United States and the Philippine-American War, 1899–1902.* Chapel Hill: Univ. of North Carolina Press, 1979.

Weston, Rubin Frances. *Racism in U.S. Imperialism: The Influence of Racial Assumptions on American Foreign Policy, 1893–1946.* Columbia: Univ. of South Carolina Press, 1972.

Wharton, Vernon Lane. *The Negro in Mississippi, 1865–1890.* 1947. Reprint, New York: Harper and Row, 1965.

Wheeler, Marjorie Spruill. *New Women of the New South: The Leaders of the Woman Suffrage Movement in the Southern States.* New York: Oxford Univ. Press, 1993.

Whitaker, Walter. *Centennial History of Alamance County, 1849–1949.* Charlotte: Dowd Press, 1949.

Whites, LeeAnn. *The Civil War as a Crisis in Gender: Augusta, Georgia, 1860–1890.* Athens: Univ. of Georgia Press, 1995.

Wilkerson, Marcus Manley. *Public Opinion and the Spanish-American War: A Study in War Propaganda.* New York, Russell and Russell, 1967.

Williams, Eric. *The Negro in the Caribbean.* Washington: Associates in Negro Folk Education, 1942.

Williams, Linda M., and Victoria L. Banyard, eds. *Trauma and Memory.* London: Sage Publications, 1999.

Williamson, Joel. *The Crucible of Race: Black/White Relations in the American South since Emancipation.* New York: Oxford Univ. Press, 1984.

Wilson, Charles Reagan. *Baptized in Blood: The Religion of the Lost Cause, 1865–1920.* Athens: Univ. of Georgia Press, 1980.

Wilson, Edmund. *Patriotic Gore: Studies in the Literature of the American Civil War.* New York: Oxford Univ. Press, 1962.

Wilson, Forrest. *Crusader in Crinoline: The Life of Harriet Beecher Stowe.* Philadelphia: J. B. Lippincott, 1941.

Wilson, James Harrison, *Under the Old Flag: Recollections of Military Operations in the War for the Union, the Spanish War, the Boxer Rebellion, etc.* New York: D. Appleton and Company, 1912.

Wilson, John Frederick. *Public Religion in American Culture.* Philadelphia: Temple Univ. Press, 1979.

Wink, Amy L. *She Left Nothing in Particular: The Autobiographical Legacy of Nineteenth-Century Women's Diaries.* Knoxville: Univ. Press of Tennessee, 2001.

Winter, Jay. *Sites of Memory, Sites of Mourning: The Great War in European Cultural History.* Cambridge, U.K.: Cambridge Univ. Press, 1995.

Wood, Forrest G. *The Arrogance of Faith: Christianity and Race in America from the Colonial Era to the Twentieth Century.* Boston: Northeastern Univ. Press, 1990.

———. *Black Scare: The Racist Response to Emancipation and Reconstruction.* Berkeley: Univ. of California Press, 1968.

Woodward, C. Vann. *Origins of the New South, 1877–1913.* 1951. Reprint, Baton Rouge: Louisiana State Univ. Press, 1971.

———. *Reunion and Reaction: The Compromise of 1877 and the End of Reconstruction.* Boston: Little, Brown, 1966.

———. *The Strange Career of Jim Crow.* 1955. Reprint, New York: Oxford Univ. Press, 1974.

Wyatt-Brown, Bertram. *Yankee Saints and Southern Sinners.* Baton Rouge: Louisiana State Univ. Press, 1985.

Zelinksy, Wilbur. *Nation into State: The Shifting Symbolic Foundations of American Nationalism.* Chapel Hill: Univ. of North Carolina Press, 1988.

Index

Abbott, Lyman, 46

abolitionists, 1, 5, 41, 113, 121, 125, 129, 175, 182, 241

Acklen, Joseph, 166

Acts of the Apostles, 45, 58–59

Adam: as white, 43

Adams, M. Pardee, 227

Adams, Samuel, 4

Advice to Freedmen (Brinckerhoff), 56

Africa, 202, 210, 212, 220, 225

African Americans: advice literature for, 56–57; in Civil War, 5, 42, 46–48, 51, 57, 68–69, 75, 109; class issues within, 54, 82, 84; depictions of, 5, 11–12, 15, 43, 61–78, 92, 96–97, 100–104, 116, 168–69, 174, 195–96, 199–202, 236–37; education of, 4, 46, 51–86, 99–100, 102–3, 109, 175–77, 180, 206, 214, 217, 247; and holidays, 48–49, 74–75, 150; and imperialism, 213–14, 240–43; medical neglect of, 148, 170–71; on northern Protestants, 22–23, 70, 75–76, 84–86, 119, 124, 142–44; religious beliefs of, 62, 65–67, 248–49; responses to Abraham Lincoln's assassination, 21, 51; responses to Dwight Lyman Moody, 119, 124, 141–44, 204; on sectional reconciliation, 17–19, 30, 86, 90, 95–96, 108–11, 117–19, 142–43, 150, 171, 206–7, 241–42, 247–49; on segregation, 3, 18, 142–44, 203–8, 244, 247–49; and sexuality with whites, 73–75, 106; status of, 1–4, 32, 38–50, 53, 55, 59, 88, 90, 92, 110, 116, 126, 150, 173, 232, 244–45, 264n20; violence against, 2–3, 17–18, 76, 79–82, 88, 102, 108–9, 125–26, 132, 135–36, 143, 179, 199, 204–7, 211, 218, 246, 249; and Woman's Christian Temperance Union, 178–79, 203–8; and yellow fever, 148, 167–72

African Methodist Episcopal Church, 21, 48, 51, 55, 63, 76–77, 108, 142–43, 150, 248

African Methodist Episcopal Zion Church, 51

Agassiz, Louis, 43

Agnew, Samuel, 153

Ahlstrom, Sidney, 9, 126, 215

Alabama Baptist, 198

Alcott, S. M., 112–13

Allen, Horace N., 221

Alvord, John W., 56, 58–59, 65, 79

Ament, W. S., 229

American Baptist Home Mission Society, 55, 106–7

American Bible Society, 105

American Board of Foreign Missions, 229

American Freedmen's Union Commission, 52, 55, 106

American Historical Association, 10–11

American Missionary, 81, 169, 203, 218

American Missionary Association, 51, 55, 56, 59, 73, 75, 84–85, 107–8, 169

American Protective Association, 199

American Tract Society, 56, 57

Amherst College, 215

Amonson, Louis, 234

Anderson, Benedict, 15

Anderson, D. W., 48

Andover Theological Seminary, 25–26

Andrew, John, 41, 46

Andrews, Sidney, 29, 170

angels: images of, 1, 28, 115, 209

antebellum era, 4, 7, 43, 49, 90, 101, 104, 138, 182

Anthony, Susan B., 178

anti-imperialism, 213–14, 229–30, 237–43

Anti-Imperialist League, 241

Argonaut, 223

Argyll, Duchess of, 99

"Ariel," 93

Arnold, Benedict: images of, 95

Asia, 210, 212, 220, 225

"Athena Hygeia," 173

Atkins, Gaius Glenn, 128, 216

Atlanta Constitution, 106, 140

Atlanta University, 82, 107

Atlantic Monthly, 75, 97, 98, 100

Augusta Constitutionalist, 140

Australia, 210

Bailey, Hannah, 239

Bain, George, 198

Bancroft, George, 127

Banneker, Benjamin, 57

Baptist Courier, 228

Baptists, 13, 26, 34, 40, 51, 55, 78–79, 105–7,
    129, 131, 140, 165–66, 228

"Battle Hymn of the Republic" (Howe), 19, 134

Battles and Leaders of the Civil War, 130

Bederman, Gail, 204

Beecher, Edward, 94–95, 99

Beecher, Henry Ward, 13–14, 30, 37–38, 43, 87–
    88, 91–100, 103–4, 108, 111, 116, 123–24, 127,
    129, 135–37, 146–47, 171, 247

Beecher, Lyman, 91

Been in the Storm So Long (Litwack), 75

Bellamy, Edward, 17, 244–46

"beloved community," 86

Benade, W. H., 41

Bengal, 210

Berle, A. A., 229

Berlin Africa Conference of 1884, 220

Beveridge, Albert, 16, 213, 230, 233, 237–38

Bible View of Slavery (Hopkins), 35

Bird, Arthur, 17, 244–46

Birth of a Nation (Griffith), 2, 236

Bishop, Richard, 158

"black codes," 32, 63

black liberation theology, 67

Black Reconstruction in America (Du Bois), 19

Blair, Henry, 198

Bledsoe, Albert Taylor, 130–31

Blight, David, 8

"Blue and the Gray, The," (Finch), 112, 189–90

Boardman, George Dana, 40

Boardman, Henry, 33

Booth, John Wilkes, 21, 31, 246

Bordin, Ruth, 177

Boston Daily Globe, 128

Boston Earthquake, 107

Boston Evening Transcript, 128

Boston Herald, 229

Boston Sunday Times, 132, 134–35

Botome, Elizabeth, 54, 67, 75

Boxer Rebellion, 225–26, 229

Brazil, 217, 225

Brewer, David J., 10

Brinckerhoff, Isaac, 56

Britain, 10, 123–24, 143, 204, 206, 210–11,
    228, 245

British Guiana, 83

Brooks, Phillips, 127, 129

Brooks-Higginbotham, Evelyn, 83–84

Brown, Benjamin Gratz, 114

Brown, Helen, 56

Brown, John, 95, 103

Bryan, William Jennings, 232, 243

Bryce, James, 10

Buck, Paul, 8, 113

Bulgaria, 210

Bureau of Refugees, Freedmen, and Abandoned
    Lands, The (Freedmen's Bureau), 56, 58–59,
    61, 63, 65, 79, 86, 94, 108, 122

Burns, Anthony, 121

"businessmen's revival," 121, 131–32. *See also*
    revivals

Butler, Benjamin, 29

Butler, J. G., 30, 46

Calhoun, John C., 1

Call, The, 226

Camus, Albert, 53

Canada, 210

Capers, Will, 64–65

Carey, Isaac, 27

Cargill, J. M., 171

Carnegie, Andrew, 230

Carroll, Charles, 223, 248

Catholicism, 9, 16, 146, 157, 198–200, 207, 217, 224

centennial celebrations, 137

Central Presbyterian, 105

Century Magazine, 130, 220

Chamberlain, Daniel, 206

Chamberlain, George W., 217

Chapin, E. H., 117

Chapin, Sallie F., 191, 194–95, 198, 200–201

Charlottesville Chronicle, 79–80

Chase, Lucy, 62, 64, 65, 67–69, 75, 78, 81, 85

Chase, Salmon, 113

Chase, Sarah, 62, 67–69, 75, 78, 81

Cheever, George, 41–42

Cheever, Henry, 42

Chesnut, Mary, 28

Chicago Fire, 107, 123, 151

Chicago Herald, 128

Chicago Tribune, 125, 130

Child, Lydia Marie, 57–58, 75

Chile, 210, 224

China, 210, 215, 219

Chinese Crisis from Within, The, 226

Christian Advocate and Journal, 32, 41–42, 46, 157, 172, 184, 194

Christian Index, 228

"Christian Nation," 4, 10, 18, 206–7, 212, 220, 231, 233, 248–49

Christian Recorder, 21, 48, 63, 141, 171, 242

Christian Statesman, 194

Christian Union, 100, 198

Christmas, 70, 74–75

Church of Scotland, 51

Church of the Holy Trinity v. The United States (1892), 10

Churches. *See* Protestants; *and specific denominations*

Cincinnati Gazette, 24

Cincinnati Star, 155

civil rights bills, 88

Civil Rights movement, 86

civil service reform, 113

Civil War, 1–2, 7, 11, 23, 51, 70, 104, 111, 113, 120, 122, 138, 142, 148–49, 160, 165, 176, 180, 195, 214; African Americans in, 2, 5, 41–42, 46–48, 51, 57, 68–69, 75; chaplains in, 122, 146; in historical memory, 8, 14, 97–98, 109, 111–12, 123, 127, 129–30, 132–37, 161–62, 166, 173, 179, 185, 187–90, 197–200, 228, 234, 241

Clark University, 82

Clarke, Alida, 72

Clarke, Frances E., 219, 225

Clarke, James Freeman, 46

class issues, 9, 13, 54, 82, 84, 123–24, 134, 199, 211, 217

Cleveland Gazette, 206, 241

Cleveland Leader, 128

"Cleveland letter" (Beecher, Henry Ward), 93–94, 99

Cole, Chester C., 47

Collyer, Robert, 122

colonial era, 4

Columbia Seminary, 139

Compromise of 1877, 149–50

Cone, James, 67

Congregational Home Missionary Society, 217

Congregationalism, 25, 31–32, 41, 51, 115, 121, 129, 217

Congregationalist, 81, 92, 229

Congress, 23–24, 38, 42, 52, 56, 88–89, 125, 172, 200–201, 245, 248

Constitution, 3, 56, 88, 116

contact theory, 60, 63–76, 85–86

Corliss, Alonzo B., 79

Corliss Engine, 137

Cotton States, The (Nordhoff), 126

Crane, C. B., 26, 42

Crane, Steven, 135

Creegan, Charles, 218–19

Crummell, Alexander, 18, 108, 110

Crusade of 1873, 179–80, 185, 194. *See also*
Woman's Christian Temperance Union
Cuba, 16, 208, 212, 225–44. *See also* War of 1898
currency, 196
"curse of Canaan," 43, 131–32. *See also* racism:
and religion
Cuyler, Theodore, 239

Dabney, Robert Lewis, 106
Darwin, Charles, 102, 222
"David and Goliath," 116–17
Davis, Jefferson, 1, 28–29, 34, 98, 131, 153
Davis, Jefferson, Jr., 153
Davis, Mrs. Jefferson, 191
Dawson, L. O., 216
Day, William Howard, 48
de Hauranne, Ernest Duvergier, 10
de Trobriand, Philippe R., 125–26
"de Trobriand affair," 125–26
Decoration Day, 141, 191
Deming, Henry, 40, 44
Democrats, 23, 30, 34, 37, 39, 47, 71, 74, 93–94,
113–15, 125, 131, 140, 149, 183, 186, 197–98.
See also politics
Denby, Charles, 221
Denmark, 210
denominations. *See* Protestants; *and specific*
denominations
depressions, economic, 107, 124, 128, 137,
149, 211
Detroit Evening News, 151
Dewey, George, 212, 244
Dixon, A. A., 171
Dixon, Thomas, Jr., 2, 16, 213, 230, 236–37
"Do Everything" policy, 181, 199, 209. *See also*
Woman's Christian Temperance Union
Dodge, William E., 127, 129
Douglas, Mary, 136
Douglass, Frederick, 18, 21–23, 27, 49, 57, 90,
95–96, 108, 117–18, 142–43, 150, 206–7, 249
Dred Scott v. Sanford (1857), 4, 45
Dromgoole, J. P., 162

Drummond, Henry, 130
Du Bois, W. E. B., 2–3, 18–19, 52, 59–60, 84,
110, 143, 243–44, 248–49, 262–63n5
Dunbar, Paul Laurence, 24
Dunning, William, 8
Durkheim, Emile, 66
Dutch Reformed Church, 51
Dutton, Samuel, 46

Easter, 20, 24–25
Easton-Sentinel, 27
economic depressions. *See* depressions,
economic
Ecumenical Conference on Foreign Mis-
sions, 231
Eddy, Richard, 41, 44
education, of African Americans, 4, 12, 46, 51–
86, 99–100, 102–3, 109, 175–77, 180, 206,
214, 217, 247, 264n29
Edwards, Laura F., 8
Edwards, Rebecca, 178, 196
Edwards, Richard, 43
elections, presidential, 59, 74, 89, 113–18, 135,
149–50, 156, 213–14, 232
Eliot, George, 100
Ellis, E. John, 166
Ellis, John, 172
emancipation, 2, 4, 38, 40, 57, 101–2, 116
Emancipation Proclamation, 40, 57, 74–75
Emory University, 188
Engels, Friedrich, 123
England. *See* Britain
Enlightenment, the, 45
Epidemic of 1878, The, 159
Epidemics. *See* yellow fever
Episcopal Church, 11–12, 34–37, 70, 94, 105,
111, 129, 137
Epstein, Barbara, 178
Equality: A Novel (Bellamy), 17, 246
Eustis, James, 172
evolution, 102. *See also* science, racism in
existentialism, 53

Fahs, Alice, 111, 132–33
Federal Elections Bill (Force Bill), 201
Federal Writers' Project, 128
Felton, Rebecca, 240
Fifteenth Amendment, 2–3, 56, 88, 90, 104, 114, 201
Finch, Frances Miles, 112, 118, 189–90
Findlay, James, 126
Finney, Charles Grandison, 56, 175
Fish, Hamilton, 126
Fisk University, 82, 85, 143
Fitzmaurice, John W., 234–35
Florida, 98–104, 247. *See also* tourism
Flynt, J. Wayne, 78
Foner, Eric, 8
Fool's Errand, A (Tourgée), 77, 192
Ford's Theatre, 23, 25
Forman, Henry, 223
Fort Sumter, 176
Forten, Charlotte, 62, 67, 75, 77, 87, 110
Foster, Gaines, 8, 177–78
Foster, Judith, 184
Foster, Sarah Jane, 62, 64, 67–68, 70, 72–73, 80
Fourteenth Amendment, 3, 56, 88, 104, 114
Fourth of July, 48–49, 74–75, 150, 215
Fowler, Henry, 44
France, 210, 244
Frank, Henry, 224
Frank Leslie's Illustrated Newspaper, 28–29, 154–57, 159–61, 170
Franklin, John Hope, 8
Fredrickson, George, 43
Free Methodist Church, 51
Freedman, 57
Freedman's Third Reader, 57–58
Freedmen's Book (Child), 57–58, 75
Freedmen's Bureau. *See* Bureau of Refugees, Freedmen, and Abandoned Lands, The
Freewill Baptist Church, 64
"Frontier." *See* West, the
Fugitive Slave Act, 121
funerals, 20–21, 25–26, 66, 117, 209

Gannett, William, 66, 75
Garfield, James, 126, 127
Garland, A. H., 166
Garrett Biblical Institute, 25
Garrison, William Lloyd, 125–26
Genesis, Book of, 43
genocide, 148, 168
Georgian, 246
Germany, 210, 244
Giddings, Joshua E., 241
Giles, J. L., 1–3, 17, 19, 246, 249
Gilmore, Glenda, 84, 288n14
Godkin, E. L., 126, 132, 229
Goen, C. C., 138
gold standard, 196
Goldberg, Michael, 196
Golden Age, 115
Good Friday, 20
Goode, John, 166
Goodnow, Josephine, 218–19
Goodspeed, E. J., 137
Gordon, Anna, 194, 209
gospel hymns. *See* hymns
Gospel in All Lands, 218
Gracey, J. T., 219, 222
Graham, Billy, 141
Grant, Ulysses S., 1, 108, 113, 115–17, 122, 125–27
Graves, John Temple, 246
Great Awakening. *See* revivals
Great Britain. *See* Britain
Great Depression, 128
Great Missionaries of the Church (Goodnow), 218–19
Great South, The (King), 126
Greeley, Horace, 1, 13, 96, 99, 113–18, 124, 137
Greenback Party, 186
Grey, William H., 49
Griffith, D. W., 2, 19, 236
Grimké, Francis, 110
Guam, 208, 212

Guiness, Lucy E., 222, 224
Guiteau, Charles, 127

Haiti, 83, 244
Hale, Grace Elizabeth, 7
Hall, Edward Payson, 80
Hamilton, J. Taylor, 223
Hancock, Cornelia, 61–62, 71, 78, 81
Hannibal Morning Journal, 189
Harper, Frances E. W., 18, 57, 90, 109, 203–4, 249
Harper's New Monthly Magazine, 111, 154, 161
Harper's Weekly, 29, 46–47, 87, 128, 159, 173
Harris, C. R., 104
Harris, I. G., 166, 172
Harrison, Benjamin, 220
Haven, Gilbert, 40–41, 46, 61, 73–74
Haviland, Laura, 64, 68, 75
Hawaii, 210
Hawks, Esther, 51–52, 62, 68–70, 73–75, 77, 102
Hawley, Bostwick, 38
Hayes, Rutherford B., 149–50, 157, 172
Haymarket Tragedy, 199
Hayne, Paul Hamilton, 130, 153, 165, 191
Haywood, Atticus Green, 188–89, 206
Heathen Woman's Friend, 218
Higginson, Thomas Wentworth, 75
Hoar, George F., 238
"Hold the Fort," 134–35
holidays, *See* rituals, religious; *and specific days*
Holland, Elihu, 45
Holmes, Oliver Wendell, Sr., 153
Homestead Strike, 199
Hopkins, John H., 34–36, 39, 258n60
Horsman, Reginald, 43
Hose, Sam, 240
House, John, 166
Howard, John, 155
Howard, Oliver Otis, 56, 122
Howard University, 82
Howards, the, 155, 163, 169
Howe, Julia Ward, 19, 134

Howells, William Dean, 19, 97
Hunt, Mary, 200
hymns, 134, 182, 200

Iceland, 210
immigration, 9, 173, 177–78, 195–96, 198–208, 211, 217
imperialism, 3–4, 16, 18–19, 207–49
industrialization, 127
Ingersoll, Robert, 142–44
Interior, 228
Irish, depictions of, 29
Islam, 140
Italy, 83

Jackson, Thomas "Stonewall," 34, 142, 194
Jacobs, Harriet, 80
Jacobson, Matthew Frye, 225
Jameson, J. Franklin, 10–11
Janes, Edmund, 104
Japan, 219
Jefferson, Thomas, 4
Jeffrey, Reuben, 44
Jenkins, John, 37–38
Jesus Christ, images of, 1–2, 6, 61, 92, 99, 111, 113, 115, 136, 143, 175–77, 181, 195, 203–4, 209, 216, 220, 223, 232, 238, 249
Jim Crow. *See* segregation
John Freeman and His Family (Brown), 56
Johnson, Andrew, 24, 31, 42, 93–96, 108
Johnson, Martha, 66, 69–70
Jones, Jacqueline, 52
Jones, Sam, 143
Judaism, 9, 199
Judas Iscariot, images of, 95
Julian, George, 113

Kearney, Belle, 174–78, 181, 195, 209–10
Keating, J. M., 163–64
Keating, M. T., 157
Kidder, Daniel P., 25
King, Edward, 126
King, Martin Luther, 86

Kipling, Rudyard, 19, 234, 238, 242–43
Kirk, Edward N., 121
Kittredge, A. E., 227–28
Knights of the White Camellia, 76
Korea, 210, 221
Ku Klux Klan, 76, 81, 102, 108, 115, 143, 192, 236

Lamar, L. Q. C., 166, 172
Lanier, Sidney, 130
Lasch, Christopher, 239
Laurie, Thomas, 31
Lee, Fitzhugh, 230
Lee, Robert E., 1, 21, 34, 96, 98, 103, 142, 146, 194, 246
Leonard, A. B., 172–73
Leopard's Spots, The: A Romance of the White Man's Burden, 1865–1900 (Dixon), 236–37
Lewis, Diocletian, 179
Leyburn, John, 105
Liberal Republicans, 113–18
Light and Life for Heathen Women, 218
Lincoln, Abraham, 5, 74, 122, 176; with African Americans, 5, 44–45, 57, 71; assassination of, 11–12, 20–51, 88–89, 128, 246–47; and Emancipation Proclamation, 40; in historical memory, 40, 44, 57, 99, 128, 135, 209; as national redeemer, 21–22, 30
Lincoln University, 82
literature: African Americans in, 96–97, 109, 126, 242–43; and Civil War, 97–98, 109, 129–30; and religion, 26, 89, 111–13, 216–18, 230, 234–38; and sectional reconciliation, 96–98, 111–13, 117–18, 126, 164–65, 192–93, 213, 227, 230, 234–37, 244–46; utopian, 17, 244–46; War of 1898, 17, 213, 227, 230, 234–38; during yellow fever, 153
Litwack, Leon, 75
Livermore, Mary A., 194
Lodge, Henry Cabot, 201
Logan, Rayford, 84
Long, Kathryn, 121

Looking Backward, 2000–1887 (Bellamy), 244–46
Looking Forward: A Dream of the United States of America in 1999 (Bird), 17, 244–46
Lost Cause, 8, 17, 131, 142, 146, 162–67, 191
Louisville Courier-Journal, 29
L'Ouverture, Touissant, 57
Lutherans, 30
lynching, 3, 18, 143, 199, 202, 204–7, 225, 232, 240–41, 246, 247–48. See also violence

Macrae, David, 43, 92, 103–4
Mahan, Asa, 115
Manila Bay, 212
Martin, Sella, 6, 55
Marty, Martin, 9, 126
"Martyr, The" (Melville), 20–21
Massachusetts Fifty-Fourth Regiment, 68–69, 73–75
May, Henry F., 9
McCauley, James, 40
McClintock, John, 30
McComb, Samuel, 228
McGiffert, Joseph N., 91
McGuffin, John B., 221
McKinley, Ida, 231
McKinley, William, 16, 213, 230–33, 237, 241, 243
McKitrick, Eric, 8
McLean, Curtis, 45
McLeod, Georgia Hulse, 190–91, 194–95
McLoughlin, William, 92, 126
McMinnville New Era, 152
McPherson, James, 8, 115
Mead, Sidney, 126
Melville, Herman, 20–21
Memphis Appeal, 152, 163–64
Men of Our Times; or Leading Patriots of the Day (Stowe), 99
Merinsky, Svobodin, 116
Merrick, Caroline, 190
Methodists, 13, 30–32, 34, 38, 40–42, 45, 51, 61, 78–79, 104, 106–8, 129, 131, 143,

Methodists (*continued*)
150, 176, 182, 186, 206, 215, 218, 222, 227, 230
Mexico, 4, 244
Millard, E. C., 224
Miller, Kelly, 236, 241
Miller, Samuel, 33
Miller, Stuart Creighton, 220
Milton, Hattie A., 169
Milwaukee Index, 104
missionaries: abroad, 16, 212–26, 245; perceptions of African Americans and other people of color, 61–76, 212, 214, 221–26; during Reconstruction, 12–13, 49, 51–87, 99, 102, 106–7, 109, 125, 132, 135, 141, 159, 169, 191, 247; support for interracial marriage, 73–75
Mississippi Daily Clarion, 193
Moody, Dwight Lyman, 13–14, 119–45, 146, 147, 148, 149, 154, 167, 171, 176, 182, 187, 199, 204, 215, 216, 228, 242, 247
Moorhead, James, 40
Morehouse College, 82
Morgan, J. Pierpont, 127, 129, 156
Morgan, Matt, 114–15
Mormonism, 217
Morton, Samuel, 43
Mott, John R., 216

Nation, The, 126, 132, 149–50, 229
National Baptist Sunday-School Convention, 105
National Convention of Soldiers and Sailors, 93–94
National Woman Suffrage Association, 178
nationalism, 6–7, 10, 12, 15–16, 18, 27, 40, 53, 90–91, 97, 111, 118, 124, 129, 148, 168, 170, 192, 207, 213, 218, 239, 244, 246–47
Native Americans, 4, 224–25
nativism, 198–208, 224
natural selection, 102
"Negro, The: What is His Ethnological Status?" 93
New Deal, 128

New England Freedmen's Aid Society, 81
New Englander and Yale Review, 92
New Era, or the Coming Kingdom (Strong), 221–22
New South, 8, 163
New Year's Day, 74–75
New Year's Eve, 137
New York Advocate, 160
New York Baptist Register, 87
New York Draft Riots, 135–36
New York Herald, 104, 128
New York Independent, 32, 37–38, 41, 81, 87–88, 92, 108, 115, 118, 125, 157, 160, 192–93
New York Star, 87
New York Sun, 229
New York Times, 37, 81, 97, 102, 125–26, 130, 154, 157, 158, 160–61, 228
New York Tribune, 81, 113, 116, 125, 130, 135
Newman, J. P., 41
newspapers, 26, 29, 81, 83, 87–88, 91, 125, 127–28, 159–60, 264n20
Nordhoff, Charles, 126
Norfolk Virginian, 78
North American Review, 81, 152, 230
"North Carolina, #2," 203
Northwestern University, 176
Norwood; or Village Life in New England (Beecher), 96–97, 135
Nott, Josiah, 43

Oberlin College, 56, 115
O'Leary, Cecilia, 8
Omi, Michael, 7
Oriental Consolidated Mining Company, 221
Origins of the New South (Woodward), 8
Our Country (Strong), 217–18, 221–22

Padduck, Wilbur F., 44
Palmer, Benjamin Morgan, 5, 148, 160–61, 165
Palmetto Leaves (Stowe), 100–101, 191
Pan-African Conference of 1900, 243
Panic of 1873, 107, 124, 128. *See also* depressions, economic

Paris Commune, 124

Peking Oriental Society, 221

Pennsylvania Freedmen's Association, 63

Pennsylvania State Equal Rights' League, 48

Perry, William Stevens, 224

Phelps, Austin, 25–26

Philadelphia Divinity School, 249

Philbrick, E. S., 61–62

Philippines, 16, 208, 210, 212, 225–44. *See also* War of 1898

Phillips, Wendell, 41, 99, 116–17, 121, 125–26

Piers, Craig C., 148

Pierson, A. T., 216, 219–20, 222

Pike, James S., 126

Pixley, Frank M., 223

Platt, Orville, 233

Plessy v. Ferguson (1896), 143

Plumer, William, 137–40

political cartoons, 9, 28–29, 89, 173

politics: and African American education, 46, 55–56, 59; ; considering land redistribution, 2, 24, 41, 71; religion in, 10, 22, 32, 37, 41–42, 46–47, 55, 59, 89–90, 111, 113–18, 128–29, 176–77, 181–82, 213, 220, 225, 230–34, 237–43

polygenesis, 43

Poole, W. Scott, 8

Populists, 196, 211

Power, J. L., 159

Pratt, Julius W., 231

Presbyterians, 5, 13, 26–27, 32–33, 35, 45, 51, 59, 104–5, 107, 110, 113, 128–29, 137, 138, 139, 147–48, 153, 160–61, 165, 182, 215, 221, 228

Princeton Review, 45

Princeton Theological Seminary, 32, 138

Prioleau, George W., 242

Proctor, Henry Hugh, 85

"Prodigal Son, The," 109–10, 117

Prohibition and Home Protection Party, 197–98

Prostrate South, The (Pike), 126

Protestant Reformation, 25, 272n31

Protestants: and African American education,

46, 49, 51–86; and civil rights, 3, 6, 22, 38–50, 55–56, 61, 63–76, 87–88, 91, 98, 170, 201, 247; and imperialism, 210–30; and interracial sexuality, 73–75, 106; in print culture, 26, 56–59, 87, 89, 92, 137, 216–19; responses to Abraham Lincoln's assassination, 12, 22–52, 240, 246–47; and sectional schisms, 5, 31–33; and segregation, 3, 15, 64–65, 107–8, 124, 141–46; 178, 202–8, 242, 262n54; support for sectional reconciliation, 23, 30, 34–37, 89–111, 119–45; support for slavery, 34–37, 39; on the theatre, 31; views of African Americans, 6, 38–50, 61–62, 64–76, 124; views of southerners, 22, 26–28, 54, 76–77, 87–88, 91, 93–98, 129–30, 140–47; on violence, 202, 219–20, 229; and the Woman's Christian Temperance Union, 182, 198; during yellow fever outbreak, 147–48, 157

Puerto Rico, 208, 210, 212

Pullman Strike, 199

Putnam's Monthly Magazine, 92, 112–13

Quakers, 52, 64, 72, 79

race: blurring of, 12, 53, 69–70; constructions of, 6–7, 11, 22, 27, 29–30, 39–50, 102, 224, 235–36, 260n111; and contact, 52–53, 60, 63–76, 85–86; "one blood" argument, 44–45, 58–59, 61

racism: and federal government, 4, 74; and medical issues, 148, 167–72; and religion, 18, 34–37, 39, 43–45, 55, 61, 63, 72–76, 78, 88, 90, 93, 108, 123, 143–45, 212, 218–26, 236–37, 242, 244–49; scientific, 29, 40, 43–45; and sexuality, 73–75, 168, 205, 223

Randolf, Anson D. F., 137

"rebels," 53, 86

"Reconstruction" (Giles), 1–3, 17, 246

Reconstruction Amendments, 2–3, 56, 88, 104, 114

Red Badge of Courage, The (Crane), 135

Red Record, A (Wells), 205

"Redeemer Nation." *See* "Christian Nation"

Reese, John, 95

Republican Party, 2, 23, 47, 59, 113, 115, 117–18, 123, 125–26, 131, 149–50, 176, 183, 186, 197–98, 201, 206, 241; radicals in, 2, 22, 24, 37, 41–42, 54, 87, 89, 92, 126

"Reunited" (Ryan), 146–47

Revelation, Book of, 100

revivals, 13, 119–45, 146, 148, 149, 154, 167, 176, 182, 204, 247; of 1857–58, 121, 131–32

Revolutionary era, 4, 137

Reynolds, John, 37

Richardson, Heather Cox, 8

Richardson, Joe, 52

Richardson, W. J., 66

Richmond Theological Seminary, 84

"ring shout," 62, 67

rituals, religious, 20, 24–25, 48–49, 66, 70, 74–75, 91, 110–11, 117, 137, 150, 209

Roach, Clara L., 193–94

Road to Reunion, The (Buck), 8

Robinson, Charles, 27, 40, 44

Robinson, John, 222

Roediger, David, 7

Roosevelt, Theodore, 16, 213, 230, 233–34, 237, 243

Ross, Emmett, 164–65

"Rough Riders," 233, 240

Rousseau, 45

Russel, Edmund, 235–36

Ryan, Abram J., 146–47, 150, 191

Sample, Robert, 26, 31

Sankey, Ira, 123

Satan, images of, 28, 92, 95, 223, 238

Satter, Beryl, 200

Savage, Frederick, 128

Savannah Tribune, 242

Saxton, Alexander, 7

Schlesinger, Arthur, Sr., 9

Schurz, Carl, 113, 238

science, racism in, 29, 40, 43–45, 102

Scotia Seminary, 82, 84

Scott, Tom, 127

Scribner's Monthly, 132, 137

segregation, 3, 6, 18, 65, 107–8, 124, 143–44, 178–79, 199, 202–8, 225, 242, 246

Seiss, Joseph, 45

"Sermon on the Mount," 115, 249

Seward, William, 21

Seymour, Caroline, 111–12

Shadwell, Bertrand, 238

Shaw, Stephanie, 84

Sheridan, Philip, 125, 180

Sherman, William Tecumseh, 134

Sibley, Jane Elizabeth, 193

Sigourney, Lydia H., 57–58

Silber, Nina, 8, 178

Singleton, J. W., 163

Sins of the Father, The (Dixon), 236

Slaughter, Linda, 61, 71

slavery, 35, 39, 91, 96, 116, 121, 123, 134, 138, 141, 174–75, 190, 201, 225

Smalls, Robert, 71

Smedley, Martha, 77

Smiley, Sarah F., 136

Smith, Gerrit, 37, 96

Smith, Henry, 143

Snay, Mitchell, 138

Somerset, Lady Henry, 210

Souls of Black Folk (Du Bois), 52, 248

South: and churches, 5, 31–32, 78–80, 165–66, 216; and Confederacy, 1, 5, 17, 21, 33–34; feelings toward the North, 13–14, 17, 22–23, 28, 54, 70, 76–82, 89, 130–31, 140–43, 147, 161–67, 186, 188–90, 195–96; northern perceptions of, 1–2, 5, 11–12, 14, 22, 26–29, 31–32, 96–98, 100–104, 116, 125–26, 129–30, 147, 154, 158–61, 190–93, 200, 217–18, 224–25, 247; responses to Abraham Lincoln's assassination, 33–34; use of violence, 2–3, 17–18, 76, 79–82, 88, 102, 108–9, 125–26, 132, 135–36, 143, 179, 199, 204–7, 211, 218, 246, 249; in the War of 1898, 212, 228, 230–34

South America, 212, 225, 244

Southall, James G., 79–80

Southern Baptist Convention, 165–66

Southern Baptist Theological Seminary, 216
Southern Review, 131
Spahr, Charles, 238–39
Spain, 83, 212, 224, 231, 241, 244
Spanish-American War. *See* War of 1898
Spear, Samuel, 27
Springfield Republican, 94, 125
St. Louis Medical and Surgical Journal, 163
Stampp, Kenneth, 8
Stanton, William, 43
Stead, William T., 210–11
Stevens, P. F., 189
Stevens, Thaddeus, 24, 41–42, 47, 59, 71, 87, 92, 95, 109
Stevenson, Hannah, 81
Stewart, Eliza "Mother," 183–87, 199–200
Stokes, Missouria, 193
Storrs School, 203
Stowe, Harriet Beecher, 13–14, 91, 97–104, 108, 111, 123, 137, 147, 191, 200, 247
Strong, George Templeton, 24, 27
Strong, Josiah, 217–18, 221–22, 224, 240
Student Volunteer Movement for Foreign Missions, 215–17, 219, 223
suffrage, 2–3, 6, 41–42, 88, 126, 178–79, 181, 190, 196, 198, 201–2, 232, 249
Sumner, Charles, 38, 41–42, 57, 113, 115, 118, 241
Sunday schools, 64, 105–6, 122, 214
Supreme Court, 4, 10, 45, 127, 143

Taney, Roger, 4, 45
Tappan, Lewis, 73
Taylor, Bayard, 117
temperance. *See* Woman's Christian Temperance Union
Thanksgiving, 74, 91, 110
theology, 9, 25, 40, 43–44, 53, 67, 78, 93, 128–29, 131–32, 216, 222–23
Thirteenth Amendment, 56, 88, 104, 114
Thomas, Gertrude, 29
Thomas, Jacob, 30
Thornton, Montrose, 248

Thorpe, Margaret Newbold, 69, 77–78, 109
Tilden, Samuel J., 149
Tillman, Benjamin, 239
Tilton, Elizabeth, 127
Tilton, Theodore, 87, 115, 127
"To the Person Sitting in Darkness" (Twain), 230
Todd, Elbert S., 219, 222–23
Torrey, R. A., 228
Tourgée, Albion, 50, 77, 85–86, 192–93
tourism, 98–104
Towne, Laura, 62, 64–68, 70–72, 82, 109
Townsend, E. D., 35–36
trauma, theories of, 148–49, 167
Trinidad, 83
Trollope, Anthony, 10
Trumbull, Lyman, 113
Tucker, H. C., 222, 225
Turkey, 244
Turner, Frederick Jackson, 217
Turner, Henry, 150
Twain, Mark, 229–30
Tyng, Stephen Higginson, 94

Uncle Tom's Cabin (Stowe), 97–98, 103
Underwood, John C., 114
Union Signal, 203
Union Theological Seminary, 106
Unitarianism, 51, 121–22
United Brethren, 51
United Presbyterians, 51
United States Christian Commission, 122
Universalism, 41
urbanization, 9, 127, 217
USS *Maine,* 231

Venezuela, 245
Victoria, Queen, 123
violence, 2–3, 17–18, 54, 76, 79–82, 88, 104, 108–9, 125–26, 132, 135–36, 143, 179, 199, 204–7, 211, 218, 229, 246, 249
visitors to the United States, 10, 43, 92, 103–4

Vogell, H. C., 77
Voice, The, 190–91, 201–2
Voltaire, 45

Walker, Clarence, 55, 84
Walker, George, 24–25, 41–42
Wall Street, 25, 107, 124
Wanamaker, John, 127–29
War of 1898, 3–4, 16–17, 19, 208, 212–14, 224, 226–45, 251n4
Washington, Booker T., 85
Washington College, 138
Washington National Republican, 150
Washington Post, 142, 152, 153, 163, 168
Washington University, 96
Waterbury, Marie, 61, 65
Watterson, Henry, 29–30
"waving the bloody shirt," 125, 149
Weber, Max, 96, 272n31
Webster, Daniel, 1
Wells, Ida B., 18, 124, 143, 199, 204–6, 249
West, the, 211, 217
Western Theological Seminary, 138
Westminster Gazette, 206
Wheatley, Phillis, 57
Wheeler, Joseph, 230, 232
White, George, 248
White, George H., 248
"White Man's Burden" (Kipling), 19, 234, 238
whiteness. *See* race

Whitman, Walt, 123, 127, 132, 136
Whittier, John Greenleaf, 86, 127
Willard, Frances, 14–15, 129, 175–210
Williamson, Joel, 236
Wilmington Race Riot, 240
Wilson, Charles Reagan, 8, 131
Wilson, Woodrow, 216
Winant, Howard, 7
Wittenmyer, Annie, 180–81
Woman and Temperance, 191
Woman in the Pulpit (Willard), 182
Woman of the Century, 191
Woman's Christian Temperance Union, 14–16, 173–210, 288n14; and African Americans, 16, 198–208, 239; and immigrants, 16, 198–208
Woman's Work for Woman, 218
Woodward, C. Vann, 8
World's Woman's Christian Temperance Union, 210
World-Wide Missions, 218, 222

Yale College, 136
Yale Divinity School, 85
Yard, Robert, 45
yellow fever, 14, 80, 144–74, 247
Yoder, Jacob, 61, 80, 87
Young Men's Christian Association, 121–22, 155

Zion's Advocate, 64